STATE AND SOCIETY IN IRAN

To Mina and Amir
fruits of my life

STATE AND SOCIETY IN IRAN

THE ECLIPSE OF THE QAJARS AND THE EMERGENCE OF THE PAHLAVIS

Homa Katouzian

I.B. TAURIS

LONDON · NEW YORK

Acknowledgement
I.B.Tauris thank Kaveh Moussavi for his
generous support in the publication of
this book

New Paperback Edition published in 2006
by I.B.Tauris & Co Ltd
6 Salem Road, London W2 4BU
175 Fifth Avenue, New York NY 10010
www.ibtauris.com

In the United States and Canada distributed by St. Martin's Press
175 Fifth Avenue, New York NY 10010

First published in 2000 by I.B.Tauris & Co Ltd

Library of Modern Middle East Studies 28

ISBN 10: 1 84511 272 5
ISBN 13: 978 1 84511 272 1

A full CIP record for this book is available from the British Library
A full CIP record for this book is available from the Library of Congress

Library of Congress catalog card: available

Typeset by The Midlands Book Typesetting Company, Loughborough, Leicestershire
Printed and bound in India by Replika Press Pvt. Ltd.

Contents

Acknowledgements

I began working on this book late in 1989. Besides completing some writing on other topics, both in English and Persian, there were several reasons why it took so long to finish, even though much of the subject had been familiar to me from my youth. In particular, I had to find, read, interpret and correlate a large number of British official documents, as well as primary and secondary sources in both Persian and English. Nevertheless, this book would have been ready for publication much earlier had not disaster struck in the form of a fire which destroyed my study, together with the six chapters that had already been written, and all the back-ups, documents and notes.

I would not have given up the work, but the tremendous moral and material support I received from friends in three continents made it much easier to turn the catastrophe round and start again. Aziz and Azizeh Cameron, Azar Ebtehaj, Jaleh Gohari, Habib Ladjevardi, Ali and Jamileh Razavi and Banafsheh Ziadloo made very generous contributions towards the reconstruction of my study.

I also received valuable gifts of books from Parvin Alizadeh, Mohsen Ashtiany, Mehdi Askarieh, Saeed and Ladan Barzin, Ali Dehbashi, Cyrus and Caroline Ghani, Houshang and Farzaneh Golshiri, John and Faraneh Gurney, Koorosh and Shohreh Homayounpour, Bozorgmehr Kasravi, Shahrokh Meskoob, Reza and Susan Moussoli, Nasser Pakdaman, Amir Pichdad, Hossein and Roya Shahidi, Reza and Shahrzad Sheikholeslami, Shahran Tabari as well as my English and Persian publishers, I.B.Tauris and Nashr-e Makaz. Other friends – Shahram and Sorour Aghili, Anna Enayat, Eprime and Linda Eshag, Ali Gouché, Roy Mottahedeh, Manuchehr and Shirin Rassa, Floreeda Safiri, Houshang and Sherie Sayyahpour, and others too numerous to mention – gave me sympathy, support and encouragement in various ways. I am greatly indebted to the Library of the Middle East Centre at St Antony's College, Oxford for their remarkable permission, granted without a formal request from me, to borrow their books for as long as other readers did not require them.

Bozorgmehr Kasravi's efforts in helping me to recover many of the lost documents and references were invaluable. So were the technical advice and assistance from Saeed Barzin and my son Amir, to someone who was a mere novice in word processing and computer skills when he began the present task.

Words fail me in expressing my gratitude to all of them, especially as they are living proof that one may still have friends even when one lacks power.

Preface to the Paperback Edition

The period which extends from the death throes of the Qajar monarchy, past the accession of Reza Shah and onto his abdication following the Allied invasion of Iran in 1941, is a fascinating chapter in the long and discontinuous history of Iran. It also contains the seeds of virtually all the major social, political and cultural issues that have faced the country since.

It all began with the Tobacco Revolt of 1890–1892, followed especially by the death of Naser al-Din Shah in 1896. This period led to the onset of chaos both in the centre and in the provinces, in parallel with a growing campaign for the rule of law – in sharp contrast to Iran's traditional system of arbitrary government. The triumph of the Constitutional Revolution, which resulted in 1906 during this uncertain phase, produced the first Majlis in the following year. But matters did not end here. Ongoing confrontation between royalist and constitutional radicals led to the coup of 1908 and the arbitrary government of Mohammad Ali Shah, after which the country degenerated into civil war which in turn ended with the deposition of the Shah in 1909. There followed a period of increasing chaos which had always characterized the aftermath to the fall of an arbitrary state in Iranian history. This chaos occurred despite the fact that the historical reasons which had always alienated the population from the State and created confrontation with it – namely the effect of arbitrary rule – had for the first time in Iran's history been brought to an end. Nevertheless, once again a state of chaos was found both in the centre of politics in Tehran and in the provinces. The onset of the First World War merely intensified this chaos.

The Anglo–Iranian agreement of 1919 – which was a brainchild of Lord Curzon and hardly supported by the rest of the British government – might have led to greater peace and stability but it was vehemently rejected by the Iranian public and condemned by the other Great Powers. The 1921 coup was a consequence of persisting chaos and, within a few years, led to considerable public support for the transformation of Reza Khan, the military officer, to Reza Shah the autocratic ruler. This was especially true among the modern social and political elite. Chaos came to an end as the new regime embarked on a programme of modernizing policies. But from 1930 onwards it was arbitrary government which returned in the pursuit of modernization.

The abdication of Reza Shah in 1941 once again plunged the country into disorder. On the surface the country looked very different from 45 years earlier when Naser al-Din Shah had been assassinated. But deep down in society, in its political and cultural dynamic, many key factors remained the same.

If law, order and parliamentary government had taken root before or even after 1941 it is quite likely that there would not have been a revolution in 1979. The events of the 1979 revolution and its aftermath were in many ways a consequence of the developments that this book describes and analyses, both in the broader context of the historical sociology of Iran and within the specific period of history under review.

The main issues in this period were conflicts between society and state, the clash of arbitrary power and trends towards chaos, struggles for law and liberty, conflicts over traditionalism and modernism, and the proclivity for conspiracy theories in both domestic and international politics. A century has passed since these issues surfaced in Iranian society. Much has changed since then. But the issues are still well in place.

HK
St Antony's College, Oxford
October 2005

Preface

This book integrates two studies into one volume. The first is a general study of state and society in Iran, with specific application to the period beginning with the assassination of Naser al-Din Shah Qajar in 1896, and ending with Reza Shah Pahlavi's abdication in 1941. The second is a detailed, document-based, blow-by-blow account and analysis of the 1919 Agreement and the Coup d'Etat of 1921 which was a direct result of the failure of that Agreement. The two studies are clearly combined, if only because the latter forms part of the former. Yet it would not have been necessary to conduct such a long and detailed study of the Agreement and the Coup merely as part of a study of state and society in Iran at this time. The former study was needed – especially in the face of so many contradictory accounts and interpretations which still persisted over those issues – for a comprehensive analysis of state and society during the period. The six chapters (four to nine inclusive) which contain the study of the Agreement and the Coup could, with some modification, have been published separately.

The whole book, integrated as it now is, has precedents in my writings on Iranian history, society, politics, literature and political economy. I began to formulate the theory of arbitrary rule in the late 1960s and early 1970s in studies of land reform and Iranian agriculture, and of Iran's economy as an oil-exporting country and 'petrolic society'. I developed the theory further, with more supporting evidence, in subsequent studies of Iranian culture and society written in both English and Persian.

In the present book I have tried to do two things. Firstly, I have put forward the most comprehensive version so far of the theory of arbitrary rule – of the arbitrary state and the arbitrary society – with comparative analysis and evidence from the histories of Iran and of Europe in regard to property ownership, law, legitimacy, rebellion and social mobility. Secondly, I have applied the theory of arbitrary rule (as a paradigm of the historical sociology of Iran) to a study of events from the end of the nineteenth century to late 1941. This relatively short period provides ample evidence for the theory while, at the same time, the theory helps make historical sense of the events themselves and of subsequent social and political developments in Iran. Ideally, I might have extended the study to the end of the twentieth century, but decided against doing so both on grounds of length, and because I had already applied the theory to later periods in my works on Musaddiq, Hedayat and the Iranian political economy.

The period under study is almost unique in Iran. The sequence of rebellions, revolutions, Coups, civil and foreign wars, chaos and arbitrary government make it relatively unusual even in this country's long and turbulent history. What renders it unique, however, are the apparently modern features of these events, even while they are rooted in age-old traditions.

Assassination had always been a well-worn technique for dispatching rulers both popular and unpopular, but there was no precedent for a middle-class trader-cum-intellectual such as Mirza Reza to assassinate a ruler like Naser al-Din, and, moreover, to do so in the name of law, justice and political reform. Rebellions in Iranian history date back to the reigns of Darius I and Xerxes, but no previous revolution had aimed to bring down the arbitrary state in order to replace it with the rule of law. Chaos had always followed the collapse of arbitrary rule, but had never been justified in the name of freedom, let alone law, and had never taken the form of destructive parliamentary conflicts, confrontation between legislative and executive powers in the name of constitutional government and the separation of powers. The chaos following the overthrow of an arbitrary state had always eventually been ended by a strong regime which had soon created another arbitrary state; it had never been ended in the name of saving the 'motherland' from disintegration, 'catching up with the trail of civilization', or bringing 'progress' and 'modernization'.

The period covered by this book thus reveals an authentic and traditional Iranian pattern of historical change: a cycle of arbitrary rule to rebellion to chaos and back to arbitrary rule. But it does so in completely new ways – in the clash of the country's traditional experience with a new influence, the political culture of a dynamic, modern and much more powerful Europe. The old pattern emerges within forms of revolution aimed at establishing law, chaos in the name of freedom, and restoration of the old order for the sake of the motherland and modernization, none of which had any precedent in Iranian history. This book is an attempt to show the logic of this peculiar mixture of traditional structures and modern forms in recent Iranian history.

The 1919 Agreement and the 1921 Coup make up a fundamental part of this process. The reason for giving them special attention is twofold. On the one hand, they bring to a climax the problem of chaos in the period. This includes the real and imagined role of foreign powers, and the complete triumph of the modern conspiracy theory of politics in Iran, resulting both from the Agreement and the disillusionment that followed the establishment of dictatorship and arbitrary rule.

On the other hand, few detailed and comprehensive studies of the Agreement or the Coup exist, and given their great impact on Iran, it was necessary to combine evidence and analysis to explain events for readers interested in this period.

Cyrus Ghani's recent book, *Iran and the Rise of Reza Shah: From Qajar Collapse to Pahlavi Power*, does contain an extensive study of this topic. While it is a valuable contribution to the subject, my account differs significantly in various ways and is therefore complementary.

In writing this book my principal motive was the same as in previous studies. I intended not only to make sense of the past, but also – and especially – to offer an analytical framework through which to make sense of the present.

A Note on Method

The claim itself of the need for a specific theory of society and social change in Iran may pose questions at the very conceptual and methodological levels of the argument. In this brief note it will be shown that such a claim, and such a requirement, is entirely consistent with – indeed called for by – received methodological doctrines in both social and natural sciences.

There have been many theories of state, politics and society in the history of European political thought and social analysis. The most successful and influential of modern European theories include the variety of social contract theories, other liberal theories, Hegelian and Marxian theories, and the totalitarian theories of the twentieth century. Yet it must be emphasized that although many of the European theories disagree with each other in their basic premises, implications and predictions, sometimes almost irreconcilably, all of them reflect the background of European history and experience: they reflect European systems of government, social structures and relations, public and private institutions, and so on, and their changes through time as a result of socio-economic, technological and ideological developments. European theorists such as Plato, Aristotle, Aquinas, Machiavelli, Locke, Rousseau, Vico, Herder, Hegel, Marx, J.S. Mill, Spencer, Lenin, Hayek, Rosenberg, *et alia*, had the background of European political culture and civilization in mind so that, although they may disagree with each other's approaches as being 'materialistic', 'idealistic', 'atomistic', 'institutional', 'sociological' – or downright 'liberal', 'racist', and 'totalitarian' – none would argue that the social framework to which they refer is alien to the experience of European society from the classical age to modern times.

Marx may describe the state as representing the interest of the propertied classes which would 'wither away' after the socialist state has presided over the abolition of private property in society. Hayek may describe this process as 'the road to serfdom'. Yet, it is clear even from much of their terminology, that they both have in their premises the general background of European society and its developments. In other words, the disagreement and dispute is much less about the facts and much more about theories which give them analytical significance for a description of the past and prediction of the future.

It is perhaps not surprising that (except in rare moments of reflection) European theories of state and society were usually applied to the historical experience of non-European societies like Iran in the nineteenth and (especially) twentieth centuries: European analysts took the facts as corresponding to seemingly similar facts from European history; Iranian analysts did not have theories of their own, and what they understood from European theories they applied – more or less uncritically – to the facts of Iranian history and society. They saw Iranian land assignees, tribal chieftains and state officials as an aristocracy, merchants as bourgeoisie, peasants as serfs, and so on. It follows that they also saw the state as the representative of the ruling classes.

There is a basic methodological aspect to this matter which goes beyond the point in hand. It is the confusion between *generalization* and *universalism* in natural as well as social sciences. Scientific theories are characteristically *abstract* and *general*, but for that very reason they are incapable of universal application. Moreover, the more abstract and general a theory, the narrower its scope of application. Abstraction enables a theory to specify the conditions in which it claims to hold. Thus, it excludes the many more situations in which it would be inapplicable. The resulting theory is nevertheless general in the sense of explaining the relevant events or phenomena in all the circumstances which correspond to those specific conditions. If the theory is borne out in those circumstances then it may be correct; if not, then it is false.

This author has elaborated on this point elsewhere at some length*. Here, the example of a fundamental physical theory may suffice. Galileo's Law of Inertia states that, given a force of gravity, freely falling bodies will accelerate at the rate of 9.81 metres per second in a state of vacuum. In other words, outside a vacuum the rate of acceleration would be different, although not so much as to make the Law generally invalid. The important qualifications, however, are that where in the universe there is no gravity nothing would fall; and where (as on the moon) the force of gravity is significantly different from the earth, the law of inertia would be invalid. Therefore, the law of inertia is generally valid where there is a force of gravity, and it is the same as the earth; but it lacks universal validity.

What is true of theories of physics can scarcely be untrue of theories of state and society. In fact, it is likely to be more true of the latter because usually there are many more variables involved, and the pace of their change is more rapid. Human society is the universe of social and historical theory: therefore theories which are generally valid for some of its parts may not be valid for the rest. For example, theories which explain European revolutions as being essentially due to conflicts among the social classes cannot satisfactorily be applied to the case of Iran, because Iranian states have not been representative of any social classes in the sense which is rendered by the experience of Europe (see 'The Basic Theses', below).

The Law of Inertia itself contains the reasons for its universal inapplicability, that is, the reason why it may not be valid everywhere. Likewise, a successful theory in the case of a given society or group of societies would normally contain the reasons why it may not be valid elsewhere. The analytical logic and scientific techniques (being products of the human mind) could be applied everywhere, but the meaning, significance and functions of the social categories to which they are applied may be different, thus resulting in different theories. Hence, there is no need for a separate social science in the case of different societies, only different theories pertinent to significantly different societies, within a uniform social science.

This brief note on the methodological aspects of the argument was intended to forestall some basic misunderstandings which may result from the theory of Iranian state and society presented in the rest of this chapter. Of course, no theory (in any science) is the description of things as they are. If the Law of Inertia was a mere description of the acceleration rate of falling bodies, it would have suggested innumerable rates in countless places. Likewise, the theory presented below is no more a

---

* See Homa Katouzian, Ideology and Method in Economics (London and New York: Macmillan and New York University Press, 1980). Ch.7 especially.

pure description of the long Iranian history than are theories of European feudalism – with all its spatial and temporal varieties – pure descriptions of their subject.

Finally, some of the basic observations and arguments presented here could be more or less relevant to some other societies as well, be they ancient Sumer, Egypt and Assyria, or the much more recent Moghul India and Ottoman Turkey. It is no part of our purpose, however, to present a general theory of the history of all such societies because there are important differences among them through time and space, and a competent general theory would require extensive knowledge of them all, which may be beyond the capacity of a single theorist. If such theories are formulated by competent analysts in the case of each of these societies, it may then be possible to use all of them in suggesting a general theory which could also contain within itself the reasons for the remaining variations among them.

1

Arbitrary Rule:
A Theory of State,
Politics and Society in Iran*

Supreme rule

Modern studies of Iranian history and society have often been based on theories developed for European society. This has led to important anomalies, such as why the growing prosperity in Iran and apparently rapid economic development along capitalist lines, in the 1960s and '70s, should result in massive social revolt to bring down the state. These anomalies can be resolved by recognising the fundamental differences between the two societies in such basic principles as property ownership, social class, the nature of state power and questions of law.

In Iran, agricultural property was owned by the state, which assigned or farmed out tracts of it to individuals or groups as a privilege, but not a right. There was social stratification, but the social classes did not enjoy any rights independently from the state. Hence there was no aristocracy, and the make-up of social classes changed rapidly over time. There was no law outside the state, which stood above society, despite a body of rules that were subject to rapid and unpredictable change. Unlike Europe, the state's legitimacy was not founded in law and the consent of influential social classes, and the mere success of a rebellion was sufficient for its legitimacy. This explains the frequent crises of succession in Iranian history. Until modern times, revolts and revolutions were led against an 'unjust' arbitrary ruler to replace it with a 'just' one. The result was generalized chaos until a new arbitrary rule was established. Notwithstanding their many differences, the two revolutions in the twentieth century were massive revolts by the society against the state and for lawful government. In spite of some temporary successes, the entrenched historical experience of Iranian society proved to be more powerful than newly acquired political ideas.

The following section entitled 'The Basic Theses' presents a comparative theory of Iranian state, society and politics, developed by applying social science models and techniques to Iranian society. It compares and contrasts the Iranian experience with that of Europe, laying bare the important – but often concealed – differences between them. It offers evidence from both sides to support the need of a new interpretation of Iranian history and society, and ends with a brief application of the theory to major social and political trends in twentieth century Iran.

This shows how effective it is in explaining events, ideas and personalities which have often confounded commentators using traditional theories and approaches.

The basic theses

Some of the following theses have been extensively covered in the author's earlier publications. They are summarized here and the reader may consult the references for further explanation. Others, such as the notions of law, legitimacy and centralization, are discussed more fully.

Thesis 1

Historically, Iran has been an arbitrary society where there has been no state, social class, law and politics as observed in European history and explained and analysed by European theorists. The system of arbitrary rule was based on the state monopoly of property rights, and on the concentrated – although not necessarily centralized – bureaucratic and military power to which it gave rise. There could be no rights of property ownership in land, only privileges which the state granted to individuals (and some clans and communities), and which it could therefore withdraw at any time.

Thesis 2

The state directly owned large, though varying, amounts of agricultural land. It assigned much of the latter to individuals, usually members of the royal household, state functionaries and other magnates. There was no contractual security of title to ownership and no automatic rights of bequest. Apart from this, various systems of tax-farming were in use which were different in time and space. (It is noteworthy that the class of tax farmers in Moghul India whom the 1808 British Act of Land Settlement turned into independent landlords were known as *Zamindars*, a Persian word meaning landholders.)

This did not mean that the state was constantly engaged in appropriating or reallocating landed property. Indeed, it was possible for some families to hold on to their titular possessions for several generations. The important point is that this was possible only so long as the state did not wish, or did not have the physical power at the time, to repossess their entitlement or give it to others. Apart from that, Iranian history abounds in examples of how property might be taken away even from notables who had not fallen from grace, before or after their death. This was so even in the latter half of the nineteenth century, when the authority of the state was declining because of the impact of European powers and European ideas.

The state monopoly of property ownership was formally in land alone, which until recent times was the most important form of property. But the arbitrary power to which it gave rise resulted in a similar insecurity and fragility of ownership for merchant capital, both when the owner lived and after he died. Merchant capital was more obviously earned, although here, too, good relations with the state and its functionaries were very helpful. It could also be more easily realized in monetary form, spent, hidden or even buried. On the other hand, the commercial classes were generally more distant from the state, and their property ran the risk of violation by state officials, local governors and magnates.

Thesis 3

It follows that social classes always existed in terms of differences in official position, occupation, type of property, wealth and income. They consisted of royal persons, state functionaries, religious dignitaries, merchants, traders, artisans, town labourers, peasants and so on. But the nature of their relationship vis-à-vis the state (as well as each other) was basically different from European society. In Europe, it was the social classes that were functional; in Iran it was the state, while the social classes were empirical (see below).

There was in Iran no peerage and aristocracy founded on the feudal class monopoly of landownership as an independent and individual right, maintained and reinforced by such laws as primogeniture and entail, and perpetuated over time. As in Europe, the peasant had to surrender his surplus product to some agent of exploitation: in feudal Europe, it was to aristocratic landlords and, in later periods, to rural gentry as well; in Iran, it was to state officials, land assignees, tax farmers and the like. The important difference was that landlords did not have the right of independent ownership, could not be certain of enjoying the benefit of their privilege throughout their own lifetime, and could not perpetuate it through generations of their descendants (see thesis 2 above). Therefore they did not constitute an aristocratic or gentry class, and hence did not have any political rights independent of the state.

Thesis 4

Iran has always been a trading nation. The Persian words *bazar* and *bazargan* are as ancient as the country's domestic and international trade. There is much evidence in classical Persian texts of countrywide banking and credit facilities long before they emerged in Europe. Naser Khosraw alone attests to the existence of two hundred *sarrafs* in Isfahan which he witnessed on a visit to that city in the eleventh century.[1]

But there was no long-term accumulation of commercial capital (which might have led to the accumulation of physical capital in agriculture and manufacturing) as in Western Europe. The accumulation of commercial capital requires postponement of present consumption – i.e., saving. And long-term saving requires a minimum degree of security over a reasonable time. Property must not be threatened with arbitrary violations in the owner's lifetime and beyond, and there must be a certain expectation of future peace and stability.

The European bourgeoisie was given protection from feudal encroachments by the free towns and the emerging 'new monarchies', that is, absolutist states. The Iranian monied classes could not count on such protection from any powerful social group.[2]

Thesis 5

In Europe, the state was more or less dependent upon, and more or less represented, the interests of the social classes. The higher the social class, the higher the dependence of the state on it, and the greater the state's representation of its interest.

In Iran, by contrast, the social classes were generally dependent on the state. And the higher the social class, the greater its dependence on the state. In other words, in Iran the state was functional and the social classes were empirical. In Europe it was the other way round.

This explains the great differences in social mobility between the two societies. Absence of the functional social classes which were associated with the transitory nature of private ownership and the state's monopoly of all independent power meant that, in principle, any individual or family however humble could rise to the highest position and greatest fortune even within their own lifetime; and the most prominent people in society could likewise lose everything, even their lives, in a single generation. These could include chief ministers, departmental secretaries, provincial governors, army commanders, men of science and letters, and even rulers and entire dynasties.

In a word, both the mighty and the humble rightly understood that anything was possible. Just as a chief minister's life and property could be taken at the will of the ruler, the humblest person could become chief minister at the ruler's pleasure.

Thesis 6

Iran had no law in the sense of basic rules setting a boundary to the exercise of state power and making it generally predictable. Where there are no rights there is no law. That is, where the law is little more than the arbitrary decisions of the lawgiver, the very concept of law becomes redundant, even though a body of public rules and regulations exists, because these may change at any moment and without following established procedures. This is indeed the literal meaning of *estebdad*, of arbitrary government.

It is hard for a Westerner to understand this concept. In Europe, the law was regarded as a binding force which regulated – brought order and discipline to – the relationship between state and society, as well as within the society itself. It could change either as a result of organized efforts at reform through existing legal procedures or, in the last resort, by rebellion and revolution. The law was generally inviolable and difficult to change. This was particularly true of those fundamental (later described as constitutional) laws which defined the rights and obligations of individuals, social groups and the state. Such laws, written or unwritten, contracts or established traditions, did not exist in Iran. This is what made the arbitrary exercise of power possible, and indeed normal.

In judicial matters, a body of rules must have existed before Islam, and in Islamic times the Shari'a supplied an extensive and elaborate civil and criminal code. These were far from systematic in interpretation, and could vary considerably in application even at the same time and place. Yet the most restrictive factor was that they could be applied only insofar as they did not conflict with the wishes of the state. That is why the state could deal out punishments against persons, families or whole towns which had no sanction in Shari'a law; and how the condemned could sometimes escape execution on such grounds as making the Shah or local ruler laugh at the right moment.

In Europe's feudal society there were written or unwritten laws which were seemingly unchanging, and which greatly inhibited social and geographical mobility, perpetuated monopoly and class privilege, and restricted the emergence of new techniques and ideas. The liberal thinkers of the modern age attacked both the extent of these laws and customs and their resistance to change. They advocated a 'negative' concept of freedom – freedom from traditional legal restraints – which became prominent in the nineteenth century and is once again claiming precedence.

It was the European concept of law that the leaders of the constitutional movement of Iran had in mind when they campaigned for *qanun* as opposed to *estebdad*. They did not have a theory, but clearly saw the stark fact, the *differentia specifica* between the two societies. *Qanun* was the title of the opposition newspaper published by Malkam Khan in London. It was also intended by the title of Mostashar al-Dawleh's book, *One Word (Yek Kalameh)*, published before in Iran, for which he was jailed and tortured, and his house was looted.[3] A Perso–Arabic word of Greek origin – usually used in philosophy and science – *qanun* had a long lineage. What had been absent in Iranian society were 'canons' of law which could make life and labour a good deal more secure and predictable.

This comparison is not only with feudal Europe but with European society in general. European society, whether ancient, medieval or modern, had always been founded upon some kind of written or unwritten law, or deeply entrenched customary relationship, between state and society. Greek city-states had differed greatly from modern democracies in terms of the scope and limits of state power, the extent of its social base and political legitimacy, and the administration of justice as it affected social groups and classes. Such rights were different in space as well as time, both among the social classes and between them and the state. But they always existed, and hence there was always law of one kind or another. This was the 'one word' which had been lacking in Iranian society (see also chapter two).

Thesis 7

Since law was absent, so was politics. Politics existed only in the tautological sense that even the most primitive or elementary human associations such as tribes and households involved activities on the part of their members for promoting their own interest, in the sense of communal exchange. Otherwise, politics cannot exist without law, because it is only within a legal framework where rights and obligations are defined that independent thoughts and actions become possible.

Up to the 1900s, the word *siyasat* had two interrelated meanings. Firstly, it meant the art of governing the realm successfully, as in the title of Nezam al-Molk's *Siyasatnameh* (its alternative tide is *Siyar al-Muluk* which, significantly, had been the title of the Arabic translations, from the Pahlavi original, of *Shahnameh*). Secondly, it was used to mean the punishment (usually execution) of fallen notables and state officials – of the 'politicians'! Since politics did not exist, there was no appropriate word for it. Increasing contacts with Europe in the nineteenth century led the Shah, state functionaries and intellectuals to use *polteek* and *polteeki* (both of them corruptions of the French word politique)[4] in reference to European political affairs. They even constructed the term *polteek-chi* for European politicians.

Those words were later translated into *siyasat*, *siyasi* and *siyasatmadar* during and after the Constitutional Revolution, when it looked as if politics had at last come to Iran.

Thesis 8

The implication of all this for long-term socio-economic development may be summed up as 'lack of continuity'.

Iranian states could be strong or weak; rulers could be intelligent or dim, prodigal, frugal or miserly, just or unjust, bringers of peace, security and prosperity, or merely feeble and ineffectual. The exercise of arbitrary power did not mean that the consequences of the state or rulers were the same throughout history. On the contrary, precisely because power was arbitrary, much depended on the personality of the ruler (and his organization of the state), and this is perhaps the most important factor in explaining the large and rapid fluctuations in social life and national fortune. The trend of events in the Achaemenid empire after Darius I (and possibly Xerxes), in the Sassanian empire after Shapur I, and Khosraw I (Anushiravan), under the Ghaznavids after Soltan Mahmud (and possibly Mas'ud), and the Seljuqs after Malekshah (and possibly Sanjar), under the Safavids after Isma'il I and Abbas I (and possibly Abbas II), under the Afsharids after Nader, under the Zand after Karim Khan, during the Qajar rule after Aqa Mohammad (and possibly Fath'ali), and Naser al-Din, are just a few examples of frequent, swift and substantial discontinuities in Iranian history.

The persistence of arbitrary rule resulted in greater and more frequent changes than is observed in the history of Europe. And the absence of law, the high social mobility, and the absence of organized and continuous social institutions, were the most important factors behind it. These same factors also greatly inhibited continuous and cumulative social, economic, scientific and technological development.

Thus, Iran may be described as a *short-term society* as opposed to Europe's *long-term society*. Her long history, and that of its institutions and social classes, look more like a series of short-term achievements and failures than continuous accumulation. Even though European continuity involved long-term changes – changes which, precisely because of that continuity, took much time and effort to occur – once they did take place they were fundamentally irreversible.

Thesis 9

There were inter-related problems affecting legitimacy and succession. Because the state was independent of the social classes – being above the society – it did not enjoy a legitimacy comparable to European states. The absence of such a legitimacy rendered indeterminate the question of succession.

The issue of lack of legitimacy needs further explanation. As in the case of law and politics, there will always be a kind of legitimacy attached to the rule of even a tribal chief. The 'legitimacy' of an arbitrary ruler depends on his relative ability to keep the peace, put down rebellion and perform his other social and economic functions. But for all the reasons described above, it was not rooted in law, tradition and socio-political rights. In other words, rebellion was, in principle, as 'legitimate' as arbitrary rule, and the ultimate test of 'legitimacy' was in the ability to seize and maintain power. Rebels seldom became rulers through any legal or traditional right to rule, but because they succeeded in gaining power. It would be difficult to find counterparts in European history to Saboktegin, Nader, Karim Khan or Aqa Mohammad, let alone to Mahmud and Ashraf of the Ghalzeh tribe who were crowned after the fall of Safavid Isfahan.

Therefore, we speak not of the 'legitimacy' enjoyed by an Abbas I, because of his strong and successful government, which eluded a Soltan Hossein because of his feeble and incompetent rule, but of the legitimacy enjoyed by Louis XIV – the 'Sun King' and absolutist French ruler who, according to legend, once claimed 'L'état c'est moi' – which even Abbas I did not possess.[5]

The possession of 'God's Grace' (*Farrah-ye Izadi*), sometimes literally translated as *Divine Effulgence* legitimized the position of ancient Iranian rulers in the heroic and legendary as well as historical ages. A close study of the subject in Ferdawsi's *Shahnameh* has shown that the grace was bestowed on the person of the ruler, and it was not necessary for him to be first in line of succession.[6] For example, Kaikhosraw succeeded his grandfather Kaikavus in preference to his uncle Fariborz, because he was believed to hold the grace. For the same reason, the claim of Tus – army commander-in-chief and grandson of a former Shah – was brushed aside.[7]

In some cases (as in those of Feraidun, Bahman and Ardashir Babakan) the grace was revealed through feats of supernatural acts performed by its holder. For example, Faridun's magical passage, in his campaign against Zahhak, through the River Ervand (Tigris). Or Kaikhosraw's magical passage (together with his mother Farangis, and his brother Behzad in the shape of a black horse) through the Oxus, while running away from his grandfather Afrasiyab, and the account of his magical conquest of Dezh-e Bahman (Bahman Fortress) all of which proved his possession of God's Grace. These examples belong to the early, heroic and mythological periods of the *Shahnameh*. The best and most elaborate example from the historical period is when the Grace accompanies Ardashir Babakan – and this time in *physical form, in the form of a ram* – while he is running away from Ardavan.[8] But in most other cases it was not clear how the grace was acquired by the ruler except by virtue of succeeding to win power. He who ruled must have had the grace because he held the reins of power: *post hoc ergo propter hoc*. It is noteworthy that not only Iranian but also Turanian rulers, such as Afrasiyab, were held to possess the grace.[9]

The term 'Farrah' (Grace) was also used to confirm the divine legitimacy of post-Islamic rulers (for example, by Ferdawsi in the case of Mahmud),[10] but its content and implications were later expressed more often in such titles as 'Shadow of the Almighty' and 'Pivot of the Universe'. The Qur'anic verse which orders the believer to obey 'God, the Prophet, *and the holders of authority (ul al-'Amr) among you'* (emphasis added) and was often invoked to legitimize earthly rule, is ambiguous, and has been subject to various conflicting interpretations.[11] However, it is not clear from the text itself how the legitimacy bestowed by God's command to a ruler may be known except by virtue of the fact that he holds authority. Therefore, from the point of view of the subject, its implications are similar to those of the concept of God's Grace.

It is clear that, however the grace may have been acquired, the Shah was God's vicegerent on earth and his will extended beyond human limits. That is, his rule was divinely ordained, and he was legitimate by virtue of God's Grace. He was not bound by any earthly contract. His legitimacy was not even derived from primogeniture or some other established rule of succession. He was above, and not just at the head of, the society.

Succession almost invariably presented a problem. It was never clear who would succeed to the throne after the ruler's death. The Shah himself might have his own candidate, usually one of his sons, though not necessarily the eldest. But this did not guarantee his succession because there was no legal sanction behind it. For example, Mahmud of Ghazneh nominated his younger son Mohammad and did everything he could before his own death to ensure his succession. Shortly after Mohammad succeeded, his elder brother Mas'ud, the governor of Isfahan, rebelled, fought and defeated him and thereby became the legitimate successor.[12]

The problem persisted down to the nineteenth century. Fath'ali Shah chose his grandson Mohammad Mirza as his successor after the death of his son

Abbas Mirza, the Prince Regent and Mohammad's father. Yet some of Mohammad's uncles rebelled against him when he succeeded to the throne.[13] Later, Mohammad Shah himself favoured his younger son Abbas Mirza (Molk Ara) in preference to his eldest son, Naser al-Din, the heir-designate. When the latter managed to succeed his father, the nine-year-old Abbas Mirza would have lost his life, or been blinded, if foreign envoys had not intervened on his behalf. But his court was looted on official orders, and he spent much of his life as a refugee in Mesopotamia and Russia. Permission for him to go to Mesopotamia as an exile was obtained as a result of persistent interventions of both the Russian and particularly the British ministers in Tehran to stop him being killed at the age of thirteen by his brother the Shah, on the mere supposition that he might be regarded as their alternative candidate for the throne by some unknown, imagined intriguers.

The correspondence between the two foreign envoys and the chief minister makes fascinating reading. At one stage, when the British minister wrote that they should not sacrifice 'fairness' to mere imagination (that there was a plot centred around the boy), the chief minister revealed the logic of arbitrary injustice by pointing out that in his country one should act on mere supposition, otherwise one may lose the game. This was so precisely because 'legitimacy' always belonged to the winner. The chief minister wrote that he had reported the British minister's letter to the Shah. The Shah had agreed that the British minister meant well, but had added that:

> Your excellency must pay attention to some peculiar Iranian customs
> and traditions and realize that, in Iran, the things that your excellency
> has in mind will not work, and one cannot be immune from the evil
> intent of seditious and rebellious people. If the leaders of the Iranian
> state wish to act on the basis of fairness and justice to maintain order
> and security for all their subjects, *they would have no choice but at the slightest
> thought, imagination or supposition of rebellion, irrespective of who it might be, to try
> to put it down forthwith and not to hesitate even for a moment.*[14]

As it turned out, the problem of royal succession eventually came to an end as a result of British guarantees of the succession of the heir-designate to the throne.

Nevertheless, it is extremely instructive that Naser al-Din Shah – who was by no means the worst example of an arbitrary ruler of Iran – almost withdrew the right of succession from his son and heir-designate, Mozaffar al-Din Mirza (the governor-general of Azebaijan), and sold it to his other son, Zel al-Soltan, the governor-general of Isfahan. He wrote to the former that the latter had offered him two Persian crores (roughly one million tomans) for the position. Zel was well known both for his shrewdness and lack of scruple. Mozaffar was lucky, therefore, that in reply to his father the Shah, his able secretary, Amir Nezam Garrusi, warned that Zel might well spend another ten crores for the Shah's position itself. It was, of course, an open secret that Zel was doing

everything possible (including offering subservience to the British) to overthrow his father.[14a] But regarding the implications for our theory, there could be
no better evidence than, little more than a hundred years ago, it was quite
normal for the Shah to sell the succession for money.

This being the case, it is not surprising that there was so much filicide, fratri-
cide and parricide within the royal household. Apart from outright killing, the
blinding and/or permanent incarceration of princes within the women's
compound (*Haram* or *Andarun*) was a favourite Safavid device. It was from the
Andarun that Shah Safi emerged to claim the throne of his grandfather, Abbas I,
and ruled with exemplary cruelty. And it would not take much imagination to
think of the magnitude of insecurity in which ministers, chieftains and magnates
lived and worked – and sometimes died. The familiar story, from ancient to
modern times, of the long line of powerful persons who (alone or together with
their family and clan) perished on the order of their rulers, told in detail, would
fill several volumes of chilling history. With regard to our theory, however, the
most important point is that, irrespective of whether they were prince, minister,
or army commander, there was no procedure, no hearing, no defence, no law
when they fell. To incur the Shah's displeasure, suspicion and wrath was all that
was necessary for their destruction.

It follows, therefore, that rebellion, when it succeeded, was as legitimate as
the state. In Ferdawsi's *Shahnameh,* when an 'unjust' ruler is about to fall, we are
informed that he has lost the Grace, whereas there are other 'unjust' rulers who
do not fall at all. In other words, the ruler is deemed to have lost the Grace by
virtue of being overthrown, and the successor or rebel to have gained it by
virtue of his victory.

The ideal concept of the 'Just Ruler' (in the Islamic period, *Malek-e Adel*)
became the test of the ruler's legitimacy. There can be no clear and precise
notion of justice without reference to a legal framework. In its absence, justice
may be perceived to exist only in relation to the existing social expectations. The
evidence shows that the just ruler corresponding to the ideal concept was one
who ran the country well, maintained peace and security within as well as
without his realm, employed able officials and governors (and punished them
for injustice, that is, for actions not permitted by the ruler himself), and thus
promoted peace and prosperity.[15] Khosraw I (Anushiravan) in ancient times and
Abbas I in the sixteenth century are perhaps the best prototypes of the 'Just
Ruler' in that sense, although hardly in any other sense. The unjust ruler,
however, was contrary to that, and therefore rebellion against him was
legitimate. But many unjust rulers were not overthrown, and so – in theory –
they still had the Grace and remained Shadow of the Almighty.

At this point we should make brief reference to the period of absolutist or
despotic 'New Monarchies' in Europe. For the continent as a whole this lasted
about four centuries, though it had an appreciably shorter lifespan in its western
parts – specifically England, France and Prussia, but also the Austrian (Holy
Roman) empire because of its highly decentralized nature.

The power of the absolute ruler was based in law. The strong absolute ruler exercised extensive powers in laying down the law by virtue of the 'royal prerogative'. But there were definite limits to the royal prerogative, and the king (or queen) was not entirely free from legal bond and constraint. Whatever his personal motives for reforming the church, Henry VIII's Reformation in the sixteenth century was wholeheartedly approved by the English parliament,[16] as were the religious settlements of his daughter Elizabeth I, who was probably the most powerful absolute ruler in the history of England.[17] Absolute government in England was severely checked at the Restoration of Charles II, after the English civil wars and revolution of 1641–60, and came to a complete end in the Glorious Revolution of 1688, which overthrew James II and established William and Mary on the throne.[18]

In France, where absolute monarchy was established roughly with the reign of Francis I (Henry VIII's contemporary), it took almost a century and a long period of religious and civil war – with the houses of Guise and Bourbon each claiming the throne of the Valois – until the Bourbon Henry IV re-established peace, religious tolerance and absolute government at the turn of the seventeenth century.[19] His early assassination by a Catholic fanatic, and the succession of his very young and feeble son, led to further turmoil until the able, strong and dedicated Cardinal Richelieu built the French state and ruthlessly imposed absolute government.[20] Yet his death, which was followed by that of Louis XIII, led to the Regency of Queen Anne and Cardinal Mazarin, which was seriously threatened by the revolts (known as the *frondes*) of the 'forces of feudal anarchy', led by the great aristocratic magnates and the *parlement* (judicial authorities) of Paris.[21] Only when Louis XIV began his direct rule after Mazarin's death did he manage to re-establish absolutist Bourbon rule, which, while declining in force, continued until the French Revolution of 1789.[22]

Far from lacking a social base, the absolute monarchies extended it to the lower gentry and the bourgeoisie, and became known as protectors of the 'people' from the power of the aristocratic magnates. The aristocracy and many of their rights and privileges remained, but they lost some of their power and it became easier for lower orders to join their ranks. Private ownership of land remained as strong as ever, and in capital it became much stronger than before. Church law was observed, and the church retained much, though not all, of its power and privileges. Judicial processes – which included the prerogative courts – were respected, and any act of doubtful legality by the state was the exception which proved the rule. It occasionally led to massive revolts, as in the case of the English civil wars and revolution.[23] In no sense, therefore, did *estebdad* or arbitrary rule exist in the European absolutist state, although in Russia the absolute ruler wielded much more power than in other parts of Europe.

The theory of the Divine Right of Kings was developed in the sixteenth and particularly seventeenth centuries as the basis for the legitimacy of absolute monarchy. There were many, sometimes conflicting, versions of this theory. In general, they cited the divinely ordained kingship of biblical rulers such as David as the source of their argument (Filmer being an important exception to this), but it is sometimes believed that their real model was that of ancient Persian kingship, which they knew about from classical European sources.[24] Yet the divine right theory is neither the same as the Persian God's Grace theory, nor is the practice of absolute monarchy similar to arbitrary government. James I of England came closest to the God's Grace theory when he wrote that kings were God's vicegerents on earth.[25] And in a conflict with the judges of the prerogative court he wrote that to put in doubt what belonged to the 'mystery' of the king's power was against the law.[26]

Yet the very fact that he had to argue with judges about his prerogatives, and even to invoke 'the Law' against them, gives the lie to any supposition of the right of arbitrary rule. Besides, James himself was emphatic about the rule of primogeniture as the basis of his own legitimacy, and his son Charles I took his stand in 1649 against his revolutionary accusers solely on the basis of the law of the land. He soon became known as the Martyred King, because his trial and execution had been unlawful.[27]

Thesis 10

Lack of recourse to independent judicial procedures – outside the civil and criminal cases in which the Shah and his officials had no interest – led to the development of the tradition of intervention by great officials, the Shah's or governor's favourites, or indeed leading religious divines, in order to save the lives, limbs and/or property of those who had fallen victim to the suspicion and/or wrath of arbitrary rulers. A tradition also emerged of taking sanctuary or *bast* in a sacred place, although, under the Qajars, even the royal stables were sometimes used as sanctuary for relatively minor cases. These traditions were sometimes effective in preventing or reducing the scale of punishment. At other times, however, they were of little or no use, as in the case of Nader Shah's blinding of his eldest son, or Naser al-Din's summary execution of the ten or twelve young soldiers who had demonstrated in demand of their unpaid wages. There can be numerous examples, and, like some of the other theses presented in this chapter, a detailed study of this one alone could run into volumes.[27a]

Thesis 11

Arbitrary rulers and states sometimes fell as a result of palace Coups, massive revolts or foreign invasions. Mention has already been made of palace Coups, the fear of which took a toll of potential successors. Foreign invasion has been a common cause of the fall of the state in all societies. But in Iran, invasions were not seriously resisted, and were sometimes even invited and supported, if the ruler was believed to be unjust or simply doomed. For example, Baihaqi says that the people of (Greater) Khorasan invited the Seljuq of Transoxiana, who came and conquered it with their support, because the Ghaznavid governor systematically plundered 'both the rich and the poor', and sent half his booty to the court so that he would not be dismissed for unjust behaviour against the people of the province.[28]

Local revolts usually spread and proliferated when the degree of perceived injustice was felt to be beyond endurance, and the chance of success reasonably good. Since the arbitrary state had no permanent or traditional social base (and no legitimacy based in law), it was natural for many – of high as well as low status – to join the revolt, and for few (often including state officials) to resist it.

In Europe, massive rebellions divided the society itself. In the English civil wars and revolution some social classes and regions of the country sided with the king, and others with the parliament (although, of course, such divisions were not entirely neat). And after the king was defeated, the Presbyterians, the House of Lords and most of the Commons (and the people and classes they represented) parted company with the Puritans (or Independents), the Army and the Levellers long before the revolution was over.[29]

In the early stages of the French Revolution (1789–99), Louis enjoyed considerable legitimacy and support. Radicalization alienated constitutional monarchists such as Lafayette and Barnave, and later led to the fall of the Girondins and even of 'moderate' Jacobins like Danton, until the Thermidorians overthrew the radical purists led by Robespierre and put the *Directoire* in power. In Russia, the whole of the opposition was united in the February revolution, but the October Revolution which followed it rapidly led to the alienation of the Kadets, the Mensheviks and the right Social Revolutionaries, not to mention the Tsarist aristocracy and upper bourgeoisie. The Bolsheviks had to fight three years of massive and bloody civil war to defeat the opposition and the social classes they represented.[30]

The point is that in these revolutions, firstly, there was a massive revolt against the existing law and social order in order to establish new ones. In the case of England it is true that Charles had misused the law, but when the revolutionaries tried and executed him they put themselves outside the existing legal framework; secondly, the society was divided along recognizable lines for and against the revolution; and thirdly, the revolt was not only intended to overthrow an unpopular or unjust regime, but to replace it with a new constitutional structure, about which there was disagreement among the revolutionary parties depending on their socioeconomic background and interest.

In the absence of detailed studies of at least the more important Iranian revolts and rebellions (there is little reliable historical evidence for many of them), it would be difficult to formulate a general theory of revolutions in Iran.[30a] Yet it can be observed with confidence that the basic features of European revolutions as outlined above would not apply in their case: there was no established law to rebel against, much less to replace with by a different legal framework; the society was not divided between the state's socioeconomic base (which it represented) and the opponents of that base. Instead, the basic aim of the revolt was to bring down an 'unjust' ruler or state, and replace it by another which would be hopefully 'just' or less 'unjust'. They were not revolts by a part of the society against the rest; they were revolts of the society (*mellat*) against the state (*dawlat*). There was conflict between as well as within the social classes as in any other society. But the most fundamental dichotomy – even antagonism – was between the state on the one hand, and the society on the other.[31]

There were great differences between traditional Iranian revolts and the two revolutions in the twentieth century, the Constitutional Revolution and the revolution of 1977–79. There were also important differences between these two revolutions. Yet they shared the basic features of traditional Iranian revolts: both were massive uprisings of the urban social classes – almost irrespective of occupation, rank, wealth and income, education or degree of religious commitment – against the state. Peasant participation, where and when it occurred, was merely a function of the urban movement and leadership, as had been true of traditional revolts as well. Moreover, although (contrary to the past) there were more or less clear objectives, or more accurately, slogans, for replacing the existing state – constitutional monarchy, democracy, republic, Islamic government, and so on – the collective energy expended over the negative programme of bringing the state down at any cost was far stronger, and its social bond more cohesive. It is well known that during the revolution of 1977–79, when the modern-educated activists and sympathisers were questioned about their programme and the chances of its success, they responded by saying 'let him [the Shah] go, and let there be flood afterwards'.[32]

Thesis 12

The history of arbitrary rule is therefore punctuated by palace Coups, periodic rebellions and occasionally massive revolts, which may or may not have been successful. But when they were, the breakdown and fall of the state resulted in general disorder, the division of arbitrary power and its exercise by one party against another and by all parties against society. As with feudal and capitalist states and societies, an arbitrary state represented an arbitrary society. Indeed, unaccountable state and ungovernable society are two sides of the same coin.

In a European revolution, when the existing state was overthrown, its particular law ceased to be binding, but the sense of law as such, and the idea of legal propriety (albeit according to a new code of conduct) did not altogether vanish. But the fall of the state in an arbitrary society was a licence to any and all who had a certain amount of power to use it in an arbitrary way. Hence, a single centre of arbitrary power was replaced by many, resulting in much greater insecurity and lawlessness in the society. The repetitive looting and destruction of Isfahan by conflicting forces after the fall of the Safavid state is a well-documented example of such disparate and uncontrolled use of arbitrary power.

Given the generalised lawlessness – reminiscent of the Hobbesian concept of the state of nature – it is not surprising that, within a short space of time, the society felt nostalgic about the loss of stability under the former regime, and prayed for the rise of a 'strong man' who would put an end to the use of divided and disorganized arbitrary power, and bring peace, stability and better material standards by establishing a new arbitrary state. Despite the ruthlessness and cruelty with which Aqa Mohammad Khan founded the Qajar state, the people – and especially the humblest among them – were grateful to him for bringing an end to the devastating disorder and insecurity of many decades in the eighteenth century. It was nothing new: Am'aq Bokhara'i, the classic poet, had observed several centuries earlier that long years of harsh government were better than a few years of chaos.

The history of arbitrary society is thus characterized by the cycle of an arbitrary state, overthrown by rebellion and being replaced by disorder and chaos, until a new state brings this to an end and restores arbitrary rule.[33]

Thesis 13

The concentration of arbitrary power was not necessarily accompanied by centralization of the state administration. For example, it is well known that there was no extensive countrywide or centrally organized bureaucratic network in Qajar Iran.[34]

To begin with, administrative centralization is itself relative to given systems of government. It is probably true that even the liberal democratic, let alone totalitarian, states of the twentieth century were in many senses more interventionist and centralized than many of the arbitrary or absolutist states of the past. Generally, this has been the result of great changes in technology, social organization and political programmes in the recent past. That aside, however, there is no reason why concentration of power must necessarily result in central bureaucratic organization, intervention and control.

The association of concentration of power with bureaucratic centralization is (vaguely) based on the experience of absolutist states, or 'New Monarchies', which replaced the feudal states of Europe, and which, relative to the feudal period, were often more centralized. But there has been much exaggeration about administrative centralization in absolutist states. As Emile Lousse has succinctly put it:

> Absolutism does not invariably entail the centralization of power and administration. To be sure, it favours centralization and uses it, and centralization is itself consonant with its interests. But the one can exist without the other. Absolutism adjusts perfectly well to a federal state, or to a simple commonwealth with a monarchial constitution, as Spain, Austria and Prussia were until the end of the *ancien regime* ... It is in some cases only, and even then only in a specific period, as for example in France, that absolutism and centralization advance side-by-side ... [Yet], the high point of administrative centralization in France is not reached during the period of absolute monarchy at all, but after its demise. In the case of France – the

most favourable example so far – royal absolutism is an important but an intermediary stage in the evolution of centralization.[35]

J. Russell Major carefully distinguishes between the Renaissance and the seventeenth- and eighteenth-century states:

> I have described the Renaissance Monarchy as being a decentralized state with confused boundaries and jurisdictions, but motivated by the force of dynasticism, legality and tradition. Its strength lay not in the size or loyalty of its army, but rather in the support of its people ... Medieval decentralization was derived largely from the activities of the great feudal nobles and their vassals. Renaissance decentralization was essentially bureaucratic ... The break between the Renaissance Monarchy and that of the late seventeenth and eighteenth centuries is more pronounced. Dynastic politics did not completely disappear, but national and economic considerations became more important. Armies became larger and the kings won effective control over them.[36]

The same basic principle applies to the arbitrary state. The hallmark of the arbitrary state is that power is concentrated and used arbitrarily, although the state may not be centralized and interventionist. The provincial governor who was appointed to run the affairs of the province used his power just as arbitrarily, within the general norms set by the central ruler, and could be sacked or punished. He did not have freedom of action in an autonomous way, outside the general policy of the state. There did not have to be direct bureaucratic centralization.

Some Iranian states were centralized in a manner which was relative to the prevailing technology and the cost of transport and communications. Others were not. The Achaemenid, Sassanian and Safavid states are examples of the former; the Arscid, Seljuq, Zand and Qajar, of the latter. Apart from differences in technology, many factors explain the relative differences in the degree of their administrative centralization. The Arscid state – usually regarded as being philhellenic – might have been particularly influenced by the tradition of the Alexandrian Greek states in Western Asia, including Iran. There can be little doubt that their administration was looser and less centralized than the Achaemenid state before them, and the Sassanian state after. They were described by early Arab historians after the advent of Islam as the *Muluk al-Tawa'if*, which may be roughly translated as 'rulers of the [various] communities'.

Regarding the implications of the term itself, it could describe any multi-ethnic or multi-national state or empire, although the decentralized character of the Arscid state may have had something to do with it. At the turn of the present century the term was used by the Iranian intelligentsia to describe the Qajar realm, which was also a decentralized arbitrary state. It is very likely that an important reason behind bureaucratic decentralization under the Qajars was the high cost of bureaucratic centralization, in view of the decline of the country's economic fortunes since the eighteenth century.

However, the European term 'feudalism' was then translated into the '*Muluk al-Tawa'ifi* system'. At one stroke, this gave rise to three eventful confusions: thatEuropean feudalism was such a system; that Iran had always been a decentralized state; that Iran had been a feudal society throughout its history.[37]

The point, in a word, is that – centralized or not – Iran was always an arbitrary state and society.

Thesis 14

There remains the question of the origin of the arbitrary state. In this connection, two basic points should be raised: firstly, the theory sketched above explaining the basic features of the arbitrary state and society is completely independent of any theory (or knowledge) of the factors which brought it about; and secondly, it is notoriously difficult, if not foolhardy, to supply definitive answers to such massive historical questions, partly because of the great paucity of reliable evidence. Subject to these important qualifications, the following hypothesis seems reasonable.

Aridity probably played a basic role in shaping the structure of the Iranian political economy. There are two main reasons for this. Firstly, it served to create isolated and autonomous village units of production, none of which could produce a sufficiently large surplus to provide a feudal power base; and secondly, given the expanses of the region, the collective surplus of all or most of the isolated villages was so large that, once taken by an 'external force', it could be used as the economic base of a countrywide arbitrary state or empire.

The arbitrary system could then be used to prevent the subsequent fragmentation of power until such time as a combination of internal and/or external pressures would destroy it and replace it with another state. The size of the direct and indirect collective agricultural surplus was so large as to enable the state to retain the monopoly of power, and to prevent the later emergence of feudal autonomy in agriculture, or bourgeois citizenship in towns. Apart from that, it created its own pre-legal and pre-political culture which – as in the case of other systems anywhere – grew their own independent roots in the society through time, and provided powerful cultural and 'superstructural' explanations and justifications for their existence.

This martial and mobile force was originally provided by invading nomads, and thereafter both by the existing and the incoming nomads who succeeded in setting up strong and arbitrary states, and who almost invariably gave way to their successors (in the end) through a short, sharp and general upheaval: the Medes, the Persians (Achaemenids), the Greeks (Seleucids), the Parthians (Arscids), the Persian Sassanians, the Muslim Arabs, the Ghaznavid Turks, the Seljuq Turks, the Ilkhan Mongols, the Teimurid Turks, the Safavid Turkamans, the Afsharid Tukamans, Zand Lor-Persians, and the Qajar Turkamans.[38]

Twentieth-century Iran

In the following chapters, the above theory will be applied to a close study of state and society in Iran from the Constitutional Revolution to the abdication of Reza Shah. However, for a variety of theoretical and practical reasons, it will be useful to end this chapter with a short application of the theory to the history of twentieth century Iran.

The Constitutional Revolution was the first general upheaval in the history of Iran which, in contrast to past revolts against arbitrary rulers, not only intended to bring down a given arbitrary rule but also had a clear positive programme – suggested by an awareness of the experience of Europe – of ending such rule altogether and replacing it by the rule of law in the form of a constitutional monarchy. It eventually succeeded by establishing a constitution which, in addition to providing a legal basis for the state (as opposed to ancient arbitrary rule) created parliamentary government along basic democratic principles. It benefited both the landlords and the commercial classes by securing the basis of their property ownership, and by affording them a large amount of political power, as opposed to mere privileges (see also chapter two).

Ideally, this could have resulted in the formation of a new state representing a powerful social base. Yet the radically new situation had no cultural roots, and the ancient traditions of chaos resulting from the fall of the state were as strong as ever. Therefore, the years which followed the victory of the revolution witnessed growing division and instability both at the centre and in the provinces, such that a cool observer might have predicted the complete disintegration and fragmentation of the country, as had happened after the fall of the Safavid state in the eighteenth century. Increasing foreign – especially Russian but also British – intervention had much to do with this, and the activities of the armies and agents of Russia, Turkey, Britain and Germany during the First World War greatly strengthened the process towards disintegration (see chapter three).

Nevertheless, domestic factors in favour of the disintegrative trends were also at work, and had their roots in the long tradition of disorders following upheavals. The fall of an arbitrary rule had always been followed by chaos until another strong (and arbitrary) state was formed to bring domestic peace and security. Thus, although the intervention of alien powers played a very important role, the pattern was familiar, and the domestic forces of destructive conflict needed little encouragement to bring chaos to the country. These were not just nomadic, ethnic and regional; they existed at the centre as well, in the Majlis, among the factions and parties, and within the ranks of the competing political magnates.

The rule of law (*hokumat-e qanun*), constitutional monarchy (*saltanat-e mashruteh*) and even democracy (*hokumat-e melli*) had apparently been established. Yet the public response was similar to the age-old pattern of the fall of an arbitrary government followed by the arbitrary behaviour of the society at large. The terms law (*qanun*) and freedom (*azadi*) were used almost synonymously, because law was associated with freedom from arbitrary rule. Therefore, in practice, both law – and especially freedom – came to mean freedom from all restraint, that is, from the law itself. It was the (much more familiar) traditional practice clad in modern forms. That is how, much as it had happened in the past after the fall of a powerful ruler, nostalgia broke out for the strong rule of Naser al-Din, whom they now began to call the 'Martyr Shah' (*Shah-e Shahid*).[39]

It was this threat of civil war and disintegration more than any other factor which finally resulted in the 1921 Coup, even though it was helped and organized – without the British government's knowledge – by British officers and diplomats in Tehran (see chapters four to nine). The Coup was greeted with joy by modern nationalist intellectuals; and Reza Khan's military leadership, and later government, attracted a good deal of support from an even larger public because of the peace and stability which it brought (see chapter ten).

Seen from this angle, the foundation of the Pahlavi state was in line with the emergence of a strong state after chaos which had characterized Iranian upheavals throughout the country's history. If Reza Khan/Reza Shah's rule had remained firm, but basically constitutional, as in its early years, socioeconomic development would have taken place, and the history of twentieth century Iran would have been different. But, from the late 1920s, power was exercised with increasing arbitrariness, not only alienating landlords and merchants, traditional politicians and young democrats, but even the state's own bureaucratic and military chiefs (see chapter eleven).

In 1941, Reza Shah's rule was ended by the invading allies. Had he had a reasonably strong and committed social base, however, his abdication would have been both unnecessary and unlikely, as he was then prepared to cooperate with Britain and Russia (see chapter 11, below).[40]

The years 1941–53 were once again a period of interregnum, displaying the same old tendencies towards social and political upheaval after the fall of an arbitrary regime. If the foreign powers had not been there, first in full force, then by force of influence, it is likely that there would have been much greater chaos than was in fact experienced. Yet the same trends which always followed the fall of a strong state were present, not least in the capital and within the Majlis itself. Freedom, once again, meant destructive conflict and absence of restraint. A growing number of people began to wish that another Reza Shah would restore order and discipline, and only six years after his abdication amid public rejoicing, the fifteenth Majlis passed a private members' bill that he should be officially described as Reza Shah the Great. Mosaddeq's popular government, at least in its first 18 months, created a strong sense of public solidarity if only because the main adversary was foreign, although even in that period destructive conflict was still much in evidence. This was followed by a much wider and more powerful domestic struggle in which the forces opposed to the popular government were eventually helped and organized by the American and British governments to bring it down in the 1953 Coup.[41]

This led to an authoritarian or dictatorial, but not arbitrary, government whose main power base was the landlords and the religious establishment. There was therefore a significant degree of political participation and constitutional restraint. This did not take long. Within a few years power began to become concentrated, but the process was interrupted by the economic crisis of 1959–60, just at the time when the regime had lost the goodwill of the Soviet Union and the undivided support of the United States. The failure of attempts to initiate democratic control, and even mere participation at the level of the first few years after the 1953 Coup, led to the riots of June 1963 which were put down with considerable severity.

From 1963 to 1977, power became concentrated at an accelerating rate because all opposition had been defeated, oil revenues were accruing to the state at a rapidly increasing (and later exponential) rate, and foreign powers, Western as well as Soviet and Eastern European, became more and more uncritical towards the regime, not least because of the absence of an organized opposition and the increasing oil wealth. When in 1977, at the height of such domestic power and foreign support, a combination of economic dislocation and foreign criticism led the regime to allow a certain amount of political openness, this quickly led to its downfall by early 1979. There was a massive revolt, true to the ancient pattern, of the society against the state. No social class resisted the revolution, and no organized political force defended the regime.[42]

It is difficult to know how the chaos and destructive conflict which followed the victory of the revolt would have come to an end had there not been a long foreign war to establish and consolidate the exclusive power of the Islamic state. But many of those who actively supported the revolution gradually came to regret it, and large numbers of people began to refer to Mohammad Reza Shah as 'The Blessed One' (*Khoda Biyamorz*). The pattern was indeed familiar.[43] Yet the presidential election of May 1997 has led to trends for political dialogue across both the Islamist and non-Islamist spectrum. And if this is not bought to an abrupt end either by traditions of arbitrary rule, or by traditions of chaos, and persists over a reasonably long period towards a lawful and tolerant society, it may be the beginning of a fundamentally new era in Iranian history.[44]

Notes

*   This chapter is a revised and extended version of the author's paper of the same title published in *British Journal of Middle Eastern Studies*, 24 (1), 1997.

1   See his travelogue *Safarnameh-ye Naser Khosraw*, Raynold Nicholson (ed.), (Tehran: Donya-ye Ketab, 1982), p. 138.

2   Theses 1–4 above have been discussed and documented at some length in the author's following works: 'The Aridisolatic Society, A Model of Long Term Social and Economic Development in Iran', *International Journal of Middle East Studies* (July 1983), pp. 259–81; *The Political Economy of Modern Iran* (London and New York: Macmillan and New York University Press, 1981); 'Radd-e Olguy-e Bardehdari-Feodalism-Kapitalism dar Tahavvolat-e Jameh'eh-ye Iran', *Payam-e Emruz* (July 1994), reprinted in the author's *Chahardah Maqaleh dar Adabiyat, Ejtima', Falsafeh va Eqtesad* (Tehran: Nashr-e Markaz, second

edition, 1996); 'Tarh-e Kutahi as Nazariyeh-ye Estebdad-e Tarikhi-ye Iran' and 'Estebdad, Hokumat-e Qanun ...' in *Estebdad, Demokrasi va Nehzat-e Melli* (Tehran: Nashr-e Markaz, second edition, 1996); the author's introduction to the second edition of *Eqtesad-e Siyasi-ye Iran*, M. Nafissi and K. Azizi (trans.), fifth impression (Tehran: Nashr-e Markaz, 1996), pp. 5–41; *Musaddiq and the Struggle for Power in Iran* (London and New York: I.B.Tauris, 1990). For a scholarly study of the systems of land assignment and tax farming, see A.K.S. Lambton, *Landlord and Peasant in Persia* (London: Oxford University Press, 1953; reissued London and New York: I.B.Tauris, 1991). For different responses to the theory of arbitrary state, see John Foran, 'The Modes of Production Approach to Seventeenth-century Iran', *International Journal of Middle East Studies* (August 1988), and *A Century of Revolution* (Minneapolis: University of Minnesota Press, 1994); Abbas Vali, *Pre-capitalist Iran* (London and New York: I.B.Tauris, 1993). For an alternative explanation for lack of capitalist development in Iran, see Ahmad Ashraf, 'Historical Obstacles to the Development of a Bourgeoisie in Iran' in M. A. Cook (ed.), *Studies in the Economic History of the Middle East* (London: Oxford University Press, 1970).

3   Mostashar al-Dawleh was much more of a reformist than a revolutionary. His concept of law – similar to that of early loyal reformers such as his mentor Mirza Hossein Khan Sepahsalar – was meant to bring order and discipline as well as responsibility to the administration of the state. See Abdollah Mostawfi, *Sharh-e Zendegani-ye Man*, vol. 1 (Tehran: Zavvar, 1981), pp. 120–27. The failure of this reformist attempt later led to the radicalization of the campaign for the rule of law. Thus, it was to evolve, first in emphasis, then in substance, from the establishment of official order and discipline to the attainment of freedom from arbitrary rule, constitutional monarchy, popular sovereignty, and even (ultimately) freedom from the state itself, i.e. the traditional Iranian chaos as the antithesis of arbitrary government.

4   *Politique* is both noun and adjective: it means both 'politics' and 'political'.

5   See H. Katouzian, 'Barayeh Inkeh Bahaneh-yi Namanad', in *Payam-e Emruz* (September 1995).

6   See H. Katouzian, 'Farrah-ye Izadi va Haqq-e Elahi-ye Padshahan', *Ettela't-e Siyasi-Eqtesadi*, 12, 9 and 10, July 1998.

7   See Ferdawsi's *Shahdameh*, Sa'id Nafissi (ed.), vol. 3 (Tehran: Berukhim, 1935), pp. 752–54.

8   See, *ibid.*, vol. 1, for the story of Feraidun, and vol. 3 for those of Kaikhosarw. See vol. 7 for the case of Ardashir Babakan, and *Karnameh-ye Ardashir Babakan*, translated from the Pahlavi original by Sadeq Hedayat, in *Zand-e Vohuman Yasn* (Tehran: Amir Kabir, 1963), pp. 179–81.

9   Ferdawsi, *Shahnameh*, vol. 4, p. 1029, and vol. 5, pp. 1290–91.

10 *Ibid.*, vol. 6, p. 1554.

11 See also A.K.S. Lambton, 'Islamic Political Thought', in Joseph Schacht and C.E. Bosworth (eds), *The Legacy of Islam*, 2nd edition (Oxford: University Press, 1972).

12 See Ali Akbar Fayyaz (ed.), *Tarikh-e Baihaqi* (Mashhad: The University Press, 1971); also H. Katouzian, 'The Execution of Amir Hasanak the Vazir', *Pembroke Papers*, 1990, pp. 73–88.

13 See for example Mehdi Bamdad, *Sharh-e Hal-e Rejal-e Iran*, vols 1–6 (Tehran: Zavvar, 1992), on the killing, blinding and/or imprisonment of his brothers and uncles, either because of their open rebellion or because of mere suspicion against them. See for example the entries, in vol. 1, for Hasan Ali Mirza (p. 377), Khosraw Mirza (p. 485) and Jahangir Mirza (p. 284), but there were a few others as well. Mohammad Shah also had his able minister, Mirza Abolqasem Khan, the younger Qa'em-maqam, suddenly arrested and strangled to death a few months after mounting the throne with the latter's indispensable help. This incident is famous. What is not so well known is that Qa'em-maqam had also played a leading role in the demise of those princes, whether guilty or merely suspected. It must be emphasised that Mohammmad Shah was one of the least bloodthirsty of all Iranian rulers. Indeed, he displayed strong Sufi sympathies.

See Abdolhossein Nava'i, *Iran va Jahan,* vol. 2 (Tehran: Homa, 1990) which, together with its first volume (1987), is a very good single source on specific instances of arbitrary government over a long period. For just one significant example, see vol. 2, pp. 147–50. It recounts that when Isma'il I, the founder of the Safavid State, entered Tabriz without resistance, he nevertheless massacred 'his opponents' and plundered the city. And in order to avenge his father, Shaikh Haidar, he had the corpses of his dead opponents exhumed, and set fire to them in public, together with the bodies of 200 prostitutes and 400 thieves whom he had ordered to be slaughtered for the purpose. When he came to Tabriz the second time, he ordered twelve of the city's prettiest boys (who must have been from the upper classes) to be rounded up. He then raped them all personally, and turned them over to his generals to do the same. It goes without saying, of course, that not only were these acts religiously sinful, but – much more significantly – they were in stark violation of Shari'a law. On the troubles over Mohammad Shah's succession, see also Mohammad Ebrahim Bastani Parizi, 'Asiya-ye haft sang' in *Asiya-ye Haft Sang* (Tehran: Donia-ye Ketab, 1988); and Denis Wright, *The Persians Amongst The English: Episodes in Anglo-Persian History* (London and New York: I.B. Tauris, 1985).

14   See Abdolhosain Nava'i (ed.), *Sharh-e Hal-e Abbas Mirza Molk Ara,* 2nd edition (Tehran: Babak, 1982). The letters have been published from the Iranian archives in Abbas Eqbal-e Ashtiyani's introduction to the book; see pp. 29–31, emphasis added.

14a   See Bastani Parizi, *Asiya-ye Haft Sang,* p. 644.

15   The concept of the 'Just Ruler' is to be found, with some variations, in a few Persian classical texts, especially Ferdawsi's *Shahnameh* and Nezam al-Molk's *Siyasatnameh* (or *Siyar al-Muluk*). See also H. Katouzian, 'Demokrasi, diktatori va mas'uliyat-e mellat' in *Estabdad, Demokrasi va Mehzat-e Melli,* pp. 52–63.

16   See for example S.T. Bindoff, *Tudor England* (London: Pelican Books, 1952), chapter 3; Walter Cecil Richardson, 'The "New Monarchy" and Tudor Government', and Geoffrey Rudolph Elton, 'The Tudor Revolution: The Modern State is Formed', in Arthur J. Salvin (ed.) *The New Monarchies and Representative Assemblies: Medieval Constitutionalism or Modern Absolutism?* (Boston: D.C. Heath, 1964).

17   Bindoff, *Tudor England,* chapters 6 and 7.

18   See, for example, Maurice Ashley, *England in the Seventeenth Century* (London: Pelican Books, 1952), chapters 6, 7 and 12.

19   See for example H.A.L. Fisher, *A History of Europe, From the Earliest Times to 1713,* Vol. I (London: Fontana, 1964), chapters 30, 33 and 49; Herbert Butterfield *et al., A Short History of France,* Part 3, 'Centralization and Expansion' (Cambridge: University Press, 1959).

20   See for example C.V. Wedgwood, *Richelieu and the French Monarchy* (London: The English Universities Press, 1949).

21   See for example Arthur Hassall, *Mazarin* (London: Macmillan, 1903).

22   See for example Maurice Ashley, *Louis XIV and the Greatness of France* (London: The English Universities Press, 1946); David Ogg, *Louis XIV* (London: Oxford University Press, 1967).

23   See for example Heinz Lubasz (ed.), *The Development of the Modern State* (London: Macmillan, 1964); Perry Anderson, *Lineages of the Absolutist State* (London: New Left Books, 1974).

24   For a comprehensive study of the Divine Right of Kings, see John Neville Figgs, *The Divine Right of Kings* (Cambridge: Cambridge University Press, 1914). For a classical version of the theory, see Jacques Beningne Boussuet, 'The Divine Right of Kings' in William F. Church (ed.), *The Greatness of Louis XIV* (Boston: D.C. Heath, 1959). For arguments over the divine right theory among Robert Filmer, Algernon Sidney, John Locke *et al.,* see for example F.J. Hearnshaw (ed.) *The Social and Political Ideas of Some English Thinkers of the Augustan Age, 1650–1750* (London: Harrap, 1928), chapter 2 especially.

25   See C.H. McIlwain (ed.), *The Political Works of James I* (Cambridge, MA: 1918), p. 307.

26 *Ibid.*, p. 333.

27 See for example C.V. Wedgwood, *The Trial of Charles I* (London: World Books, 1964), especially chapters 6–13.

27a See for example Nava'i, *Iran va Jahan*, vols. 1 and 2; Mokhber al-Saltaneh, *Khaterat va Khatarat* (Tehran: Zavvar, 1984), and *Gozaresh-e Iran* (Tehran: Noqreh, 1984).

28 Ali Akbar Fayyaz, *Tarikh-e Baihaqi*, pp. 530–31.

29 See for example Maurice Ashley, *England in the Seventeenth Century*, chapters 6 and 7; C.V. Wedgwood, *The King's Peace 1637–1641* (London: Collins, 1955), *The King's War, 1641–1647* (London: Collins 1958), *The Trial of Charles I;* Christopher Hill, *The English Revolution*, 3rd edition (London: Lawrence & Wishart, 1955), and *The Century of Revolution, 1603–1714,* 2nd edition (London: Van Nostrand Reinhold (UK), 1988).

30 See for example E.L.Woodward, *French Revolutions* (London: Oxford University Press, 1965); Leo Gershoy, *The Era of the French Revolution (1789–1799)* (Princeton: D. van Nostrand, 1957), and *From Despotism to Revolution* (New York: Harper & Row, 1963); E. H. Carr, *The Bolshevik Revolution*, vols. 1–3 (London: Macmillan, 1951–1953).

30a See, nevertheless, H. Katouzian, 'Towards a General Theory of Iranian Revolutions, *Journal of Iranian Research and Analysis*, 15, 2, November 1999.

31 For the dichotomy of *mellat* and *dawlat*, see H. Katouzian, 'The Aridisolatic Society …', and 'Yaddashti darbareh-ye 'mellat', 'melli', 'melli-gara' va 'nasionalism' in *Estebdad, Demokrasi va Nehzat-e Melli*.

32 In Persian: 'In beravad va har cheh mikhahad beshavad.'

33 On the cycle of arbitrary rule-chaos-arbitrary rule, see also H. Katouzian, 'Demokrasi diktatori va mas'uliyat-e mellat'.

34 See also Ervand Abrahamian, 'Oriental Despotism: The Case of Qajar Iran', *International Journal of Middle East Studies* (1974), pp. 3–31.

35 Emile Lousse, 'Absolutism', in Heinz Lubasz (ed.), *The Development of the Modern State*, p. 44.

36 Russell Major, 'The Limitations of Absolutism in the "New Monarchies"', in Arthur J. Salvin (ed.), *The New Monarchies and Representative Assemblies: Medieval Constitutionalism or Modern Absolutism?* pp. 83–84.

37 See also H. Katouzian, 'The Aridisolatic Society …' and 'Farrah-ye Izadi va Haqq-e Elahi-ye Padshahan'.

38 See H. Katouzian, *ibid.*

39 See also Ervand Abrahamian, *Iran between two Revolutions*; John Foran (ed.), *A Century of Revolution*; Katouzian, *The Political Economy of Modern Iran*.

40 See also Homa Katouzian, 'Problems of Political Development in Iran: Democracy, Dictatorship or Arbitrary Government?', *British Journal of Middle Eastern Studies*, 22 (1995), pp. 5–20; *Musaddiq and the Struggle for Power in Iran* (London and New York: I.B. Tauris, second edition, 1999); and 'The Pahlavi Regime in Iran', in H.E. Chehabi and Juan J. Linz (eds.), *Sultanistic Regimes* (Baltimore and London: Johns Hopkins Press, 1998).

41 See also Fakhreddin Azimi, *Iran: The Crisis of Democracy, 1941–1953* (London and New York: I.B. Tauris and St Martin's Press, 1989); Katouzian, *Musaddiq and the Struggle for Power in Iran*.

42 For the history of the period as a whole see, for example, Abrahamian, *Iran Between Two Revolutions*; Foran, *A Century of Revolutions*; Nikki Keddie, with a section by Yann Richard, *Roots of Revolution* (New Haven and London: Yale University Press, 1981), and Katouzian, *The Political Economy of Modern Iran*.

43 For some analytical discussions of the revolution of 1977–79, see Katouzian, *The Political Economy of Modern Iran*, chapters 17 and 18, 'Problems of Political Development in Iran', and 'The Pahlavi Regime Iran'; Said Amir Arjomand, *The Turban for the Crown* (Oxford and New York: Oxford University Press, 1988). John Foran, *A Century of Revolution*, chapter 7; H.E. Chehabi, *Iranian Politics and Religious Modernism: The Liberation Movement of Iran under the Shah and Khomeini* (New York: Cornell University Press, 1990); Valentine

Moghadam, 'Iran: Development, Revolution and the Problem of Analysis', *Review of Radical Political Economics*, 16 (1984), pp. 227–40; and 'Populist Revolution and the Islamic State in Iran', in *Revolution in the World System*, Terry Boswell (ed.), (New York and London: Greenwood, 1989), pp. 147–63. Mansoor Moaddel, *Class, Politics and Ideology in the Iranian Revolution* (New York: Columbia University Press, 1993); Keddie, *Roots of Revolution*, Ch.9; Abrahamian, *Iran Between Two Revolutions*, chapter 11.

44 See also Katouzian, *Musaddiq and the Struggle for Power in Iran*, preface to the second edition.

2

Liberty and licence
*in the Constitutional Revolution**

This chapter discusses the Constitutional Revolution – its causes, agents and consequences – in the light of the theory of state and society suggested in the previous chapter. There will be no attempt to produce a detailed account of events, programmes and personalities because this has been done in various Persian and English works, both primary and secondary, some of which will be cited. Nevertheless, a short narrative is included as a reminder of the main ideas and events, classes and individuals involved on both sides of the movement.

Prelude to the revolt

As we have seen, it is characteristic of Iranian revolts and rebellions that they occur when the state is perceived to be weak and unable to enforce its authority. Naser al-Din Shah was an arbitrary ruler like all before him. But, as previously noted, the consequences of arbitrary rule were not all alike either for the ruler or for the country. Much depended on their personalities as well as on the circumstances of their rule. For example, the fall of the Safavid state and its dreadful consequences for Iranian society and economy were largely due to the personality of Shah Soltan Hossein, who combined extreme promiscuity and intemperance with superstition, susceptibility to influence, and timidity and indecisiveness at moments of crisis. Otherwise, the state would not have fallen so swiftly and miserably in the face of rebellion by some of the poorest and most backward nomads of the far eastern provinces of the empire.[1]

For all his love of women and hunting – neither of which was unusual among Iranian rulers – Naser al-Din was no Soltan Hossein. On the contrary, he was intelligent, self-confident, upright and strong.[2] The decline of the state – especially, though not exclusively, during the last three decades of his reign – was much more a result of the long-term trend of the rise of industry and empire in Europe than of any unusual weakness in his character. Throughout his reign he managed both to maintain and exert his authority in the centre and provinces and to preserve his dignity towards foreign powers. And he managed the

* This chapter is an extensively revised and edited version of 'Liberty and Licence in the Constitutional Revolution of Iran', *Journal of the Royal Asiatic Society*, 3, 8, 2, July 1998.

increasing weakness of Iran's political, economic and military power (compared to Europe) better than many other arbitrary rulers might have done.

The relative erosion of Naser al-Din's own authority towards the end of his reign was partly due to the publicly evident fact of his growing weakness vis-à-vis European powers, and to the increasing belief that all the county's ills were due to arbitrary rule – a belief which entirely resulted from direct and rather simplistic comparisons with Europe. The Tobacco Revolt of 1890–92 had some obvious economic motives, but it was the first political movement of its kind in the country's history inasmuch as the society challenged the state on a specific issue: it was an attack on arbitrary government, not just on an arbitrary ruler; and it succeeded in reversing an arbitrary decision without the complete destruction of the regime itself. It could thus be described as the first political movement in the country's history, because there was a struggle over a specific major issue which was resolved by a political decision, and although it badly damaged the Shah's authority, he still managed to minimise his losses.

When he had begun to back down, he wrote in his first letter to Hajj Mirza Hasan Mojtahed-e Ashtiyani, the movement's leader in Tehran:

As for the tobacco question, no one is infallible, and – among human beings – perfect knowledge belongs to the pure person of our prophet, peace be unto him. There are times when one takes a decision which he later regrets. Just on this tobacco business I had already thought of withdrawing the domestic monopoly ... such that they would not be able to complain and ask for a large compensation while, at the same time, the people |would| be rid of the European monopoly of internal trade which was truly harmful. We were about to take action when the edict (*hokm*) of Mirza-ye Shirazi ... was published in Isfahan and gradually reached Tehran ... Would it not have been better if you had petitioned us – either individually or collectively – to withdraw the monopoly ... without all the noise and the stopping (*tark*) of *qalian'*.[3]

These words show the Shah's astuteness in recognising and dealing with a dangerous situation, and his strength of character in backing down with as much tact as possible. Large-scale historical speculation is usually of little consequence, but it would seem eminently reasonable to suggest that if someone like his son and successor had ruled in his place in the second half of the nineteenth century, the country might have been ripped apart from within if not from without.

It was not just the enlightened public who saw arbitrary government as the source of the country's backwardness and decline. The Shah himself shared this belief, which was why, in the early 1870s, he had lent his own authority to Sepahsalar-e Qazvini's reformist measures towards the creation of an orderly and responsible government. After Sepahsalar-e Qazvini submitted his draft constitution to the Shah for the creation of a responsible Council of Ministers, the Shah wrote beneath it:

Jenab-e Sadr-e A'zam, I very much approve of this account which you have written concerning the Council of Ministers. With God's blessings make the necessary arrangements and put it into action soon, since any delay would result in a loss to the state.[4]

He could see the benefits of an organized and orderly administration to himself as well as the country, but it took no more than a little while for him to recognize the implications of responsible government for his own position and role in the country. Nevertheless it is significant that he came back to the theme many years later, immediately after returning from his third visit to Europe, when he ordered state luminaries to set up a council of state. His brother, Abbas Mirza Molk Ara, who was present in that fruitless meeting, even quotes him as saying:

[A]ll the order and progress which we observed in Europe in our recent visit is due to the existence of law. Therefore, we too have made up our mind to introduce a law and act according to it.[5]

The main reason why this gesture too came to nothing – indeed it came to far less than the Sepahsalar attempt – may have been the conflict between his interest in social progress and his reluctance to give up his arbitrary power. But there may well have been another factor equally at work in his mind against a genuine reform of the state along constitutional lines.

The problem had once been echoed by his great-grandfather when he expressed amazement to his European visitors as to how it would be possible to run a country where others had a share in the ruler's decision-making.[6] His disbelief would appear to be perfectly understandable once we remember that in Iran's historical experience chaos and disorder had been the only alternative to arbitrary government, and that he would only have had to look back to the eighteenth century after the fall of the Safavid state. Indeed, the assassination of his uncle Aqa Mohammad, the subsequent turmoil, and the perennial rebellions in his own reign, would have provided more immediate evidence for scepticism about the efficacy of responsible government.

Down to the present day, most Iranians and many, if not most, Iranian intellectuals use the terms *estebdad, hokamat-e motlaqeh* (absolutism or despotism) and *diktatori* interchangeably, and believe that *demokrasi* is a weak and ineffectual system which would inevitably result in rebellion, chaos, disorder and disintegration – in *fetneh, ashub, harj-o-marj* and *khan-khani*. That is, they identify Iranian *estebdad* with European dictatorship, and Iranian *ashub* or *khan-khani* with European democracy.

The fear that lawful government would simply result in chaos was genuine and still prevalent in the second half of the nineteenth century. It is doubtful if Zel al-Soltan had much real love for constitutional government, but his astonishment at discovering order and discipline in Paris seems genuine:

Although they say there is freedom and republic, and there is absolute licence (*har keh har keh ast*), this is not the case … In this country, it looks as if everyone – whether king or beggar, rich, boss or lackey – has the book of law under his arm and in his view, and he knows that there is no escaping from the claws of the law … The power of the police must be seen, it cannot be gauged from the description of others.[6a]

Fath'ali Shah may therefore be excused for his lack of faith in responsible government, but Naser al-Din had seen for himself that, in Europe, government based in law was orderly, efficient and successful. He may have been worried about losing grip precisely because Iranian society had known no alternative to arbitrary government except chaos. The story put forward by his daughter, Taj al-Saltaneh, that his assassination was arranged by Amin al-Soltan and his associates who knew that he was determined to inaugurate a constitutional regime immediately after the celebration of his golden jubilee, cannot be taken seriously.

She quotes her step-mother, Anis al-Dawleh, that shortly before his fateful visit to Hazrat-e Abdol'azim the Shah had told her that, after the golden jubilee celebrations, 'I would abolish the tax, establish a consultative assembly, and call for elected deputies from the provinces. I don't think that my assassination would serve the *r'aiyat*'s interest'.[7] Indeed, he had already abolished taxes on meat and bread in Tehran in order to prepare the public mood for the jubilee celebrations. Yet there is an insight in her view that the Shah had been mindful of the possible ungovernability of society if he gave up his arbitrary power. At any rate, that is what increasingly happened during and after the Constitutional Revolution (see below and chapter three).

In fact, the process began shortly after Naser al-Din's own assassination in 1896. As mentioned in chapter one, mass rebellion in Iran normally began and succeeded at times of crisis, and when the government was weak, divided and ineffectual. The country had already been in a state of crisis for some time, when Naser al-Din's assassination both demonstrated and exacerbated the extent of the rift between state and society. The new Shah, Mozaffar al-Din, was timid and feeble, and a relentless power struggle ensued among courtiers, ministers and state officials. Slowly, the process of disintegration began both at the centre and in the provinces several years before widespread public agitation started for lawful and responsible government.

Almost every contemporary source cites 'the hungry and frustrated Turks' as quickly setting about looting the treasury immediately after the arrival of the new Shah from Tabriz. The 'Turks' in question were the Azerbaijani and other courtiers, favourites and entourage of Mozaffar al-Din who had endured many years in his service as governor in Tabriz eagerly counting the days till the end of his father's long reign.[8] They were uncouth and inexperienced, and could influence his decisions much more successfully than the more able and experienced state officials at the centre. The latter in their turn were at loggerheads, and – as usual – engaged in mutually destructive rivalry. At first, Amin al-Soltan was retained as chief minister. He was dismissed about six months later, but it took another four months before Amin al-Dawleh was appointed chief minister (*vazir-e a'zam*) in February 1897 and, in June, chancellor (*sadr-e a'zam*).[8a]

Talebof believed that Amin al-Dawleh could have saved the situation in the interests of both *dawlat* and *mellat*, and succeeded in bringing about orderly constitutional reform.[9] Another contemporary, who knew Amin al-Dawleh personally, held similar views.[9a] However, he was dismissed early in the summer of 1898, mainly – some contemporary sources say wholly – because he put a stop to the financial gains and overweening powers of the 'Turks' as well as of many others. It is nevertheless true that the Russians saw him, along many other Iranian reformists of the time, as leaning towards Britain and added their weight to the campaign for his dismissal.

Amin al-Dawleh was replaced by his much more cunning and self-interested, but also more able, predecessor, Amin al-Soltan, the Atabak, who then was pro-Russian. Amin al-Soltan lasted until September 1903, far longer than the man whose downfall he had facilitated, and over time earned the hostility both of the reformers and the general public. He in turn was replaced by one of the 'Turks', the Qajar nobleman (shahzadeh) Ain al-Dawleh, who was unsuited to the management of the growing crisis both within the state and among the people. He was to remain at his post until the triumph of the constitutionalists succeeded, in August 1906, in obtaining the *farman* for constitutional monarchy.

Before discussing the campaign for constitutional government it would be helpful to present some evidence of the growing chaos which, according to our comparative theory, usually prepared the ground for major revolts.

Growing chaos

To show the extent of confusion, chaos and inability to deal with day-to-day matters within the state and government itself, I shall cite a few examples from two important contemporary sources, both by the same author. They report on daily events between Mozaffar al-Din's succession in 1896 and 1906 just after the struggle began, first for 'justice', then for an independent judiciary, and finally for constitutional government. These are the *Mer'at al-Vaqaye'-e Mozaffari* and the *Notes and Diaries of Abdolhossein Khan Sepehr*. The author, known both as Malek al-Movarrekhin and Lesan al-Saltaneh, was no revolutionary hothead. A grandson of the famous Lesan al-Molk, author of *Nasekh al-Tavarikh*, he was not a political activist and even dedicated and formally presented the first book to the Shah.

In 1897 Amin al-Dawleh becomes Vazir-e A'zam and declares that letters written to him should exclude the customary flattering addresses or he would not read them. Otherwise he would read *in toto* every letter which he receives (after his fall these practices are discontinued). Later in the year there is unrest among Tehran's notables, ulama and privileged people because the Vazir plans to cut off their privy purses. Besides, he is very much in control of the seal of his office, does not seal any written order without reading it first, does not grant money to anyone without good reason, pays no attention to the contradictory edicts of the ulama, and to some extent has blocked their ways of making illicit money. Amin al-Soltan, his predecessor, is busy promising to reverse all this if he replaces the incumbent. Not long afterwards this happens.[10]

Aziz Mirza is a Qajar nobleman and 'one of the noblest ruffians of Tehran'. In August 1899 together with his band he causes a great public mischief, and the governor of Tehran – apparently ignorant of his being a *shazdeh* – has the soles of his feet beaten with a stick. While the governor is watching the beating, Aziz Mirza pulls a 'revolver' out of his pocket and fires a bullet, which misses him. The governor reports the incident to the Shah and the latter orders them to cut off his hand. This causes unrest among other young *shazdehs*, the Shah sacks the governor and orders him to pay 600 hundred tomans compensation to the mutilated man. He also orders the expulsion from town of the officer who had arrested him.[11]

In the same month in the royal *farman* for the new chief minister it is mentioned that 'he is an expert in the affairs and *polteek* of the state, be they domestic or foreign' (cf. chapter one on the absence of politics in traditional Iran).[12]

Early in October 1899 bread is short in Tabriz. The landlords are suspected of hoarding, there are riots in the city, shops strike, and many people take *bast* at a shrine. Enemies of Nezam al-Ulama, a leading landlord and religious figure, declare him to be the main culprit. A mob attacks his house and there are a few deaths and injuries. The exceptionally able and respected Hasan Ali Khan Garrusi, the Amir Nezam, twice intervenes and humours the mob and public to relent. Nezam al-Ulama leaves for Tehran. Next day, 'the hooligans and ruffians' (*ashrar va awbash*) attack his house again, and loot and set fire to it. They also attack and loot the homes of his brother and his nephew, the latter of whom is *chef de cabinet* to the heir-designate and governor of Azerbaijan.[13]

In April 1903 Ain al-Dawleh, Tehran's governor, receives a regular bribe of about 1000 tomans a day from the bakers and butchers. Bread as well as meat are short and expensive. Some women stop the Shah's and the governor's carriages and complain. The governor orders them to be beaten up. There is an ongoing struggle between the chief minister – Amin al-Soltan – and 'the Shah's Turkish lackeys'.

In the same month Salar al-Dawleh – one of the Shah's sons, and governor of Borujerd and Arabistan (later Khuzistan) – is behaving very unjustly towards the people and families there, and rapes the women. Also a brother of the Shah who rules Kashan has behaved so unjustly that the people have taken *bast* in Qom's shrine. When the Vazir is told that money is so short and injustice so great that the state is about to fall, he answers that he is so busy defending his own position that he has no time to see to these problems. In the following month 'the Shah's Turkish lackeys' together with Ain al-Dawleh are agitating against Amin al-Soltan. There is a great shortage of bread in Kashan.[14]

In May the governor of Mashad, a grandson of Fath'ali Shah, has angered the people so much that they strike and go on the rampage. The governor runs away. The Shah sends 300 troops without success. Then the Shah backs down and sacks the governor. This does not satisfy the people who set fire to his father's grave. Shortly afterwards they riot again and kill Hajeb al-Tawlieh ('one of the town's rabble'). The Russians send word that unless the government quells the unrest they would send troops to protect their subjects. The Shah is frightened, but the Vazir says he is unable to act successfully unless he is given real power. The Shah agrees. This happens just at the time when 30 men closest to the Shah have conspired against the Vazir, and he is about to fall. Next month one of the Shah's sons who was governor of Araq, Golpaigan and Khansar is removed because he has done grave injustice to the people, taking their money, raping their women, and accumulating 100,000 tomans over a short period.[15]

In June 1903 there are riots in Azerbaijan. They say there should be no Armenians in Tabriz, and the heads of post and customs offices should be Muslim. The ulama of Tabriz are behind 'the rabble'. The governor of Gilan, Mirza Mahmud Khan Hakim al-Molk, has died. Some say he has been poisoned. He was a favourite of the Shah and an enemy of the chief minister and chancellor. Within a short period he made two-and-a-half million [tomans]. After his death the government orders his house to be sealed off on 'the pretext' that his accounts would have to be investigated'.[16] [Other sources also report that Hakim al-Molk had been a shameless money grabber and an enemy of Atabk. It was widely believed that Atabak had had him poisoned].[16a]

Still in the same month the governor of Fars summons the Qashqa'i chiefs. They refuse, and say if it is for taxes someone should be sent to them and they would pay up. The governor is angered and sends troops against them. They shoot 40 of them down, and the government is now helpless against the Qashqa'i's.[17] The Bakhtiyaris refuse to pay their tax. Mounted troops are sent from Tehran to collect it. They kill a few of them and the rest run away.[18]

The chief minister, Amin al-Soltan is dismissed (in September 1903), and four months later Ain al-Dawleh replaces him.[19] 'The Shah has told those around him that he likes three things in life and regards all other things as worthless: eating, hunting and copulation'.[20]

December 1904, a note of obituary for a grandson of Fath'ali Shah: there was a rumour that the late Shah used to have illicit relations with him. When he was governor of Astrabad (later Gorgan) he subdued the rebel Turkamans, and then killed and looted the property of the loyal Turkamans who had helped him subdue the rebels. As governor of Khamseh he also killed and looted the property of many innocent people. Although the Shah had been told of all this, he was made head of the armed forces and took much of their pay for himself. They say his estate is worth five million tomans.[21]

In January 1905, Qavam al-Dawleh has become Vazir-e Lashkar despite the fact that the year before he had been publicly flogged and imprisoned, because he has paid 20,000 tomans for the post.[22] March, in Russian Azerbaijan Shi'as and Armenians have clashed. 'They say *Ingilis-ha* have been behind it so as to destroy the Russian government completely'[23].

In July 1905 a prominent Qajar nobleman quarrels with a merchant over property and seeks the help of Sayyed Abdollah Behbahani whose students beat up the police (*farrash*), and the nobleman in question breaks the rib of one of them. The heir-designate, Mohammad Ali Mirza [who is acting as regent in the absence of his father in Europe] has him brought before himself, personally beats him, orders that the soles of his feet be heavily beaten by a stick, and throws him into jail. Next morning he orders his release, apologises to him, and gives him a ring.[24] For years now the Lor nomads around Behbahan have looted the towns people's property, rape their women and sell the men into slavery at lucrative prices.[25] The people of Quchan run away to Akhal over the Russian border to escape from the injustices of local rulers and, being destitute, sell their daughters to Turkamans.[26]

November 1905, political agitation begins in mosques. The sermons of Sayyed Jamal al-Din Isfahani and the activities of Tabataba'i and Behbahani are noted.[27] The Russian revolution of 1905 is also noted, as is the decision of the Tsar to grant constitutional government. It is described as *hokumat-e mashruteh* in Persian.[28] December 1905, Vazir Nezam 'takes for himself' one toman of the pay of every soldier under him [as a rule they gave the soldiers' pay to their commanders to distribute among them]. The soldiers get together and give him a good beating. The Shah dismisses him and gives his regiment to someone else.[29] The Imam Jom'eh gives the home of a dead prostitute to a prayer leader. The relatives of the deceased complain to Ala al-Dawleh, the governor of Tehran. The governor sends for the prayer leader, swears at him as well as the Imam Jom'eh, and restores the property to the beneficiaries of the dead woman. Shaikh Fazlollah Nuri intervenes, but the governor sends him a message full of invective, saying that he has no authority, is neither the Shah nor the chief minister, and even if the latter likes him he does not.[30]

Also in December 1905, a Zoroastrian has had illicit relations with a married sister of the Shah. The governor arrests him but lets him go after he pays 25,000 tomans. The go-between is also arrested and the soles of his feet are heavily beaten, but he is released after he pays the governor more than 1,000 tomans.[31] Bread is short and expensive in Tehran. The bakers' leader (*Nanva Bashi*) is ordered to be brought before the chief minister, Ain al-Dawleh and the governor, Ala al-Dawleh. To frighten him, the minister tells the executioner 'to tear off his belly', but the governor pretends to intervene on his behalf. Instead, they have the soles of his feet heavily beaten and obtain a pledge that he would solve the bread problem. Next day the price of bread rises even further.[32]

Two days later occurs the famous heavy flogging of the sugar merchants on the governor's orders which results in angry public reactions and ends in the *bast* of many of the leading ulama and their supporters in the shrine of Hazrat-e Abdol'azim, until they return honourably when the government promises to take action on their demands.

Malek al-Movarrekhin's *Yaddashtha* come to a sudden end with his note on the meeting of the royal council convened on the Shah's orders to set up an independent judiciary, and in which Ehtesham al-Saltaneh – former head of Iran's legation in Berlin – famously attacks Amir Bahador-e Jang, the Shah's 'Turkish lackey' par excellence, for opposing legal justice.[33] (See below).

The campaign for constitution

The realization of Iran's fundamental weakness vis-à-vis European powers began early in the nineteenth century, especially in the wake of the Russo–Iranian wars. This brought Iran into closer contact not only with Russia but also with Britain and, for a brief period, France as actual or potential countervailing powers. Later expansion of European empires made the situation more acute and more obvious.

Throughout the nineteenth century, Iranian reformers saw two factors in particular as the cause of Europe's power and prosperity: modern technology and government based in law. Efforts began in both directions, though eventually, it was thought – not unrealistically – that responsible and orderly government was the more important. The unrealism was, firstly, a belief that the abolition of arbitrary rule was simpler than it was, and, secondly, that it would quickly result in modernization. In spite of efforts made, little result was obtained. Meanwhile the country's position declined further in power and prosperity.

The Tobacco Revolt of 1890–92 may be seen as the culmination of this process. Modern intellectuals began to put much emphasis on constitutional government; in some cases they also began to formulate a new sense of Iranian patriotism, even – though much less obviously – of nationalism. The merchants became more conscious of their interests, although the interests of different groups of merchants were not always the same. The Ulama were an even more heterogeneous group. But most of them felt that, in their role as 'leaders of the people' (*ro'asai-ye mellat*), they had to respond to the calls of the society.[33a] The revolt thus succeeded as a dress rehearsal for the constitutional movement of early 1900's.

The death of Naser al-Din resulted in growing erosion of authority both in the centre and provinces, and chaos became rife everywhere. The weakness of his successor increased hostile competition among the officials, as well as greed. The Constitutional Revolution was not inevitable: it became inevitable largely because of these circumstances.

Several specific events and issues brought matters to a head.[33b] Foreign trade merchants were angry with Iran's newly appointed chief customs officer, a Belgian, Joseph Naus, who was thought to be in the pocket of the Russians. Later, a photograph showing him dressed as a mullah provided fresh material for public anger. There was a deadly conflict between Ain al-Dawleh and Amin al-Soltan; even when the latter lost (in September 1903) and was replaced by the former as chief minister and chancellor and went abroad, his party was still quite active against Ain al-Dawleh.

Given the highly decentralized nature of shi'a institutions, competition, and at times vilification, among the ulama was familiar. After the death of Mirza Hasan Ashtiyani, who had been the most prominent *mojtahed* in Tehran, which was followed by the death of Sayyed ali Akbar Tafreshi, both Shaikh Fazlollah Nuri and Sayyed Abdollah Behbahani wished to be recognized as the top *mojtahed* in the city. Nuri, Imam Jom'eh and a few other important divines tended to support Ain al-Dawleh. On the other hand, Behbahani and his partisans favoured Amin al-Soltan. Behbani's circle included the Ahstiyanis and the Tabtaba'is, except that Sayyed Mohammad Tabtaba'i, who himself was a leading *mojtahed*, did not have a personal stake in the conflict. The personal rivalry between Behbahani and Nuri began to take shape along political lines, although Nuri acted in concert with the other ulama at crucial moments before the campaign for constitution bore fruit.

As we have seen from the chaotic events described in the extracts above, here were reports, from the four corners of the country, of tyrannical behaviour by local governors resulting in protests which developed into vociferous and demonstrative campaigns. The defeat of Russia in the Russo–Japanese war had a very significant impact. Constitutionalists believed that 'Japan defeated Russia, because the former was a constitutionalist regime, the latter, a despotic one'. The outbreak of the 1905 revolution in Russia was more potent, both in providing a model from the dreaded Big Bear itself, and by spreading radical ideas and campaign methods – sometimes embodied in fighters arriving from the Caucasus – especially among the modern intellectuals, many of whom, like Taqizadeh, Dawlat-Abadi, Mosavat, were still in religious dress. Young radicals – democrats and social democrats, particularly in Tehran, Tabriz, Gilan and Mashad – began to form groups and launch campaigns for radical revolutionary programmes.

What triggered the first explosion was the flogging of some respectable sugar merchants of Tehran by the governor, Ala al-Dawleh, in an attempt to end the scarcity of sugar in the market. Sayyed Jamal al-Din Isfahani's subsequent fiery denunciation of arbitrary government to a mosque congregation led to a clash, which resulted in the departure of many ulama, students, merchants and shopkeepers to the sacred shrine of Hazrat-e Abdol'azim in a traditional demonstration of anger against the government. The 'migration' happened at the end of 1905, and was led by Behbahani, Tabataba'i and a few other important divines, whom Nuri joined a couple of days later. Within a month, on 12 January 1906, the protesters had returned to Tehran after the Shah's agreement to meet their central demand of instituting independent judicial courts, which they called *Edalatkhaneh*.

This did not work, because Ain al-Dawleh and others like him at the court were not committed to implementing the Shah's promise. Letters by the ulama, notably a long and important one by Tabataba'i, had little effect, although the publication of usually clandestine revolutionary leaflets continued along with mosque gatherings. Meanwhile, Ain al-Dawleh convened a high council in the court, at which Amir Bahador passionately opposed the institution of the independent courts promised by the Shah. He was opposed, equally passionately, by Ehtesham al-Saltaneh, but the outcome was continued stalling of the reform process.

Once again an incident detonated the powder keg. Persecution of individual dissidents by the government led to the arrest of a leading preacher. Attempts by the people to release him en route to jail resulted in bloodshed, and the following *bast* in a major mosque finally ended with the 'migration' of dissident ulama and their supporters, late in June 1906, to Qom. Others, led by leading merchants such as Hajj Mohammad Hossien Amin al-Zarb and Hajj Mohammad Taqi Bonakdar, took sanctuary in the compound of the British legation in Tehran. Within a few weeks the number of the 'migrants' to Qom reached 2000, and the *bastis* in Tehran 12,000. They were now aiming for no less than the establishment of constitutional monarchy and the dismissal of Ain al-Dawleh. On 5 August the Shah agreed to their demands, and this inaugurated the era of constitutionalist government.

The Shah and his heir-designate, Mohammad Ali Mirza, signed the constitution in December. The former died in January 1907, and the latter succeeded to the throne shortly afterwards. The confrontation between the new Shah and the Majlis eventually resulted in the Shah's Coup in June 1908, when detachments of the Cossack brigade bombarded the Majlis, and arrested many leading constitutionalists including Bahbehani and Tabatba'i. There followed widespread arrest and persecution of constitutionalist activists and intellectuals, including the execution of Jahangir Khan Shirazi, Malek al-Motekallemin and Jamal al-Din Isfahani. Azerbaijan led the resistance, and this had a positive impact on resistance elsewhere.

A year later, in June 1909, the Bakhtiyari army in Isfahan, led by their chieftains, and the army of the Gilan *mojahedin*, led by big landlords like Sepahdar-e Tonokaboni and Fathollah Khan (later entitled Sepahdar, after the former's title was elevated to Sepahsalar), made a successful attack on Tehran. The Shah abdicated and was exiled from the country, and the constitutionalist regime was restored, predictably in a more radical form. The resistance of the Tabriz revolutionaries in the wake of Mohammad Ali's Coup had played a decisive role in encouraging resistance in the capital and elsewhere, which ended in the capture of Tehran by constitutionalist armies.

The Shah had wished to restrict the powers of the first Majlis, while the radicals had wanted to extend it. Those in-between had tried, unsuccessfully, to forge a compromise. Among them were some of the ulama, led by Nuri, who, for both doctrinal and personal reasons, had broken ranks with the constitutionalists and campaigned for *mashru'eh*, or lawful government, firmly based on the *Shari'a*. Meanwhile, no fewer than seven cabinets had come and gone in the less than two years between the fall of Ain al-Dawleh and the Coup of June 1908.[33c]

What the revolution meant

Throughout most of the last century, the dominant analytical view of the Constitutional Revolution was that it was a bourgeois revolution. This view was held not only by Marxist intellectuals, but by the great majority of modern educated Iranians. The only alternative explanation attributed the whole of the Movement to a British plot to put an end to Russian influence in Iran. This view was popular among those generations who had actively or passively supported the revolution, but later regretted it, partly because their utopian hopes were dashed, but mostly as a consequence of the chaos which prevailed and the threat of disintegration the country faced shortly after the victory celebrations were over. Not even the growing indifference of the British legation in Teheran towards the revolution after the Anglo–Russian Convention of 1907 – to the great dismay, if not anger, of the revolutionaries and their leaders – was seen by the conspiracy theorists to require an explanation.[33d] Their attitude was analogous to that of so many ardent supporters of, and participants in, the revolution of 1977–79, who later maintained that it had been the work of America, Britain or both; that the hostage-taking of US diplomats in Tehran was engineered by America herself; that America and other Western powers had instigated the Iraq–Iran war; and that the worldwide American campaign against the Islamic government has been no more than a camouflage.

The fact that later generations did not advocate this convenient conspiracy theory about the Constitutional Revolution – that it was conceived and organized by Britain – was due to four main reasons:

- they had little experience of 'constitutional' disorder and chaos;
- they contrasted the aims of the constitutional revolution with the reality of dictatorial or arbitrary regimes under which they lived;
- they lived at a time when revolutions and revolutionaries were highly respectable in Iran and in many other third world countries;
- the attractive alternative explanation that it was a bourgeois revolution was both high-sounding and associated with an ideology which was politically powerful and intellectually stimulating.

In my previous writings on the subject I have challenged the conventional Marxist interpretation of the Constitutional Revolution, but since some readers are still sceptical I offer a short analysis which includes some additional arguments and evidence.

Marx's concept of bourgeois revolutions is a product of his theory of (European) history or his historical sociology (of Europe). This in turn was based on his philosophy of social change in the wider sense. The two concepts are often believed to be synonymous, which has given further support to the view that Marx's theory of European history has universal application. The philosophy of social change is universal in scope because, like all such philosophies, it is in the nature of a grand metaphysical conception (the appellation 'metaphysical' is not intended to be pejorative; it defines all universal categories which are inherently untestable, but may nonetheless be useful in formulating testable general theories with limited application). In his philosophy of social change Marx disagreed with Hegel and Hegelians – often described as Idealists – who held the view that ideas alone determined the course of events, and he stressed the role of natural environment, productive technology and social institutions in influencing individual and social existence. But he also rejected Materialism, which denied any independent role for human consciousness (as in Feuerbach's 'man is what he eats'), although most of his followers in the twentieth century accepted it. He argued that the extent of human knowledge and the scope of further discovery at each stage of history was limited because, at every stage, humans set themselves such problems as they can possibly solve. Or, what is the same thing, problems which demanded solutions bore a definite relationship to the changing needs and requirements of human existence. Social and material constraints did not prevent speculation into the nature of any conceivable problem. But when a problem was too abstract, too irrelevant to the contemporary environment, it would be very difficult to resolve satisfactorily; and if somehow (by accident or genius) it was resolved, it would languish for want of application and would be generally ignored until later, when socio-environmental relevance would force it to be uncovered or rediscovered.[34]

In this context, Marx drew a distinction between the base (or infrastructure) of a social system – broadly characterised by the state and nature of its existing technological achievements – and its social edifice, or superstructure, that is, the existing social relations which provide the framework for social, political and legal conduct, and the institutions of public and private morality. There are at least three interpretations of Marx's theory of social change. One makes superstructural change a rigid function of basic, infra structural transformations; another allows superstructural changes (and, in particular, changes in sociopolitical constitutions and norms of moral behaviour), even on the basis of the existing infrastructure; and a third regards social change (including major infrastructural changes) as a consequence of the interaction between the basic and infrastructural forces.[35] The first interpretation, favoured by most twentieth century Marxists, was put forward by Engels, Kautsky and their Russian followers, and others who have followed them.[36] The only clear evidence for it in the works of Marx occurs in an unusually simplistic passage in the preface to his *Introduction to the Critique of Political Economy* (1859). Marx's own view oscillated between the second interpretation (as in the first volume of *Capital,* 1864) and the third, as in his earlier works such as *The Eighteenth Brumaire of Louis Bonaparte* (1852), *Poverty of Philosophy* (1847), *The German Ideology* (1845) and *The Economic and Philosophical Manuscripts* (1844).

Marx argued that, in their conception of social reality, humans were strongly influenced not only by their personal history and self-interest but notably by their social history and class interest. Here he had in mind the independent, functional, classes of European society: classes which were ruled by, but were independent from, the state, and movement in and out of which was rare and unusual: they were solid, not malleable, social entities. He saw European history as a process of struggle between social classes – masters and slaves, patricians and plebeians, feudal lords and serfs, the nobility and the bourgeoisie, industrial capitalists and the proletariat – and their various subdivisions. He cited as his major evidence the revolt of the Spartacist slaves in ancient Rome, the European peasant revolts in the Middle Ages, the peasant revolts in sixteenth-century Germany after Luther's attack on the church of Rome, the English revolutions and civil wars in the seventeenth century, the French Revolution at the end of the eighteenth century, and the European revolutions of 1848 which he himself witnessed and supported.[37] Whereas, as we saw in chapter one, although there always were social classes in Iran, unlike Europe they were neither functional nor independent.

It was against such empirical and historical evidence from European history and society that Marx put forward his sociology of history. And he expressly excluded Asiatic societies from this theory because he realized that both the sociology and the pattern of historical change in Asian societies, including Iran, had been fundamentally different from the experience of Europe. In this, of course, he had been long anticipated, from classical Greeks to Montesquieu, Adam Smith and Hegel.[38]

Marxist analyses of the Constitutional Revolution have run along the following lines. Economic development in the nineteenth century, especially as a result of increasing trade with Russia and Western Europe, led to the growth of an urban bourgeoisie which could not be accommodated within the existing feudal or 'semi-feudal' system. In the well-known Marxist terminology, the forces of production – that is, the combined effects of capital accumulation and technical progress – had developed to the extent that the relations of production (i.e., the prevailing class structure and the social, legal and moral institutions corresponding to it), could no longer contain them. The resulting conflict between the technological base and the institutional superstructure – in other words, the clash of socio-economic reality with ideological appearance – eventually manifested itself in a political upheaval for the establishment of a new (and historically relevant) institutional framework.

This is a brief and basic statement of a familiar model whose original formulation was based on much empirical data from the French Revolution. Explicitly or implicitly, it has been used by many, if not most, historians and sociologists of Iran, sometimes with (occasionally significant) qualifications. For example, the more adaptive versions have tended to put greater emphasis on the accumulation of financial as opposed to physical (i.e. industrial) capital in nineteenth-century Iran, or they have considered the political and economic impact of imperialism, and of European ideologies, to be important. There is no doubt that all these factors and others must be included in any analysis of the Constitutional Revolution, but the question is whether or not the Marxist model would make sense in this case. Was it indeed a bourgeois revolution?

I have shown in chapter one that Iran was not a feudal society, and that the arbitrary system did not allow long-term accumulation of capital and investment in expensive and extensive means of industrial production that could not be quickly realised in monetary form. Further, a close statistical and historical study of the Iranian economy in the nineteenth century has not revealed a pattern of development consistent with the Marxist model.[39] It is true that the impact of the rise of industry and empire in Europe jolted the Iranian economy out of its traditional equilibrium and opened it up to international trade more than ever before. This led to a decline in the country's production and export of traditional manufactured goods, and a steady increase in its production and exports of primary cash crops, while its import of modern manufactured goods grew rapidly.[40] Apart from this, loss of territory reshaped the map of the country, at times robbing it of some of its best natural and human resources, diminishing both its productive capacity and its internal market, and reducing its military and political power.

Among other causes, the process of relative weakening resulted in preferential tariff treaties which left the economically weak and technologically underdeveloped industries unprotected against the import of cheap and fashionable machine-made products. This in turn led to a loss of manufactured exports, a shift to primary cash crop production, a possible decline in production of staple foods and a general rise in imports.

The balance-of-payments deficit and the inflationary consequences were reinforced, as if by the wrath of God, by a dramatic fall in the international price of silver – on which most of Iran's money was based – in the last three decades of the century. Meanwhile the slow but fairly steady growth of population tended to depress living standards still further.[41]

There was no significant technical progress, in the economic sense of the term, in either industry or agriculture. One could even observe economic regress in the sense of loss of traditional knowhow, refined over centuries, without the acquisition of a suitable substitute which, in economic terms, would be at least as useful as the older techniques. The 'technical progress' to which political historians usually point almost invariably refers to minority consumption of the products of modern European technology, aside from the introduction of the telegraph. Likewise, there could not have been any significant increase in the accumulation of financial capital and rise in the stock of physical capital. There are no statistics for these important economic categories, but indirect evidence makes it very improbable that there was a significant increase in either of them. There had been no progress in productive technology; both the internal and the external markets for Iran's manufactured goods had declined; taxes and other extortions had become more and more oppressive; the domestic debasement of the currency coupled with the severe fall in the international price of silver had reinforced persistent inflation; and the traditionally strong Iranian sense of social and economic insecurity had increased even more as a consequence of these and other depressing events.[42] It is commonplace that long-term investment is dependent on technical progress, an expanding market and – above all – a reasonable degree of security.

Foreign trade grew, and was the main force behind the tendency for the concentration as well as centralization of financial capital. But this was not the same as a genuine growth and accumulation of capital; it represented shifts between different trade sectors as well as between individual merchants. Trade with Europe benefited the big merchants, and by increasing their personal fortunes it increased their potential political power at the expense of the state. European trade also played an important role in weakening the arbitrary system in a number of indirect ways. Firstly, the growing role and influence of imperial powers exposed the weakness of the Iranian state and robbed it of the traditional public belief in its omnipotence. Secondly, their illicit payments to the Shah and state officials helped weaken the structure of arbitrary rule from within. Thirdly, the greater specialization in the production and export of raw materials, the relative decline of traditional manufacturing, the use of modern means of communication such as the telegraph, the endemically rising inflation, the crippling deficit in foreign payments and the resulting accumulation of foreign debt, led to a structural disequilibrium in the economy which the traditional state apparatus could not comprehend, let alone cope with.

Mainly through Russia, Britain and France, Europe was presented to the eyes and ears of Iranians as a magic model of power, prosperity and progress. The intelligentsia, who included many Qajar noblemen and state officials, looked for the key to this great and wonderful secret, and found it – writ large – as LAW.[43] They saw law first as responsible and, especially, as orderly government, and later as freedom. It would make private property safe and powerful, official positions less insecure and more responsible, and would protect life and limb against arbitrary decisions. And they almost believed that this alone would turn the country into a powerful and prosperous state.

When Sayyed Jamal al-Din Isfahani, the famous radical preacher and thinker of the Movement, asked his audience in a sermon what the country needed most, a few individuals shouted slogans such is 'unity', 'patriotism', etc. Admitting the desirability of all of these, the Sayyed nevertheless said that first and foremost there was need for *qanun*. And, in the traditional style of teachers trying to teach the Persian alphabet to small children, he began to spell out each letter, then two letters together – q, a, qa etc. – asking the entire audience to repeat it after him. He then launched the following, which must be the most intensive single eulogy ever sung in praise of law in the annals of the Constitutional Revolution (and in reading the following it must be remembered that, in Persian, *qanun* both means 'law' and 'the law'):

> People! Nothing would develop your country other than subjection to law, observation of law, preservation of law, respect for law, implementation of the law, and again law, and once again law. Children must from childhood read and learn at schools that no sin in religion and the *shari'a* is worse than

opposing the law ... Observing religion means law, religion means law, Islam, the Qur'an, mean God's law. My dear man, *qanun, qanun,* children must understand, women must understand, that the ruler is law and law alone, and no-one's rule is valid but that of the law. The parliament is the protector of law ... the legislative assembly and legislature is the assembly which legislates the law, the sultan is the head of the executive which implements the law. The soldier is defender of the law, the police is defender of the law, justice means law, riches means implementing the law, the independence of the monarchy means rules of the law. In a word, the development of the country, the foundation of every nationality, and the solidarity of every nation arises from the implementation of the law.[44]

The nature of any revolution may by discerned by an examination of its aims, its supporters, its opponents, and its results. Here the central objective – indeed the very desideratum and password – was *mashruteh,* that is, government conditioned by law. Before the coining of this the Persianized term 'qonstitusiyun' was almost invariably used. Nearly all merchants, artisans and shopkeepers, most of the ulama and religious community, many if not most of the landlords and nomadic chieftains, most of the ordinary urban public, and the entire modern intelligentsia either actively or passively supported it. In particular, the triumph of 1909 would not have been possible without the full support of the great religious leaders such as Hajj Mirza Hossein Tehrani, Akhund Mullah Kazem Khorasani, Shaikh Abdollah Mazandarani and others, as well as such powerful landlords and nomadic chieftains as Sepahdar-e (later, Sepahsalar-e) Tonokaboni, Fathollah Khan Akbar (later, Sepahdar-e Rashti), Aliqoli Khan Sardar As' ad and Najafqoli Khan Samsam al-Saltaneh, the paramount Bakhtiyari chiefs. What is more revealing, perhaps, is that not a single social class *qua* class resisted the revolution, in total contrast to all the minor as well as major European revolutions since the seventeenth century. And finally, in regard to its aims and objectives, the most important achievement of the revolution was *mashruteh* itself, that is, constitutional government, as understood by its campaigners and supporters.

It is clear from all this that the Constitutional Revolution was not a bourgeois, nor indeed any other European, type of revolution.

Mashru'eh versus Mashruteh

Mashru'eh was a vague term hastily thrown into the argument by Nuri and his followers to describe constitutionalism firmly based on the *Shari'a.* It was not a clear political concept as it lacked both form and content as an alternative to constitutional government, and the identification and cooperation of its advocates with the Shah's arbitrary rule left little credit for them as constitutionalists. The hindsight provided by the present Islamic republic into the thinking of the proponents of *mashru'eh*, although not unreasonable, is misleading. It gives them even more credit than they deserve: they were traditionalists who, at best, claimed that they wished to replace arbitrary rule with an authoritarian government based on the *Shari'a* while at the same time maintaining the existing traditional social framework intact; they were even hysterical about the publication of newspapers. For all its so-called fundamentalism, the Islamic republic is much influenced – in its own fashion – by modern European ideas and experiences (including Marxist and liberal which it formally denounces) both in its discourse and in its conduct. In a word, past *mashru'eh* was traditionalist, whereas present *Islamism* is revisionist.

At a turning point in their confrontation with the Majlis and constitutionalist ulama, Nuri and his followers took *bast* (in the summer of 1907) in the shrine of Hazrat-e Abdol'azim outside Tehran. There they issued a number of statements and shed much light on their views, exposing their fears and forebodings about the consequences of *mashruteh's* triumph. They are full of propagandist diatribes about Jewish men raping Muslim boys and women, allowing 'a bunch of Zoroastrians' to enter a mosque, etc.[45] Yet they retain the essentials of their views and show that they were much more concerned about the application of modern European culture than the mere abolition of arbitrary government. In one of these *layehahs*, which they describe as 'an account of the views of … Hajj Shaikh Fazlollah … and the other migrants to the sacred shrine', they say that 'a year ago an idea was introduced from Europe that in any state where the Shah, ministers and governors could do what they like (*beh del-bekhah-e khod*) to the people, the government is the source of injustice, transgression and plunder; that [in such a country] there could be no prosperity, and that the inevitable persistence of the people's poverty would result in the country's loss of independence …' Therefore:

> The people should combine and ask the Shah to change the arbitrary rule (*saltanat-e delkhahaneh*) … and enter a contract so that, from then onwards, the Shah and his officials would strictly abide by that contract … They called that arbitrary rule – in the current parlance – *saltanat-e estebdadi*, and this contractual rule *saltanat-e mashruteh'*.[46]

The ulama then combined, the statements add, to make this possible. No sooner had the Majlis been convened, however, than ideas began to circulate about the necessity of changing and improving some of the less fundamental *Shari'a* laws, and adapting them to contemporary needs and requirements:

> … such as … the education of women and the founding of schools for girls, and the usage of funds hitherto used for *rawzeh-khani* and the pilgrimage of sacred shrines for investment in factories and the paving of roads and streets, and in constructing railways and acquiring European industries …[47]

After a long diatribe against the Anarchists, the Nihilists, the Socialists, the Naturalists, and the Babists, they list their demands as follows:

- The word *mashru'eh* should be added to *mashruteh* in the constitution;
- It should be stated in the constitution that all legislation would have to be vetted by a group of the ulama who would be specially chosen by the leading *maraje'* and no-one else;
- The articles of the constitution, such as that which declared the 'absolute freedom of all publications' and was suitably amended by the ulama, be revised and made consistent with the *Shari'a*.[48]

It follows from this statement that they were opposed to such modernizing policies as the education of women, and the encouragement of saving and investment for economic development instead of contributing funds for the religious purposes mentioned by the statement; and that they were afraid of the adaptation and modernization of the less basic *Shari'a* rules, and fearful even of such things – which they described as *farangi* – as shouting 'long live', displaying fireworks, and inviting foreign emissaries in the company of their wives to be present at the official ceremony of the first anniversary of the issuance of the *farman* for constitutional government. The strong fear, arising from a total sense of alienation, of an imminent onslaught of a wholly strange culture, and of losing their entire grip – becoming outmoded and *dépassé* – is evident from their texts, and it was probably no less, and perhaps more, potent than all the other factors in shaping their hostility towards their opponents.

The statements mentioned above were issued before the Shah's Coup, when Nuri and his followers were on the defensive. After the Coup of 1908, the Shah appointed a council of state. This council, which included a number of state dignitaries, Qajar noblemen, Nuri, Imam Jom'eh and other ulama of their persuasion, addressed a letter to the Shah begging him to disband 'the public [*omumi*] consultative assembly' which it described as being 'contradictory to the rules of Islam'. The Shah duly replied that 'now that you have declared that the Majlis contradicts Islamic rules ... we too have decided totally against it, and such a Majlis will not be heard of again, but – under the guidance of the Lord of the Time ... we shall give the necessary orders for the extension of justice'.[49]

It will appear from this as well as from what followed that, whatever Nuri's real convictions may have been, and despite his proclamations in favour of *mashruteh-ye mashru'eh* before the Coup, he was all in favour of disbanding *mashruteh* itself, perhaps as a price of preventing secularization as well as social and cultural modernization. It was the attack on constitutionalism itself which prompted the great *maraje'* at Najaf, led by Akhund-e Khorasani, to take the field against Nuri as well as the Shah with much greater vehemence than before, especially after the Coup of 1908.[50] And it was from these quarters that the reply to the theoretical statements of Nuri and his followers came.

Two articles written by a Najaf Mojtahed, Mohammad Isma'il Gharavi-e Mahallati, and confirmed and countersigned, the first by the Akhund, and the second by he and Shaikh Abdollah Mazandarani (Hajj Mirza Hossein Najl-e Mirza Khalil-e Tehrani had recently died), may be seen as a direct reply to the views put out by Nuri and his associates quoted above, as well as a refutation of the grounds put forward by the Shah and his state council for abolishing constitutional government. The first and shorter article argues that the meaning of *mashruteh* is that the Shah and the government would be bound by written laws (*qavanin-e mazbut*), in contrast to *estebdadi* monarchy and government, which means government based on the arbitrary (*khodsari*) 'decisions, passions and whims' of the Shah. This system has been responsible – the article added – for the country's decline such that it is even in danger of losing its independence. Therefore 'given the necessities and requirements of our time' there is no choice other than the election by the people of their representatives to establish laws within whose limits the Shah and the government would run the country's affairs.[51]

The second article is in much the same spirit, but longer and more elaborate:

> Statements have been put out in Tehran claiming that *mashruteh* and the existence of a poplar consultative assembly contravene the Islamic faith and the rules of the Qur'an. As a result, the state has seized this false pretext and declared that what is against the Qur'an will never be established in the Islamic realm of Iran ... But those who are familiar with *mashruteh* and its implications realise that this slander and defamation is but a pretext for the destruction of the country and the abolition of the rights of the Muslim people. Otherwise, there is no conflict between Islam and the Qur'an, on the one hand, and the limitation of governmental power, on the other. This is in conflict only with personal interests of the ruler, and is vehemently opposed to the destruction of the peoples' lives, property and dignity.[52]

The article goes on to elaborate these points, forcefully and at some length, until it produces a mature and sophisticated description of constitutional government which most contemporaries and later generations did not fully absorb:

> The meaning of freedom in constitutional states is not absolute licence, which would permit everyone to do what they like to the point of violating the lives, property and dignity of others. Such a thing has never existed and will never exist in any community of human beings, as it would result in none other than absolute disruption and general anarchy in the affairs of the people. On the contrary, the meaning of freedom is the liberty of the general public from arbitrary and unaccountable government by force, so that no powerful individual – i.e. the Shah – could use his power so much as against the least powerful member of the community, and impose

anything on him except that which is permitted by the law of the land, and before which all the people – be they Shah or beggar – would be equal. And freedom in this sense is a rational precept and one of the pillars of the Islamic faith.[53]

Two points are worthy of emphasis here: firstly, the explicit definition of liberty as freedom from arbitrary rule, which, as argued below, was the interchangeable concept of both law and freedom implicitly held by all; and secondly, the clear distinction between liberty and licence in a constitutional regime which, at least in practice, many if not most of those who were both for and against *mashruteh* did not make.

Thus, when the battle lines were drawn, the Najaf ulama declared Nuri to be a *mofsed*: 'Since Nuri is a *mofsed* and disrupter of peace, his authority in the Affairs [of Islamic Faith] is *haram*'.[54] And in response to the Shah's humble pleadings that he was not anti-constitutionalist, they wrote him increasingly hostile and aggressive letters, saying, for example:

[N]o matter how hard we tried to bring peace and unity between *dawlat* and *mellat* ... and called on *dawlat* to get in line with *mellat* ... on the contrary, *dawlat* has merely responded by making hypocritical promises ... and although we knew that all the ills are due to the provocations of the treacherous *dawlat* and *dawlatis*, nevertheless preferred to ignore it ... until what we wished to avoid happened, and the unity of *dawlat* and *mellat* was completely disrupted.[55]

And when the civil war began, they issued a statement in which they declared fighting on the government side to be the same as taking orders from Yazid:

Now we openly declare to [all the armed forces] that following orders, and shooting at the people and supporters of the Majlis is the same as taking orders from Yazid son of Mo'avieh, and is a negation of Islam.[56]

Thus both Nuri and the Shah lost the 'religious' argument to the constitutionalist ulama, whose weight of authority, both in size and importance, was much greater than Nuri and others of the ulama who agreed with him.

Liberty and licence

The constitution of 1906 did not end the ancient sense of alienation of the society from the state, of *mellat* from *dawlat*: it simply gave it a respectable legal definition and institutional dressing (see chapters one and three). Here, it is intended to show that the roots of the problem lay in the period before the complete triumph of the revolution in 1909, and that the civil war and even the fall of Mohammad Ali could have been avoided had there been a realistic under-standing of European constitutionalism among all the main parties concerned.

Although it was seldom understood by any of the protagonists, their concepts of law and freedom – beyond an independent judiciary and respon-sible government – were different from those which had developed in Europe. In fact, they were strongly influenced by the culture of the ancient arbitrary society itself. The original concept of freedom in Europe had meant *freedom from the law*, including from entrenched and apparently irremovable social traditions and customs. The 'individualist' theories and movements of the seventeenth and eighteenth centuries were opposed to the extensive as well as discriminatory laws and traditions which governed the society and the economy. They were not opposed to law as such. They were against absolutist government and the extent of state interference in the society and economy, and were in favour of the indi-vidual's right to the pursuit of his own interest as well as equality before the law.[57] Thomas Carlyle later caricaturized their view (with specific reference to Adam Smith) as 'anarchy plus the constable'. John Stuart Mill, on the other hand, formulated their concepts of law and freedom succinctly as the freedom to pursue one's interest to the extent that it would not deprive others of the freedom to do the same.[58] Still later, Isaiah Berlin described their concept as 'the negative concept of freedom'.[59]

The eventual triumph of the movements (in Europe) for negative freedom and politico-judicial equality before the law, exposed their limitations for the social and economic rights of the property-less classes, and led to demands for new laws – or social legislation – to protect their rights and enable them, too, to benefit from the fruits of legal equality and individual freedom. Harold Lasky later summarized their concept of liberty as the freedom to 'realise one's best self'.[60] Still later, Berlin described their concept as 'the positive concept of freedom'.[61] Both socialists and anarchists campaigned for it: the socialists, in different ways, tried to use the state, while the anarchists hoped to replace the state with popular administration, in pursuit of that goal.

Iran's constitutionalists, especially the radical democrats among them, saw no conflict between law and freedom. Indeed, they virtually identified one with the other because they saw them both as freedom from arbitrary government.

This was most clearly and explicitly stated at the time by Sayyed Mohammad Reza Shirazi (later known by the name of his newspaper, *Mosavat*), a religious figure as well as radical democrat. Explaining to his readers the meaning of 'a few novel political terms such as liberty, equality, etc.', he described liberty as freedom from arbitrary rule:

Whenever [the terms] liberty and equality are used in civilized countries, they render certain clear meanings which have been gradually obtained as a result of the passage of ages and centuries. For example, liberty is used in the sense of political freedom, and whenever the word is uttered it means the same thing, i.e. [freedom] from the arbitrariness of the state ...[62]

Therefore, not only their concept of freedom, but also their concept of law was negative in Berlin's sense, insofar as it meant the removal, rather than active application and imposition, of something else; that is, law meant the absence of arbitrary rule and little besides. In practical terms this was consistent with the ancient dialectic in Iranian society between *mellat* and *dawlat*, and the periodic cycle of arbitrary government-rebellion and chaos–arbitrary government throughout its history. Down to the present time such notions of freedom, democracy and law are still much the most dominant among Iranians both in and out of the country, and not least in the educated communities, including those who favour Western democracy as well as those who dislike it.[63]

Once the constitution was granted and the Majlis elected, the confrontation was transferred from the streets, mosques and *madresehs*, sacred shrines and foreign legations to the first Majlis. There were two interrelated reasons for this: the extensive powers which the constitution had granted to the legislature, leaving little for the task of governing the realm by the executive; and the persistence of ancient suspicion and alienation between state and society. There still was no politics, and therefore no room to compromise. The Majlis was literally described as 'The Peoples' House' (*Khaneh-ye Mellat*) and the implications of this for the relationship between the state and society were the same as they had been under arbitrary government. The state was still held in great suspicion as an alien force; and the popular understanding was that the Majlis was the countervailing power to the executive whose only role and function was to carry out the wishes of the Majlis on both minor and major matters for running the country. In effect, the Majlis was both legislature and executive, and the executive was at best seen as the equivalent of a European civil service. This attitude continued after the triumph of 1909, so that the cabinets were increasingly unable to govern the country (see chapter three).

The Majlis itself was divided among many irreconcilable trends and tendencies whose only common cause was to assert its right to supreme power. The only prominent and popular leader of the revolution whose motives could not be doubted and who grasped the problem well and spoke his mind openly was Abd al-Rahim Talebof. He declined his election to the first Majlis because he felt that the turn of events was different from that which a few enlightened intellectuals like himself had intended. After Mirza Ali Akbar Khan Qazvini (later, Dehkhoda) had gone to Istanbul in the wake of the Shah's Coup, he wrote to Talebof seeking his assistance in resurrecting *Sur Esrafil* outside the country. Talebof reacted in anger and frustration to the prevailing idealistic radicalism, although he was still emotionally sympathetic towards the sufferings of the revolutionaries:

> I hope that Iranian emigrants would soon go back and, instead of fighting and killing, work along the line of moderation ... It is wonderous that in Iran they are supposedly fighting for the freedom of thoughts and ideas and yet no one cares about another person's views, and if someone

expresses [independent] views he would be treated as if he had committed a capital offence ... And the charge is brought by those who ... neither have intellect nor knowledge nor experience; all they have is guns.[64]

Does Dehkhoda remember, he goes on to add, that Talebof had written to him wondering ' what kind of animal is Tehran to be able to deliver a hundred and twenty [political] societies in a single night?'[65]

I am seventy-one and have known Iran for fifty years. What lunatic would try to erect a building without the aid of a builder; what madman would call up a builder without providing the material; what insane person would expect a change of the Iranian regime overnight?[66]

He goes on to ask what prophet could possibly put the country on the path of incredibly rapid progress that 'Hossein the Clothier or Mohsen the Taylor ...' were supposed to be doing.

The letter is long and very instructive about the clash of subjective ideals and objective realities in almost any revolution. But his words addressed to a Tabriz newspaper were more specifically applicable to Iran, and turned out to be prophetic. They reveal his instinctive insight into the working of not only the arbitrary state but the arbitrary society as well:

Up until now Iran was captive to the double-horned bull of arbitrary government, but from now on – if it does not succeed in bringing order to itself – it will be struck by the thousand-horned ox of the rabble and the mob. Supporters of the arbitrary government (*mostabeddin*) would then laugh at our immaturity ... I openly declare that I see this as being inevitable.[67]

The assassination of Atabak is perhaps the clearest example of the refusal of both sides to compromise, that is, not to be satisfied with any outcome other than the complete elimination of the other side as a political force. The rejection of the principle of compromise is a clear sign of the persistence of 'pre-politics' as discussed in chapter one. On the one hand, it indicates a state of distrust between the conflicting parties; on the other, it shows their willingness either to win or to lose completely and at any cost. This has been a persistent pattern in twentieth century Iranian politics down to the present time, when on almost every occasion compromise has been denounced as *sazeshkari*, which is regarded as little short of surrender and betrayal.[68]

The plot to assassinate Atabak has not yet been fully uncovered. Both the radicals and the Shah's men were around in and out of the Majlis on that fateful night. The balance of probability is that Abbas Aqa – the agent of the revolutionary Secret Committee (*Anjoman-e Ghaibi*) – fired at the chief minister, although it is not clear whether he then turned the gun on himself or was shut by his own comrades as part of a cover-up. But there can be little doubt that both parties wanted Amin al-Soltan out of the way because any settlement reached by him – which was likely to have the backing of both Russia and Britain – would have been short of the maximum demands of either party.

This was as true of the Shah as of Haidar Khan (Amuoqlu), the leading Secret Committee activist in making and throwing bombs; but it was also true of many who were a good deal less radical.[69] And it is not as if Atabak's survival would have seen the end of the problem, even if he had managed to put a package together which the two uncompromising parties somehow would have felt obliged to accept. Just as any agreement reached by Mosaddeq short of the ideal over the oil dispute would have been condemned as a sell-out. And any compromise in the revolution of 1977–79 would have been described as a betrayal by bourgeois liberals (committed on the orders of their foreign masters) by most of those who later criticized democratic leaders for accepting the leadership of the radicals despite their own fears of the consequences of the disorderly collapse of the former regime.

Atabak was unpopular, and he was not trusted by either the constitutionalists or the radicals. But there were others with much better credentials among political and revolutionary leaders who were trying to arrange a compromise along basic constitutionalist principles. Men like Mokhber al-Saltaneh, Naser al-Molk and Behbahani – and even, to a lesser extent, Mostawfi al-Mamalek, Moshir al-Dawleh and Mo'tamen al-Molk – still look dull, grey and suspicious in the annals of Iranian historiography on account of their conciliatory attitudes and their attempts at forging a compromise, although there can be no doubt about their commitment to the general principles of constitutional government. The Shah did not want a compromise so long as he hoped to crush the movement; the radicals responded in like manner by attacking him and his family with unprintable verbal abuse, even to the point of publicly accusing his mother, the daughter of Amir Nezam (Amir Kabir), of highly promiscuous behaviour; and the crowds were, as usual, loud and hysterical.

Kasravi cites some evidence of the obscene personal attacks on the Shah published in Sayyed Mohammad Reza Shirazi's *Mosavat* (a direct translation of the French revolution slogan *égalité*), and says that when the Shah turned to the courts for protection the Sayyed refused to answer the summons of the court and published a special issue making fun of it. Kasravi the moralist has the better of Kasravi the revolutionary when he comments that 'if some in the ranks of the freedom party deserved to be killed this man was the first among them'.[70]

When at long last the Shah saw no alternative but to sue for a compromise solution before the battle of Tehran, the radicals would accept no accommodation short of his deposition (khal') from the throne. Once again we may be reminded of events of an Iranian revolution which is far closer to living memory. Decades later, Taqizadeh had confided his deep regrets to a close friend for his insistence that there should be no solution short of the Shah's deposition at that historic moment. No wonder that he of all the commentators praised Behbabhani – in his memoirs – in great admiration, especially emphasizing the latter's political insight and courage.[71]

To sum up this chapter's discussion, the Constitutional Revolution was basically one in a long line of historic revolts by Iranian society against the ancient arbitrary state. To a different degree, all the urban classes participated in the revolution and not a single social class (*qua* class) fought against it. In this case, however, there was a specific and very important difference which was due to what had been learnt from the experience of Europe: the revolution was fought not just against the existing arbitrary rule but clearly against the arbitrary regime itself; that is, for law and – what was meant to be almost the same thing – freedom.

As in previous Iranian revolts, it occurred when the state was very weak and the ruler feeble and incompetent, so that the arbitrary government's minimum but vital traditional function of maintaining physical order and security was being rapidly eroded. Yet, despite its modern European trimmings, the consequences of the revolution were more in line with the traditional clash of *dawlat* and *mellat* – of unaccountable government and ungovernable society – so that neither side was prepared to reach a modus operandi (let alone a modus vivendi) along the lines of constitutional governments in Europe. The result was a war of elimination in which the revolutionaries triumphed. But the age-old problem of the rift between the government and the governed continued such that, among large sections of the society, *qanun* came to mean little but liberty, and liberty was seldom distinguished from licence. No wonder that constitutionalism did not last for more than fifteen years, during which this tendency towards chaos and disintegration became daily more powerful, and it looked increasingly unlikely that the country would last at all.

Notes

1   For a detailed description of events in the specific case of the collapse of the Safavid State see Lawrence Lockhart, *The Fall of the Safavid Dynasty and the Afghan Occupation of Persia* (Cambridge University Press, 1958); *Nadir Shah*. London: Luzac, 1938. See also David Morgan, *Medieval Persia 1040–1797* (London and New York: Longman, 1988), chapters 15 and 16.

2   See Abbas Amanat, *Pivot of the Universe, Nasir al-Din Shah Qajar and the Iranian Monarchy, 1831–1896* (London and New York: I.B.Tauris, 1997).

3   See Nazem al-Islam-e Kermani, *Tarikh-e Bidari-ye Iraniyan*, (ed.) Sa'idi Sirjani, vol. 1. (Tehran: Agah, 1983), pp. 22–39. For a history of the revolt see Nikki Keddie, *Religion and Rebellion in Iran, The Tobacco Protest of 1891–1892* (London: Frank Cass, 1966).

4   Quoted in Abdollah Mostawfi, *Sharh-e Zendegani-ye Man*, vol. 1 (Tehran: Zavvar, 1981), p. 123.

5   See Abdolhosain Nava'i, (ed.) *Sharh-e Hal-e Aabbas Mirza Molk Ara* (Tehran: Babak, 1982), p. 175.

6   See Abdolhossein Nava'i, *Iran va Jahan*, vol. 2 (Tehran: Homa, 1990).

6a   Quoted in Ebrahim Bastani Parizi, *Zir-e In Haft Asman* (Tehran: Javidan, 1983), p. 55.

7   See *Khaterat-e Taj al-Saltaneh*, (eds) Mansureh Ettehadiyeh and Sirus Sa'dvandiyan,

(Tehran: Nashr-e Tarikh-e Iran,1983), p. 60. E'temad al-Saltaneh, who died before the Shah, thought that Amin-al Soltan (Atabak) was disloyal towards his master (See *Ruznameh-ye Khaterat-e E'temad al-Saltaneh,* (ed.) Iraj Afshar (Tehran: Amir Kabir, 1971). Both the claim of the disloyalty of Amin al-Soltan towards the Shah and the rumour about notes by the Shah on future reforms left with 'one of his wives', are found in some other sources as well, e.g. Yahya Dawlat-Abadi *Hayat-e Yahya* (Tehran: Ferdawsi and Attar, 1983), vol. 1, chapter 21. Atabak and E'temad al-Saltaneh were great enemies to the extent that when the former died, Atabak and Hajj Amin al-Zarb, his close friend and collaborator, were accused of having arranged his death using a Florentine technique. See, for example, Khan Malek-e Sasani, *Siyasatgaran-e Dawreh-ye Qajar* (Tehran: Hedayat, n.d. [date of preface1959]), and Nava'i, *Iran va Jahan,* vol. 2, who go on to add that they then contacted Mirza Reza to prepare for the assassination of the Shah. The allegations cannot be taken seriously and look typical of Iranian conspiracy theories. According to Mehdi Bamdad, the assassination of the Shah as well as of Atabak was arranged by Britain. See his *Sharh-e Hal-e Rejal- Iran,* vol. 2 (Tehran: Zavvar, 1992), pp. 409–10. See further *Khaterat-e Siyiasi-ye Mirza Ali Khan-e Amin al-Dawleh,* (ed.) Hafez Farmanfarmayan (Tehran: Amir Kabir, 1991).

8　Two very good contemporary sources on the 'Turks' are *Khaterat-e Taj al-Saltaneh* and *Khaterat-e Ehtesham al-Saltaneh,* (ed.) S. M. Musavi (Tehran: Zavvar, 1988), although rarely does a contemporary source omit to mention them and their deeds.

8a　Dawlat-Abadi *Hayat-e Hahya,* vol. 1; Bamdad, *Sharh-e Hal-e,* vol. 2 (entry on Mirza Ali Khan Amin al-Dawleh); E. G. Browne, *The Persian Revolution* (London: Frank Cass, 1966), ch. IV.

9　After Amin al-Dawleh's death, Talebof wrote in a private letter, 'God immerse him in his blessings. It is extremely sad that he is not alive now to end the problem of our lack of statesmanship. A long time would have to pass before anyone of his calibre could emerge …' See *Yaghma,* vol. 15, no. 4, p. 1 79.

9a　See Dawlat-Abadi, *Hayat-e Yahya,* vol. 1, various chapters.

10　*Yaddasht-ha-ye Malek al-Movarrekhin va Mer'at al-Vaqaye'-e Mozaffari,* ed. Abdolhossein Nava'i (Tehran: Zarrin, 1989). See *Mer'at,* pp. 127–247. It is worth emphasising that evidence of increasing disorder and chaos may be found in almost all the contemporary sources and those written later by authors with first-hand experience of the events. Indeed, in his voluminous memoirs Abdollah Mostawfi occasionally refers to the period between the turn of the twentieth century and the Coup d'état of 1921 as 'the twenty-year chaos'. Here we shall cite the evidence from Malek al-Movarrekhin's two books because they have recently come to light; they cover the years immediately before the onset of the revolution, and they have systematically recorded the events at the time of their occurrence. For corroborating evidence, see for example Mostawfi, *Shah-e Zende-gani,* vols. 2 and 3, (Tehran:Zavvar, 1964); Yahya Dawlat-Abadi, *Hayat-e Yahya,* vols. 3 and 4; Mokhber al-Saltaneh (Hedayat), *Khaterat va Khatarat* (Tehran: Zavvar,1984); S. M. Musavi, ed., *Khaterat-e Ehtesham al-Saltaneh.*

11　*Mer'at,* p. 267.

12　*Ibid.,* p. 270.

13　*Ibid.,* pp. 306–07.

14　See *Yaddasht-ha,* pp. 20–22.

15　*Ibid.,* pp. 23–26.

16　*Ibid.,* pp. 26–27.

16a　See Bamdad, *Sharh-e Hal-e,* vol. 3, entry on Mahmud Khan Hakim al-Molk, Mokhber al-Saltaneh, *Khaterat va Khatarat,* and Browne, *The Persian Revolution.*

17　*Ibid.,* pp. 27–28.

18　*Ibid.,* p. 29.

19　*Ibid.,* pp. 30–32.

20　*Ibid.,* p. 92.

21 *Ibid.*, pp. 102–03.

22 *Ibid.*, p. 113.

23 *Ibid.*, p. 121.

24 *Ibid.*, p. 184.

25 *Ibid.*, p. 231.

26 *Ibid.*, p. 248.

27 *Ibid.*, pp. 251–52.

28 *Ibid.*, p. 260. Incidentally, this should end speculation about whether or not the term *mashruteh* had currency before the constitution was granted. The traditional term, of course, was *qonstitusiun*. This became a matter of dispute between Mohammad Ali Shah and the Majlis, when the former insisted that his father's *farman*, which he too had endorsed at the time, had specifically granted *qonstitusiun*, not *mashruteh*. See, for example, Mokhber al-Saltaneh, *Gozaresh-e Iran: Qajariyeh va Mashrutiyat* (Tehran: Noqreh, 1984), who had told the Shah that the former could even have a more radical meaning than the latter.

29 *Yaddashtha*, p. 269.

30 *Ibid.*, p. 271

31 *Ibid.*, pp. 271–72.

32 *Ibid,*. p. 273.

33 For other sources, see *Khaterat-e Ehtesham al-Saltaneh*, Nazem al-Isam *Tarilkh-e Bidari-ye Iraniyan*, Dawlat-Abadi, *Hayat-e Yahya*, vol. 2, and Ahmad Kasravi, *Tarikh-e Mashruteh-ye Iran* (Tehran: Amir Kabir, 1994).

33a For the historical meaning of 'mellat', 'melli', etc., see Homa Katouzian, 'Yaddashti darbareh-ye "melat", "melli", "melli-gera" va "nasionalism"', in *Estebdad, Demokrasi va Nehzat-e Melli*, second edition (Tehran: Nashr-e Markaz, 1997).

33b The brief narrative that follows in this section will be based on the primary sources cited in the notes above, notably those by Nazem al-Isalm, Dawlat-Abadi, Mostawfi, Mokhber al-Saltaneh, Bamdad, Kasravi and Browne. The more recent sources include Janet Afary, *The Iranian Constitutional Revolution, 1906-1911* (New York: Columbia University Press, 1996); Vanessa Martin, *Islam and Modernism: The Iranian Revolution of 1906* (London and New York: I.B. Tauris, 1989); Mangol Phlipp Bayat, *Iran's First Revolution, Shi'ism and the Constitutional Revolution of 1905-1909* (New York: Oxford University Press, 1991).

33c Apart from sources cited in (33b) above, see Abdolhossein Nava'i, *Dawlat-ha-ye Iran Az Aghaz-e Mashrutiyat ta Ultimatom* (Tehran: Babak, 1976).

33d Few indeed of the younger generations of the Constitutional Revolution did not later firmly believe that they had been thus deceived by Britain and her agents (such as Taqizadeh!) into campaigning against arbitrary rule. The view is regularly expressed in comments on the Constitutional Revolution in Mehdi Bamdad, *Sharh-e Hal-e Rejal-e Iran*, vols. 1–6.

34 See among other sources Herbert Marcuse, *Reason and Revolution*, second edition, (Routledge and Kegan Paul, 1955), W. A. Kaufman, *Hegel*, (New York: New American Library, 1957) and *From Shakespeare to Existentialism* (New York: Doubleday, 1960). David McLellan, *Young Hegelians and Karl Marx* (London: Macmillan, 1969). Bertrand Russell, *Philosophy and Politics* (Cambridge: Cambridge University Press, 1947).

35 See Homa Katouzian, *Ideology and Method in Economics* (London and New York: Macmillan and New York University Press, 1980), pp. 151–52.

36 See for example Friedrich Engels, *Herr Eugen Dühring's Revolution in Science: Anti-Dürhing*, ed. C. P. Dutt (London: Lawrence, 1943); *Dialectics of Nature*. (Moscow: Progress Publishers, 1964); Nikkolai Bukharin, *Historical Materialism* (New York, International Publishers, 1928). Joseph Stalin, *Dialectical and Historical Materialism* (London: Lawrence and Wishart, 1941).

37 See for example Katouzian, *Ideology and Method in Economics*; George Lichtheim, *Marxism* (London: Routledge and Kegan Paul, 1962); John Plamenatz, *German Marxism and*

Russian Communism (London: Longman, Green and Co., 1954); Isaiah Berlin, *Karl Marx* (Oxford University Press, third edition, 1963); David McLellan, *Karl Marx* (London: Macmillan, 1973).

38 The more important primary references are to be found in Marx's contributions to the American newspaper *Daily Tribune* in the 1850s, and his brief analytical classification of societies in the *Introduction to the Critique of Political Economy* (1859). For detailed bibliographical references see Perry Anderson, *Lineages of the Absolutist State* (London: New Left Books, 1974) and Karl Wittfogel, *Oriental Despotism* (New Haven:Conn.: Yale University Press, 1957). The general view that there had been basic differences between modes of development in Europe and Asia had of course a long precedent, the more recent prominent contributors being Montesquieu, Adam Smith, James Mill, Hegel and Richard Jones. See also Katouzian, *Political Economy,* chapter 2.

39 See Katouzian, *ibid.,* chapter 3, text and appendix.

40 See *ibid.,* tables 3.2 to 3.8. The structural change in favour of primary production and exports, and against manufacturing, may be particularly seen in table 3.7.

41 For the extent and effects of debasement, depreciation, inflation. etc. see *ibid.,* text as well as tables 3.2 to 3.5.

42 For detailed analysis and evidence, see *ibid.*

43 There were many nobles and notables who raised the issue of law and responsible government before younger middle class intellectuals stepped in, for example Abbas Mirza Molk Ara, Sepahsalar-e Qazvini, Malkam Khan, Mostashar al-Dawleh, Amin al-Dawleh, E'temad al-Saltaneh, Sa'd al-Dawleh, Mokhber al-Saltaneh, Sani' al-Dawleh and Ehtesham al-Saltaneh.

44 See Sayyed Mohammad Ali Jamalzadeh, 'Sayyed Jamal al-Din Va'ez-e Isfahani va Ba'zi Mobarezat-e U' in Ali Dehbashi, (ed.), *Yad-e Mohammad Ali Jamalzadeh* (Tehran: Nashr-e Sales, 1998), pp. 51–52. The quotation from Sayyed Jamal's Sermon is direct from a report in the *Al-Jamal* newspaper, no. 35, 1905.

45 See Kasravi, *Tarikh-e Mashruteh-ye Iran,* pp. 415–23.

46 *Ibid.,* pp. 415–16.

47 *Ibid.,* pp. 416–17.

48 *Ibid.,* pp. 432–38.

49 See Nazem al-Islam-e Kermani, *Tarikh-e Bidari-ye Iraniyian,* pp. 241-43.

50 See their numerous statements, their correspondence with the ulama in Iran, and their aggressive and uncompromising letters to the Shah himself in Kasravi's *Tarikh-e Mashruteh* and Nazem al-Islam's *Tarikh-e Bidari.* For a couple of short examples, see below.

51 See *ibid.,* pp. 365–71.

52 *Ibid.,* pp. 365–67.

53 Ibid., pp. 367-371.

54 Quoted verbatim in *ibid.,* p. 528.

55 See Nazem al-Islam, *Tarikh-e Bidari,* p. 229.

56 *Ibid.,* p. 214.

57 The most famous of them are leading social contract theorists such as John Locke, and liberal economists such as Adam Smith, David Hume and the French Physiocrats.

58 See in particular his famous essay on liberty, and his other works on the subject, in John Gray (ed)., *On Liberty and Other Essays* (Oxford and New York: Oxford University Press, 1991).

59 Isaiah Berlin *Two Concepts of Liberty* (Oxford: The Clarendon Press, 1959).

60 See Harold Lasky, *A Grammar of Politics* (London: Allen and Unwin, 1963).

61 See Isaiah Berlin, *Two Concepts of Liberty.*

62 See his newspaper, *Mosavat,* no. 1, 13 October 1907, p. 2. See further below on him and his newspaper.

63 See Homa Katonzian, 'Demokrasi, Diktatori va Ms'ullyiat-e Mellat' in *Estebdad,*

Demokrasi va Nehzat-e Melli, second edition (Tehran: Nashr-e Markaz, 1996).
64   See, Yahya Ariyanpur, *Az Saba ta Nima*, vol. 1 (Tehran: Zavvar, 1993), pp. 289–290.
65   *Ibid.*, p. 290.
66   *Ibid.*
67   *Ibid.*, p. 291.
68   For specific examples see Homa Katouzian, *Musaddiq and The Struggle for Power in Iran*, second edition (London and New York: I.B.Tauris, 1999); 'Introduction' to *Musaddiq's Memoirs* (London: Jebhe, 1988); and *The Political Economy of Modern Iran*.
69   Of the contemporary sources, Mokhber al-Saltaneh (*Khaterat va Khatarat*, and *Gozaresh-e Iran: Qajariyeh va Mashrutiyat*) believed that Atabak had been murdered by the Shah's hatchet men – Movaqqar al-Saltaneh, Mafakher al-Molk and Modabber al-Soltan – who were certainly around when the Majlis adjourned on that fateful night; Dawlat-Abadi (*Hayat-e Yahya*, vol. 2) points out that the Shah did not want Atabak and hints that he may have been planning to have him assassinated, but still believes that Abbas Aqa was the sole assailant; Nazem al-Islam, too (*Tarikh-e Bidari*, vol. 2.), says that Arshad al-Dawleh was intent on arranging Atabak's assassination on behalf of the Shah when Abbas Aqa relieved him of the task. Of the later historians, Kasravi (*Tarikh-e Mashruteh*) insists that it was the work of the young revolutionary and none other, although he also is aware of the Shah's hostility towards Atabak; Shaikholeslami ('Majera-ye Qatl-e Atabak' in *Qatl-e Atabak va Shanzdah Maqaleh-ye Tahqiqi-ye Digar*, Keyhan: Tehran, 1988) also believes that it was the work of the young man and the secret committee behind him but emphasizes – along Nazem al-Islam's lines – that the Shah, too, was intent on ridding himself of Atabak. The argument between him and Taqizadeh over this subject has been published in full, where the latter has categorically denied any previous knowledge of the assassination of Atabak, and, somewhat unconvincingly, has added that he even disapproved of it when it happened.
70   See Kasravi, *Tarikh-e Mashruteh*, pp. 593–95. He also displays awareness of the fact that not even *Sur Esrafil* was immune from such misdemeanours. For obscene personal attacks on the Shah see also Abdollah Mostawfi, *Sharh-e Zendegani*, vol. 2, p. 258.
71   See *Zendegi-ye Tufani, Khaterat-e Siyasi-ye Taqizadeh*, (ed.) Iraj Afshar, Tehran: Elmi, 1993. Taqizadeh probably did not know of the plan to assassinate Behbahani before the event, but it is not very likely that he regretted it when it happened. His own later development into a sophisticated modern politician earned him the suspicion and distrust of all the main parties, and that – as he told Iraj Afshar in his old age, who in turn told this author – must have reminded him of his own radical idealism as a leader of the constitutional revolution.

3

Constitutionalism and Chaos

The twelve years which separated the triumph of 1909 and the Coup d'état of 1921 were marked by chaos both at the centre and in the provinces. Revolutions everywhere show a pattern of early unity of revolutionary forces breaking up into destructive conflicts and factional struggles. In the English civil wars and revolution the rift became almost complete when it was decided to put the king on trial. In the French Revolution, the conflict began in the National and Legislative Assemblies, grew much more fierce and deadly in the Convention, when St Just's 'despotisme de la liberté' was reigning supreme, came to a climax in the Thermidor of 1794, and was forcibly abandoned as a result of Bonaparte's Coup of Brumaire 1799. The revolutions of 1830, and especially 1848, also ended in serious conflict among the liberators themselves. In Russia, the February revolution quickly led to confrontations between Liberals and Mensheviks on the one hand, and Bolsheviks and Left Social Revolutionaries on the other, resulting in the October Revolution, which led to the civil war, the one-party state, and the struggle between the communist Right, Left and Centre, until Stalin's faction triumphed and eliminated its rivals. The fierce civil struggles during China's Cultural Revolution began more than a decade after the communist triumph in 1949, but involved the elimination of such leaders as Lio Shao-Chi, Lin Piao and nearly Chou En-Lai, until the overthrow of the Gang of Four and the accession to power of Deng Xiao-Ping.

On the other hand, the factional struggles in those revolutions did not result in chaos, disorder and near disintegration in comparison with Iran's Constitutional Revolution. If anything – at least within a short period of time – central government became stronger and more effective, and the civil as well as military achievements of the revolutionary governments were often spectacular, and sometimes almost miraculous. To mention one famous example: in the midst of the Terror the French managed to win the battle of Valmy, and to stamp out domestic rebellion in the provinces, notably in Vendée.

Anatomy of the chaos

It would be easy to blame the Iranian chaos on foreign interference. Such intervention had existed increasingly since the early nineteenth century, but it had never been associated with the sort of domestic chaos that overtook the country after 1910. The recent extension of the Entente, and the Anglo–Russian

Convention of 1907, had made the Iranian government weaker in that it could no longer play off Britain against Russia, but had not made it more likely that these nations would induce chaos in the provinces. Apart from that, it was mainly the influence of the two foreign powers that discouraged massacres, vendettas or a deadly power struggle among the revolutionaries themselves, after the Shah was overthrown. This was also true after the fall of Reza Shah in 1941.

After the 1907 Convention, the Russians were hated not only because of their enhanced presence in their Sphere of Influence, but perhaps even more for the brutal and often inhuman behaviour of their forces in the northern provinces of the country. The British began to be distrusted, resented and then also hated largely because of their acquiescence in the Russian behaviour. The First World War had a devastating effect on the whole of the country, in part because of the occupation and/or serious interventions of the Russian, Turkish, British and German powers.

So much is well known and hardly a matter for disagreement. What is not so widely appreciated is the important contribution of domestic forces and factors, both in the centre of politics and in the provinces, towards discontinuity, insecurity, rift and threat of disintegration. Indeed, if the main political forces in Tehran had worked within the constitution for governability rather than ungovernability, the fate of the country might well have been different in the twentieth century. It was more like the traditional Iranian chaos following the fall of an arbitrary ruler, as predicted by the comparative theory suggested in chapter one, even though this time the revolution had been for law and against arbitrary rule, and not just an arbitrary ruler. As early as 1910, poet-laureate Bahar, then a young radical Democrat in Mashad, addressed a long and desperately emotional *mosammat* to all the constitutionalists, begging them to abandon destructive conflict amongst themselves. Significantly, it was entitled 'The Motherland is in Danger':

> Agreed we not from the outset not to sew division?
> Were we not united in making for unity?
> Whither then that pact and whereto that agreement,
> Why is it that you have all now changed your minds? ...
> Try to save the motherland, for God's sake,
> Let there be no more rift, for God's sake,
> Destroy the enemy [instead] for God's sake,
> O' people try to help, for God's sake ...[1]

Chaos following the fall of an arbitrary rule had been familiar from Iranian history, although – to make just one comparison – the chaos following the fall of Soltan Hossein had not taken quite the same form, or had quite the same consequences, as that which followed the fall of Khosrow II (Parviz). Likewise, the chaos that developed quickly after the Constitutional Revolution also took its own contemporary form and had its own specifically contemporary causes and pretexts. Indeed, much of it took place in the name of law and freedom.

To begin with, there was the problem of the extraordinary powers of the Majlis, as mentioned briefly in chapter two. The letter of the constitution was by itself sufficient to make the task of governing very difficult. If the British parliament today had the power over the executive that the Majlis had then in Iran, it would find the task of governing a good deal more problematic, even though the society it rules is one of the most governable in the world. Yet the problem went far beyond the letter of the constitution. Firstly, there was the notion that the Majlis was *khaneh-ye mellat* (as opposed to *dawlat*), as if the two were still as contradictory as in the defunct arbitrary system. The Majlis was not seen to be part of the state; rather, it was seen as the force of the society (*mellat*), which would virtually give order to the 'state' (*dawlat*) – that is, the executive cabinet – even on the small detail of its work. The misunderstood doctrine of the separation of powers, which had been written in the constitution, merely provided a modern rationalization for the traditional Iranian confrontation of powers after the fall of an arbitrary state. The same thing happened in the period 1941–1953.[2]

Secondly, there was no proper parliamentary party system through which longer lasting cabinets could try to make the best of a difficult job in managing the Majlis. The parties which sprang up were somewhat malleable and lacked the kind of programmes that could be translated into executive policy. Apart from issuing statements of ideals (which radical sentimentalists were particularly good at) they tended to know what they did not want more clearly than what they did want.

The Democrat party's programme included 'the complete separation of the political from the religious power', 'distribution of land among the peasantry', 'opposition to Senate', etc.[3] Their top leadership consisted of Taqizadeh, former *talabeh* turned radical modernist intellectual, Sayyed Mohammad Reza Mosavat, former *talabeh* turned reckless revolutionary; Solaiman Mirza, a Qajar nobleman whose dead brother (Yahya Mirza) had been a hero of Bagh-e Shah; and two other radicals, Hosseinqoli Khan Navvab and Vahid al-Molk, who were somewhat less colourful than the other three.

The Moderate party (*E'etedalliyun*) was led by Sayyed Mohammad Sadeq Tabtaba'i[4] (eldest son of the great Tabatab'i), Ali Akbar Dehkhoda, the radical intellectual, the Dawlat-Abadi brothers – Babi/Azali religious types and intellectuals – and Shokrollah Khan Qavam al-Dawleh, a landlord-politician from Tehran. They were gradualists. For the conditions of the country at the time, their programme may be described as radical reformist, but Democrats denounced it, along with its authors, as 'reactionary'.[4*] The Democrats often had the backing of the Bakhtiyari leaders of the revolution. The Moderates had the blessing of the *Sayyedain* – Behbahani and Tabatab'i – and the goodwill of Naser al-Molk when he became regent. On the whole, the younger and more radical urban activists supported the Democrats, and the older and more conservative were behind the Moderates. The divisions were far less along class lines than they were of ideas and allegiances: Solaiman Mirza was a nobleman, and Mostawfi al-Mamalek a high *divani* landlord and one of the richest men in Tehran, while Dehkhoda was a middle-class intellectual who was no better off than Taqizadeh, and almost as radical as him during the revolution.

Thirdly (among the factors contributing to chaos), there was the traditional rush towards autonomy, rebellion and pillage – *khan-khani, fetneh va ashub,* and *gharat* – in the provinces and border regions, as discussed in chapter one above. This process, as noted in chapter two, had already begun under Mozaffar al-Din, whose feebleness and lack of interest outside 'eating, hunting and copulation' left the country's affairs to the insatiable appetite of the central and provincial ministers and governors. Thus, Malek al-Movarrekhin's reports (cited in the previous chapter) of killing, raping and looting by the governors were matched by his reports of Lor and Turkaman tribesmen looting, raping and selling both men and women into slavery, the Qashqa'is and Bakhtiyaris refusing to pay tax and putting government troops to flight, and so on. They show the beginning of a trend that was naturally accentuated by revolution and civil war, and got almost completely out of hand during the First World War.

But it must be emphasized that chaotic and lawless behaviour was not exclusive to local and tribal leaders. It was found on the part of government representatives and commanders as well, just as had been the case during the rapid decline of central authority after Naser al-Din. Indeed, the new rulers' arbitrary behaviour was sometimes the cause of similar responses by the local people. Within a few years, when tribal and provincial people wanted to say there was looting and killing somewhere they said 'it was constitutitonalised' (*mashruteh shod*). To give but one example, Abdolhossein Khan Mo'ez al-Soltan (further entitled Sardar Mohayy, after the fall of Mohammad Ali) was a young revolutionary hothead, if not hero, who had distinguished himself in the Battle of Tehran as a commander of the Gilan forces. A couple of years later he was made governor-general of Kurdistan. According to a contemporary local historian, he behaved with great injustice towards the local people. He says that once the Sardar tried to sell the semi-official position of Shaikholeslam for as much as 7000 tomans, although the incumbent was only offering 300. In the end, by selling various sub-offices they managed to raise the 7000. He sold the governorship of one town to two different people and received the money from both, but obviously the job could only go to one of them. 'Sardar Mohayy was extremely interested in two things: first, money, second, pretty boys'. The historian goes on to pass the general comment:

There was loss of faith in constitutionalism and constitutionalists alike. Indeed, among the people, the word constitutionalism (*mashruteh*) came to mean killing and looting, so that whenever anyone killed anyone and anywhere was looted, they said it was constitutionalised.[4a]

Soon it became a habit in Tehran itself to describe anyone who got good posts or made good money under the new regime as having 'achieved his constitutionalism' (*'beh mashruteh-ash resid'*). For decades later, the expression was to persist as a metaphor for describing anyone who had succeeded in anything not altogether by fair means.[4b]

Putting aside the specifically contemporary factors, the pattern was familiar from Iranian history whenever a crack in the resolve and/or apparatus of the state had occurred. Yet if, (after the revolution) there had been a relatively cohesive government at the centre, the provincial and regional situation would have been considerably less unstable, which in turn would have reinforced the central government's position. The fact remains, however, that the politics of confrontation at the centre – both within the Majlis, and between it and the rapidly changing cabinets – itself represented old patterns from the arbitrary society, from the lawless society after the fall of a lawless state, except that it was now justified in apparently modern and constitutional terms. Government based on law quickly began to mean little but licence and absence of restraint by many of the modern lovers of 'freedom and law' (*'azadi va qanun'*) as well as by the traditional forces of anarchy. In other words, the tendency described in chapter two as characteristic of the period of revolution and civil war (1906–09) was strengthened even further after the revolution.

Contemporary evidence

In March 1910, Sepahsalar-e (formerly Sephdar-e) Tonokaboni forms the first post-victory cabinet.

In July, four masked men enter Sayyed Abdollah Behbahani's home and shoot him dead. His murder is an indirect result of the feud between the Democrats and the Moderates, both of which have representatives in the Majlis. The militant Haidar Khan and four others are blamed as the culprits, and Taqizadeh, the Democrat leader, is accused of being behind the plot. 'The jurist on whom Islam was leaning, Taqizadeh ordered and *shaqizadeh* assassinated', is the verse shouted by angry crowds in the bazaar.[5] In Najaf, Khorasani and Mazanderani attack Taqizadeh and ask the Majlis to expel him. A compromise formula is reached, and the Majlis votes a three-month leave of absence for him to go to Europe. This he does, though he was not to return to the country until some time after the Coup of 1921. The young Ali Mohammad Tarbiyat – a radical Democrat – who had been suspected of being one of the four assassins is killed in the street, together with another young Democrat, by a band of armed men. Haidar Khan is found and arrested, but released without charge after spending six weeks in jail.[6]

Also in July – less than five months after he had become the first constitutionalist prime minister – Sepahsalar resigns over conflicts with the Bakhtiyari khans, and the Democrats' candidate, Mostawfi al-Mamalek, forms a cabinet.

In August, the government orders Sattar Khan and Baqer Khan, the two heroes of the Azerbaijan resistance to Mohammad Ali's Coup, to lay down their arms together with the band of *mojahedin* under them. They refuse. They are Moderate supporters, and are in competition with the Bakhtiaris who are also armed and support the Democrats. Troops led by Yeprem Khan (a revolutionary hero as well as the police and security chief) and armed Bakhtityaris led by Sardar Bahador (later, Sardar As'ad III) jointly attack and arrest them. The fight leaves 30 dead and 63 wounded on both sides.[7]

In September, the regent, Alireza Khan Azad al-Molk, dies and the Moderates' candidate, Naser al-Molk, then in Europe, wins twice as many votes in the Majlis as Mostawfi, the prime minister, to become the new Regent. In the same month, a large Bakhtiyari force from Isfahan encircles Kashan to arrest Nayeb Hossein Kashi who has led an armed rebellion since 1907, and frequently plunders the rich and poor alike. There are many dead and wounded, but the Nayeb and his 1200-strong force manage to escape to the desert.[8]

In November, 500 bandits attack the Bandar Abbas area and loot all the villages and caravans, including substantial British merchandise. In Shiraz a Muslim girl is killed and 'the Jews' are blamed for it. The mob first attack and loot the courts, then the Jewish ghetto. Troops sent to defend the ghetto together with some Qashqa'i tribesmen join the mob. Eleven Jews are killed and 15 wounded.[9]

In January 1911, the Isfahan police chief shoots the city's governor in the latter's office. The governor is wounded but his nephew is killed.

In February, Sani' al-Dawleh, Majlis speaker and a Moderate leader, is assassinated by two Russian subjects who then take advantage of the capitulation agreement and are handed over to the Russian legation in Tehran.

In March, less than ten months after he had taken office, Mostawfi resigns as prime minister and Sepahsalar takes over once again.

In May, women rioters protesting the bread shortage attack the mayor's office in Isfahan, loot it, kill the mayor and hang his body in the Shah Square, attack and loot other government offices and release prisoners from jail. The governor orders the opening of fire on them, a few are killed and the rest scatter.[10]

August and September, Mohammad Ali Shah and his brother Sho'a' al-Saltaneh invade Iran and attack Gomesh Tappeh in the Turkaman region; there are demonstrations in Mashad in favour of the deposed Shah, which leave some dead and wounded. Their other brother, Salar al-Dawleh, attacks in the west and comes as far as Soltan-Abad (Arak). Mohammad Ali's force is defeated at Varamin as is Sho'a's in Mazandaran, while Salar's is pushed back. Meanwhile, just a few months into his second premiership, Sepahsalar is dismissed by the Majlis on suspicion of sympathy for the old Shah, and Samsam al-Saltaneh Bakhtiyari, a Democrat favourite, is appointed.[11]

Between October and December, Morgan Shuster, Iran's Treasurer-General, tries to enforce a Majlis decision to confiscate Sho'a's and Salar's property in retaliation against their rebellion. The Russians oppose his decision, he insists, the Majlis backs him, and it all ends in his own dismissal and the closure of the Majlis. This episode will be discussed in more detail below.

March 1912, the regent orders the banishment from Tehran of Democrat leaders Solaiman Mirza, Navvab and Vahid al-Molk.

In April, Salar al-Dawleh takes Kermanshah once again, and prepares to take Hamadan. A force led by Farmanfarma and Yeprem Khan defeats and pushes him back, but Yeprem is killed in action.[12]

In September, Salar returns to Kermanshah and, in another pitched battle, he is defeated and pushed back once again. Nayeb Hossein loots seven villages between Yazd and Kerman, and takes women and children into slavery. In Fars, there is another clash between government and tribal forces. In Azerbaijan, the Shahsavan nomads rebel, and the governor-general (Sepahsalar) asks Eqbal al-Saltaneh, the Khan of Maku, to assist him in putting it down.[13]

In the same month, a large number of Democrats in Tehran issue an *E'lamiyeh* demanding elections for the third Majlis which have been overdue for several months since its closure at the end of the Shuster affair. There is a newspaper campaign against Samsam's government, and he orders the press to be censored.

In November, Sa'd al-Dawleh – the old constitiutionalist hero turned ogre by defecting to Mohammad Ali – returns from Europe to a glorious public welcome in Tehran. They say that he is grooming himself to replace Naser al-Molk as Regent, and has the support of both Russia and Britain. Newspapers attack Samsam again and demand that Sa'd should replace him.[14]

In the same month, the British consul in Bushire complains of the inertia of the governor-general of Fars in dealing with bandits who regularly loot British and Indian merchandise.[15]

Also in November, there are irreconcilable conflicts within the cabinet and some ministers stop attending its meetings. Samsam resigns as prime minister.

In January 1913, the Regent appoints Ala al-Saltaneh, and he forms a mixed cabinet which includes Vosuq al-Dawleh, a right-wing Democrat; Mostawfi al-Mamalek, a centrist Democrat; Mostashar al-Dawleh, a left wing Democrat; and the brothers Moshir al-Dawleh and Mo'tamen al-Molk who are popular pro-Moderates.[16]

In February, armed Bakhtiyari horsemen demonstrate in the bazaar against Ala and in favour of their own chief Samsam, the former prime minister, leaving several dead and wounded.

In April, a company of the Iranian Cossack Brigade clashes with Kurdish rebels near Kermanshah. Thirty Cossacks are killed and the bodies of 20 rebels are recovered.

In August, armed Bakhtiyaris in Tehran refuse to give up their arms. The gendarmes disarm them on government orders. There are more than 100 casualties. The Bakhtiyaris, it should be emphasised, are a pillar of the constitutional regime, and their own chief has been recently prime minister.

In the same month, Ala resigns and Mostawfi forms a cabinet.

In September, the British minister in Tehran sends a strongly-worded note to the government protesting against the insecurity of roads in the south of the country which results in the regular plunder of British and Indian merchandise.

In November, there is a battle between the Cossacks and the Shahsavans in Ardebil, and the Cossacks ask for reinforcements from Tabriz.[17]

In July 1914, Ahmad Shah comes of age and is formally crowned amid lavish celebrations.[18]

In August, war breaks out in Europe, Ala's government, which meanwhile had replaced Mostawfi's, resigns, and Mostawfi once again becomes prime minister.[19]

It must be emphasized that within four years there had been eight premierships and five prime ministers. The same pattern was to repeat itself until 1923, when Reza Khan became prime minister, apart from Vosuq's attempt to build a strong government between 1918 and 1920. It was to be repeated yet again between Reza Shah's abdication in 1941 and the Coup d'état of 1953.

The above selected events are a small sample of the chaos both at the centre and in the provinces before the First World War. To do justice to this period of history would need a long study in its own right. Kasravi's voluminous *Tarikh-e Hijdahsaleh-ye Azerbaijan*, a single source, is proof of that.

The case of Morgan Shuster

Before the Anglo–Russian Convention of 1907, the constitutionalists had sought and obtained sympathy and support from Britain. After their triumph in 1909 they increasingly began to look elsewhere for help. Modern Iranians were culturally close to France, but France was then a very eager member of the Entente. Whatever the real hope of attracting help from Germany, it was unlikely that, after the Russo–German agreement at Potsdam, the Germans would annoy the Russians over Iran. The new Iranian regime often recruited military and civilian personnel from smaller European powers, especially Sweden and Belgium. All things considered, however, they managed to employ a young, efficient and zealous adviser from the United States, to organise the country's financial system. He was Morgan Shuster.

Shuster's mission was deemed to be so important that he was appointed Treasurer-General by no less than an act of the Majlis, with extensive powers to reorganise public finance and collect revenues. It is clear from his book that he was opposed to old school imperialism and felt much in sympathy with Iran in her relationship with her two imperialist neighbours.[20] It is also clear that as a young, liberal American he had little understanding of the traditional methods of bargaining and exchange with which things were somehow managed in Iran. He set out to create an island of financial efficiency and propriety in the midst of a traditional ocean, which was still going through a revolutionary storm and was still subject to interference by Russia and Britain.

Under the powers given to him by the Majlis, he organised the Treasury gendarmerie as an instrument for collecting overdue or other revenues. Shuster nominated Major C.B. [Claude] Stokes, a British officer, to head the gendarmerie on secondment. Stokes was very sympathetic to Democrats; he had been the British diplomat who had allowed Taqizadeh and the others to take sanctuary in the British Legation compound after Mohammad Ali Shah's Coup.[21] Apart from that, the Russians would not allow a British officer to command a military force in their sphere of influence. In the face of Russian opposition, the British, who had agreed to let Stokes take on the task, backed down.[22] Thus Shuster's mission began with a major clash with the Russians in Iran.

Predictably, he began to make powerful Iranian enemies as well, but he still had the support of the Majlis and the public. For example, his gendarmes tried to collect Ala al-Dawleh's overdue taxes without success. Ala al-Dawleh was the fierce old arbitrary governor of Tehran, whose flogging of the sugar merchants had triggered the campaign for independent judicial courts, and who had later turned coat and become constitutionalist, although he no longer had a government position. He had the gendarmes beaten up and thrown out. There was a public outcry, and shortly afterwards Ala al-Dawleh was gunned down outside his own house by unknown assassins.[23]

After the deposed Shah and Sho'a' al-Saltaneh were defeated and driven out of the country, and while their brother Salar al-Dawleh was still leading a rebellion in the west, the Majlis ordered the confiscation of the property of Sho'a' and Salar. On the other hand, Mohammad Ali and Sho'a' were dependent on Russia, and so under Russian protection.

Neither Naser al-Molk, the regent, nor Samsam, the prime minister, nor Yeprem Khan, the powerful police chief, was pro-Russian. The regent was pro-Moderate, and Samsam and his Bakhtiyaris, as well as Yeprem, had had good relations with the Democrats. But all of them, besides other cabinet members and magnates, knew that the Russians would seriously oppose the confiscations. They also realised that they could not resist the Russians without British support, which since the 1907 Convention was no longer available.

The Russians claimed that Sho'a's property near the Bastiyun, north of the then Tehran, was a collateral for his debt to the Russian Loan Bank in Iran. The government and many Moderates were weary of implementing the confiscation order in the face of Russian opposition. Outraged by the Russian attitude and encouraged by Solaiman Mirza and other Democrat leaders, Shuster decided to act. The Russians posted a few of their own soldiers outside the garden park of Sho'a's property. Ignoring them, Shuster's Treasury gendarmes went into action, sent the Russian soldiers packing and occupied the property. The same operation was carried out against another property of Sho'a's near Hazrat-e Abdol'azim. The Russian minister protested to Vosuq al-Dawleh, the minister of foreign affairs. The latter reported to a private session of the Majlis and advised them to shelve the matter for the time being. The Democrats, who were in minority, loudly rejected Vosuq's advice and won enough Moderates to their side to make a solid majority. The Russian legation then sent a formal note to the government demanding the evacuation of Sho'a's property. Given the defiant mood of the Majlis – and the general public, who had discovered a cause for giving vent to their anti-Russian feelings – Shuster refused to call off his gendarmes.

Until then, the issue had been an explicitly legal one of who had the right to claim the property; and a tacitly political – but limited – one of showing the Russian resolve to protect Sho'a'. Both the refusal to comply by the Russian note and the heat which the conflict generated against Russian arrogance turned the issue into a confrontation as to whom – the Russians, or Shuster and the Majlis – had more muscle to flex in the matter. The result was disaster for Iran and its infant constitutional regime.

The Russians presented the government with an ultimatum demanding Shuster's dismissal as well as a pledge not to appoint any foreign advisers without the approval of Russia and Britain. Far from retracting their position, the Majlis and public responded with angry speeches and articles, and the Majlis unanimously rejected the ultimatum. The Russians then moved some of their forces in the north to Qazvin and threatened to occupy Tehran. There were angry demonstrations in the capital and some other major cities. There was the threat of jihad in the *atabat,* and Akhund-e Mullah Kazem decided to lead it personally, but shortly afterwards died of a sudden illness. There was a general belief that he had been poisoned by Russian agents.

Samsam's government saw no alternative to the Russian occupation of the capital but to accept their ultimatum. Yet, in line with the public mood, the Majlis Democrats – followed, willy-nilly, by most of the Moderates – were still defiant. The government then accepted the ultimatum and, together with an assembly of the notables, appealed to the regent to dissolve the Majlis. The deputies refused to break up, and – helped by Samsam's Bakhtiyaris – the revolutionary hero Yeprem Khan, as head of the *Nazmiyeh,* forced them out of the House.

It looked rather like the Thermidor of 1794 and the Brumaire of 1799 combined. But this was December 1911, and unfortunately not the end of the matter. Angry public reaction in Tabriz led to massacre, plunder and executions by the Russian troops, who then installed their own Iranian governor – the pitiless Samad Khan (Shoja' al-Dawleh) former governor under Mohammad Ali – in the city. Even that did not end the catastrophe. In the following March, there were major clashes between the Russian troops and the people of Mashad. Many were killed and wounded when the troops fired at them in the shrine of Imam Reza where they had taken sanctuary, hoping for immunity. And it was heart-rending for the Shi'a community to learn of the damage caused to the dome of the shrine by the Russian bombardment. Meanwhile, the regent banished a few Democrat leaders, including Solaiman Mirza and Navvab, from Tehran to try and stem the tide of public agitation; and the Russians encouraged another rebellion by Salar al-Dawleh in the west.[24]

Predictably, the matter did not pass without numerous angry laments being written by poets and songwriters. One of the most popular was the song by the radical nationalist poet and musician Abolqasem Aref-e Qazvini about Shuster's enforced dismissal. He writes in a prefatory note to the song that he had been witness to students shouting 'Independence or Death' in Baharestan, the parliament square:

> Shame upon a home when the guest leaves the table unfed,
> Give him your life and do not let him leave,
> If Shuster goes from Iran, Iran will go with the wind
> O' young people do not let Iran leave.
> You are life to a dead body!
> You are life to the whole world!
> You are an immense treasure!
> You are life eternal!
> God let you stay, God let you stay.[25]

Poet-laureate Bahar, then a leading young Democrat in Mashad, wrote a long *tarkib-band* vehemently attacking Naser al-Molk, the regent, calling him, among other things, a 'Europe worshipper' and a 'gutless' and 'duplicitous' man. He wrote that the regent had plotted with the Russians to bring Mohammad Ali back to the throne. That was foiled by the heroes who fought and defeated the old Shah. Then Shuster – 'that highly esteemed Consultant' – went to work against him, and so the regent arranged for the Russian ultimatum, which led to Shuster's dismissal:

> Traitors have no shame of their deed,
> May they go blind and blind in speed,
> Slaves and agents of Russia are they,
> From the general to the colonel indeed …[26]

He also wrote a longer *tarkib-band*, entitled 'The Gun of Russia', when Russian troops opened fire on the crowd who had taken sanctuary in Imam Reza's shrine and damaged the dome in the process:

Why is the prophet of God wailing?
He thinks of his honourable descendant's tomb!
Reza the Shah, the Martyr of Khorasan, the Foreigner of Tus,
Whose pure heart was set alight by the guns of Rus.[27]

Appraising the Shuster affair

Let us now try and assess the Shuster affair in all its aspects. The Anglo–Russian Convention of 1907 had declared the north of Iran as Russia's sphere of influence, and Russian troops rode their iron horses in the northern provinces.

Mohammad Ali and Sho'a' could not have led their rebellion deep inside the country without Russia's approval. This angered the Iranians, but they managed to defeat the intruders while Russian troops did not intervene to defend them. Then the Majlis decided to confiscate Sho'a's (and Salar's) property as a retribution for their rebellion. The Russians opposed this on the seemingly legal pretext that Sho'a's property was mortgaged to the Russian Loan Bank in Iran.

At this point it might have been possible to negotiate a face-saving formula with the Russian minister. Shuster and the Majlis remained adamant against the government's advice. Then came Russia's formal protest note. It was clear that the Russians would not relent, and it would have been wise to look for a compromise. At least, the Majlis might have adjusted its tone so as not to hurt the pride of an arrogant and chauvinist power. But neither the Majlis, nor the public, nor even Shuster himself, were in such mood. None of them explained *how* they and the government could resist the Russian force – knowing that Britain would not intervene to support them – especially now that the matter had become a battle of wills, and a question of prestige and credibility. The Russians moved their troops to Qazvin and sent the humiliating ultimatum. It was unanimously rejected by the Majlis, with greater indignation than before. The government, however, saw no alternative but to comply with it. The Majlis was cleared by troops, and Shuster was dismissed and had to leave the country. There followed the anti-Russian agitation and demonstrations with disastrous consequences as mentioned above.

Twenty years ago, the writer compared the Iranian disaster of 1911 with the Thermidor of 1794 in the French Revolution.[28] The analogy is fair insofar as the idealists had a major setback on both occasions. But it must be observed that in both cases idealists played an important role in bringing the full catastrophe upon themselves. It should also be emphasised that, unlike France, the conflict in Iran over the Russian ultimatum was not a domestic matter, so that no domestic political force engineered the 'Thermidor'. It was Russian oppression, and the emotionally charged public response to it, which led to an unnecessary domestic struggle and the worst possible outcome for the country.

The highly arrogant and oppressive behaviour of Russia and its occupying forces in Iran was stark, and against all norms of behaviour towards an independent country. It was the reason behind the great emotional outburst of Democrats, Moderates and the urban crowds in defence of their country's – indeed, their own – dignity and integrity. On the other hand, it was clear that every act of Iranian defiance would simply raise the stakes, escalate the crisis and result in a much greater defeat, as in fact happened.

Thus the conflict was not a domestic one, and the government of Samsam al-Saltaneh was trying to make the best of a bad job vis-à-vis a very powerful foreign foe whom Britain would no longer move to contain. Yet the Majlis and the crowd were facing the cabinet almost as if they were responsible for the Russian threat, and as if they or anyone else in Iran might put an end to Russian aggression. There was therefore a destructive conflict between the Majlis and the cabinet, out of which both bodies, as well as the country at large, would end up as losers.

It would not be possible to present even a brief outline of the debates and disagreements within the present compass. The most fundamental point, however, is that the Majlis saw itself as the representative of the people or society (*mellat*), as opposed to the state (*dawlat*), along lines discussed in previous chapters. Indeed, much of the long parliamentary debate, which ran over several meetings, was about the relative powers of the Majlis and the government. For example, on one occasion Vosuq, the foreign minister, bitterly complained of the cabinet's lack of power to act, and Shaikh Mohammad Khiyabani, the Tabriz Democrat leader, replied by saying that any more executive power would bring the former regime back in a new guise[29] – although he was to change his mind about domestic conflict and chaos years later, when he tried to bring some order to Azerbaijan (see chapter five). Unless it is seen in this historical context, the conflict would make no sense at all, for the result was a total and unmitigated defeat for both the state and the society.

This was anticipated at the very time by no less a radical Democrat than Taqizadeh, who – as noted above – had recently been in effect driven out of the country because of his radical views. He sent as many as 13 telegrams to leading figures of different views, including Solaiman Mirza, Vosuq, Sayyed Mohammad Reza Shirazi (Mosavat) and Mo'tamen al-Molk, imploring them to come to terms with Russia so as to avoid a disastrous defeat. For example, in his telegrams to Solaiman Mirza, who had replaced him as the parliamentary Democrat leader, he wrote:

I am absolutely astonished at the attitude which the Majlis had adopted towards the question of the [Russian] ultimatum ... At this moment, hostility and stubbornness would result in eternal damnation.[30]

And he went on to say that 'the Majlis and the government' must act as one, form a crisis committee and meet the Russian demand of a formal apology.

In his telegram to Mo'tamen al-Molk, the Majlis speaker and head of the Legislature, he wondered whether 'there was no-one among the country's leaders to comprehend the delicacy of the situation, and realise that the whole world would reproach us for showing such stubbornness over a mere apology'.[31] In yet another telegram to Mo'tamen, he 'begged [him] in the name of the motherland to give courageous advice in this dangerous situation, so that the cabinet withdraws its resignation, the apology is made, and the motherland is saved from the risk of destruction'. He even asked Mo'tamen to present his telegram to the Majlis.[32] And again:

The situation is very tight ... apologising to Russia is in fact the very essence of patriotism ... Having considered, and completely studied all aspects of the issue, I submit that the [political] parties must unite in one form or another and help the government. Otherwise, it would be treasonable. The motherland is in danger.[33]

To say that Iran was right, is to state the obvious but miss the point. The question is what the Majlis and cabinet should have done to serve the country's best possible interests in the situation. Perhaps it was right to resist and test the ground in the first instance, especially if this could have been done without aggravating Russian feelings. But once the Russians stiffened their resolve and made it clear that they would act, was it right for the Majlis – and especially Democrat leaders who were shouting the loudest – merely to give vent to their emotions?

Here we observe both an example of 'pre-politics', of the continuation of the pre-constitutional distrust and lack of cooperation between *mellat* and *dawlat*, and the wider problem of the absence of politics in the normal sense of the term, as discussed in chapter one.

Other, more ancient but perhaps less obvious, insights may be gained into the event. During the millennia of arbitrary rule, the practice and theory of righteousness, self-sacrifice and martyrdom, which belonged to the realms of religion and mysticism, had also been extended to resistance against unjust arbitrary rulers. People would fight for a cause, often without regard to the worldly interests of themselves and others, and defeat, death and even total annihilation would not matter at all because they too were seen as means, if not the only means, of redemption. There was no politics and no notion of conflict management: there was either win or lose. If the rebels won, they would probably become oppressors themselves and lose their previous legitimacy. If they lost, they would be regarded as martyrs irrespective of the mistakes that they had made. Now that constitutionalism had made public participation (in the affairs of the state) possible, and in the absence of any real political tradition, the rich and powerful traditions of mysticism and martyrdom were extended to the sphere of righteous politics.

A similar attitude motivated the popular, but usually powerless, causes and movements; a similar language and literature were used and created both through the struggle and after its failure and defeat; and a similar oral and written history justified almost every decision and action – especially those which had led directly to disaster. It was the old tradition of mystical martyrdom in the new garb of political action, and was therefore bound to have devastating consequences in disputes which were political rather than mystical, and which could only be resolved advantageously by the use of real political methods and instruments, including the hated solution of compromise.

By the early 1960s, this mystic attitude towards dissident political activity was succinctly described by the slogan, suitably attributed to Imam Hossein, 'Life is nothing but Idea and holy war for its realisation' (*Inna 'l-hayat 'aqidat-i wa Jihad*). This slogan was invented first by religious dissidents, but it was fully embraced by the entire opposition to Mohammad Reza Shah's regime for almost two decades. It was somehow overlooked that politics is meant to be for life, not life for politics.

This pattern was to be repeated in the twentieth century, when the control of movements with good causes was allowed to fall in the hands of an emotional public which would shout for death or the delivery of the ideal, for which, however, there often was not even a clear and practical definition, so that *any* achievement might be construed as being short of the ideal. There have been similar experiences in Europe and elsewhere. What makes the Iranian case look exceptional is the great dominance and persistence of such attitudes to politics, and the fact that such patterns became typical of Iranian dissident political movements in the twentieth century, when, as mentioned in the previous chapter, any and all political compromise was held to be tantamount to treason.

The second Majlis was not far from completing its term when it was cleared of deputies by Yeprem's troops. But elections for the third Majlis were postponed for more than two years, during which the regent was relatively more powerful than before, although that does not mean he was a dictator or indeed that he had much power. At any rate, the Shah came of age, elections were held and the third Majlis began its short career a couple of months after war broke out in Europe.[34]

War and disintegration

By the time the third Majlis met in December 1914, the Turks had entered the European war on the side of the two German empires. They entered it late in October, and attacked the Russians in the Black Sea shortly afterwards. Until then the war had not yet come to the Iranian borders, and although the German cause had many passionate well-wishers, especially among the Democrats, there was no urgency to take up an official attitude towards the war. As soon as the Turks joined the hostilities, Mostawfi's government declared Iran neutral, but the Turks would not recognise such neutrality while Russian troops still occupied Azerbaijan. Persistent attempts by the Iranian government, with some sympathy, but no real support, from Britain, to persuade Russia to evacuate its northern provinces was of no avail. Instead, the Russians brought back the notorious Samad Khan from Tiflis, who raised some Iranian levies to supplement Russian troops.[35] The Turks invaded Azerbaijan in December, and by early January 1915 they had almost driven the Russians out of the whole of that province.[36]

Russia's forces were in Iran, and Russia herself was as arrogant and moody as ever. Britain, who disembarked troops in Bahrain and Abadan to meet the Turkish threat, was also there, now with greater emphasis on her alliance with Russia. The Turks entered the war, and would not tolerate Russian occupation of the Iranian territory, which was also the best route to their own eastern provinces. The Germans wished to use the Afghans against British India, while at the same time inflaming religious and nationalist sentiments in Iran, India and elsewhere in the region. They therefore began to contact Iranian nationalists and Democrats, and send agents to nomadic chieftains and other magnates in the southern regions in Britain's sphere of influence.

All this looks sufficiently straightforward to explain Iran's predicament during the First World War. But there was another factor, which served both as a good excuse and an effective instrument for the violation of Iran's integrity by the warring powers. It was the chaos, and especially the fact that the government could not speak with one voice for the whole country, and that, mainly as a result, it had very little means of enforcing its decisions on domestic and foreign issues. It is doubtful whether the Russians would have evacuated Azerbaijan except by force. But (at the beginning) when the government told them they should withdraw their troops and let Iran raise a local levy for the defence of the province, the Russians refused, arguing that the government lacked the ability to do that.

From the beginning of the war until their defeat in January 1915, the Russian mood underwent several changes, in which the Russian government considered bribing Iran with territorial gains at the expense of the Turks, or persuading it to join the war on the side of the Entente, or demanding 'benevolent neutrality' as in the Russo–Ottoman war of 1877. But the Russians remained in occupation, and when the Ottoman army forced them to retreat, they tended to blame their failure on Mostawfi's government. The British minister, Sir Walter Townley, summed this up in a dispatch to the Foreign Office:

> It is unfortunate that the Russian Government is so suspicious of the present Cabinet ... I can understand that Petrograd has been annoyed by repeated requests ... that the Russian troops should be withdrawn from Persia ... but it is but fair, I think, to bear in mind that the Persians have for long been endeavouring to get the Russians out of Persia, and that it is only human to seek to profit from a chance occasion. There is very little to prove the Russian contention that there would be disorders if the Russian troops were withdrawn ... That the presence of foreign troops in the country was provocative of disorder was, I think, abundantly proved in our case in Shiraz, where the withdrawal of the Central Indian Horse had the best possible effect.

And he went on to add:

> In any case, had the [Russian] troops been withdrawn last October [1914] when the Persian government first asked that they might be, our position and that of Persia would have been a much better one than it is today. We have a mighty weight to carry here in our Russian ally, which makes it no easy task to guarantee that Persia will not listen to Turco-German blandishments ...[37]

The Foreign Office, on the other hand, put much more emphasis on keeping the Russians happy than appeasing the Iranians. When it became clear that the war would not end shortly, the British attitude, though not quite the country's behaviour, began to parallel that of Russia, trying to install as friendly a cabinet as possible in Tehran, and sympathetic government officials in the provinces; entering secret deals and bribing tribal leaders and provincial magnates. This had its consequences for Anglo–Iranian relations – and especially the 1919 Agreement – after the war, when Tsarist Russia had fallen, and Soviet Russia kept issuing most benevolent declarations of friendship and sympathy for Iran (see chapter five).

For a moment in January 1915, Russia contemplated handing over Azerbaijan to the Iranians now that it was largely occupied by the Turks, but the fortunes were quickly reversed and the Russians withdrew their verbal offer. In March, the ulama in the *atabat* sent the Shah a formal *fatva* against the allies,[38] while the expulsion of German diplomats from the Russian sphere of influence had driven yet another hole into Iran's profession of neutrality.[39] Mostawfi's government fell under Entente pressure, and the more flexible Moshir al-Dawleh formed a ministry that, nonetheless, did not satisfy either Russia and Britain, or the pro-Germans of the Majlis.

Russia and Britain were lobbying for Sa'd al-Dawleh, but the Majlis agreed to a compromise on Ain al-Dawleh, whose cabinet included the pro-British Abdolhossein Mirza Farmanfarma.[40] This left the Democrats unhappy and when, in June, Farmanfarma, as minister of the interior, sent some Kurdish forces to brush with Turkish troops in the west, they managed to bring down Ain's government. There followed a typical example of rift at the very centre of politics when many Moderates, led by Sayyed Hasan Modarres, refused to have Mostawfi, and the Democrats, led by Solaiman Mirza, would not accept Ain's conditions for forming a new cabinet. Yet, after an unsuccessful attempt by Moshir, they agreed on Mostawfi.

Meanwhile, the British and Russian ministers in Tehran had been discussing with their respective governments the use of a financial lever to oil the rusty wheels of the Iranian government in return for their commitment to some form of 'benevolent neutrality'. The pro-German party in the Majlis being strong, it was decided to disguise the financial aid in the form of a moratorium on Iran's servicing of her existing debts to the two powers. It took too long to negotiate, experienced much ebb and flow, and came too late to avert a major crisis.

Bushire had been put under British occupation as a result of a raid by local tribesmen, apparently organised by Wassmuss, the legendary German agent, which had led to the death of two British officers.[41] Shiraz, the seat of the governor-general of Fars, was in turmoil; both British and German consulates were involved, although the Germans had public sympathy on their side. All four warring parties were violating Iran's neutrality, but in general the Iranians saw the Russians and British as the aggressors, while the Germans and (less so) the Turks were seen, if not as liberators, then as merely responding to the Anglo–Russian activities.

Regarding the troubles in Fars, Sir Charles Marling, who had replaced Townley as British minister, blamed Mokhber al-Saltaneh (later, Mehdiqoli Hedayat), the governor-general, for taking sides against Britain. He even wrote directly to Mokhber warning him to remain neutral, to which Mokhber replied with a challenge to Marling to name any specific act of doubtful neutrality on his part.[42] This happened before the Bushire incident which, Mokhber says, he could have dealt with satisfactorily if the British had not declared the town under occupation. In the end, Mostawfi agreed to dismiss Mokhber in order to get British occupation lifted.

The powers were at war, and inevitably pursued their interests with any means at their disposal. Nevertheless, if there had been a significant amount of unity and cooperation among leading politicians in Tehran, the government would have been in a much stronger position to deal with the warring powers. On the other hand, the fact that the Russians would not withdraw their troops – thus giving cause to the Turks to invade Iranian territory – made it much more difficult for the cabinet and Majlis to come up with a united policy.

Far from withdrawing, in November 1915 the Russians moved their considerable troops in Qazvin towards Tehran. This spread panic and there was talk of the capital being moved to Isfahan where – in the centre and south – the Entente position was less strong, and it was outside Russia's sphere of influence. About half of the Majlis deputies moved to Qom, causing that body to cease to function, which is probably just what the Russians had intended by their ominous threat. They took control of the gendarmerie, which had moved with them, and set up the National Defence Committee led by Solaiman Mirza. The young Shah was adamant that he would move the capital unless the Russian troops pulled back, and a deal was eventually struck for the Shah to remain, the Russian troops to pull back by stages, and Farmanfarma and Ain al-Dawleh to enter Mostawfi's cabinet. Yet in December this cabinet fell and Farmanfarma became prime minister with British backing.[43]

The Russian show of force had apparently secured Tehran for the Entente. When Russian troops took Qom, and the *melliyun* fell back on Kashan, and then Isfahan, Nezam al-Saltaneh (Rezaqoli Khan Mafi), governor-general of Arabistan (later Khuzistan), Loristan and Borujerd, threw in his lot with them. He attacked and took Kermanshah and Hamadan – the Russians retook the latter fairly soon – and formed the pro-Central Provisional Government in which both Solaiman Mirza (though not as a minister) and Modarres took part. They received money from the Germans and some help from the Turks, but did not become very effective, not least because of conflicts among themselves. Men like Modarres were much more sober in their political judgement and action than many of the Democrats, and they would not have been driven so far if the Russians, backed by their British allies, had not effectively chased them out of Tehran.

On the lighter side, though significant in other ways, a son of Farmanfarma who was married to Nezam's daughter had accompanied his father-in-law to Kermanshah. While the two prime ministers were exchanging threatening telegrams, Nezam wired Farmanfarma that he had taken his son hostage. The latter told his secretary to wire a raspberry back. And when the Secretary asked how, Farmanfarma simply drew a line on a piece of paper to be wired.[44]

In the spring of 1916, the surrender of the British to the Turks at Kut in Mesopotamia released Turkish troops for deployment in Western Iran, thus boosting the Provisional Government. At about the same time, Farmanfarma was replaced by Sepahsalar. The latter was considered to be more pro-Russian than pro-British, although careful consideration makes these conventional labels seem less meaningful than usual: some politicians were idealistic, some altruistic, some pragmatic, still others amenable to personal favours from one or another of the big powers, and, in a few cases, they had a large appetite for such favours. Yet the Entente did not manage to form a single government in Tehran during the war that they could truly claim as being entirely their own. And not even the Provisional Government, which was more obviously dependent on the central powers for its existence, could be described as being in the pocket of the Turks and Germans. To a large extent this was a product of internal disunity and mutual suspicion: each group – in some cases each magnate even within the same group – watching the other, and each being anxious not to arouse too much suspicion.

In the same period, the British South Persia Rifles was organised in Fars, and the Jangal Movement, led by Kuchik Khan and his followers in Gilan, declared their affiliation to the Union of Islam movement, just launched by the Turks to boost their popularity in Muslim countries. The Entente stiffened their resolve in Tehran. They had considered entering an alliance with Iran under Mostawfi, but his extensive demands had not been met and he had resigned office. The negotiations had been renewed under Farmanfarma, who had demanded no less a price – and probably more – than his predecessor: it amounted to the complete restoration of Iran's sovereignty, including return of the Persian Gulf islands and revision of the Torkamanchi treaty, as well as financial and military aid.[45] The negotiations dragged on as usual, and the attempt gave way to a much less ambitious scheme when Sepahsalar replaced Farmanfarma as prime minister. This dragged on even longer. The Russians, and to a lesser extent the British, were not prepared to give much ground, but suddenly – to their astonishment – in August 1916 the government informed them of their agreement. This was the so-called Sepahdar (i.e. Sepahsalar) agreement, the main provisions of which were the raising of a local force under British and Russian officers, and the setting up of a mixed commission of the three countries to supervise the country's finances, in return for a monthly subsidy of 200,000 tomans for the government.

But a few days later the cabinet fell, and it took a while for Vosuq to form a new ministry. The new cabinet simply claimed that they could not find the relevant Anglo–Russian notes in the foreign ministry, although they also explained privately to Marling that it was a very unpopular measure, and unwise to implement it in any case.[46] So the Entente powers were astonished once again, although in the Persian text of the 'agreement' it had been mentioned that the government agreed to the proposal 'in the present circumstances ([i.e.] *force majeure*)'.[47] It was further explained in the Persian press that only Sepahsalar and his foreign minister had agreed to the proposals, although Marling had been given to understand that it had been a unanimous cabinet decision. This is a major example of the observation made above that, although the attitude and relationship of leading politicians was (sometimes markedly) different towards the foreign powers, the differences were often not so great as they appeared at the time, and have been believed to be since.

The advance of the Turks from Hamadan towards the capital influenced the fall of Sepahsalar'e cabinet, and possibly even the 'disappearance' of his 'agreement'. An assembly of notables summoned by the Shah advised against leaving the capital in the face of the Turkish advance, though it looks as if, this time, the Russian and British envoys were not averse to the idea. Vosuq became prime minister in a familiar factional contest with Ala al-Saltaneh. The public saw his success as the work of the Entente, especially the British, and it is no wonder that his government effectively refused to enforce the Sepahdar agreement, for fear of being accused of taking orders from the Entente.

It was then, in September 1916, that the Committee of Punishment (*Komiteh-ye Mojazat*) came into being, and began to assassinate pro-British public figures. Some of these were small fry, and in a few cases private feuds had much to do with the operations of the Committee. But, despite some suggestions to the contrary, its political purpose cannot be doubted. It included naive romantics such as Hossein Khan Laleh, who lost his life in the process, and shrewd adventurers such as Ehsanollah Khan.[48] The former was caught and executed; the latter fled to Gilan to join Kuchik, and later dropped him in favour of the Iranian Communists, whose alliance with Kuchik, in June 1920, was very short-lived (see chapter six).

Iranians received the news of the February revolution in Russia rather like a terminal patient receiving news of the discovery of a cure for his illness, and the October revolution which followed looked little short of a miracle for Iran. Kasravi has recorded both the feeling of despondency and depression in Tabriz before these great events, and the sense of joy and optimism when they took place.[49] The term Bolshevik became so respected among the Iranian public that Aref-e Qazvini, who knew very little about them, likened his beloved, in a verse, to 'the Bolshevik, spreading plenty wherever you go'. In another verse, he described them as 'the Guide of the Way to Salvation'.[50]

Several other cabinets – Ala al-Dawleh, Ain al-Dawleh, Mostawfi al-Mamalek, Samsam al-Saltaneh – came and went until 1918, when the defeat of the central powers was in sight and, with active British backing, Vosuq formed an eventful government. Thus, between 1914 and 1918, there had been 12 premierships (though some prime ministers formed cabinets more than once). Hence, between 1910 and 1918 there were 20 premierships with an average life of five months. The same pattern was to be repeated over the period 1941–51, when chaotic trends re-emerged after the fall of Reza Shah's rule.

Vosuq's 1918 government was to last longer than any other between 1906 and 1926, except Reza Khan's cabinet of 1923–25. In retrospect, it was the last chance that the Iranians had for reaching a workable political settlement in accordance with the rules established by the constitution of 1906. The alternatives were revolution, disintegration and/or the establishment of a dictatorial regime, which could easily and quickly turn into arbitrary government. In the event, it was the last option that succeeded.

In October 1917, the fourth Majlis elections for Tehran had been held. The deputies-elect were pro-Central almost to a man. Most of them were radical Democrats such as Taqizadeh and Mosavat (who, at the time, were leading the *Komiteh-ye Melliyun* and publishing *Kaveh* in Berlin) and Solaiman Mirza (then in enforced British exile in India). Others included more moderate leaders such as Moshir, Mokhber and Samsam.

All this while the country was in turmoil. The central government's hold over the provinces was little more than nominal representation by a governor-general, and even this was not the case on some occasions in some regions. The financial system had all but collapsed and – apart from excise duties that brought in little revenue – customs were the only significant source of government revenue. The military situation was, if possible, even worse. The traditional *nezam* and tribal levies had virtually ceased to exist. The gendarmerie, which had been created as the constitutional government's own force, had ceased to be effective both for lack of money and because they had defected to the pro-Central cause. The Cossack Brigade – later, Division, which was led by its Russian officers and was answerable to the Shah alone – would have been in a similar situation after the Russian Revolution if Britain had not stepped in to pay for most of its monthly keep. As mentioned above, Britain also organised the South Persia Rifles, which was led by British officers and used to maintain security in the south.[51]

Yet it would be a mistake to measure the importance of Tehran to the rest of the country, simply because of its lack of money and men to enforce its writ in the provinces. It was soon to be shown, and shown time and again, that whoever held Tehran would be well placed to hold the rest of the country. The fact is that there was no effective central government even at the centre, and in the centre, of politics. Even in regard to its relations with the provinces, many of the difficulties of the so-called central government arose from its weakness, division and lack of authority in Tehran. Everything else remaining the same, if there had been a significant amount of unity in Tehran the country would have been in a much better position both to deal with the great foreign problem and with the forces of disintegration in the provinces. As may be predicted from the theory in chapter one, the chaos at the centre was more crippling and destructive than the chaos in the 'impassable roads and immeasurable distances' (as a Russian politician put it in the case of Russia, after swift German victories during the war).

Few political leaders saw the fundamental problem of weakness and disunity at the centre as starkly as Modarres. That is why he – who had just returned from Istanbul, where he had taken refuge after the collapse of the pro-Central Provisional Government – surprised many by actively campaigning for a Vosuq ministry (see chapter four). Vosuq's government was intended to provide just that degree of strength and continuity at the centre which might make it possible to return the country to some workable degree of order and stability. Its weakness was that its cabinet was seen by the public, even before the 1919 agreement, as thoroughly pro-British, so that it lacked the degree of public trust and cooperation that was necessary to bring about cohesion. Still, he had some notable successes in restoring order. The most celebrated examples were the destruction of the Committee of Punishment, and the termination of the eleven-year-old rebellion and brigandage of Nayeb Hossein Kashi at the head of a band of marauders, both of which had a wide measure of support among the people and the politicians. Kasravi is full of praise for these steps, which were taken by Vosuq's government.[52]

Either a strong government such as Vosuq's, or a Coup of the kind that was led by Reza Khan and Sayyed Zia could have saved the country from continued chaos and final disintegration. This is clear not only in hindsight; it was clear to a few leading politicians even at the time.[53]

The rise of Iranian nationalism

The origins of much that happened in Iran in the decades following the Constitutional Revolution lay in two distinct, but closely related, features of state and society since 1909: domestic chaos and foreign intervention. A third factor, that became entangled with the other two, was the conflict over modernization, or more especially how, in what sense and at what speed it might be achieved.

Almost all Iranian politics in the twentieth century – conservative, constitutionalist, democratic, nationalist, Marxist-Leninist and Islamist – had its roots in these problems, which intermittently produced chaotic trends and arbitrary governments.

There had been no 'nation' in Iran before the Constitutional Revolution, just as there had been none in Europe before nations were built between the Renaissance and Reformation, and the 1848 revolutions. At the onset of the French Revolution about half of Louis XVI's subjects spoke no French at all, and only five per cent spoke the language of the court and Voltaire. At the beginning of the nineteenth century, it would have been very unlikely to predict the Italian Risorgimento of the1860s. It would have been equally remarkable to predict the emergence of a unified German state before the rise of German romanticism and counter-enlightenment (both philosophical and literary) in the latter half of the eighteenth century.[54]

It would, of course, be a mistake to think that before the rise of modern nations and nationalism, a sense of communal identity and belonging – often giving rise to shared feelings, experiences, legends, myths, etc. – had not existed among various peoples in various places. There has always been a clear distinction between 'us' and 'the others', whether in the household or tribe or religious community or the whole country. The Greeks were as much conscious of being Greek as the Persians of being Persian and the Chinese of being Chinese. And there have been legends about heroes and heroines such as Leonidas, Abu Moslem Khorasani, Alexander Nevsky and Joan of Arc sacrificing themselves for the sake of their fellow countrymen. But they and their ideas cannot be projected as nationalist and nationalism in any social and historical sense that is rendered by these terms and concepts in modern times. To give a passing reference to one famous example from medieval Europe, Joan of Arc was the heroine of a dynastic, rather than 'national', war. And she was destroyed as much by the English as by their French allies who delivered her to them to be tried – by French judges – and burnt, not as a French 'nationalist', but as a witch and heretic.

To repeat the point, there had been no nations and no nationalism anywhere until, both in theory and practice, they began to take shape in Europe (and later elsewhere) from the end of the Middle Ages until our own time. At present, we are observing the emergence and effects of nations and nationalisms in Africa, Eastern Europe and Asia, which are often as emotional, heroic and self-indulgent as those which, both in Europe and beyond, have long since spent their passions.

By the beginning of the twentieth century many, if not most, Iranians still thought of their village, town or province as *vatan*, or homeland. There certainly was a sense of Iranian community and culture, largely centred on the Persian language and literature, and a sense of what most of that community held in common, including religious beliefs and passions. But there was no sense of Iranian nationalism as described above, except among a small intellectual and educated elite who, under the direct influence of Europe, had begun to build and promote it. These were men, of whom Fath'ali Akhundzadeh (Akhundof) and Mirza Aqa Khan Kermani – in two successive generations – are probably quintessential examples, although the latter was, if anything, somewhat less radical in his nationalist and modernist enthusiasm than the former.[55]

It is sometimes thought that an Iranian nationalism existed before the Islamic conquest and had been suppressed by the Arab conquerors. The evidence offered for this belief is *Shahnameh*, when it is read and interpreted anachronistically, as if its authors were modern Iranian nationalists of the twentieth century. *Shahnameh* is a compendium of ancient Iranian myth, heroism, legend, and stylized history which brings together the collective cultural experience of a large community (indeed, communities), as do similar works which have survived from other ancient and classical civilisations. It is hardly evidence of modern notions of nationalism when an ancient people boasted about their military successes or denigrated their enemies in their myths, legends or historical accounts. Every tribe in four continents has been doing so since time immemorial.

Something of these ancient tribal sentiments still survives in the pride that is taken in the family, the town, the school, the university, even in a given field of academic study, sometimes with negative effects for others. There is as little substance in the claim that *Shahnameh* is evidence of ancient Iranian nationalism as there was in the myth, consciously invented by the Nazis, locating the origins of their own ideas and sentiments in the pagan and Teutonic age. The Greeks and Romans were certainly proud of their civilizations (as were the Chinese) and they often belittled the outsider; but they cannot be described as nationalists, nor were the Italian communities which remained scattered for such a long time after the fall of the Western Empire, although they were all aware of their great Roman origins.

While Persian was the language of administration and high culture, other – Iranian as well as non-Iranian – languages and dialects were spoken in many provinces. High literature was almost invariably in Persian, and was the main channel for communication in lands as far apart as Samarqand and Bokhara, Isfahan and Fars, the Caucuses and Lahore. As the language of administration as well as high literature, Persian was probably the strongest factor making for a communal identity among the peoples who belonged to the Iranian cultural region.[56]

But there is no evidence, before the twentieth century, of the Pan-Persianist theory and practice that became the official ideology in Pahlavi Iran. For example, under the Safavids the language spoken at the court was a Turkic dialect; under the Qajars the language of the heir-designate's court at Tabriz was Turkic, and this was also spoken at the court in Tehran alongside Persian.[57] Down to Mozaffar al-Din, the Qajar Shahs often took pride in the claim that they descended from Genghis Khan, and this they would not have done if the Iranians had then looked upon Genghis as a wild and barbaric conqueror who had destroyed their motherland. As late as the mid-nineteenth century, Lesan al-Molk's voluminous *Nasekh al-Tavarikh* begins with the fall of Adam, and reaches its climax with the advent of Islam, including its conquest of Iran; and its greatest heroes are the Islamic *ghazis* and Shi'ite martyrs.

In Persian poetry there had been a good deal of *habsiyat* (prison ballads) and, even more, *ekhvaniyat* (fraternal exchanges) but what had existed of *vataniyat* (laments, usually nostalgia, for the poet's home town or province) underwent revolutionary change at the beginning of the twentieth century.

Sayyed Hasan Ghaznavi, the twelfth-century poet, had expressed nostalgic feelings for his homeland *Korasan*:

Every breeze which brings me the scent of Khorasan
It brings life into my body like the breath of Jesus ...

Hafiz wrote, two centuries later, on a rare occasion of being away from *Shiraz*:

> Remembering my friend and my home, I shall weep hard
> Such that I would demolish the ways and means of travel from the world.

However, within the first couple of decades of the twentieth century, most fervent *vataniyat* were written not for the poet's home town or province but for *Iran*, the likes of which had seldom existed in the annals of Persian literature. And they were written by the most famous poets of the day. Not only by ardent nationalists such as Ashraf (Nasim-e Shomal), Aref, Lahuti, Eshqi and Farrokhi, but even by more traditional figures such as Bahar and Adib al-Mamalek, with Iraj being the major exception that proves the rule. Ashraf's and Lahuti's works are less well known in this respect. Ashraf wrote:

> A cock was singing in the cloister, cock-a-doodle-do
> Addressing the unconsciously inebriate, cock-a-doodle-do
> Where is Bahman, where Rostam, cock-a-doodle-do
> Alas, autumn hit the rose garden, cock-a-doodle-do
> > Help, the winter is too cold, cock-a-doodle-do ...[58]
> > (The last line is the poem's refrain)

Lahuti wrote:

> You are a child of Iran, and Iran is your motherland
> Your life is to put your good body to work, *balam-lai* [lullaby]
> > *Lailai, balalai-lai; lailai balalai-lai* ...[59]
> > (The last line is the poem's refrain)

This nationalism emerged suddenly with the onset of the Constitutional Revolution and set alight the hearts of most of the young Europe-conscious (though not necessarily modernist), educated Iranians. Its greatest expositors were men like Mirza Aqa Khan Kermani, who themselves had been greatly influenced by that seminal social and literary critic, Fath'ali Akhundzadeh (Akhundof). In his writings almost all the elements of modern Iranian nationalism – romantic glorification of ancient Persia, fervent desire to become European overnight, intense anti-Arab and anti-Islamic feelings, derision of classical Persian literature, etc. – are to be found.[60] Indeed, the only remaining major element was anti-Turanianism, which, with the collapse of the Ottoman Empire and release of strong Pan-Turanian forces and passions in that country, completed the main elements of modern Iranian nationalist ideology at the end of the First World War.

Even Akhudzadeh's anti-Islamic and anti-Arab thoughts and feelings had to wait until after the War to bear full fruit. The forerunners of modern nationalism during the Constitutional Revolution were not anti-Islam, but argued that it had been distorted by selfish mullahs who had most influence within the religious establishment, a view which was extended and followed to the bitter end by the then youthful Ahmad Kasravi. It is possible that men like Mirza Aqa Khan, and even Dehkhoda, were being tactfully cautious, given the support that constitutionalism needed and received from the bulk of the religious faithful and the community; although, even then, the fact that they did not attack Islam in the name of nationalism or constitutionalism reflects the mood of the wider revolutionary outlook. It is, however, clear from Zail'abedin Maragheh'i's *Siya-hatnameh-ye Ebrahim Baig* that he has a genuine regard for 'true' Islam.

Europe was clearly the source of this ideology of Iranian nationalism as far back as Akhundzadeh, who died in 1878 and, as indicated above, was even more comprehensive and less compromising in his nationalist sentiments than his immediate followers. Yet he had died before some of the more radical, chauvinist and racist theories, nurtured and expounded by men such as Comte de Gobinaux and Stewart Chamberlain, had had time to have a large practical impact in Western Europe in general, and Germany in particular.

In terms of pure romantic sentiments and sense of national superiority there was little difference between Iranian, Turkish and, later, Arab nationalism of the twentieth century. The European Aryanism that developed and spread at the end of the nineteenth century was, if anything, an affront to Semitic Arabs and Turanian Turks. But it became the strongest instrument of romantic Iranian nationalism and Pan-Persianism: the Iranian nation was not just superior on account of its real and imagined ancient glories, but even more so because it belonged to the master European race which had created the great social and scientific civilization that was contemporary Europe. And the frustration, not to say depression, of fervent nationalist intellectuals was the greater because of the glaring contrast between Iran's obvious contemporary backwardness and Europe's modern achievements, which they believed their country had failed to emulate, mainly – if not solely – because of Arabs (later also Turks) and Islam. Alexander I and the Greeks were also given their share of the blame for Iran's decline, but, although it persisted in history books for decades, it did not persist as much and as long as the others, partly because they were European, and partly because they were no longer Iran's neighbours.[61]

The most outspoken, and a most sincere, poet-laureate of this ideology of Iranian nationalism was Aref-e Qazvini, whose passionate songs and poems are, ironically, in the genres and styles of traditional mourning for religious tragedies and martyrs, thus reflecting their hidden cultural and psychological affinities. He was either for sudden and miraculous delivery or for total destruction and death:

Naught but death would relieve my pain,
Alas that which would relieve my pain did not arrive,
I am mourning Alexander's adventure in Iran,
You wonder why at the Spring of Life he did not arrive ...
When the Arabs found their way into Iran and since,

A word of happiness from the land of Sassan did not arrive ...
That is why Aref has arrived wondering
Why the news of the total destruction of Tehran did not arrive.[62]

The Turks were soon to go down the same path in Aref's nationalist poetry, although the provocation came from their own quarters when Turkish writers and journalists began to claim that Iran had been ruled by Turks for a thousand years. When the waves of Turkish pan-Turanianism began to touch the coasts of Azerbaijan, Aref addressed a song, 'This Cradle of Zoroaster', to his Turkic-speaking compatriots, asking them to 'avoid the Turks and Turkish language':

Do not forget the [Persian] language
Zoroaster said:
Do not extinguish fire by water![63]

And he must have been extremely angry at the chauvinistic proclamations of some Turkish nationalist intellectuals when he wrote:

The Turkish tongue is good for pulling out,
It must be cut out of this country.[64]

The swift early victories of the Germans during the war were a great source of joy and hope, at least for the non-Arab people of the Middle East (because the Germans were allied to the Ottomans, Arabs seeking independence could not have been enthusiastic about German victories). They also became a source of pride for the modern Iranian elite, because of the belief that the Germans were of the same race as themselves.

Adib-e Peshawari, the Persian-speaking Indian Muslim who had moved to Tehran, wrote twelve *qasidehs* in honour of the Kaiser and the German people, in his excruciatingly difficult language. He wrote in a *mosammat*, where he described Britain as a mouse and a blackbird:

The English Channel came to boil,
Lightening struck London,
Because of the work of the Emden [German battleship].
There was turmoil where the sandal grows [India],
The mouse which used to sit on the barrel of wine [i.e. Britain],
Fell from the top of the barrel ...[65]

In a powerful *qasideh* entitled 'The Conquest of Warsaw', and characteristically written in the Khorasani style, Bahar wrote:

The Kaiser captured the realm of Warsaw,
He broke the might of the Slav ...

His offensive cut the Tsar's army,
Just like the gardener's sheers do the weed.
Soon as a result of another onslaught,
The Muscovite must give up Moscow.
That Centre which has turned into a wasteland
The pleasant land of Xerxes and Khosrow,
The Big Bear which never considered
The begging and imploring of its exhausted pray,
Now fear has made it look like a rabbit,
Who watches the greyhound from a distance ...[66]

Writing in a mixture of *mosammat* and *tarji'band*, Vahid-e Dastgerdi went even further, boasting openly about the common racial origins of Germans and Iranians:

From two sides are they destroying the land of Jamshid,
The ugly fox from the South and the cunning bear from the North...
The Slav's head was beaten with the German mace,
O' Iran, O' remainder of Kay and Sassan,
Rise and join the battlefield like your forbears...
Iran and Germany are of the same race,
They are both elephantine and lion-like in battle ...[67]

Such was the cultural and ideological background to the great emotional rejection of the 1919 Agreement. The official Pahlavi nationalism which began from the mid-1920s did not add much to the intellectual basis of these sentiments. It was their forceful and comprehensive application by the state to the society that spread it far, wide and deep under the two Pahlavi Shahs. The nature and implications of this official nationalism are discussed in chapter eleven.

Positive achievements

The main purpose of this chapter was to show how revolution quickly led to chaos – chaos being endemic in Iranian culture each time an arbitrary regime became weak and/or collapsed. It continued until the intrusion of the First World War, when the activities of the belligerent powers brought the country to the brink of disintegration.

It was not as if there had been all losses and no gains. The Constitutional Revolution had two main objectives, which were somewhat related to each other. Firstly, the abolition of the arbitrary regime and its replacement with a constitutional one based on the rule of law. Secondly, the modernization of the administrative machinery – especially in matters regarding finance, justice and law and order – and introduction of modern education, modern transport facilities, etc. Among a small modernist elite, hopes and aspirations were a lot more lofty, amounting to an earnest wish to turn the whole country into a modern western European society within a short space of time.

Mass revolutions everywhere have been highly optimistic and voluntaristic in character. The elation brought by united action, and the victory in bringing down the existing regime, tend to widen the horizons of hope and aspiration well beyond the realm of possibility, when it looks as if the mere will of a group of idealists can surmount any difficulty on the way to the longed-for salvation. That is how revolutions get out of hand and tend to lose even that which was gained. For example, in the French Revolution the concepts of 'the people's sovereignty', 'virtue' and 'nature' were pushed to such limits that, for a long time, some of the real political advancements of the first couple of years of the revolution were lost to the country, and had to be regained through other struggles and revolutions later in the nineteenth century.

Regarding the first objective of the Constitutional Revolution, we have shown that little was achieved towards creating a constitutional state, because destructive conflict among the constitutionalists themselves made normal governance extremely difficult. In the absence of such destructive distrust and conflict, slow but real long-term political progress would have been possible. Even the interfering foreign powers, and the unruly nomadic khans and provincial magnates, would have been more effectively dealt with if there had been the minimum necessary cooperation at the centre. The most important achievement of Reza Shah was that he brought order and stability after the chaos. But the fact that his achievement arose from the iron rule of a single individual ruler meant that his unconstitutional rule did not result in long-term political development.

Two points need to be emphasised to avoid confusion and misunderstanding. Firstly, political unity or order does not imply the absence of conflict or lack of pursuit of different programmes by different social groups and parties. On the contrary, it means that such conflict would be almost impossible to manage in the absence of an orderly framework: without it, the result would be not constitutional government but chaos. Secondly, political development does not necessarily have to begin with modern democracy, which in fact has been its end product. But there can be no continuous and cumulative political development in the absence of some sort of constitutional framework that sets a definite as well as predictable limit to the exercise of power, and makes possible a certain degree of political participation, thus leading to further advancement and participation (see chapter one).

This said, the rudimentary notions of law and legal justice, elections, parliamentary representation, cabinet, ministerial responsibility, etc., that came into being after the Constitutional Revolution, were useful gains and certainly improvements on traditional arbitrary rule and traditional chaos. They were of some value even in the last phases of Reza Shah's and Mohammad Reza Shah's rule, when it had become almost completely arbitrary, because there still was the shadow of a parliament and an administrative system. More significantly, the judicial machinery that came into being and evolved from the Constitutional Revolution through the early period of Reza Shah was, despite its serious limitations, incomparably better than anything that had existed before.

Regarding the second major objective of the revolution – state-building and modernization – there was perhaps more lasting progress, partly because there was greater unity about them in the centre of politics and among leading political trends and figures. Here, the main restraints were the sheer paucity of resources coupled with the fact that the chaotic government and society described above made it difficult to achieve even what was potentially possible. A body of civil servants came into being who began to learn the modern methods of running a country. The gendarmerie and police forces – both of them organised and led by Swedish officers – were definite improvements on what had existed before. Judicial courts became organized and were more accessible to larger numbers of people. There was a quick and continuous development of a modern legal profession, including judges, lawyers and notaries public. Modern schools, which had begun to appear before the revolution mainly through private and civic effort, increased in number and capacity, and a growing number of middle-class families paid serious attention to the education of girls as well as boys.

Education had always been valued in Iran. Its social origin is likely to be in the absence of a continuous propertied aristocracy, which made possible elevation to the highest administrative positions by virtue of learning, since meritocracy was not characteristic of societies in which the state depended on independent ruling classes (see chapter one on the high social mobility characteristic of an arbitrary state and society). That motivation was now even more at work when 'state-building' offered greater opportunities for government employment. Yet, whatever the historical origin and the practical motive, education and learning had always been a source of social prestige, and modern education added to that tradition. Indeed, the faith in education was now – and in following decades – so enhanced that many pinned their hopes for continuous political development on the spread of education. It was seldom appreciated that political development is not possible without long- term practice and participation, and that in its absence even a highly educated person would have a less realistic understanding of political processes than the common man in a politically advanced society.

Such achievements provided the basis for further and more rapid developments under Reza Khan and Reza Shah, in part because (as before) there was little conflict over their desirability, but mainly because both the concentration and the centralization of power made it much easier to pursue these aims speedily.

Notes

1   See *Divan-e Mohammad Taqi Bahar, Malek al-Sho'ra*, (ed.) Mohammad Malekzadeh, vol. 1 (Tehran: Amir Kabir), 1956, pp. 202–05.

2   For the latter period, see for example Homa Katouzian, *Musaddiq and the Struggle for Power in Iran* (London and New York: I.B.Tauris), second edition, 1999; Fakhreddin Azimi, *The Crisis of Democracy, 1941–1953* (I.B.Tauris and St Martin's Press), 1989.

3   See Malek al-Sho'ara Bahar, *Tarikh-eMokhtasar-e Ahzab-e Siyasi dar Iran*, vol. 1, (Tehran: Jibi, 1978), p. 9. For a detailed account of the Democrat party programme see Gholam-reza Varahram, *Nezam-e Siyasi va Sazmandehi-ye Ejtema'i-ye Iran dar Asr-e Qajar* (Tehran: Mo'in, 1988), pp. 426–35. See also Janet Afary, *The Iranian Constitutional Revolution, 1906–1911* (New York: Columbia University Press, 1996).

4   It is noteworthy that this Tabtaba'i joined Solaiman Mirza in the early 1920s in launching the Socialist party. It is just an example of the great malleability of political leaders and parties between the two Iranian revolutions of this century.

4* For a detailed discussion see, Gholamreza Varahram, *Nezam-e Siyasi*, pp. 435–45.

4a See Shaikh Mohammad Mardukh Kordestani, *Tarikh-e Mardukh*, quoted directly in Mehdi Bamdad, *Sharh-e Hal-e Rejal-e Iran* (Tehran: Zavvar, 1992), vol. 6, pp. 133–35. See also p. 293, on another case of 'constitutionalising [i.e. looting] the people'.

4b Numerous examples of the use of this expression in the more specific sense of 'having made it good through constitutionalism' are to be found in Bamdad's entries for many constitutionalist leaders in his encyclopaedia of the notables. See for example *ibid*, vol. 1, p. 349.

5   See Ebrahim Safa'i, *Rahabran-e Mashruteh*, vol. 1 (Tehran: Javidan, 1984), p. 201.

6   See Safa'i, *ibid.;* Iraj Afshar (ed.), *Zendegi-ye Tufani, Khaterat-e Sayyed Hasan Taqizadeh* (Tehran: Elmi, 1993); Abolqasem Kahhalzadeh, *Dideh-ha va Shenideh-ha, Khaterat-e Mirza Abolqasem Khan Kkahhalzadeh*, (ed.) Morteza Kamran (Tehran: Kamran, 1984), which includes quotations from the memoirs of Mahmud Mahmud, with whom Haidar Khan had taken refuge for a time; Baqer Aqeli, *Ruzshomar-e Tarikh-e Iran* (Tehran: Nashr-e Goftar), third edition.

7   See Esma'il Ra'in, *Yeprem Khan-e Sardar* (Tehran: Ra'in, 1971. Kasravi); *Tarikh-e Hijdah-saleh-ye Azerbaijan* (Tehran: Amir Kabir, 1992), part 1, chapter 1; Baqer Aqeli, *Ruzshomar*, p. 75.

8   Almost all of the period's sources describe Nayeb Hossein as a brigand who was a rebel against the government and terrorized the villages around Kashan, Isfahan and Yazd, near the great desert. See for example Kasravi, *Tarikh-e Hijdahsaleh*, Abdollah Mostawfi, *Sharh-e Zendegani-ye Man*, vols. 2 and 3 (Tehran: Zavvar, 1963). Kahhalzadeh, *Dideh-ha va Shenideh-ha*. For a recent account, favourable to Nayeb Hossein, see Mohammad Reza Khosravi, *Toghyan-e Nayebiyan*, ed. Ali Dehbashi, (Tehran: Beh Negar, 1989).

9   See, Aqeli, *Ruzshomar*, p. 77.

10 *Ibid.*, pp. 78–81.

11 See Mostafi, *Sharh-e Zendegani*, vol. 2, pp. 352ff.; Kasravi, *Tarikh- Hijdahsaleh*, chapters 20–22; Yahya Dawlat-Abadi, *Hayat-e Yahya*, vol. 3 (Tehran: Attar & Ferdawsi, 1983), chapters 22–24; Aqeli, *Ruzshomar*, pp. 82–85.

12 See for example Ra'in, *Yeprem Khan-e Sardar*. Kasravi, *Tarikh-e Hijdahsaleh*, part 2, chapter 17.

13 See Aqeli, *Ruzshomar*, pp. 92–93.

14 *Ibid*, p. 93.

15 *Ibid*, p. 94.

16 *Ibid.*

17 *Ibid*, pp. 94–96.

18 See for example Mostawfi, *Sharh-e Zendegani*, vol. 2, p. 458.

19 See Aqeli, *Ruzshomar*, pp. 97–98.

20 See Morgan Shuster, *The Strangling of Persia, A Record of European Diplomacy and Oriental Intrigue* (London: T. Fisher Unwin, 1912).

21 See Taqizadeh, *Zendegi-ye Tufani*, pp. 77–80. For Stokes's correspondence, decades later, with Taqizadeh in London, see *ibid*, Appendix 25.

22 See Mostawfi, _Sharh-e Zendegani-ye Man_, vol. 2, pp. 357–58; Edward Browne's introduction to his _Letters from Tabriz_, where he attacks Russian arrogance over Shuster's proposal to appoint Stokes as the commander of his Gendarmerie, as well as their following ultimatums; see its Persian translation _Nameh-ha'i az Tabriz_, trans. Hasan Javadi, as it contains the letters in the Persian original (Tehran: Kharazmi, 1982). Malcolm E. Yapp, '1900–1921: The last Years of the Qajar Dynasty', in Hossien Amirsadeghi and F. W. Ferrier eds., _Twentieth Century Iran_ (London: Heimemann, 1977).

23 See Mostawfi, _Sharh-e Zendegani-ye Man_, vol. 2, p. 359; Aqeli, _Ruzshomar_, p. 86.

24 The references can be numerous. See for example Shuster, _The Strangling of Persia_; Mostawfi, _Sharh-e Zendegani-ye Man_, vol. 2; Kasravi, _Tarikh-e Hijdahsaleh;_ Browne, _Letters from Tabriz_, Afary, _The Iranian Constitutional Revolution._ Ervand Abrahamian, _Iran between Two Revolutions_ (Princeton NJ: Princeton University Press, 1982).

25 For the full text of the song, see _Divan-e Aref-e Qazvini_, ed. Abdorrahamn Saif-e Azad (Tehran: Amir Kabir), pp. 365–66.

26 Se, _Divan-e Bahar_, pp. 217–20.

27 _Ibid_, pp. 221–24.

28 See _The Political Economy of Modern Iran_ (London and New York: Macmillan and New York University Press, 1981), p. 68.

29 For the full texts of their speeches, see S. A. Azari, _Qiyam-e Shaikh Mohammad Khiyabani dar Tabriz_ (Tehran: Safi'ali Shah, 1983). See further, Homa Katouzian, 'The Revolt of Shaykh Muhammad Khiyabani', _IRAN_, 1999.

30 For the full text of the letter, see Taqizadeh, _Zendegi-ye Tufani_, Appendix 5, p. 459.

31 _Ibid._ p. 458.

32 _Ibid._ pp. 458–59.

33 _Ibid_, p. 463. Altogether, Taqizadeh sent 13 telegrams to various authorities and influential people. For their full texts, see _ibid._, pp. 457–64.

34 For a discussion of the long recess and the elections of the third Majlis, see Mansureh Ettehadiyeh (Nezam Mafi), _Majlis va Entekhabat, Az Mahsruteh Ta Payan-e Qajarieyeh_ (Tehran: Nashr-e Tarikh-e Iran), 1996, chapter 5.

35 See, for example, Ahmad Kasravi, _Tarikh-e Hijdahsaleh_, part 3; and _Qiyam-e Shaikh Mohammad Khiyabani_, (ed. and intro.) Homa Katouzian, Tehran: Nashr-e Markaz, 1998.

36 See also Wm. J. Olson, _Anglo-Iranian Relations during Wold War I_ (London: Frank Cass, 1984).

37 Townley to Grey, 18/1/15, Grey Papers, FO 800/70, quoted in _ibid._ pp. 45-46.

38 See Dawlat-Abadi, _Hayat-e Yahya_, vol. 3, p. 283; Aqeli, _Ruzshomar_, p. 103.

39 See Dawlat-Abadi, vol. 3, chapter 32.

40 _Ibid.,_ p 278 and Aqeli, _Ruzshomar_, p. 103–04.

41 Most contemporary Iranian sources cover one or another aspect of Wassmus's operations. See in particular Kahhalzadeh, _Dideh-ha va Shenideh-ha_, and Ahmad Akhgar, _Zendegi-ye Man_ (Tehran: Akhgar, 1987). See also Christopher Sykes, _Wassmuss, The German Lawrence'_ (London and New York: Longman, Green & Co., 1936).

42 See Mokhber al-Saltaneh, _Khaterat va Khatarat_ (Tehran: Zavvar, 1984), p. 279.

43 See, _ibid.;_ Mostawfi, _Sharh-e Zendegani-ye Man_; Kasravi, _Tarikh-e Hijdahsaleh_; Olson, _Anglo-Iranian Relations_; Aqeli, _Ruzshomar_.

44 See Abdolhossein Nava'i, _Iran va Jahan_, vol. 2.

45 See Olson, _Anglo–Iranian Relations._

46 Marling felt that this was a piece of 'truly Persian trickery', though it is familiar from situations where a party to a transaction is in great material disadvantage relative to the other. See Marling to Grey, 16/9/16, FO 371/2736, quoted in _ibid_, p. 150.

47 For the Persian text of the Sepahdar agreement see Bahar, _Tarikh-e Mokhtasar_, vol. 1, p. 25.

48 On the Committee of Punishment and its operations, see, for example, Javad Tabrizi, _Komiteh-ye Mojazat_ (Tehran, Iran va Islam, 1983). 'Ebrahim Khan Monshizadeh' (a

founder of the Committee) in Mehdi Bamdad, *Sharh-e Hal-e Rejal-e Iran*, vol. 1 ('Tehran: Zavvar, 1992, pp. 29–31). Mostawfi, *Shar-he Zendegani-ye Man*, vol. 2; Kahhalzadeh, *Dideh-ha va Shenideh-ha*; Aqeli, *Ruzshomar.*

49   See Ahmad Kasravi, *Qiyam-e Shikh Mohammad Khiyabani*, and *Tarikh-e Hijdahsaleh.*
50   See *Divan-e Aref*, pp. 235 and 300.
51   For detailed and comprehensive studies of the Cossacks, the gendarmes and the SPR's, see Stephanie Cronin, *The Army and the Creation of the Pahlavi State in Iran*, (I.B.Tauris, London and New York, 1997); Florida Safiri, *Polis-e Jonub-e Iran*, Tehran: Nashr-e Tarikh-e Iran, 1986.
52   See, *Kasravi, Tarikh-e Hijdahsaleh*, part 4, chapter 2. Also, 'Vosuq al-Dawleh', in Ebrahim Safa'i *Rahbaran-e Mashruteh*, vol. 1; Kahhalzadeh, *Dideh-ha va Shenideh-ha*.
53   See especially Bahar (who, in his politics, was close to Modarres), *Tarikh-e Mokhtasar*, vol. 1.
54   Sources on the origins and nature of European nationalism are very numerous. For analytical insights into the subject from the point of view of the history of ideas, see Isaiah Berlin, 'The Counter-Enlightenment' and 'Nationalism: Past Neglect and Present Power', in *Against The Current, Essays in the History of Ideas*, (ed.) Henry Hardy, (London: Pimlico, 1997); Isaiah Berlin, *Vico and Herder, Two Studies in the History of Ideas* (London: Hogarth Press, 1976). For historical developments involving the appearance of the nation-state, and of nationalism, see for example G. R. Elton, *Reformation Europe, 1517– 1559* (London: Collins, 1966); G. N. Clerk, *The Seventeenth Century* (London: Oxford University Press, 1960). Christopher Hill, *The English Revolution* (London: Lawrence & Wishart, 1955); and *The Century of Revolution* (London: Van Norstrand Reinhold, 1988). Maurice Ashley, *Louis XIV and the Greatness of France* (London: English Universities Press, 1966). E. L. Woodward, *French Revolutions* (London: Oxford University Press, 1965). Irene Collins, *The Age of Progress, A Survey of European History between 1789 and 1870* (London: Edward Arnold, 1970). David Thompson *Europe Since Napoleon* (Harlow: Longman, 1962). H. A. L. Fisher, *A History of Europe* (London: Edward Arnold & Co., 1936).
55   For a discussion of the nationalist ideas of Akhundof and Mirza Aqa Khan, and the nationalist trends following their ideas, see Homa Katouzian, *Sadeq Hedayat, The Life and Legend of an Iranian Write* (London and New York: I.B.Tauris, 1991), chapters 1 and 5. See also the primary references therein, including Feraidun Adamiyat, *Andisheh-ha-ye Mirza Aqa Khan Kermani*, Tehran: Payam, 1978.
56   See also Homa Katouzian, 'Problems of Political Development in Iran: Democracy, Dictatorship or Arbitrary Government?', *British Journal of Middle Eastern Studies*, 22, 1995.
57   For a wider discussion, see *ibid.*
58   See Edward G. Browne, *The Press and Poetry of Modern Persia* (Cambridge University Press, pp. 213–17).
59   *Ibid*, p. 185
60   See for example, M. Sobhdam (Mohammad Ja'far Mahjub), (ed.), *Maktubat-e Fath-Ali Akhundzadeh*, (Paris: Mard-e Emruz, 1985).
61   For a fictional demonstration of this nationalism in relation to Alexander's conquest, the Arab conquest and the Mongol conquest, by young Iranians of the period, see the three short stories by Sadeq Hedayat, Bozorg Alavi and Sheen Partaw in *Aniran*, discussed in Katouzian, *Saedq Hedayat*, chapter 5.
62   See *ibid.*, pp. 69–70 for this English translation. For the Persian original see *Divan-e Aref*, ed. Saif-e Azad, pp. 262–63.
63   See Katouzain, *Sadeq* Hedayat, p. 70, *Divan-e Aref*, p. 390.
64   *Sadeq Hedayat*, p. 280; *Divan-e Aref*, p. 384.
65   See Yahya Aryanpur, *Az Saba ta Nima* (Tehran: Zavar, 1993), p. 320.
66   See *Divan-e Bahar*, vol. 1, pp. 267–69.
67   See Aryanpur, *Az Saba ta Nima*, p. 323.

4

The campaign for the 1919 Agreement

If there was one thing that all leaders of public opinion held in common towards the end of the First World War, it was the need to restore the country to a tolerable degree of order and discipline. And if they felt this at a rational or emotional level, the ordinary people felt it in its most existential sense as a question of survival from one day to the next. They saw the chaos as a product of the constitutional regime, rather than as something with deep historical roots in the country's history (see chapter one). Hence their faith in constitutional government was severely shaken, and they now identified it with disorder and generalized lawlessness, through which they had lost the stability and relative predictability of arbitrary rule. They even began to pray for the soul of the Martyr Shah (Naser al-Din), whose strong rule they now recalled with greater realism, if not with romantic nostalgia. A popular new verse on the lips of many middle-class people of older generations was: 'Iran still needs the sticks of arbitrary rule.'

It was about this time that some more educated Iranians began to develop the theory that the whole constitutionalist movement had been a product of Anglo–Russian rivalry in Iran, which had come to an end by the 1907 convention through which Russia had joined the Anglo–French Entente. The great *bast* in the British legation was now viewed in a very different light, not as the purely selfless support of a freedom-loving country (as they had then believed), but as an artful plot of a great power – Britain – to reduce its main rival in the area. The view that Britain had engineered the Constitutional Revolution was to persist for a long time in the twentieth century, especially among older generations (see chapter two).

Apart from their common agreement on the need for order and stability, Iranian politicians were also agreed that trying to achieve that would require a major reorganization of public finance and the creation of a unified military force. The connection between the two was obvious; therefore, both tasks had to be implemented at one and the same time. There was thus complete unity among Iranian conservative, liberal and radical constitutionalists, as well as modern nationalists, about the country's most pressing political ends. But there was also great divergence of opinion on how best they should be achieved.

The British Foreign Office, on the other hand, and more specifically Earl (later Marquis) Curzon, also wanted to see a more stable, as well as pro-British, Iran, and sought this in the reorganization of Iran's finance and military with close – almost exclusive – British involvement and participation. But just as there was strong conflict of opinion in Iran on how to reform the civil and military administration, in Britain too there was serious disagreement about the most desirable type of relationship between the two countries. Curzon's Persian Policy, which was accepted by Vosuq and his supporters, initially met with strong resistance from within the British government, and the critics later renewed their scepticism after the solid and persistent Iranian opposition to it began to justify their initial misgivings (see chapter five). It would be no exaggeration to claim that Curzon imposed his policy almost single-handedly on the British as well as on Iranian governments: David Lloyd George and Arthur Balfour, then still Foreign Secretary, were at the Paris Peace Conference, dealing with much more important European issues, and giving almost a free hand to Curzon, the acknowledged Eastern – and especially Persian – expert to deal with Iranian (and Arab) problems. This strengthened his position vis-a-vis the Treasury, the India Office and the Government of India, and (to a lesser extent) the War Office, all of which were, for different reasons, weary of high-profile British involvement in Iran.

We shall show in the following chapters that Curzon's policy failed for three inter-connected reasons. Firstly, the massive and impassioned Iranian opposition to it; secondly, the campaigns of America, France and (both Red and White) Russia against it, in particular the Bolshevik landing at Enzeli and the establishment of the Soviet Republic of Iran in Gilan, which threatened a Bolshevik thrust towards the capital; thirdly, the fact that the other British government authorities – India, the India Office, the Treasury and the War Office – were by no means prepared to give the policy the degree of material support which the circumstances required, especially when the extent of both Iranian and foreign opposition to the Agreement became evident. Curzon's fatal mistake was that he grossly underestimated the Iranian opposition to the Agreement, and barely anticipated the strong reaction of America and France. Most of all, he seriously underrated the trouble that the Russians could still cause despite the upheavals in which they themselves were caught. In other words, when he insisted on his own Persian Policy and eventually won the argument within the British government, he never expected that he would need a great deal of support from other British government departments for it to succeed (see chapter five).

Early in 1918, after the Bolshevik Revolution and the onset of civil war in Russia, and while Iran was gripped in ever-increasing disorder, Britain sought to establish a pro-British government there, which would also bring a certain degree of stability and normalize the social and political situation. Vosuq passed the test on both criteria as few leading politicians did: he was both pro-British and able to lead a strong government. It was Balfour, not Curzon, who was then Foreign Secretary. Curzon became interim Foreign Secretary in the wake of

Balfour's mission to the Paris Peace Conference late in 1919, and was confirmed in that office a year later. But as the chairman of the powerful Eastern Committee of the War Cabinet, he was nevertheless concerned with the Eastern issues at close quarters.

Sir Charles Marling, then British minister in Tehran, began to lobby for a Vosuq cabinet in 1918, and reported that the Shah would support the idea if he was paid a subsidy of 20,000 tomans per month. It was eventually agreed to pay him 15000 tomans.[2] The Shah's great appetite for money is not in doubt, but it would be a misreading of history to regard him as willing to sell his country short for a bribe. Iran was still occupied by British forces in the north, east and south and, as part of that, it depended heavily on these troops for a certain degree of domestic order. It also owed considerable debts to Britain and was still receiving British money for its day-to-day administrative expenses. A strong cabinet was needed to deal with the chaotic situation both at the centre and in the provinces, and, in the circumstances, there were not many politicians who could compete with Vosuq in dealing with the formidable problems confronting them.

Vosuq was not a popular politician, but, in 1918, he had a certain amount of support which, at least in qualitative terms, was considerable. The old Democrat party, of which Vosuq had been a member, had effectively disintegrated as a result of the vicissitudes of the war. A group of old Democrats now wished to reorganize the party, mainly as a lobbying force for a Vosuq ministry. Other active Democrats – probably the majority – were opposed to party reorganization at the time, also mainly because they were opposed to a government led by Vosuq. They were thus divided into the Pro-reorganization (Tashkili) and the Anti-reorganization (Zedd-tashkili) groups of Democrats.[3] An able and effective figure among the former, pro-Vosuq, Democrat group was poet-laureate Bahar, the young radical Democrat of the Constitutional Revolution, who had sided with the central powers earlier in the War, and now believed that a strong government was needed to save the country from disintegration.[4] Many powerful conservative politicians and notables, for example, Fathollah Khan Akbar (entitled Sepahdar-e A'zam) who was to join his cabinet, also supported Vosuq. But perhaps most important of all, he had the active support of Sayyed Hasan Modarres, who had been a minister in the Mohajerin govenment in Kermanshah, had spent some time in Turkey after the collapse of that movement, and had just returned to Tehran.

Modarres was an unusal politician for his time and place, for he always combined a commitment to his basic (popular and constitutionalist) principles with a mature sense of political realism, and a good understanding of political choices and constraints in any given situation.[5] It was for these reasons that he was often misunderstood by well-meaning but emotional and less sophisticated individuals who saw in his political realism signs of inconsistency, 'collaborationism' and even duplicity. The poet and journalist Farrokhi Yazdi once described him in a quatrain as a 'turkey'[6] which is a symbol for a turncoat in

Persian literature. Aref[7] and Eshqi[8] likewise did not spare Modarres from occasional abuse, although in the end Eshqi changed his mind. Unlike many politicians of his time, he had no contact with foreign legations, and was content to deal directly with the domestic political forces. Years later, Sir Percy Loraine, then British minister in Tehran, who did not know Modarres personally and was not much in favour of his political position, described him both as 'of course the leading people's tribune',[9] and as 'the figurehead of constitutional conservatism, and of Tory democracy'.[10]

In spite of the Shah's agreement, the active campaign by Modarres, the tacit or explicit support of conservative politicians, and the lobbying of the Pro-reorganization group of Democrats, the installation of Vosuq was not an easy task. The conflict of opinion came to a head when the incumbent prime minister, Samsam al-Saltaneh, refused the Shah's bidding to resign, and the Shah appointed Vosuq in mid-August 1918 while Samsam still claimed to be the lawful prime minister.[11] The formal argument of Samsam and his supporters – in fact, Vosuq's opponents – was that he could only be dismissed by an address of the Majlis to the Shah, but the parliament had been in long recess since 1915, and all subsequent governments. including Samsam's, had been nominated by the Shah after consultation with leading political figures. Whichever side was right or wrong, the conflict itself was characteristic of chaos and the politics of chaos (see chapters one to three).

Apart from the monthly subsidy of 15000 tomans paid to the Shah, the British government agreed to pay 350,000 tomans a month to the Iranian treasury to keep the government afloat in the interim period until financial and other reforms would enable it to use Iranian resources. They were also paying 100,000 tomans directly to the Cossack Division towards the upkeep of that force, although a few months after Vosuq formed a cabinet they decided to pay the Cossack subsidy through the cabinet.[12]

Shortly after Vosuq became prime minister, Marling's mission in Tehran came to an end. He was replaced – though only as interim minister – by Sir Percy Cox, who had had long service with the government of India and was closely familiar with the situation in the Persian Gulf.

The 1919 Agreement

Now that a strong and pro-British government was in possession of what reins of central government power there were in Iran, it was time for Britain to formulate a Persian policy which at once brought stability and security to Iran and safeguarded British interests in the region. Civil war was raging in Russia, and its outcome was far from certain. There were great conflicts both within and between the imperial Russian colonies of the Caucasus, on the northwestern borders of Iran. The Arab lands which had been previously ruled by Turkey were in a state of flux. And Afghanistan was in turmoil.

Conflict of opinion over an appropriate Persian policy surfaced as early as November 1918. Cox outlined a policy proposal for discussion involving the possibility of obtaining a British mandate on Iran from the Paris Peace Conference, which prompted outright rejection by the government of India. To ask the Paris conference for a mandate on Iran without such a request from Iran herself, wrote the Viceroy, would be 'a flagrant departure from our oft-repeated guarantee of Persia's integrity'. Apart from that, he detailed five reasons why a mandate would commit Britain to large and unacceptable financial and military commitments in the country. India's alternative proposal was almost exactly what popular politicians in Iran – men like Mostawfi-al Mamalek, Moshir al-Dawleh and Modarres – dearly wished to see:

> Our view is that we should maintain our influence in Persia by regaining Persian confidence by liberal policy and removal of causes of irritation; that we should continue some assistance in arms and money; that Persian government should be provided with financial adviser, *whether British, American or other*, that for the rest we should give Persia a real chance which she has not had for years past since Russian domination began, of putting her house in order and administering her provinces herself through Governor Generals.[13]

If the possibility of obtaining a mandate had indeed been entertained more seriously than a mere sounding-out by Cox, India's reaction firmly placed it outside further consideration. Indeed, in a telegram to the Viceroy the following January Cox withdrew the idea, describing it as 'perhaps a Council of Perfection', or what in modern parlance might be described as a maximum possible programme.[14]

These were just the opening shots, however, of the conflict within the British government and Empire over the proper course of action to follow in Iran. It was to continue for months before the Agreement was reached, and to be renewed later when it became evidently doubtful to succeed. The issue was debated through the Eastern Committee of the British War Cabinet, which was chaired as well as greatly influenced by Curzon. The idea of obtaining a mandate having been rejected by all the parties concerned, the Committee then debated the kind of relationship with – and therefore the degree of commitment to – Iran which they felt was appropriate for Britain to pursue. Both the government of India and the India Office were looking for a policy along the lines quoted above from the Viceroy. Curzon (and his Foreign Office staff) were seeking a much closer involvement which eventually took shape in the 1919 Agreement.

The differences of opinion in the Eastern Committee meeting of 19 December 1918 led to the submission of two memoranda for further discussion, one by the Foreign Office and one by India. The Iranians were about to dispatch a delegation to the Peace Conference seeking financial and military assistance and advice, reparations for war damage by the forces of the belligerent powers, and the recovery of some of the territories lost to the Russian and Ottoman empires over the previous century.

The Foreign Office was opposed to the delegation's admission to the conference from the very beginning, and this was clearly stated in the memorandum by Marling which broadly reflected Curzon's position, although both tacitly and explicitly one can discern Marling's personal stamp on it. Instead, he advocated bilateral Anglo–Iranian negotiations leading to binding commitments on both sides.

The Iranian notion of open assistance, he argued was, 'You advance the money for us to spend as we like, without control of any kind'. As the country was currently dependent on British money and arms to remain upright, and she owed Brtiain considerable sums of money, it could be persuaded to accept British terms. The only other power which had the resources to help Iran was America, and given her current political mood, Marling suggested, she would not want to get involved. The British offer to Iran should include the creation of a uniform military force – by the amalgamation of the existing Cossacks, South Persia Rifles and gendarmerie – led by a British officer who would select staff from British as well as other nationalities. It should also include financial reorganization with a British adviser 'with very large powers' who could likewise choose his assistants from British and other nationalities. He concluded by saying that Russia would eventually 'recover from her present madness', and he therefore made some suggestions to make the policy tolerable by a future non-Bolshevik Russia.[15]

India's very different views on the other hand, were elaborated in the long and critical memorandum written by Sir Hamilton Grant. He outlined four possible options: to clear out of Iran completely, which he rejected for several reasons; to obtain a mandate for Britain, which he likewise rejected on the same grounds as the Viceroy's comments on Cox's proposals; to obtain a mandate for another power, which he regarded as neither possible nor desirable. This brought him to the final option: 'to assist Persia on a limited scale', which he expounded and recommended. He referred to the rise in Iran of 'a curious kind of patriotism and nationalism which is neither to be bought nor overawed'. It might look out of place with the country's stage of development, 'but whatever may be its psychology this feeling exists, and we must allow for it'. He therefore proposed that Britain should make a public declaration to the Iranian government along the following lines, the preamble to which comes close to making an official apology:

> The exigencies of the war ... have compelled His Majesty's Government, during the last four years, reluctantly to take action in Persia which has not unnaturally aroused suspicions as to our intentions in regard to that country. Now that the war has been successfully terminated in our favour, His Majesty's Government are anxious to regain the confidence of the Persian people, and to prove the sincerity of their oft-repeated declarations

that the independence and integrity of Persia are their desire, and that they sincerely wish to have as their neighbour in the East a friendly and prosperous Persia.

Nonetheless, the declaration went on to say, Britain had given considerable loans to Iran without insisting on quick repayment; and it was now their firm policy to try and make Turkey to withdraw completely from Iranian territory, to abrogate the Anglo–Russian convention of 1907, to withdraw their troops from Iran as soon as the circumstances (including Iran's security and stability) made it possible, and to continue their financial subsidy to the Iranian government until law and order was reasonably restored in the country. They would even surrender the South Persia Rifles to Iran to use in any unified army which she herself would organize, and would be prepared to assist Iran in organizing the uniform force only if she herself so wished. The only condition they would set was that Iran would employ British advisers in organizing their financial situation. This was a reasonable demand, said the declaration, in view of Iran's substantial debt to Britain, without which they would have to stop the current subsidies and ask for the repayment of their loans. But it was 'not intended in any way to infringe the sovereign rights or liberties of Persia'.[16]

The two rival British outlooks on their Iranian policy were thus far apart. The only concession India had made to the other Foreign Office was the employment by Iran of British financial advisers, but even that did not specify any conditions regarding their powers and position, the rest of the proposals being unequivocally in line with popular Iranian sentiments and aspirations.

Curzon summed up his own view in the following Eastern Committee's meeting of 30 December 1918. To disengage completely from Iran would be 'immoral, feeble and disastrous'. To obtain a mandate was neither likely nor practicable. The policy suggested by India, which he described but did not name, theoretically looked attractive, but unworkable. Instead, they should talk to the Persian delegation (whom he knew from Cox were on their way to Paris) with complete frankness, assure them most explicitly of Iran's independence and integrity, and abrogate 'the hated Anglo–Russian Convention'. They should offer assistance for organizing a unified military force on the condition that a British officer is put at its head (though officers of other nationalities could also be employed by Iran); and for organizing her public finance, likewise on the condition that a British financial adviser is employed for the purpose. If this was not accepted by the Iranians, then Britain should stop paying the current subsidies, demand a settlement of all of Iran's outstanding debts to her, and leave them to settle their affairs without British assistance.[17] Thus, at that time, Curzon was ready to engage in serious (though bilateral) negotiations with the delegation that he knew Iran was sending to the peace conference. But a couple of months later he gave up the idea, when it became clear that Cox could negotiate an agreement with Vosuq and his two close cabinet allies in Tehran (see below). Likewise, he did not object to Iran's employment of non-British military advisers as well, but – encouraged by Cox – he changed his mind about that too, during the negotiations for the Agreement. As we shall see in chapter five, Curzon's snubbing of Iran's peace delegation, and his insistence on exclusively British advisers, were two of the most important reasons for the anger aroused by the agreement.

This was Curzon's policy outlook at the time, and formed the basis for Cox's negotiations in Tehran, which ended in the 1919 agreement. But India and the India Office were far from convinced and would not give up the fight. In the minutes of the committee meeting it had been stated that 'the Committee were generally in favour of the policy recommended by the Chairman and Lord Robert Cecil.' This was seized by Edwin Montagu, Secretary of State for India, who wrote in a hard letter addressed to Curzon a few days later:

> I am sorry to have to bother you with further correspondence, but I really feel so alarmed about some aspects of Eastern affairs that I am compelled to write to you … I notice in the draft Minutes [of the Eastern Committee] a statement that the Committee agreed with the Chairman. Surely you will not allow this to stand, for the situation was this. Mr Balfour was away; I was away; I do not see it recorded that the C.I.G.S. was present; Lord Robert Cecil (I do not know whether he is a member of the Committee or not now) had left before he had heard either Sir Hamilton Grant or Sir Arthur Hirtzel, and therefore the Committee consisted of the Chairman [i.e.Curzon]; and the Chairman, of course, not unnaturally agreed with the Chairman.

Montagu objected to Curzon's insistence on a British commander for the proposed uniform Iranian army as being 'unnecessarily offensive to the Persian Government and national feeling' and went on to add:

> Lastly I cannot regard the policy of the Eastern Committee with regard to Persia on a footing satisfactory to the Persians by re-establishing their confidence in us as being anxious to help but not desirous to control.

And he finished by the threat of stopping India's financial contributions to British policy in Iran:

> I have warned the Eastern Committee more than once of the grave diffi-culty which I am experiencing, and which I shall experience more and more in the future, of getting contributions from Indian revenues to expenditure in Persia. I cannot honestly make the attempt in future if the policy is one in which neither the India Office nor the Government of India concur.[18]

Curzon was not to be cowed by such strong words into giving up a policy, the realization of which he was increasingly regarding as a principal achievement of his career, although it is clear that these statements were effective in modifying the policy in the shape of the final agreement (see below). Indeed, within a few days of Montagu's highly discouraging letter, he wired Cox with a five-point plan frame for negotiation:

- Unqualified reassurances on Iran's independence;
- Abrogation of the 1907 convention;
- Creation of a uniform force, although 'command and officering the force *would be subject for discussion*';
- Appointment of a British financial adviser;
- Withdrawal of British forces as soon as advisable.

Curzon told Cox not to communicate the plan frame to the Iranian government straight away, but to try and 'induce atmosphere' that the proposals were very generous, and that if they were rejected Britain might completely end its assistance to Iran.[19]

Cox responded forthwith with good news. The three most important cabinet ministers – Vosuq, Firuz Mirza Nosrat al-Dawleh (then justice minister, later foreign minister) and Akbar Mirza Sarem al-Dawleh (minister of finance) – were eager to negotiate. The Shah had also been brought into line; he would stop his 'persistent intrigues against the Cabinet', and had openly declared his full support for Vosuq's government. The situation looked ripe for presenting more definite British proposals, he added, unless the discussion of Iranian affairs by the Paris peace conference got in the way.[20]

Curzon found Cox's encouraging news as 'a source of great satisfaction', but was still anxious about the attitude of the Iranian peace delegation in Paris. Accordingly, he gave Cox careful instructions to ensure that the policy would have the unequivocal backing of Tehran. The delegation, he wrote, seemed to have different instructions from those pursued by the three ministers in Tehran, and there could not be one policy negotiated directly with Britain and another advocated by the delegation in Paris, 'possibly backed by the Shah'. If the Peace Conference was to be presented with a 'fait accompli' on the Iranian question, an agreement reached in Tehran must not be disowned by their spokesmen in Paris. Curzon would consult Arthur Balfour to see whether or not they should tell the Iranian delegation that 'we are in consultation with their Government and prefer to settle matters with latter not regarding it as case for Peace Conference at all'.[21]

He promptly wired Balfour in Paris, sending him a copy of the telegram to Cox, and suggesting that no discussions should be entered into with the Iranian delegates (who had just arrived in Paris) which could upset Cox's work in Tehran. Whatever Balfour's reply was to Curzon's specific question about the wisdom of informing the delegates of the Tehran negotiations, 'fait accompli' became a recurrent phrase in the Cox-Curzon-Balfour correspondence, and the decision was very quickly made to keep the Iranian delegation in the dark about the bilateral proceedings in Tehran. This prolonged secrecy was to be seized on later by the opponents of the Agreement (in Iran as well as America, France and elsewhere) as clear proof that it concealed sinister motives and designs which were not apparent from its published text (see chapter five). It was to be echoed by none other than James Balfour, the senior assistant financial adviser to Iran as a result of the 1919 Agreement, no later than three years after the event.[22]

Now that Cox had 'induced atmosphere' for working towards a bilateral agreement – as opposed to an international deal for which the delegation in Paris was looking – the three Iranian ministers (Vosuq-Firuz-Sarem, who became known as 'the triumvirate') sought British help to 'create an atmosphere conducive to favourable reception' of the results of the negotiations so far achieved. They asked for permission to announce Britain's willingness 'to employ and encourage Persian Capital' for railway construction, road building, the creation of modern urban municipalities, and supplies of arms and munitions for the proposed uniform army. These were indeed some of the urgent desires of Iranian reformists and modernizers of all colour and creed, but the British declaration would not bring short-term results, and would not, by itself, bring about 'the atmosphere' that the ministers wished to create. On the other hand, the one request of the triumvirate which would have had an immediate propaganda effect was the most controversial.

The Iranian delegation in Paris was, among other things, looking for the return of much of the territories lost to the Russian and Ottoman empires since the end of the eighteenth century. This was an over-optimistic project, likely to get nowhere and in fact it did not. But it was a major part of the dream of the rising tide of modern nationalism in Iran. The triumvirate felt that if they were to compete, perhaps even to outdo the Paris delegation – which so far had not even been admitted to the Conference – they should obtain public British support for these 'desiderata', another term which became recurrent in the correspondence as a summary reference for this particular Iranian demand. They asked for British support for a joint guarantee of Iran's independence 'by all of the Allies'; a revision of the Treaty of Turkamanchai; the return of parts of Kurdistan; the revision of customs treaties which had been cast much in favour of Russia as well as Britain; and reparations from Russia and Turkey for war damages to Iran.[23]

Curzon's response to the other requests – except the request for arms, to which he readily agreed – was non-committal but not discouraging. He was prepared to view favourably the issues of customs revisions and Iran's demands for reparations from Russia and Turkey. But he found the rest of the Iranian demands, the hard core of their requirements for creating a favourable atmosphere, 'open to gravest objections'. In later correspondence with Cox, and conversations with Firuz, he was to emphasize the unrealism of some of the Iranian demands, and the difficulties which Britain would face in giving them its active support. At this point, however, he was also concerned that a multinational – as opposed to British – guarantee of Iran's independence as well as pursuit of territorial rearrangements would open up the whole case to the Paris

Conference and to the participation of other powers, which was contrary to his policy of entering an exclusive, bilateral, agreement with Iran.[24]

This was early in March 1919. Having received Curzon's clear views on these issues, Cox continued his work in Tehran, and within a month sent a draft agreement to Curzon which became the basis for the final document. Before discussing this, it would be useful to review the development of Cox's pursuits in Tehran more closely. It was mentioned above that Cox's first discussion paper on the subject sent in November 1918, two weeks after the Armistice, had envisaged the possibility of obtaining a mandate from the world powers (the normal vehicle for which would have been the Paris conference and the League of Nations it later created). This had been rejected both by the Foreign Office and – most vehemently – by the Viceroy and the India Office, and was later explained away by Cox himself as a maximum programme.

Next, in mid-January 1919, he sent an outline of a new discussion paper to all the relevant departments, this time about entering a bilateral agreement with the Iranian government. It was broadly along the five-point framework suggested to him by Curzon a couple of days earlier (see above), but was much more ambitious than perhaps even Curzon would have expected. Cox himself described it as a 'moderate scheme between the two extremes' – that is, his own earlier suggestion of a mandate, and India's alternative policy along the memorandum submitted by Sir Hamilton Grant. He proposed the appointment of a British financial adviser and staff, and advisers for other key ministries as well, while adding that it would be 'much better, if possible, [to] have Advisers associated with the governors of each major province to supervise expenditure and advise in administration'. The new army should be headed by a British officer with the same powers of administration as those enjoyed by the then Swedish commander of the Iranian gendarmerie. He also made some suggestions about ways of financing the scheme through a British loan to Iran. Yet he ended his telegram by emphasizing that 'the above suggestions are necessarily crude' and were intended to enable the British government to instruct him on the definite lines of policy that he should pursue.[25]

India opposed Cox's 'moderate scheme' almost as vehemently as it had rejected his earlier maximum proposal. The Viceroy saw no wisdom in having British advisers attached to various government departments or the provincial governors. Such measures would open them 'to the charge (not merely in Persia, but in England and the world at large) that we are treating Persia as a British protectorate.' It would be better to suggest the employment of non-British (for example, French Swiss) officers, but failing that, a British advisory military mission might be appointed for the training – not command – of the Iranian army. The Viceroy's prophetic remarks about the fate of the Agreement proved so accurate that it must be quoted in full:

Cox's full programme of reform ... is so thorough that it may well prove too strong meat even for ultra pro-British triumvirate of the Cabinet. In any case, as we know from experience pro-British optimism of men so bound up with us as Vossuk [Firuz, and Sarem] are a very uncertain barometer of public opinion. In a matter of such moment we cannot afford a repetition on a large scale of our experience over the South Persia Rifles whose recognition by Vossuk was closely followed by his downfall, and repudiation of his recognition by successive cabinets contributed greatly to our troubles in South Persia. It is not enough that the proposed reforms would be readily acceptable to present Cabinet; it is essential that they should run so little counter to public opinion that the present Cabinet will be able to carry them into effect, and that their successors in office will accept them as a matter of course.[26]

Cox was not convinced of these fears since he believed that India's views were six months out of date, and felt sure that – as of February 1919 – they had 'all the cards in our hand'.[27] India's attack was, nevertheless, another turning point in the process of formulating British policy, and had noticeable effect on the final agreement, as may be readily observed from the draft which Cox communicated to Curzon in April:

1. British Government reiterates in the most categorical manner the understanding which they have repeatedly given in the past to respect the independence and integrity of Persia.

2. British Government will supply at the cost of Persian Government the services of such expert advisers as may be necessary for the several Departments of the Persian administration. These advisers shall be engaged on contracts and endowed with adequate powers, the nature of which should be a matter of agreement more or less between the Persian Government and advisers.

3. British Government will (group omitted) provide at the cost of Persian Government such officers and munitions and equipment of modern type as may be adjudged necessary by a Joint Commission of military experts, British and Persian, which shall assemble forthwith for the purpose of estimating the needs of Persia in the direction of a uniform force which the Persian Government proposes to create for the establishment and preservation of order in the country and on its frontiers.

4. British Government in consultation with Persian Government shall seek in customs revenue or other sources of income at the disposal of the Persian Government adequate security for a substantial loan to be provided or arranged by British Government for Government of Persia for the purpose of financing the reforms indicated in clauses 2 and 3 of this agreement, and pending the completion of negotiations for such a loan, British Government shall advance such funds as may be necessary to provide personnel and equipment for initiating the said reforms.

5. British Government, fully recognizing the urgent need which exists for the improvement of communications in Persia, both with a view to the extension of trade and prevention of famine, are prepared to cooperate with Persian Government for encouragement of Anglo-Persian enterprise in this direction both by means of railway construction and other forms of transport, subject always to examination of the problems by experts, and to agreement between the two Governments as to particular projects which may be most necessary, practicable, and profitable.

6. British Government agree, in principle, in so far as they are concerned, to the examination of existing treaties with a view to their revision in conformity with the present-day requirements, and will be prepared to enter into special negotiations for the purpose as soon as, in the opinion of the two Governments, a suitable moment has arrived.

7. The two Governments agree to appointment forthwith of a joint committee of experts for examination and revision of the existing customs tariff with a view to its reconstruction on a basis calculated to accord with the legitimate interests of the country and to promote its prosperity.

8. British government will lend their full support to Persian Government for the establishment of her position as a member of the League of Nation.[28]

Apart from the principal agreement, the draft proposal included a subsidiary agreement which, it specified, 'shall for the present remain secret': '(a) it being hereby mutually agreed and decided between the parties that British and Persian Governments will make no claims against one another for losses incurred by one Government against the other resulting from the recent World War, the British Government undertakes to support the claims of Persia to obtain compensation for material damage suffered by Persia from action of other belligerents; (b) it being understood that Persian Government is anxious to obtain a rectification of the frontier of Persia in certain localities, the British Government accordingly agree to receive confidentially the detailed explanations of the desires of the Persian Government and to examine them with an open mind; furthermore in the case of any particular item the justice or expediency of which in the interest of the people concerned they may become convinced, the British Government will endeavour to the best of their power to assist the Persian government to attain their object in such manner and by such means as may be decided between the parties to be possible and convenient'.[29]

Cox had no comment to make on articles 1, 3, 4, and 5 of the principal agreement. Article 6, a barely visible hint at the 'desiderata' regarding the return of former Iranian territories, he rightly described as 'innocuous and vague'. Article 7 was intended to increase Iran's revenues from customs. Article 8 was included to 'captivate public excitement'. Regarding article 2, he had wanted the power of the expert advisers to be determined by both governments. He had also wished to insist that Iran would be bound by the Agreement not to employ any other advisers or obtain any other loan from other countries. The triumvirate had resisted these demands on grounds of adverse public reaction, saying that the conditions would be fulfilled in practice. Cox realized, however, that the most sensitive part of the draft proposal was the two secret clauses which could create a British obligation to support actively 'the Persian desiderata'. But he was generally sympathetic to them, especially as they would make the Agreement more acceptable to the Iranian public opinion. It was he who had insisted on the secrecy of the subsidiary agreement, he explained to Curzon a few days later, not the Iranian ministers who would have preferred its clauses to be included in the principal agreement.[30]

There were other secret Iranian demands which Cox supported as best he could, and which were to cast a shadow on the Agreement both then and later. The Shah asked for a monthly subsidy of 20,000 tomans for life, and British guarantee of the perpetuation of the Qajar dynasty. The triumvirate asked for a secret service fund of 500,000 tomans – 'palm oil', as Cox described it in a later dispatch – to be used for dividing the opposition and persuading the public; they explained that the alternative was to use coercion against the opposition. The triumvirate also asked for guarantees of their income and property as well as asylum by Britain if they failed badly and had to leave the country.[31] These demands led to a host of troubles which will be discussed below.

Looking at the draft proposal, one can clearly discern the influence of India's opposition to Cox's earlier probings: instead of his British commander for the uniform force, there was now to be a joint military commission for organizing it; instead of so many advisers for so many departments and provinces, there were now to be 'such expert advisers as may be necessary'. Besides, India had been proven right in anticipating resistance even by the triumvirate themselves to the more outlandish conditions of Cox, as explained in his comments on article 2 of the principal draft proposal.

Still, the Viceroy was as unhappy with the whole scheme as before:

> For demands of Shah and triumvirate ... and suggestion that we might see scheme through by coercion are highly significant corroborations of our warning that this ultra pro-British triumvirate is very uncertain barometer of [Iranian] public opinion.

He warned about the prospect of facing 'wave of [Iranian] nationalism', about rising anti-British feelings among Muslims everywhere, about never being able to disengage from Iran, and about considerably more financial and military costs than was envisaged, if 'Cox's latest scheme' was approved. And he emphasized that India would not be prepared to increase its financial commitments to the British policy in Iran.[32]

Neither Cox nor Curzon was impressed with India's forebodings. Curzon had already expressed his general satisfaction with the draft proposal.[33] Cox responded to India with vigour as well as rigour, defending the draft proposal (which he said was British policy, not his 'latest scheme'), trying to allay India's fears, and arguing that the differences between his and India's views were more apparent than real. But he did hint that the onset of a 'Bolshevik movement' in Iran might upset the policy.[34]

What played a crucial role, perhaps, in the debate was the agreement of the India Office with the new proposal. In his letters both to the Foreign Office and to the Viceroy, Montagu stressed the dangers of Iranian instability to the British Empire, and said that the new scheme no longer contemplated to 'force tutelage upon Persia'. The risks mentioned by the Viceroy were real, but he was prepared to take them since the benefits seemed to outweigh the costs. He was opposed to the Shah's personal demands, and he would not agree to more financial commitments by India unless it was in the form of an interest-bearing loan. He proposed an urgent meeting of the Inter-Departmental Conference on Eastern Affairs (the 'ad hoc' conference which had replaced the standing Eastern Committee), which duly met on 7 May and signalled the go-ahead to Cox, subject to amendments which were communicated to him by Curzon.[35]

Meanwhile there was a profuse correspondence between Cox and Curzon – continued until August when the final agreement was signed – on several queries and amendments. For example, regarding article (2) Curzon suggested the insertion of 'all' before 'such experts'.[36] Later, a compromise was found in the form of 'whatever expert advisers may, after consultation between the two Governments, be considered necessary',[37] which entered the final text of the agreement. The secret clauses, on the other hand, were not acceptable to Curzon in their existing form, and occupied a good deal of the argument on points of substance. He suggested that their contents could be covered by (a much more vague and far less binding) exchange of letters between the two governments, and that was accepted by the triumvirate.[38] Negotiations in Tehran, and between Tehran and London, did not drag on such points of substance, mainly because the draft proposal met Curzon's essential requirements, and partly because both sides displayed flexibility in dealing with contentious points.

The final agreement, which was signed and published in August 1919, consisted of six articles. There was no substantive change in the first five articles of the draft proposal, except for the amendment to article 2 mentioned above, and the insertion of 'absolutely' before 'the independence and integrity of Persia' in article 1. Article 7 of the draft proposal – on the creation of a modern transport system – became article 6 of the final agreement, while articles 6 and 8 of the draft proposals, both of which would have created international obligations for Britain, were completely dropped. In the same spirit, the proposed confidential subsidiary agreement was also dropped and replaced by a public exchange of letters, as mentioned above. Apart from that, a separate contract was signed at the same time for a British loan of £2 million for a period of 20 years at an annual interest rate of 7 per cent. Britain had suggested 15 years and

8 per cent interest, but they accepted the more favourable terms to Iran suggested by the triumvirate.[39]

Much of the Curzon-Cox correspondence for finalizing the agreement, in fact, fell on the thorny issue of the Shah's and the triumvirate's private demands. In his initial response to Cox's telegrams on these matters Curzon was very discouraging:

> His Majesty's Government could not commit themselves to maintenance in perpetuity of Kajar dynasty, or to pay subsidy to Shah, which would amount at a present rate to 120,000 l. a year ... Further payment of 500,000 tomans would, *if ever approved*, have to be merely an advance out of any prospective loan.[40]

Trying to play down the financial costs of the perpetual subsidy the Shah had asked for, Cox wrote that the Shah's life may not be long on account of 'his increasing obesity'. He also suggested some verbal amendments which would make the guarantee for the dynasty less binding.[41] Curzon refused 'gambling' on the Shah's life.[42] However, the Shah's demands proved much easier to deal with as neither Cox nor the triumvirate pressed them too hard. It was finally agreed that his present subsidy of 15000 tomans be maintained for as long as he gave loyal support to Vosuq's government.[43] In place of British guarantee of the Qajar dynasty that the Shah had asked for, Cox addressed a confidential letter to Vosuq that the Shah and his successors would enjoy friendly British support so long as they were friendly towards Britain. As for the demands of the triumvirate for the protection of their property, etc., Cox addressed an identical confidential letter to each of them, promising that they would have Britain's 'good offices and support in case of need', and, if necessary, asylum 'in the British Empire'.[44]

The Iranian ministers' demands – especially the money for 'oiling the wheels' – proved much more agonizing for Curzon and his colleagues, largely because, if ever found out, they could give the impression of impropriety regarding the Agreement. Cox wrote that it could not be put down as an advance on the British loan to the government because it would then have to be accounted for.[45] Curzon replied that British parliamentary scrutiny was likely to be more thorough than that of the Iranian ministry of finance, and suggested that the money might be accepted as an advance on the loan 'before their Ministry of Finance is reorganized'.[46] After the Inter-Departmental Conference of 7 May, Curzon could pass comprehensive comments on the whole proposal, including the ministers' demands. As a way out of the dilemma, Cox had suggested that, instead of 500,000 tomans, 350,000 could be paid, which was equal to the amount of monthly subsidy that the British government was currently paying to the Iranian treasury. It could be regarded, he explained, as a one-off extra-monthly subsidy to the Iranian government. Curzon replied that this was not possible, because it would not be authorized by the (British) Auditor-General. Furthermore:

Our view is that proposed agreement will be of utmost advantage to Persia, who gain much while losing nothing. Idea of compensating Ministers [for loss of personal property in case of failure] appears therefore to be out of the question. We could hardly go beyond guarantee of asylum. If Ministers are so frightened of proposed agreement to fear expulsion, agreement itself would not rest on very secure foundation. Similarly, no British Government would employ coercion to obtain or enforce compliance [with the Agreement], which must be either freely given or not at all.[47]

Cox explained that the reference to coercion had been misconstrued, that the triumvirate were convinced of the merits of the policy, and that they were merely afraid that some future Iranian government might try to persecute them for other reasons if they did not have British protection, adding, nevertheless, that they did not wish these issues to delay the progress of the negotiations. But the money was necessary and would be acceptable 'as advance on account of loan'.[48]

Curzon now saw the risk of paying the money as an advance on the official loan, and for once was prophetic:

I gravely doubt wisdom of such action. Should this Cabinet fall and be succeeded by Mushaver [currently foreign minister, leading the peace delegation in Paris] or others, fact that first 200,000l [500,000 tomans] of loan had been expended for such purpose would become known in Persia, would effectively damn career of Triumvirate, and if made public would excite severest criticism here.[49]

Cox insisted that the money was necessary, but they might agree on a smaller sum, Vosuq's cabinet would not fall in the next two years, and otherwise the purpose of the money could be explained away as 'education of public opinion' or 'costly initiation of reforms'.[50]

By early July almost all the other points had been hammered out but the issue of the money had not yet been resolved. Curzon suggested paying £20,000 (= 50,000 tomans), that is, ten per cent of the sum asked for. The triumvirate turned it down, saying that if an adequate amount was not to be paid, they would rather fight for the Agreement on its merits. Cox once again insisted.[51] Curzon thought the sum demanded was too large 'for suggested purposes', but, emphasizing his 'intense dislike of this phase of the transaction', he threw in the towel and left the matter to Cox's discretion.[52] He had already vented his frustration in a minute he had written to Cox's previous dispatch on that subject:

We have offered 20,000. They ask for 200,000. This is not merely exorbitant it is corrupt. I thought I had said this to Cox a dozen times over but I cannot get it into his head.[53]

Cox's haggling about the money in Tehran resulted in an agreement on 400,000 tomans (slightly more than £131,000). Reporting the conclusion of the deal, he added that Vosuq had not been pushing for the money:

> In justice to Vosugh I feel bound to tell you in confidence that it was not he but the other two members of the Triumvirate who gave me all the trouble in this connection and Prime Minister was doubtless not in strong enough position to risk a split with them over it.[54]

Sarem al-Dawleh cashed 200,000 tomans from the Imperial Bank of Persia (half of which was the share of Firuz) immediately upon approval, and the balance was accredited to Vosuq's account at the Bank in September.[55] But if Cox had not managed to strike a better bargain over the sum to be paid, he had been successful in obtaining a letter from Sarem as minister of finance acknowledging receipt of the sum as 'the first instalment on account of 2000,000 stipulated in Agreement signed today'.[56] In appearance at least, this would save the British government embarrassment if the deal was ever exposed. But it would make it even more difficult for the triumvirate to account for it.

Curzon's great battle over the issue was entirely justified when, in November 1920, and several months after Vosuq's government had fallen, the deal became public as a result of a parliamentary question in Britain. Before then, rumours had been rife in Tehran about 'the British bribe' to the triumvirate, but there had been no proof nor any knowledge of the sum in question. Herman Norman, who had replaced Cox as British minister from June 1920, reported the strong reaction in Tehran to the news of the exposure in London.[57] Sepahdar, who had been a member of Vosuq's cabinet, was then prime minister, and he had rightly denied any previous knowledge of it. In reply to Norman, Curzon wrote that that aspect of the matter had been 'extremely repugnant to' him, and that they had a letter from the then finance minister acknowledging the receipt of the money as the first instalment of the loan:

> Present Prime Minister was at that time a member of the Cabinet ... We must therefore hold him jointly responsible with his colleagues for the official act of that Cabinet, and you should speak to him very strongly in this sense.[58]

But he rejected the Iranian view, related as well as shared by Norman, that the British government had 'bought Vossugh's cabinet'.[59]

Sepahdar repeated that he had had no previous knowledge of the matter, and that 'as money was never paid into Treasury, Government could not accept contention that they had received it as a first instalment of loan'. He asked for a copy of Sarem al-Dawleh's letter (which Norman felt he could not refuse) as well as British assistance in an effort to recover the money. Given the very difficult situation in which Sepahdar's government was at the time (see chapter seven), Norman suggested to him that the matter would be best forgotten for the moment.[60] Sepahdar agreed, but nevertheless wrote and protested to Vosuq, who was then in London, mentioning the sum of £250,000 which had been quoted by mistake when the news first had come out. Vosuq visited Curzon at the Foreign Office and said that he had replied to Sepahdar that 'any such sum' must have been received in connection with the purchase of arms, etc. He asked Curzon, however, to inform Norman that:

[the]sum paid by Sir P. Cox on conclusion of agreement was advanced at instigation of Sarem-ed-Dowleh and Prince Firouz who each received 100,000 tomans: the remainder was put at His Highness' [i.e. Vosuq's] own disposal by Sarem-ed-Dowleh but was not touched as Vossough was opposed to procedure.

Subsequently His Highness used the remaining sum of tomans 200,000 to help Tomanianz but firm nevertheless became bankrupt. His Highness received from firm title deeds of lands in North Persia as security and is prepared to hand these over to you or 'a qui de droit' or to repay that sum on his return. In any case he wishes Sepahdar to be enlightened that it was never question of 250,000.[61]

In chapter seven I shall have occasion to return to this subject in the context of Sepadar's ministry. However, more than a decade later, when Taqizadeh was finance minister, Reza Shah ordered him to take back the money from the triumvirate for the Iranian treasury. Sarem returned the money in four instalments. Vosuq either returned the title deeds of Tomaninantz's lands or the 200,000 tomans, it is not clear which. Firuz at first denied having been paid, but 'I heard that they eventually got it back from him as well'.[62]

But in August 1919 all that was a long time in the future. And now that the Agreement had been finally signed, Curzon could heave a sigh of satisfaction and write in a personal letter – and with a considerable degree of truth – that he had 'done it all alone'.[63] At the same time, he wrote a long memorandum, addressed to his cabinet colleagues and especially aimed at India, the India Office, the Treasury and the War Office, explaining the Agreement and why it was concluded:

What they mean in practice is this: not that we have received or are about to receive a mandate for Persia ...; not that Persia has handed over to us any part of her liberties; not that we are assuming fresh and costly obligations which will place a great strain upon us in the future; but that the Persian Government realizing that we are the only neighbouring Great Power closely interested in the fate of Persia, able and willing to help her, and likely to be disinterested in that object, have decided of their own free will to ask us to assist Persia in the rehabilitation of her fortunes.

And he went on to explain the reason for Britain's special interest in the country:

> If it be asked why we should undertake the task at all ... the answer is that ... now that we are to assume the mandate for Mesopotamia ... we cannot permit the existence, between the frontiers of our Indian Empire in Baluchistan [of India] and those of our new Protectorate [Mesopotamia], of a hotbed of misrule, enemy intrigue, financial chaos, and political disorder. Further, if Persia were to be left alone, there is every reason to fear that she would be overrun by Bolshevik influences from the north. Lastly, we possess in the south-western corner of Persia great assets in the shape of the oilfields, which are worked for the British navy and which give us a commanding interest in that part of the world.[64]

More than a year later, in November 1920, when criticism of his policy was mounting in Britain as well as Iran and elsewhere, Curzon said in the House of Lords:

> In our Persian policy there has been no element whatsoever of wild or reckless adventure such as has sometimes been ascribed to us. On the contrary, there has been a deliberately thought out plan ... to solve the Persian problem in a manner consistent, not so much with British interests (though naturally we have not forgotten them) as with the continued national existence and independence of Persia herself. There was no attempt to suggest anything of the nature of a British protectorate over Persia. We never thought of going to the League of Nations to ask for a mandate over Persia. We preferred to treat her as a friendly and independent State in the position of equality with ourselves.[65]

The reasons described by Curzon for Britain's special interest in Iran could not be doubted by any British department of state or the government of India. His clear, even emphatic, reassurance about Iran's independence – especially in the confidential memorandum addressed to his own cabinet colleagues – would be difficult to dismiss as a ploy to mislead the Iranian public. Yet there is no clear explanation here or elsewhere why there had to be an extended involvement of this magnitude with Iran, rather than a more limited policy along the lines suggested by the government of India. It is, however, fair to note Curzon's emphasis in his memorandum on the danger of continued chaos and/or Bolshevism on the borders of the British Empire in India and Iraq (Mesopotamia).

It would be a fruitless exercise to speculate about Curzon's secret motives. But, on the basis of the evidence in this and the following chapters, it would appear that, now Russia seemed to be out of the way, he felt there was a real chance for Britain to establish a special relationship with Iran free of competition from any other great power in or out of the region. And, as part of that, there seems to have been a psychological motive, a wish for a great personal achievement as the architect of the new Iran and of a close relationship between the two countries. It would be difficult to explain his singlemindedness and the time and energy he devoted to creating the Agreement, trying to make it work, and then ignoring the evidence of its failure for a long time while all others were convinced of it, and being so personally hurt when it did fail, without allowing for some deep psychological motive.

Harold Nicolson, who had known Curzon personally, had worked under him, and – like so many British officials of the time – was critical of his Persian Policy, perhaps came closer than many others in discerning Curzon's motives and intentions. 'As a romanticist', he wrote, Curzon could not remain immune 'to a phenomenon familiar to all those who have travelled or have lived in Persia ... those plains of amber, those peaks of amethyst, the dignity of the crumbled magnificence, that silence of two thousand years':

> Essentially, however, his constant preoccupation with Persia arose from the 'main love' of his political life, [which] was centred on his Indian obsession ... Always he had dreamt of creating a chain of Vassal states stretching from the Mediterranean to the Pamirs and protecting, not the Indian frontiers merely, but our communications with our further Empire ... In this chain of buffer states Persia was to him at once the weakest and the most vital link.[66]

However that may be, the fact remains that, as Nicolson himself points out, Curzon both misunderstood the mood of the Iranian public at the time (confusing it with three decades before, when he had travelled in Iran), and conducted his policy such that it seemed to confirm their worst fears.

The campaign in Iran

Immediately after the signing of the Agreement, Vosuq published a long statement about it and about his government's work since its inception almost exactly a year before. He said that he had accepted office when the country was in a chaotic state. The world war was still on, while the country was struck by brigandage, rebellion, terrorism, famine, an empty treasury and the disintegration of the armed forces. Yet he put the country's interest before his own and risked both his life and reputation by accepting the heavy burden of office. He was now happy that he had done as much as possible to improve the situation towards which British financial and military assistance had been helpful. It was however clear, the declaration continued, that short-term injections from abroad would not solve the country's problems, and there was dire need for administrative as well as military reorganization, which without the assistance of foreign experts and technicians would be impossible.

No-one doubted the need for this, he explained. The question was whence the assistance should be sought, so that it would be both 'possible and practical' and ' would not put in doubt the independence of the country'. Various opinions were put forward, but they seldom met the test of practicality. It was not practical to try and receive assistance from several countries at the same time, because none of them would then be prepared to make the kind of commitment which was needed, and even assuming that they would, the political, cultural, and techincal differences among themselves would make the task difficult:

> For these reasons, and in view of the country's internal and external realities, recourse to any country other than Britain was not justified, both because of Britain's past assistance and the keen interest which she showed during negotiations in Iran's future development, and because, otherwise, the condition of practicality would not be fulfilled.

He concluded his long statement by explaining the articles of the Agreement, emphasizing that it guaranteed the country's independence and integrity, and pointing out that, in all circumstances, the best of agreements could be beneficial only when they are implemented wisely and by a competent government.[67]

In chapter five we shall see why and how such expositions and explanations were of no consequence in allaying public fears that the country had been sold out to the British empire. The supporters of the Agreement made up a small minority, both in quantity and in quality. Many of the journalists, public speakers and preachers who advocated its case did so for reasons of personal benefit. Years later, Modarres – who went over to the opposition when the agreement was announced – put their number at 800 men in the whole of the country.[68] According to a prominent contemporary opponent of the Agreement, a considerable amount of money was paid to some journalists and preachers to expound the virtues of Vosuq and the Agreement in the press and from the pulpit.[69] As the opposition intensified and spread, the government increasingly resorted to coercion, imprisonment and banishment (see chapter five).

The two most prominent younger journalists and intellectuals who supported the government and the Agreement were Sayyed Zia (later, Tabataba'i) and poet-laureate Bahar. The poet-laureate edited the semi-official newspaper *Iran*. He believed in the need for a strong government, and was – and always remained – friendly towards Vosuq (and his brother Qavam). But, although a political type, and a sophisticated one at that, he could not be described as a politician. He gave loyal support to Vosuq, but his role as well as degree of involvement was not such as to taint him either then or later, whereas even at the time Sayyed Zia was being described by otherwise moderate figures like Abdollah Mostawfi as 'this wheeler-dealer of yours [Vosuq's], this paid public agent of the British'.[70]

Sayyed Zia was indeed a journalist-politician, an ardent supporter of the Agreement, openly in regular contact with British diplomats and other ex-patriates in Tehran, and his loyalty to Vosuq was entirely political rather than personal. Born in 1889, he was the son of a prominent preacher, Sayyed Ali Aqa Yazdi, who first sided with the Constitutional Revolution, then went over to Shaikh Fazlollah's campaign for *mashru'eh*, but changed his mind before it was too late.[71] Zia received both a traditional and modern education in Shiraz and Tabriz, including acquaintance with French and English, and as a youth joined the constitutional movement. In 1908, after Mohammad Ali Shah's Coup, he was suspected of involvement in a bomb-throwing incident. And as neither the Ottoman nor the British legation allowed him to take *bast*, he was admitted by the Austrian legation. When the constitutionalist and government armies were fighting outside the gates of Tehran, he actively participated in the agitations inside the city.[72] It was from this period that he got to know some pro-constitutionalist British diplomats and officers, notably Walter Smart and C.B. [Claude] Stokes (see chapters seven to nine).

After the revolutionary triumph, he launched the newspaper *Sharq*, then *Barq*, but kept falling foul of the authorities on account of his radical pronouncements. In the end, he was unofficially advised to leave the country for some time, and spent two years in Paris. He returned to Iran in the wake of the first world war, launched the newspaper *Ra'd*, and unlike other radicals who supported the central powers now that Britain and France were on Russia's side in the war, he advocated the cause of the Entente, and it was from then onwards that he lost the confidence of his old radical friends and was increasingly regarded as a pro-British, therefore also pro-Russain, activist.[73]

Late in 1917 or early in 1918, an organization known as the Committee of Iron (Komiteh-ye Ahan) was set up in Isfahan with the support of the British consulate and the active involvement of Colonel Haig, a British officer whom we shall meet again at the time of the 1921 Coup (see chapter nine). Very little reliable information exists on this Committee. Dawlat-Abadi, who became a member for a time, says that within a short period it had enlisted as many as 2000 members in Isfahan. The impression he gives is that it had been created as an organizational base for a modern political movement and programme.[74]

In 1919, the Committee's centre was transferred to Tehran, and because its meetings were usually held in a house – apparently belonging to Sayyed Zia – in the Zargandeh suburban village, it was sometimes known as the Kommiteh-ye Zargandeh.[75] The Sayyed became known as its leading figure, but the other members were not publicly known. As a result, its full membership has remained unknown, but it is virtually certain that Major Mas'ud Khan (Kahyan), Captain Kazem Khan (Sayyah), Modir al-Molk (later, Mahmud Jam), Adl al-Molk (later, Hossein Dadgar), Soltan Mohammad Khan-e Na'ini (Ameri) and Mirza Karim Khan-e Rashti (later known among the elite as Khan-e Akbar), were among them.[76] Kahyan and Sayyah were directly involved in organizing the 1921 Coup. They as well as Jam, Dadgar and Ameri were members of the Sayyed's short-lived government after the Coup. Dadgar became speaker of the Majlis for several sessions under Reza Shah, before falling out of the Shah's favour and being exiled to Europe. Jam became prime minister under Reza Shah and minister of the royal court under his son. Ameri and Khan-e Akber remained highly influential people until their deaths in the Pahlavi era.

Sayyed Zia led a vigorous campaign in support of the Agreement and Vosuq's government in his newspaper, was closely in touch with Vosuq, and, in November 1919, was sent by him at the head of a delegation to conclude a treaty with the newly formed Republic of Azerbaijan before it fell in Bolshevik hands (see chapter five). After the departure of Cox and the fall of Vosuq, he increased his direct contacts with the British legation, and under Sepahdar's cabinet – which fell as a result of the 1921 Coup – he virtually became the liaison and courier between the legation and the government (see chapters six and seven).

The Shah in Europe

Soon after Cox had opened negotiations for the Agreement, the Shah began to express an urgent desire to visit Europe for the first time. This was to be expected from a young Iranian of means, let alone the Shah. Since the second half of the nineteenth century it had become a strong desire for rulers, dignitaries and men of means to follow up the fabulous tales they heard about 'Farangestan' by visits to the continent which was increasingly thought of as paradise on earth. By the time the war ended, it became almost mandatory for any ambitious young man of the higher families to do the same. The Shah would probably have acted sooner had it not been for the outbreak of war shortly after his accession. Now that the war had ended, the first real opportunity had arrived, though he still needed British help in arranging it because of the chaotic post-war conditions in Russia and Eastern Europe. But both the triumvirate and Cox in Tehran and, even more so, Curzon in London, were afraid that he might 'get into bad hands'.

The Shah was an insecure young man who had been a boy when the constitutionalists had deposed his father and put him on the throne. All his life he had experienced nothing but revolution, conflict, chaos, war, foreign pressure and domination, and the threat of the country's disintegration. His great-grandfather had been assassinated, his grandfather forced into accepting constitutional monarchy, his father and two of his uncles deposed and banished from the country as rebels. He had been so attached to his father that, at the time of his abdication in 1909, the Shah at first intended to take him with himself to exile and let his second son succeed him. And when he changed his mind, the boy himself was extremely unhappy, repeatedly trying to hide himself in the hope of leaving the country with his parents, rather than remaining behind and occupying the throne.[77] He had been brought up in his royal capacity by conservative constitutionalists such as his two regents (Alireza Khan Azad al-Molk and Abolqasem Khan Naser al-Molk) and – even more so – by popular and deomocratic constitutionalists such as Mostawfi al-Mamalek and Moshir al-Dawleh. The latter were the kind of men whom he trusted and whose opinions he respected and, if possible, heeded. Otherwise, he was an inexperienced politician among many, in a society where politics often meant little more than the art of feathering one's nest as much and as quickly as possible, and turning even more quickly than the direction of the wind. Such were the background and circumstances which explain his commitment to constitutional government, his desire for public approval, his duplicitous conduct and his large appetite for money.

Cox had had several occasions to report on ill-feeling between the Shah and Vosuq with occasional 'temporary reconciliations.'[78] In February, he informed Curzon of the Shah's request regarding his proposed visit to Europe. By March he wrote that the Shah was very upset about not receiving a reply, and suggested that an encouraging reply would be 'very helpful' even though the actual visit could be deferred to an opportune moment.[79] Curzon was concerned that, once in Europe, the Shah would be used by the Iranian peace delegation in Paris against the negotiations in Tehran. He could therefore give 'no encouragement to the proposal'.[80] Cox persisted, adding that the Shah had now come completely into line, and unless he received some reward in acknowledgment, he might change his attitude.[80a] A few days later, the Shah 'complained bitterly of the unfriendliness' of the British government, and accused Vosuq as well as Cox for putting a 'spade in his wheel'.[81]

This was the end of March. Curzon relented, on the condition that he would keep off trouble in Europe, would not go to Paris before the end of the Peace Conference, and would grant full powers to Vosuq for the signing of the Agreement in his absence.[82]

That condition was probably the reason why the Shah promptly changed his mind and decided to postpone his visit to 'the autumn'.[83] It was only a few days later that Cox had sent the draft proposals for the Agreement, and the Shah would not have let the process to be completed in his absence. In fact, the Shah began his journey to Europe in mid-August, only a few days after the Agreement had been signed in Tehran.

The timing could hardly have been worse for the Agreement, because it coincided with the French and Swiss press campaigns which described it as proof that Iran had become a British protectorate (see chapter five). He was accompanied, among others, by Firuz – who had just replaced Moshaver, the chief delegate in Paris, as foreign minister – and Colonel Wickham, an officer in the British forces in Iran. Moshaver was made ambassador to Turkey (which was an unpaid post), replacing Ehtesham al-Saltaneh, who hated both Firuz and the Agreement, though the Shah gave Ehtesham a high medal as consolation.[84]

After a short visit to Istanbul, they journeyed via Italy (though not Rome) and Switzerland to France and eventually to England. While they were on their way there were rumours that the Shah might extend his visit to America. The rumours were dismissed as unfounded,[85] but in the meantime the American embassy in London first confirmed and then denied to the Foreign Office that an invitation would be sent to the Shah if he decided to visit America.[86] More worrying for Curzon were the effects of the anti-Agreement European press campaigns and the activities of discontented Iranians in Europe which began to affect the nerves not only of the Shah, but even of Firuz. He was due to go to London before the Shah in preparation for his state visit, and it was felt that he should avoid going to Paris on his way from Switzerland. But he feared that this would be held by the 'clique of Persians in Paris' as further evidence of his subservience to Britain.[87] The atmosphere in Paris was so hostile that Curzon confidentially advised the British embassy there that it was not desirable for Firuz 'to remain long in Paris on this occasion'.[88] In fact, his stay in Paris was short, but long enough for him to send a long and 'pessimistic' telegram to Tehran about the attacks on the Agreement in Paris.[89]

Firuz arrived in London in mid-September. Curzon threw a banquet for him on 18 September, where he gave a speech calculated to encounter the hostile interpretations put abroad by the opponents of the Agreement:

> I was never an ardent admirer of the Anglo-Russian Convention [of 1907]. On the contrary, I criticised it severely in Parliament and elsewhere ... I regard that Agreement as dead.

He then came to his central point about the nature of the new 1919 Agreement:

> I have always been a sincere and outspoken friend of Persian nationality. I regard Persia as a country with a great history and a romantic past ... I know that country and that people to be possessed of marked individuality and national spirit, too ardent to be suppressed, too valuable to be submerged ... It is an obvious interest to us to have a peaceful and prosperous Persia; and, as regards Persia herself, if it be true – and I do not think that the most ardent Persian patriot would deny it – that external assistance of some sort is necessary for her, is it not unnatural that it should be to this country that she should turn.[90]

Shortly afterwards, Cox reported to Curzon that the speech was translated and published in Persian, and received with unbounded satisfaction.[91] Meanwhile Firuz returned to France in order to accompany the Shah on his state visit in November.

The Shah was received in England with pomp and circumstance. No less a royal person than Prince Albert (later George VI) led the welcome party in Dover, only because the Prince of Wales was absent from the country. The King himself was at Victoria Station to welcome the Shah to London. He was given a royal banquet, where both the King and the Shah gave ceremonial speeches. In his banquet speech, the King welcomed the Shah with 'a most cordial greeting on an occasion fraught both with happy memories and with even happier prospects', and concluded with an allusion to the Agreement:

> We welcome [the Shah's visit] more especially at the present moment ... when we are about to embark upon a collaboration in the field of material and administrative progress which should ensure to your country a future not unworthy of its famous past.[92]

The Shah's reply to the King's speech – given in French – was commensurate in its warmth and its gratitude for the reception he had been given, and likewise alluded to the Agreement, though not in an exclusive sense: he spoke about Iran's need for help from 'Western democracies, and particularly Great Britain, whose friendly relations with my country already go back a long time'.[93]

Years later, after the fall of Ahmad Shah, a legend grew about this speech, and the more Reza Shah and Mohammad Reza Shah became unpopular, the more widely and firmly it was believed by the public, not least by politicians and intellectuals of almost every colour and creed. According to the legend, the Shah had been opposed to the Agreement and was advised by Firuz (Nosrat al-Dawleh) or his uncle Nosrat al-Saltaneh – who was very close to him, and was among his suite in London – to mention the Agreement with approval in his banquet speech. But he vehemently rejected that advice. After the speech, he was told by either of the two Nosrats (the confusion is due to their titles, but the reference must be to Firuz) that he had thus forfeited his throne. The legend went even further. It maintained that the moment the Shah refused to mention the Agreement in his speech, the British decided to overthrow the Qajar dynasty: the Coup d'état of 1921, the rise of Reza Khan and the emergence of the Pahlavi state and dynasty, were merely the stages by which that initial decision was masterfully (though 'magically' may be a more accurate term) implemented.[94]

It is true that the Shah did not mention the Agreement as such. It is also true that the Agreement did not have his wholehearted support. Yet the fact that, in its stark simplicity and improbability, this conspiracy theory was believed by most of the country's highly educated and sophisticated individuals (who were indeed responsible for its formulation and propagation) is strong evidence for much of the theoretical outlook about the state, politics and society in Iran on which this book is based (see chapter one). It may be explained briefly. The Shah was weak, greedy and unpopular with much of the country's modern elite, and constitutionalism had fallen into disrepute because it had been confused with chaos both at the centre and in the provinces (see chapter two). There was longing for stability and progress. Therefore, even among Reza Khan's opponents, very few shed tears for the fall of Ahmad Shah and the Qajars when it happened. But no sooner had Reza Shah alienated the public as an arbitrary ruler, than Ahmad Shah was turned into a martyr in the cause of Iranian independence and democracy, and legends such as the above were believed to be undeniable historical fact.

The Shah left England apparently very satisfied with his treatment there,[95] to continue his visit to Europe until a few months later when his urgent wish to return to Iran became another obsession for himself and another source of worry for the triumvirate and the Foreign Office (see chapter five). On his earlier visit to London in September, Firuz called on Curzon at the Foreign Office for talks about matters of mutual interest. They clearly reflected the effect of the negative comments he had read and heard on the Agreement in Europe. He insisted that the British advisers for Iran should be of the highest calibre, and should not have experience of service in India or elsewhere in the East, i.e., a background of colonial service. He also insisted that the financial adviser should be the best available regardless of cost. Curzon agreed, but it gave him an opportunity to wonder about the recent appointment by Iran of four French judicial experts. He was concerned that, given French hostility towards the Agreement, they would use their influence against it as well as against Vosuq's government. Firuz replied that if they abused their position they would be asked to leave.

Firuz also probed the idea of reconstituting the Iranian peace delegation to the Paris Conference, led by himself, and wondered about the possibility of claiming reparations from Turkey and Russia for war damages to Iran. Curzon responded with sympathy but could not give concrete answers in view of the unsettled situation of the two countries at the time. Furthermore, Firuz expressed unhappiness at the fact that the British Caspian flotilla had been handed over to the White Russian Admiral Deninkin rather than to the Iranian government. Curzon regretted that Britain had not received a request from Iran in time, and pointed out that in any engagement between Denikin and the Bolsheviks the latter were likely to win, and there would be no point in Iran losing a couple of 'useless vessels' in any such conflict. But he added that the question of Iran's having ships in the Caspian should be considered independently. Finally, Firuz raised the urgency and importance of road and railway construction and economic and industrial development, and Curzon thought that the Iranians should take the initiative in suggesting what they desired to be done.[96]

On his visit of 13 November to Curzon, after the Shah had left England, Firuz came to the most important point, and 'startled' Curzon by producing a map that showed Iran's claims for frontier rectifications which included parts of territories lost to the Russians – both in the Russian Azerbaijan and outer Khorasan – as well as parts of Kurdistan. This must have been a copy of the same map taken by the Iranian peace delegation to Paris. Mention has already been made of the importance of the issue for the triumvirate, especially as an effective means of making the Agreement popular. Now, in view of the negative reactions and responses to the Agreement both in Iran and abroad, the issue had acquired much greater urgency than before. Curzon's response was very brief and not very encouraging. In relating the matter to Cox, however, he was much more open and wrote that if these were the kinds of demands for which the Iranians hoped for British backing, 'I am afraid that they will be exposed to very considerable disappointment'. In the same visit, Firuz also referred to dangers of a Bolshevik intrusion into Iran, to which Curzon responded in a reassuring manner, though he was to change his tune when it actually happened. There followed a long exchange of views about the projected railway construction as well, and at the end of the meeting Firuz handed a detailed memorandum to Curzon on Iran's claims for territorial compensation.[97]

Despite Curzon's initial evasion over Iran's territorial claims, Firuz vigorously persisted with his justification of Iran's claims, and his demand for British support. He followed the above memorandum by two long letters to Curzon, both dated 17 November 1919, which he personally handed to the Foreign Office. They contain long and elaborate arguments for the return of much of Iran's lost territories on historical, linguistic, racial and religious as well as geopolitical grounds.[98] Having done that, in their following meeting two weeks later – before Firuz left England for France – he returned to a long and detailed discussion with Curzon about Iran's claims. Curzon responded 'with absolute frankness' this time. In his view, the first Iranian peace delegation (that led by Moshaver) had wrecked their chances by making extravagant territorial claims. The present demands were of a different scale, but still had no chance of being approved by the Peace Conference. He had no right to veto the Iranian demands, and they could submit them to the Conference if they so wished, but they should not expect British support for the majority of the claims. Alternatively, they could submit a more modest case with British backing. Firuz parted by saying that he would report on their meeting to his government.[99] But Firuz was to raise the subject with Curzon again, when the ship of Vosuq's government began to head for the rocks (see chapter five).

Firuz intended to remain in Europe as Iran's foreign minister and head of the Paris delegation until the end of the Paris Conference. But his stay took much longer than he could imagine at the time, and he returned to Iran shortly before the Coup of 1921 (see chapter eight). In the meantime, he travelled to London on several other occasions to confer with Curzon and the Foreign Office on matters which increasingly arose from the campaign against the Agreement. That campaign is the subject of the next chapter.

Notes

1 In Persian: Molk-e Iran chub-e estebdad mikhahad hanuz.
2 Eastern Committee, 10th meeting, 28/5/19, Cabinet Papers, cited in Houshang Sabahi, *British Policy in Persia, 1918–1925* (London: Frank Cass), 1990, p. 11.
3 See for example Mohammad Mosaddeq, *Musaddiq's Memoirs*, (ed. and intro.) Homa Katouzian, tr. S.H. Amin and H. Katouzian (London: Jebhe, 1988), Book I and Editor's Introduction. Malek al-Sho'ara Bahar, *Tarikh-e Mokhtasar-e Ahzab-e Siyasi dar Iran*, vol. i (Tehran: Jibi, 1978); and vol. ii, (Tehran: Amir Kabir, 1964), especially chapter 1, p. 9ff.

4   Bahar, *ibid.*, vol. ii, chapter 1.

5   This author still maintains his view of Modarres as a politician, first presented in 1976, in a seminar presented to the Middle East Centre of St. Antony's College, Oxford: 'Mudarris was an accomplished parliamentarian, with electrifying oratorical powers, who on a number of important occasions turned the parliamentary tide in his own favour by the sheer weight of a speech or two full of commonsense, wit and sometimes moral intimidation. He was in contact with people of all classes and, if anything, was noticeably less warm in his attitude towards the nobility than he was towards the common people. He was democratic in his political attitude, and he had no use either for high posts or for worldly possessions. Indeed, Flaubert's remark about Renan – 'if a man is someone why should he want to be something' – fits his case perfectly. But at the same time he loved to enjoy personal power, especially in a 'king making' capacity. He was self-assured to the point of being incautious and even tactless at times, and this was an important factor in his downfall. He was a man of principles, but [unlike men like Mostawfi al-Mamalek] he was not too particular about the means he employed to attain his objectives. However, even when he used tactics which could be easily taken as evidence of hypocrisy and inconsistency, he applied them in a way that would largely pre-empt such accusations. For example, he surprised many by his defence of Nusrat al-Dawleh [Firuz]'s credentials for commission to the Majlis barely six month's after the latter's activities in favour of the 1919 agreement. But, at the same time, he spoke with such contempt both of him and of his role in that episode that it was difficult to accuse him of inconsistency. Or when, in a moment of despair, he made the tactical mistake of contacting Khaz'al, the Shaikh of Muhammareh, who stood accused of being a separatist, a tyrant, and an agent of imperialism all at once, he still made no bones about his [negative] sentiments towards him ...' See Homa Katouzian, 'Nationalist Trends in Iran, 1921–1926', *International Journal of Middle East Studies*, November, 1979, p. 546; and H. Katouzian, *The Political Economy of Modern Iran*, (London and New York, Macmillan and New York University Press, 1981), pp. 86–87.

6   See Hossein Makki (ed.), *Divan-e Farrokhi Yazdi*, (Tehran: Amir Kabir, 1978), p. 259.

7   See Saif-e Azad (ed.), *Divan-e Aref-e Qazvini*, fourth edition (Tehran: Amir Kabir, 1963), for example, p. 325.

8   See Ali Akbar Salimi (ed.), *Kolliyat-e Mosavvar-e Eshqi*, first edition, (Tehran, n.p., n.d.), for example, pp. 325–34 and 396.

9   Loraine to Chamberlain, 15/1/26, FO 371/11841.

10 Loraine to Chamberlain, 15/6/26, FO 371/11841.

11 See for example Abloqasem Kahhalzadeh's memoirs, *Dideh-ha va Shenideh-ha*, (ed.) Morteza Kamran (Tehran: Kamran, 1984); *Musaddiq's Memoirs*, Book I; Baqer Aqeli, *Ruzshomar-e Tarikh-e Iran*, vol. 1 (Tehran: Nashr-e Goftar, 1995).

12 Cox to Curzon, 15/1/19, 371/3858.

13 Viceroy (Foreign Department) to Secretary of State for India, FO 371/3262, emphasis added.

14 Cox to Viceroy, 13/1/19, FO 371/3859.

15 Memorandum by Marling, 20/12/18, FO 371/3262.

16 Memorandum by Grant, 20/12/18, FO 371/3858.

17 See the Earl of Ronaldsheay, *The Life of Lord Curzon*, vol. iii (London: Ernest Benn, 1928), pp. 213–15.

18 Quoted directly in *ibid.*, pp. 216–17.

19 Curzon to Cox, 11/1/19, FO 371/3858.

20 Cox to Curzon, 13/1/19 and 14/1/19, FO 371/3859; 15/1/19, FO 371/3858.

21 Curzon to Cox, 23/1/19, FO 371/3858.

22 See James Balfour, *Recent Happenings in Persia*, (Edinburgh and London: William Blackwood & Sons, 1922), chapter V.

23 Cox to Curzon, 25/2/19, FO 371,1859.

24 Curzon to Cox, 5/3/19, FO 371/3859.
25 Cox to Curzon, 13/1/19, FO 371/3859.
26 Viceroy (Foreign Department) to Secretary of State for India, FO 23/1/19, 371/3858.
27 Cox to Curzon, 25/2/19, FO 371/3859.
28 Cox to Curzon, 10/4/19, 371/3860.
29 Cox to Cruzon, *ibid.*
30 Cox to Curzon, 17/4/19 and 19/4/19, FO 371/3860.
31 Cox to Curzon, 11/4/19, FO 371/3860.
32 Viceroy to Secretary of State for India, 20/4/19, FO 371/3860.
33 Curzon to Cox, 17/4/19, FO 371/3860.
34 Cox to Curzon, 30/4/19, FO 371/3860.
35 I.O. to F.O.3/5/19; Secretary of State to India, 9/5/19; Curzon to Cox, 9/5/19, FO 371/3860.
36 Curzon to Cox, 17/4/19, FO 371/ 3860.
37 Curzon to Cox, 9/5/19, FO 371/3860.
38 Curzon to Cox, 17/4/19; Cox to Curzon, 19/4/19; Curzon to Cox, 23/4/19; Curzon to Cox, 9/5/19; Cox to Curzon; 13/5/19; Cox to Curzon, 14/5/19; Curzon to Cox, 17/5/19, FO 371/3860; and Cox to Curzon, 21/5/19, FO 371/ 3861.
39 For the full text of the final agreement (and the separate contract for the British loan of £2 million) in English, see James Balfour, *Recent Happenings in Persia,* pp. 123–25. For the full text (and Cox's letter to Vosuq) in Persian, see Abdollah Mostawfi, *Sharh-e Zendegani,* vol. 3 (Tehran: Zavvar, 1962), pp. 18–20.
40 Curzon to Cox, 17/4/19, FO 371/3860, emphasis added.
41 Cox to Curzon, 19/4/19, FO 371/3860.
42 Curzon to Cox, 23/4/19, FO 371/3860.
43 Curzon to Cox, *ibid.* Curzon to Cox 9/5/19 and Cox to Curzon, 13/5/19, FO 371/3860. Cox to Curzon, 12/8/19, *British Documents on Foreign Policy,* vol. iv, no. 715, text as well as n. 2.
44 Curzon to Cox, 9/5/19, FO 371/3860. For the secret letters of assurance, see *BDFP,* vol. iv, no. 734, text as well as n. 2 and enc. 6, and n.3 and enc. 7.
45 Cox to Curzon, 19/4/19, FO 371/3860.
46 Curzon to Cox, 23/4/19, FO 371/3860.
47 Curzon to Cox, 9/ 5/19, FO 371/3860.
48 Cox to Curzon, 13/5/19. FO 371/3860.
49 Curzon to Cox, 17/5/19, FO 371/3860.
50 Cox to Curzon, 21/5/19, FO 371/3861.
51 Cox to Curzon, 17/7/19, FO 3861.
52 Curzon to Cox, 30/7/19, FO 371/3861.
53 Minute by Curzon to Cox to Curzon, 17/7/19, 371/3861.
54 Cox to Curzon, 14/8/19, *BDFP,* vol. iv, no. 720.
55 These details came out when the matter of British money became public in November, 1920. See Norman to Curzon, 19/11/20, *ibid.,* vol. xiii, no. 583.
56 Cox to Curzon, 15/8/19, *ibid.,* vol. iv, no. 721.
57 Norman to Curzon, 18/11/20, *ibid.,* vol. xiii, 582.
58 Curzon to Norman, *ibid.,* 22/11/20, no. 585.
59 *Ibid.,* and no. 582.
60 Norman to Curzon, 25/11/20, *ibid.,* no. 587.
61 Curzon to Norman, 1/12/20, *ibid.,* no. 593.
62 See Sayyed Hasan Taqizadeh, *Zendegi-ye Tufani, Khaterat-e Sayyed Hasan Taqizadeh,* (ed.) Iraj Afshar (Tehran: Elmi, 1993), pp. 195–96.
63 See Ronaldsheay, *The Life of Lord Curzon,* p. 217.
64 Memorandum by Earl Curzon on the Persian Agreement, 9/8/1919, *BDFP,* vol. iv, no. 710.

65 See Harold Nicolson, Curzon: *The Last Phase, 1919–1925* (New York: Houghton Mifflin & Co., 1934), p. 145.
66 *Ibid.*, pp. 121–22.
67 For the full text of this long statement, see Mostawfi, *Sharh-e Zendegani*, Vol. 3, pp. 12–18.
68 In a parliamentary speech quoted in Hossein Makki, *Tarikh-e Bistsaleh*, Vol. 4 (Tehran: Elmi), pp. 158–68.
69 See Mostawfi, *Sharh-e Zendegani*, p. 24.
70 *Ibid.*
71 See for example Ahmad Kasravi, *Tarikh-e Mashruteh* (Tehran: Amir Kabir, 1994).
72 See Ja'far Mehdi Niya, *Zendegi-ye Siyasi-ye Sayyed Zia al-Din Tabtab'i* (Tehran: Mehdi Niya, 1990), pp. 17–22.
73 See *ibid.* and Malek al-Sho'ra Bahar, *Tarikh-e Mokhtasar*, vol. 1.
74 See Yahya Dawlat-Abadi, *Hayat-e Yahya* (Tehran: Attar, 1983), vol. 4, chapter 12.
75 See *ibid.*, and *Mokatebat-e Firuz Mirza*, (eds.) Mansureh Ettehadiyeh (Nezam Mafi) and Sirus Sa'dvandiyan, (Tehran: Nashr-e Tarikh-e Iran, 1990), pp. 36–37
76 See for example Makki, *Tarikh-e Bistsaleh*, vol. 4, pp. 155–56.
77 See Javad Shaikholeslami, *Sima-ye Soltan Ahmad Shah Qajar*, vol. 1 (Tehran: Nahsr-e Goftar, 1993), pp. 20–22; Taqizadeh, *Zendegi-ye Tufani*.
78 Cox to Curzon, 30/11/18 and 12/12/18, FO 371/3263.
79 Cox to Curzon 12/3/19, FO 371/3859.
80 Curzon to Cox, 13/3/19 FO 371/3859.
80a Cox to Curzon 20/3/19 FO 371 3859.
81 Cox to Curzon, 25/3/19, FO 371/3859.
82 Curzon to Cox, 28/3/19, FO 371/3859.
83 Cox to Curzon, 5/4/19, FO 371/3859.
84 Ehtesham al-Saltaneh, *Khaterat-e Ehtesham al-Saltaneh*, (ed.) S. M. Musavi (Tehran 1988).
85 Sir R. Rodd (Rome) to Curzon, 3/9/19, *BDFP*, vol. iv, no. 755.
86 Notes by G. P. Churchill (28/8/19 and 5/9/19) of conversations with Mr Williams of the American embassy in London, *ibid.*, nos. 739 and 758.
87 Sir H. Rumbold (Berne) to Curzon, 7/9/19, *ibid.*, no. 761.
88 Curzon to Sir G. Grahame (Paris), 9/919, *ibid.*, no. 764.
89 Cox to Curzon, 19/9/19, *ibid.*, no. 784.
90 *The Times*, 19/9/19.
91 Cox to Curzon 30/9/19, ibid. no. 798. See further Vosuq's long and measured letter of 15/10/19, addressed to Cox, expressing great satisfaction at Curzon's speech, while at the same time quoting and emphasizing his words of guarantee for Iran's independence and liberty, and, inter alia, citing his 'explicit' support for 'Persia in putting her claims forward at the Peace Conference in Paris' (see further below on this bone of contention between the two sides). *BDFP*, vol. iv, no. 816. See also parts of Curzon's grateful reply to Vosuq through Cox in *ibid.*, n.1.
92 For the full English text of the King's speech, see Shaikholeslami, *Sima Soltan Ahmad Shah*, vol. 1, pp. 435–36.
93 For the full text of the Shah's speech in French, see *ibid.*, pp. 439–40.
94 There are few Persian memoirs, notes, histories, etc., of the period which omit to mention this legend as hard fact, according to one or another version. In a few sources, Naser al-Molk, the former regent, has been mentioned as the man who advised the Shah to mention the Agreement in his speech, and then prophesied his own as well as his dynasty's doom since he had refused to do so. For a recent and less well-known source, which claims that the British had instigated the Shah's journey to Europe in order to obtain his consent for the Agreement, and at the same time mentions Nosrat al-Saltaneh and Naser al-Molk (rather than Firuz) in connection to his speech, see Abolqasem Kahhalzadeh's memoirs, *Dideh-ha va Shenideh-ha*, pp. 421–23.
95 Curzon to Cox, 14/11/19, vol. iv, no. 847.

96 Note by Earl Curzon of a conversation with the Persian Minister for Foreign Affairs, 23/9/19, *ibid.*, no. 789.
97 Curzon to Cox, 13/11/19, *ibid.*, no. 845, and the full text (in French) of Persian Memorandum, *ibid.*, no. 846, and Enclosure in No. 846.
98 The Persian Minister of Foreign Affairs to Earl Curzon (long letter in French), 17/11/1919, *ibid.*, no. 849; and the Persian Minister for Foreign Affairs to Earl Curzon (another long letter in French), 17/11/1919, *ibid.*, no. 850.
99 Curzon to Cox, 28/11/19, *ibid.*, no. 854.

5

The campaign against the
1919 Agreement*

As with most historical events, the failure of the Agreement had a number of important causes, some of which have been noted in the previous chapter. The vehement campaign against it was the most significant cause of its failure, but that too was due to several factors. Outstanding among them was the manner in which Cox and Curzon had conducted the negotiations – the thick veil of secrecy, the exclusion of the Paris peace delegation both from the conference and from negotiations, which angered the French and American delegations as well. It ignited the dynamite of surging Iranian nationalism and aroused the anger and suspicion of the other great powers that Iran had lost her independence, and would henceforth be ruled by a combined dictatorship of Britain's Iranian agents and her technical advisers.

There would have been some opposition to the Agreement – perhaps even considerable – as the triumvirate themselves had anticipated, even if the foreign reaction had not been so vehement and widespread. But the unanimously negative response of America, France and Bolshevik Russia could have left no doubt in the minds of even the most moderate Iranians – outside the small group of politicians and journalists who supported the triumvirate – that their rulers had sold out the country to the British Empire.

The internal campaign

Rising Iranian nationalism was in itself not yet sufficiently strong to loose such a wide and deep outburst of emotions in every layer of Iranian political society. They were no longer afraid of Russia, whose two successive revolutions they had greeted with unbounded relief and optimism. On the contrary, they had received the news of the fall of the Tsarist regime as well as the Bolshevik declarations of friendship and goodwill towards their country with unmitigated joy and satisfaction. They viewed France as a disinterested and friendly nation with which Iran had already developed a close cultural bond. They regarded America

*This chapter is a revised version of the author's paper, 'The Campaign Against the Anglo-Iranian Agreement of 1919', published in *British Journal of Middle Eastern Studies*, 25 (1), 1998.

as an almost selfless power – 'the protector of world peace', as Iraj put it in a verse[1] – helping the weak and the vanquished.

This left Britain as the master of the region and, which was also securing an international mandate on Mesopotamia, a largely Shi'a land which housed the most sacred Shi'a shrines and colleges and had large numbers of Iranian residents in its towns and cities – where there soon was to be an anti-British revolt supported by the Shi'a ulama there as well as in Iran. (For reasons which are not difficult to understand, the French mandate on Syria did not create much excitement among Iranians.)

Thus, not only the modern nationalists, but the ulama and religious community, the democrats and popular constitutionalists, the gendarmerie and some of the Cossack officers were united in the belief that Iran had become a British protectorate. The nationalist poet Eshqi joined forces with Hajj Aqa Jamal Isfahani – a famous Tehran *mojtahed* of conservative views who was not normally involved in politics – because of their active opposition to the Agreement. Hossein Saba, the owner-editor of *Setareh-ye Iran*, later to become a staunch supporter of Reza Khan, was banished to Qazvin together with a few other journalists. Five political notables, including Hajj Mo'in Bushehri and Momtaz al-Dawleh (one-time Majlis peaker and head of the Legislature, and brother of Momtaz al-Saltaneh, Iranian minister in Paris) were likewise banished to Kashan. Dawlat-Abadi, a respectable and moderate constitutionalist, was opposed to the Agreement, as he said to Cox himself, although he did not have any strong objections to its published text. Mokhber al-Saltaneh (Hedayat) another moderate constitutionalist who had been a minister or provincial governor for much of the preceding 20 years was likewise against the Agreement.[2] The three most respected and publicly trusted politicians – Mostawfi al-Mamalek and the brothers Moshir al-Dawleh and Mo'tamen al-Molk – did not campaign against it, but their criticism of it was well known. Indeed, the brothers, together with other important notables such as Ain al-Dawleh and Hajj Mo'in al-Tojjar, met with Vosuq shortly after the Agreement had been signed, saying that they were convinced of his good intentions, but the Agreement was against the country's interest and should not have been concluded without wider discussion. Vosuq's replies to their points reportedly convinced Moshir, Mo'tamen and Ain, but not the others.[3] A week later, Cox addressed a letter to Vosuq (because, he said, some self-seekers might mislead the public), with emphatic and repeated reassurances of Britain's good intentions. The following is an extract:

[The] essential objects of this agreement ... are: the complete internal and external independence of the Persian State; the preparation of means of strengthening the power of the Persian Government to enable them to maintain internal order and guard against frontier dangers; and finally to devise means for the development and progress of the country. In no way has it been the aim of the British Government by this agreement to limit the independence and authority of Persia, on the contrary, it is their desire that this ancient kingdom that has so long been in jeopardy and discord should be made capable of preserving its independence, and (having regard to the important geographical position of Persia) that the mutual interests of the two States should be better respected and safeguarded.[4]

It was translated and published in the Persian press, but it did not work. Many of the opponents did not trust Vosuq's government even before the Agreement was announced, but its announcement threw Modarres – who had done so much to install Vosuq in power – as well into uncompromising opposition. The matter was very important not only for that reason but because Modarres was a shrewd and level-headed politician who carried a great deal of weight in every political circle outside the radical democrats. He was aided by Imam Jom'eh Kho'i (father of Jamal Imami, a famous politician from the 1940s onwards), another powerful religious and public figure in Tehran. Cox evidently regarded their opposition as sufficiently important to be reported to London.[5]

The list of famous figures who campaigned against the Agreement is lengthy. One of them, Abdollah Mostawfi, wrote a long pamphlet against it – entitled *Ibtal al-batil* or *Refuting the Falsehood* – as well as against Vosuq and his government. It now covers over 100 pages of his memoirs. Mostawfi was a moderate constitutionalist and high civil servant who had benefited from both traditional and modern education, had been a diplomat both in London and in Moscow, and was at the time head of a department in the ministry of finance. He wrote, addressing Vosuq:

> You may have imagined that Iran has other things too, which you have not given as a gift to the British … Do not worry. The present level of service which you have rendered to the British has made them the owners of everything in Iran, and you can rest assured that – as a satirical magazine in Paris has put it – you have sold this country to the British for fifty centimes.[6]

He wrote that previous prime ministers, 'because they did not accept bribes', were not able to spend money on propagandists and makers of false public opinion.[7] Elsewhere in the pamphlet he repeatedly referred to 'the British money' and the uses to which it was being put to beef up support for the government. Fourteen consecutive times he opened a sentence by saying, 'if it had not been for the British money', then this and that would not have been possible for Vosuq to do.[8]

Inevitably, poets and poetry were drawn into the campaign, and poems and songs – often of the most vehement and venomous nature – poured from the tongues and pens of both famous and not-so-famous poets. The prime minister, who was a poet of some note, published a lyric which, in the tradition of 'esteqbal' writing, encouraged a number of poems in the same metre, rhyme and 'radif', by friendly poets, including Bahar. Iraj wrote one that was respectable and another (apparently unfinished) which was an attack on Vosuq, though he did not mention his name[9] Aref, wrote another addressed to Vosuq which was extremely scathing, and opened with the verse, 'Thou, the door of whose home is open to whores.' He wrote in another poem:

> God damn to everlasting shame
> He who betrayed the land of Sassan
> Tell the zealous Artaxerexes the Long-armed
> The enemy annexed your kingdom to England.[10]

Eshqi wrote several poems, some of which are very long and include invective. The most venomous contained the verse: 'O' Vosuq al-Dawleh, Iran was not your daddy's estate ...' In a long poem against the Agreement, he wrote:

> It is the story of cat and mouse, our pact with Britain,
> Once it catches the mouse, how would the cat let it go?
> Even if we be lion, she is the fox of our time,
> The fox famously defeats the lion.[11]

Farrokhi Yazdi felt that the share of Firuz must be also acknowledged:

> Nosrat al-Dawleh is busy in Europe
> Annihilating the motherland – look and see ...
> Like a dealer for the sale of the motherland
> Constantly finding customers – look and see ...
> To deliver the motherland to Britain
> He is even keener than her – look and see ...

And in a poem he wrote in jail for his campaign against the Agreement:

> Take this message to Vosuq al-Dawleh, O' morning Breeze,
> It is not nice to treat Iranian patriots badly.
> He whose only offence is love of the motherland
> No creed would condemn to a dark cell ...
> The one who affairmed our independence in the Agreement
> Means none but to appropriate [Iran] by those ominous points [of the Agreement][12]

In 1926, Vosuq had a chance of defending himself and his policy at length in the Majlis, the only public occasion he used to do so after his fall from office. This was when Mostawfi al-Mamalek introduced his cabinet to the Majlis, in the first administration under Reza Shah after the few months of Forughi's caretaker cabinet. This cabinet had been the product of an accord between

Modarres and the Shah, and it was Modarres who had insisted on Vosuq being included, first as minister of finance, then of justice (see chapter eleven). Mostawfi had offered the foreign ministry to Mosaddeq, which the latter had emphatically declined, saying that it was not possible to work with the Shah in a constitutional framework.[13]

When the new cabinet was being introduced to the Majlis for approval, Mosaddeq delivered a very long speech against it, reasoned as well as impassioned, only because it included Vosuq and Forughi (as minister of war, who happened to be absent on a foreign mission). It was a scathing attack on the two men for different reasons, but Vosuq and the 1919 Agreement took up almost all his attention. His attack on Vosuq covered many points, but the Agreement was its central theme. He spoke about the British money – quoting the figure of £131,000 – and about betrayal. He quoted Secretary of State Lansing, as well as the American Legation's communiqué against the Agreement (see below). He detailed the arrest and the banishment of the Agreement's opponents. He warned the highly popular Mostawfi not to 'commit suicide with Vosuq's hand, because for patriots patricide (*mamlekat-koshi*) was as bad as suicide'. He cited both secular and Shari'a law that the crime befitted capital punishment. He shouted:

> Deputies! The people's eye tuned dark as it saw so much wrongdoing and betrayal.
> Tribunes! The same eye went white in the hope of seeing the trial of political leaders who sell out their country. In a country in which ministerial responsibility is more apparent than real, and where the people are so forgetful, the treason of the traitors infects every individual.[14]

Modarres rushed to the rescue. He said at the outset that he knew nothing about the British money and no doubt Vosuq himself would reply to that point. He explained that he had helped install the Vosuq ministry in 1918, which managed to bring a semblance of order to the country. He had opposed him when the 1919 Agreement had been signed. It was – in jurisprudential terms – an 'unauthorized contract' ('aqd-e fozuli') because it did not have parliamentary sanction. Yet he had not said a single insulting word against any of its supporters, because the matter was political and 'God only knows who was right.' He himself had joined the others in 1916 to form the provisional government of Kermanshah which accepted money from the Germans while telling them that 'we would not give [you] a receipt', and spent it without betraying the country. The 1919 Agreement was wrong, but it was now dead and buried. The country faced great problems of reconstruction and needed the cooperation of all of her able politicians. If everyone was rejected for one reason or another no-one would be left for the tasks ahead.[15]

Vosuq then took the tribune, and delivered a long, cool and reasoned speech. He began with a lengthy preamble familiar from the communiqué (quoted in chapter four) about the dreadful circumstances of the country when he had formed his ministry. He had been aware of the great risks of unpopularity, yet ready to put the country's interest above his own. He did not claim to be fault-less, but he had never consciously wronged the country.

The Agreement had provided for the employment of British advisers and experts by Iran, their scope of action being determined jointly by them and the Iranian government. He had emphasized from the outset that the full imple-mentation of the Agreement would be subject to parliamentary ratification, and the few steps which – because of the country's urgent needs – were taken in the meantime, were beneficial, and, in any case, could have been reversed by the Majlis. 'The philosophy behind the Agreement' and all that happened after-wards, he could not expound, he said – in a clear reference to the 1921 Coup and its aftermath – because the circumstances made it inexpedient. But, in a fleeting remark, he mentioned 'the difficulties of one of the two contracting governments in fulfilling its commitments'. For reasons which will become clear later in this chapter, he was referring to the British government. 'As for the £131,000, I can only submit that if Dr Mosaddeq has received any of it then so have I, and if it is proven that I have taken such a fund, apart from being ready to return it twice over, I would accept the whole of Dr. Mosaddeq's criticisms'.

The speech was measured and polite throughout, but he ended it with a parting shot:

> There is one other point of which I wish to remind him [Mosaddeq]. Most of the students and novices of politics regard a course in public popularity as being necessary. And if, at present, he is now at that stage of his studies, I, of course, do not object to his criticisms. But I would like to submit that in my student days I completely avoided that course, and moved up to the next stage. Thus, I may lose the contest for demagogy and popularity. I would only ask him that, at least when the higher interests of the state are at stake, would it not be better for him to go beyond the exercises of that course, or become my pupil.[16]

Firuz was a deputy in the same Majlis, and joined Mosaddeq and ten others in abstaining when the House divided on the endorsement of the cabinet.

The external campaign

The campaign against the Agreement outside Iran was led by France, the United States and Bolshevik Russia as well as Iranian expatriates in Western Europe, including members of Iran's peace delegation and diplomatic legation in Paris.

On 12 January 1918, Karl Bravin, an unofficial Soviet representative to Tehran, had brought an official message from Lenin declaring the repudiation of 'all Tsarist privileges and agreements that are contrary to the sovereignty of

Persia'. Two days later, Trotsky issued a formal diplomatic note on behalf of the Bolshevik government which declared that 'the Anglo–Russian convention of 1907, in view of its inconsistency with the freedom and independence of the Persian nation, is completely and irrevocably annulled'. This was months before Vosuq formed his cabinet. But less than two months before the 1919 agreement was announced, Georgi Chicherin, now foreign commissar after Trotsky, sent another diplomatic note to the Iranian government which unilaterally cancelled all Iranian debts to Russia and renounced all Russian privileges and concessions in the country. It even added that the Russo-Iranian boundary will be determined by the wishes of the peoples living along the frontiers.[17] Three weeks after the announcement of the 1919 agreement, however, Chicherin issued a very different kind of statement:

> At this moment when the triumphant victor, the English robber, is trying to lassoo the Persian people into total slavery, the Soviet ... Russian Republic solemnly declares that it does not recognize the Anglo–Persian Treaty which carried out this enslavement ... . [It] regards as a scrap of paper the shameful Anglo–Persian Treaty by which your rulers have sold themselves and sold you to the English robbers, and will never recognize their legality.[18]

Nevertheless, the statement repeated the abolition of the Tsarist treaties and privileges as in the June declaration.[19]

Some of the intemperate language may be attributed to familiar revolutionary zeal, but the rest must be because Britain was then at war against the Bolsheviks, and they saw the Agreement as turning Iran into a permanent British military base against Bolshevik Russia. Curzon and Cox did not appreciate the extent to which the Bolshevik's unilateral gestures of goodwill had enchanted the Iranians, nor how much their violent attack on the Agreement and Vosuq would encourage opposition among young political activists and radicals. Apart from that, the White Russian government of Admiral Kolchak were also annoyed because they had not been consulted, particularly as the Anglo–Russian convention of 1907 had been effectively set aside.[20] This had its impact on the attitude of the Russian officers of the Cossack Division (see below).

The impact of American and French deprecation of the Agreement, however, was much greater, because it came from seemingly disinterested great powers which, together with Britain, were leaders of the then world, and the Iranian peace delegation had been initially sent to Paris to try and obtain financial and technical help from them. Among the major mistakes that Curzon and Cox made in pursuit of their policy, perhaps the biggest blunder was the fanaticism with which they managed to exclude the delegation both from the Paris conference and from the bilateral negotiations. The evidence shows that Curzon had allowed for the possibility of talking to them, and later believed that it was unnecessary because the government in Tehran was willing to negotiate directly with Cox. And, instead of correcting this impression, Cox – who ought to have known better – kept reinforcing it (both directly and indirectly) in his dispatches. He thus turned out to be too efficient an emissary, who would win the battle and lose the war.

In November 1918, Vosuq had intended to lead the Paris delegation himself. This had been 'vetoed' by the Shah on the pretext that he 'could not be spared', but in fact because he distrusted Vosuq. Both Moshir al-Dawleh and Naser al-Molk declined the offer,[21] and the Shah insisted on Moshaver al-Mamalek (Aliqoli Khan Ansari), then foreign minister, who was more of a diplomat than a politician. The other two members of the delegation were Zoka' al-Molk (Forughi) and Mo'in al-Vezareh (Hossein Ala), who were described respectively by Cox as 'an independent Nationalist of not very extremist views', and 'an honest patriot with visionary ideas'. But he thought that Moshaver was 'a time server' who, though not genuinely friendly towards Britain, 'will probably think it in his interests to keep the right side of us'.[22] Events, however, did not justify that belief.

According to a long (private) letter written by Forughi in May 1919 from Paris to Tehran, the subject of their mission had been discussed before their departure. It had been agreed that they should seek advisers from France and America. There was some doubt as to what adviser should be employed from which country, Vosuq's own view being that the financial adviser should be sought from France, and the military adviser from America. In Paris, Forughi wrote further, they managed to obtain the goodwill of the American delegation in particular, so that Robert Lansing, the Secretary of State, in a banquet given by Iranians in his honour, publicly promised them support on behalf of the US president. But Vosuq – having heard the news – wired them not to jeopardize the country's chances.[23] (See below.) On the other hand, their efforts to get a sympathetic hearing from the British delegation did not succeed. They said that they were negotiating with the government in Tehran. The Iranian delegation offered to go to London for negotiations, but the British told them the Iranian government must either negotiate with the British government or take their case to the Conference; they could not do both at the same time (see below).

But even before the delegation reached Paris, Curzon was determined not to let them be admitted to the conference. He wrote to Cox that because Iran had been a non-belligerent, 'her position at the Peace Conference is more than questionable', but he might be prepared to discuss future Anglo–Iranian relations with the delegation if they had authority from Tehran to do so 'with complete candour.'[24] At that very time, Cox reported the triumvirate's readiness to negotiate with him, so a delighted Curzon responded by saying that since the Paris delegation had been sent with 'very different instructions', there could not be 'one policy agreed upon by Persian Cabinet and ourselves, and another advocated at Paris and possibly backed by the Shah'.[25] This he followed by a telegram to Arthur Balfour in Paris, asking him not to enter any discussions with the Iranian delegation which would prejudice Cox's negotiations in Tehran.[26]

By March 1919, when the Tehran negotiations were well under way, Curzon still envisaged the possibility of the delegation – finding 'their position [in Paris] untenable' – coming to London to coordinate the talks.[27] But he turned down Balfour's suggestion that he might receive Moshaver, unless the delegation regarded their mission to the conference as abortive, and wrote to Cox that he had told the Iranian minister in London that 'the Persian Government could not ride two different horses in this fashion'[28] (see Forughi above). Shortly afterwards, he opposed the Shah's visit to Europe before knowing the definite intentions of the Paris delegation.[29]

No sooner had Curzon sent this telegram, than Cox wired him some definite information about those intentions. Moshaver had sent a long telegram to Vosuq asking 'urgently for authority to enter forthwith into relations with American financiers'. With 'the concurrence of the Shah', Vosuq had replied that the government had no intention of 'ruining the enemies [sic; it must be "country's"] future by substituting America for Germany'[30] (see Forughi above).

From that moment onwards the possibility of talking to the peace delegation in London was discarded, and Moshaver's own suggestion of doing so was turned down.[31] Immediately after the signing of the Agreement in August Curzon sent him a formal invitation to come to London, which he in turn declined to accept, on the grounds that he was no longer foreign minister and chief delegate to the Conference, and was about to go and meet the Shah in Istanbul as the new ambassador to Turkey.[32]

Yet, back in April, Moshaver did not give up his efforts for admission to the conference. He sent another long telegram to Vosuq. The Americans were very encouraging on all scores – he wrote – including 'help in commerce', and the disagreements between the French and the British over Syria could be used to gain the support of France. This was 'absolutely reliable' information which Curzon had received from Paris.[33] Cox's information from Tehran was that Moshaver had wired that the French would not help without British concurrence, but the Americans were ready to do so 'provided they receive a formal request from the Persian Government'.[34]

A few days after Cox had sent the draft proposal of the Agreement to London (see chapter four), Vosuq received another telegram from Moshaver. He had asked Lord Hardinge (permanent under-secretary at the Foreign Office) in Paris if Britain would support their admission to the conference. Hardinge had replied that it would depend on the results of the Tehran negotiations. In his telegram to Vosuq, Moshaver had asked for the details of the negotiations, and the latter had replied that, as he had been informed, it was about the employment of advisers. Vosuq had asked Cox whether they wished to inform America and France of the nature of the proposed agreement 'before the fact, or when it was a "fait accompli"'.[35] Curzon wrote to Balfour in Paris that, given the negotiations in Tehran, Moshaver's activities in Paris should logically be curtailed by his government, 'but this would be contrary to Persian methods'. In his view, they should wait and present Moshaver 'with "fait accompli"', simultaneously informing America and France.'[36] Thenceforth, the Tehran negotiations proceeded apace until the Agreement was announced in August (see chapter four).

The French campaign

This was the background to the American (direct) and the French (indirect) attacks on the Agreement, and to the campaigns of Iranian diplomats and expatriates, along with the European press, that the country had been sold out to Britain. The Anglo–French Entente had much weakened during the Paris Conference for a number of reasons, partly, though not mainly, on the question of Syria.[37] As early as March 1919, Paul Cambon, the distinguished French ambassador to London (and descendent of the famous Jacobin leader in the French Revolution) had written frankly to Curzon that they had received a request from the Iranians to send them a financial adviser, and were willing to do so if there was no objection from Britain. Curzon had responded, with equal frankness, that the request was inconsistent with the attitude of the Tehran government; that Britain was footing a large bill for her army in Iran as well as for the Iranian administration and the Cossack Division; and that, therefore, if Iran were to appoint a foreign financial adviser, it had to be from no other country than Britain.[38]

The French were not prepared to support the Iranian delegation without British concurrence, but were still annoyed when the Agreement was published. A French cabinet minister went so far as to say in a speech in the National Assembly that, given his regard and admiration for Britain, he could not 'remain silent in face of facts such as those which have been announced to us in regard to Persia', though he did not name the Agreement.[39] At the same time, the Iranian minister in Paris (who, incidentally, was publicly known to be against the agreement) had informed Balfour that Moshaver and Ala were engaged in 'anti-British propaganda ... largely incited by the Americans and encouraged by the French'.[40] Yet the French government made no public statements on the matter, then or later, leaving it to their minister in Tehran to lead an effective campaign against the Agreement which, in the face of repeated British protests, they promised to curtail though without avail (see below).

The French press, on the other hand, felt no such restraint in attacking the Agreement. *Le Figaro* was quoted in Tehran as having gone so far as to say that 'the half-a-centimetre Shah had sold his country for one centime'.[41] But to give only one important example, the influential Paris daily *Temps*, in a long article on 17 August, wrote that the Agreement was prejudicial – 'porte-alliente' – to the independence of Iran. True, it had reaffirmed the 'independence and integrity' of Iran, but the same declaration, using the same words, had been made in the Anglo–Russian convention of 1907. The fact that both her army and her finance had been entrusted to British experts showed that the country's independence would not be what it had been before, and it would thus not qualify for membership of the League of Nations. The Anglo–Iranian negotiations in Tehran, while the Iranian peace delegation was in Paris, were indefensible. And, alluding to the secrecy surrounding the negotiations, the paper concluded that British promises to her allies must be kept 'even when they apply to Asia'. In no time, the same points about Iran's 'integrity and independence', and the implications of using British military and financial experts, were being made by Modarres and other opponents of the Agreement in Tehran.

The press campaign in France (and Switzerland and Belgium) continued for some time, declined when the story lost its news value, but surged up again in the wake of the Bolshevik landing at Enzeli, which dealt a great blow to British prestige and policy (see below). The *Temps* led the attack on 24 May, once again rejecting the view that the Agreement was consistent with Iran's independence, and commenting that 'if we wish that the national sentiment of the Turks and the Persians should bar the way to the Bolshevists, we must first of all know how to act ourselves'. The Evening newspaper *Journal de Debats* said that the Agreement had clearly failed to protect Iran, and warned about the danger of Bolshevik 'contamination' in the country. The *Echo de Paris* described the Agreement on the following day as a 'quasi-protectorate treaty'. The *Gaulois* wrote that it was clear that Britain could not defend Iran from the Bolshevik attack: 'it is quite understandable that the Persians should turn against the authors of a policy, the errors of which they are now beginning to experience'.

The French minister in Tehran wasted no time at all going to work against the Agreement. Only two days after it had been signed, he spoke about it with anger and indignation at Firuz's first reception in Tehran as the new foreign minister.[42] This prompted a complaint by Curzon to the French ambassador in London, who explained that that was not official French policy, and that Bonin – the minister in Tehran – would be instructed to desist.[43] A month later, Hardinge complained to Cambon in person, reminding him that he had twice declared the 'complete disinterestedness of French Government in Persia'. Reaffirming that position, Cambon said that the French press reflected 'wounded susceptibilities' because of lack of prior warning to France about the Agreement, but he promised to bring Bonin's activities to his government's attention.[44] Hardinge did not mention the fact that the French government had conferred the Legion of Honour on Moshaver, the former Iranian chief delegate in Paris.[45]

The French legation in Tehran continued its campaign by supplying the hostile comments of the French press, by campaigning among Iranian press and politicians, and by encouraging key figures and forces to attack the Agreement and Vosuq's government. Bonin himself, as the European minister responsible for Sweden's interests in Iran, wrote to the three Swedish officers running the Iranian police and gendarme forces about whether the Agreement would have adverse effects on their employment, although he had never before contacted the Swedes.[46] This was followed by further inquiries made of the Swedes and the gendarmerie by the French military attaché, and the French vice-consul enticing a mullah attached to the gendarmerie to tell the Iranian officers that they would have French and American backing if they resisted the Agreement.[47]

In fact, the French legation continued its campaign in Tehran so effectively that the Foreign Office once again intervened – this time with greater vigour – through their embassy in London, so that Cambon visited Hardinge in person and read the telegram he had sent to Bonin in Tehran with instructions to 'cooperate closely' with Cox, and make no unfavourable comments on the Agreement.[48] Bonin had a pause, then resumed his offensive afterwards. The Foreign Office once again complained, and was told that Bonin had been recalled from Tehran. But he was still there in May when the Bolsheviks landed at Enzeli; and he went overboard. Curzon summoned Cambon to the Foreign Office, reminded him of the background and the current activities of Bonin, and mentioned that Firuz – then in London – had also 'complained bitterly of the implacable hostility of M. Bonin'. For good measure, Curzon also reminded the French ambassador of Britain's 'heavy cooperation with the French Government' in regard to Syria. Being somewhat embarrassed, Cambon made some excuses but promised to bring the matter to the attention of Millerand, French prime minister as well as foreign minister.[49] This was barely three weeks before the fall of Vosuq and the beginning of the end for the Agreement.

Much alarmed, as well as encouraged, by the European press campaign against the Agreement, pockets of Iranian expatriates in Europe ranging from the remnants of the Iranian National Committee in Berlin, such as Taqizadeh, Jamalzadeh and Kazemzadeh (Iranshahr), to Forughi, Ala and Momtaz al-Sataneh (the minister in Paris who had been sacked by Firuz despite last-minute efforts to save his job) in France, and Mosaddeq, Davar and Mahmud Afshar (the future owner and editor of *Ayandeh*) in Switzerland, launched a campaign in Persian and European languages against the Agreement.

One of their French manifestos, published in Switzerland and addressed to 'Aux Partisan du droits' and entitled 'Appel du Parti National Persan' declared that 'after five years [i.e. since the beginning of World War I] of protest against imperialism, Great Britain today wishes to annexe Iran to her empire', because – it declared – the Agreement had robbed Iran of her independence. It concluded by demanding the withdrawal of British troops from Iran, and the enforcement of the Agreement only upon the approval of the League of Nations. It was signed, 'Pour le Parti Persan, AYN-LAM-BER', the pseudonym of Davar, who was then known as Ali Akbar Modd'i al-'Omum. This is clear from a French journal article entitled 'Le Sentiment National Persan', which describes an interview with Davar, 'le fondateur du parti national Persan ... Tres aimablement, M. Ali Akbar (Ayn-Lam-Ber), ancien procureur general de Teheran'. There is also a report on Davar's activities in an article – in *Tribune de Geneve* – entitled 'contre l'accord anglo-persan'. A recently published book in Iran reflects the extent of the anti-Agreement activities of the Iranian expatriates in Europe.[50]

The American Campaign

The United States, like France, did not lodge a formal protest against the Agreement. But her opposition to it came from the highest official levels, was the loudest and most explicit, and was by far the most effective, although it was launched a month after the agreement had been signed. Indeed, having watched the French reaction in the early days, Curzon rushed to talk to John Davis, American ambassador to London, mentioned the French annoyance, and asked for the support of the American minister in Tehran. Davis passed very positive remarks on the Agreement, and said that he 'would gladly act upon' Curzon's suggestion.[51]

Three weeks later, the American legation in Tehran published a communiqué which exploded like a bomb over the heads of Cox and Vosuq. It was the Persian translation of a statement by the State Department, bearing instructions that it should be published in Tehran. It had been issued, it read, 'in view of misrepresentations contained in an article in *Raad* of August 19th last with reference to attitude of President Wilson, American peace mission [in Paris] and America towards Persia.'[52] This referred to a report received by the State Department from Tehran (which, incidentally, betrays a poor translation) quoting Sayyed Zia's newspaper as follows:

> America, the only Government able to assist Persia, abandoned her. The Four Great Powers at Paris decided that Persia should be under protection and that it is a part of Great Britain's portion. Persia has been deceived by President Wilson's good words and Persia is in the same position as Egypt.[53]

This, it later turned out, was not a quotation from the very long article in defence of the Agreement in *Ra'd*, but a misleading summary. The article had referred to America at two stages. First, it said that, though America speciously displayed benevolence towards all nations, it had nevertheless made no move in support of Iran when Russia demanded Shuster's expulsion. None of the great powers had supported Iran's admission to the Peace Conference or offered it anything but resignation to a mandatory arrangement. They had divided the globe into three zones of influence, Iran falling into the British zone, and her destiny was settled here. Thus the weak nations had misinterpreted President Wilson's fourteen points which had prompted Egypt into revolt for complete independence, but America had then declared that British control of Egypt was not inconsistent with Wilson's fourteen points.

The most tactless reference to America came at a later stage of the article, which referred to Iran's peace delegation having been misled by 'President Wilson's pious words of justice'.[54] The article reflects Sayyed Zia's zeal to defend the Agreement against critics who argued that America would have given Iran a better deal had she been approached. But in the circumstances it was wide open to misunderstanding. The damage was done.

The official US communiqué declared that she had not refused aid to Iran; that America's peace delegation in Paris had tried to obtain a hearing for Iran but had not been supported by others (i.e. Britain), and this was probably explained by the present Agreement; that the Iranian government itself had not supported their own peace delegation which had openly sought urgent American aid and assistance; and that the Agreement – having come as a surprise to America – indicated that Iran did not wish her aid or support.[55]

The next day, Curzon addressed a long letter, couched in very polite terms, to the American ambassador. Reminding him of his earlier talk with him on the Agreement, and Davis's positive remarks on it, he said that, while on a visit to Paris before the Agreement had been concluded, he had informed President Wilson of the Tehran negotiations through one of his aides, Colonel House.

He had now heard about the communiqué issued in Tehran which, 'while hardly in accord with the ordinary forms of diplomatic procedure, would undoubtedly be regarded locally, and indeed was regarded, as a challenge to the Anglo–Persian Agreement of an unfriendly and almost a hostile character.' There was nothing in the Agreement that should make a friend of Iran suspicious; indeed it was very similar to the agreement which America had lately been negotiating with Liberia. Curzon was not responsible for the misrepresentation of the *Ra'd* article, but he hoped that America would immediately inform the Iranian government that their communiqué had been intended to correct misunderstandings caused by *Ra'd* rather than 'cast any aspersion on the Anglo-Persian Agreement'.[56]

Davis promptly replied that his favourable comments had been a reflection of press reports. The American government was not favourably impressed with the 'secrecy and lack of frankness' surrounding the negotiations for the Agreement, and were not able to take action which would indicate their approval of 'the treaty thus negotiated'. He had also contacted Colonel House, whose recollection was that Curzon had suggested the inadvisability of receiving the Iranian delegation before the conference, but did not recall any reference to the nature and implications of 'the instant treaty'.[57] Curzon responded with equal promptness. He had in fact told Colonel House, he wrote, that he was negotiating an agreement directly with the Iranian government, and that was his sole reason for asking the Colonel to pass on the information to the President, whom he himself had not found available in his brief visit to Paris.[58]

A lull of four weeks was followed by something of a diplomatic storm. Davis had contacted Colonel House again, who said that 'there was no discussion of details and I was left with no impression as to what the agreement with Persia was to be', adding that 'it was so casual that I am sure it made no impression upon the President either.' Accordingly, Davis had been instructed by his government to point out that they did not have any foreknowledge of the Agreement, that they had always been willing to assist Iran as shown by their recent famine relief operation in the country, and that not only *Ra'd*, but also the highest Iranian officials, had openly said that America had refused to help Iran.

Therefore, they had thought it essential to put the facts right, and the responsibility rested with the British government who, without their knowledge, had entered an agreement 'with the Government of the Shah which promises to affect so materially the relations between Persia and the United States'.

Much of Davis's long letter was about Curzon's reference to the US–Liberian treaty negotiations which had clearly added insult to the American injury. The Liberian republic had been founded with American assistance a century before, he wrote, and ever since she had received American help against attempts by 'foreign nations to infringe for their own ends the sovereignty of Liberia'. But, as they had once written to the French government, they exercised 'no "*protectorate*" over Liberia'. Therefore, there was an underlying dissimilarity between the two agreements because Britain had entered an agreement 'with the Shah' without American knowledge, whereas America had informed and extensively negotiated with Britain for her approval of the proposed treaty with Liberia. He concluded that the American government could not give its approval to the Agreement 'unless and until it is clear that the authorities and people of Persia are united in their approval and support of that undertaking'.[59]

Curzon noted in minutes that, in a private letter accompanying the official one, Davis had offered to meet him for a discussion of the issue, adding bitterly that he did not 'feel much inclined for polemics on a question on which the US Govt. have gone out of their way to be nasty. Perhaps on some future occasion they may find us less enthusiastic about some proposal of theirs than they would desire'.[60]

Nevertheless, he was shortly to note his 'friendly conversation' with Davis, in which he had fully explained the reasons for having kept the negotiations with Tehran confidential, and had the impression that the American government would 'not wish to reopen the case.'[61] In fact, the American government did not reopen the case, but the damage done to the Agreement in Iran by their communiqué, and by the persisting negative attitude of their legation in Tehran, was enormous. Apart from that, the argument persisted through the American press, Congress and public opinion for some time. On 5 October, two days before the date of Davis's last letter to Curzon, an article in *Washington Post* described the Agreement as a blow to the League of Nations, whose creation was being discussed in Paris, because it involved the surrender of Iran's independence and the control of the Iranian people by Britain.

Meanwhile, Lord Grey, British ambassador to Washington, wrote to Curzon that he would try and explain that the purpose of the Agreement had been none other than to 'encourage a strong and independent Persia as a buffer State on Indian frontier'. But he was worried about the repercussions of the American communiqué in Iran, and suggested an open invitation by Britain to America for participation in financial and technical assistance to that country.[62] Curzon did not agree. While pointing out that the Agreement had not postulated 'a monopoly of British employment and assistance in Persia' – as there were French and Belgian experts already in the country – he thought that a deliberate invitation to America would 'open the door to similar pressure from other Powers' and 'would merely drive Persia back into the rut of international rivalry in Tehran from which it was main object of agreement to relieve her'.[63] The allusion is clearly to the traditional Anglo–Russian rivalry in Iran, and it comes close to explaining both the political and psychological motives of Curzon in the secrecy with which he had negotiated the Agreement, and the jealousy with which he wished to guard his special relationship with Iran – motives which, had they been less obsessive, might well have avoided the abject failure of his policy (see chapter four).

Predictably, Cox entirely endorsed Curzon's view.[64] Grey accused Cox of 'in effect' advocating 'a virtual British protectorate of Persia'.[65] Curzon wrote back that if the Iranian government wished to employ American experts 'with our approval', there would be no obstacle.[66] Grey retorted that if he repeated that point in Washington 'it would confirm impression that we treat Persia as a Protectorate'.[67] Curzon threw up his hands and minuted that 'nothing we can say or do will give satisfaction to Lord Grey & I propose to desist from the attempt. He was not sent to America with a view to making trouble about the Persian agreement. But he seems to regard that as his main preoccupation'.[68] Cox later reported that the new American minister in Tehran had claimed that he had achieved some modifications of the Agreement, which was probably an allusion to his contacts with Lord Grey and the latter's correspondence with London.[69] Curzon replied that there had been no further discussion with the American government, and he did not 'contemplate any modification whatever in the agreement'.[70]

Early in 1920, the American government inquired if Curzon intended to reply to Davis's letter of 10 October, and whether there would be any objection to the publication of the two letters already exchanged between him and Davis.[71] Curzon was almost indignant. He had privately told Davis, he wrote, what he thought of that letter, but 'on grounds of friendship' he was not going to write a reply. He strongly objected, however, to the official publication of 'this unofficial correspondence'.[72] Thus, America did not alter her public posture about the Agreement, which was proof for the growing number of its Iranian opponents that their worst fears had been justified.

The Russian campaign

Yet none of this would necessarily have spelt doom for the Agreement. It could have succeeded either if it had not been rejected so widely and so categorically by its internal/external opponents, or if the British government as a whole – specifically the government of India, the India Office, the Treasury and the War Office – had been prepared to provide the means, i.e. sufficient financial and military support, to defend the Agreement in Iran itself. Curzon had pushed it through against the opposition, or serious doubts, from these departments in the belief that he would not require more than the basic and modest price they had eventually agreed to pay for their acquiescence. The real requirements turned out to be of a considerably taller order than Curzon (greatly encouraged by Cox's optimistic reports during his negotiations in Tehran) had foreseen, and, when this became obvious, neither India nor the other British government departments were prepared to draw Curzon's chestnuts out of the fire.

The internal and external opposition to the Agreement culminated in the Bolshevik landing of May 1920 at Enzeli, which led to the declaration in Rasht of the Soviet Socialist Republic of Iran, with the express objective of marching to Tehran and toppling the Qajar dynasty. This could only be met with much greater military/financial capability than Curzon and Cox had at their disposal. By the time Cox's interim mission to Tehran terminated in June 1920, many important British officers on the ground – and most important of all, the military and financial advisers who were there to implement the Agreement itself – had serious doubts about how it was concluded and enforced, and quickly converted the new British minister, Herman Norman, to their position (see chapter six).

The Russian opposition to the Agreement took three forms. Most effective was the strong reaction from Moscow, which was largely motivated by the fear that Iran would become a British military base. Another effective Russian opposition emanated from the White Russian officers of Iran's Cossack Division, both for patriotic reasons and out of self-interest. The third source of opposition was the government of the Whites based in Paris – they were still recognized by Iran, as well as Britain, and maintained a small legation in Tehran. The outcome of the civil war in Russia was still uncertain when the Agreement, and the abrogation of the 1907 convention, were announced. Clearly, the Whites were much in need of British support, and would not upset Curzon over the loss of their privileges in Iran. But their legation in Tehran quietly encouraged the activities of the Russian Cossack officers against the Agreement.

In 1878, the Tsar had agreed to Naser al-Din Shah's personal request to create a force similar to his own Cossack army, financed by Russia and led by Russian officers, as a favour to the Shah and a useful instrument of Russian interest in the country. It thus became the Shah's own personal force, and was used as such by Mohammad Ali, his grandson, against the first Majlis, when the loyalty of the traditional Iranian 'provincial levies' (*afvaj*) had become increasingly doubtful. In time, Iranian officers were also trained and coopted into the force, but the Russian commander and other officers remained in full control of the brigade and were directly answerable to the Shah himself. Because of its Russian finance and command, the brigade was regarded by the constitutionalists with much fear and suspicion, and they rushed into creating a countervailing gendarme force led by Swedish officers. This was a much more modern and democratic force, and by 1921 had developed so far that Mohammad Taqi Khan Pesyan's provincial gendarmerie in Khorasn had become an efficient force of 6000 foot, horse and guns. But in 1919 they were still much less effective than the Cossacks, and in any case as a 'melli' (popular/constitutionalist/national) force were less reliable than the Cossacks in defending an unpopular policy. During the war, they had been known to be pro-German, while the Cossacks had fought on Russia's side against the Turks and the pro-Central Provisional Government of the *Mohajerin* in western Iran.[72a]

The February revolution in Russia divided the Russian officers of the Cossack Brigade into Tsarist and democratic camps. Colonel Clergé, the commander put in charge of them by Kerensky's government, was naturally loyal to the new regime in Russia, but most of the officers under him were still loyal to the Tsar, though they put up with him only as long as that regime survived as the legitimate government of Russia.[73] That was changed by the October revolution, when, in opposing the Bolsheviks in Russia, the democratic element quickly faded into the background, and the Tsarist generals and admirals took charge of the campaign against Bolshevism. Clergé was still loyal to the February regime, and the Tsarist officers decided to overthrow him.[74] The 'Coup against Clerge' – as it is often called in Iranian sources – was organized by another senior Russian officer, Colonel Starosselski, and led by Colonel Filartov and Reza Khan's 'atriad' of Cossacks, who surprised and disarmed him in his barracks in Tehran and forced him to leave the country.[75]

Whether or not the Shah had been privy to the move is uncertain, but it could not have succeeded against the serious disagreement of Russian, and especially British, diplomats in Tehran. With the benefit of hindsight, this is sometimes cited as 'Reza Khan's first Coup'. But Reza Khan would not even have conceived of such a move without the prior decision of his senior Russian officers. It is even highly doubtful if he would have (or indeed could have) led the Coup of February 1921, had it not been organized by General Ironside and some other British officers, and supported – at least immediately after the event – by the British legation in Tehran (see also chapters seven to nine).

The Shah, at any rate, put Starosselski in charge of the force. The Bolsheviks having already repudiated Tsarist interests and privileges in Iran, Britain felt that they should take on most of the force's finance, now upgraded to a division. They paid a monthly subsidy of 100,000 tomans, to be added to the Iranian contribution of 60,000. The pay of the men and the NCO's was low, and often pocketed in part or whole by their superior officers. They survived partly by plundering and looting the villages around their posts, if not with the encouragement, then with the acquiescence of their commanding officers.[76]

The Agreement had envisaged the organization of a unified Iranian force based on the existing Cossacks, the gendarmerie and the British South Persia Rifles in the south. Whatever their patriotic feelings, the Russian Cossack officers could see the writing on the wall for their own careers and privileges, the likes of which was hard to predict in the post-war chaos of their own country and much of Eastern and Central Europe. They were therefore intent on working against the implementation of the military plan. The Shah did not trust the triumvirate, Britain and the Agreement; besides, he wished to retain, for as long as he could, the Cossack Division as his personal force under his own supreme command. Thus he lent quiet support to Starosselski's resistance to the change, and to his campaign against the Agreement in secret contact with leading anti-Agreement politicians.

Starosselski, indeed, had begun active opposition shortly before the Agreement had been signed. The Shah having left for his visit to Europe a few days after it was signed, Cox had an interview with Starosselski, trying to reassure him that no precipitate action was envisaged, and that there would be full consultation in reaching any decision. Likewise, he tried to allay any misgivings of the Tsarist Russian minister in Tehran. Both these men told him that, ultimately, any decision had to be made by the (White) Russian government in Paris, and Cox optimistically concluded that he would have no more trouble from Starosselski.[77] His optimism was short-lived. A month later, he reported that both Starosselski and the Russian legation, as well as Bolshevik elements, were active against Vosuq and the Agreement.[78] Starosselski had presented a long report to Vosuq about a serious Bolshevik threat to the Northern provinces, and suggested that the scattered Cossack detachments be brought together under his own command in the North to meet any Bolshevik action with effective force.[79] Cox (and Vosuq) were suspicious of Starosseski's motives – perhaps including the possibility of a 'Coup d'état' – but they took the factual side of the report seriously, and Vosuq suggested reinforcing Norperforce in Qazvin as well as sending a British force to Tabriz.[80]

While still in London to prepare for the Shah's impending state visit, Firuz told Curzon that Starosselski was working in the interests of Tsarist Russia, that he was trusted by the Shah who regarded the force as his own bodyguard, and that he had already shown 'what a serious menace he might become.' Firuz and his colleagues were seriously discussing the possibility of sacking him, which they thought they could easily do, but Curzon passed no comment because it was a matter 'for the Persian Government rather than for ourselves'.[81] They would soon discover that Starosselski's dismissal was far from easy.[82] Meanwhile, Curzon contacted the War Office on Vosuq's proposals for British reinforcements, which they did not accept.[83]

Cox did not wish to sound alarming, he wrote to Curzon, but his report on (and his response to) the situation in the north and north west might well fit that description. Norperforce at Qazvin, he reported, was barely adequate for its present task. There was no British force in Tabriz. There might be serious Bolshevik trouble in Khorasan, where General Malleson's East Persian Cordon Field Force was still deployed. Despite the recent successful operation of Iranian and British troops against the Jangalis in Gilan, 'the behaviour of Cossack detachments ... has been so atrocious and incompetency of Persian (administrative) officials so complete that the peasantry would welcome the return of the Jangali regime, and the movement is gathering head[way] again in close collusion with Bolshevist and Turkish elements in Baku'. Moreover, it was certain that the moment (the White Russian) General Denikin came back to the

Caspian coast, they would 'once again establish their old control on Persian coast of Caspian'.

Cox was now beginning to see his erstwhile optimism flying in the face of the facts, and was ready to acknowledge this when he concluded his long and detailed dispatch:

> In view of effect of recent agreement are we called upon to sit still and watch this process which has only been made possible owing to our assistance[to Denikin] with our ships and money? Are we not now rather under an obligation to assist Persia to re-establish her rightful position on her Caspian coast and prevent restoration of Russian influence?[84]

This was followed by a further report on ominous contacts and activities by Denikin's men, asserting that 'there can be no doubt that these activities are part of Denikin, in communication with Russian legation and Starosselski, to restore and strengthen Russian position in Northern Persia'.[85] Denikin was defeated in the Russian civil war before he could make such a move; instead, the Bolsheviks landed at Enzeli a few months later. And by now both Vosuq and Cox were keenly aware of that possibility. As the beginning of 1920 was fast approaching – a fateful year for Russia, Iran and Curzon's 'Persian Policy' – Cox received a slap in the face in the form of a short and sour telegram from Curzon that the India Office would 'refuse categorically' to pay the monthly Cossack subsidy as from the end of December.[86] As it turned out, the British subsidy continued to be paid for another six months, but it would not be difficult to guess some of Cox's Christmas prayers for the New Year.

The 'Bolshevik menace' was growing by the day as the Red Army pushed south through the Whites' position. Anticipating a Bolshevik landing at Enzeli soon after the fall of Petrovsk and Krasnovodsk, Vosuq, and increasingly Cox, began to press harder for a British military and naval presence to hold the Caspian coast.[87] But the War Office would not be moved. The situation was 'thoroughly understood and exhaustively considered' in London, wired Curzon:

> We should have liked to replace British flotilla and personnel ... But Admiralty were unable to sanction the venture unless War Office would guarantee the security of Baku, and War Office would not do the latter unless two Allied divisions with a third in reserve would be provided to hold the Batoum-Baku line.

These were not forthcoming, and the scheme was reluctantly dropped. They were trying to help Iran as best they could, but he was 'a little tired of their constant attempt to make us responsible for the consequences of their own inertia and incapacity in the past, and think that they are disposed both to ask and to complain over much'.[88] Such are the early signs of Curzon's irritability at being constantly reminded that he lacked the proper instruments to implement his policy. Cox did not let that pass without comment. Vosuq's government had been a success, but 'against active aggression now the Government is powerless and as our own interests are involved as well as those of Persia, it is incumbent on me to ensure that His Majesty's Government are under no illusion as to outlook.' Bolshevik agents had helped organize pro-Bolshevik committees inside Iran, and the government were trying to contain them. The crucial factor, however, was the control of the line going through the Caspian coast up to Tabriz. He asked again for the issue to be reconsidered.[89]

The Bolsheviks were looking to an already existing guerrilla base in Gilan. It was the force of the Jangalis led by Mirza Kuchik Khan. Son of Mirza Bozorg, he had been born and educated in a *madreseh* in Rasht, became a constitutionalist fighter (*mojahed*), fought with the fighters of Gilan in 1909, when Tehran fell to the constitutionalists, and had become disillusioned with the new regime, not least because of the Russian ultimatum of 1911 and the dissolution of the second Majlis. In 1915, when the Russians threatened to march on Tehran, which led to the flight of many politicians and Majlis deputies and the effective dissolution of the third Majlis, Kuchik decided to organize a guerrilla movement against the Russian forces and pro-Russian landlords in Gilan. This he did with significant effect, later joining the pro-Turkish Union of Islam (*Ettehad-e Islam*) and receiving some material support from them. His forces were based in the thick forests of northern Gilan, from which they assumed their popular name of Jangali (*jangal* meaning 'forest' in Persian).

Kuchik was in contact with popular politicians in Tehran, and sometimes sought their advice for his decisions. Typically, he lay dormant whenever there was a popular (*melli*) cabinet in Tehran, but became active under pro-Russian or pro-British cabinets. Predictably, he opposed Vosuq's government in 1918, launched a series of guerrilla operations, and – at one stage – held Rasht as well as other major towns in northern Gilan.[90] In the spring of 1918, when General Dunsterville's Dunsterforce was trying to move through Enzeli to Baku to meet the Turkish forces in the Caucasus, it had to negotiate its passage with the Jangalis. Eventually, the two sides entered an eight-point agreement for a peaceful passage. In September, Dunsterforce had to evacuate Baku back through Enzeli to Iran, and was stationed in Qazvin as North Persia Force, or Norperforce, under a new commanding general.[91]

There was another Jangali upsurge in the wake of the announcement of the 1919 agreement, but a major offensive by Cossacks, helped by Norperforce, forced them into retreat, though (as mentioned in Cox's report, cited above) the atrocious behaviour of the Cossacks made the peasants wish for Kuchik's return. From mid-1919 the Bolsheviks had sent missions to Kuchik to woo him for combined operations.[92] But he had remained noncommittal, and even entered into serious negotiations for a possible settlement with Vosuq's government. In November 1919 he offered terms to the government – through the acting governor, Mirza Ahmad Khan Azari – on which he was prepared to settle, along with a signed copy of the Quran 'for endorsement'. By January

1920, Kuchik and some of his fighters had entered Rasht peacefully, reported Major Edmonds, the British army political officer, amid shouts of 'long live Kuchik Khan' by the people, but 'the return of the Cossacks a few days later failed to arouse any enthusiasm'. 'Comment is unnecessary', added Edmonds. Edmonds did not know the exact terms offered by Kuchik to the government, but believed that they included the absorption of most of Kuchik's men into the gendarmerie, and financial compensation (to the people?) for damages caused by government troops. 'With Bolshevism knocking at the door, commented Edmonds 'the solution of the Jangali question has come none too soon'.[93]

By March, Edmonds was reporting that the deal seemed to be heading for the rocks because of Azari's duplicity. He had discovered that Azari had entered two agreements with Kuchik, but then 'devoted all the resources of his vulpine nature to evading fulfilment of his part of the obligations'. The Jangalis 'naturally became suspicious', and Azari tried to use this as an excuse to resume hostilities towards them. The matter was brought to Vosuq's attention. He recalled Azari and sent a high court judge on a fact-finding mission. Edmonds's assistant had received 'a most cordial reception' by Kuchik, who had promised him to try and prevent any Bolshevik movement in Gilan. Edmonds believed that the immediate appointment of a 'substantive' governor was needed.[94]

In the same month (March 1920), the joint military commission of British and Iranian officers, which was chaired by General Dickson and included the Cossack senior officer Amir Movassaq (later General Mohammad Nakhjavan) and the gendarmerie Colonel Aqevli, submitted its report for the creation of a unified military force. As anticipated, its main point was to merge the Cossack, gendarmerie and SPR under a unified command.[95] Starosselski stepped up his campaign against the proposal. The Cossack force had been created by a treaty with Russia, he argued, and the Shah himself (who was then still in Europe) had reassured him that it would remain an independent force. Vosuq asked the British government to prompt the White Russian authorities in Paris to tell Starosselski to desist.[96] Soon after the Commission's report was submitted, Colonel Aqevli committed suicide. It was widely believed by the public that it was because of his opposition to the report.[97]

Meanwhile, the Iranian cabinet, in consultation with Cox, sought other ways of dealing with the Starosselski problem in the light of the additional fear of 'the Bolshevik menace'. One alternative was to stop paying the British subsidy to the Cossacks, thereby reducing it to a much smaller force financed by the 60,000 tomans paid by the government. Another – couched in very cautious terms, in view of Curzon's susceptibilities – was to approach Soviet Russia directly.[98] A couple of days earlier, Vosuq had wondered whether, 'if seriously pressed', Britain would contemplate 'retiring from Persia and simply defending frontiers of India, thus leaving Persia to be overrun'.[99] Cox concluded that, apart from getting reinforcements from India and Baghdad:

[The best way] of protecting our own interests and of responding to Persians' moral claims to our protection and support now is to regain the (?control of) Caspian, and we earnestly hope possibility of doing this may again be considered.[100]

Curzon felt that he needed support from his colleagues, and discussed the matter at length in a meeting of the occasional Inter-departmental Conference, which had replaced the standing Eastern Committee of the Cabinet. It was not possible, he wrote, to ask the White Russian authorities in Paris to intervene with Starosselski. The best alternative among those communicated by Cox was to stop the British subsidy and reduce the Cossack force. Military opinion in London was that a Bolshevik attack on Iran was very unlikely, and that the infiltration of small Bolshevik groups could not be prevented by a stronger military force. Reinforcements from Baghdad and India would not be forthcoming, but there was a consensus that the resumption of British naval command in the Caspian would be of the utmost benefit. However, the Admiralty refused to consider that option without the necessary military base, and the army could not accept that condition. Having had no satisfaction from his own colleagues, Curzon decided to vent his frustration on Vosuq's (and Cox's) inquiry as to whether Britain would let Iran be overrun by the Bolsheviks:

[S]uch remarks are both ungracious and uncalled for, and when made should be resented ... [The Agreement had provided for] no obligation to defend the present frontiers of Persia against all attack. We accepted a moral obligation to do our best on Persia's behalf, and this we are doing and shall continue to do ... While, therefore, we are keeping such troops as possible in the country and are furnishing all available officers as advisers, and munitions, &C, we cannot be subjected to perpetual whines and complaints that Persian Government are being left in the lurch.[101]

In despair, Vosuq repeated the possibility of sending a mission to Soviet Russia, and Cox advised him to ask Firuz in Europe to discuss it with Curzon.[102] Firuz saw Curzon in London and 'startled' him by testing his view about 'the Persian Government entering into direct relations with the Soviet Government of Russia and concluding a treaty with them'. Curzon replied that communications with Bolshevik forces who were threatening Iran's frontier was understandable, but to send a mission to Moscow to enter formal relations with the Soviet government was a very different question, 'on which I could not possibly give any favourable advice to the Persian Government and which I could not recommend them to pursue except on their own responsibility':

I was indeed rather painfully impressed by the fact that whereas the Persian Government had recently made an agreement with us, which we were doing our best to carry out, Persia now appeared to be running about in every direction trying to make herself secure by all sorts of arrangements with other people.[103]

Curzon had also been alarmed by a recent letter by Firuz to *The Times*, hinting of the possible recognition of Soviet Russia by Iran. '[I]t was not my business', he had told Firuz, 'to impose veto upon their action', but he could not sympathize with such actions by Iran 'when she was beginning to reap first fruits of Anglo–Persian Agreement'.[104] It all sounds like a jealous lover who is suspecting a new relationship, and reflects the same psychology – now in the face of such grave and unforeseen difficulties – which had led to the Agreement being concluded with such secrecy.

The idea of talking directly to Moscow was eminently sound, and would almost certainly have avoided the Bolshevik landing and occupation at Enzeli and altered the course of history for Iran, as well as for the Agreement. Moshir al-Dawleh, who replaced Vosuq in July 1920, pursued that policy despite Curzon's great annoyance, although his government had fallen by February 1921, when Sayyed Zia signed the resulting Irano–Soviet agreement a few days after the Coup. Thus Reza Khan became its real beneficiary, when the Bolsheviks withdrew from Gilan (which led to the collapse and defeat of both the Iranian Bolsheviks and the Jangalis), and the Soviets entered friendly relations with the Iranian government and increasingly with Reza Khan himself. The problem of Vosuq's government was not only that it depended entirely on the existing British financial and military support, but that – unlike Moshir's that followed it – it could not afford to incur Curzon's wrath when it was so isolated both inside and outside the country (see chapter six). Curzon would not – and could not – veto their proposal to recognize Soviet Russia, but it was enough for him to tell them that they would do so entirely 'on their own responsibility'.

Meanwhile, Vosuq and Firuz were grasping at every possible straw to improve their internal and external position. If, through the Paris Peace Conference, they could obtain some rectification of past territorial losses to the Russian and Ottoman Empires, it would directly improve their image at home. If they could involve American capital in Iranian investment projects, this would do the same as well as prove to the world that Iran was not a British protectorate. If they established close relations with the new (and as yet non-Bolshevik) Republic of Azerbaijan, it would make the western Caspian coast safer from Bolshevik operations. If they could get the Shah in Europe to order Starosselski to submit, it would help the situation, and, if not, it was best to try and keep the Shah in Europe until the government's position was stronger in the country. They tried all of these options, and failed in all of them.

At the end of March the Shah complained to Lord Derby, British ambassador to Paris, that Vosuq's government – which he said he was keeping out of loyalty to the British government – were being unfriendly to him by creating obstacles for his return home. He required 400,000 franks for his travelling expenses, and British arrangements to convey him back to Iran.[105] Vosuq was of the opinion that the Shah's early return would add to the existing problems, and predicted – rightly as things turned out – that he himself would not be able to continue in office. Besides, the Shah had taken 120,000 tomans of government money for his European visit, had had five million franks since, and was constantly pressing for more.[106] Firuz tried to persuade the Shah to stay in Europe 'till after hot weather',[107] but the latter thought that this was a British plot 'to get rid of him', and alternately said that he would abdicate, or would ask the French or Americans to convey him home. Firuz and Derby felt that it would be better to comply with his wishes. The Shah told them that he would support Vosuq and 'loyally adhere to the Anglo–Persian agreement'.[108] In the meantime, Vosuq had telegraphed the Shah, with no success, asking him to order Starosselski to conform with government policy. He now asked Curzon, through Cox, to tell the Shah that unless he put an end to the Cossack chief's intrigues his monthly British subsidy would be stopped and facilities for sending him home would not be made. Cox added: 'If he refuses we shall be justified in doing the necessary before he returns; if he complies we can similarly go ahead but with less trouble' (see below).[109]

Curzon asked Derby to try.[110] The Shah obstinately refused, in spite of Derby's and Firuz's insistence, saying that he was only prepared to send a telegram – to Vosuq – of general support for government policy, and even then Starosselski must not be informed of its content.[111] Two weeks later, the Shah was in Cairo on his way home, from where (on 7 May) Herman Norman informed Curzon, through Field Marshal Allenby, that he had given 'categorical assurances' of loyalty to Vosuq's government as well as of cooperation over the Cossack issue once he reached the Iranian capital.[112] He did not keep either of these promises, but before he had received Allenby's telegram, Curzon had wired Cox that: 'In view of Shah's obstinate attitude, there appears no harm in action being taken as anticipated in penultimate paragraph of your telegram No. 219 (of 21st April)'.[113]

This is the paragraph quoted above, in which Cox had referred to 'doing the necessary'. What was it? It could not have been getting rid of the Shah in one way or another, because Cox had written that if the Shah agreed to cooperate in the matter of Starosselski, 'we can similarly go ahead but with less trouble'. And in any case it would have been easier to dispatch the Shah while he was still in Europe. It could conceivably be any number of things, but, given the context, the most likely possibility was that they were thinking of dealing with Starosselski's trouble by force. There was obviously no plan, because Cox replied to Curzon that Vosuq was temporarily indisposed, but that he would 'discuss plans with him as soon as possible'.[114] Whatever it was, nothing came of it.

The Shah later told Vosuq in Tehran that, before leaving Iran, he had told Starosselski not to follow any orders sent by him from Europe, even if he was certain of their authenticity.[115]

The issue of frontier rectification had been extensively discussed with Curzon when Firuz was in London, before and during the Shah's state visit (see chapter four). Firuz took the matter up again with equal vigour and persistence in later visits to London. This time he enlisted Vosuq's personal support and intervention in the form of a long telegram to himself, a copy of which he duly handed to the Foreign Office. Vosuq pointed out that both the letter and the spirit of the Agreement, as well as Curzon's subsequent speeches, had projected 'a strong position [for Persia] in the Middle East' and 'the restoration of Persia to her former greatness and to the important position due to her in Asia'. And if the Iranian people became conscious of the fact that these objectives were being ignored, he said pointedly, then friend as well as foe would combine against them, and the least result would be the demise of the Agreement. If the spirit of the Agreement was what they had been given to understand during the negotiations, and by Curzon's public pronouncements, then it could make Iran a strong link between East and West, and would enable them 'to procure progress and policy for the country with Great Britain's assistance'. But if this was not the case – and here he was prophetic:

[W]e shall be deprived of the means of resisting the fierce onslaughts of the opponents of the Agreement and of those who encourage an opposite policy to Persia, for it cannot be denied that with a half-hearted and hesitating attitude not only will the interests and rights of the country be jeopardized but all that we have been anxiously at pains for a long time to set up will only have served to expose your highness and myself to everlasting recrimination and execration.

He combined this very strong plea with a detailed and reasoned argument for the case of Iran's frontier rectifications, and said in response to Curzon's noncommittal replies to Firuz:

Your Highness says that Lord Curzon assures you that he himself and the British delegates will not oppose the claims of Persia when they are submitted to the [Paris] Peace Conference. An indifferent attitude on the part of the representatives of Great Britain would not suffice; their active support will be essential to our cause, more especially as our requests are quite moderate and justifiable.[116]

Having handed in Vosuq's telegram, Firuz discussed Iran's claims at length with Lord Hardinge, in Curzon's absence from the Foreign Office. Hardinge pointed out that the claims went far beyond the question of rectification of frontier infringements by other powers; that the aim of the Agreement had been to 'make Persia strong and independent within her frontiers' and resist 'any infringement by any other Powers of her existing territories'; and that it would not be right for Britain to support actively the recognition of Iran's claims by the conference, when it did not have the means of helping Iran to enforce the claims and annex the territories in question. Firuz said that he understood Britain's position, and would settle for a discussion of Iran's claims by the conference with active British support for a conference resolution along the following lines:

> The Conference recognizes that the territorial claims of Persia in Trans-Caspia are well founded, but that the whole of this question, depending as it does upon the solution of the Russian problem, cannot be decided at present.[117]

He emphasized that such a resolution would greatly strengthen the hands of the Iranian government at home. Hardinge replied that he would refer the matter to Curzon, but was not very hopeful.

Curzon commented to Cox that he found the Iranian claims 'utterly unreasonable', and that it had not occurred to him during the negotiations for the Agreement that by supporting frontier readjustments 'we were to dig into bygone history'.[118] He also wrote a formal reply to Firuz, reiterating his previous pronouncement on the issue: it was not for him to veto Iran's full claims which she could submit to the Conference on her own; alternatively, they could submit 'a more moderate assertion of the Persian desiderata backed by the support of His Majesty's Government'.[119]

From the discussions and the correspondence it would appear that there had been a mutual misunderstanding of the nature and implications of 'the Persian desiderata'. However that may be, it was considerations arising from *realpolitik* which divided the two sides. Curzon and the Foreign Office must have anticipated strong opposition from the French and, especially, the Americans, to Iran's claims if only because of their opinion about the Agreement. They must also have been mindful of the implications of these claims for the White as well as Red Russian governments, and for the whole question of future relations of Western powers with Russia. Last but not least was what was briefly and subtly pointed out by Hardinge to Firuz: it was already difficult for them to obtain (from the Treasury, the War Office, the India Office and the government of India) the means of keeping the Agreement afloat; if the Conference did affirm Iran's territorial claims with their active support, they would be in no position to provide the instruments – directly and indirectly – for her to recover and maintain those territories. The Iranians, on the other hand, were desperately cornererd by a strong internal and external opposition, which declared that the Agreement had turned Iran into a British protectorate. They needed not just public announcements by Curzon and themselves about Iran's independence and strength, but spectacular proof of their sincerity. There could thus be no resolution of the issue which was satisfactory to both sides.

Curzon's position on the question of territorial claims was not unreasonable. But, while he could not deliver the means of protecting the Caspian coastline, his opposition to an attempt by Iran to come directly to terms with Moscow was unreasonable. So was his jealous reaction to Iran's attempt to obtain domestic and international approval by involving American capital and skill in her development. The matter was introduced to Curzon by the hapless Firuz in a further meeting with him. Curzon saw no possible objection to the employment of 'two or three [Americans] here or there'. Firuz 'startled' him by vague references to various projects and then 'dropped in world oil'. Curzon took the hint to mean that the American Standard Oil Company 'was endeavouring to secure a foot-hold on Persian soil', and 'warned him [Firuz] strongly against' such a project.[120] It was in the same meeting that Curzon objected that, while they had entered an agreement with Iran and were trying to do their best to carry it out, the Iranians 'were running about in every direction': 'One day it was a treaty with Azerbaijan and another day a financial arrangement with the Americans, and now it was a proposal to come to terms with the Soviet Government'.[121]

Curzon, at least, had not objected to the negotiations with the newly founded Republic of Azerbaijan for a cultural and commercial treaty. As early as October 1919, the Norperforce political officer had reported that restive elements in Iranian Azerbaijan were relying on support from the republic.[122] At the same time, the Iranians floated the idea of recognizing the new republic on grounds of providing protection for Iranian subjects – merchants, professionals and oil workers – in that country. The White Russian chargé d'affaires in Tehran had objected, and dropped a hint about the possibility of Denikin's adopting an 'unfriendly attitude towards Persians within his reach'.[123] Firuz, in any case, was not much enamoured of the presence of the White Russian representative in Tehran; but, independently of that, he believed that the recognition of Azerbaijan would also contain the Pan-Turanian movement, which the Turks had encouraged there as well as in Iranian Azerbaijan.[124] Curzon did not make any remarks on the idea, but still asked Oliphant to write to the White Russian chargé d'affaires in London to warn them in friendly but firm terms about the threat they had made to the Iranian government over their wish to recognize Azerbaijan.[125]

In November, Vosuq sent Sayyed Zia to Baku at the head of a six-man official mission which included the gendarmerie captain, Kazem Khan Sayyah, his future collaborator in the Coup of 1921. They left for Baku on 28 November, 1919, and were going to be met there by Colonel C. B. [Claude] Stokes,[126] an old friend of Sayyed Zia's from 1911, when the Russians had rejected his nomination by Shuster to command the latter's Treasury gendarmes,[127] and who was later to try to obtain, though without much success, Foreign Office support for Sayyed Zia's abortive government after the Coup.[128] Apart from all other matters, Iran and the new republic needed each other's cooperation to meet the threat of Bolshevism. By the end of March, the Sayyed had concluded a treaty with the Azerbaijan government and sent it to Tehran for ratification.[129] In April, he returned to Iran, warned Tehran about recent Bolshevik successes in the Caucasus, and suggested ways of making it clear to Soviet Russia that Iran was not hostile towards them[130] (see also below). But by the end of the month the Republic of Azerbaijan fell to Bolshevik forces, and matters took a decisive turn against Vosuq's government.

Khiyabani's Revolt

Before that happened, however, Shaikh Mohammad Khiyabani had taken charge of Tabriz and most of Iranian Azerbaijan at the head of the Tabriz section of the Democrat party. Hitherto, it has been firmly believed by almost all shades of political opinion that the Shaikh's primary motive had been to oppose the Agreement and Vosuq's government; even Mokhber al-Saltaneh (Hedayat), who later put down the revolt under Moshir al-Dawleh's government, was under that impression.[131] There was also a strong suspicion, both then and since, of separatist motives either for independence from Iran or, more likely, an arrangement with Turkey or Soviet Russia. The alleged Turkish connection was extremely far-fetched (see below) and quickly faded out of account. But the pro-Bolshevik legend was later spread by Iran's first communist party, and by leaders of another revolt in Azerbaijan 25 years later as well as the Tudeh party. It became an article of faith among all the Marxist-Leninist tendencies, and spread across the political spectrum.

However, recent evidence virtually discards all these theories. It shows that Khiyabani's revolt had been intended to establish a strong autonomous rule in Azerbaijan as a part of Iran; to stamp out the chaos and disorder in the province; and to promote modern projects, especially in the fields of education, culture and administration. It also shows that, far from being pro-Bolshevik, the Shaikh and his men outlawed the Tabriz Bolsheviks and took up arms against them, and that Vosuq's government acquiesced in their rule in Azerbaijan. The evidence in question is provided by Ahmad Kasravi's recently published manuscript of 1923 on the Shaikh's revolt; Major Edmonds's (weekly as well as monthly) reports on the north-western provinces of Iran and the Caucasus for 1919 and 1920; reports by Ottoman and Bolshevik secret agents in Iran on Khiyabani and his movement; reports of the British consul in Tabriz; and the recently published memoirs of Abolqasem Kahhalzadeh and some additional notes by Mokhber al-Saltaneh.

At the time of his uprising, Khiyabani was about 40. He had been an educated prayer leader at a Tabriz mosque, though not a *mojtahed*, and a teacher at the Talebiyeh College of Tabriz, where Kasravi had been taught by him. A constitutional revolutionary, he had joined the Democrat party at its very inception, and had been elected a deputy for Tabriz to the second Majlis. In 1911, the Shuster crisis led to the dissolution of the Majlis and the Russian occupation of Tabriz (see chapter three). Fearing the Russians, Khiyabani took refuge in the Caucasus until the Imam Jom'eh of Tabriz obtained immunity for him to return to his home town where he first became a prayer leader, once again, and then opened a shop in the bazaar and quietly maintained contact with his fellow Democrats.

After the Russian Revolution, the Tabriz Democrats resumed activity but soon divided into two factions, the Tajaddodiyun (Tajaddod Faction), because they were responsible for the party newspaper of that name), and the Tanqid-iyun (Critical Faction). The former was led by Khiyabani, and the latter by Dr Zainol'bedin Khan (Kazemzadeh-ye Iranshahr's brother). From the start, Kasravi belonged to the Critical Faction, who were particularly critical of what they described as Khiyabani's 'dictatorial' style of leadership. For about a year, he and the Democrats were increasingly active in running the town and – as much as possible – the rest of the province, and the two successive governors were quite helplessly in their hands. They appropriated about half of the arms and ammunitions left by the Russians (leaving the rest for the government), and efficiently organized the famine relief by stamping out hoarding and speculation and assisting the poor and hungry. But Kasravi also attributes the assassination of some 'undesirable' as well as a few 'innocent' community figures to the Khiy-abani faction.[132]

When the Turkish army occupied Tabriz in the name of the Unity of Islam movement, they banished Khiyabani to Marargheh, but released him when they pulled out their forces in 1918. A following report by Isma'il Haqqi, the leading agent of Envar Pasha's *Teshkilat Mahsusa*, confirms both the conflict between Khiyabani's movement with the Ottomans, and his rapport with the povincial government:

In Tabriz, next to the Democrat party which is run by Khiyabani, Nobari and Hariri, who incidentally enjoy the support of the police force, there exists a few trivial parties ... On the other hand, the Democrat party with its clear Iranian xenophobic stance is the most serious and popular party, which not only enjoys the good graces of the people, but also has the support of the police, Gendarmerie and regular soldiers.

The Turkish secret agent further reported a coincidence of interest between the Democrats and the British in the region which – as we shall see later – was strengthened after Khiyabani's revolt:

Furthermore our explicit support of the Mojahedin's Pan-Turkist policy allowed the British to launch a counter-campaign in the city ... the campaign has bolstered the Democrats' anti-Ottoman position.[132a]

Khiyabani's return to Tabriz once again resulted in the supremacy of the Democrats and the renewal of the disagreements among them over Khiyabani's style of leadership. After the announcement of the 1919 Agreement, the Tabriz Democrats responded in their newspaper by emphasizing that it would not be valid without Majlis approval, although they did not discuss it again, even when they took power.[133]

In November 1919, Sardar Entesar (later Mozaffar A'lam) was sent to be military commander of Azerbaijan, and Khiyabani established good relations with him. This was followed by the appointment of the aged Ain al-Dawleh who – it appears both from Kasravi and Edmonds – was in no hurry at all to reach Tabriz, and after slowly reaching Zanjan remained there until quite some time after the revolt. Meanwhile, two Swedish gendarmerie officers were sent from Tehran to run the police force. For different reasons, neither Khiyabani nor Sardar Entesar was pleased with their arrival, especially as it seems that they had taken their duties seriously. According to Kasravi, the Sardar had secretly given the green light to Khiyabani for his revolt. The incident which triggered the uprising occurred a few days before *Nawruz* (21 March 1920) when, on Kiyabani's orders, armed Democrats forcibly removed a prisoner from a police station, and the Tabriz police laid siege to their headquarters. At this point Sardar Entesar appeared on the scene and ordered the police to disperse. Next day the Democrats declared a general strike, which was observed by some policemen as well, and the acting governor ordered the two Swedish officers to leave town. Thus, the Democrats took over the government, with the help of Sardar Entesar, with hardly a shot being fired.[134]

It is therefore clear that the Democrats had been effectively in control for much of the time – other than the period of Turkish occupation – since the departure of the Russians, and also that the tendency towards complete takeover had existed since the Autumn of 1919. That must be one of the reasons why Vosuq's government did not react in anger, fear or surprise to the event. But there were other, more important, reasons. Khiyabani issued a brief but broad statement in favour of effective and orderly constitutional government in Azerbaijan, in which he said nothing against Vosuq, Britain and the Agreement.[135] And even when he and his men were specifically asked about these issues they were evasive and non-commital.[136] Kasravi notes that some time after the uprising Major Edmonds visited Tabriz, met Khiyabani in private, and reached an understanding with him.[137] This is entirely borne out by Edmonds's reports at the time and afterwards.

Edmonds saw the Shaikh in Tabriz, on 1 May, 1920, and reported that he 'spoke with conviction that he had Tabriz in his hands and that his decisions could admit of no discussion'. He reiterated their public demands for constitutional and orderly government; he categorically denied allegations of separatism, emphasizing that Azerbaijan was an integral part of Iran; he said that 'his first duty was to preserve order and he was determined to do it'; he explained the restrictions imposed on political meetings by referring to the danger arising from the activities of Bolshevik and pro-Turkish elements; he said that he and his men were hostile only to Germany and Turkey, the latter of which had caused much damage to, and had campaigned for the annexation of, Azerbaijan. He further told Edmonds that:

... his party did not oppose the Anglo–Persian agreement as such but they would expect the people to have some voice in controlling its interpretation ... An instrument like the agreement was necessary and inevitable but it should not be between two or three men but between peoples.

And while even some moderate constitutionalists had condemned both Vosuq and the Agreement, he said about the latter:

'Poor Vusuq he [sic] has handicapped himself hopelessly by electing to play a lone hand. He is distracted from the administration of the state by those around him ... I think you may tell higher [British] authority that your relationship with Persia would be on a much firmer basis if the Prime Minister would take the country into his confidence.[138]

The matter was so important that Edmonds sent a special report on the lengthy interview. In his general report for the month of May, in the briefing item on Tabriz, he mentioned this report and commented further:

In P[olitical] O[fficer]'s opinion the movement started as a genuinely patriotic agitation for the restoration of the constitution, there was nothing Separatist or Bolshevik about it. It is of course impossible to foresee the results of mishandling by the Central Government. This view is rather confirmed by latest news of step taken by the Democrats, since the Russian descent on Enzeli, to suppress bolshevik [sic] activity in Tabriz and prevent communication the German Consul (who was endeavouring to profit by the situation) with the outside world.[139]

The reference to 'mishandling' must be an allusion to Edmonds's earlier reports on the case of the Jangalis, cited above. However that may be, Cox must certainly have informed Vosuq of Edmonds's reports and comments on the situation in Tabriz, and Vosuq could only have been pleased that, while the Democrats were not attacking him or the Agreement, they were trying to bring order to the town and parts of the province, and were suppressing Bolshevik agitation as well. There is some fairly direct evidence for this in connection to the affair of the German consul in Tabriz.

Edmonds mentioned in his report for May that the Democrats had surrounded the German consulate. This was true, and it ended with the death of the consul. A very excitable young man, the consul had been in league with Bolshevik agitators in town, more likely from anti-British rather than pro-Bolshevik motives. In the wake of the Bolshevik landing at Enzeli (see also below) the Tabriz Bolsheviks became very active, and 'it was generally believed that Wustrow – the German Consul – was at the bottom of it'.[140] The Democrats decided to arrest their leaders, and Wustrow gave them refuge in the consulate. When Khiyabani's men surrounded the building, Wustow, whose staff 'refused to follow his orders', began to shoot from the roof-top, but he was quickly hit in the mouth and died. It was not clear whether he had committed suicide or had been hit by a bullet.[141] Khiyabani's own violent death was described with exactly the same ambiguity in September of that year (see chapter six).

A couple of days later, Vosuq asked Kahhalzadeh, the Persian Secretary at the German legation in Tehran, to his office and told him to inform the legation that Wustrow had committed suicide. Next day, the German minister, accompanied by Kahhalzadeh went to the foreign ministry and was officially informed of the consul's death. They were told that it was 'widely believed that he had taken his own life', and that in any case 'it was his own fault'. The German minister did not take the last comment at all comfortably.[142] In a report sent to Moscow, a Bolshevik secret agent in Tabriz compared the Democrats with the Kadet (liberal) party, clearly implying that they were no separatists, and confirmed their hostile attitude towards the Bolsheviks, although he thought they were anti-British as well:

> The Democrats, while stressing Iranian nationalism and seeking changes and reforms for the whole of the country, have extended their struggle along two fronts, an anti-British and an anti-Bolshevik one.[142a]

It is clear that, at least for the time being, Vosuq was not losing any sleep on account of Khiyabani and the Tabriz Democrats. This was shortly after the Bolshevik landing at Enzeli, which was not welcome by them; indeed, Khiyabani did not approve of Kuchik Khan's subsequent deal with the Bolsheviks in declaring the Socialist Republic of Iran in Rasht.

The Bolshevik landing at Enzeli

On 19 April, Sayyed Zia, en route from Baku to Tehran, visited Major Edmonds in Qazvin. He said that the Baku government was in chaos, and he believed that the Bolshevik committee was planning a 'Coup'. Bolshevik ships had set out from the Baltic for the Caspian via the Volga, and he took 'a very pessimistic view of the situation at Enzeli'. The Bolsheviks believed, he further explained, that in the event of their invasion of Iran, British forces would withdraw to the Indian frontier. He was going to impress the need for urgent decisions upon the government in Tehran.[143] Ten days later, the Revolutionary Committee of Baku proclaimed the Soviet Socialist Government of Azerbaijan. The following day, the Russian Bolshevik army began to enter the city, and soon numbered 20,000. The Edalat committee of Iranian Bolsheviks then began to take possession of Iranian property.[144] Vosuq's and Cox's worst fears were about to be realized.

During the first week of May intelligence reports began to pour in about Bolshevik troop and naval reinforcements, and on 8 May Starosselski received intelligence about an impending Bolshevik landing at Enzeli, which included attempts to woo the Cossack garrison at Astara to their side. They had emphasized that they had no quarrel with Iran, only with the British.[145] Curzon, though concerned, was still not very convinced of the likelihood of an actual attack.[146] Vosuq made an urgent appeal through Cox, and suggested some detailed measures for meeting the situation:

> If they are not taken he [Vosuq] fears that unfavourable developments must supervene involving fall of present Government ... He argues, *and I agree*, that failure to take measures to keep situation under control, will be short-sighted economy and that infinitely greater loss or expenditure will result from failure to do so.[147]

Three days later, on 17 May, Vosuq instructed Firuz in Paris to make urgent and strong representations through Derby to Curzon.[148] On 18 May, Curzon replied to Cox that the proposals had been 'exhaustively examined at meeting of Eastern Committee [i.e. the Inter-departmental Conference]', but were not endorsed. 'Position at Enzeli does not appear to be exposed to immediate danger either by land or sea ...'.[149]

On that very day, a Bolshevik fleet of 13 ships, including a destroyer, appeared at Enzeli, bombarded Qaziyan, and landed.[150] General Champain, the Norperforce GOC, who was present at Enzeli for inspection, ordered the withdrawal of his considerably inferior force to Rasht. Wires began humming between Tehran, London and Paris. Cox immediately informed Curzon that Champain had withdrawn to Rasht partly because 'no instructions had reached him', a view which was to persist in comments, books and articles,[151] though there was no foundation to it[152] (see below). Firuz was 'very much perturbed' at the news. He told Derby that 'the Persian Cossack force is not dissolved and frankly hostile. French Minister [in Tehran] also hostile and evidently pleased at Persia's present difficulties'. He made three suggestions for reinforcements, failing all of which he renewed the question of talking to Moscow.[153]

Champain's withdrawal from Enzeli had been far from hasty or due to lack of instructions. On the contrary, as early as 28 February (almost three months before the Bolshevik landing) he had received clear instructions to withdraw if attacked in force. The telegram sent by the War Office to General Headquarters in Baghdad, and copied by them to Champain in Qazvin, reads as follows:

> The Cabinet has approved of the following telegram ... The South Russian military Situation renders it probable that the Bolshevicks [sic] may shortly gain naval command of the Caspian ... [T]he role outlined for Norperforce is that of an outpost which if attacked in force will fall back to the main line of resistance which must be within reach of railhead. In case of an attack: [T]he detachment now at Enzeli would probably provide such a deterrent to the naval forces of the Bolshevicks as to prevent their

attempting a serious landing … Arrangements should therefore be made to offer a bold definite front to Bolshevicks … should they threaten ENZELI and by bluff endeavour to prevent the port being seriously attacked by them. *At the same time, there is no intention of holding on to ENZELI should it be seriously attacked, and you should make arrangements to assure the withdrawal of your detachment at ENZELI.*[154]

Cox's reference to lack of instructions is a source of puzzle, because the above telegram had been repeated to him at the same time.[155] Curzon was obviously aware of the cabinet decision.

The retreat from Enzeli was a major blow to British prestige. The French press, as noted in chapter 4, enjoyed a field day. On 20 May, *The Times* attacked the assumption of 'enormous responsibilities' by ministers 'with light-hearted eagerness, without counting the costs, without reckoning up their resources, and without considering where they will be if something unexpected happens'. There were bitter recriminations within the British cabinet. In a letter written to Curzon on 20 May, Churchill, Secretary of State for War, attacked both him and his policy. He intended to seek cabinet approval to withdraw all the British forces in Iran to Mesopotamia, and to dissolve the 'Eastern Committee' which, he implied, was Curzon's captive instrument. The evacuation of Enzeli, he pointed out, had been contemplated by the War Office shortly before the Bolshevik landing, but had been stopped by a decision of the 'Eastern Committee' from which Churchill had been absent:

I do not see that anything we can do now within the present limits of our policy avert the complete loss of British influence throughout the Caucasus, Trans-Caspia, and Persia. If we are not able to resist the Bolsheviks in these areas, it is much better by timely withdrawals to keep out of harm's way and avoid disaster and the shameful incidents such as that which has just occurred.[156]

In the following crisis meeting of the cabinet on 21 May, Curzon led a 'violent attack' on the General Staff for not having made clear the gravity of the situation at Enzeli. There was much pressure for withdrawing all the British forces to Mesopotamia. This was successfully resisted by Curzon.[157] The day before, Hardinge had written a long memorandum to Curzon, warning of dire consequences for the British position in the region if this happened:

Once the evacuation of Tabriz and Kasvin is effected the fall of Tehran is inevitable, but before that happens the Government of Vossouk-ed-Dowleh will have disappeared. The Anglo–Persian Agreement will have become a scrap of paper, the Europeans of Tehran will be obliged to fly towards the south, and anarchy and destruction will prevail. If and when a large Bolshevik force is concentrated at Kasvin and Tehran, the flanks of both India and Mesopotamia will be exposed and the Bolsheviks will be in a position to choose whether to attack in the east or in the west.[158]

This being a small sample of Foreign Office opinion, the cabinet reached a compromise on keeping Norperforce at Qazvin.[159] Accordingly, orders were sent out by the War Office for a retreat from Rasht to Qazvin, but a small force was stationed on the elevations of the Manjil pass as a first line of defence.

The retreat from Rasht was probably an eventful mistake. Raskolnikov, the Bolshevik naval commander (and namesake of the anti-hero in Dostoyevsky's *Crime and Punishment*) had said that his mission was only to appropriate the vessels which had been interned at Enzeli, and he had negotiated for the retreat of the British garrison from there to Rasht. This had been repeated by another Bolshevik commander, Kayanov, who 'stated that his object was simply to recover Russian property at Enzeli, chiefly the Volunteer Fleet, and that he had no immediate intention of going further'.[160] On 27 May, Chicherin replied to Firuz's formal protest at the landing in a friendly tone, citing his very favourable declaration towards Iran of June of the previous year, and saying that the Soviet commander had landed at Enzeli on his own local initiative and would leave after further negotiations.[161]

A careful study of the Russian archival material may show exactly what the thinking had been on the Bolshevik side. The present evidence would seem to indicate that they were wary of a massive military operation in Iran. Indeed, their column at Ardebli was attacked by Shahsavan and other local forces, losing many men, all their guns, and many of their rifles before retreating into Russian territory.[162] However, if Rasht had not been evacuated, it is unlikely that Kuchik Khan would have thrown in his lot with the Bolsheviks, as he did for a short but crucial period which provided the basic local legitimacy for the declaration of the Soviet Socialist Republic in Gilan. Kuchik was a patriotic constitutionalist and a Muslim believer who looked up to political leaders like Moshir al-Dawleh and Mostawfi al-Mamalek. Edmonds's reports, cited above, tend to support the view that he would not have been too eager to join hands with the Bolsheviks. At the end of May, his entry on 'Kuchik Khan and the Bolshevik's was as follows:

> Kuchik Khan went to Enzeli on 22nd and received an ovation. He had several interviews with Kajanoff [Kayanov] but is stated to have differences with them over their programme. He left on May 29th. He was subsequently interviewed by the governor-general, Gilan, and promised to assist in the preservation of order in Resht area.[163]

On 4 June, just as Norperforce evacuated Rasht, Kuchik entered the town and, together with Iranian Bolsheviks and their Soviet advisers, declared the Socialist Republic in a coalition headed by himself. It is unlikely that the Bolsheviks would have made such a move merely on the strength of Soviet support, and against the opposition of the Jangalis, especially when Khiyabani's popular movement in Azerbaijan was actively against them. Predictably, the coalition lasted less than two months, but that was sufficient to establish the Bolshevik hold in Gilan, and not only spell doom for Vosuq's government and the Agreement, but also pave the way for the Coup of 1921 (see chapters six to eight).

Meanwhile Firuz had rushed to London to talk to Curzon, and had sent his note of protest (drafted by Vosuq himself in Tehran) to Moscow with Curzon's approval, who in their reply played the matter down as a local incident. The crisis cabinet meeting in London had recommended that the Iranians should talk directly to Moscow. But Curzon clearly did not make that suggestion to Firuz, despite the repeated representations they had been making (both before and after the Enzeli landing) for just such a move, which, if it had been made in time, is very likely to have altogether averted the event. Indeed, on 27 May, the very day on which Firuz and Curzon had a meeting, Leonid Krassin had arrived for negotiations in London at the head of what was officially described as a Soviet trade delegation. Firuz asked Curzon if he should meet with Krassin. Curzon said that he had no objection to that, but thought it would be better if he himself first raised the issue with Krassin. Curzon's old fear of Iran 'playing one side against the other' was still as strong as ever, yet there was still no inkling that it was wreaking havoc with his own Persian Policy. Far from it, Curzon was in an optimistic mood, telling Firuz that they 'should not be over-much disturbed by local or partisan intrigues, should deal firmly but quietly with Starasselski [sic], and should fight the battle of Anglo-Persian Agreement with renewed vigour':

> Indeed I said I could not understand why they had not already convened the Mejilis, place the agreement before it and openly challenged a verdict. I could not myself conceive that any Persian Assembly would prefer to exchange the enhanced stability and security which Persia had already begun to enjoy for the chaos which would follow the abandonment of this policy, and if I were in the position of the Persian Government I would feel tempted to adopt a bolder line.

Reporting the conversation to Cox, he concluded that Firuz had left him in a 'far from despondent mood'.[164] This must have increased Cox's admiration for Firuz's skills at the art of the stiff upper lip.

After the Gilan Republic was declared, Firuz lodged a formal complaint at the newly constituted League of Nations. That created an embarrassing situation for both Britain and France because a full hearing of the case would have involved the presence of Soviet representatives, and therefore the international recognition of the Soviet government. Neither of the two European powers was yet ready for that, especially as at that time Baron Wrangel's Polish armies had penetrated deeply into Russia, and the Iranian situation could not be discussed at the League with Soviet representatives in complete isolation from the Polish invasion of their country. In the end, in view of Iran's ongoing 'negotiations' with the Soviet government – that is, the exchange of telegrams between Moscow and Tehran – and the projected meeting between Firuz and Krassin in London, the League's Council decided to commend Iran's action in lodging her complaint and asked to be kept informed of further developments.[165]

The Curzon-Krassin negotiations finally led to a British 'ultimatum' that they would not continue the talks unless Moscow promised to refrain from any attempts by whatever means of encouraging any of the peoples of Asia against the interests of the British empire. This was accepted by Checherin, and Curzon apparently believed – as he wired Herman Norman – that it was helpful 'for protection of Persia'.[166] By then it was three weeks that Vosuq's government had fallen, and the Agreement had been officially declared by the new Iranian government as being 'in abeyance'.

Notes

1   See Mohammad Ja'far Mahjub (ed.), *Divan-e Kamel-e Iraj Mirza,* sixth edition, (America: Sherkat-e Ketab, 1989), p. 125.

2   See, for example, Abdollah Mostawfi, *Sharh-e Zendegani-ye Man,* vol. 3 (Tehran; Zavvar, 1964); Yahya Dawlat-Abadi, *Hayat-e Yahya,* vols 3 and 4 (Tehran; Attar & Ferdawsi, 1983); Mokhber al-Saltaneh (Hedayat), *Khaterat va Khatarat* (Tehran: Zavvar 1984); Mohammad Mosaddeq, *Musaddiq's Memoirs,* Homa Katouzian (ed. and intro.), tr. S.H. Amin and H. Katouzian (London: Jebhe, 1988).

3   Cox to Curzon, 1/9/19, *British Documents On Foreign Policy* (hereafter *BDFP*), vol. iv, no. 749.

4   Cox to Vosuq, 9/9/19, *ibid.,* no. 785.

5   Cox to Curzon, 22/8/19, *ibid.,* no. 732.

6   See Mostawfi, *Sharh-e Zendegani,* p. 20. The pamphlet was not published at the time, but is the most comprehensive and articulate source on the subject.

7   *Ibid.,* p. 24.

8   *Ibid.,* pp. 45–46.

9   See *Divan-e Bahar,* Mohammad Malekzadeh (ed.), vol. 2, (Tehran: Amir Kabir, 1956), pp. 395–96 for Bahar's contribution, and the *matla'* of Vouq's lyric which is as follows: Thou who plunder the tribe of the heart and the faith/Who transgresses against the harvest of the hearts; *Divan-e Kamel-e Iraj Mirza,* Mohammad Ja'far Mahjub (ed.).

10 See *Divan-e Aref,* (ed.) Abdorrahman Saif-e Azad (Tehran Amir Kabir: 1977), pp. 325 and 246–47 respectively. Aref has another *esteqbal* for Vosuq's poem which contains critical asides but no invective. See, *ibid.,* p. 235.

11 See *Kolliyat-e Mosavvar-e Eshqi,* Ali Akbar Salimi (ed.), first edition (Tehran: n.p., n.d.), pp. 305–08.

12 See *Divan-e Farrokhi,* Hossein Makki (ed.), (Tehran: Amir Kabir, 1979), pp. 194 and 196 respectively.

13 See Homa Katouzian, *Musaddiq and The Struggle for Power in Iran* (London and New York: I.B. Tauris, 1990); Katouzian (ed. and intro.), *Musaddiq's Memoirs.*

14 The full text of the speech is quoted in Hossein Makki, *Tarikh-e Bistsaleh-ye Iran,* vol. 4, (Tehran: Elmi, 1995). See pp. 142–58. See also *idem, Doktor Mosaddeq va Notq-ha-ye Tarikhi-ye U* (Tehran: Elmi, 1985).

15 For the full text of the speech, see Makki, *ibid.,* and *Tarikhh-e Bistsaleh,* pp. 158–67.

16 For the full text of the speech, see Makki, *ibid.,* pp. 167–76, and *Doktor Mosaddeq,* pp. 209–19.

17   See Martin Sicker, *The Bear and The Lion* (London: Praeger, 1988), chapter 2.
18   *Ibid.*, p. 39.
19   Curzon to Cox, 4/9/19, *BDFD*, vol. iv, no. 756.
20   Cox to Curzon, 22/8/19, *ibid.*, no. 732.
21   Cox to Curzon, 30/11/18, F.O. 371/3263.
22   Cox to Curzon, 6/12/19, F.O. 371/326. The three-man delegation also took two Iranians and a French assistant with them, though this is not mentioned in Cox's telegram.
23   For the full text of Forughi's long letter, see Habib Yaghma'i, ed., *Maqalat-e Forughi*, Tehran: Yaghma'i, 1975–76.
24   Curzon to Cox, 12/1/19, F.O. 371/3858.
25   Curzon to Cox, 23/1/19, F.O. 371/3858.
26   Curzon to Balfour, F.O., 25/1/19, 371/3858.
27   Curzon to Cox, 5/3/19, F.O. 371/3859.
28   Curzon to Balfour, 11/3/19, and Curzon to Cox, 12/3/19, F.O. 371/3859.
29   Curzon to Cox, 17/3/19, F.O. 371/3859.
30   Cox to Curzon, 18/13/19, F.O. 371/3859.
31   Curzon to Cox, 21/3/19, F.O. 371/3859.
32   Sir G. Grahame (Paris) to Curzon, *BDFP*, vol. iv, no. 722.
33   Curzon to Cox, 6/4/19, F.O., 371/3860.
34   Cox to Curzon, 14/4/19, F.O. 371/3860.
35   Cox to Curzon, 19/4/19, F.O. 371/3860.
36   Curzon to Balfour, 23/4/19, F.O. 371/3860.
37   See for example Alfred Cobban, *A History of Modern France*, vol. 3, 1871–1962 (London; Pelican Books, 1965), part II, pp. 1871–1962.
38   Curzon to Cambon, 11/3/19, F.O. 371/38.
39   Grahame to Curzon, 30/8/19, *BDFP*, vol. iv, no. 747.
40   Grahame to Curzon, 21/8/19, *ibid.*, no. 730.
41   Mostawfi, *Sharh-e Zendegani*, vol. 3, p. 20.
42   Cox to Curzon, 13/8/19, *BDFP*, vol. iv, no. 716.
43   Curzon to Cox, 19/8/19, *ibid.*, no. 728.
44   Curzon to Cox, 25/9/19, *ibid.*, no. 793.
45   Curzon to Cox, 11/9/19, *ibid.*, no. 773.
46   Cox to Curzon, 28/8/19, *ibid.*, no. 738.
47   Cox to Curzon, 13/9/19, *ibid.*, no. 779.
48   Curzon to Cox, 1/11/19, *ibid*, no. 832.
49   Curzon to Cox, 31/5/20, *ibid.*, vol. xiii, no. 448.
50   See Mahmud Afshar, *Nameh-ha-ye Dustan*, Iraj Afshar (ed.), *Tehran: Mawqufat-e Doktor Mahmud Afshar Yazdi*, especially, pp. 170–76. A copy of the 'Appel du Parti National Persan' was sent by the British legation in Georgia to Curzon. See Wardrop (Tiflis) to Curzon, 28/11/19, *BDFP*, vol. iv, no. 855, and its Enclosure 1.
51   Curzon to Lindsay (Washington), 18/8/19, *ibid.*, no. 727; Curzon to Cox, 1/9/19, *ibid.*, no. 748.
52   Cox to Curzon 10/9/19, *ibid.*, no. 770.
53   Davis to Curzon, 9/10/19, no. 808.
54   Cox to Curzon, 8/11/19, *ibid.*, no. 840.
55   Cox to Curzon, 10/9/19, *ibid.*, no. 770.
56   Curzon to Davis, 11/9/19, *ibid.*, no. 774.
57   Davis to Curzon, 12/9/19, *ibid.*, no. 778.
58   Curzon to Davis, 14/9/19, *ibid.*, no. 780.
59   Davis to Curzon, 7/10/19, *ibid.*, no. 808, emphasis added.
60   Minute by Curzon, *ibid.*
61   Curzon to Grey, 21/10/19, *ibid.*, no. 824.

62 Grey to Curzon, 28/9/19, *ibid.*, no. 794.

63 Curzon to Grey, 1/10/19, *ibid.*, no. 803, emphasis added.

64 Cox to Curzon, 9/10/19, *ibid.*, no. 812.

65 Grey to Curzon, 17/10/19, *ibid.*, no. 818.

66 Curzon to Grey, 21/10/19, *ibid.*, no. 824.

67 Grey to Curzon, 27/10/19, *ibid.*, no. 826.

68 Minute by Curzon, *ibid.*

69 Cox to Curzon, 21/12//19, *ibid.*, no. 876.

70 *Ibid.*, n. 2.

71 Lindsay to Curzon, 13/1/20, *ibid.*, vol. xiii, no. 366.

72 Curzon to Lindsay, 20/1/20, *ibid.*, no. 368.

72a There are a few English and Persian sources on the Iranian Cossacks, their origins, organization and development. For the most recent and comprehensive account, see Stephanie Cronin, *The Army and the Creation of the Pahlavi State, 1910–1926* (London and New York: I.B. Tauris, 1997), which is also the best source on the government gendarmerie.

73 See General Hassan Arfa, *Under Five Shahs,* (London: John Murray 1964), chapter 5.

74 See *ibid.*, and Richard H. Ullman, *Anglo–Soviet Relations, 1917–1921*, vol. 3, 'The Anglo–Soviet Accord' (Princeton: Princeton University Press, 1972). Bahar's account of the reason behind the overthrow of Clergé is both extensive and explicit. Arfa too is fairly explicit on the matter. See further, Malek al-Sho'ra Bahar, *Tarikh-e Mokhtasar-e Ahzab-e Siyasi dar Iran*, vol. 1 (Tehran: Jibi, 1978), chapter 20. See also Cronin, *The Army and the Creation of the Pahlavi State*.

75 See Bahar, *ibid.*; General Ahmad Amir-Ahmadi, *Khaterat-e Nakhostin Sepahbod-e Iran* (ed.) Gholamhossein Zargarinezhad, vol. 1 (Tehran: Mo'sseheseh-ye Pazhuhesh-ha-ye Farhangi), pp. 117–18.

76 The Cossacks were notorious for looting and plundering peaceful villages. For first-hand neutral reports of the attitude of the peasants and common folk towards them, see The Edmonds Papers, Middle East Centre, St Antony's College, Oxford (the papers consist of a considerable amount of intelligence and – occasionally – diplomatic reports in English, and copies of letters, public and press statements, newspapers, etc., written and published in Persian in the area at the time).

77 Cox to Curzon, 29/8/19, *BDFP,* vol. iv, no. 741.

78 Cox to Curzon, 30/9/19, *ibid.*, no. 798.

79 Cox to Curzon, 30/9/19, *ibid.*, no. 799.

80 Cox to Curzon, 1/10/19, *ibid.*, no. 800.

81 Curzon to Cox, 21/10/19, *ibid.*, no. 822.

82 Curzon to Cox, 4/12/19, *ibid.*, no. 861.

83 Cox to Curzon, 29/10/19, *ibid.*, no. 828.

84 Cox to Curzon, 21/11/19, *ibid.*, no. 852.

85 Cox to Curzon, 4/12/19, *ibid.*, no. 860.

86 Curzon to Cox, 20/12/19, *ibid.*, no. 873.

87 Cox to Curzon, 17/1/20, *ibid.*, vol. xiii, 367; 29/1/20, no. 371; Cox to Curzon, *ibid.*, 18/2/20, no., 374.

88 Curzon to Cox, 7/2/20, *ibid.*, 373.

89 Cox to Curzon, 21/2/20, *ibid.*, 375.

90 The sources on Kuchik and the Jangalis are now numerous. See for example Ebrahim Fakhta'i, *Sardar-e Jangal, Mirza Kuchik Khan* (Tehran: Javidan, 1978); Mohmmad Ali Gilak, *Tarikh-e Enqelab-e Jangal (beh ravayat-e shahedan-e aini)* (Rasht: Nashr-e Gilak, 1990); Gholamhossein Mirza Saleh, (ed. and tr.), *Jonbesh-e Mirza Kuchik Khan* (Tehran: Nashr-e Tarikh-e Iran, 1990); Ahmad Kasravi, *Tarikh-e Hijdahsaleh-ye Azerbaijan* (Tehran: Amir Kabir, 1992); Cosroe Chaqueri, *The Soviet Socialist Republic of Iran* (Pittsburgh; Pittsburgh University Press, 1995); Y. Yodfat, *The Soviet Union and Revolutionary Iran* (London;

Croom Helm, 1984); Sicker, *The Bear and The Lion*; Ullman, *The Anglo–Soviet Accord*. For a very informative contemporary source on the period, see The Edmonds Papers.

91 For the text of the agreement. see Fakhra'i, *Sardar-e Jangal*, pp. 153–55. See further, Ullman, *The Anglo–Soviet Accord*; Arfa, *Under five Shahs*.

92 See Major Edmonds's report for January 1920, The Edmonds Papers.

93 *Ibid.*

94 See Edmonds's report for March 1919.

95 Cox to Curzon 13/3/20, *BDFP*, vol. xiii, no. 387. For details of the report see Cox to Curzon, 9/4/20, *ibid.*, no. 403.

96 Cox to Curzon, 13/3/20, *ibid.*, no. 387.

97 This is mentioned in most contemporary sources, e.g. Bahar, *Tarikh-e Mokhtasar.*

98 Cox to Curzon, 13/3/20, *BDFP*, vol. xiii, no. 387.

99 Cox to Curzon, 12/3/20, *ibid.*, no. 386.

100 Cox to Curzon, 13/3/20, *ibid.*, no. 387.

101 Curzon to Cox, 22/3/20, *ibid.*, no. 395.

102 Cox to Curzon, 5/4/20, *ibid.*, no. 401.

103 Curzon to Cox, 10/4/20, *ibid.*, no. 406.

104 Curzon to Cox, 11/4/20, *ibid.*, no. 407.

105 Derby to Curzon, 30/3/20, *ibid.*, no. 397.

106 Cox to Curzon, 9/4/20, *ibid.*, no. 402.

107 Derby to Curzon, 13/4/20, *ibid.*, no. 408.

108 Derby to Curzon, 15/4/20, *ibid.*, no. 410.

109 Cox to Curzon, 22/4/20, *ibid.*, no. 414.

110 Curzon to Derby, 24/4/20, *ibid.*, no. 415.

111 Derby to Curzon, 26/4/20, *ibid.*, no. 416.

112 Allenby to Curzon, 7/5/20, *ibid.*, no. 418.

113 Curzon to Cox, 27/4/20, *ibid.*, no. 417.

114 *Ibid.*, n.2.

115 Norman to Curzon, 13/6/20, no. 461.

116 Vosuq to Firuz, *ibid.*, vol. iv, Enclosure in no. 877.

117 Curzon to Cox, 30/12/19, *ibid.*, no. 877. Recently published documents show that Firuz was considerably more active over the issue of the rectification of frontiers than is revealed by the Foreign Office documents alone. See Mansureh Ettehadiyeh and So'ad Pira (eds.) *Nosrat al-Dawleh, Majmu'eh-y-e Mokatebah ...*, Tehran: Ketab-e Siyamak, 1999, various documents, including letters by Firuz to leading European politicians and diplomats.

118 *Ibid.*

119 *Ibid.*; Curzon to Firuz, 19/12/19, *ibid.*, no. 871; Note by Oliphant of a conversation with Firuz, 20/12/19, *ibid.*, no. 872; Firuz to Curzon, 20/12/19, Annex. to no. 872.

120 Curzon to Cox, 10/4/20, *ibid.*, vol. xiii, no. 406.

121 *Ibid.*

122 Edmonds's report for October 1919, The Edmonds papers.

123 Cox to Curzon, 19/10/19, *BDFP*, vol. iv, no.820.

124 Curzon to Cox, 21/10/19, *ibid.*, no. 822.

125 Oliphant to Sabline, 29/10/19, *ibid.*, no. 829.

126 Edmonds' report for November 1919, The Edmonds Papers; Arfa, *Under Five Shahs.*

127 Stokes was a young pro-Constitutionalist officer at the British legation, who, at the time of Mohammad Ali Shah's Coup, had allowed Taqizadeh and few others to take refuge in the legation compound, thus saving their lives. It was partly because of his popularity with the Constitutionalists, and hostility towards the Russians that, in 1911, Shuster tried to put him in charge of the Treasury gendarmes (see chapter 3). He figures in quite a few primary Persian sources. See, for example, Iraj Afshar (ed.), *Zendegi-ye Tufani, Khaterat-e Sayyed Hasan Taqizadeh* (Tehran: Elmi, 1993), various pages. See also Malcolm E.

Yapp, 'The Last Years of The Qajar Dynasty', in Hossien Amirsadeghi and R.W. Ferrier (eds.), *Twentieth Century Iran* (London: Heinemann, 1977), p. 15.

128 Stokes (Tiflis) to Curzon, 3/3/21, F.O. 371/640.

129 Edmonds's report for April 1920, The Edmonds Papers.

130 Edmonds's special report on his meeting with Sayyed Zia in Qazvin, 19/4/20, The Edmonds Papers.

131 See Mokhber al-Saltaneh, *Khaterat va Khatarat*; Mostawfi, *Sharh-e Zendegani*; Bahar, *Tarikh-e Mokhtasar*; Dawlat-Abadi, *Hayat-e Yahya*; Abolqasem Kahhalzadeh, *Dideh-ha va Shenideh-ha, Khaterat-e Abolqasem Kahhalzadeh*, (ed.) Morteza Kamran, (Tehran: Nashr-e Farhang, 1984).

132 This brief on the background to Khiyabani and his revolt is based on the above-mentioned manuscript of Ahmad Kasravi, written in 1923 and put at this author's disposal by his family for publication. See Ahmad Kasravi, *Ahmad Kasravi: Qiyam-e Shaikh Mohammad Khiyabani*, Homa Katouzian (ed. and intro.), (Tehran: Nashr-e Markaz, 1998). In two other sources Kasravi has discussed Khiyabani's revolt, but the manuscript is much more extensive and comprehensive in coverage and throws important new light on the whole affair. See his *Tarikh-e Hijdahsaleh* and *Zendegani-je Man* (Tehran: Nashr va Pakhsh-e Ketab, 1976). See also Homa Katouzian, 'The Revolt of Shaykh Muhammad Khiyabani', *IRAN*, 1999.

132a The Turkish General Staff Military History and Strategic Studies (ATASE), Ankara, K. 1859, D. 88/142, 9/5/1918.

133 Cf. Hajj Mohammad Ali Aqa Badamchi, 'Shaikh Mohammad Khiyabani', in *Sharh-e Hal va Eqdamat-e Shaikh Mohammad Khiyabani*, special issue, *Iranshahr*, Berlin, no. 14, 1926, reprinted in *Entesharat-e Iranshahr* (Tehran: Eqbal, 1972).

134 See Kasravi, *Qiyam-e Shaikh Mohammad*; Katouzian, 'The Revolt of Shaykh Muhammad'.

135 See Kasravi, *Tarikh-e Hijdahsaleh*, p. 868.

136 *Ibid.*, p. 846.

137 Kasravi, *Qiyam-e Shaikh Mohammad; Tarikh-e Hijdahsaleh*.

138 C.J. Edmonds, 'Note on an Interview with Shaikh Muhammad Khiyabani,' sent on 12 May together with a memorandum to the British minister in Tehran, the British civil commissioner in Baghdad, and assistant political officer in Tabriz, The Edmonds Papers.

139 Edmonds's report for April–May, 1920.

140 See Ernest Bristow, British consul in Tabriz, 'Report on Azerbijan during 1920', The Edmonds Papers. It appears that the German consul in Tabriz had been active long before Khiyabani's revolt. See Mansureh Ettahadiyeh and So'ad Pira (eds.) *Nosrat al-Dawleh, Majmu'eh-ye Mokatebat ...*, Tehran: Katab-e Siyamak, 1999, document no. 50, pp. 150–151.

141 *Ibid.*, and Kasravi, *Qiyam-e Shaikh Mohammad.*

142 See Kahhalzadeh, *Dideheh-ha va Shenideh-ha*, pp. 432–33; Katouzian, 'The Revolt of Shaykh Muhammad'.

142a Russian Central State Archives, Archive of October Revolution, Found 5402, Invente 1, File 514, list 4.

143 Edmonds's special report of 19/4/20 on his meeting with Sayyed Zia in Qazvin, The Edmonds Papers.

144 Edmonds's report for April–May, 1920.

145 Cox to Curzon, 9/5/20, *BDFP*, vol. xiii, no. 422.

146 Curzon to Cox, 11/5/20, *ibid.*, no. 423.

147 Cox to Curzon, 14/5/20, *ibid.*, no. 425, emphasis added.

148 Derby to Curzon, 20/5/20, *ibid.*, no. 436.

149 Curzon to Cox, 18/5/20, *ibid.*, no. 433.

150 Cox to Curzon, 18/5/20, *ibid.*, no. 434; Edmonds's report for April–May 1920; Martin Sicker, *The Bear and the Lion* (New York: Praeger, 1988), p. 40.

151 See, for example, Lord Ironside (ed.), *High Road to Command, The Diaries of Major General Sir Edmund Ironside*, 1920–22 (London: Leo Cooper, 1972), p. 138; Ullman, *The Anglo–Soviet Accord*, p. 362.

152 Cox to Curzon, 18/5/20, *BDFP*, vol. xiii, no. 434.

153 Derby to Curzon, 20/5/20, *ibid.*, no. 438.

154 War Office to Baghdad, 25/2/20, copy to Champain, 28/2/20, W.O. 158/697, emphasis added.

155 *Ibid.*

156 Churchill to Curzon, 20/5/20, Curzon MS box 65, quoted in Ullman, *The Anglo–Soviet Accord*, p. 363.

157 Wilson MS diary, quoted in Ullman, *ibid.*, p. 364.

158 Curzon to Cox, 18/5/20, *BDFP*, vol. xiii, no. 433, n.4.

159 See Ullman, *The Anglo–Soviet Accord*.

160 Edmonds's report for April–May 1920.

161 Cox to Curzon, 27/5/20, *BDFP*, vol. xiii, no. 446.

162 Edmonds's report for April–May, 192

163 *Ibid.*

164 Curzon to Cox, 27/5/20, *BDFP*, vol. xiii, no. 445.

165 Explaining the French objections, Balfour wrote that, among other reasons, 'they think that if the Council is forced to apply Article 17 (which allows them to invite Soviet Government "under conditions", to take part in their deliberations) this would be a long step towards such a consummation' [i.e. recognition of the Soviet Union]. See Balfour to Hardinge, 5/6/20, *ibid.*, no. 452; minutes by Curzon and Hardinge, *ibid.*, n.3; Oliphant's memorandum on his conversation with Firuz, 10/6/20, *ibid.*, no. 458. See further, Ullman, *The Anglo–Soviet Accord*, pp. 368–69, who discusses the problem arising from the ongoing Polish–Soviet war with reference to Sir Eric Drummund's memorandum of 26 May 1920.

166 Curzon to Norman, 13/7/20, *BDFP*, no. 510.

6

The Fall of Vosuq

The threat of disintegration

In the year 1920, the continuing increase in conflict and chaos finally confronted the country with a stark choice between military dictatorship on the one hand, and disorder and disintegration on the other. The chaos which began after Naser al-Din Shah's death had continued up to, during and even after the Constitutional Revolution, had peaked during the War and was now reaching new heights in peacetime (see chapters two and three). It became increasingly clear that Vosuq's attempt to stabilize the situation within the existing framework had failed, especially after the status quo had been under-pinned by the 1919 Agreement. The rise of Bolshevik power in the Republic of Azerbaijan and its impact on revolutionary forces in northern Iran, particu-larly the province of Gilan, was an unanticipated event which greatly exacerbated political instability and fear of disintegration. Vosuq's cabinet fell, but (for reasons discussed in the following two chapters) it was not possible to create a minimum level of political stability and cohesiveness, despite the efforts made in the following six months. The result was the Coup of February 1921.

Norman and the fall of Vosuq

The period June 1919 to February 1920 saw the gradual demise of the Agree-ment and the final peak of the post-revolutionary chaos, which began to decline rapidly thereafter, ending with the establishment of modern arbitrary rule within ten years (see chapters seven to eleven). Thus, neither Iranian politics nor Curzon's Persian Policy proved capable of changing the situation such that both constitutionalism and order and stability could be achieved within the existing framework.

In its modern form, this pattern was familiar from the long span of Iranian history, as we saw in chapter one.

The Shah returned to Iran at the beginning of June via Mesopotamia, over which Britain had now obtained an international mandate, much to the conster-nation of the Shi'i leadership and community. In Karbela, Mirza Mohammad Taqi Shirazi, sometimes known as the second Mirza (after Mirza Hasan of the Tobacco revolt fame), who was the senior *marja'*, refused to see him. But in

Najaf he had a meeting with Shari'at-e Isfahani (sometimes known as the Shaikh al-Shari'a, a renowned, but relatively apolitical, teacher) who, on behalf of the senior ulama advised him to ditch the Agreement.[1]

When, after the official reception, the Shah and Vosuq drove in state slowly around the centre of Tehran, student demonstrators shouted 'Long live the Shah, death to English [*ingilisi*, meaning Vosuq] and Agreement'.[2] Three days later Cox sent a desperate plea to Curzon:

> Three valuable weeks have ... elapsed and in absence of any solid assurances from His Majesty's Government in matter of provision of funds for financing proposed precautionary measures no forward action has been taken or been possible ... Simultaneous withdrawal of our detachments from [?Rasht] Tabriz and Meshed coupled with delay in reply of His Majesty's Government is making Prime Minister's position so impossible that it is only with great difficulty that I can prevent him from resigning.[3]

This was followed by another plea from Norman, who presented his credentials to the Shah on 10 June as the new British minister,[4] replacing Cox who was leaving to become High Commissioner in Baghdad. Meanwhile, Firuz sent word through Curzon that the Shah should be urged to prove publicly that Vosuq had his support, and should dismiss Starosselski'[5] The Shah, on the other hand, had put strong pressure on Vosuq for the government to repay him the one million French francs which he had spent from his own purse in Europe (in addition to the public monies already given or sent to him), as well as the £8,000 he had borrowed from Firuz for the same purpose, and the 50,000 tomans that was owed to him by a now insolvent company.[6] He told both Norman and Vosuq that he no longer wished to keep the Russian officers of the Cossack force, but he adamantly refused to agree with the plan offered by Vosuq for their dismissal on flimsy grounds. 'Fact is', wrote Norman to Curzon, 'the Shah is so very nervous for his personal safety that he is no longer accessible to argument.'[7]

Vosuq was on the verge of resigning office. He believed that the Shah – who was 'extremely fond of money' – was in league with his enemies. He explained that he had not carried out his previous resignation threats because the Shah kept promising that he would give him loyal support when he returned home. As late as 14 June the Shah told Norman that he was 'perfectly satisfied' with Vosuq, while on 23 June, a few days after Vosuq had tendered his resignation, he told the British minister that he 'disliked and distrusted' Vosuq 'extremely'.[8] Norman spared no effort to persuade the Shah to grant Vosuq his conditions for staying in office, and withdraw his own demand for money at least for the time being. It did not work. The Shah formally accepted Vosuq's resignation on 25 June.[9]

The search for a new prime minister had already begun in earnest. Norman had put forward the names of the popular brothers Moshir al-Dawleh and

Mo'tamen al-Molk,[10] and Curzon had advised against them.[11] The day Vosuq's cabinet fell, Esmond Ovey of the Foreign Office wrote a long memorandum on the situation in Iran. Reviewing developments since the Agreement was signed, he concluded that Vosuq's fall was 'almost a *fait accompli*' and that Norman should support a 'strong and friendly Prime Minister':

> On paper Mr Norman's views – a more popular Minister with Nationalist connections ... are unexceptionable ... it may appear undesirable in these days of democracy to suggest any form of absolutism during the period of transition, but a Persia left to itself can only fall under one of two absolut-isms – that of the past or that inaugurated by the Bolshevists in Russia. It would be better it should fall under a temporary executive absolutism tempered by the advice of the imperial English advisers.[12]

The analysis in London was a reflection of the argument among the British diplomats, officers and advisers in Tehran. While Vosuq's resignation was still being processed, General Dickson, the British military adviser, told Norman that 'the Nationalist Party' were willing to form a government.[13] Norman was shortly to enlist the support of Dickson as well as Armitage-Smith, the financial adviser, against Curzon for his choice of Moshir as prime minister (see below). Almost a year later, having returned to London after the February 1921 Coup, Dickson was to write about the argument within the British community in Tehran early that summer on the kind of individuals and cabinets it was best for Britain to work with. In his long letter to Curzon he said he had believed that the success of British policy lay in working with popular politicians, whereas there were others who thought that Iranians were not yet ready for parliamen-tary government:

> It was in this spirit ... that I sought the acquaintance of those who are commonly termed the nationalist party [*melli*] in Persia and it has been my privilege to secure the friendship and confidence of many of them ... [T]he genuine patriotism and honesty of purpose of many of these men, and particularly such as Mushir-el-Dowleh, Motamin-el-Molk and Mostawfi-el-Mamalik was in a striking contrast to that of those who professed openly pro-British and pro-agreement views and whose fulsome adulation of everything British appeared to me to ill conceal a simple desire to personal advancement and gain.

The former were neither anti-British nor pro-German, but they were pro-German during the War out of fear and hatred of Russia and of the Anglo–Russian agreement of 1907:

> They were, however, very uneasy regarding the Anglo–Persian agreement of 1919, not from anything in the provisions of that instrument, but from

the manner in which, and the individuals with whom it had been concluded ... The Anglo–Persian agreement, they asserted, could have been concluded in a constitutional manner and would then have been supported by all patriotic Persians.[14]

In his letter to General Sir Percy Radcliffe, Dickson was more explicit and succinct about his own role in supporting a Moshir cabinet:

It will probably be no news to those who have read between the lines of events ... that the situation in Teheran at the time of Mr Norman['s arrival] was a serious one in itself apart from the Bolshevik invasion. Anti-British feeling was very strong, the result of what was believed to be the manner in which the Anglo–Persian agreement policy had been initiated and that in which it was being carried out.

Given the circumstances:

Two alternatives lay before Mr Norman. The first was the continuation, in an accentuated form, of the so-called 'vigorous' policy hitherto pursued, the second was to conciliate popular feelings and attempt a rapprochement with the Nationalist Party ... The chief of those who advocated conciliation and cooperation with the nationalists was myself, and any claim I had to express an opinion was based not so much on my recent service in Persia as the fact that I had spent a great part of my boyhood in that country and had thereby acquired a facility in speaking their language and getting an insight into the inner character of [the] Persian ...

Norman accepted his view rather than the opposite one, which advocated continuation of the 'vigorous' policy:

The views which I advocated at the time were adopted by Mr Norman and I believe that it was due to Mr Norman's courage ... that the difficulties which the army had to deal with [as a result of the revolt] in Mesopotamia in the summer of last year were not intensified by an outbreak of a similar nature in Persia.[15]

As we shall see in the following chapters, the views of Norman and Dickson were to diverge increasingly after the arrival of General Ironside and the fall of Moshir's cabinet, ending with bitterness on both sides after the Coup. In the summer of 1920, however, they were both optimistic that a popular government would diffuse the public tension, finish the suspended Majlis election, and call it to pronounce on the Agreement. On the day the Shah accepted Vosuq's resignation he sent for Moshir.[16] Curzon wrote to Norman that Firuz believed Moshir did not have the courage to convene the Majlis and carry through the

Agreement policy, but he would be ready to support him or any other prime minister who was loyal to the Agreement.[17] Norman, nevertheless, went ahead and lent support to the formation of Moshir's government, saying that the matter was so urgent that there was no time for him to consult Curzon.[18]

This was the beginning of an usual conflict between Curzon and the Foreign Office, on the one hand, and the British diplomats and other British personnel in Tehran, on the other, which was to continue until sometime after the Coup of 1921 when Norman was recalled to London. Increasingly, the men on the ground realized that Curzon's policy was causing harm rather than good to British interests, and they placed loyalty to their country above loyalty to their political masters. Inevitably, Norman was caught in the middle and took most of the blame. The correspondence between London and Tehran became often dramatic and sometimes acrimonious.

Moshir was in no hurry to form a cabinet before driving a hard bargain with Norman and, through him, with Curzon. He said he would have to declare the Agreement as suspended pending the decision of the Majlis. Norman objected to the word 'suspended', and they eventually agreed on saying that its execution was in abeyance until the Majlis decision. He planned to include Mostawfi al-Mamalek and Mokhber al-Saltaneh – neither of whom was liked in the Foreign Office – in his cabinet, because the former was very popular and the latter had influence in Azerbaijan (for Khiyabani's revolt see chapter four and below). He also insisted that the full 350,000 tomans monthly subsidy to the government and 100,000 tomans for the Cossacks – the latter of which had been already stopped – should continue to be paid for a few more months. He concurred with the view that the Russian Cossack officers should be dismissed at the first opportunity, but said that it would be dangerous to do so at the moment. He also probed the possibility of talking directly to Moscow, which Norman told him London would not approve. Meanwhile, the Shah was nervous and impatient for the new cabinet to be formed.[19]

Curzon was far from amused. He viewed a Moshir government, he wrote, with 'considerable misgivings'. He particularly objected to Mokhber's joining the new cabinet. Britain would no longer pay the Shah's personal subsidy (as he had said before), which was conditional upon Vosuq being prime minister. They would pay the government's subsidy for another four months, but Curzon would not authorize further payments to the Cossacks, although part of the £2 million loan could be authorized to be used for this purpose.[20] Norman spoke to Moshir, who told him that he had not known of the Shah's subsidy, nor about his demand for repayment of his additional travel expenses which Moshir would not authorize. Reporting to Curzon, Norman thought that the curtailment of subsidies to the Shah and to the Cossacks was a mistake. He asked for the maintenance of the Shah's subsidy, which Curzon was soon to firmly decline.[21] As for the Cossack finance, Norman defied his chief's policy and obtained the agreement of the Imperial Bank of Persia to postpone, for a couple of months, receipt from the Iranian government of the monthly 100,000 toman interest on a loan taken out by them the previous January, which would thus be released for payment to the Cossacks. 'I regret', he wrote to Curzon tongue-in-cheek, 'that this measure should be necessary'.[22] In a following telegram – which must have added insult to injury – he pointed out that Moshir would not use any part of the £2 million loan attached to the Agreement while the Agreement itself had not been approved by the Majlis. He also defended Mokhber's appointment as minister of finance.[23]

Having obtained his conditions from Norman, Moshir formally accepted office on 4 July. But London was still unhappy. A memorandum written by G. P. Churchill at the Foreign Office discussed the recent developments. It was fairly measured in its presentation of the facts and accurate in its predictions. After the landing at Enzeli, it recalled, Vosuq 'had asked for considerable British support which he did not get'. Instead 'we decided to withdraw our forces [i.e., the East Persia Cordon Field Force] from Eastern Persia, and our western forces withdrew to Kasvin in the face of the Bolsheviks'. Vosuq then fell, the memorandum continued, because the Shah did not like or support him and he was tired of office, although it ignored the fact that none of that might have happened if Vosuq had been given adequate British support, or at least if Curzon had not effectively opposed his (and Firuz's) decision to speak directly to Moscow. Moshir was a 'Statesman of Western ideas and Education, but greatly lacking in determination'. It was not likely either that the Majlis would meet in that year, or that the new cabinet would last long. Much depended on the extent of military and financial assistance that Britain would give Moshir's government.[24]

A week later, Curzon described the position to Norman as being 'most unsatisfactory'. He was especially angered by the fact that Moshir would not use the loan which was tied to the Agreement:

> You should see Prime Minister and explain to him that Persian Government cannot have it both ways, i.e. treat agreement as in existence, so far as advantages to Persia are concerned, and as cancelled in so far as it involves obligations ... If Prime Minister declines to recognize his predecessor's commitments, he must not be surprised if consequences are withdrawal of British advisers financial and military, and stoppage of monthly subsidy [to the government treasury]. You should explain position to Mushir-ed-Dawleh and point out to him anomalies and dangers of situation.[25]

Norman did not let that pass without a very long comment in three continuous parts. 'A Nationalist and Constitutional Government' had to rule by consent. He did not 'believe, with some, that [Moshir's] government are merely trying to get out of us all they can and will abandon us in the end, and with others that though their intentions are good they lack energy and courage to carry them out'.[26] The most important thing, he continued, is that this government is financially honest, they stop their subordinates 'from robbing', and they have the confidence of the public. A radical cabinet would be altogether hostile to the Agreement. A conservative one would not do better than Vosuq's without strong military support by Britain, and unless Britain would accept the extra expenditure required it would be better to keep a government which did not face a rebellion in the capital.[27] Besides, if Britain supported a 'Conservative Government of old type' it would lose her the good will of 'enlightened and progressive elements in the country':[28]

> If course which I here advocate, having been approved, turns out in a few months to be impracticable, for which I must, of course, take the blame, it will still be possible to revert to our former policy of working with more conservative elements, though it may be necessary to do this under the auspices of another [British] Minister [in Tehran].[29]

Curzon launched a full-scale attack:

> Time has come to take stock of the Persian situation so far as it can be deduced from telegrams received here from Tehran. This seems to be required both for your guidance and for information of Persian Government. Prior to your arrival and return of Shah, the policy pursued by British and Persian Governments was support of Vossugh [sic] Ministry and execution of Anglo–Persian Agreement, which was already in effective operation. Since then there has been complete revulsion, in circumstances over which His Majesty's Government have been powerless to exercise control. Vossugh has disappeared; a nationalist minority has been installed; prominent Persians who had distinguished themselves by unfriendliness to Great Britain and to the agreement have been recalled; Starosselsky, whom it had been decided to dismiss is master of situation; and position occupied by Great Britain appears to be one of no small humiliation. As regards agreement, the position is one which is impossible to defend.

Chief among the 'prominent Persians' mentioned by Curzon were Taqizadeh and Solaiman Mirza, whose purported return to Iran – respectively from Germany and Mesopotamia – he had found especially undesirable.[30] The Agreement, however he went on to say, 'is apparently in a state of suspended animation':

> At the very moment when Persian territory is being invaded, and efforts of British Military Commission are pre-eminently required for organization of national forces, the brigade which it had begun to organize is broken up, and a large number of capable British officers are left with nothing to do ... The Financial Adviser ... is not permitted to work ... Further the Persian Government, inspired by some punctilio, which it is difficult to

understand, decline to use loan upon which it has already without hesitation indented with supply of munitions for elementary needs of the country.

Nevertheless, the Iranian government went on asking for more help. They could not have it both ways. They should summon the Majlis forthwith and decide on the Agreement. In the meantime they could not behave 'as though it [the Agreement] were dead'. They should either put British officers and advisers to work, or expect them to be withdrawn by Britain.

> You should speak to Mushir-ed-Dowleh in sense of these instructions, explaining to him that His Majesty's Government have extended to him, and are still willing to extend to him, every consideration that is demanded by difficulties of the situation, but that he cannot play fast and loose with international obligations or expect us to give unmurmuring support to a Government which treats the Power upon whom it depends for its continuance with such scant respect.[31]

Curzon did not stop at that. He quickly followed it by another – short – telegram to Norman, 'for your private guidance':

> I think you ought to know that length and frequency of your telegrams are a source of unfavorable comment in Cabinet ... You would much facilitate our task by observing greater proportion and conciseness in your messages which exceed in dimensions those received from any half a dozen storm-centres in the world.[32]

Before launching his counter-attack, Norman enlisted the support of both Dickson and Armitage-Smith, especially (though not entirely) since Curzon had linked the suspension of the Agreement to the suspension in their work as advisers. Dickson sent a long communiqué signed jointly with Armitage-Smith to Norman, which the latter duly communicated to Curzon, adding that they had sent it 'because they feel as I do' that the only policy which would safeguard British interest would be to give total support to Moshir's government, and that to take any other course would be disastrous.

The communiqué said that the British government were apparently unaware of the degree of hostility they had provoked in Iran on account of the secretive negotiations for the Agreement and because the Iranian signatories had received British money. Anti-British feeling ran high, the previous situation was leading to anarchy and revolution, and to revive that policy would lead the same way. 'The only way ... is to go with open hands to our old friends national and constitutional party', reassure them that Britain wished to have a strong and independent Persia as her neighbour, and ask them 'to take the reins, summon an honest Medjliss, and lay matter frankly before it'.

They were the only people, Dickson continued, who could assure the public of Britain's good will and get Majlis approval for the Agreement, but for that very reason – and in view of existing suspicions – they had to keep it in abeyance for the moment. And although this put the advisers in a disagreeable situation, 'I fully realize necessity for line taken by Cabinet, members of which are quite open and frank, and in fact exceedingly friendly'.[33]

This was followed by Norman's rebuttal to Curzon. The Agreement was in fact less in operation under the previous government, because while they allowed the financial commission to work they did not enforce their recommendations, 'nor removed one single thief from public service, which nevertheless was more corrupt under them than ever before even in the history of Persia'. Nor did they accept and implement the report of the Joint Military Commission, saying it was not possible before Majlis approval, and yet adding that it was inopportune to summon the Majlis. The prominent persons whose recall Curzon had derided were not anti-British; they had been left with no choice but to turn to Germany against Russia. Starosselski could no more be dismissed by the previous than by the present cabinet. The present situation was a direct result of orders of the War Office to Norperforce, and the retreat from Enzeli.

If there had been any British humiliation, he continued, it was due to that policy rather than anything affecting the Agreement at the time. Armitage-Smith and Dickson were constantly consulted by Moshir's government who had put most of the existing recommendations of the former to use. Moshir's refusal to use Agreement-related funds might be somewhat pedantic but it was logical; in any case, contrary to Curzon's contention, this was evidence that they were not trying to derive every possible benefit from the Agreement. And regarding Curzon's threat of the withdrawal of British advisers:

> I doubt whether His Majesty's Government have right to withdraw members of Financial Commission. They have contracts with Persian Government who pay them and whose servants they are.

Even if Curzon maintained his present attitude towards Moshir's ministry, it would be 'unwise' for Norman to take steps that would lead to his resignation. Moshir had laid down his conditions from the outset and had so far fulfilled his obligations. 'I therefore hesitate to charge them with a breach of faith'. There were only two ways of putting the Agreement into operation. One was by this government with public consent and parliamentary approval; the other was 'its imposition on a reluctant country by a reactionary government in which we must be prepared to cooperate by force'.[34]

Norman followed this strong material by another lengthy telegram making much the same basic points but in a more conciliatory tone.[35] He did not even stop at that. A couple of days later, Norman sent Curzon the financial adviser's further extensive remarks to his joint communication with Dickson, which he had likewise asked Norman to communicate to London. Armitage-Smith was a distinguished British financial expert, who was later to become secretary-general to the important Reparation Commission created by the Versailles peace treaty. 'A scholarly, energetic and meticulous man', wrote Nicolson years later, 'he was much respected by the Persians who, had he not been a symbol of the Anglo–Persian Agreement, would have liked to retain his services'.[36] This is completely borne out by Mokhber, Moshir's first finance minister, under whom Armitage-Smith's work was in fact suspended, as well as Bahar who knew him from some distance.[37] He served Iran with loyalty and commitment, not least in the negotiations which he conducted on her behalf in financial disagreements with the Anglo–Persian Oil Company.

'I am happy to say', he wrote, 'that I have found a formula satisfying both scruples of Persian Government and my own'. He had proposed, and they had agreed, to send him as their representative to London to settle all their outstanding differences with the Anglo–Persian Oil Company. He would rather do this than resign his position, because he believed that his financial reforms would be useless unless they had the sanction of the Majlis. Moshir was sincere and friendly and had put into operation his existing proposals, whereas the previous government had achieved no actual results 'because they dared not dismiss thieves, mostly their own adherents, who conspired to block reforms'. The prime minister's character was 'beyond reproach', and an honest government deserved at least as much consideration 'as a corrupt Government relying on bribery and violence'.

The alternative to Moshir's government, he continued, would be either an extreme anti-British one, or a corrupt and reactionary government which 'I refuse to serve'. The government's handicap was due to the 'secrecy, bribery and violence' with which the former government negotiated and upheld the agreement. The rest was due to the withdrawal of troops from Enzeli, which had encouraged the Bolsheviks and strengthened Starosselski, with whom they should either make a frank and friendly settlement, or strengthen the British military force to reduce his effect.[38]

Given the barrage from this united front, Curzon felt he had to beat a quick retreat, at least for the time being. The British government, he wired Norman, 'appreciate the ability and sincerity with which you have explained position and given your views'. They did not intend to change the Iranian government. All they wanted was for Moshir, with least possible delay, to make the Agreement effective with the assent of the Majlis, or by rejection show that Iran did not want British help. There was no point in digging into 'bygone history' about Vosuq's government. He had not accepted the Agreement being in abeyance for four months, but he agreed to continue paying the monthly subsidy for the period within which he expected a decision to be made on the Agreement:

Our policy remains unchanged, but our adherence to it is in Persia's hands much more than in our own. With regard to suggested modifications of agreement when it comes before Medjliss ... we shall be quite willing to meet views of Persian Government.[39]

Moshir had formally accepted office on 4 July. The above telegram was dispatched on 13 August. Much had happened in the meantime and much was going to happen soon to keep a hapless Norman constantly on his toes.

Moshir's government

To recapitulate briefly the circumstances in which Moshir took office: the Soviet Socialist Republic in Rasht was backed by material and military support and advice from Soviet Russia and the Caucasus, and had the declared aim of extending its rule to the whole of Iran. Norperforce was stationed at Qazvin, with a detachment in the Manjil pass as a first line of defence against a possible Bolshevik thrust, and with orders not to advance beyond that point. The British East Persian Cordon Field Force in Khorasan was about to be withdrawn. The South Persia Rifles were designated to be handed over to Iran as part of the projected unified Iranian force. Currently, they were engaged against a nomadic uprising in Fars province. There were many other, relatively less important rebellions and marauding bands elsewhere in the country so that not only ordinary roads, but even many of the highways, were not safe for travel and transport. Khiyabani's rule was still in force in Azerbaijan. There was thus a classic state of chaos as predicted by the comparative theory suggested in chapter one, the continuation and intensification of the rising tide of chaos since the revolution (see chapters two and three).

Starosselski's position had been greatly strengthened, because the retreat of Norperforce from Enzeli and Rasht had left a vacuum which only the Cossacks could possibly fill. In any case, the Shah was opposed to his dismissal. As noted, the monthly British subsidy of the Cossacks had been officially stopped, although Norman had managed to find a replacement for it. The subsidy to the government treasury had been promised for only another four months, until October, by which time Curzon expected the Majlis to have been convened and a final decision taken on the Agreement. The political public was in revolt against the Agreement and extremely suspicious of British aims in the country. The elections partially carried out under Vosuq were believed to have been rigged, and there was much public pressure for new elections everywhere. Moshir thus needed an instant pocketful of miracles to deal with the situation, and he failed because he did not get it. He might have succeeded had the pressure from Curzon on Norman and, therefore, on himself not been so great, especially in regard to the impossible haste with which he was required to convene the Majlis and obtain a final decision on the Agreement.

His right- as well as left-wing critics have portrayed Moshir as a well-intentioned but ineffectual politician, but the record of his premiership in those four months reveals that he was both able and firm, although he would not act outside the broad confines of his constitutional powers. He saw his immediate tasks as what followed, and set about it as best he could in the circumstances. First and foremost was the Republic in Gilan, because it received help from a powerful foreign power across Iran's border, had declared a full-scale revolution for the whole of the country, and was a strong psychological as well as material base for Bolshevik agitation elsewhere in the country.

Secondly, there was the Azerbaijan problem which, though less ominous, had created real fears of separatism and/or Bolshevik connections. Then came the problems of diffusion of political tension and agitation at the centre itself, restoration of law and order in the rest of the country, administrative reform (especially at the ministry of finance) and elections for the new Majlis. Meanwhile he had to keep his government together by consent, manage the financial situation as best he could, and keep Norman on his side.

He saw rightly that the first major step for solving the Gilan problem was to woo Kuchik. The Gilan republic drew much of its popular legitimacy both within Gilan and elsewhere in the country from Kuchik and his movement, which were entirely native as well as local, had good constitutionalist, anti-imperialist and religious credentials, and whose militia was completely independent from foreign powers. For the very same reasons, Kuchik identified himself with popular constitutionalists at the centre to the extent of sometimes privately seeking their advice over important decisions.[40] It would have been very difficult for him to have remained a rebel against a government led by one such as Moshir al-Dawleh, and including another such as Mostawfi al-Mamalek.

There was little doubt at the time – although no proof – that Moshir contacted Kuchik and asked him to part company with his unlikely bedfellows. At any rate, he sent Sardar Fakher (later Reza Hekmat, the future Majlis speaker) to Gilan on an unofficial fact-finding mission who personally met with Kuchik. It was believed at the time in Gilan that the Sardar had delivered a message from Moshir to Kuchik to break up his coalition with the Iranian Communists party (first formed in Baku as the Edalat party).[41] This is now confirmed by British documents in a telegram from Norman to Curzon who wrote: 'An emissary left Tehran several days [before 22 July] to negotiate with Kuchik Khan'.[42]

As noted, Moshir formally took office on 4 July. On 8 July, Kuchik left Rasht for Fuman in protest, even before Sardar Fakher had met him. He was genuinely unhappy about the zeal with which his Communist partners had begun to attack private property and had taken other actions which were offensive to the cultural and religious sensibilities of ordinary people. He had entered the coalition early in June, with the understanding that there would be no social reforms along strict ideological lines, but increasingly felt that this condition was being systematically violated. By the end of July the coalition fell apart in a clash of forces which each side blamed on the other, and Kuchik and his men retreated into the thick forests.[43]

A week before that event, Moshir had told Norman that he hoped to persuade Kuchik to desist, but if his peaceful approach failed he would move against him. Meanwhile, he declared martial law in Tehran, and asked for British arms and ammunition in preparation for the force that he was planning to send to Mazandaran.and Gilan.[44] An advance party of gendarmes, led by Major (later, General) Habibollah Khan had been already active against the combined operations of Gilan revolutionaries and some local magnates in Mazandaran.[45] Being in his uncooperative mood, Curzon steadfastly refused to 'make recommendations for these supplies' of arms and ammunition requested by Moshir.[46]

At the same time, the evacuation of Mashad by the East Persian Cordon Field Force had begun. Indeed, the War Office had intended to withdraw them in May but had agreed to postpone it against Cox's pleas that, in the circumstances, it would have damaging propaganda effects. As it happened, the circumstances were hardly better now than before, so that, in a telegram to Curzon via Norman, Armitage-Smith wrote: 'We shall never recover military prestige lost at Enzeli, and withdrawal from Meshed will complete our disgrace'.[47] But there was much worse to come. At the very time that Curzon refused to agree to the supply of arms, and Kuchik's and the Communist forces fell apart and clashed in Gilan, came the shocking news of the withdrawal of the Norperforce detachment from the Manjil pass. By all accounts, including Armitage-Smith's, it was a bigger shock even than the retreat from Enzeli and Rasht, and a greater blow to British prestige than those events, although in practice it barely changed the military situation between the two sides.[48] On 28 July, Norman had received early warning of the move from the Norperforce commander, General Champain, and he had found the Shah much depressed at the news of the prospect which he said 'must infallibly produce panic here'. 'I pointed out the military advantages of movement as described to me by G. O. C. Norperforce but His Majesty replied with perfect truth that such an explanation would entirely fail to reassure the public'.[49] Evacuation began on 30 July,[50] and as Norman reported a couple of days later:

> News of the sudden evacuation of Menjil came as a complete shock to the Persian Government … I did indeed warn them that such a step would probably be necessary but they were expecting a further delay of two or three weeks which would give them time for other arrangements of defence of Capital … As was to be expected political effect of withdrawal, following as it does on the evacuation of Enzeli and Resht, has been deplorable.

The British government had not been at all encouraging to the Iranians in response to their requests for money and arms:

> They now feel present withdrawal is merely preliminary step which will be followed in due course by complete abandonment of their country to a Bolshevik invasion …

Norman then pointed out the most important implication of the event, which would have been predicted by anyone knowing the country even if he had no factual knowledge of the specifics: that the public interpreted the withdrawal from Manjil as an anti-Moshir move by Britain:

> In a country like this where official secrecy has no existence apprehensions of Government are shared by thinking public ... in an exaggerated form, and it is, moreover, being said by influential people that His Majesty's government have ordered their force to leave Menjil to mark their disapproval of policy of the Cabinet and bring about its fall.[51]

James Balfour, chief assistant to Armitage-Smith and present in Tehran at the time, was to write as early as two years after the event that the incident 'did more than any foreign intrigue could possibly achieve to injure the British position, and ... had an even more disastrous effect than the Enzeli episode ...'[52]

Champain had ordered the evacuation of Manjil apparently on his own initiative and out of extreme caution to avoid contact with the forces of the Gilan communists and their Soviet allies. He explained to Sardar Fakher, who was on his way back from his mission to Kuchik, that the Gilan militia had been attacking the detachment in Manjil, and it was tactically advisable that they were withdrawn to their headquarters at Qazvin.[53] Balfour explains in some detail that an advance party of the insurgents had shelled the British position by a single gun and then retreated, giving Champain the incorrect impression that they were about to launch a major attack.[54] General Ironside, who took over command from Champain in October, was also of the opinion that the withdrawal had been unnecessary.

Curzon, at any rate, wired back to Norman that he had contacted the War Office and that 'any instructions for [the detachment's withdrawal] did not, I understand emanate from here'.[55] This leaves open the question as to whether or not orders had been sent from General Haldane at the British military headquarters in Baghdad, as Norperforce was under his overall command. However that may be, within two weeks of the evacuation Champain received orders – no doubt prompted by Curzon – to reoccupy Manjil.[56] But the damage to British prestige, and to Moshir's credibility, had been done.

It is interesting to note that Curzon gave Norman the news of orders for the reoccupation of Manjil in the same telegram in which he beat a retreat from his bellicose attitude towards Norman's policy and Moshir's government. Before that happened, however, his reaction was almost cynical, expecting to benefit from the panic that the evacuation had spread in Tehran, and especially the fear that it had instilled in the Shah:

> With reference to the evacuation of Menjil ... it appears to me that attitude of Shah furnishes such a favourable opportunity for plain speaking to His

Majesty as has not hitherto occurred … To judge by your description of the Shah's feeling at the present time, it ought not to be difficult for you to exercise your influence with His Majesty to secure the active cooperation of his government …[57]

Having got Kuchik out of the way, Moshir then took the other two logical steps to deal with the Gilan 'insurgents' (*motejaserin*), as he came to call them: talking to Moscow, and sending troops to Gilan. In his early negotiations with Norman, Moshir had mentioned the possibility of direct contact with Moscow, which Norman had said London would not favour, although there can be little doubt that he personally thought it was a necessary move. Moshir, at any rate, went ahead with the idea and instructed Moshaver al-Mamalek, then ambassador to Turkey, to lead a mission to Moscow. Moshaver was one of the ablest and most senior Iranian diplomats. He was popular in the country for his role as chief delegate to the Paris Peace Conference and was known to be critical of the manner in which the Agreement had been made (see chapters four and five). As noted, Curzon did not favour the policy of talking directly to Mocow, but Moshir's move was right, although it was not to bear fruit until long after he had left office. On the other hand, Curzon suspected Moshaver of being anti-British, and – assuming that Moshir did not wish to upset Curzon without good reason, which in fact he did not – it might have been more tactful to choose someone other than Moshaver to lead the delegation to Moscow.

Moshaver's negotiations in Moscow got off the ground very slowly and bore fruit months later, in the wake of the Coup in February 1921, when the resulting agreement was signed by Sayyed Zia (see chapter nine). If Curzon had not effectively prevented Vosuq and Firuz from contacting Moscow much earlier, it is very likely that an arrangement would have been reached fairly quickly which would have avoided the Soviet landing at Enzeli and, perforce, the declaration of the Soviet Republic in Gilan. After the latter events, however, the situation had markedly changed both against the Iranian and against the British position vis-à-vis the Soviets. The British had retreated, Gilan as well as parts of Mazandaran were in the hands of the insurgents and their Soviet allies, Iranian radicals were looking to Soviet Russia as their potential liberator, and both conservative and popular constitutionalists were anxious to reach a settlement with the Russians. In other words, there was little incentive for Moscow to arrive at a quick agreement with Iran and, incidentally, to draw Britain's chestnuts out of the fire there.

As noted above, Curzon refused to recommend delivery of the arms and ammunitions which Moshir had asked for in order to launch a full-scale attack on the Insurgents. This happened when he was sending his threatening anti-Moshir telegrams to Norman, though it is still difficult to know why he would refuse help for a successful operation against the insurgents. Perhaps he wanted to play on the Shah's and the government's fear of a quick decision on the

Agreement, and indeed he hoped that the evacuation of Manjil might have that effect, although he had not been behind the incident. Perhaps he did not much like the prospect of a victory by the indomitable Starosselski using further British supplies. Whatever the truth, despite Curzon's lack of cooperation, and despite the shock of the Manjil withdrawal, Moshir decided to send a relatively large force, led by Starosselski himself, to meet the insurgents. At first there was resounding success; afterwards, abject failure. It played a decisive role in the fall of Moshir's cabinet, and for that reason its full discussion shall be postponed to the following chapter.

The fall of Khiyabani

The Azerbaijan problem must have looked incomparably easier than that presented by the Caspian insurgents. Moshir and his colleague had personally known and respected Khiyabani as an old constitutionalist democrat from his time as a Tabriz deputy in the second Majlis (see chapters three and five). Two weeks after Moshir formed his cabinet, he told Norman that negotiations with the Tabriz Democrats 'were proceeding satisfactorily'.[58] Kasravi writes in his manuscript on the revolt of Khiyabani:

> We all know Mr Moshir al-Dawleh, who took over the realm after Vosuq al-Dawleh's cabinet, to be a renowned freedom-seeker (*azadikhah*). And there can be no doubt that he did not wish to resort to fighting and blood-shed with the revoltees (*qiyamiyan*) of Tabriz, who belonged to the freedom-seeking public ... And so it was that for over two months the government was making conciliatory gestures and overtures to Khiyabani. But Khiyabani and his lieutenants were in no mood to listen to such words, and it was not easy for them to step down from the elevations to which they had ascended.[59]

From early July to the end of August, Moshir tried to come to terms with Khiyabani. He sacked Ain al-Dawleh – the non-interfering governor – who certainly was not a 'freedom-seeker'. The latter left Tabriz 'early in July', but not before his caravan was held up a few miles outside the town by an unofficial party of Democrats 'until he had disgorged forty thousand tomans of his ill-gotten gains during the five weeks of Governor-Generalship', as the British consul reported.[60] Khiyabani then occupied the Government House which had been rendered vacant by Ain's departure. They had also created a 'Khiyabani Guard', according to Kasravi, of 300 men, whose significance was probably more symbolic than real. After a few weeks, Moshir named Mokhber as the new governor of Azerbainjan, which (as he had told Norman) he had planned to do from the beginning. Mokhber was an old constitutionalist of the moderate tendency, several times minister and governor, and twice previously governor of

Azerbaijan. He did not carry quite the same weight among constitutionalists and democrats as Moshir, but he was a respected political figure with impeccable credentials, especially as he had been openly critical of the 1919 agreement.

Mokhber's account of events from then until the fall of Khiyabani is very similar to Kasravi's independent narrative, except that – as Kasravi was no longer present in Tabriz when Khiyabani fell – Mokhber's description is more detailed and occasionally more precise. For example, Kasravi writes that he heard that when Mokhber's appointment was announced to Khiyabani, he first wired back that Mokhber was not needed, and, later, that the people did not want him. He had also insisted that the province must be recognized as Azadistan (which was probably an indirect plea for recognition of his own rule there). Nevertheless, he asked the government to send him money for the maintenance of the services of the provincial government.[61]

According to Mokhber, Moshir twice sent Khiyabani 20,000 and once 15000 tomans.[62] He further says that when he was named as governor, he got a message from Khiyabani through a third person that if he wanted to go to Tabriz he must go alone, and that 'Azerbaijan is now Azidistan, and it has its own military force'.[63] Before all this, when Mokhber had become minister of finance in Moshir's cabinet, Khiyabani, who knew him personally, had sent him a telegram of congratulations,[64] and in a following letter – couched in highly respectable terms, and addressing him as his 'esteemed and exalted fellow democrat' – he said that Mokhber's 'wise, learned and true' view of the political situation was entirely consistent with his own.[65]

At the end of August, Mokhber left for Tabriz, 'alone', as Khiyabani had suggested, i.e. without new civil or military personnel for the province. Years later he described the chaotic situation he encountered on his way there:

> Everywhere on the way the harvest had been left unthreshed, herds were inside the village walls, and – fearing the Shahsavan [nomads] – the peasants were sitting in the watch towers with guns in their hands ... In Tikma Dash we came across a group of Shahsavans. They had thirty riders, I had seventy led by two Garmrudi khans. A horse was killed from either side, but they passed and so did we. At Jangavar peasants began to shoot at us, thinking that we were Shahsavans. We put the carriages in the front and the shooting stopped.[66]

Kasravi writes in the manuscript that 'in those very days, lawlessness in Azerbaijan had become so bad that the Tabriz-Miyaneh road was cut off ... and the Shahsavan were looting the villages up to a few miles from Tabriz'[67] – all of which is consistent with developments discussed in chapters one to five.

At Basmenj, near Tabriz, Mokhber dismissed his Garmrudi guards. Sa'ed al-Saltaneh (not to be confused with the much more famous Sa'ed al-Vezareh, later Mohammad Sa'ed), a Tabriz community leader and go-between, met him there and said that he should attend Khiyabani's regular meetings at the Government

House. Mokhber agreed, but Khiyabani telephoned Sa'ed back to say that he did not wish to see Mokhber. Neither would he be allowed to take up residence in Ali Qapu (Government House) or in the other two government buildings. Mokhber declined the Tabriz Cossack's suggestion to send a welcoming party, and arrived at Sa'ed's house in the town.

On the third day Sayyed al-Mohaqqeqin and Badamchi (the Khiyabani lieutenants mentioned in chapter five) went to see him. He told them that Vosuq had gone, the Agreement was in abeyance, members of the cabinet (as they knew) were honest men, and civil war and separatism would be destructive; that is, all the reasons that he and most others believed had motivated the revolt. They replied and went on repeating – as, according to Kasravi, they had done since the beginning – that they had a great ideal which they were not yet ready to reveal.

Mokhber then asked the British and American consuls to try and bring Khiyabani into line, he says, so that 'if things got far' he would have witnesses that he had tried his best for a peaceful resolution of the problem. Khiyabani told the British consul that Mokhber was a fast-talker and would get the better of him if they met and talked. And whatever he replied to the American consul, the consul told Mokhber that he was now a 'rebel'.[68]

The Russian Cossack chief had visited Mokhber and told him that Khiyabani's men could be easily reduced. The commander of the less important but more popular gendarmes had also sent friendly word to him, whereas the gendarmes are likely to have defended Khiyabani against Ain al-Dawleh and Vosuq. It was Khiyabani who made the first move. On 13 September, the tenth day of Mokhber's arrival in Tabriz, Sayyed al-Mohaqqeqin brought word from him to Mokhber that he should leave town. He wrote in his inimitably telegraphic style:

On Sunday 13 September Sayyed al-Mohaqqeqin saw me and said 'Khiyabani says, What are you waiting here for?' I said I am waiting for you to give up your stubbornness. He said our position is unchangeable. I said I have not come on my own initiative so that I could leave on my own initiative; I must speak to Tehran. He said the telegraph is under censorship. I said if I lie do not communicate it. He said have it done *hozuri* [i.e. when the two correspondents were personally in the respective telegraph offices]. I said tomorrow is a holiday [because of Moharram]; I shall have it done *hozuri* on Tuesday. I then told the Sayyed, assuming I was to leave what about my security on the road. He said we would send riders with you. I said I do not trust your riders. He said take Cossacks with you. I said that makes sense.[69]

Kasravi writes in his manuscript:

For ten days Mokhber al-Saltaneh was there and no matter how many times he sent messages to Khiyabani that he had been appointed governor of the province and wished to talk to him, he would only reply through some of his collaborators that the people did not want Mokhber … Eventually, Khiyabani sent a message to Mokhber, saying 'leave town or you would be thrown out.'[70]

Meanwhile, the Cossack chief and his Iranian assistant, Zafar al-Dawleh (later, General Hasan Moqaddam) had contacted Mokhber again and declared their readiness for action. That Sunday afternoon there was, as usual, an open-house tea party at the Cossack headquarters on the outskirts of the town. Mokhber went there 'two hours before the sunset' and stayed behind after all other guests had left. He ordered the Cossacks to get ready for action during the night and move early in the morning. On the other hand, Khiyabani and his men – as Kasravi pointedly notes – were completely surprised, probably because they were sure that Mokhber would soon leave town.

Both Mokhber and Kasravi write that by sunrise the Government House and other government buildings and offices were in the hands of the Cossacks after very little resistance, which had resulted in only a couple of deaths on either side. Both also say that late on that very Sunday the Cossacks had recognized Khiyabani going home alone, but did not arrest him because, according to Mokhber, he had ordered the Cossack chief against it.

The movement thus collapsed within a few hours with hardly a shot being fired. Khiyabani and most of his lieutenants went into hiding, and the Cossacks – as was their habit – looted their homes, though Mokhber managed to stop the looting of the homes of Sayyed al-Mohaqqeqin and a few others.[71] Mokhber says that, since he could not find Sa'ed al-Saltaneh by telephone, he told another intermediary to tell Khiyabani that he could go home and remain there unmolested, and when the intermediary asked him to write the message down he did so. There is no reason to doubt this, because Mokhber did not take severe measures against any of the others. The accounts of Kasravi and Mokhber about the manner of Khiyabani's death on the following day are consistent. Khiyabani was hiding in the basement of a neighbouring house. A couple of Cossacks on regular beat were told by a little girl that he was hiding at the home of Shaikh Hossein Miyanaji. Instead of a little girl, Kasravi says a beggar, but in his *Iranshahr* article (cited in chapter five), Badamchi refers to 'that child of a dog'.[72] Perhaps it was a child beggar. At any rate, the Cossacks entered the house, there was an exchange of fire, and Khiyabani was killed. It was not clear who opened fire first, and there was a theory that, having been hit in the foot or leg, Khiyabani had then shot himself in the head. Both Kasravi and Mokhber mention these conflicting rumours without insisting on any of them. Indeed, Mokhber concludes by saying *Wa al 'Imu 'indu Allah* (God knows best).[73] Nonetheless, Mokhber quotes verbatim a suicide note, allegedly found in Khiyabani's pocket, which had been handed to him:

Farewell comrades. Since I was all on my own, and determined not to be arrested, I committed suicide. Follow my principles. Do not forget my people. I have no one. They looted my home. So much for Mokhber al-Sataneh's love of freedom (*azadikhahi*).14 September [1920], Mohammad Khiyabani.[74]

Once the man was killed, the rabble, most of whom, says Kasravi, had been applauding his public speeches until a few days before, followed the corpse in dancing and jubilation as it was being carried to the police headquarters, and were thinking of taking it round the bazaar in triumph. Mokhber heard the noise, discovered its source, put a stop to it and ordered the body to be buried in a local Imamzadeh.[75] Kasravi gives the same account, as does even Badamchi who – not sparing Mokhber his anger – bitterly complains that he 'did not arrange a respectable funeral' for 'that blessed martyr'.[76] Mokhber says that he repaired Khiyabani's home, replaced his looted furniture, and paid 6000 tomans (which up to then had been collected from an entry-and-exit tax for Tabriz under Khiyabani) to his family. Kasravi writes in the manuscript:

> And of Khiyabani's lieutenants the only one who was killed was Mirza Taqi Khan Raf'at. On the day that the Cossacks occupied the town, he and a few others had escaped to a village near Arvanaq. One day they hear that a few riders have come to arrest them. The others manage to escape, but as he does not succeed in running away, the poor young man, driven by fear, pulls his pistol and kills himself ... Some of the others had already obtained immunity for themselves from Hajj Mokhber al-Saltaneh, while the remainder hid away and when they were found were banished from town.[77]

Raf'at was the editor of *Tajaddod*, organ of the Tabriz Democrats, and is especially known for his radical views as a modern literary critic. Mokhber says that there was much pressure on him from the town notables to banish some leaders of the revolt, and in the end he had to banish three of them, including Badamchi, to a village, but lifted the ban 'after a few months'.[78]

Predictably, meetings were held in Tehran, and elegies and other poems were written in mourning for the violent death of Khiyabani. But this time the reaction was mixed. While hardly any one received the news of Khiyabani's death with joy, constitutionalists, and many popular politicians and activists – certainly all the supporters and well-wishers of Moshir's cabinet – did not blame the government for it. The government allowed a public memorial meeting of the Tehran Democrats, called by Solaiman Mirza (later Eskandari), in which Moshir and Mokhber were blamed and attacked for Khiyabani's death. The Democrats brought those charges in their newspapers as well. In a number of ways the most significant published material of that kind was a long and impassioned *tarji'band* by poet-laureate Bahar, of which the refrain was:

If the blood of the innocent [*mazlum*] Khiyabani comes to boil
Iran would wear a red shroud from one end to the other.[79]

Hasan was the first name of both Vosuq and Moshir. Bahar, who had
supported Vosuq's government, compared Vosuq's execution of a couple of
leaders of the rebel band of Nayeb Hossein Kashi (Kashani) with the death of
Khiyabani in this verse; 'If that Hasan killed a couple of Kashis for the sake of
the motherland/This Hasan killed like beasts the freedom-lovers of the
motherland'.[80]

Kasravi makes a brief reference to the hagiographies which were published at
the time – 'someone wrote that Khiyabani had become a *mojtahed* at Najaf,
another, that he had graduated in law from Istanbul' – and also mentions
Bahar's poem. He points out that, in an article, Bahar had attacked Khiyabani
and the revolt at the beginning (to which Khiyabani had reacted in great anger)
and says that the real motive behind Bahar's poem was to attack Moshir, who
had replaced Vosuq.[81] There may be something in this, though the fact that –
even if indirectly – some kind of understanding had been reached between
Vosuq and Khiyabani soon after the rising must also explain Bahar's apparent
change of heart. But almost a quarter of a century later, writing about the political history of that period, his verdict was very different:

> These actions of Moshir al-Dawleh were very brilliant and – though it hurt
> the feelings of the sentimentalists *(manfi-bafan)* and even some popular
> constitutionalists *(melliyun)* – there can be no doubt that the appropriate
> course of action had been taken. And the prime minister enjoyed such a
> high esteem that the criticisms did not shake his position.[82]

From new as well as old evidence used in this and the previous chapter, it is
clear that Khiyabani was neither a separatist nor pro-Bolshevik, and his revolt
was not a reaction to the 1919 Agreement. He wished to govern Azerbaijan with
a firm hand, bring order and discipline to it, and inaugurate modernizing
reforms. That explains the rather intriguing fact that Khiyabani could live with
Vosuq but not with Moshir. Had Vosuq tried to topple Khiyabani by force,
there would have been a strong popular resistance in Tabriz with unpredictable
consequences; there would also have been a great outcry in Tehran and elsewhere. Moshir's 'weakness' as a strict constitutionalist was also his strength as a
popular and legitimate prime minister who could deal with Kuchik and Khiyabani with incomparably greater ease, even though their different responses led
to different outcomes for themselves.

No doubt there were many factors working towards the decline of Khiyabani's authority before his fall. But by far the most effective was that this time
he had to reckon with Moshir and Mokhber, not Vosuq, Sardar Entesar and
Amin al-Molk. His great mistake, perhaps, was that he overlooked that, thinking
that his previous tactics would work again, perhaps even more easily. But it was

not as easy to tell Mokhber to leave town as it had been to tell Amin al-Molk and Sardar Entesar, for he and his political master enjoyed the kind of political legitimacy, and hence self-confidence, that they and their political master did not.

The restoration of central government rule in Azerbaijan was no mean achievement for Moshir. But he had to meet a deadline at the end of October to hold elections and convene the Majlis, and that would have been wellnigh impossible without a notable success in the military campaign against the Gilan insurgents. This he did not achieve, and that is why his cabinet fell.

Notes

1   See Yahya Dawlat-Abadi, *Hayat-e Yahya* (Tehran: Attar and Ferdawsi), 1983, vol. 4, p. 146.
2   Cox to Curzon, 3/6/20, *BDFP*, vol. xiii, no. 449. For an eyewitness account of the incident by a student who participated in the demonstration, see Farhad Kazemi (ed.), *Khaterat-e Natamam-e Doktor Parviz Kazemi* (New York, 1995).
3   Cox to Curzon, 6/6/20, *BDFP*, no. 453.
4   *Ibid.*, n. 5.
5   Curzon to Cox, 7/6/20, *ibid.*, no. 455.
6   Cox to Curzon, 8/6/20, *ibid.*, no. 456.
7   Norman to Curzon, 13/6/20, *ibid.*, no. 461.
8   Norman to Curzon, 13/6/20,*ibid.*, no. 462; 14/6/20, no., 463; 23/6/20, no. 483.
9   Norman to Curzon, 15/6/20, *ibid.*, no. 466; 18/6/20, no. 468; 23/6/20, no. 483; 25/6/20, no. 486.
10 Norman to Curzon, 15/6/20, *ibid.*, no. 466; 20/6/20, no. 475; 23/6/20, *ibid.*, no. 483.
11 Curzon to Norman, 23/6/20, *ibid.*, no. 481.
12 Memorandum on the Persian Question by Mr Ovey, 25/6/20, *ibid.*, no., 490.
13 Norman to Curzon, 20/6/20, *ibid.*, no. 475.
14 Dickson to Curzon, 14/5/21, F.O. 371/6427.
15 Dickson to Radcliffe, 8/10/21, F.O. 371/6427.
16 Norman to Curzon, 25/6/20, BDFP, vol. xiii, no. 486.
17 Curzon to Norman, 25/6/20, *ibid.*, no. 487.
18 Norman to Curzon, 26/6/20, *ibid.*, no. 491.
19 Norman to Curzon, 26/6/20, *ibid.*, no. 492; 27/6/20, no. 493; 28/6/20, no. 494; 28/6/20, no. 495; 30/6/20, no. 496.
20 Curzon to Norman, 1/7/20, *ibid.*, no. 497.
21 Curzon to Norman, 19/7/20, *ibid.*, no. 508.
22 Norman to Curzon, 3/7/20, *ibid.*, no. 499.
23 Norman to Curzon, 3/7/20, *ibid.*, no. 500.
24 Memorandum on the Persian Question by G. P. Churchill, 9/7/20, *ibid.*, no. 507.
25 Curzon to Norman, 19/7/20, *ibid.*, no. 515.
26 Norman to Curzon, 24/7/20, *ibid.*, no, 522.
27 Norman to Curzon, 24/7/20, part II, *ibid.*, no. 523.
28 Norman to Curzon, 24/7/20, part III, *ibid.*, no. 524.
29 *Ibid.*
30 Curzon to Norman, 30/7/20, *ibid.*, no. 527.
31 Curzon to Norman, 31/7/20, *ibid.*, no. 531.
32 Curzon to Norman, 6/8/20, *ibid.*, no. 535.
33 Norman to Curzon, 6/8/20, *ibid.*, no. 534.
34 Norman to Curzon, 6/8/20, *ibid.*, no. 537.

35   Norman to Curzon, 9/8/20, *ibid.*, no. 538.

36   See Harold Nicolson, *Curzon, The Last Phase, 1915–1925, A Study in Post-War Diplomacy* (London: Constable & Co., 1934), p. 141, n. 1.

37   See Mokhber al-Saltaneh (Hedayat), *Khaterat va Khatarat* (Tehran: Zawar 1984), p. 311; Malek al-Soh'ara Bahar, *Tarikh-e Mokhtasrar-e A.hzab-e Siyasi dar Iran*, vol. 1 (Tehran: Jibi, 1978), p. 39; Mokhber expresses much the same view in *Gozaresh-e Iran* (Tehran: Nashr-e Noqreh, 1984).

38   Norman to Curzon, 11/8/20, *BDFP*, vol. xiii, no. 539.

39   Curzon to Norman, 13/8/20, *ibid.*, no. 540.

40   See, for example, Dawlat-Abadi, *Hayat-e Yahya*, vol. 4.

41   See Ebrahim Fakhra'i, *Sardar-e Jangal, Mirza Kuchik Khan* (Tehran: Javidan, 1978), p. 269.

42   Norman to Curzon, 22/7/20, *BDFP*, vol. xiii, no. 517. And report by Fetan al-Dawleh (later, Mahmud Fetan) to Farmanfarma in Mansureh Ettehadiyeh (Nezam Mafi) and Sirus Sa'dvandiyan, (eds), *Mokatebat-e Firuz Mirza*, vol. 1 (Tehran: Nashr-e Tarikh-e Iran, 1990), pp. 28–29.

43   See further, Fakhra'i, *Sardar-e Jangal*; Mohammad Ali Gilak, *Tarikh-e Enelab-e Jangal* (Rasht: Nashr-e Gilak, 1990); Cosroe Chaqueri; *The Soviet Socialist Republic of Iran* (Pittsburgh: Pittsburgh University Press, 1995); Martin Sicker, *The Bear and The Lion* (London: Praeger, 1988); Nasrullah S. Fatemi, *Diplomatic History of Persia, 1917–1923: Anglo–Russian Power Politics in Iran* (New York: Russell F. Moore Co., 1952).

44   Norman to Curzon, 22/7/20, *BDFP*, vol. xiii, no. 517.

45   Norman to Curzon, 2/8/20, *ibid.*, no. 532. For a detailed account of the advance campaign by the gendarmes in Mazandaran, see General Hassan Arfa (himself fighting in that campaign as a young officer), *Under Five Shahs* (London: John Murray: 1964), chapter 5.

46   Curzon to Norman, 27/7/20, *BDFP*, vol. xiii, no. 525.

47   Norman to Curzon, 21/7/20, *ibid.*, no. 516.

48   Norman to Curzon, 11/8/20, *ibid.*, no. 539. See further, James Balfour, *Recent Happenings in Persia* (London and Edinburgh: Blackwood and Sons), 1922, chapter IX.

49   Norman to Curzon, 30/7/20, *ibid.*, no. 528, n. 1.

50   Norman to Curzon, 31/7/20, *ibid.*, no. 529.

51   Norman to Curzon, 2/8/20, *ibid.*, no. 532.

52   See Balfour, *Recent Happenings in Persia*, p. 198.

53   See Ettehadiyeh and Sa'dvandiyan, *Mokatebat-e Firuz Mirza*, pp. 28–29.

54   Balfour, *Recent Happenings*, p. 199.

55   Curzon to Norman, 31/7/20, *BDFP*, vol. xiii, no. 530.

56   Curzon to Norman, 13/8/20, *ibid.*, no. 540. See also Bahar, *Taikh-e Mokhtasar*, vol. 1.

57   Curzon to Norman, 5/8/20, *BDFP*, vol. xiii, no. 533.

58   Norman to Curzon, 20/7/20, *ibid.*, no. 515.

59   Ahmad Kasravi, *Qiyam-e Shaikh Mohammad Khiyabani*, (ed. and intro.) Homa Katouzian, Tehran: Nashr-e Marksz, 1998, p. 163; and *idem*, 'The Revolt of Shaykh Muhammad Khiyabani', *IRAN*, 1999.

60   That is, the five weeks since he had actually arrived in Tabriz, since (as we saw in chapter 5) he had been appointed a long time before that, and had been moving extremely slowly to reach Tabriz. See the report by Ernest Bristow, British consul in Tabriz, for the year 1920, The Edmonds Papers.

61   Kasravi, *Qiyam-e Shaikh Mohammad*, p. 164.

62   The three sources in all of which – at different lengths – Mokhber relates and discusses the fall of Khiyabani are his *Khaterat va Khatarat, Gozaresh-e Iran*, and the little known booklet *Bar Man Cheh Gozasht*. This was recently reprinted in *Ayandeh* under the title 'Nokteh-ha-'i dar Tarihk-e Mashrutiyat', January–March, 1993. The figures for the money sent by Moshir to Khiyabani are quoted in this last source, p. 966. In *Khaterat va Khatarat*, he mentions one 20,000 tomans only, although it is clear from the context that that was not necessarily the only money sent by Moshir to Khiyabani.

63 Mokhber al-Saltaneh, *Khaterat va Khatarat*, p. 313.

64 *Ibid.*

65 *Ibid.*, pp. 313–14.

66 *Ibid.*, p. 315.

67 Kasravi's, *Qiyam-e Shaikh Mohammad*, p. 161.

68 Mokhber, *Khaterat va Khatarat*, pp. 315–16. The point about using the two consuls as intermediaries is also in 'Nokteh-ha-'i dar Tarikh', p. 966.

69 *Khaterat va Khatarat*, p. 316. This is repeated more briefly in 'Nokteh-ha-'i dar Tarikh', p. 967.

70 Kasravi, *Qiyam-e Shaikh Mohammad*, p. 165.

71 *Khaterat va Khatarat*, p. 317.

72 See Badamchi, 'Shaikh Mohammad Khiyabani', in the Khiyabani special issue of *Iranshahr*, no. 14, Berlin 1926, p. 38, reprinted in *Entesharat-e Iranshahr* (Tehran: Eqbql, 1972).

73 'Nokteh-ha-'i dar Tarikh', p. 968.

74 *Khaterat va Khatarat*, p. 318, n. 1.

75 'Nokteh-ha-'i dar Tarikh', p. 968.

76 *Iranshahr*, p. 38.

77 Ahmad Kasravi, *Qiyam-e Shaikh Mohammad*, 168.

78 *Khaterat va Khatarat*, p. 320, and 'Nokteh-ha-'i dar Tarikh', p. 968.

79 In the Persian original, 'Gar khun-e Khiyabani-ye mazlum bejushad/Sartasar-e Iran kafan-e sorkh bepushad'. See *Divan-e Bahar*, (ed.) Mohammad Malek-zadeh (Tehran: Amir Kabir, 1956), vol. 1, pp. 313–315.

80 In the Persian original; 'Kosht an Hasan az bahr-e vatan gar do seh Kashi/Kosht in Hasan ahrar-e vatan ra cho mavashi'. See *ibid*.

81 Kasravi, *Qiyam-e: Shaikh Mohammad*, pp. 169–70. In Kasravi's *Tarikh-e Hidahsaleh-ye Azerbaijan* (Tehran: Amir Kabir, 1992), p. 883, Bahar's earlier criticism and Khiyabani's anger to it has also been mentioned, but his elegy for Khiyabani's death has been omitted.

82 See Bahar, *Tarikh-e Mokhtasar*, vol. 1, p. 54.

7

The Fall of Moshir

The Campaign in Gilan

Towards the end of July, the main body of the Cossacks, led by Starosselski himself, went out to topple the Gilan Republic. They had lightning success. Following the gendarme operation led by Colonel Habibollah Khan (Shaibani), they cleared Mazandaran quickly and then moved into Gilan. It happened just at the time that the British detachment at Manjil was retreating to Qazvin, and resulted in unfavourable comparisons being made between the retreating British and advancing Cossack forces.[1] General Ironside, who took over the Norperforce command in October, noted in his diary: 'I hear that as our men sulkily withdrew, the Persian Cossacks going forward jeered at them. What a thing to happen …'[2] By 11 August, Armitage-Smith said in a telegram (sent via Norman) to Curzon:

When His Majesty's Government immobilised their troops before Bolshevik attack and retreated from Enzeli they made Starosselsky master of North Persia. He alone commanded the troops capable of taking the field …, he cleared Mazanderan, and if he does not go over to enemy he can pose as saviour of Persia …[3]

Having cleared Mazandaran, the Cossacks went to Qazvin, where Norpreforce was stationed, and made it a base for an attack on Rasht. On 20 August, the Insurgents pulled out of Rasht and retreated towards Enzeli. Starosselski entered the town on 24 August and ordered hot pursuit. Delighted by the news, the Shah rushed to honour him with the title of Sardar, and sent him a jewel-studded sword as a mark of his satisfaction.[4] Norman reported to Curzon that the Cossacks had captured papers which 'afforded conclusive proof that Bolshevik invasion of Persia was deliberately planned by Soviet Government of Azerbaijan'. Starosselski had asked the government to warn the Azerbaijan Republic that, unless they discontinued their intervention he would send a force to occupy the other side of the border, north of Ardebil. Norman had concurred in Starosselski's suggestion to the government, but London warned him not to encourage any provocation against the Azerbaijan Republic. Norman, at any rate, hoped that London would induce Moscow to prevail on Baku to pull out their naval and military forces from Iranian territory.[5]

Whatever the thinking was in Moscow – and the evidence suggests that there was a division of opinion regarding the involvement in Gilan[6] – the position on location was far from what Norman and Starosselski had hoped. The Cossacks, in pursuit of the revolutionaries, at first scored further successes at Khomam and Pirbazar, but between Hasan-rud and Ghaziyan their luck turned. The Soviet fleet at sea, and their gunboats in the Enzeli lagoon, began to pound them with heavy artillery fire, and they fled in panic and dismay.[7] It was firmly believed that the force led by Reza Khan of 700 men, the *atriyad* of Hamadan, had been completely annihilated, although much later it turned out that most of them had in fact dispersed through the forest, and that perhaps only ten per cent had been killed by enemy action.[8]

Starosselski then ordered his troops to evacuate Rasht. Panic broke out and many fled the town. A biographer of Kuchik and historian of the Jangal movement, who had witnessed the events, wrote:

> In the wake of the evacuation of Rasht many of the civilians began to run away in large numbers. They were afraid of Bolshevik reprisals because when the Reds had retreated some of them had attacked them in the rear, killed a few and disarmed some of the others. Besides, they had given every possible help to the government army by way of supplying food and other necessities and looking after the injured.[9]

This was a 'catastrophe', because it was so sudden that they did not even manage to take much of their cash and valuables with them:

> Mother separated from child, sister from brother, they madly took the road to Qazvin, mounted and on foot. They were in such hurry and so unprepared that some of them died of exposure and hunger.[10]

The news of the defeat, the evacuation and the sudden flight was received in the capital with horror, and for the first time panic spread in Tehran itself that the Bolsheviks would soon be running their lives.[11]

Although it was a great reversal of fortune, it was not as bad as it seemed at the time, and there was still reason to hope that, with a certain amount of help and support from Norperforce, the Cossacks would be able to launch another serious offensive. Norman, who described the setback as a 'disaster', nevertheless thought that if such support was given they could have a good chance of bouncing back. He attributed the disaster, realistically it seems, to three factors: the character of partisan warfare, the support of the Russian gunboats, and the poor training and lack of discipline of the Cossacks.[12]

Predictably, rumours flying round about the causes of the Cossack retreat were very different from Norman's sober and informed assessment. There were two theories – or, rather, two rival sets of 'facts'. One was that the British were in league with the Soviets: they had evacuated Manjil shortly before the

Cossack move, and had ordered Starosselski, who was their man, first to pretend that he was genuine, then to concoct defeat and retreat; that was why Norperforce did not participate in the operations and did not support the Cossacks when their luck apparently turned.[13] This was the favoured account of the event among Iranians at the time. A short while later, especially when Ironside and Norman finally toppled Starosselski, the other set of 'facts', put out by the defeated and demoralised Iranian Cossack officers, gained currency: Starosselski had entered into a secret pact with the Soviets for reasons of Russian loyalty and/or, especially, material gain. He therefore made sure that the Insurgents and their Soviet allies would beat the Cossacks. Recent memoirs of one such officer – who also makes it plain that he did not like Starosseslki for more personal reasons – gives an extensive as well as colourful account of this 'fact', to the extent of claiming that Starosselski had plans of taking all the money and emigrating to America.[14]

It would not be worth mentioning these theories if they did not help bring to life the atmosphere of intrigue, suspicion and paranoia in the midst of which a handful of level-headed men, be they Moshir or Norman, were trying to deal with the situation, each according to his own duties. Apart from that, the accounts usually given of the Cossack evacuation, both in Persian and foreign sources, contemporary and more recent, is that they quickly fell back to Manjil in dismay and disarray. That is incorrect. The Cossacks evacuated Rasht on 27 August, but their final retreat (of which more below) began several weeks later. They regrouped shortly afterwards and, by 11 September, were again in touch with the enemy ten miles north of Imamzadeh Hashem. Just at that time Norperforce received orders from Haldane (GOC in Baghdad) to send some of their forces to Mesopotamia. This was because of the anti-British uprising in Iraq in the summer of 1920. Poor Norman was desperate:

> Political effect here of withdrawal of British troops at this juncture will be absolutely disastrous … Our enemies have been making capital out of our retirement from Manjil and out of inability of General Champain to move beyond (? that) place and have been doing their utmost to create impression that we are (?us)ing Bolsheviks to destroy Persian troops after which we shall expel former and seize the country for ourselves.

It was even worse than that:

> It is even widely believed that we are financing and working in collusion with invaders with above objects. Withdrawal of troops at this juncture will appear to (? justify) these accusations and it is not too much to say that even without any further advance on the part of Bolsheviks serious disorders are likely to break out in the (? capital) … In these circumstances it will be impossible to restrain the Shah and Government from evacuating capital in anticipation of invasion.[15]

Faced with this desperate plea, Curzon acted quickly and had the cabinet instruct Haldane not to withdraw troops from Norperforce unless the situation in Mesopotamia made it absolutely imperative, and even then not without prior cabinet approval.[16] But this incident again shows how the War Office and, perforce, GOG Mesopotamia, were wary of their reluctant, ill-defined and undermanned Iranian mission, and of making the kind of commitment that would have been absolutely necessary for the survival of Curzon's Persian Policy. It goes a long way to explain the mission of General Ironside, who was sent to Iran as the new GOC Norperforce barely two weeks later (see below).

Far from acknowledging defeat, Starosselski felt strong enough to have a long and frank talk with Norman about the future of the Cossack Division. He told Norman that, while the force was now defending British interests against the Bolsheviks, it was clear that it would be dissolved as an independent body once it won the war. This made the officers reluctant to fight, while ordinary troopers saw the Bolsheviks simply as enemies of England. Under Vosuq, he had learned about plans to eliminate the Division as an independent body, and had intended to resist this by force, including the disruption of Norperforce communications with Mesopotamia. It would facilitate their cooperation, he added, barely concealing the implied threat, if they were given some assurance about the force's future survival. Moshir was 'considerably impressed' when Norman gave him this account of Starossleki's attitude, which he said he had had no previous knowledge of, because the Colonel was not in the habit of confiding so intimately to Iranians.[17]

Curzon was far from impressed. He pointed out that since the Agreement was at present in abeyance, no definite view could be taken of the future of the Cossack Division. But it was supposed to be the Shah's own bodyguard, and they must be loyal both to Iran's and to Britain's interests, as British forces were there to defend Iran. Norman should tell the Shah to tell the Colonel that his duty was to act with whole-hearted loyalty in the defence of their common interests. He also issued an open threat that, if the Iranians concurred in the Colonel's attitude, Britain would withdraw its forces to parts of the country where it could serve only her own interests in Iran as well as in Mesapotamia.[18]

Problems of finance and elections

In the meantime, the tug of war between Norman and Curzon continued almost unabated. The main issues were the question of the Iranian government's financial needs, the Majlis elections to decide on the Agreement, and now, north Iranian oil. In 1916, A subject of the Tsarist Russian empire by the name of Khoshtaria had obtained a concession from the Iranian government for oil exploration and extraction in the country's northern provinces, and a second concession for other minerals, both of which he had recently transferred to the Anglo–Persian Oil Company. The issue of the Khoshtaria's concessions had come up a couple of times in the correspondence between Curzon and Cox when the latter was minister in Tehran and wished to obtain the Iranian government's recognition of the transfer.[19]

It may be recalled from chapter five that Firuz had once 'startled' Curzon by referring to 'world oil' in the course of a conversation about possible American investment in Iran. Indeed, Curzon had been alarmed into thinking that the American Standard Oil Company – 'that omnivorous organisation' – was 'endeavouring to secure a foothold on Persian soil'.[20] Now, in August 1920, Norman received information from 'an absolutely sure source' that American investors had expressed interest in north Iranian oil on favourable terms, and that this had been followed up by the American Secretary of State offering his help in arranging a concession through the Iranian minister in Washington. However, the Iranians had not responded to these inquiries.[21]

Norman, it appears, communicated this information to Curzon in order to demonstrate Iranian loyalty. Curzon responded, in a telegram marked 'most secret', with a very different story. He had been assured by 'a most reliable informant' that the Iranian minister in Washington had told the State Department that the Iranian government would rather give the north Iranian oil concession to Americans than to any other nationality. Curzon had been further informed that the American minister in Tehran had been instructed to contact the ministry of foreign affairs and report on their response.[22]

It was clear from Norman's earlier telegram that the Iranians did not recognise the transfer of Khoshtaria's concessions to the Anglo–Persian Oil Company, and regarded it as null and void. They argued that the concession had been obtained before the Russian Revolution, when parts of Iran were under Russian occupation; that the Bolshevik (later, Soviet) government had unilaterally cancelled all such concessions; and it was doubtful if Khoshtaria had the right to transfer the concession to a third party.

Curzon did not see it this way. He asked Norman to inform the Iranian government 'categorically' that the British government did not accept their view and intended to support the Anglo–Persian Oil Company, which had obtained the concessions from Khoshtaria by proper legal means. They had already twice informed the Iranian legation in London of their view and would take up the matter again in due course.[23] In the end, the Iranians replied that the Khoshtaria concessions themselves lacked legal basis because they had not been approved by the Majlis, which had been in recess at the time and since its being granted.[24] The issue was to come up again later, in the early 1920s, when American companies pursued their interest more actively, though they did not obtain concessions for north Iran's oil, nor did Iran ever recognise the claim of the Anglo–Persian Oil Company. But for the moment it was yet another point in Curzon's books against Moshir's government.

The government's financial situation was dire. They had borrowed £500,000 from the Imperial Bank of Persia in Tehran in order to finance Starosselski's campaign in the north and, by the end of August, this had been all but spent.

They were not prepared to take an advance on the £2 million loan negotiated with the 1919 Agreement, on the grounds that it was in abeyance pending the decision of the Majlis (see chapter six).

Instead, they were anxious to negotiate another, independent, loan of 2 million tomans (not pounds) from Britain. This had the sympathy of both Norman and Armitage-Smith, who was about to go to London as their plenipotentiary to settle their outstanding accounts with the Anglo–Iranian – then called Anglo-Persian – Oil Company. Norman came up with a plan (to which the Iranians agreed) for Armitage-Smith to negotiate the loan for them in the City of London at 7 per cent interest for a period of 40 years.[25] Curzon was not unsympathetic to the idea, but would not agree to it unless 'it be repayable out of the loan based on 1919 Agreement'.[26] He wished to keep the Agreement somehow in the picture, being angry at the attempts by Moshir's government to keep it out.

Armitage-Smith and Norman arrived at a formula which would explain to a future Majlis why the proposed £2 million loan should be deducted by the new 2 million toman loan, emphasising the fact that it was a separate loan, repayable over 40, not 20, years. Having done that, Norman, nevertheless, showed his cheek to Curzon by adding in brackets that, in any case, there was likely to be trouble when the money paid out of the £2 million 'to late Government for purposes of corruption' became known to the Majlis.[27] At any rate, Curzon awaited Armitage-Smith's arrival in London for a final decision. But the Tehran government were in dire financial straits there and then. The gendarmerie's pay was two months in arrears, and even the Cossacks in the front were not fully paid, while reinforcements were arriving from across the Caspian sea to shore up support for the Insurgents.[28]

They suggested that the Anglo–Iranian Oil Company give them an advance on the arrears of royalties which they claimed. The company did not accept this, arguing that it could prejudice the negotiations which they were due to begin shortly in London, with Armitage-Smith representing the Iranian government. Instead, they were prepared to pay £350,000 in current royalties which normally would have been paid two months later.[29] The Iranians were delighted at the offer, and asked the Company to pay the sum through the Imperial Bank of Persia in London, which would then authorize payment by its branch in Tehran.[30] The Company did so,[31] but a week later Moshir's government fell as a result of the new Ironside-Norman policy (see below). Just before that event, Curzon telegraphed Norman that if the Majlis did not meet and/or take a quick decision on the Agreement, no more British government money (including loan) would be given, and 'to hold out further hopes [from commercial British sources] wd. be misleading'.[32]

To hold speedy Majlis elections was indeed a thorny issue. Norman was missing no opportunity for pressing the matter to Moshir, if only because of the pressure from Curzon on himself. Moshir's dilemma over the subject was manifold. The obvious problem was that the government was not in control of considerable parts of the country. Apart from Gilan, and Azerbaijan, where

Khiyabani continued to run the show until mid-September, the government's writ was not exactly operative in some other regions, especially in nomadic and distant rural areas. There was also conflict of opinion in the very centre of politics, on whether Vosuq's unfinished elections should be continued or there should be new elections everywhere. The argument was that in many of the constituencies where members had been elected, there had been intimidation and elections had been rigged. On the other hand, the annulment of those elections would have led to new conflicts, and apart from that, it would have prolonged election of the necessary quorum for the opening of parliament.

At the bottom of all this, let it be emphasized, was the stark fact that constitutionalism had failed in its most basic practical objective of creating a constitutional framework within which all the major political forces and trends were prepared to work, run the country, and settle their disputes. That is, unlike any constitutional regime that is workable in practice, a framework had not emerged within which all major political powers genuinely recognised each other as legitimate, and within which they would compete with their various political programmes. It was in this sense, and for this reason, that there was still chaos in the centre of politics itself, and among political groups and magnates.

In the midst of all this came the Cossack campaigns in Mazandaran and Gilan, and Mokhber's mission in Azerbaijan. At the same time, government coffers were empty, and there was little money to finance countrywide elections in a vast land with a sparse population and poor means of transport. By mid-September, few steps had been taken to complete the elections, although the government had virtually decided not to repeat those which had been previously held under Vosuq. To complete the government's dilemma, the season of Moharram mournings had just started.[33]

The gates were thus wide open for another round of combat between Curzon and Norman. Curzon declared his deep disappointment with the situation, accusing Norman of not having thrown his weight about sufficiently over the issue in time, and saying that a long delay would mean the failure of the policy with which Norman had associated himself – a failure resulting in a situation 'of which Persia will be the chief sufferer'.[34] Characteristically, Norman responded first with better news about the specific issue in question,[35] and then with a long telegram pointing out the difficult circumstances, attacking Vosuq's government and stressing Moshir's achievements:

> Cabinet is composed with one exception of financially honest men, it has made a beginning of reforms, it has saved Mazandaran and Azerbaijan for Persia, it has organized out of very unpromising materials ... an expedition which with little help from us bids fair to re-conquer Gilan from Bolsheviks, from whom it has also succeeded in detaching a very influential ally, Kuchik Khan ... it has also taken steps ... to summon Mejlis, and it has made it possible to convince not only all moderate people, but also many

extreme democrats of honesty of Great Britain's intentions towards Persia and of necessity of some kind of agreement between the countries.[36]

Curzon wasted no time, equally characteristically, in countering Norman's contention that, in the matter of the succession of Moshir's government, he had acted in the absence of clear instructions from London. In a short, sharp and pointed telegram he barraged Norman with numbers and dates of relevant telegrams which he believed refuted Norman's claim.[37] The storm was soon to break out again over the Coup against Starosselski and the consequent fall of Moshir's government.

General Ironside and the Coup against Starosselski

Late in September, Major General Sir Edmund (later Field Marshal Lord) Ironside arrived in Qazvin via Baghdad, to take over command of Norperforce from Brigadier General Champain. Ironside did not merely have a higher rank and a knighthood. At 39, he had already distinguished himself in active command and – in particular – had displayed considerable ability in dealing with emergency situations. Readers of his *Diaries*, as perhaps also of the following appraisal, would recognise him as an able, intelligent, tough and daring military commander whose name seems to have been justified by the reputation of his namesakes – 'the ironsides' of Cromwell's New Model Army noted for their dazzling successes during the English civil war.

Unfortunately, only parts of Ironside's *Diaries* have been published, and the present author did not succeed in gaining access to the manuscript. However, from the quotations, attributions and allusions of two authors who have seen it, it is clear that part III of the published *Diaries* (which describes Ironside's mission in Iran) has been heavily edited, to the extent that some seemingly important parts of the manuscript have been completely left out. In fact, the published version is in the form of memoirs, whereas it is clear from quotations by those who have seen the original that it is indeed a diary.[38] This is borne out by the portion of the original which has been published in Tehran.

In December 1973, the editor of the published *Diaries*, the present Lord Ironside, sent a copy of the relevant parts of the manuscript diary to Asadollah Alam, the Iranian minister of the royal court, hoping that they 'will find a number of suitable extracts' from it 'to be placed on record in time for the 50th anniversary of the Pahlavi dynasty'. Whether or not this took place, the copy of the manuscript was discovered after the Iranian revolution, and a portion of it, mainly in Persian translation but including photocopies of a few pages of the original, was published in Tehran as an appendix to the Persian translation of the published *Diaries*.[39]

Why the whole of what they had of the manuscript diary has not been published in Iran, either in English or in Persian translation, or indeed both, is a

matter for speculation. Certainly, it could not be due to any copyright considerations, if only because Iran does not subscribe to the international copyright
convention. Although the complete history of Ironside's activities while he was
in Iran for the five crucial months before the Coup – and especially his role in
organising the Coup itself – cannot be written without access to all relevant
pages of the manuscript, what is available from it in print, and from the quotations of those who have seen the full manuscript, and the portion which has
been reproduced in Iran, in addition to available British documents, make a very
good approximation possible.

Having met and conferred with General Sir A. L. Haldane – GOC Mesopotamia – in Baghdad before taking up his new command, Ironside had been 'given
a free hand to act as he thought fit'.[40] Haldane had explained his difficulties to
him in regard to Norperforce, which are familiar from the evidence discussed in
the present and preceding chapter:

> Though the North Persian force was under his [Haldane's]command, the
> policy there was directed by the Foreign Office and the War Office,
> through the British Minister in Tehran. He had pressed the War Office
> hard to get a policy from the Foreign Office, but with no success.[41]

Haldane had told Ironside that he had been picked for the post 'because of his
reputation as a resourceful leader of independent, isolated forces, and that,
unlike his predecessor, Champain, he would be given a free hand'.[42]

Ironside assumed command of Norperforce on 26 September. On 6 October
the War Office sent a telegram to Haldane (repeated to India and Tehran) as a
guide for dealing with the situation in Iran. It emphasised that Ironside 'must
clearly understand that we are not in a position to reinforce him in the event of
a serious military invasion of North Persia by the Russians'. He should also bear
in mind that any position of importance occupied by Norperforce would be
very difficult to evacuate, owing to resistance by the Iranian government,
backed by the Foreign Office. He should deal with Starosselski with 'tact and
firmness', and use his personal influence with him and any other forces so that
their energies are used 'to the best advantage in order to meet the wishes of our
Political authorities in Tehran'. He should also send Haldane an appreciation of
the situation as soon as possible, and the latter 'should telegraph to the War
Office as early as possible this appreciation and proposals for action with your
remarks'.[43]

It is clear from all this that both Haldane and the War Office gave Ironside a
free hand to deal with the situation, so long as he would not ask for further reinforcements and did not occupy any new and important position from which it
might be difficult to withdraw Norperforce later. For good measure, the telegram referred to 'the wishes of our Political authorities in Tehran', but it is
evident from the text that Ironside's decisions were not constrained by a need to
promote Curzon's Persian Policy, even though it was the official policy of the

British government. As noted, his instructions had been repeated to India and Norman, both of whom were far from happy with that policy. All that Ironside needed to do was to win Norman over to his new line, and Norman was quite willing to be won over. The War Office and the GOC in Baghdad thus actively came forward to make the best of a bad job, in order to rid themselves of Curzon's constant attempts to keep them in Iran against their own best council, and to withdraw their troops from the country. It was Curzon's turn now to be presented with *faits accomplis* (see chapter 4).

Meanwhile, Starosselski had recaptured Rasht, and his Cossacks had advanced as far north as Hasan-rud, near Enzeli. Ironside met Norman in Tehran and 'explained to him the orders I had received from General Haldane', but it is not clear from the published *Diaries* if they reached a clear understanding on the future course of action.[44] Fortunately, an official document makes good the deficiency. When Ironside went back to Qazvin, he saw the War Office telegram of 6 October (cited above) instructing him to send a full report on the situation, and, three days later, wired his report, which laid out fully his immediate plans for getting rid of Starosselski, and taking over the command of the Cossacks. It is a revealing document:

> The formation of a Persian army under British supervision is in abeyance. H.M. Minister in Tehran [i.e. Norman] informs me that the Mejliss cannot give its sanction to this portion of the Agreement until about February at the earliest. With allowance for Oriental diplomacy this means until the moment of withdrawal of Norperforce [early in the spring].[45]

This, at any rate, would be impossible with the opposition of Starosselski. Therefore:

> Given that the withdrawal of Norperforce in April [19]21 will take place, it is essential to commence the formation of a British-controlled Army at once. New units are out of the question. I do not recommend northwards of a nucleus of South Persian Rifles.[46]

The alternative was to take over the Cossack Divsion itself:

> There remains therefore the substitution of British control in the Persian Cossacks for the Russian [sic] control of Starosselsky. This should be done at the earliest convenient moment …. The present successful campaign against Resht and Enzeli has enhanced the prestige of Starosselsky, but the Oriental mind is easily turned … I think the active intervention of Norperforce to carry this substitution out would be fatal to our Agreement … Starosselsky must be legally dismissed by the Persian Gov., and continuous political pressure must be exerted from now onwards … A good successor [to Starosselski] ready at hand is Colonel Huddleston [the British military

attaché in Tehran]. Whoever is selected must be a soldier … Care must be taken to avoid an administrative officer without such experience.[47]

General Dickson, the report continued, had become involved in Iranian politics and 'in the event of the present [i.e. Moshir's] Gov. being forced out, Brig. Gen. Dickson would not be of much value for the construction of an Army':

> I have informed H.M. Minister [Norman], that with his Military Attaché [i.e. Colonel Huddleston], I become his military adviser and that the position of Brig. Gen. Dickson is thus affected … If he is really much mixed up in politics he should withdraw from Tehran.[48]

Someone had to be responsible for the work of the Joint Military Commission (which, though in abeyance, was still led by Dickson). If Ironside himself was not given the responsibility for it, he would give every help to whoever was given it to make preparations 'for the British-controlled Army':

> No time is to be lost during the precious period of the presence of Norperforce, and I wish to make it clear that I do not consider that preparations are being made of an adequate nature.[49]

It must be emphasised that Ironside drew up these plans and sent the above report when it looked as if Starosselski and the Cossacks had been thoroughly successful in beating the Insurgents in Gilan, in their second offensive. On 10 October, the day after he sent the above report, Ironside inspected the British troops at the Manjil pass, and two days later he went back to Tehran for further conferment with Norman. A few days afterwards, Starosselski's Cossacks once again faced fierce resistance and a counter-offensive near Enzeli, backed up by Soviet gunboats and reinforcements. According to his published *Diaries*, Ironside had ordered wire-tapping at Qazvin, so that he was able to see copies of telegrams exchanged between the Shah and Starosselski. The latter wired the Shah, he says, for permission to withdraw from Rasht for refitting, and both he and Colonel Philipov, who was in Tehran, were 'loud in their abuse of the British and everything to do with them'.[50]

Starosselski began evacuating from Hasan-rud, for the second time, on 21 October 'entirely due to bad morale'.[51] His forces were pursued by the Insurgents and their Soviet allies, and evacuated Rasht the next day. On the same day, 22 October, the British detachment at Manjil asked Ironside for clear instructions: 'What help may I give Col. STAROSSELSKY if he asks for it'. Ironside wired back with clear instructions:

> From a political point of view it would be very advantageous to us to leave Col. STAROSSELSKY to make a mess of things as it would then be more easy for me to get rid of him. In view of this you will give him no

assistance forward of your present position but will, if they so desire, allow the Cossacks to fall back behind you.[52]

Such a response must be the origin for the firm belief – so extensively discussed by Dawlat-Abadi, who is one of the more sober and reliable contemporary sources – that, in addition to the Soviet gunboats, English planes had actually bombarded the Cossacks near Enzeli.[53]

Ironside saw his opportunity. He got Norman's agreement to press for Starosselski's dismissal at all costs, even that of Moshir's resignation, without consulting the Foreign Office. On 24 October, Ironside sent a long report to Haldane, describing Starosselski's withdrawal from Rasht and accusing him of financial corruption:

> I think the moment has now arrived when we should assume some sort of control of the Persian forces in order to supply local defensive but to do this means that I must have some officers with which [sic] to begin.

He suggested Huddleston and a couple of others, did not think Dickson was suitable (though he would help him if he was chosen) and asked for specific orders to take control of the Cossacks:

> It is important to know whether we are to start control of the Cossacks however nominal or it is useless to depose Starosselski, who however bad would be better than a Persian leader uncontrolled by British. The moment has arrived to make a decision and I think the matter is urgent. Are we to depose Starosselski and assume control & who is to exercise that control, myself or Dickson.

He ended by reporting Norman's agreement and cooperation:

> The minister Tehran agrees that Starosselski should be deposed [and afterwards] he tries winning the foreign office [sic]. Minister & I interviewed Prime Minister and told him that Starosselski must go. Will inform you later of results.[54]

They had indeed met Moshir and pressed him extremely hard to agree to Starosselski's dismissal. The following is from Ironside's manuscript diary:

> ... I had gingered up Norman and an ultimatum was delivered by us both as to Staros[selski]. I insisted on his being recalled, dismissed and called upon to render an account of the money he had spent in the so-called campaign. I told the [Prime] Minister that he had asked me not to interfere and I had refrained, but now the Persian Cossacks had collapsed and we could waste no more money on them.

The wretched man was up against it. He wriggled in his chair like an eel at the end of a line. He said that his head would be chopped off if he went to the Shah and asked for the dismissal of his own special favourite. He suggested other names. Anything to escape. I felt like a bulldog with a small dog in front of me. I was told that to institute British control in the Persian Cossacks now would make the Agreement impossible. I told him he made no effort to make it possible and that I had no intention of instituting British control [this contradicts Ironside's report, cited above, where he argues for British control]. I merely refused to have British money embezzled and wasted by the Russians ...

The Prime minister wept and wrung his hands, and short of kneeling at my feet he did everything to attempt me [sic] to change. I left him exhausted, but not too impolite to forget the departure coffee. Norman tells me that I frightened him thoroughly and that he will get Starosselski dismissed.[55]

In fact he had not. On the contrary, when Norman frightened the Shah directly into agreeing to dismiss Starosselski, Moshir resigned, despite the Shah's insistence that he should remain in office. He explained that he would not do so while knowing that an important decision had been imposed on the Shah by representatives of a foreign power against the advice of the prime minister.[56] Obviously, then, he had not been fearful of the Shah 'having his head chopped off' if he agreed with Starosselski's dismissal. He was a correct, urbane and self-respecting man.

The resignation of Moshir

Moshir resigned on 26 October. According to Norman's long account of his and Ironside's visit to him, he had not opposed the dismissal of Starosselski, but the appointment of British officers to the Cossack Division:

Prime Minister said that he personally concurred in opinion that moment had come to dismiss Colonel Starosselski but as I foresaw he demurred to appoint British officers to Division as being certain to weaken position of government with whose policy it would be inconsistent and would react unfavourably on prospects of agreement. Another solution must be found and he would have to consult Shah and some of his colleagues. General Ironside and I both replied there was no other solution and demonstrated impracticability of some which he proposed.[57]

Next day Moshir told Norman that the Shah did not agree to dismiss Starosselski. But he still insisted that the appointment of British officers to the force would be very unpopular, and would harm both his government and British interests. Norman said that if this was not done, British troops might be withdrawn from Iran. Moshir replied that if Norman insisted on the appointment of British officers 'the Government would be bound in conscience to resign'.[58]

Norman then sounded out Sepahdar-e A'zam (later Fathollah Akbar) as a successor to Moshir, and found him willing. Next day he saw the Shah and found him unwilling to dismiss Starosselski and appoint his own uncle 'to nominal command of division with British officers under him'. Norman threatened that he would refuse to allow any more British money to be paid to the Cossack Division, and it would be unlikely that British troops would remain in Iran.[59] The message was loud and clear: with no money for the Cossacks and no British troops in Iran, the gates of Tehran would be wide open to the forces of the Insurgents and their Soviet allies. The Shah surrendered. He consulted Moshir, who tendered his resignation. Next day he accepted Norman's nomination of Sepahdar, and asked for two favours, which Norman agreed to recommend to London: repayment of the 15,000 toman monthly personal subsidy, and British assistance for a six month visit to Europe from next April.[60]

Starosselski still had an army at his command which Norperforce would not have fought if – as it was very likely – it resisted. Therefore while he was on his way to Tehran to report to the Shah, and his troops were retreating south towards Manjil, Ironside interceded and edited their telegrams to his own advantage:

> The operation had so far been executed most successfully, but there remained the tricky business of shepherding the Cossacks into a camp at Aga Baba [Aqa Baba, or Aqababa] some miles from Kazvin … Luckily for me Starosselski played into our hands. As soon as he saw his men into the second defile he set off in his car to Kasvin and Teheran. He stopped at the post office in Kasvin long enough to wire to the Shah that he was motoring there at once, and a long wire to his Brigade [sic] to camp to the north of Kasvin. Our wire-tappers suppressed his wire to the Shah and altered the order for camping to Aga Baba.[61]

Once they arrived there, the Cossacks were disarmed by Norperforce, and ceased to exist as an independent entity.[62] Starosselski reached Tehran and met the Shah on 29 October. Norman had told the Shah to receive, reprimand, and dismiss him in severe terms, and this – Norman understood – the Shah did.[63] He then appointed a harmless little desk officer, Sardar Homayun (later Major General Qasem Vali), as the nominal head of the Division, and who left for Qazvin the next day. Starosselski tried to organize some kind of feeble resistance, which is sometimes described as his attempted 'Coup'. Norman asked the Shah to order him to go back to Qasvin, which he obeyed.[64] Once he reached Qazvin, he met Ironside for the first time, saying 'I am not armed', and then, 'I congratulate you, you have won'.[65] 'On the date of the liquidation', Norperforce later reported, 'total number of Russian on the list of the Persian Cossack Division was, officers 87, other ranks 120'.[66]

All this while Curzon had maintained silence. On 29 October, he exploded. It had all been done without his prior knowledge and approval, especially as it was such a sudden as well as radical policy reversal on Norman's part:

> I find some difficulty in forming and expressing an opinion on a situation in which there appears to be a complete *volte face* in Persian policy, and in which I am again presented, in this case without the slightest warning, with a *fait accompli*. Till a week ago I had been led by you to believe that success of British policy in Persia was inseparable from Premiership of Mushir-ed-Dowleh ... Now all this has changed, and the leading actors are in the course of voluntary or compulsory disappearance from the scene without any previous consultation with His Majesty's Government.[67]

He felt he had to leave it to Norman to deal with the situation, which was such that 'no instructions from this end can avail to control'. He was anxious that the deposition of the Russian officers might run into serious trouble. He rejected the Shah's demand for the renewal of his subsidy, and ended his telegram with the following warning:

> In deciding upon new policy in the manner which you have described, you will doubtless recognise that General Ironside and yourself have assumed no slight responsibility, which will require the justification of success, This I trust that you may obtain, while asking you to bear in mind that the intentions and objects of His Majesty's Government, as to which you have been frequently informed, remain unaffected by these vicissitudes. I shall await further information from you with anxiety.[68]

Once he received the news of Starosselski's bloodless dismissal, however, Curzon supported the change, and attacked Moshir's government forcefully in a speech in the House of Lords, thus convincing the Iranian body politic that London had been behind it all. This prompted the writing of a *tarj'band* by the fiery Farrokhi Yazdi, with the refrain:

> His temper, Lord Curzon has lost
> He has resorted to elegy recitals.[69]

Sepahdar and Sayyed Zia

Sayyed Zia had become more active behind the scenes after the fall of Vosuq. His Committee of Iron, now known as the Committee of Zargandeh (see chapter five) was holding regular meetings, which other political activists, such

as poet-laureate Bahar, also occasionally attended. A group of radical Democrats, led by Solaiman Mirza, and some leading figures of the old Moderate
party, notably Sayyed Mohammad Sadeq Tabataba'i – the influential eldest son
of the revered constitutionalist leader – having got together and describing
themselves as socialists, also began to coordinate their activities with the
Zargandeh Committee. Indeed, it had been initially proposed that Sayyed Zia
and Tabataba'i join Sepahdar's cabinet. But the idea had been abandoned
because both of them were still wearing the turban, and at that the time it
would contradict the Shi'a tradition that religious figures should not join the
government.[70]

Increasingly, the Sayyed became known as the link between the British legation and the political circles in Tehran, although as long as Moshir was prime
minister he did not play that role between the government and the legation.[71]
He had close personal friends among the diplomatic staff of the legation, particularly Walter Smart, the new Oriental Secretary, Godfrey Havard, and Colonel
Huddleston, the military attaché. Smart had known Sayyed Zia well from the
years of the Constitutional Revolution and after, as had Colonel C. B. [Claude]
Stokes who was then posted in Tiflis. Colonel Haig, the original founder of the
Iron Committee of Isfahan, was also in Tehran and – as we shall see in the
following chapter – he was to play a role in the Coup, as did Colonel Smyth and
all the others mentioned above.

Zia became much more active, important and powerful during Sepahdar's
term of office. It was he who had sounded out Sepahdar on Norman's behalf,
when it looked likely that Moshir would resign. Indeed, this might be the origin
of the rumours after the 1921 Coup that Sayyed Zia had first contacted Sepahsalar-e Tonokaboni (Mohammad Vali Khan Khal'atbari), on behalf of the
British legation, to lead the Coup. According to this legend, Sepahsalar might
have agreed to play that role, but when he understood that the Sayyed was to
join his cabinet he declined the offer in contempt, and it was then decided that
the Sayyed himself should lead the Coup.[72]

The legend might be due to either of the following confusions. It is not
impossible, though not very likely, that the Sayyed had first sounded out Sepahsalar – a much stronger man than Sepahdar – as a possible successor for
Moshir, and, when the possibility of the Sayyed himself joining his cabinet had
been mentioned, the old and extremely proud man – a very large landowner,
former supreme military commander, prime minister, etc. – had rejected the
offer with disdain. Alternatively, the legend may simply be due to a confusion,
not infrequent in contemporary historiography, between Sepahdar, on the one
hand, and Sepahsalar, on the other. The latter's title used to be Sepahdar until
he was given the much more exclusive title of Sepahsalar after he successfully
led the Gilan revolutionary forces which captured Tehran in 1909. The tide of
Sepahdar was then given to Fathollah Khan Akbar, who used to be known as
Sardar Mansur. The fact that the Sayyed sounded out the latter for premiership
but, for the reason mentioned above, himself failed to join his cabinet, might

have been the origin of the bizarre legend which certainly has no veracity in regard to the Coup.

At any rate, after his appointment, Sepahdar, a well-meaning but simple and weak man, increasingly relied on Sayyed Zia as a go-between, especially whenever he wanted to plead with Norman about his government's parlous financial position. The Sayyed, like many others, regarded Sepahdar's cabinet as a caretaker government during the search for a more permanent solution to the country's political crisis. He told Bahar at the time, referring to Sepahdar, 'none of these men are worth much. We ourselves ought to do something'.[73]

It was at this time that Sardar Mo'azzam-e Khorasani – later Abdolhossein Taimurtash – got closer to Sayyed Zia and became involved in the search for a political settlement. He was about 40 years old, born in Khorasan into a rich and influential family, a modernist and pragmatic nationalist who had seen military training in Russia, spoke Russian as well as French, was very intelligent, able, good-looking, arrogant, and with few moral scruples. He had a reputation for harshness – even cruelty – which had been enhanced by his governorship of Gilan under Vosuq.[74] He was destined to play an important role both in the ascendancy of Reza Khan to the throne and in the establishment of his dictatorship in the first crucial years of his reign, before being destroyed by him when Reza Shah's arbitrary rule commenced in earnest.

The basic, well-hidden weakness of Taimurtash's personality revealed itself only when he fell from the pinnacles of power in 1932. Legends regarding 'the reasons' for his demise do not bear serious examination. He died without being disloyal to Reza Shah. His fate was consistent with those of the long line of able and strong ministers throughout the history of Iran's arbitrary rule (see chapter one).

Sepahdar's ministry got off on the wrong foot. The dismissal of Starosselski and the virtual takeover of the Cossacks by British officers, the resignation of Moshir in protest, the formation of the new cabinet with Sayyed Zia's active role as go-between, and Curzon's speech against Moshir in the Lords, had left little room for the political public to doubt that this was all British policy directed from London, and that Sepahdar was no more than a British agent. Suddenly, the news of the 'corruption money' paid to the triumvirate over the 1919 agreement exploded like a bombshell in Tehran.

In reply to a parliamentary question in the Commons, the minister of state at the Foreign Office admitted that some of the £2 million associated with the 1919 Agreement had already been paid to the triumvirate before the Agreement had been approved by the Majlis. The implications were clear, and it shows the strength of opposition to Curzon's policy within the British government that the matter should have been leaked. At the time, Reuters reports, which were the only reliable source of international news in Iran, used to be vetted by the British legation in Tehran to prevent or delay the release of particularly embarrassing news.

Norman claimed that the matter 'unluckily escaped my notice', so that the full news 'has appeared in the Persian press'. It is more likely that he purposefully let the cat out of the bag, thus exposing the triumvirate as well as undermining Curzon's policy in a single stroke[75] (for details of the exposure and its impact in Iran, see chapter four). The British personnel in Iran, both diplomatic and military, had known about the matter and strongly disapproved of it as well as of the government of the triumvirate. The exposure left little chance, such as there was, of the Agreement being approved by a future Majlis, because scarcely any deputy would now risk being accused of having received British money by voting for it.[76] That, at any rate, was what Taimurtash told Norman.[77]

It is also likely that Norman released the news specifically in order to expose and discredit Firuz, and spoil his chances for a comeback. Firuz was still in Europe, frequently visiting London, and Norman might have guessed that Curzon's hostility to Moshir's government had, in no small measure, been due to the influence of Firuz, whose bid to remain foreign minister under Moshir had been unsuccessful. Besides, Norman must have known that the young, intelligent, rich, ambitious and ultra-pragmatic politician was biding his time and preparing the ground for forming a government in the near future. Neither Norman nor his colleagues in Tehran liked or trusted Firuz, largely because of his previous record, including his great unpopularity with the public, who more or less saw him – unfairly – as a puppet of the British government. In forming this opinion about Firuz, Sayyed Zia must also have played a part, since he did not like Firuz and did not rate his own chances highly under a Firuz regime, apparently because of the latter's social snobbery.[78]

But for the time being there was the question of keeping Sepahdar's cabinet afloat, not least in its ability to meet its urgent financial obligations. This led to the same tug-of-war between Norman and Curzon as before. Upon the formation of the cabinet, Norman asked that the monthly subsidy of 350,000 tomans, which was due to be stopped at the end of October, to be paid for two more months, and a part of it would be used by Ironside for the 'maintenance and re-organisation of the Cossack Division.'[79] Curzon replied that British financial constraints would not allow that, especially as there was the continuing financial commitment to the South Persia Rifles. They could pay 60,000 tomans for the Cossack Division, and the Iranian government would somehow have to find the balance of 290,000 tomans, while the SPR's were going to be disbanded at the end of 1920.[80]

Norman's understanding of Curzon's attitude had been different. He had promised Sepahdar accordingly and now thought he would be accused by him of bad faith. He was horrified at the thought of a premature closure of SPR, and painted the darkest picture of what would follow if these policies were not revised. But, rather than attracting sympathy from Curzon, it provoked him into the comment that 'Mr Norman and we are now beginning to reap the fruit of his policy'.[81] Norman might well have thought the same about the fruit of Curzon's own policy. The argument over money was, however, to continue in various forms, until Armitage-Smith's skilful negotiations in London with the

Anglo–Iranian Oil Company bore fruit, and agreed arrears due to Iran began to be paid by the company.[82]

Predictably, another – and related – thorny problem was the issue of the completion of the elections, the opening of the Majlis, and its pronouncement on the wretched agreement. As Norman realized and kept explaining, there was virtually no question that the Majlis would meet before the end of the year. Some of the elected provincial deputies were even refusing the summons to Tehran on feeble excuses,[83] for fear of being associated with the Agreement. On the other hand, it is clear that Curzon, being now in a weak position in the cabinet over his Persian Policy and the Agreement, wished to be rid of the whole problem quickly, one way or another. He had lost much credibility among his colleagues in dealing with it, was suspicious of Norman as well as the Iranians, and had little energy left to consider fresh approaches – which Norman did not tire of proposing one after the other – in the hope of finding a possible as well as successful outcome to the impasse.

Norman even put to Curzon the suggestion by Sepahdar that they might resort to bribery. Sepahdar had argued that most of the influential opponents of the Agreement cared only about lining their own pockets, and if something like a million tomans was distributed among them they would come into line. Sepahdar himself did not want any money, and insisted that it should be distributed by Norman himself. Norman does not seem to have been much in favour of paying corruption money, but passed on the idea to Curzon.[84] It 'filled' Curzon with 'great surprise'. After all that had been said about the money paid to the triumvirate, he said, they were now proposing bribery. The British government wished to secure the Agreement only by 'open and legitimate procedure', and unless a decision was pronounced on the Agreement by the end of the year, it would be regarded as having lapsed.[85] Norman did not insist, but once again defended both himself and Sepahdar.[86]

The creation of an Iranian military force under the executive command of British officers was the main preoccupation of both Norman and Ironside, who were mindful of the fact that Norperforce must leave in the spring, and firmly believed that, without an effective Iranian force to face 'invasion' from Gilan, the government would collapse, and anarchy would be followed by a soviet government at least in the northern regions of Iran. A couple of weeks after Sepahdar's cabinet was formed, Norman and Dickson – in his official capacity as head of the British Military Mission – presented Sepahdar with a detailed plan to organize an army under the authority of the Iranian ministry of war, but with British executive command. It was to be raised to the strength of 7000 by the spring of 1921, organized and trained in Qazvin, and officered by a select group of Cossack and Central Brigade officers. The Central Brigade was a poorly trained force in Tehran for keeping the peace, and the unselected officers were to be absorbed in it.

Sepahdar was wary of the unpopularity of the scheme, given that Moshir had resigned precisely over that issue. But Norman did not relent, and took reinforcements with him to the prime minister in the shape of Ironside and Huddleston. Sepahdar retreated, suggesting that Norman would put his proposal in writing so that he could take it to the Shah, and suggested that he calls an assembly of the notables – something which had had precedent – to decide the issue in the absence of the Majlis.[87]

The Assembly met shortly afterwards, and Norman's letter to Sepahdar was read out at the request of its members. The Assembly did not feel competent to decide on such an important issue, and urged the quick opening of the Majlis to pronounce on that and, indeed, on the Agreement. Norman was pleased that the tone of the debate had been moderate, and that no one had made anti-British statements. He also felt that it was 'perhaps lucky' that his proposal had not been approved, in view of the fact that (as noted above) he had meanwhile learned from Curzon that Britain would not finance the project.[88] Dawlat-Abadi, himself a member of the Assembly, gives a detailed account of its proceedings, which reveal the extent of the suspicion with which most of its members had viewed Norman's proposal, although he too does not report any openly anti-British remarks being made in the meeting.[89]

This did not deter Ironside from going ahead with the task within the existing framework and resources. It may be recalled that, while he was organizing the dismissal of Starosselski and British control of the Cossacks, he had asked GHQ in Baghdad and the War Office whether he or Dickson or another officer should be in command of the Cossacks. The War Office wrote that he should leave the matter to Dickson, as this was a Foreign Office matter and Dickson had been on loan to the latter in his mission in Tehran.[90] At the end of October, Ironside wrote to Dickson that he would be 'at the head of all work of that kind', that General Lamont and Colonel Huddleston were going to Qazvin, that Colonel Smyth was already there, and that Dickson should also pay a visit to talk to the 'new commander of the Cossack Division', that is, the nonentity Sardar Homayun.[91]

In practice, Dickson, who was not privy to Ironside's plans, did not have a role in the matter, Lieutenant-Colonel Henry Smyth, frequently assisted by Haig and Huddleston, became the executive commander of the Cossacks at Aqababa, and began their training and reorganization into a more effective force. This did not require any formal approval by the Iranian government, because Sardar Homayun – who had no active role in the matter, and was to be eased out of Qazvin later and returned to Tehran – was nominally commander of the Division, and the Cossacks were kept in Aqababa, well out of public sight. By late January 1921, Norman was to report that Smyth 'has for past two months or so been unofficially and almost secretly working amongst Cossacks, with results that their efficiency has been greatly increased'.[92]

Back in December 1920, however, Norman and his Iranian advisers had not given up the idea of creating an Iranian army, independently of the Agreement, with British military and financial support. After the assembly of notables refused to sanction Norman's proposal, Zia and Taimurtash talked firmly to

Sepahdar, warning him of the disaster that would ensue when Norperforce and SPR were withdrawn, and convincing him to send a note to Norman saying that the Iranian government accepted his proposal for organising a new force. But their plan was much more bold and comprehensive. They believed that, to be effective, such a force had to be 15,000 strong and on a more permanent footing, rather than 7000 on a year's contract as Norman had suggested. They were also thinking of reorganizing the police and gendarmerie, and incorporating SPR after the departure of its British officers. There was to be a cabinet reshuffle as well, with the Sayyed and Taimurtash themselves joining the cabinet (the Sayyed no doubt taking off his little turban and replacing it by a *kolah*, as he was later to do when he formed a cabinet after the Coup). The proviso was that Britain would supply a £1 million loan for financing the project. Norman was very excited by Sepahdar's final agreement to this project, which, after all, had been essentially his own brainchild. The whole of the assembly of notables had been called to approve of something less than this, and he pleaded with Curzon to agree to it.[93]

Curzon received the suggestion with 'bewilderment'. The scheme of creating a 15,000 strong force paid by the British government 'would be impossible to defend'. Two cabinets had been 'torpedoed' and now the third one was to be 'jettisoned' so that a reinforced cabinet 'may feel strong enough to arrest its opponents' – the very procedure that Norman had denounced as the greatest crime of Vosuq's government:

> Persia is now paying the penalty for her own vacillation and folly, and, if she cannot extricate herself by the only legitimate means, namely by constitutional action of Mejilis summoned for the purpose, no other expedient can save the situation.[94]

Curzon's emphasis on proper legal procedures reflects both his own bad conscience about the past and, perhaps more specifically, the criticisms he had had to endure recently on that account. But, perhaps more important, he was unable to grasp the significance of what Norman had achieved in obtaining Sepahdar's approval for the proposal. He had become 'very suspicious' of the Iranian government's 'financial tactics',[95] and doubtful if any of their proposed plans would in fact see the light of the day even if the required money was paid. He was also suspicious of the reports he was receiving about the progress of Moshaver al-Mamlek's negotiations for a treaty in Moscow,[96] the nullification by Iran of the Khoshtaria concessions, and Iran's encouragement of Americans, as he believed, 'to fish in troubled waters'.[97] Yet, if he had approved this scheme, it might have altered the course of Iranian history, and with it Anglo–Iranian relations.

Norman defended himself and Sepahdar's government, saying that Curzon's suspicions were unfounded, that there were no financial tactics, that the negotiations with Moscow were a direct consequence of Iran's military weakness, which

Britain was not willing or able to remedy, and that the insistence on the deadline for the Agreement at the end of the year would have disastrous results.[98] Yet he kept laying emphasis on the Zia-Taimurtash-Norman proposal, which he believed would redeem the situation and allay Curzon's suspicions and fears.[99] He must therefore have been deeply disappointed to receive Curzon's attack on himself and on the latter proposal. There was no analogy between the present proposal and what happened under Vosuq, he wrote, because the idea was to 'seize a few terrorists and agitators'; he had not torpedoed two cabinets, and he was fully supporting the existing one, to 'which addition of two men of courage and energy [i.e. Zia and Taimurtash] can only strengthen, even if it leads to resignation of one or two of present Ministers, a contingency by no means certain'.[100]

On the same day that this telegram was dispatched, but three days before it was received by Curzon, Norman received a letter from the India Office informing him of the government of India's decision to disband the two British levy corps in Khorasan and Sistan, unless they received contrary instructions by that same day. Curzon sourly minuted: 'if the Govt of India like deliberately to expose the E. borders of Persia, I should let them do so. The result in a short time will be a fine chaos'.[101] It both indicates the position of his Persian Policy within the British government and empire, and his own resignation to the fact that it was almost completely in ruins. Hence perhaps his final, short, and probably fatal rejection of Norman's scheme in the following, single-sentence, telegram:

> You should defer taking action with regard to formation of a force under British officers until the Medjliss meets, and either accepts or rejects the agreement, which provides for the formation of a uniform force under such officers.[102]

It was after the failure of all these various schemes and proposals that thoughts began to turn towards the creation of a strong government in Iran outside the existing framework, which would be able to face the Gilan revolutionaries and bring a measure of stability to the country. On 20 December, the day after Curzon sent his final rejection of the Zia-Taimurtash-Norman scheme, G. P. Churchill, at the Foreign Office, made a 'gloomy forecast' of the short-term prospects, which included the likelihood of 'a Bolshevik menace in the Spring' when Norperforce was firmly due to leave the country. He concluded that 'all idea of governing Persia with and through a Mejliss, or by employing the advanced Democrats should, at this dangerous stage in Persia's affairs, be entirely abandoned'. A government of strong men, 'whose names are known and feared among the great tribes', should be formed, led by someone such as Ain al-Dawleh:

> The broad lines could be laid down, however, for the guidance of H.M Minister [i.e. Norman] who will be best able to carry out the details according to local requirements and the fluctuations of the situation.[103]

South-western tribes were to be contacted directly in preparation for the defence of Iran's central and northern regions in case of chaos or the establishment of a soviet government in the north.[104] This was immediately echoed in a wire to Norman from Curzon, who wrote that 'the only thing now left to be done is to consider how best to deal with the situation probable by a complete collapse in the north, and to secure our interests elsewhere [in the country]'.[105] Obviously, this was not the line of thinking that Jed to the 1921 Coup.

Ironside, unlike Norman, was not responsible to Curzon and the Foreign Office. His mission from the War Office and GHQ in Baghdad was to deal with the situation as best he could, so long as he did not take any decision which might require, or possibly lead to a need for, reinforcements from Baghdad. Thus his thoughts began to be directed towards a 'military dictatorship which would impose sufficient order on the Persian armed forces to prevent a Soviet invasion'.[106] He wrote in a 'situation report' to the War Office on 8 December that: 'That would solve many difficulties and enable us to depart in peace and honour'.[107] A few days after the dispatch of the 'situation report', Ironside was summoned by Haldane to Baghdad and spent three working days there, 12 to 15 December, reviewing the situation and the time and manner of the Norperforce's withdrawal, with Ironside being 'treated very much as an expert in risky withdrawals'.[108] On 15 December, Winston Churchill, Secretary of State for War, said in the House of Commons that 'we are trying to rouse Persia of its responsibility', and that 'we are giving Persia another and final chance to put their house in order by the spring' [when Norperforce was set to leave Iran].[109] Churchill was referring to the fact that, under pressure from the Foreign Office, they had agreed to delay the departure of Norperforce to April 1921, though Churchill is likely to have been aware of the recent communications between Ironside, Haldane and the War Office. This provoked another round of argument between Norman and Curzon, Norman claiming that the Iranians were indeed ready to take responsibility by agreeing to organize a new military force for which Britain would not lend them money, and Curzon retorting with his familiar list of grievances.[110]

As 1921 rapidly approached, plans and decisions began to take shape regarding the Iranian situation, about which Curzon and the Foreign Office had no idea and the War Office did not care, as long as it meant that Norperforce would leave Iran in April 1921 at the latest. So strong were their views that they described '*the necessity for the early reduction of expenditure by the withdrawal of military forces as entirely over-ruling any considerations for the internal security of the country after our troops have left*'.[111]

Sayyed Zia and his close lieutenants in the gendarmerie were in touch with Smyth, Haig, Smart and others, hoping to be able to use the Cossacks in Aqababa in organising a Coup before Norperforce left the country (see chapter eight). Smyth was working closely with Ironside in giving shape and discipline to the Cossacks. Ironside and Norman, each in his own way, were still trying to beat the deadline without leaving either chaos or a soviet government behind them. In the end, Norman failed in his own approach and had to acquiesce in Ironside's surgical solution.

Notes

1 See James Balfour, *Recent Happenings in Persia* (Edinburgh: Blackwood & Sons, 1922), p. 209.
2 Ironside's manuscript diary quoted in Richard H. Ullman, *Anglo–Soviet Relations*, vol. 3, The *Anglo–Soviet Accord* (Princeton: Princeton University Press, 1974), p. 379.
3 Norman to Curzon, 11/8/20, *BDFP*, vol. xiii, no. 539.
4 See for example Ebrahim Fakhra'i, *Sardar-e Jangal* (Tehran: Javidan, 1978), and Balfour, *Recent Happenings in Persia.*
5 Norman to Curzon, 26/8/20, *BDFP*, no. 543, and *ibid.*, n. 3.
6 See for example Martin Sicker, *The Bear and the Lion* (New York: Praeger, 1988), chapter 3.
7 See General Ahmad Amir Ahmadi, *Khaterart-e Nakhostin Sepahbod-e Iran*, (ed.) Gholam-hossein Zargari-nezhad (Tehran: Bonyad-e Mostaz 'fan-e Iran, 1994), vol. 1, pp. 146–47; Fakhra'i, *Sardar-e Jangal*, p. 304; Balfour, *Recent Happenings in Persia*, pp. 201–02.
8 See Fakhra'i, and Balour, *ibid.*
9 Fakhra'i, *ibid.*, p. 304.
10 *Ibid.*
11 See for example Balfour, *Recent Happenings.*
12 Norman to Curzon, 29/8/20, *BDFP*, no. 544.
13 Norman to Curzon, 11/9/20, *ibid.*, no. 549.
14 Amir Ahmadi, *Khaterat*, vol., pp. 140–53.
15 Norman to Curzon, 11/9/20, *BDFP*, no. 549.
16 Curzon to Norman, 15/9/20, *ibid.*, no. 551.
17 Curzon to Norman, 13/9/20, *ibid.*, No. 550, n. 2 and n. 3.
18 *Ibid.*
19 See for example Curzon to Cox, 9/4/20, *ibid.*, no. 404.
20 Curzon to Cox, 10/4/20, *ibid.*, no. 406.
21 Norman to Curzon, 18/8/20, *ibid.*, no. 541.
22 Curzon to Norman, 21/8/20, *ibid.*, no. 542.
23 Curzon to Norman, 30/8/20, *ibid.*, no. 546.
24 Norman to Curzon, 6/10/20, *ibid.*, no. 560.
25 Norman to Curzon, 3/9/20, *ibid.*, no. 547.
26 Curzon to Norman, 10/9/20, *ibid.*, no. 548.
27 Norman to Curzon, 3/9/20, *ibid.*, no. 547.
28 Norman to Curzon, 21/9/20, *ibid.*, no. 554.
29 Curzon to Norman, 30/9/20, *ibid.*, no. 558.
30 Norman to Curzon, 19/10/20, *ibid.*, no. 563.
31 *Ibid.*, n. 4.
32 Curzon to Norman, 20/10/20, *ibid.*, no. 565.
33 Norman to Curzon, 16/9/20, *ibid.*, no. 552.
34 Curzon to Norman, 20/9/20, *ibid.*, no. 553.
35 Norman to Curzon, 24/9/20, *ibid.*, no. 555.
36 Norman to Curzon, 25/9/20, *ibid.*, no. 556.
37 Curzon to Norman, 29/9/20, *ibid.*, no. 557.
38 See Ullman, *The Anglo–Soviet Accord*, and Denis Wright, *The English Amongst the Persians* (London: Heinemann, 1977).
39 See Mo'asseseh-ye Motale'at-e Farhangi, *Khaterat-e Serri-ye Ironside* (Tehran: Rasa, 1994).

40 See, *High Road to Command, The Diaries of Major-General Sir Edmund Ironside, 1920-1922*, (ed.) Lord Ironside (London: Leo Cooper, 1972), p. 118.

41 *Ibid.*, p. 128.

42 Ullman, *The Anglo–Soviet Accord*, based on Ironside's entries in his MS diary for 28 and 29 September 1920.

43 W.O. to Haldane, 6/10/20, *BDFP*, no. 561

44 Ironside, *High Road to Command*, pp. 137–38.

45 Ironside to Haldane, 9/10/20, W.O. 158/687.

46 *Ibid.*

47 *Ibid.*

48 *Ibid.*

49 *Ibid.*

50 Ironside, *High Road to Command*, pp, 140–41.

51 Manjil to Norperforce, 22/10/20, W.O. 158/697.

52 *Ibid.*

53 See Yahya Dawlat-Abadi, *Hayat-e Yahya* (Tehran: Attar and Ferdawsi, 1963), vol. 4, chapter, 17.

54 Ironside to Haldane, 24/10/20, W.O. 158/687.

55 Quoted from Ironside's entry in his MS diary for 24 October, 1920, in Ullman, *The Anglo–Soviet Accord*, p. 381.

56 See Nasrollah Seifpur, Fatemi, *A'ineh-ye Ebrat* (London: Nashr-e Ketab, 1989), chapter 4.

57 Norman to Curzon, 25/9/20, *BDFP*, no. 566.

58 Norman to Curzon, 25/9/20, F.O. 371/4914.

59 Norman to Curzon, 26/10/20, F.O. 371/4914.

60 Norman to Curzon 27/10/20, *BDFP*, no. 570.

61 Ironside, *The Road to High Command*, p. 145.

62 See Amir Ahmadi, *Khaterat*, pp. 152–57; Ullman, *The Anglo–Soviet Accord*, p. 382.

63 Norman to Curzon, 1/11/20, *BDFP*, no. 574.

64 *Ibid.*

65 Quoted from Ironside's entry for 31 October in his MS diary, in Ullman, *The Anglo–Soviet Accord*, p. 383.

66 Norperforce to GHQ, 21/1/21, W.O. 158/684.

67 Curzon to Norman, 29/10/20, *BDFP*, no. 573.

68 *Ibid.* For Norman's defence of his volte face, see his telegram to Curzon on 5/11/20, *BDFP*, no. 577.

69 See Homa Katouzian, 'Nationalist Trends in Iran, 1921–1926', *International Journal of Middle East Studies*, 1979.

70 See Dawlat-Abadi, *Hayat-e Yahya*, vol. 4, chapter 19.

71 See Malek al-Sho'ara Bahar, *Tarikh-e Mokhtasar-e Ahzab-e Siyasi dar Iran*, vol. 1 (Tehran: Jibi, 1978); *Mokatebat-e Firuz Mirza*, (eds.) Mansureh Ettehadiyeh (Nezam Mafi) and Sirus Sa'dvandiyan, vol. i (Tehran: Nashr-e Tarikh-e Iran, 1990).

72 Various versions of this legend are to be found in numerous memoirs and accounts. For an elaborate form of the story, see, for example, Abdollah Mostawfi, *Sharh-e Zendegani-ye, Man*, vol. 3 (Tehran: Zavvar, 1964), pp. 202–05; Hossein Makki, *Tarikh-e Bistsaleh-ye Iran* (Tehran: Elmi, 1995), vol. 1, pp. 173–77.

73 See Bahar, *Tarikh-e Mokhtasar*, p. 64.

74 See for example Fakhra'i, *Sardar-e Jangal*, 'Taimurtash' in Ebrahim Khajeh Nuri, *Bazigaran-e Asr-e Tala'i* (Tehran: Jibi,1978); *Yaddasht-ha-ye Doktor Qasem Ghani*, (ed.) Cyrus Ghani, vol. 1 (Tehran: Zavvar), pp. 168–77; Baqer Agheli, *Taimurtash dar Sahneh-ye Siyasat-e Iran* (Tehran: Elmi, 1992); *Khaterat-e Sadr al-Ashraf*, (Tehran: Vahid), p. 240, who also recounts the execution of five innocent men by Taimurtash in Gilan.

75 Norman to Curzon, 19/11/20, *BDFP*, no. 582.

76 Norman to Curzon, 25/11/20, *ibid.*, no. 588.

77 Ibid, and Norman to Curzon, 7/12/20, no. 599.

78 On the personal relationship of Zia and Firuz, see Bahar, *Tarikh-e Mokhtasar.*

79 Norman to Curzon, 28/10/20, *BDFP,* no. 571.

80 Curzon to Norman, 9/11/20, *ibid.,* no. 584.

81 Norman to Curzon, 25/11/20, *ibid.,* no. 586, and Curzon's minute in n. 4.

82 Curzon to Norman, 1/1/21, *ibid.,* no. 625.

83 Norman to Curzon, 5/12/20, *ibid.,* no. 597.

84 Norman to Curzon, 2/12/20, *ibid.,* no. 594.

85 Curzon o Norman, 8/12/20, *ibid.,* no. 604.

86 Norman to Curzon, 12/12/20, *ibid.,* no. 610.

87 Norman to Curzon, *ibid.,* no. 586, and n. 4.

88 Norman to Curzon, 1/12/20, *ibid.,* no. 591.

89 See Dawlat-Abadi, *Hayat-e Yahya,* vol. 4, chapter 21. See also Stephanie Cronin, *The Army and the Creation of the Pahlavi State in Iran* (London and New York: I.B.Tauris, 1997), chapter 2.

90 Haldane to Ironside, 1/11/20, W.O. 158/687.

91 Ironside to Dickson, 30/10/20, W.O. 158/687.

92 Norman to Curzon, 24/1/21, F.O. 371/6400.

93 Norman to Curzon, 7/12/20, *BDFP,* no. 599.

94 Curzon to Norman, 10/12/20, *ibid.,* no. 607.

95 Curzon to Norman, 8/12/20, *ibid.,* no. 603.

96 Curzon to Norman, 26/11/20, *ibid.,* no. 589.

97 Curzon to Norman, 8/12/20, *ibid.,* no. 603.

98 Norman to Curzon, 11/12/20, *ibid.,* no. 609, and 12/12/20, no. 610.

99 *Ibid.,* no. 610.

100 Norman to Curzon, 13/12/20, *ibid.,* no. 611.

101 Curzon to Norman, 16/12/20, *ibid.,* no. 612, and n. 1.

102 Curzon to Norman, 19/12/20, *ibid.,* no. 614.

103 Memorandum by G. P. Churchill, 20/12/20, *ibid.,* no. 616.

104 *Ibid.*

105 Curzon to Norman, 23/12/20, *ibid.,* no. 618.

106 See Ullman, *The Anglo–Soviet Accord,* p. 384.

107 Quoted in Ullman, *ibid.,* from a copy of Ironside's 'situation report' in his Ms diary.

108 See Ironside, *High Road to Command,* pp. 154–55.

109 Norman to Curzon, 21/12/20, *BDFP,* no. 617.

110 Curzon to Norman, *ibid.,* no. 617, 23/12/20, no. 618; and Norman to Curzon, 27/12/20, no. 622.

111 War Office to Haldane, 23/12/20, *ibid.,* no. 619.

8

The road to the 1921 Coup

As 1921 dawned, conflict, disorder and the threat of disintegration were coming to a peak, comparable, in many ways, to the last months of Shah Soltan Hossein's reign and the eclipse of the Safavids in the first couple of decades of the seventeenth century (see chapter one). Soltan Hossein himself fell in 1722, but his line survived until 1736, when Nader became Shah. Ahmad Shah, on the other hand, did not lose his throne to the forces of chaos or revolution, but four years later, to the man who – rather like Nader – stamped them out (see chapters ten and eleven). What happened in 1921, therefore, was not new: it was typical of Iran's long and troubled history, of a prolonged crisis eventually leading to hopes that 'a strong man' would save the situation and restore order and stability (see chapter one).

Yet, early in January 1921, it was by no means clear what fate lay in store for Iran. The Gilan revolutionaries and their Soviet allies had shown little sign of activity outside their own domain. Iranian officials, led by Moshaver al-Mamalek (Ansari) were still negotiating for a comprehensive treaty in Moscow. It could have borne fruit sooner than it did (a few days after the Coup), had it not been for Tehran's deference – for a short but crucial period – to both Norman's and Curzon's suspicions of Soviet motives. If the same accord had been reached and signed before February, the Coup might well have been avoided.

The Cossacks near Qazvin were under the command of Colonel Smyth, who was also their paymaster, although Reza Khan was increasingly allowed to play the role of field commander. In Tehran, the Shah was fearful both of the Russians and of the British, fearful of losing his throne – perhaps even his life – and wished to leave the scene as quickly as possible by another visit to Europe, to recover from his 'mental fatigue'. The government was virtually dependent on the British legation for its day-to-day decisions, largely because of its reliance on Norperforce to defend Tehran against a much feared attack from Gilan. Curzon and the Foreign Office had by now given up almost all hope that the Majlis, even if called, would approve the Agreement, and – along with India and Baghdad – were keen to secure the central and southern parts of the country as a last resort, if Tehran fell to the Gilan forces. The War Office was set on withdrawing Norperforce in April, and had no inclination to help save Curzon's Persian Policy. Nor did the Treasury, who believed that their money had been wasted, and were in any case under pressure from the public to cut such expenses. India, like Norman, believed that the British government should publicly repudiate the 1919 Agreement. Nothing angered Curzon more at the time than this suggestion.

The policy crisis

The whole of British policy had been thrown into a melting pot, with various suggestions being made but no clear course of action being followed. Late in December, G. P. Churchill in London had circulated the idea (see chapter seven) that a strong conservative government might be formed to hold the fort either in Tehran, or, if that was not feasible, in the centre and south of the country, leaving the northern parts, including Tehran, to a soviet government or to chaos.

Both Norman and Ironside were absolutely convinced that the withdrawal of Norperforce in April would be followed by a full-scale 'invasion' across Manjil and on to Tehran. 'All Persians and most Europeans whom I have consulted', Norman wired Curzon on 8 January, 'have expressed conviction that whether Persian–Soviet treaty is signed or not, removal of our troops will be immediately followed by a Bolshevik occupation, or at least by arrival of numerous Bolshevik agents', followed by anarchy, lawlessness and a panic flight of anyone who had anything to lose.[1] An attack on a Norperforce outpost by Gilan forces (many of them Russian) seemed to confirm this view, although Ironside saw the attack itself as an attempt to test the Norperforce resolve. In fact, Norperforce inflicted heavy casualties on the assailants while losing none on their side, took 21 prisoners, one of them Georgian, one Armenian and the rest 'Russians of 244th regiment'. This strengthened Ironside's opinion that a 'revolutionary army will come on when we evacuate Kasvin, and that they have no intention of evacuating Gilan according to their agreement'.[2] The reference is to the draft agreement between Iran and the Soviet Union, which was still being negotiated.

According to a Norperforce intelligence report, the Gilan forces were about 7000 in number (including Soviet fighters) with many heavy guns, field guns, machine guns and transport facilities.[3] They had also received intelligence that 30,000 Soviet forces had assembled in Baku, which they believed were intended to support the Gilan forces when the march to Tehran began. On the other hand, the Soviets said they refused to withdraw their forces from Gilan because they feared that Norperforce would then attack Baku.[4] It was, as Norman noted, preposterous that Norperforce would take such action, especially in view of its numerical weakness, and lack of necessary equipment and naval support. Yet it shows the degree of mistrust and miscalculation from which all the parties suffered. On the one hand, Norperforce had been forbidden to move towards Rasht for fear that this might result in the intervention of official Soviet forces, which the British cabinet was not prepared to contemplate at any cost. On the other hand, the Soviet Union was fearful of the possibility of a British attack across the border into the Azerbaijan Republic.

Norman, Ironside, the Shah and almost everyone else concerned in Iran were also suffering from the same sense of high suspicion, which led them into misunderstanding and miscalculation. When the draft Irano–Soviet agreement negotiated by Moshaver al-Mamalek reached Tehran, Norman – and possibly many of the Iranians concerned – felt it was too good to be true. The Soviet Union had given almost all the former Tsarist privileges away, as they had repeatedly said in their earlier unilateral declarations, and were demanding merely that their Caspian fishing concession be renewed when it fell due. The only serious bone of contention was the secret agreement, which they proposed to accompany the open one.

This proposed the right for the Soviet Union to send troops to Iran if British forces attacked it from the country. It also gave them the right to demand the dismissal of any Briton employed by Iran, if he was actively hostile towards the Soviet Union. Lastly, it proposed that Iranians should also grant a general amnesty to the Insurgents, and allow trade unions to be formed and socialist politics to be pursued, so long as their activities were lawful.[5] Most significantly, however, the Russians said nothing about the 1919 Agreement, which shows that the safeguards they were demanding was on the assumption that the Agreement would be upheld. This was rejected by Sepahdar on Norman's advice, on the flimsy argument that, as a member of the League of Nations, Iran should not enter any secret agreements. Iranian notables, including some leading popular politicians supported Sepahdar in rejecting the secret clauses, and therefore the draft proposal.[6]

Curzon was somewhat less suspicious, although he generally shared Norman's 'scepticism as to Soviet motive'. Yet it is remarkable that he was ready to envisage a simultaneous withdrawal of Norperforce and Soviet forces in Gilan, although he would not yet contemplate entering into a tripartite agreement with Iran and the Soviet Union to arrange this, as their 'intentions and undertakings', he felt, 'were equally to be mistrusted.'[7]

The Soviet government were offended by Iran's lukewarm response to their liberal advances, complaining that Iran was 'entirely subservient to Great Britain.'[8] The Iranians insisted that the Soviet forces in Gilan should be withdrawn at the very time that the agreement was signed. The Soviet Union, now so obviously eager to normalize her relations with Iran (and accommodate Britain as well) said in the end that their forces were ready to evacuate Iran, but suggested that 'as each of the parties makes the withdrawal of its troops dependent on that of the troops of the other, a mixed commission should be appointed to arrange the matter immediately'. At long last, Norman seemed to believe the Soviet intentions, but by then it was ten days before the Coup commenced.[9]

Back in January, the fear of a serious 'Bolshevik invasion' – that is, an attack from Gilan – was still very much alive and keenly felt by all concerned. Curzon kept repeating that the Agreement had lapsed, that they should try and safeguard British interests in the direction of the centre and south, and that there was no point in wasting any more time on the possibility of reorganizing Iranian forces under British officers.[10] He was now inclined to agree with Norman that if the Majlis met it would be unlikely to approve the Agreement. 'The time limit which I have given the Persian Government on various occasions for the acceptance of the agreement by the Medjiliss, viz., 31st December, has expired', he wired Norman:

I do not, however, see any necessity, to inform Persian Government officially that His Majesty's Government regard the agreement as at an end. We signed it and were prepared to carry it out. The Persians, however, put it in abeyance, in which state it is at present, and to judge by all the omens is likely to remain.[11]

This seems to have left the door not entirely closed. But Curzon's attitude rapidly hardened. He refused either to annul the Agreement publicly and formally – the failure of which, he insisted emotionally, must be put squarely at Iran's door – or to contemplate a modified form which would be more acceptable to popular sentiment in the country.

Alone among the participants appraising the situation, the government of India had a clear, realistic and workable policy, which was entirely consistent with the view they had held when the Agreement was being negotiated, and was a suitable remedy for its disastrous effects which they had anticipated. They did not share the fears of the others, and specifically Norman, about the Soviet intentions. 'It is not for us to intervene', wrote the Viceroy to Montague, 'but we cannot help feeling that Persia's best chance is to gamble on the sincerity of Soviet proposals.'[12] They argued that, rather than making Britain popular for trying to help Iran as well as safeguarding their own interest, the Agreement had in fact led to suspicions in Iran, Afghanistan and among Muslim Indians that it was designed to submerge the Muslim people of the Middle East, while the Soviet Union, an officially atheist power, was now being seen as their liberator. They believed that the Agreement should be formally repudiated by Britain, and, if the Iranians so desired, a financial adviser be supplied to them. Both the South Persia Rifles and the Cossacks should be handed over to Iran, 'to be officered as she likes', to keep internal order. Regarding any external threats, 'our own disappearance into the background will rob Bolshevism of her one valid excuse, and possibly remove temptation for open aggression':

These proposals are devoid of attractiveness of elaborate proposals under the Anglo–Persian Agreement. But they have at least this to commend them. They are designed to square with the facts. To us [the government of India], at any rate, it seems that we have failed because we have tried to do too much … Persian nationalism, however, has proved too strong for Persia to accept this willingly. In short we should leave Persia to work out her own salvation, simply providing her with assistance which she needs most, and which is the only assistance she is likely, of her own free will, to accept from us, *viz*, a Financial Adviser.[13]

This telegram had been sent as early as 6 December, prompting Norman to reply, in apparent disagreement, directly to the Viceroy, although it is clear he is complaining that if Curzon had not bamboozled Sepahdar's eventual agreement to raise a force under British officers, the situation both for Iran and for the Agreement would have been very different. He wrote in conclusion:

Opportunity lost will never recur in so favourable a form, but if His Majesty's Government consent to give promised help with least possible delay, to keep British troops where they are at least till the autumn, and to maintain South Persia Rifles for at least another year, it may be possible to save situation.[14]

The postponement of Norperforce's departure, at any rate, was out of Curzon's hands, and would not be contemplated by the War Office or indeed by the cabinet. But both Norman and, especially India, had a very good point, and India could be heeded without need for any financial and military commitment. It is difficult to avoid the conclusion that Curzon's emotional involvement in his policy, both when he more or less imposed it on his colleagues, and now that it was falling apart, made it impossible for him to see sense, even to his own advantage.

The Shah, paralysed by fear as well as by contradictory advice, was unable to take any decision at all. Early in January he was still insisting on leaving for Europe. This is explained both by his fear of what might happen after Norperforce's departure, and of taking any unpopular decision. He wished to be absent from the scene, so that, if it ended up the wrong way, at least his physical survival would be guaranteed. This same psychology led him to leave for Europe three years later, when the British no longer had any say in the matter, because of his fear of Reza Khan coupled with inaction against him either for fear of failure or unpopularity. This move was to the detriment of both the Shah and his dynasty. A similar psychology may be detected in Mohammad Reza Shah, both when he clashed with Musaddiq and before the revolution of February 1979, though Ahmad had been much less unpopular than Mohammad Reza was on those occasions.

There was a real and widespread scare that 'the Bolsheviks' would show up in the wake of a departing Norperforce. The Shah told Sepahdar that if Norman did not agree with his journey to Europe, he would commence it nonetheless, hoping to convince the British government on arrival. This was probably a bluff, and in any case Sepahdar asked Norman and Curzon to discourage him. Norman read the Shah's mind well:

Shah is doubtless in a nervous state, but I believe it to be solely the effect of fear. Real motive of his anxiety to leave the country probably is wish to be in safety when impending crisis occurs. If His Majesty's Government stand by Persia and danger therefore passes, he hopes to return, while if they leave her to be overrun by the Bolsheviks he will remain in Europe.[15]

But, Norman added, the Shah had become so unpopular, being preoccupied only by his own interest, that in any case he might not be able to return. His deposition, however, would be likely to lead to revolution, 'which I believe in any case to be inevitable if British protection to Persia is not continued in some form'.[16] Norman's allusions to the protection of Iran, as part of his quarrels with Curzon, are too obvious to require emphasis.

Curzon replied that the Shah should not be encouraged, since 'to desert his country at this critical juncture ... would be inevitably interpreted as cowardice.'[17] But news of the possible evacuation of the European community was much stronger than fear of the charge of cowardice. Norman told the Shah of his 'duty to his own people and family' and the probable 'destruction of monarchy'. He finally agreed to stay when Norman promised to give him a month's notice of the date of Norperforce's departure.[18] Only a few days later the Shah came back to the theme, this time threatening voluntary abdication to quit the country 'as a private individual'. The *Vali'ahd* (his brother, and heir apparent) had opposed the idea and declined to replace him, but the Shah's mind was made up: either his youngest brother could succeed him, or a republic might be declared.[19] Yet the fact that he once again asked for Norman's and Curzon's agreement to go to Europe shows that he was bluffing, at least in part. Curzon thought that he should be 'kept on the throne, if possible', but failing that, the *Vai'ahd* might replace him.[20]

Meanwhile the talk continued about either 'strengthening' Sepahdar's government by bringing stronger men into the cabinet, or setting up a strong new ministry. Two names, those of Ain al-Dawleh and Farmanfarma, were being openly canvassed, and both of them were also willing to serve in a cabinet led by Mostawfi al-Mamalek. Predictably, neither Ain nor Farmanfarma inspired much confidence among the wider public, although Norman reported that Ain was more acceptable because he had got closer to the popular politicians, while Farmanfarma, though not very popular, was intelligent and energetic. Regarding the alternative of strengthening the existing cabinet, Norman mentioned Firuz's name, saying that he would soon arrive in Tehran and he could then discuss the situation with him.

The whole thing prompted Curzon to comment, it seems with more humour than either irony or justice, that 'Mr Norman has now accomplished the complete circle, having come back to one of the corrupt Triumvirates of the Sir P. Cox days! No further triumph is possible'.[21] Nonetheless, he wrote to Norman that he approved of his search for a strong cabinet and his proposal to consult Firuz.[22] It is unlikely that Norman and other members of the British community favoured either Ain or Farmanfarma, or indeed his son Firuz, when not even Sayyed Zia would back Farmanfarma (see chapter nine). They did not like either of them, but they would not have tried to stop them if they had a real chance to form a strong government.

The opportunity came when the hapless Sepahdar, not knowing which way to turn, offered his resignation to the Shah. The latter broke the news to Norman, who told the Shah that he did not wish Sepahdar to think that he was behind his fall, but if he insisted on resigning it was a different matter. The Shah – in high spirits for a change because the news of his intending departure had rallied support for him – confirmed that it was indeed Sepahdar's own wish, and it was decided he should send for Mostawfi.[23]

What upset the apple-cart was Curzon's insistence on not repudiating the Agreement, which he nevertheless kept repeating had lapsed since the last day of 1920. Mostwafi sent Norman a message that, if he took office, he would not be able to submit the Agreement to the Majlis for approval. Norman had no authority to agree to that condition. The Shah then suggested that he would either strengthen Sepahdar's cabinet, or nominate someone else on Norman's advice. Norman declined to make any suggestions on the basis that he could no longer arrange British financial and military support for the government. Anyone selected now on his recommendation would be known as the candidate of the British legation, and, he wrote pointedly, 'now that I am to lose moral force which I have hitherto derived from presence of British troops, I could not keep him in power in the face of attacks which would be immediately made on him by the Opposition.'[24] Curzon is unlikely to have lost much sleep by all this, especially in the case of a man such as Mostawfi, although if he had told Norman that he could accept Mostawfi's realistic condition, the new cabinet would have been formed. Attempts to persuade Mostawfi to change his mind did not succeed, and Sepahdar was asked to look for a stronger cabinet.[25]

The fact that Britain was no longer giving financial assistance to the government, and, more especially, that Norperforce was shortly due to leave the country, was by now well known. Given the resulting state of panic in Tehran, hardly anyone would be prepared to risk his name, and possibly his neck too, by upholding the Agreement. Indeed, 55 'well disposed' deputies, as Norman wired, soon issued a public declaration denouncing it, in order to dispel rumours that they had received British money to support it.[26] The news threw Curzon into yet another rage, saying that the British government had 'not the slightest intention of denouncing the agreement themselves and of accepting thereby the responsibility for proceedings the blame for which must rest exclusively upon Persian shoulders'.[27] The day after this telegram was sent, and a couple of days before the Coup, Sepahdar formed another cabinet after much consultation, but it soon proved a futile effort (see further below).

At the same time the old clash of opinion – as in the summer of 1920 – among the British personnel, both civilian and military, was renewed about the kind of government which could save the situation (see chapter six). Norman and almost all of his staff, including Smart, Havard, and Huddleston, were inclined towards a strong, even though unpopular, government. Smart went even so far as to visit Bahar – no doubt knowing that he had been pro-Vosuq – and 'repeatedly' sounded him out on the desirability of bringing 'a strong government'.[28] This gives an indication of how widely the idea was canvassed at the time. On the other hand, Dickson still supported a government by men like Mostawfi and Moshir.

Further than that, Ironside, Colonels Smyth, Haig and Huddleston, on the one hand, and Sayyed Zia, the gendarme officers in his confidence, and British diplomats such as Smart and Havard, on the other, were rapidly thinking of another possibility, of which not even Norman had any inkling. They decided to get rid of Dickson. Huddleston, the military attaché, had sent a very critical report about him to the War Office. But Dickson was in fact on loan to the Foreign Office, in connection with the Agreement, as head of the British Military Mission. Therefore Norman sent a telegram to the Foreign Office, giving 'strong support' to Huddleston's suggestion that Dickson should be recalled. Dickson, he wired, was not a man 'likely to inspire confidence in an emergency situation':

> [He] has also I learn lately been indulging in a good deal of rather mischievous talk about the gravity of the situation which is calculated still further to increase already growing panic. I am better qualified to comment on his political activity. It has always been too marked and is not at present being exercised in the same direction as that of (? Legation).[29]

It is significant that Norman sent a copy of his telegram to Ironside. The orders from London came quickly, and on 21 January Norman could write to Dickson, in a very polite and friendly letter, that he should 'return to England without delay'.[30] Poor Norman must have felt bad about the whole thing, because on the same day he also wrote a private letter to Dickson saying how much he would miss him, the sentimentality being perhaps stronger for his guilt about secretly conniving in the orders for Dickson's recall to London. He wrote in the private letter that Dickson's departure will 'leave a real void in my life', and 'my task thankless enough anyhow and now it will be worse'. But there was a brighter side to the matter:

> I can assure you that I would almost give anything to have a similar chance of getting away honourably instead of having to stay here looking on impotently while our interests and policy go to ruin.[31]

The jibe at Curzon is obvious, as is Norman's state of mind. Dickson must have felt that his recall was the work of Ironside, Huddleston and the others, but not Norman, and he was perhaps more eager to linger and see the end of the saga. He procrastinated until after the Coup, when he was told in no uncertain terms that he must leave, and left in anger (see chapter nine).

The evacuation scare

All through the fateful month of January, there was talk of evacuating the European community from Tehran before the coming of 'the Bolsheviks', which they firmly believed would follow the departure of Norperforce. The scare fuelled the wish to flee, and that further fuelled the scare. This was often combined with talks about possible removal of the capital to Isfahan, or (occasionally) Shiraz, which was understood to mean giving up Tehran to 'Bolshevism' and/or anarchy. Much of the scare was due to the propaganda work of a relatively small, but very active, group of radicals in Tehran, which convinced both the Iranians and the British personnel, including Norman. On 19 January, Colonel Smyth, the actual commander of the Cossacks in Aqababa, wrote in a situation report to the War Office:

> P. G. [Persian Government] has for the last two months been terrorised by Bolshevik committees. There is also actually a committee of officers. The committees prevent the Mejlis meeting, stop all effective Government, and are simply a preparation for actual Bolshevism.[32]

These exaggerations (by the Iranians and the British alike), like similar historical situations in Iran, were creating a state of self-fulfilling prophecy. Iranians are usually very good at exaggerating such situations even when they dread the outcome they prophesy. Rumours were flying far and wide that Britain had entered a secret accord with the Soviet Union to give up the north to them and take the south for herself. It all made sense to the Iranians, because they had resisted the Agreement (which, in their view, would have meant Britain taking the whole lot); Britain was removing Norperforce, thus 'clearing the way' for the Gilan Bolsheviks to march to Tehran; and there was the recent precedent of the Anglo–Russian convention of 1907. It certainly made much better sense than the rumours in 1978 that America (and Britain) had decided to overthrow the Shah, which not only gave a tremendous boost to the modern middle classes to actively support the revolutionary movement, but also discouraged the Shah and the army from resisting it.

The Imperial Bank of Persia – the banker and chief financier of the Iranian government – itself overtaken by the scare, far from helped matters by thinking of moving its branch from Tehran. The Iranians did not for a moment distinguish between the Bank, the Legation, the financial advisers, the military advisers, the Foreign Office, the War Office, India, etc., all of which to them were (and remained for decades to come) simply 'the British' (*inglis-ha*) taking decisions as a single body at an incredible speed and with astonishing wizardry.

When the word went round that the Bank was thinking of evacuating Tehran, it was felt there could be no better proof of how 'the British' saw the situation, and what 'decisions' they had taken about the fate of Iran. They saw the writing on the wall better perhaps than Daniel himself had seen it at the feast of

Belshazzar. Curzon minuted sourly on Norman's 'attempt to throw responsibility upon the Imperial Bank instigated apparently by the wicked apprehensions of H.M.G', whereas:

> The responsibility for the catastrophes that impend in Persia is that of the W[ar] O[ffice] to begin with, the I[ndia] O[ffice] in the second place and the Cabinet in the third. No doubt when the debacle comes the F[oreign] O[ffice] will receive the entire blame.[33]

At any rate, both Norman and Curzon intervened, and orders went out from the Bank's head office in London that they should remain in Tehran until the last possible moment.[34]

No plans were drawn up or decisions taken; not even the decision to evacuate non-essential Europeans from Tehran was fully implemented. The Shah did not wish to go to Isfahan, which, he (correctly) believed, would make him a pawn in the hands of the Bakhtiyari khans, although they were divided among themselves.[35] Two weeks later, it looked as if he might be persuaded to go after all, if the British could reach a clear understanding with the Bakhtiyaris and find the necessary money as part of a deal with them.[36] Curzon, for once, understood the situation with greater realism, and was baffled at the great scare in Tehran:

> We cannot understand here why there should be a general *sauve qui peut* [stampede] at Tehran. Shah, who is the most timid man in Persia has decided to stay. A Persian Government [the one being explored by Mostawfi] is about to be formed. It has concluded, or is in the verge of concluding, a treaty with the Bolsheviks [i.e. Soviet Russia]. Why then should the latter invade Persia or attack the capital? Why should there be a general scuttle from Tehran? It may be that our interests should be better served by a Persian Government acting under our influence at Ispahan or elsewhere. But you do not appear to regard this solution as likely. Will not damage to our prestige, of which you complain, only be enhanced by a precipitate retreat and abandonment of whole of Northern Persia to an enemy, whose advance is by no means certain, and a revolution which can probably still be avoided.[37]

India came back into the debate with its consistent clear-sightedness and sobriety. It would be wrong to abandon Tehran, wrong if the country fell to Bolshevism or anarchy, and not much better if there was a Bolshevik government in the north and a government of the Shah, under British influence, in the south. The Iranian government could stand fast in Tehran and weather the storm before April, when Norperforce would leave:

> One great obstacle to this is the universal misconception of our motive underlying the Anglo–Persian Agreement. The fact that it has not been

placed before Majlis by stipulated date gives us the opportunity of withdrawing our offer under it with good grace. Hence *we urge that no time should
be lost in disavowing the agreement publicly, and in seeing to it that our disavowal is
published throughout Persia.* Herein lies ... the best chance of starting revulsion of public opinion in our favour, and consequently of providing
antidote to Bolshevik propaganda, which at present draws most of its
force in Persia from Bolsheviks being able to pose as deliverers of Persia
and Islam generally from British domination.

And they concluded succinctly:

In short we believe that there is still chance of saving situation, provided
Persian Government stands fast in Teheran, and provided we cut ground
from under Bolshevism by scrapping Anglo–Persian Agreement ...
Without these provisos, it seems that in the end protection of British inter-
ests will have to be confined to those in the oil-fields and along Persian
Gulf.[38]

Norman must have received this opinion with a round of applause. Curzon, on
the other hand, to whom rejection of the Agreement meant little less than rejection of himself, could see nothing in it but a personal attack. He commented:

Considering that the Gov. of India decline to take the slightest interest in
Persia have steadily opposed the Anglo–Persian agreement from the start,
cut off their expenditure there without even a reference to us, and wash
their hands of all responsibility – I regard their advice which they so liber-
ally regale us as an impertinence and would not pay it the compliment of a
reply.[39]

At this point Cox joined in the debate, discussed the situation, and suggested
two alternative courses of action, but the most important part of his contribution was to agree with the abandonment of the Agreement:

As regards the Anglo–Persian Agreement. Fair and reasonable document
as it is, it has become such a red herring to the Bolshevik and such a
pretext for extremist propaganda, that I agree with the Government of
India that we must stop it in its present form as a basis of policy.[40]

This prompted another comment by Curzon: 'everyone, Mr Norman, Gov. of
India, Sir P. Cox – favours us with independent views. But as any of them who
wants anything done postulates the expenditure of money which no-one is
prepared to find – the discussion is rather futile. Of course Sir P. Cox is much
nearer the mark than any of the others'.[41] This was 10 February. The Coup came
ten days later.

Firuz: fact and legend

Firuz's activities during these months have been the subject of a good deal of speculation. This author has seen no evidence in the British archives that Firuz had been nominated in London to form a government, let alone to lead the Coup. On the other hand, indirect British evidence (of which more below), and the contemporary and subsequent Persian evidence (which is faulty in its interpretation, but useful in reconstructing the facts) show that he had been active and had obtained some promise of British support if he managed to become prime minister. Power was literally lying in the streets waiting to be picked up, and Firuz was not one who would miss or ignore the opportunity. He was able, ruthless and ambitious; he had good traditional ties in Iran; and he was acceptable to London, which had little choice. Having got some general approval for his intention to establish a strong government – either headed by himself or by his father Farmanfarma – he left in December 1920 to organise it.

This indeed must be the source of the Iranian legend that Firuz had been chosen in London to lead 'the Coup', but had failed to arrive in Tehran in time, and had thus been cheated by Sayyed Zia and his Committee of Iron. The legend is described in some detail even by those contemporary Iranian sources who are not too wide off the mark in their understanding of events. For example, in the great debate on the Coup which (in 1943) was provoked by Mosaddeq's move to prevent Sayyed Zia's confirmation as a Majlis deputy, Zia al-Molk (Farmand) said that the reason why Norman was withdrawn from Tehran after the Coup was 'because the Coup had been baked here [in Tehran] without the Foreign Office's knowledge'. They had had a vague notion, he continued, but no knowledge of the details:

And when Mr Norman informs them [of the Coup], it surprises the Foreign Office ... Whereas there had been another [Foreign Office] plan, and that plan had been related to the person of Nosrat al-Dawleh [Firuz]. This other case [i.e. the Sayyed-Zia-Reza Khan Coup] was [the result of] local wheeling and dealing. That is why Mr. Norman faced criticism by the Foreign Office, was summoned by them and left [the Foreign Office].[42]

Various versions of the legend that Firuz had been earmarked for the Coup but somehow – there are different accounts – did not succeed, are surely inaccurate but not wholly groundless. Taqizadeh speaks of Firuz's 'arrangement in London to take power for himself' but that 'fortunately ... Norman ... stopped the Foreign Office interference'.[43] Dawlat-Abadi wrote that Firuz had prepared the ground in London to make a Coup, unaware that Zia was dreaming of doing it himself, and that members of the British legation were giving him their support, at least partly because the prevailing anti-British mood did not recommend Firuz for the task. Alone among contemporary Persian sources, he displays knowledge of Firuz's visit to Cox in Baghdad, en route from Europe to Tehran, and makes some intelligent remarks on the possible purpose and result of that visit.[44] Arfa wrote a similar account, that Firuz had reached an agreement in London to lead the Coup, but that Norman, Dickson and others felt that he was 'too much compromised in the 1919 treaty business to be able to appear with a new policy', and so they went for Sayyed Zia and Reza Khan.[45] Bahar wrote that Godfrey Havard, the British consul, played a decisive role in Zia's favour because he disliked Firuz, 'otherwise he [Firuz] would certainly have made the Coup'.[46]

Almost all of the Persian sources believe that Firuz did not manage to reach Tehran before the actual Coup of 21 February, though as we shall see further below this is a mistake. The legend has also been repeated in some western accounts, most notably in that of Ellwell-Sutton who (mainly relying on Iranian sources), refers to 'Curzon himself selecting ... Nosrat ad-Dowleh Firuz', and again 'in London ... the official candidate was Nosrat ad-Dowleh Firuz who had been dispatched post-haste to Iran but arrived too late to stop the course of events'.[47]

Firuz had in fact left Europe in December, about the time when G. P. Churchill wrote his memorandum on the situation in Iran, which – we may recall – had mentioned Ain al-Dawleh as an example of a strong prime minister. The memo had been followed by a general, not specific, instruction to Norman to examine the possibility of helping the formation of a strong government within the traditional fold. Significantly, Firuz went first to Mesopotamia, and had a meeting with Cox in Baghdad. He also made a pilgrimage to Kazemain, Karbela and Najaf, met some of the leading Maraji', and obtained a *fatva*, to be used if necessary, against Bolshevism.

Cox's recommendation of him to the Foreign Office as someone both able and willing to save the situation as well as the Agreement was couched in somewhat diplomatic terms, but he clearly wished him luck. Firuz left for Kermanshah on 5 January, and Cox promised him that he would inform him there – as he informed the Foreign Office in ambiguous terms – 'if His Majesty's Government replied to his representation'.[48] It is clear from the text of this telegram that there had been another telegram by Cox about Firuz's visit. It would appear that Firuz had discussed some relatively definite courses of action with Cox, and that he had asked for specific commitments from the British government, though it is also clear that no such commitments had been made. Two weeks later, G. P. Churchill noted in a minute that 'Sir P. Cox in his telegram of January 9 ... suggests that Nosrat-ed-Dowleh (Prince Firuz) might be made use of. We subsequently approved Mr Norman's proposal to consult him on his arrival at Tehran'.[49]

Firuz went straight to Kermanshah, the seat of the governor-general of the West, who was none other than Akbar Mirza Sarem al-Dawleh (later Mas'ud), his colleague in the triumvirate who had concluded the 1919 Agreement. He stayed there, also visiting some of his own estates nearby, until he arrived in

Tehran a week before the Coup. There is no direct evidence of his activities there. There can be little doubt that he had an exchange with Sarem about his intended move, and they might have made some military preparations from the local tribal forces, as mentioned by Dawlat-Abadi.[50] If so, it is almost impossible that the idea was to capture Tehran from the west by a military onslaught, if only because Firuz went to Tehran alone, and in any case Norperforce was there to defend the legitimate Iranian government. Firuz was thinking of imposing himself (or his father) on the Shah and the establishment in Tehran as a strong, no-nonsense, government, with at least some British diplomatic pressure through the legation. It is just possible, though speculative, that Sarem was to create – but without personal involvement – a phoney diversion in the west, a tribal uprising perhaps, to force the Shah to appoint Firuz, who would then present himself as one who could solve that and other problems. On the other hand, the military preparations might have been to provide some kind of supplementary force to keep the peace and face the Gilan rebels in the wake of the departure of Norperforce, after Firuz (or his father) had taken over in Tehran. All that is assuming there had been any such preparations at all, and this is far from certain.

According to James Balfour, who was then in Tehran as senior assistant to Armitage-Smith, 'there is the very strongest reason to believe that, when passing through Kermanshah, he had plotted a Coup of his own with his former colleague, Sarem-ed-Douleh who was then governor of that town':

> Their scheme was that Firouz should proceed to Teheran, and if he considered the time ripe for overthrowing the government, should summon his fellow plotter [Sarem], who, on the plea of a visit to the dentist, should thereupon leave his post and proceed to the capital. Unfortunately for them the plans of the rival plotters were somewhat more advanced, with the consequence that, instead of dictator, Firouz found himself in jail.[50a]

Firuz had braced himself for the opportunity, as British officials both in Tehran and London were aware, although they do not seem to have known his plan, such as it might have been, in much detail. Norman wired Curzon:

> Nosrat-ed-Dowleh telegraphed to me from Kermanshah on 13th January asking me to prevent situation here from developing till he had had time to discuss it with me. I replied this was precisely what I was trying to do but that events were moving so quickly that I doubted my ability to control them. I therefore begged him to hasten his arrival. He has nevertheless twice postponed his departure, and now proposes only to start 24th January, and to stay on his way at his house near Kangavar and Hamadan. This procedure shows how impossible it is to make even for the most practical Persian to realise the value of time.

And he went on to add a historically important note about Firuz's plans:

> I gather from his brother [Abbas Mirza] Salar-i-Lashkar, that Nosrat-ed-Dowleh does not wish to enter Cabinet of Sepahdar, which he does not expect to last long. He would prefer the latter to remain in office for two or three months till he himself has overcome dislike long felt for him by the public and established his personal ascendancy in Medjliss, which he is confident of his ability to do. He will then try to become prime minister.[51]

In a following situation report at the Foreign Office, G. P. Churchill minuted on Firuz's delay:

> His delay on the road no doubt appears to be unreasonable but am not sure that it is. His father – Farman Farma – and his brother – Salar Lashkar – are at Teheran and he must be in close touch with them and probably through them with the Shah.[52]

On his way to Tehran, Firuz made a point of visiting Ironside and telling him about the dangers of an early withdrawal of Norperforce:

> Late on the evening of the 6th [of February], there presented himself a curious little figure in my office. He proved to be Prince Firouz ... He had just arrived back from Europe, and told me that he had abandoned his cars at the Aveh Pass and taken to a horse to reach me ... He was in a terrible state about our withdrawal, telling me that there would be a revolution in the country a very few days after our departure ... The little man's conversation was all in French ... I packed him off to see the British Minister [Norman], but I had little hope that he would be of any more help than had been the Sirdar Hamayun [the nominal Iranian commander of the Cossacks].[53]

Firuz was small in physical stature but far from little in personality, and he was made of very different stuff from Sardar Homayun.

On 11 February, Norman reported to Curzon that Firuz had 'at last reached Tehran, and I shall see him immediately'.[54] Sepahdar was nominally holding the fort, but no new cabinet had been announced, and now Norman was frantically active to bring a strong government to power. The Imperial Bank, being still very anxious about an imminent crash, had decided to appropriate the balance of the country's oil money in their London account to pay off the government's outstanding debts to themselves, leaving only the 350,000 tomans they had in their Tehran account. In vain did poor Norman try to dissuade them, saying that this would make matters much worse both for the Iranian government, for himself who was trying to make the best of a very bad job, and for British prestige, as the Iranians would be convinced that the matter had been instigated by the British government.[55]

Norman reported to Curzon that he had urged the Shah to appoint 'a strong reactionary Prime Minister' which would be able to open the Majlis. The Shah agreed with him, but – rightly, as Norman pointed out – said that there would be violent opposition unless the British troops postponed their departure. But that was out of Norman's – even Curzon's – hands. The chief obstacle, Norman again emphasized, was the Agreement, which, if voluntarily denounced by Britain, would clear the way for the opening of the Majlis.[56] Curzon's response, once again, was singularly unhelpful. He was 'wholly indifferent as to whether Medjliss is summoned or not' for debating the Agreement, which from the British government's point of view had lapsed six weeks before. Yet there was no question of Britain denouncing it, and the responsibility for its abandonment must be born by the Iranians themselves.[57]

Poor hapless Norman! At last he had a long meeting with Firuz, who told him he was ready to form a strong government, but it would need 'two to three weeks of well-directed activity'. The entire direction of his activity should be left to himself, and all that he demanded from the British legation was loyal support. He too believed that there was no hope left for the Agreement in its existing form. It would be very helpful if, when he became prime minister, he could announce that it had been annulled, as a result of negotiations with Britain, and then open the Majlis (exactly as did Zia when he became prime minister, which led to Curzon's unmitigated hostility towards him – see chapter nine). This would greatly strengthen his hands, and he could then make a similar agreement via a different route.[58] This last point apparently was all that Curzon saw in Norman's dispatch on his conversations with Firuz. It threw him completely off balance, as is evident from a remarkable comment minuted by him (in a handwriting even more hasty and illegible than usual) which must be quoted in full:

Nusrat-ud dowleh
'Well-directed activity' in Persia means bribes, if it is to be successful; and the cash is no longer forthcoming. I have no desire to negotiate a new agreement, and I see no reason why the Mejilis should reject or denounce the present agreement, because I see no reason why it should be submitted to them. The Persian Gov. have already strangled it. I have no intention of negotiating another treaty with Persia after April. Personally I will never propose another agreement with the Persians. Nor unless they come on their knees would I ever consider any application by them, and probably not then. In future we will look after our interests in Persia, not hers.[59]

Curzon thus washed his hands of the matter completely only a couple of days before the Coup, about which he did not have the slightest idea. It is also clear from the above document that he had made no deal with Firuz for the latter to lead a Coup, either in London or elsewhere.

Preludes to the Coup

Ironside, as we saw in the previous chapter, was thinking along different lines. Smyth had been drilling the Cossacks at Aqababa, and now – in the absence of Sardar Homayun, the nominal commander – he had entered a close relationship with Reza Khan. The idea that some kind of force should be organized to back a strong government was being widely discussed among the Iranian political elite and the British legation, as well as other British officials, including Dickson whose sympathies were with the popular politicians. Those in favour of the latter were thinking of the gendarmerie, the 'popular' (*melli*) force, and those who wanted 'one of the [Qajar] noblemen' were more inclined towards the Cossacks.[60]

But now attempts were made to bring the two forces closer together, so that there would be no conflict in the event of such a government being formed. Two gendarme officers, Major Mas'ud Khan (Kayhan) and Captain (later Colonel) Kazem Khan (Sayyah), were close lieutenants of Sayyed Zia in the Committee of Iron, and began to play an active role in bringing the two traditionally hostile forces together. Another gendarme officer, Zaman Khan was also involved, although, according to Zia, the plan of the Coup was kept secret from him.[61]

Colonel Haig, the organiser of the original Iron Committee in Isfahan (see chapter five), acted as the go-between, and it was he who, in his frequent visits to Aqababa, introduced Mas'ud, Kazem and Zaman to Smyth and the Cossacks. The three gendarme officers began to spend much time there, getting to know the Cossack commanders and acting as the liaison between them, and Zia and the Committee of Iron in Tehran. About this time Major (later General) Habibollah Khan (Shaibani), who was one of the ablest gendarme officers in Tehran, might have been brought into the new line. When the Cossacks came to Tehran for the Coup, Shaibani, who was then still a fiery nationalist did not offer any resistance[62] (see also chapter nine).

There is a good deal of legend about how the leader of the Coup was selected, and who had been canvassed for that role. Contemporary Iranian sources divide the issue between 'the civilian' and 'the military' leader of the Coup. The most celebrated story, that of Firuz, has been already discussed and rejected. It was mentioned in the previous chapter that an elaborate, but unbelievable, case has been made that Sepahsalar (Tonokaboni) had been contacted by Zia, but that he had declined the suggestion with disdain because Zia himself had wished to join his cabinet (see chapter seven). Salar Jang-e Bakhtiyari and Sardar As'ad III [formerly Sardar Bahdor] have both been mentioned. The former had led a minor rebellion about a month before the Coup, and had been defeated by a force of the gendarmes in Varamin, south of Tehran. This had been an entirely personal adventure.[63]

The story about Sardar As'ad's nomination is even more fanciful.[64] In any case, it is not even clear why these men should be regarded as projected *civilian* leaders of the Coup, and if – as it is suggested – they were supposed to lead Bakhtiyari forces to Tehran, what role the Cossacks were supposed to play?[65] It is unlikely that any such search for 'the civilian leader' of the Coup was at all made (see chapter seven). The whole idea, extensively discussed in many of the contemporary sources, arises from the belief that the entire operation had been approved and organized from London months before the event, and that Firuz had been London's premier candidate.

However, Ironside was due to leave in April, when Norperforce would be withdrawn. The idea was to release the Cossacks to march on Tehran shortly before that, assuming that no alternative solution for creating a government able to deal with chaos and or a Bolshevik revolution had been found. But Ironside was suddenly summoned to Cairo in the middle of February, and quickly decided to let the Cossacks go to Tehran (see further below). Therefore, the question of actually talking to 'civilian leaders' and telling them about the plan in January – even if contemplated – would have been premature, as well as foolishly risky.

On the other hand, there was some search for the man who should lead the Cossacks to Tehran. The name of Amirtuman (later General Abdollah) Amir Tahmasebi has been mentioned. He was one of the few Iranian Cossack officers with a higher rank than Reza Khan, had had an exceptionally good education, and was commander of the guards at the royal court. Yet he was not a field commander, and was much better at administrative and diplomatic management than military leadership, and – at the time – was too close to the court to be trusted with such a secret. It is very unlikely that he was contacted, and if Dawlat-Abadi (among some other sources) had not named him as a possible candidate the idea should have been dismissed entirely out of hand.[66]

But it is almost certain that Amir-Movassaq (later General Mohammad Nakhjavan) was asked to act, and refused. He too was one of the most senior Cossack officers, with the rank of Amirtuman. He had represented the Cossacks on Dickson's Joint Military Commission for creating a unified army, and had known Smyth from then. He was a field commander and the most senior officer at Aqababa. He himself had told a few close personal friends, including General Mohammad Ali Alavi Moqaddam, that he was first to have been approached for the task. This is confirmed by the fairly detailed and accurate account of the Coup by Colonel Qahremani, himself a Cossack officer at Aqababa and witness to the events.[67]

Sayyed Zia's own testimony lends support to the above evidence about Amir-Movassaq, especially as, regarding this particular matter, he could not have had any personal axe to grind. In May 1935, Zia read out an account of the Coup to Jamalzadeh in Geneva, who noted it down at the same time, and published it decades later (after the revolution) in 1981. It was part of Zia's famous Black Book (as he himself described it), which he told many he had written, or was writing, about the Coup and his own short-lived government, although it was never published.[68] According to Zia:

[Walter] Smart, the Oriental Secretary at the British legation, was very Irano-phile, and we were friends. Kazem and Mas'ud used to come from Qazvin to Tehran most evenings and we used to get together. One evening Kazem said 'Do you remember saying that you could overturn the situation if you had five hundred men; there are now about four thousand Cossacks in Qazvin'. I asked if they could be used. He said yes, two thousand of them could be used with good effect. We decided to go to work.

The first opportunity arose when (in January, as discussed above) the idea of moving the capital to Isfahan was contemplated:

A force was needed to take the Shah to Isfahan, and it was decided to bring 500 Cossacks to Tehran. There were already some Cossack and Gendarme soldiers in Tehran, among whose officers were Habibollah Khan Shaibani and Saifollah Khan [later, General] Shahab.

Zia and his friends thought of seizing the opportunity, and bringing 2000 Cossacks to topple the government. They tried to persuade Amir-Movassaq to lead the Cossacks to Tehran. He refused, and Reza was chosen instead:

Also, Amir-Movassaq was in Qazvin, and nominally the [field] commander of the [Cossack] force [in Aqababa]. One evening we talked to him to implement our plan and lead the Cossacks to Tehran. He said clearly that he did not have the courage to do it, and that we should leave him alone ... Therefore I asked Kazem and Mas'ud who among the officers there was capable of bringing the Cossacks to Tehran. They said Reza Khan ... Hence it fell on Kazem and Mas'ud to prepare Reza Khan ... To give the command of those Cossacks to Reza Khan who was [only] a mirpanj ... was not an easy task. So I talked to Sardar Homayun, and since I told him it was the prime minister's orders, and he was afraid of being dismissed by Sepahdar, he finally agreed to Reza Khan's appointment.[69]

Zia might have been exaggerating his own role as the man who ultimately chose Reza on the advice of Kazem and Mas'ud, and induced Sardar Homayun to make him commander. But Colonel Qahremani, who himself was a Cossack officer at Aqababa, wrote explicitly in his memoirs that 'Sayyed Zia ... came to Qazvin and talked to Amirtuman Amir-Movassaq to lead the Coup'.[70] On the other hand, Ironside writes as if he chose Reza to lead a Coup without reference to anyone else, though he does mention talking to Smyth. Smyth was of course in contact with Mas'ud and Kazem. The picture that e merges is that all of them were involved in the process, and decisions were taken by direct or indirect consultation among them.

Ironside's thoughts had been turning towards helping to establish a military dictatorship as a quick remedy to fill the vacuum before he left. In his entry for 14 January, he wrote:

> The commander of the Cossacks [Sardar Homayun] is a useless little creature and the real life and soul of the show is Reza Khan, a colonel, the man that I liked so much before. Smyth says he is a good man and I have told him to give [Sardar] Homayun leave to visit his estate. The latter is pleased to go because he has not been allowed to handle the money, and has a grievance.[71]

He then reflected on what he should do:

> I had a long talk with Smyth about the position of affairs when we go. Nobody will take any responsibility regarding these Cossacks and I cannot get any orders. I think that we have to make a decision pretty soon – even though I cannot go to Tehran with a force. Personally I am of the opinion that we ought to let these people go before I disappear. I told Smyth that I thought they could do little harm. In fact a military dictatorship would solve our troubles and let us out of the country.[71a]

By 29 January, Smyth and Reza Khan had become very good friends – as Ironside noted in his diary[72] – and the former was rapidly grooming Reza for the task ahead. Ironside saw and talked to Reza Khan a couple of more times, the last occasion being on 12th February:

> I have interviewed Riza Khan and have put him definitely in charge of Persian Cossacks. He is a man and the straightest I have seen yet. I have told him that I propose to let him go from my control gradually and that he must make preparations with Colonel Smyth when the Menjil Column goes. I had a long talk with Riza in the presence of Smyth.[73]

He made two conditions: that Reza would not attack Norperforce as they were leaving, and that he should not depose the Shah. Reza Khan agreed to both, although he did not keep the latter. But the first condition makes no sense at all unless it is a euphemism for Ironside having told Reza not to take any action against Britain's interest in the future: firstly, because Reza Khan's aim was to march on Tehran; secondly, because he would have had no conceivable motive for attacking Norperforce; thirdly, because he was in charge of a much smaller force which had been hurriedly drilled and fitted with – among other things – new English boots, by Norperforce officers.

It is important to note, however, that as late as 12 February Ironside wrote (in the above diary entry) that he had told Reza that he would 'let him go out of my control *gradually*', whereas Reza Khan and his Cossacks were released by

Ironside a few days later to march on Tehran. The reason for this, as discussed below, was something that Ironside had not at all anticipated.

This is what had been going on, and how fate or chance led to further developments. Large numbers – according to Smyth's report of 19 January to the War Office, 'half' of 'the Kasvin Cossacks have gone to Tehran by order of P. G. [Persian Government]', to be used by the government in dealing with the 'Bolshevik committees' there, though Smyth complained that the government did not have the courage to use them for the purpose.[74] These are the 500 Cossacks mentioned in Zia's notes quoted above, although he wrote that they had been summoned just in case the Shah was to move to Isfahan. On the other hand, Zia adds that:

> Rather than bringing 500 Cossacks [to Tehran] we were thinking of bringing 2000, and instead of carrying out the government's plan [of using them for the move to Isfahan] capture the city and make a Coup.[74a]

On 28 January, Dickson in Tehran wired Ironside in Qazvin that the Shah had suggested that the Cossacks still at Aqababa should be moved to somewhere nearer Tehran, such as Shamsabad. Neither Norman nor Dickson would recommend the idea, but they sought Ironside's opinion about it.[75] Ironside replied in no uncertain terms that he opposed the idea:

> On my withdrawal [i.e. the evacuation of Norperforce in April] what does the SHAH propose putting in the place of my troops. The Western defence of TEHRAN should be based on KASVIN and actually to the West of it. It is best for the Cossacks to be here under my control and I certainly do not recommend their being in TEHRAN.[76]

Ironside, as we know, had already earmarked the Cossacks for a Coup, and would therefore not send them to join the rest of the inactive Cossacks in Tehran, or allow them to be somewhere that would make the implementation of his plan very difficult. Hence his telling Reza Khan, on 12 February, that he would 'gradually' let him out of his control to march on Tehran.

This was end of January 1921, and Ironside spoke to Reza Khan on 12 February, not knowing that that was the last time he would talk to him. Then something unexpected happened. Winston Churchill, who had just moved from the War Office to the Colonial Office called a large conference in Cairo to discuss the situation in Arab lands, and, on 14 February, Haldane in Baghdad sent orders to Ironside to go there and then on to Cairo. Knowing that he would not return to his post since Norperforce would leave Iran in less than two months, Ironside told Smyth to release the Cossacks to march on Tehran as soon as he left. He wrote in the entry of his diary for 14 February:

I have given the orders for the departure of the forces to Smyth and Riza. I must allow them a certain amount of freedom of action. I must see Norman and put him in the picture. For us, a Coup d'état would be the best choice. Poor Norman would be unhappy.[77]

Ironside went to Tehran the next day specifically to arrange for the takeover of the Cossacks. According to Ullman who has had the privilege of seeing the whole of the manuscript in English, Ironside 'went to Tehran to try and persuade the Shah to bring Reza Khan to a position of power. The Shah refused'.[78] Dennis Wright, who has likewise seen the manuscript diary, writes that Ironside 'motored into Tehran for a farewell audience with the Shah whom he tried unsuccessfully to make better use of Reza Khan'.[79] Ironside's talk with the Shah took place on 15 February. It is remarkable, but both Ullman's and Wright's allusions to his conversations with the Shah (based on his diary entry, which they do not quote directly) imply that Ironside had bluntly told the Shah to make Reza military dictator. The Persian translation of some pages of Ironside's original manuscript includes an entry for 15 February, but this is obviously incomplete because it excludes Ironside's direct suggestion to the Shah to bring Reza 'to a position of power'. It reads:

Together [with Norman] we went to see the Shah. The Shah lives some six miles outside Tehran with a herd of his wives. Norman was still worried about the situation. I talked to him about Riza. He was extremely doubtful that the Shah would agree. I told him that I believed in Riza. Besides, as both of us disagree with Curzon, we should not quarrel any more between ourselves. I must let the Cossacks go sooner or later.[80]

Yet the Persian translation, as far as it goes, looks more or less authentic, for Denis Wright quotes directly from the entry in Ironside's *manuscript* diary for the same day, 15 February:

I told him [Norman] about Reza and he was very fearful that the Shah would be done in. I told him I believed in Reza ... I had to let the Cossacks go some time or other.[80a]

What now happened was this. On 15 February, the Shah had refused Ironside's suggestion to put Reza Khan in 'a position of power'. Ironside, nevertheless, was going ahead with his plan to let Reza go and take power. Reza Khan himself thought, as he believed until his dying day, that it was 'the British' who were bringing him to power (see chapters ten and eleven). The Shah could not be deposed by Ironside, and therefore by his Iranian nominee, if only because this was not British government policy; Norman and the others would have opposed it, and the Coup would have collapsed. Therefore, there had to be some kind of legitimate excuse for the march of the Cossacks on Tehran.

There was the recent precedent, as noted above, of some Cossack detachments being called to Tehran from Qazvin to deal with 'the Bolshevik committees', or accompany the Shah to Isfahan, if he decided to move the capital. There was also the background of the Shah himself suggesting, only a couple of weeks before, that the rest of them be moved nearer the capital, which Ironside had opposed because he had no idea of having to leave the country so soon. The best pretext, therefore, was to obtain an order from Tehran for the Cossacks to go there.

Something else that now played into Ironside's, Smyth's and the other Coup makers' hands was the rowdyism and indiscipline of some of the Tehran Cossacks. Norman indeed had told Smyth that some of the Tehran Cossacks – both Persian and British sources quote 500 or 600 – should be sent back to Qazvin, and some of the Cossacks there, by now drilled and disciplined, should be sent to Tehran to replace them, and this time really keep the peace.

Smyth and Zia seized the opportunity and – without Norman's knowledge or approval – asked the spineless Sardar Homayun to issue the order for the remainder of the Cossacks to come to Tehran. This was the 2000 or so men of whom Reza was now the field commander. At this point, Sayyed Zia, Walter Smart, and Colonels Haig and Huddleston played an important role. The Shah's new private secretary, Mo'in al-Molk (who had apparently been put there through the Sayyed's and Havard's influence)[81] also played a part in this, although – contrary to some Persian sources – the Shah himself was kept in the dark.[82]

The fact that the Shah had no idea of what was afoot, and almost panicked when he heard the news of the Cossack's march, is documented below. But in any case, they could not have deceived him into giving the order for the march, because he had been alerted by Ironside's open suggestion that he should bring Reza 'to a position of power'. Sardar Homayun duly sent the order to Qazvin. All this is confirmed by the above-mentioned Cossack officer Colonel Qahremani, who wrote in his memoirs (decades before any of the present documents became public):

> When they were disappointed by [Amir-Movassaq, who was the highest ranking commander in the field], they ordered Sardar Homayun to summon the Tehran *atriad* to Tehran. He too, without telling the Shah, telegraphed to Qazvin for the Tehran garrison to go to the capital.[83]

On 18 February, Ironside left for Baghdad, never to return to Iran. Colonel Qahremani, himself an officer in the *atriad* at Qazvin, clearly mentions 28 Bahman (16 February) as the day the Cossacks were released by Smyth and began their march on the capital, and he carefully accounts for every day from 16 to 21 February, when they finally entered Tehran. It follows that the Cossacks had begun their march two days before Ironside's departure, and not, as is noted in his diary, after he had left Qazvin for Baghdad on 18 February.

However, Qahramani goes on to add that, as the most senior field commander, Amir-Movassaq gave the order for the Cossacks to move, and they moved out with himself and Smyth formally at their head, while Reza Khan was the real leader charged with implementing the Coup.[84]

As soon as the Shah heard about the march of the Cossacks led by Reza Khan, he got frightened, thinking that Ironside or the British had sent Reza to depose him. Indeed, he might well have been reminded of the march of the revolutionary army from Qazvin 12 years earlier – which he might have believed had also been sent by the British – to depose his father.

On 17 February, only one day before Ironside's departure, Sepahdar at last managed to form a new cabinet. On the same day, Firuz, not having the slightest clue about the impending Coup, had told Norman that the new cabinet would not get very far, and he would then make his bid to form a government. Sephdar had suggested two alternative ways of dealing with the Agreement problem, and Norman had said he should seek London's view before commenting on them:

Nosret-ed-Dowleh suggests that reply of His Majesty's Government to Prime Minister's question should be delayed for a time. He thinks if this is done present cabinet will be unable to maintain itself, and that when it falls he himself will be able to take office.[85]

Apart from talking to Norman, Firuz had also talked to Sayyed Zia at the home of Gorfry Havard, and had made him promise that he would not oppose him if he managed to form a cabinet.[86] Norman, as we saw above, had been told of Ironside's intentions and had not approved of them, but he too did not know of the order obtained from Sardar Homayun.

It was the Shah who broke the news to Norman, and, being in a state of panic, begged him to intervene and put a stop to it. On 18 February, two days after the march had begun, Norman wired Norperforce, saying that the Shah had told Homayun to reverse the order, that Homayun had done so, but that Norperforce had claimed they had not received the new order. They should now recall the Cossacks back to Qazvin. Norperforce replied to Norman that the matter was no longer in their hands. The two documents in question must be quoted in full. Norman wired:

Shah has sent his private secretary to say that Col. Smyth when lately here asked Sardar Homayun to order Tehran aaa [sic] Hamadan detachments of Cossacks division about 2000 men who were at Kasvin to come to Tehran aaa latter did so but Shah thinking it better that these detachments should stay where they were so as to be ready to take place of British troops asked him to cancel order. This was done but new orders appeared to arrived [sic] too late as it was reported that detachment had already reached Yengi Imam aaa [I] replied that I felt sure that there must be some mistake but would you kindly do this aaa When Colonel Smyth was here I suggested to him the advisability of moving Cossacks now here [in Tehran] to Kvn [Qazvin] because they are in a very bad state, and would benefit by a little discipline aaa [sic] added that if necessary a few others might be sent to take their place but it did not occur to me that so many need be sent aaa [sic] There is however plenty of time to send the two detachments [already in Tehran] back from here to Kvn before our troops move.[87]

Norperforce waited one day, and replied on 18 February, when Ironside left for Baghdad:

Move of Cossacks was ordered by Sirdar Humayun and Colonel Smyth has no power AAA Increase in force suggested to you by Col. Smyth due to Humayun's orders AAA Understand Cossacks have been ordered remain Mirabad [Mehrabad] and not to enter Tehran.[88]

All this and more is borne out by the testimony of Colonel Qahremani, who personally witnessed and participated in the events. The Cossacks had been contacted – probably by the Shah – at Yangi Imam and ordered to return to their base. Qahremani is also aware of the contact made directly with Qazvin. On 18 February the Force's mounted regiment reached Karaj:

Early in the evening the officers were told to spread the rumour that we would march back to Qazvin next day ... But Colonel Smyth had told Amir-Movassaq [who should formally have given the order to go back] that an arrow has been shot and will not return.[89]

Ironside left Qazvin on the evening of 18 February, so he was very probably still there when Norman's telegram arrived. They decided to reply next day, when Ironside had already left, and Reza's men together with Smyth were well on the way. The reply to Norman was signed by a captain. By the time he received this telegram, Norman was at last completely in the picture.

Notes

1 Norman to Curzon, 8/1/21, *British Documents on Foreign Policy (BDFP)*, vol. xiii, no. 640; see also Norman to Curzon, 17/12/20, *ibid.*, no. 613.
2 Norman to Curzon, 1/2/21, F. O. 371/6400; see also the related minutes, *ibid.*
3 Norman to Curzon, 10/2/21, *BDFP*, vol. xiii, no. 674.
4 Norman to Curzon, 20/1/21, F. O. 371/6400.
5 Norman to Curzon, 27/12/21, *BDFP*, vol. xiii, no. 621.
6 Norman to Curzon, 6/1/21, *ibid.*, no. 635.
7 Curzon to Norman, 3/1/21, *ibid.*, no. 629.
8 Norman to Curzon, 15/1/21, *ibid.*, no. 650.
9 Norman to Curzon, 10/2/21, *ibid.*, no. 674.

10 Curzon to Norman, 3/1/21, *ibid.*, no. 630; see also Curzon to Norman, 19/12/20, *ibid.*, no. 614.

11 Curzon to Norman, 13/1/21, *ibid.*, no. 647; see also Norman to Curzon, 6/1/21, no. 637.

12 Chelmsford to Montague, 10/1/21, *ibid.*, no. 643.

13 Chelmsford to Montague, 6/12/20 as quoted in Norman to Curzon, 31/12/20, *ibid.*, no. 624, n. 3.

14 Norman to Chelmsford, fully quoted in Norman to Curzon, *ibid.*, no. 624.

15 Norman to Curzon, 3/1/21, *ibid.*, no. 626.

16 *Ibid.*, no. 626.

17 Curzon to Norman, 6/1/21, *ibid.*, no. 636.

18 Norman to Curzon, 7/1/21, *ibid.*, no. 638.

19 Norman to Curzon, 12/1/21, *ibid.*, no. 644.

20 Curzon to Norman, 13/1/21, *ibid.*, no. 645.

21 Norman to Curzon, 13/1/21, *ibid.*, no. 648, and n. 1; also see Norman to Curzon, 15/1/21, *ibid.*, no. 651.

22 Curzon to Norman, 15/1/21, *ibid.*, no. 652.

23 Norman to Curzon, 15/1/21, *ibid.*, no. 651; Yahya Dawlat-Abadi, *Hayat-e Yahya*, vol. 4 (Tehran: Attar and Ferdawsi, 1983), chapter 24.

24 Norman to Curzon, 19/121, BDFP, no. 655; Dawlat-Abadi, *Hayat-e Yahya*, chapter, 24.

25 Norman to Curzon, 24/1/21, BDFP, no. 663.

26 Norman to Curzon, 11/2/21, *ibid.*, no. 676.

27 Curzon to Norman, 16/2/21, *ibid.*, no. 678.

28 See Malek al-Sho'ara Bahar, *Tarikh-e Mokhtasar-e Ahzab-e Siyasi dar Iran*, vol. 1 (Tehran: Jibi, 1978), p. 110. The point is repeated on other pages as well.

29 Norman to Foreign Office, 15/1/21, F. O. 371/6427.

30 Norman to Dickson, official letter, 21/1/21, F. O. 371/6427.

31 Norman to Dickson, private letter, 21/1/21, F. O. 371/6427.

32 Smyth to W. O., 'An Appreciation of the Tehran Situation', 19/1/21, W. O. 158/687.

33 Norman to Curzon, 25/1/21, BDFP, no. 665, and minute by Curzon in n. 3.

34 Curzon to Norman, 21/1/21, *ibid.*, no. 660, n.3.

35 Norman to Curzon, 8/1/21, *ibid.*, no. 640.

36 Norman to Curzon, 20/1/21, *ibid.*, no. 657.

37 Curzon to Norman, 21/1/21, F. O. 371/6400.

38 Chelmsford to Montague, 22/1/21, BDFP, no. 662.

39 Minute by Curzon in *ibid.*, no. 662, n. 7.

40 Cox to Montague, 29/1/21, *ibid.*, no. 668. See also the long minutes on Cox's views by G. P. Churchill, 7/2/21, F.O. 371/6400. It is beneath this document that Curzon's minutes, quoted above, appear in his own hand.

41 Minute by Curzon in *ibid.*, n. 12.

42 See Farmand's Majlis speech in Hossein Kay Ostovan, *Siyasat-e Movzeneh-ye Manfi*, vol. 1 (Tehran: Kay Ostovan, 1948), p. 68.

43 See Iraj Afshar (ed.), *Zendegi-ye Tufani, Khaterat-e Sayyed Hasan Taqizadeh*, (Tehran: Elmi, 1993), p. 195.

44 See Dawlat-Abadi, *Hayat-e Yahya*, vol. 4, pp. 223–26.

45 See General Hassan Arfa, *Under Five Shahs* (London: John Murray, 1964), p. 110.

46 See Bahar, *Tarikh-e Mokhtasar*, vol. 1, p. 62. The role of Godfrey Havard is discussed in a few other places in this source.

47 See L. P. Ellwell-Sutton, 'Reza Shah the Great, Founder of the Pahlavi Dynasty' in George Lenchowski, (ed.), *Iran under the Pahlavis* (New York: Hoover Institution, 1978), pp. 11 and 15.

48 Cox to F. O., 9/1/21, F. O. 371/6247.

49 Norman to F. O., 23/1/21, F. O. 371/6400, minute by G. P. Churchill.

50 See Dawlat Abadi, *Hayat-e Yahya*, vol. 4, p. 225.

50a See James Balfour, *Recent Happenings in Persia* (Edinburgh and London: Blackwood and Sons, 1922), p. 227.

51 Norman to Curzon, 23/1/21, F. O. 371/6400.

52 Minute by Churchill in 'Persia: Political Situation (15)', 25/1/21, F. O. 371/6400.

53 See *High Road To Command, The Diaries of Major General Sir Edmund Ironside, 1920–22*, (ed.) Lord Ironside, (London: Leo Cooper 1972), p. 164.

54 Norman to Curzon, 11/2/21, *BDFP*, no 676.

55 Norman to Curzon, 11/2/21, *ibid.*, no. 675; and Norman to Curzon, 16/2/21, No. 2, F. O. 371/6401.

56 Norman to Curzon, 11/2/21, *BDFP*, no. 676.

57 Curzon to Norman, 16/2/21, *ibid.*, no. 678.

58 Norman to Curzon, 16/2/21, No. 1, F. O. 371/6401.

59 *Ibid.*, minute by Curzon.

60 See Bahar, *Tarikh-e Mokhtasar*, vol. 1, p. 109.

61 See Mohammad Ali Jamalzadeh, 'Taqrirat-e Sayyed Zia and his "Black Book"', part 2, *Ayandeh*, vol. 7, June 1981, p. 208. This source is important because it contains Sayyed Zia's personal account of the Coup noted down by Jamalzadeh. See *ibid.*, part 1, *Ayandeh*, March 1980, and further below.

62 See Bahar, *Tarikh-e Mokhtasar*, chapter 20; Ja'far Mehdi Niya, *Zendeginameh-ye Sayyed Zia al-Din Tabatab'i* (Tehran: Mehdi Niya, 1990), part 2, chapter 6; Dawlat Abadi, *Hayat-e Yahya*, vol. 4, chapters 25 and 26; Arfa, *Under Five Shahs*, chapter 5.

63 See Hossein Makki, *Tarikh-e Bistsaleh-ye Iran*, Tehran Elmi, 1995, vol. 1, p. 152; Bahar, *Tarikh-e Mokhtasar*, p. 61.

64 Makki, *Tarikh-e Bistsaleh*, vol. 1, p. 151.

65 *Ibid.*, p. 152.

66 See Dawlat-Abadi, *Hayat-e Yahya*, vol. 4, p. 223.

67 See Bahar, *Tarikh-e Mokhtasar*, vol. 1, pp. 79–86, and chapter 9 below.

68 See Jamalzadeh, 'Taqrirat-e Sayyed Zia', p. 207.

69 *Ibid.*, p. 210.

70 The full text of Colonel Qahremani's detailed memoirs of the Cossack march to Tehran was posthumously published (in 1942) by Bahar in *Tarikh-e Mokhtasar*. See p. 82.

71 Quoted directly from a photograph of p. 21 of Ironside's manuscript diary in, Mo'asseseh-ye Pazhuhesh va Motale'at-e Farhangi, *Khaterat-e Serri-ye Aironsaid*, Tehran: Rasa, 1994, p. 383. For a description and explanation of this source see chapter 7 above. See also Ullman, *Anglo–Soviet Relations, 1917–1921*, vol. 3, *The Anglo–Soviet Accord*, Princeton: Princeton University Press, p. 386.

71a *Ibid.*

72 See the Persian translation of p. 34 of Ironside's manuscript diary, in Mo'asseseh-ye Pazhuhesh, *Khaterat-e Serri* pp. 363–64.

73 Direct quotation from a photograph of p. 61 of Ironside's manuscript diary published in *Khaterat-e Serri, ibid.*, p. 384.

74 Smyth to W. O., 19/1/21, W. O. 158/687.

74a Jamalzadeh, 'Taqrirat-e Sayyed Zia', p. 210.

75 Britmilat to Norperforce, 28/1/21, marked secret, W. O. 158/687.

76 Norperforce to Britmilat, 28/1/21, marked secret, W. O. 158/687.

77 See the Persian translation of p. 63 of Ironside's manuscript diary in Mo'asseseh-ye Pazhuhesh, *Khaterat-e Serri*, pp. 371–72. There is a short quotation from this entry by Dennis Wright directly from the manuscript diary: 'Better a Coup d'état for us than anything else. I'll bounce old Norman'; and further: 'I told him [Norman] about Reza and he was fearful that the Shah would be done in. I told him I believed in Reza ... I had to let the Cossacks to go sometime or other.' Clearly the Persian translators of Ironside's manuscript have made a mistake in translating 'I'll bounce old Norman', into 'Poor

Norman will be unhappy'. As we shall see below, Ironside did indeed 'bounce Norman' at the 11th hour. See *The English Amongst the Persians* (London: Heinemann, 1977), p. 184.

78 Ullman, *The Anglo–Soviet Accord*, p. 387.

79 Dennis Wright, *The English Amongst the Persians*, p. 182.

80 Persian translation of the entry for 15 February, 1921 (only the parts that have been published) in Mo'asseseh-ye Pazhuhesh, *Khaterat-e Serri-ye Ironside*, p. 372.

80a See Dennis Wright, *The English Amongst The Persians*, p. 184.

81 See Seifpur Fatemi, *A'ineh-ye Ebrat*, vol. 1, p. 132

82 For example, Bahar, *Tarilh-e Mokhtasar*, chapter 17. In his fairly frank notes on the Coup (Jamalzasdeh, 'Taqrirat-e Sayyed Zia', p. 211) Zia says that he had induced Sardar Homayun to issue the order, but as will become clear below Smyth had been definitely involved in this. But Zia later claimed in his speech in the fourteenth Majlis (Kay Ostovan, vol. i, p. 76) that the Shah himself had issued the order. That is patently untrue.

83 See Qahremani's account in Bahar, *Tarikh-e Mokhtasar*, especially pp. 82–87.

84 Colonel Qahremani. quoted in Bahar, *ibid.*

85 Norman to Curzon, 17/2/21, F.O. 371/6401.

86 See Jamalzadeh, 'Taqrirat-e Sayyed Zia', *Ayandeh*, p. 211.

87 Norman to Norperforce, 18/2/21, W. O. 158/687.

88 Norperforce to Norman, 19/2/21, W. O. 158/687.

89 See Qahremani in Bahar, *Tarikh-e Mokhtasar*, p. 83.

9

The 1921 Coup

21 February 1921

The Cossacks arrived at the gates of Tehran in the small hours of 21 February 1921. No resistance was offered either by the gendarmerie or by the police, who had been told not to resist. Only a few policemen were killed or wounded in the centre of town, where they were caught by surprise and tried to resist. Sayyed Zia and Reza Khan set up temporary headquarters, and ordered the arrest of a large number of notables and politicians. Within two days the Shah had made Zia prime minister, and appointed Reza, now entitled Sardar Sapah, general commanding officer of 'His Majesty's Cossack force'. Most members of the new cabinet belonged to the Committee of Iron. Mas'ud Khan became war minister, although he was to soon lose the post to Reza Khan. Kazem Khan, Zia's other gendarme confidant, was made martial law administrator, but it soon became clear that all such administration was in fact in Reza's hands. A little more than three months after the Coup, the Sayyed was overthrown by the combined forces of the Shah and Reza Khan, and – together with Mas'ud and Kazem – was exiled from Iran, not to return until long after Reza Shah had abdicated, as a consequence of the Allied invasion of 1941.

As mentioned in chapter eight, Smyth and Zia had induced Sardar Homayun to order the transfer of the Qazvin Cossacks to Tehran. The Shah got wind of the impending putsch and tried to have the order cancelled, and the counter-order was ignored by Ironside and Smyth. And so the Cossacks marched, until, on 20 February, they reached Mehrabad, then about four miles west of Tehran, pausing before their final approach.

When the Shah had heard the news that the counter-order had been ignored, he predictably became more anxious and sent his private secretary, Mo'in al-Molk, to tell Norman and find out if he would have any objection to the Shah sending Sardar Homayun in person to meet the Cossacks on the way and order them to return. Norman said he had none.[1] The Sardar duly left Tehran on 19 February and met the advance guard of the Cossacks at Shah-Abad, east of Karaj. He spoke to Ahmad Aqa (later Amir Ahmadi) and asked to see Reza Khan. He was told that Reza was at Kalak, further back, with the 'Commander of the Division'. This probably meant Amir-Movassaq, but it must have given Sardar Homayun – still legally the commander of the whole division – food for thought. But when the Sardar saw Sayyed Zia there, he got wind of what was afoot, avoided detention by pretending that he had been duped by Ahmad Aqa's reassurance that all was well, doubled back through a different, roundabout, route and returned to Tehran to report his failure to the Shah.[2]

At Shah-Abad, Sayyed Zia met Reza Khan for the first time. Together with Mas'ud Khan, Kazem Khan and Ahmad Aqa, they swore on the Qur'an to serve the Shah and the country and never to betray one another,[3] an oath the other four must have been reminded of at various stages of Reza's ascendancy. Zia then returned to Tehran, but went back the next day to rejoin the Cossacks at Mehrabad, for the final march on Tehran. The Sayyed had already discarded his religious attire and put on a *kolah,* grooming himself for his meteoric rise to premiership.[4]

On receiving Sardar Homayun's report, the Shah almost lost his equanimity for fear of his life. He saw the events as a British plot. Only a few days before, Ironside had asked him to bring Reza 'to a position of power', which the Shah had refused to do. Now it was clear that Zia was also involved, and, in Zia's own words, everyone regarded him as 'Norman's left ball'.[5] The Shah sent Mo'in al-Molk to see Norman, no doubt to plead with him to stop the Coup. Norman, who by now was well informed about the situation, gave him the slip, reporting later to Curzon that, 'as I happened to be out of the house, I was unable to obey the summons.'

At long last, Norman had decided to throw in his lot with the plotters. Sepahdar then sent for Walter Smart, who himself had been privy to the plot, and was therefore easily available. Smart – who only a couple of days before had probingly questioned Bahar on the type of government needed for Iran[6] – found Sepahdar 'thoroughly alarmed'.[7] The latter suggested that the Tehran gendarmes, led by their Swedish commanding officer, be sent to meet the Cossacks, and, in Norman's euphemistic words, 'try to induce the latter to refrain from entering the capital.' Predictably, Smart dissuaded him from taking that step. It was then agreed that a joint deputation from the government and the British legation be sent to Mehrabad to try to stop the march.

Meanwhile, 'having been unable to find me', reported Norman, the Shah telephoned Smart at Sepahdar's house and asked him to go to his palace at Farahabad:

His Majesty was in a very agitated state and talked of immediate flight, but Mr Smart was able to calm him sufficiently to make him abandon his intention and to obtain his consent to the plan of action decided on at Sepahdar's, which he [the Shah] gave subject to my [Norman's] approval.[8]

The two government representatives in the joint deputation that was to go to Mehrabad were Mo'in al-Molk and Adib al-Saltaneh (later Abdolhossein Sami'i), assistant prime minister in the new cabinet. When the latter was told by Sephadar on the telephone to go and meet Mo'in al-Molk and the British representatives in the British legation, who were also to go on the mission, he was both angry and surprised – as he wrote in his recently published memoirs – at 'why these idiots had not even maintained the appearances.' He found Mo'in al-Molk on his own in the legation. After a few minutes:

> [S]uddenly a connecting door opened and Colonel Haig entered the room. (Whoever has seen and known Colonel Haig would know that he was a very clever, canny, witty and intelligent man. He spoke Persian very well, and had learned Iranian manners [also] very well ...). Colonel Haig approached us, shook hands with us, curtseyed and ordered tea, and incidentally said that Mr Minister [Norman] went out in the afternoon and has not yet come back. We should wait until he comes back and we see him, and then we would go to Mehrabad. It turned out that he [Haig] too would be in our company. Meanwhile General [blank space; but it must be Colonel Huddleston], a tall, broad-shouldered, reticent and serious man entered the room.

After a few minutes they came and said Norman had arrived:

> Colonel Haig ushered us to the minister's room ... After exchange of pleasantries, Colonel Haig told him the story of the march of the Cossacks from Qazvin to Tehran. He spoke, and the minister listened to him, in such a way, and with such amazement, that even we might have believed that he was completely oblivious of what was going on. Colonel Haig finished his report and then said that now the General [sic], Mo'in al-Molk and I are due to go to Mehrabad and negotiate with the commander of the Cossacks to change his mind and not come to Tehran.[9]

In his account of the same event, Norman did not feel he had to pretend to Curzon that he had been out of the legation at the time. He reported:

> Mr Smart then returned to the Legation and submitted to me the scheme [of sending emissaries to the Cossacks] which I approved, appointing as representative[s] of the Legation Lieutenant-Colonel Haig, acting counsellor, on account of his exceptional knowledge of Persian, and Lieutenant-Colonel Huddleston, acting military attaché, seeing that military men had to be dealt with.[10]

In fact, Norman had sent the original founder of the Committee of Iron and close friend of Sayyed Zia (Colonel Haig), together with the man whom Ironside had initially wanted to run the Cossacks (Colonel Huddleston) (see chapter seven), both of whom were, moreover, deeply involved in the Coup plot. The title of 'acting counsellor' for Haig seems to be an invention to justify his role as a representative of the legation. Norman did add, for good measure, that when the four men got there they saw Reza, Mas'ud, Kazem, and Zia, 'who was probably the originator of the whole movement'.

Now that Smart had stopped the government sending the gendarmes to turn back the Cossacks, Norman made sure that the police would not put up a resistance:

I then sent for General Westdahl, the Swedish chief of police, and impressed on him the importance, in case the Cossacks should enter the town, of seeing that his men confined themselves to their proper duty of maintaining public order and did not become involved in any fighting which might take place.[11]

The four men arrived at Mehrabad after 8 pm. At first they met Reza and Zia, who took off his *kolah* (in place of the old small turban) and told them who he was, prompting Adib al-Saltaneh to reply, 'We know you well no matter in what guise you may appear'.[12] Mo'in al-Molk then told Reza Khan that the Cossacks' march had frightened the people of the capital, and the Shah had ordered that they return to Qazvin. Reza became excited, boasted about the great sacrifices that the Cossacks had made, complained of lack of recognition, and said that they were going to Tehran simply to rejoin their families after long separation. When Adib al-Saltaneh said that, in fact, their services were greatly recognized, Reza remained silent. In the account that Zia gave to Jamalzadeh, he says that at that point Reza Khan was about to be persuaded.[13] Speaking passionately and forcefully, Zia then came straight to the point, attacked the political establishment, and said that they were determined to save the country from them. It is not unlikely that Zia has exaggerated his own role and under-played Reza's. But Reza Khan's silence may, in fact, have been due to the underhanded shrewdness which was to serve him so well in the future. However, Adib recounts that he then asked Hague to say his piece:

The Colonel made a move, and in his familiar mocking way uttered the following words: the prime minister has sent us to ask you gentlemen, please, to change your mind, and not come to Tehran. No reply was given to the Colonel, complete silence fell on the assembly, and after a few moments the commander of the Cossacks [Reza] and Sayyed Zia al-Din left us in the inn [where they had been meeting] and went out. We were puzzled as to what to do next. After a few minutes our two companions, the General [sic; Huddleston] and the Colonel also left us and went out of the room. We did not see them again, did not know where they had gone, and why they left us suddenly and without uttering a word.[14]

So much for the mission that – as an alternative to resistance – Smart had sold to Sepahdar and Norman had endorsed. The two British officers 'returned here at about 11 pm', wired Norman to Curzon, 'and reported their failure'.[15] Close to midnight, the frightened Adib and Mo'in were called to board one of the cars in Mehrabad and follow the march to Tehran. Before starting on the road to town, 10,000 of the 20,000 toman fund of the Qazvin Cossacks, which Kazem had taken with him, was distributed among the soldiers, although, according to Zia, the remainder was later returned to the Cossacks' fund.[16]

In the morning of 20 February, the able gendarmerie major, Habibollah Shaibani, had told Captain (later General) Arfa about the march of the Cossacks, posted him to the western walls of the city between the Qazvin Gate and the Bagh-e Shah Gate, and told him to stop the Cossacks from entering town and to return fire if they fired at his men. Later in the evening the Shah personally telephoned Arfa's post and ordered Arfa to keep him informed. An hour later, an advance party of Cossacks led by Lt.-Colonel Hossein Aqa (Khoza'i, later to become the tough commander of the Khorasan Division) approached the Qazvin Gate, was stopped by the gendarmes and, confronted by Arfa, let loose a string of obscenities (for which the Cossacks were renowned), and disappeared into the dark. Arfa tried, but did not succeed, to report the incident either to the Shah or to Major Shaibani.[17]

The main body of the Cossacks entered the city through the Gomrok (Customs) Gate in the south-west (south of the Qazvin Gate, at the bottom end of Shahr-e Naw, which was then just outside the town). The Gate was guarded by 300 men of the so-called Central Brigade, a motley group who offered no resistance. Zia and Reza set up temporary headquarters at the Cossacks' barracks (Qazzaq-khaneh), and took charge of the city.

Shortly afterwards, Farmanfarma arrived to see them. He was then regarded as an extremely important and powerful person who would be beyond molestation and intimidation. Also, Reza had once been a sergeant in an army led by him. But, as noted in chapter one, legitimacy in Iran has had much more to do with actual power than social class. The Sayyed, who had been much closer than Reza to the centre of upper Iranian society, was well aware of this. He probably had no theory about it, but knew from experience that in an arbitrary society like Iran, established figures and classes may be subjugated and even overthrown with relative ease, once the necessary minimum force is at hand. Indeed, the elites would themselves contribute towards it in the hope of saving some of their privileges, if not their necks (see chapter one).

Zia, at any rate, claims that on hearing of Farmanfarma's arrival, Reza jumped with awe and respect, but Zia ordered his arrest[18] (Norman's report that he had been arrested on the way to the American legation is incorrect).[19] If this is true, it may well have been due to Reza's customary shrewdness at difficult times, rather than timidity. However that may be, by the time he threw Zia out of office as well as out of the country, three months after the Coup, he had learned his lesson so well that nothing could shake his resolve to ride over the Iranian establishment and politicians, ultimately to the pinnacle of power.

Zia then gave orders for more arrests, which within the next two days rose to over 80 important and influential people. They consisted mainly of powerful establishment figures such as Firuz and his brother Salar Lashkar – pro-Vosuq activists such as Bahar who declined to join Zia's suite – and anti-Agreement activists, notably Modarres. On 22 February, Firuz informed Norman in writing that his father had been arrested and that he himself expected to be interned shortly. Norman, as he later reported to Curzon, intervened without success, but managed to obtain guarantees on their lives.

It is virtually certain that, had it not been for the moderating influence of the British on the ground, many if not most of those men would have lost their lives as well as their property and possessions. In fact, they did lose much of the latter to the public treasury and to private persons, most notably Reza Khan. Yet Norman's claim that he had tried to obtain their release cannot be taken seriously. Zia had quickly posted a few Cossacks outside the British legation, ostensibly to stop men trying to take *bast* in the compound, but in reality to save Norman and his other friends there from embarrassment, as he would not have put guards outside the legation without their knowledge and approval. Only Sepahdar managed to slip through the net in time and demand sanctuary from Norman, but 'after a considerable amount of argument was persuaded to return home again about noon after I had undertaken to obtain for him immunity from molestation, which Sayyed Zia-ud-Din subsequently promised to accord to him.'[20]

The next day, Zia did something quite telling. He withdrew 100,000 tomans of government money in the Imperial Bank of Persia and simply distributed it among the leading officers of the Coup, including Reza Khan.[21] He had been in the habit of acting as intermediary between Sepahdar and the Bank. But it is remarkable that now he was the leader of a military Coup, and still without any legal authority, the Bank's manager allowed him to cash this large sum of money for that purpose. However, as noted in the previous chapter, the Bank's attitude towards the current Iranian situation was usually in line with Norman's view and opposed to Curzon's.

About midnight on 20–21 February the Shah had telephoned Norman, but, according to Norman, the servant somehow did not manage 'to attract the attention of anybody in my house, so that I remained undisturbed':

> On the same morning (21 February) the Shah sent for me and asked my opinion regarding the line he should follow. He was nervous but obviously much less frightened than when Mr Smart had seen him on the previous day, presumably because no harm had come to him since the arrival of the Cossacks, and he no longer talked of flight.

At this point Norman implicitly admitted that he had been in contact with the Coup leaders and that, to say the least, he did not disapprove of their aims:

> I was able to reassure him regarding the intentions of the leaders of the movement towards himself and advised him to put himself in

communication with them, ascertain their wishes and grant whatever demands they might make. This, I pointed out, was the only course which His Majesty could possibly adopt seeing that they were masters of the situation. His Majesty readily agreed to follow my advice.[22]

Yet the Shah still hesitated. It was not until the afternoon of the next day, Tuesday 22 February, that he sent for Sayyed. Zia demanded no less than the title of dictator (*Diktator*). The Shah refused, and Zia did not insist, settling for that of prime minister.[23] Reza Khan, as mentioned before, was appointed general officer commanding the Cossacks in place of Sardar Homayun, who was to end his days as Major-General Qasem Vali in Reza Shah's army. He was also given a newfangled title – much as 'Sardar Homayun' had been – of Sardar Sepah. Shortly afterwards, Zia announced his cabinet and issued fiery statements (one signed by himself, another by Reza) about the radical changes soon to be made. At that moment all looked well for him, for the aspirations of radical nationalists, and for Norman and Anglo–Iranian relations. Hardly anyone noticed the joker in the pack.

British reactions to the Coup

Before sending his long report on the Coup – which somehow took almost two months to be received by the Foreign Office – Norman had sent a relatively short telegram to Curzon on 21 February and reported the event in some detail.[24] On the following day, G. P. Churchill noted in a comment that 'the whole thing is evidently the result of a plot and Seyyed Zia-ed-Din, the probable new prime minister, is no doubt at the bottom of it. He is a great admirer of Kerensky whom he reveres personally and endeavours to imitate'.[25] Next day, a wire received by the War Office from General Haldane said that 'General Ironside states Cossacks went to Tehran to arrest turbulent Cossack ex-officers by order of Shah and with knowledge of Mr Norman'.[26] As we saw in the previous chapter, the Shah had not ordered the Cossacks to go to Tehran. On the contrary, he had tried to stop them, and later tried to turn them back. Norman who, as late as 18 February had not yet decided to go along with the Coup-makers, had even tried to assist the Shah by sending a telegram to Norperforce that day, which had been effectively ignored. And Ironside, who left on that evening, is very likely to have known about it. However, Ironside's telegram prompted Lancelot Oliphant to comment:

We have not heard from Mr Norman [in his telegram of 21/2/21] that the Cossacks were originally sent to Tehran with his knowledge and it certainly did not require so many men to effect the arrest of a few ex-officers who could have been arrested by the Tehran police. We can, however, ignore the point.[27]

This was long before the Foreign Office received Norman's full report, cited above, which included an explanation of why and how the entire Qazvin Cossacks had marched to Tehran. The French, American, and German legations in Tehran – along with both conservative and popular politicians (though not the radical nationalists) – wasted no time in concluding that the Coup had been organized by the British legation. The Foreign Office did not place much weight on French opinion,[28] but when the news of a similar response from the American and German legations came, G. P. Churchill took it more seriously, as he minuted:

> Both the United States and German representatives believe that the recent Coup d'état at Tehran was engineered by the British Legation, but we have no indication of this in any of Mr Norman's telegrams.[29]

It is clear that the view of the foreign legations was not far off the mark, except that they further concluded that the Coup had been carried out at the instigation of the British government. This conclusion, which was shared by established Iranian politicians, although incorrect, was eminently reasonable.

At this point General Dickson's attitude became extremely embarrassing to his compatriots who had partaken in organizing the Coup, and were now supporting Zia's government. It may be remembered from chapter eight that the plotters had arranged for Dickson's recall from London, but that – probably sniffing something in the air – he had delayed his departure. Immediately after the Coup, Iranian leaders thought that he had been behind it,[30] and though he himself does not explain why, it must be for the simple reason that Smyth was formally under him in the British Military Mission. Therefore, in an attempt to defend and absolve himself to his friends – Mostawfi, Moshir and others, as well as to the American minister in Tehran – he might have given them hints as to whom he thought had been behind the plot.

Norman and his friends got alarmed, and only four days after the Coup Norman wrote him a formal letter that he should have left long before, and that, 'in view of the changed situation produced by the advent to power of a new government, I cannot but feel that your continued presence at Tehran ... may have undesirable political consequences'. It was so bad that, although the road to Hamadan (and thereby to Mesopotamia) was still blocked by heavy snow, Dickson must go to Qazvin forthwith and then leave the country when the road became passable.[31]

Once again Norman added a private letter, apologising for the tone of the other one and wondering if Dickson remembered 'something I said to you ... last summer'.[32] Dickson felt – as he wrote later in London to General Sir Percy Radcliffe – that 'the reference made by Mr Norman in the private letter can only be to a conversation [in the summer of 1920] in which he stated that my known sympathy with the Nationalists [the popular constitutionalists] would necessitate my departure from Persia should a government composed of reactionary elements again come into power' (see chapter six).[33]

Dickson had not known about the role of Smyth in the plot, or so he wrote to Curzon in May, and only learned about it from the Colonel himself in Qazvin when he got there on his way back to England.[34] According to Norman, while still in Tehran Dickson had sent him a verbal message that 'he knew for certain that Sir E. Ironside and I had organised recent Coup d'etat', though Norman denied both charges in his telegram to the Foreign Office.[35] On the other hand, in an interview with Oliphant at the Foreign Office early in May, Dickson did not implicate Norman. Reporting on their interview, Oliphant wrote:

> He said that on his way from Tehran he met at Kasvin Colonel Smyth ... and that Colonel Smyth gave him clearly to understand that the legation was privy to the advance of Riza Khan and the Cossacks on Tehran, and that General Dickson himself so informed the acting G.O.C. at Baghdad.

Oliphant asked him what he meant by 'the legation', adding that they had 'been assured categorically by Mr. Norman that he had had nothing whatever to do with it':

> The General explained that his own opinion was that the Minister had been kept in the dark by the staff and he mentioned specifically Mr Smart (the Oriental Secretary) as being privy to the whole proceeding.[36]

For good measure, and alluding to opinion expressed by Norman, Oliphant mentioned that he had found Dickson 'in no way insane or overwrought'. Both Norman and some Persian sources believed that Dickson had left Tehran thinking that he might be assassinated (perhaps even on his way back) on the order of Sayyed Zia.[37] The view that Dickson had been talking was so rife amongst the Coup makers that the United State's minister, a close friend of Dickson's who shared his views about the political situation in Iran, wrote him a formal letter denying the rumour that Dickson had told him anything about the Coup. 'My dear General', wrote John Caldwell:

> I have just this evening heard through a mutual friend that you have been accused by your Legation of having been guilty of some indiscreet political utterances and predictions to me, and that one of the 'serious crimes' of which you are accused is that of having given me a detailed written report of all facts concerning the recent revolution in Teheran. All these stories, are of course, too absurd and ridiculous to even deny ...

> As you know we have never at any time discussed Persian politics in the slightest degree, except that in casual conversation we sometimes mentioned Persians and were generally agreed as to who were the good and the bad men of Persia.[37a]

However that may be, from the present detailed study of preparations for the Coup and of the British officers and diplomats involved in it, it is clear that Dickson had a good grasp of events at the time. His only mistake (according to what he told Oliphant) was that he did not realise Norman's participation in it at the eleventh hour; but then, according to Norman's own report, Dickson had implicated him as well.

The fact that the Foreign Office soon gathered all the main facts about the Coup and how it had been organized did not mean they had any sympathy for it. On the contrary, Curzon saw it as the climax of the defiance to his own Persian Policy (by Ironside, Norman and their associates), and was in no mood to be helpful to Zia's regime. Indeed, he so displayed his personal contempt of Zia that, in his telegrams to Norman, he did not mention Zia's name even once, referring to him when necessary as the 'Persian Prime Minister'.

Within a few days of assuming office, the Sayyed had taken two radical but highly popular steps: denouncing the 1919 Agreement and signing the Irano–Soviet treaty which had been concluded by Moshaver in Moscow and awaited signature in Tehran. For Curzon, that was enough to put him beyond the pale.

As soon as he took office, Zia confided to Norman that without denouncing the Agreement the new government could not begin to work, and this view was shared by virtually everybody, both Iranian and British, in Tehran before the Coup. Zia further explained that he would employ British advisers and officers on personal contracts to organize the financial and military administration, while some American, French and perhaps other European personnel would also be employed. The new government wished to take over the South Persia Rifles (with a few of its British officers) and appoint Colonel Huddleston to raise an Iranian force of 5000 men in Qazvin. They had already reinstated James Balfour in the ministry of finance, hoping that Armitage-Smith himself would return from London soon. Meanwhile, they begged that the departure of Norperforce would be delayed for a few months:[38]

> In conclusion, he [Zia] said that if Great Britain wished to save her position here she must sacrifice shadow for substance, remain in the background, and help Persia effectively but unostentatiously. He was sure that this policy would in the end gain for Great Britain most of the advantages she had expected to obtain from an impracticable agreement.[39]

There followed another round of 'Curzon versus Norman'. Curzon replied that his attitude towards the cancellation of the Agreement was still the same as when (on 16 February) it had been proposed by Firuz to Norman (see chapter eight):

> Idea, however, of new Persian Government, that they can first denounce the agreement and then extract the main part of its advantages, seems to me fallacious. Formal denunciation ... is not disguised by statement that

no hostility to Great Britain is implied. There can at this date be no question of delaying the withdrawal of British forces at Qazvin.[40]

For the next three months Norman argued, reasoned, pleaded and begged for some degree of support from Curzon for Zia's government, to no avail. This was the more so because, sensing the British lack of will to defend the Sayyed, Reza's attitude towards the new prime minister became increasingly menacing, and as early as March 1921, when Dickson was passing through Qazvin on his way to England, 'Colonel Smyth told me that Sayyid Zia now feared his [Reza Khan's] growing power and had desired Colonel Smyth to endeavour to control him.'[41]

Norman persisted. There was no choice but to abrogate the Agreement, he wired Curzon; Zia was an honest as well as reforming nationalist, and a good friend of Britain. And the fact that he had come to power via a Coup should not be held against him since the country had hitherto been in the hands of either corrupt or incapable people, from whose hands power could not be wrested other than by force:

> New situation has been hailed with utmost satisfaction by British community here as the most favourable to British interests which could possibly have risen, and I appeal to your Lordship not to allow resentment at abrogation of agreement ... to prevent His Majesty's Government from taking advantage of present opportunity by excluding from new Government all help and encouragement which they need.[42]

At the same time, the manager of the Imperial Bank of Persia in Tehran sent a favourable report to their head office in London, and Colonel Huddleston similarly recommended Zia's regime to the War Office.[43]

On the very same day that Norman sent his appeal to Curzon, a telegram from Curzon was on its way to Tehran. It said very sternly that if the new government confirmed its abrogation of the Agreement, then:

> His Majesty's Government will hold Persian Government responsible for the repayment plus interest of first instalment paid to their predecessors [i.e. the £131,000 paid to the triumvirate] ... If present Government denounce unilaterally the 1919 agreement, it will of course be open to His Majesty's Government to denounce similarly customs tariffs ...[44]

In no time, almost the entire British personnel in Iran became active in trying to obtain British backing for Zia without, however, succeeding in making the slightest impression on the chief British policy-maker for Iran, Lord Curzon of Kedleston. According to a note by Oliphant, Winston Churchill 'was strongly in favour of supporting Seiyyed Zia-ed-Din with all the arms, munitions, etc., possible'.[45] Churchill, as noted in the previous chapter, had just moved from the

War Office to the Colonial Office, so that it was now easy for him to be generous with arms and munitions. What he might have known about the Sayyed was much less than the Foreign Office knew. It is, however, likely that he got a first-hand account of the Coup from Ironside, Haldane and Cox at the Cairo Conference, to which Ironside had been summoned from his command in Qazvin.

The day after Oliphant's note about Churchill's attitude was written, Colonel C. B. Stokes, the old pro-constitutionalist British officer whom the Russians had not allowed Shuster to put in command of his Treasury gendarmerie, and who had met Zia in Baku in the spring of 1920, came to Zia's help. He sent a telegram (from Tiflis) to Curzon:

> I have received request from Sayid Zia, new Prime Minister, Persia, to help him in any way I can ... I have known Sayid Zia for fourteen years and have repeatedly worked in closest touch with him both in Persia and last year in (? Baku). He is in fact honest patriot and a convinced Anglophile ...[46]

The Sayyed was becoming increasingly anxious about Reza Khan's growing audacity backed by military power, and Reza very soon imposed himself on Zia as minister of war as well as commander of the armed forces. One day he barged into the cabinet room, removed Mas'ud Khan from his seat, and sat in his chair. Zia badly needed a countervailing military force, and – at least in the short term – he could only get it from Britain, who still had some military forces left in Iran. This was the reason Norman kept appealing for help in the military area in particular, though he dressed it up for Curzon as if troops were still needed to meet 'the Bolshevik menace'. It is also why Zia wished to keep the SPR's, and at one stage contemplated, but did not succeed in, moving some of them to Isfahan, a move which in the debates of the fourteenth Majlis was misconstrued as having been suggested by Britain.[47] He even wrote directly to Lloyd George for help, although he later realised that it had been tactless to try and go over Curzon's head.[48]

To Norman's repeated appeals for arms and ammunition, and loan of British officers ('Colonel Huddleston is eager to lend his services immediately'),[49] Curzon replied that the (British) Army Council believed that if an Iranian force was trained by British officers it would provide a pretext for Soviet Russia not to withdraw their forces from Gilan:

> I share these views of Army Council, and in these circumstances have to inform you definitely that His Majesty's Government are not prepared to meet wishes of Persian Prime Minister.[50]

At the same time, Norman and Zia induced the Shah to appeal to the King to order a postponement of Norperforce's departure,[51] but the answer was just the same.[52] Still, these were the early, happy, days, for as soon as Norperforce moved back to Mesopotamia early in April, even the Shah realised that Zia was a spent force.

Zia's attitude was almost completely consistent with the kind of British policy the government of India had argued for since late in 1918, when Cox had begun negotiating for the Agreement in Tehran (see chapter four). It was even better than India had hoped for. Here was a reformer as well as an Anglophile, rather than any of the pro-British old guard whom they considered to be both corrupt and reactionary, who was suggesting a similar line to theirs (they were, of course, regularly receiving copies of some of the correspondence between Norman and Curzon, as before). Late in April, Zia's position, and therefore Norman's appeals, were getting desperate. It is also likely that someone – Norman, perhaps even Cox – directly asked the government of India to intervene with Curzon on Zia's behalf, and they in turn prompted the India Office to woo Curzon in London.

There was not much love lost between Curzon and (Edwin) Montague, largely on account of Curzon's bitterness over India's lack of support for his Persian Policy. It is therefore not surprising that, rather than addressing Curzon himself, Montague asked the under-secretary of state in his department (i.e. the India Office) to write to his opposite number at the Foreign Office. The under-secretary wrote in a long letter that, in Montague's view, Iranians should perhaps have welcomed the Agreement, but they had misunderstood its purpose and were against it. The policy proposed by Zia, 'who seems to combine energy and honesty to a degree unusual in the country', in involving other powers (notably America) in the country's development seemed reasonable. Apart from that, it would not be in Britain's interest to abandon Iran completely to her fate. Montague 'ventures therefore to hope that Lord Curzon ... give at least his moral support to Zia-ud-din, and to indicate informally to the Powers already approached that their cooperation would be welcome to His Majesty's Government'.[53]

But Curzon's bitterness was beyond approach, and his reply was what should have been expected. He thought, wrote his under-secretary, that the approach to the USA suggested by Montague would be counter-productive, because their minister in Tehran had reported to Washington that Britain had engineered the Coup. Regarding the French and the Swedes, past experience of their services to Iran were such that would not justify their encouragement by Britain:

> Lord Curzon therefore sees ... no valid reason to depart from opinion expressed in His Lordship's telegram ... to Mr Norman that the 'cosmopolitan policy pursued by present Persian Government is doomed to ultimate failure'.[54]

This letter was dated 12 May. Two weeks later Zia had fallen and was on the run. Norman reported to Curzon that Reza Khan, 'an ignorant but astute peasant', and the Shah had forced Zia out of office because he saw Zia as a revolutionary zealot; that the Shah was 'now entirely in the hands of Minister of War, who is, for the moment, dictator'; that Reza had promised to keep the British military and financial advisers, although 'he is … not to be trusted':

> All my efforts to dissuade conspirators from this disastrous intrigue failed, owing to fact that, since withdrawal of our troops, Minister of War no longer fears us, and Shah afraid of Prime Minister … puts his whole trust in Minister of War, who is supreme command of all military forces.[55]

It was a personal tragedy, and the end of the road for Herman Norman himself. In an extremely difficult situation he had tried to serve his country well, without working against Iran. Every scheme he had devised since assuming duty in June 1920 might have been successful if it had received some sympathy and support from his chief in London. Had he not been so keen to do his best, in view of realities which Curzon somehow failed to contemplate, he might well have been personally successful, whatever the consequences for his country and Iran. Instead, he tried hard to do well and reaped all the blame for failure. He was recalled, and withdrawn from his post soon afterwards, and offered a post in Santiago, but he was so disgusted with the whole matter that he resigned from the diplomatic service.[55a]

Having walked out of jail, Qavam al-Saltaneh became prime minister on 5 June. To the Iranian nationalists, and radicals (as well as Norman and his staff) this was little short of reaction and counter-revolution. However, Qavam quickly sent an 'extremely long message' to Curzon, delivered, on 11 June, by the Iranian minister in London and received by Oliphant at the Foreign Office, who submitted 'the gist of it' to paper. It said:

> [O]wing to the political situation throughout the East it was incumbent on the new govt. to show no bias but to remain impartial not to incur the unpopularity which the Cabinet of Seyed Zia ed Din had incurred in consequence of its pro-British attitude (!). The Prime Minister hoped that HMG [the British government] would realize this & not withdraw their moral and material support.

Oliphant doubtless put the exclamation mark because Zia had abrogated the Agreement and, as noted, was very much in Curzon's bad books. On the other hand, Qavam might also have been thinking of the pro-British government of his brother Vosuq, which Zia had supported. Oliphant had replied that, while he would give the message to Curzon, he found it strange that the Iranian government would want 'to keep their cake and yet eat it', because they both wanted to treat Britain on the same level as other powers, yet still hoped to receive the same kind of help which she had given to pro-British cabinets. And when the Iranian minister suggested that the British might directly ask 'the desiderata of the new govt.', Oliphant was unresponsive. The epitaph to the whole saga was, however, contained in minutes written by Curzon himself, in his almost illegible hand:

> Mr Oliphant's action was entirely correct for I think he realises that I am sick of this procession of Persian Ministries all taking anti-British action but all sneaking round to protest British sympathies.
>
> I do not take the slightest interest in any one of them; their appearance or disappearance from the stage excites in me no more concern than the ... fall of (British) wickets in an International test match.[55b]

It is ironic that most Iranian nationalists and radicals at the time (who were pro-Zia, and certainly against the old governing class), thought that Qavam's government had been brought to power by Britain. It is even more ironic that, for decades to come, almost all Iranians firmly believed that the British had removed their own man, Sayyed Zia, to make way for their more preferred man, Reza Khan.

Iranian reactions to the Coup

The legend about the agents and motives of the Coup handed down to future generations, and still largely – although less extensively – believed, was along the following lines. The Coup had been designed and organized by the British government to make up for the failure of the 1919 Agreement. Zia and Reza were, and remained, agents of Britain all their lives (with Reza somehow cheating in the end, and being punished by Britain, who eventually forced his abdication in 1941).

As time went by, various reasons why Britain had engineered the 1921 Coup were offered. They wanted to punish Ahmad Shah for not having mentioned the Agreement in his speech in the London banquet (see chapters four and five). They wanted to stem the tide of Bolshevism through and beyond Iran. They wanted to topple the Qajars and install Reza Shah to prepare the ground for the 1933 oil agreement.

The belief that the Coup had been British policy originated from conservative as well as popular political leaders at that time. It looks eminently reasonable for men like Firuz, Sepahdar, Modarres, Moshir and others, being involved at close quarters in the events of the previous two years, to conclude that the Coup was British-made, especially as in some ways it was. And given the fact that Norman and his staff and the British officers (except Dickson) categorically denied any knowledge of it, the Iranian politicians must be excused for not considering that it might have been devised without London's knowledge.

Some of the conservatives, indeed, were extremely angry, most of all Firuz, who was convinced that the British had led him down the garden path all the time they were hatching the plot – and then had himself, his father and his brother arrested, riches extracted from them and their lives put in serious danger. Their fear was such that Mohammad Vali Mirza (later Farman-farma'iyan), another brother of Firuz, went to Baghdad in disguise to enlist Cox's support in defence of their lives.[56]

When the Sayyed was toppled, 40 of the released prisoners, who were also deputy-elects for the fourth Majlis, put out a long statement condemning Zia in the most vehement language. Entitled 'Stating the Truth', it was written by Firuz, and signed by him, Modarres, Ashtiyani, Bahar and Tadayyon, among others. The whole thing had been a fraud, ran the statement, and was the work of 'foreign politics (*siyasat-e khareji*)'. Zia, who was a 'criminal' and 'the journalist well known for lacking conscience and being a paid agent of foreigners', had duped the Cossacks in Qazvin, who were 'temporarily under a British officer', to believe that the Shah wished them to march to Tehran, and had then joined them near the capital:

> The Iranian commander of this force [i.e. Reza Khan], unaware of the truth ... put his force at Sayyed Zia's disposal and the latter, through plot as well as pressure, managed to obtain the [Shah's] notice for premiership ...[57]

There followed martial law, arrests of notables, censorship, etc., the statement continued. Meanwhile, the Sayyed pretended to be a nationalist and reformer, but they all saw the truth beneath such pretences, and 'the respectable Iranian general [Reza Khan] also realised that his honesty and courage had advanced the foreigners' objectives and the rule of a thief and traitor'. Reza Khan then made his patriotic (i.e., anti-Zia) feeling known to the Shah, and the Shah had Zia toppled and thrown out of the country.

The statement ended with a vehement attack on British interference in Iran, though the country was not openly named.[58] This must be the origin of Curzon's remark, two years later, to Sir Percy Lorraine, that he should 'some day give a good smash between the eyes of that traitorous Firuz'.[59] Such is the irony of history that Firuz was deeply wounded, thinking that Curzon and the Foreign Office had engineered the Coup, while Curzon too was sorely hurt, perceiving Firuz as accusing him of something he had not done, and did not even support.

The younger nationalist radicals and intellectuals, both then and for some time to come, saw events very differently. The public statements put out by the Sayyed and Reza Khan immediately after the Coup (both of which had been written by Zia) used a language that was without precedent in the history of Iranian government, and was music to their ears:

> After fifteen years of a constitutionalism, which was purchased at the expense of the priceless blood of the children of Iran ... our motherland was put [in a terrible situation]. Who were the people responsible for this

situation, this lack of direction? It was those who had deceived the people
on the promise of constitutionalism, freedom, and the rule of law and
justice ... so that, in their name, they would establish chaos, personal gain
and lawlessness ...

A few hundred magnates and notables (*ashraf va a'yan*) who had taken
the reins of power, were sucking the people's blood like leeches ... and had
corrupted our motherland's political and social life so that [even] the most
patriotic elements had ... lost hope in the survival of the land and the
people ...[60]

The statement was very long, and included the new government's radical and
ambitious programme in some detail: the abolition of privy purses and unjustified payments in the administration; distribution of state lands among the
peasants; tenancy reform in private agricultural estates to protect the rights of
the peasants; reform of the judicial system; financial reform for an efficient tax
system; extension of free education; promotion of trade and industry; construction of modern transport facilities; abolition of the capitulation agreements;
abrogation of the 1919 agreement, etc., but, above all, the formation of an
adequate military force to bring security and stability everywhere in the
country.[61]

The statement signed by Reza Khan was even more vehement in its nationalism, and in its rhetoric against 'a bunch of thieves and traitors':

When we were retreating from Gilan marshlands under the barrage of
enemy guns, we felt that the origin of all of Iran's misfortunes, and the
misery and humiliation of the army [*qoshun*] were the domestic criminals.

*At the very time when we were spilling our blood before the enemy, in honour of that very
sacred blood we swore to take the first opportunity ... to uproot the selfish, comfort
seeking domestic traitors, and liberate the Iranian people from the bondage of a bunch of
thieves and traitors.*[61a]

Almost all the sentiments expressed in these two statements were shared by
the modern nationalists. And the somewhat hopeful social programme
contained in Zia's statement were shared by them as well as by popular constitutionalists, except that the latter doubted Zia's sincerity as a patriot and reformer.
What particularly convinced the modernist nationalists of his sincerity were his
abrogation of the Agreement, his signing of the Irano–Soviet treaty, and his
arrest of many of the *a'yan va ashraf*, some of whom were deeply detested as
being both rotten to the core and lackeys of British imperialism. Indeed, more
than any other single factor, this arrest of the notables accounted for the
Sayyed's continued popularity among nationalist intellectuals, especially as, after
his downfall, it looked as if the same old gang had returned to power. That is
why Aref wrote his famous song, after Zia's 'black cabinet' fell and he himself
was forced out of the country:

You whom God protect, come back!
The eye longs for your look, come back!
You whose army are the people, come back!
We die for your black cabinet, come back!

The cabinet of the *ashraf* is naught but shame,
Their colours are nothing except those of deceit,
They know no colour is thicker than black,
We die for your black colour, come back! ...[62]

Eshqi wrote a long *qasideh*, full of references and allusions to ancient Iranian glories and their imminent restoration, in praise of Zia and his regime while he was still in power. But he published it after Zia's fall to avoid suspicions that he was a sycophant:

Watch Eshqi who has cursed all cabinets,
Determined in praise of this cabinet of power.[63]

In 1923, when the Sayyed was all but forgotten, he wrote in his long *qasideh-ye mostazad* against the fourth Majlis, in which he spared very few leading politicians his invective (and, incidentally, described Firuz as 'Curzon's concubine'):

We cannot do justice to the praise of Zia, – We'll never succeed,
Words would not do justice to his praise, – Didn't you see it all?[64]

The confrontation and rebellion of Colonel Mohammad Taqi Khan Pesyan – the able and extremely popular chief of the Khorasan gendarmerie – with Qavam's government (and in favour of Zia) was especially effective in confirming the modernist and nationalist intellectuals' good opinion of Zia. Even Iraj, who was much more moderate in his opinions than the usual run of modernist intellectuals, wrote a scathing anti-Qavam poem in which he glorified Pesyan:

Who would believe that such convulsion would come about,
Every thief would be released from jail,
The age of darkness would supersede the age of Zia [=light]
The thief in chain [Qavam] would become chief minister?[65]

The Sayyed fell because of his arrogant and tactless behaviour, which had offended the Shah, frightened the conservatives, alienated the popular constitutionalists, and left himself no power base except the radical intellectuals and the British legation, neither of which wielded any significant power – the latter because it was not backed by the Foreign Office in London. With his astuteness, coupled with strong secretive cunning, Reza quickly grasped this point and used it to full advantage. He pretended to be a good servant of the Shah and a

disinterested patriot who, at the same time, did not threaten the status quo and
had no political ambition. When Zia fell – and nearly lost his life as well – the
radicals saw it as the work of the British, partly because of the record of Zia's
words and deeds as prime minister, and partly because they saw men like
Qavam and Firuz returning to power.

By the time Reza Shah had abdicated, and for decades to come, there was
hardly anyone in the country – including both the Pahlavis – who did not
believe that the Coup had been designed and executed by the British government. Indeed, Mohammad Reza Shah said in 1953 that the British had brought
down the Qajars, put his father in their place, and later overthrew him as well
(see chapter ten). It was further believed, however, that for some unexplained
reason the British had decided to remove the 'civilian instrument of the Coup'
and leave its 'military instrument' in charge. In his famous biographical essays,
Bazigaran-e Asr-e Tala'i, Khajeh-Nuri attributes Zia's fall to 'the order of *simorgh*
[the Magic Bird of the Shahnameh]', that is, the British government. Sadeq
Hedayat has the entire legend about the period 1921–1941 mapped out in an
amusing allegory, 'The Case of the Anti-Christ's Donkey' (*Qaziyeh-ye Khar
Dajjal*).[66]

The Agreement and the Coup: a summing up

When the First World War ended Iran was in the grip of chaos, both in the
centre of politics and in the provinces. Constitutionalism had acquired a thoroughly bad name, being associated with the selfish and disunited rule of the
conservatives, the inability of popular and honest political leaders to be effective
in that situation, the spread of rebellion and brigandry in the provinces, and the
breakdown of order everywhere (see chapters two and three). There was real –
and indeed realistic – fear of disintegration. The revolutions in Russia had saved
the country from the tyranny of Russian imperialism, and the likely partition of
the country between Russia and Britain after an Entente victory. Bolshevism
was so popular with modernist nationalists that Aref wrote in 1918:

> The Bolshevik is the divine guide to delivery
> – Blessed be Mohammad and his People –
> O' Lenin, O' Angel of Blessing,
> Take the trouble if you please,
> Do step in, my home is yours,
> You may nest in the apple of my eye.
> Either demolish or develop it,
> God bless your deliberations.[67]

Few lines sum up so succinctly the sense of despair, the faint glimmer of hope,
the wish for either the magical disappearance of every possible ill or for

destruction and death, and the cultural and political confusion of the sentimental radicals of the time. Though small in number, they had much influence
among the modern urban generations, but their idealism, puritanism and lack of
patience made life difficult for anyone – including and especially the popular
constitutionalists – who wished to effect a measure of possible reform and
bring some order to their troubled land.

In many ways, this political sentimentalism, born of a combination of raw
idealism and extreme political naivete, persisted and became widespread
throughout the century.

Britain, at the time the sole remaining great power in the region, had to
confront the situation. The evidence shows that, at least until the time when the
1919 Agreement was signed, Britain's main worry was to ensure order and
stability on her Indian – and now also Mesopotamian – doorstep, rather than
any great fear of the spread of Bolshevism southwards. Indeed, for much of this
time British policy-makers were convinced that the 'madness' in Russia would
soon end. The *cordon sanitaire,* which Iranian commentators sometimes make so
much of in trying to explain both the Agreement and the Coup, was conceived a
couple of years later, when it became clear that the Soviet Union was there to
stay.

Curzon saw his chance of bringing Iran into the fold of Britain's sphere of
influence in the Middle East. Even if he had been wishing to make Iran a British
protectorate, he would not have been allowed to do so by the government of
India and the India Office. Indeed, neither they, nor the Treasury and the War
Office, were prepared to help the Agreement succeed, even at a relatively small
cost. To safeguard British material interest and strategic interest alone would
then have been easy without any formal agreement, if Britain had used Khaz'al,
other Arab Shaikhs and tribes in Khuzistan, the Bakhtiyaris and some other
southern nomads to turn southern Iran into an effective protectorate. This
indeed was what their thoughts began to turn to in January 1921, as a desperate
measure, when it looked likely that Tehran would fall to Gilan Bolsheviks.
Curzon was personally more ambitious, and saw himself as the big friend and
mentor of a stable Iran, as well as the guarantor of Britain's long-term interests
in the region.

Many Iranian leaders, both conservative and popular, were also much alive to
the dangers facing the country. They were aware of the fact that Britain was now
the sole great power in the region and eager to promote political and economic
stability, and believed that the country could use British assistance (certainly
along with French and/or American) to attain those goals. The problem was
that, like Curzon and Cox, men such as the triumvirate were still in the pre-war,
and to some extent even the pre-constitutionalist, world. They therefore grossly
underrated the profound effect that constitutionalism – despite the increasing
chaos which had followed it – had had on the country's political culture, and the
great impact of the war and the Russian revolutions in fomenting nationalist and
modernist sentiments in Iran. He hoped to make Iran, not a protectorate, but a

client state of Britain and no other great power, as she had been before the fall of Tsarist Russia.

The government of India understood both those developments well. Their alternative to the Agreement was almost entirely consistent with the view of those constitutionalist leaders (like Moshir, Mostawfi and Modarres) who were not radical nationalists, who were alive to the limits of the country's political and economic capacity for development and who hoped to bring about gradual but lasting reforms with foreign help, some of which they expected to receive from Britain. Both India and the constitutionalists were overruled by Curzon and the triumvirate, who entered an agreement behind closed doors, without consultation with other important leaders and, therefore, without the Shah's real blessing and commitment. It excluded participation by other powers, specifically America and France, whom most Iranians regarded as disinterested parties. The payment of money for 'oiling the wheels', even though it was eventually described as the first instalment of the loan, was the straw that broke the Agreement's back.

The whole affair made America, France and Russia hostile to the Agreement, and their belief (which they more or less publicly stated) that the country's independence had been sold to Britain left little room for argument with the country's modern nationalists, radicals and pro-Bolsheviks. And the more emphatically Curzon and the triumvirate repeated that this was not the case, the more firmly the Agreement's opponents in and out of the country believed that it was.

There was another upsurge of revolutionary activity in Gilan which, despite Vosuq's own tactful approach, the injustice, greed and incompetence of government officials and Cossacks did nothing to moderate. Khiyabani's revolt was not a reaction to the Agreement. He too understood the logic and despised the consequences of the chaos, and hoped to bring order, at least to Azerbaijan, under his own leadership. Yet the conflict produced by the Agreement was helpful for his revolt, and it was generally believed (both then and since) that it had been a revolt against the Agreement.

The first major crack in the Agreement was caused by the Bolshevik landing of May 1920 at Enzeli, and could probably have been avoided if Curzon had not effectively stopped Vosuq and Firuz from talking direct to Moscow. Both the War Office and the British cabinet wished to avoid a long and protracted conflict with Bolshevik Russia in Iran. Norperforce had been ordered to withdraw its garrison from Enzeli if attacked by the Bolsheviks. The further evacuation from Rasht – which seems to have been entirely unnecessary – sealed the fate of the Agreement. It lost Britain a great deal of prestige, emboldened opposition to them and the Agreement, further weakened Vosuq's position, and led to the coalition of Kuchik and the Iranian Bolsheviks, backed by their Soviet allies.

At this point Cox became High Commissioner in Baghdad, and Norman arrived in Tehran at the same time as the Shah returned from Europe. The Shah neither liked nor trusted the triumvirate, and, given the blow to Vosuq's position by the events of Gilan, was strongly advised to dismiss him. Vosuq wanted certain powers – at least to bring the Cossacks into the proposed uniform force – which the Shah refused to give him. Vosuq resigned. On the other hand, the triumvirs did not enjoy a good reputation among the British diplomats and advisers in Tehran. The dominant view, as formulated by the military and financial advisers and accepted by Norman, was to back a government led by an urbane and popular constitutionalist.

Moshir's government faced many, almost insurmountable, difficulties, but it had public goodwill on its side, which is how he split Kuchik from the Insurgents and put down Khiyabani's revolt without difficulty. Money was needed to run the administration and pay the Cossacks, which Norman somehow managed to arrange for a couple of months. Also, the Agreement had to be put into abeyance, which Norman, Dickson and Armitage-Smith accepted. That was enough for Curzon to distrust both Moshir and Norman. It is true that Curzon's own hands were largely tied by India, the War Office and the Treasury, but if he had co-operated with Moshir in the same spirit as with Vosuq, Moshir would have succeeded. All Curzon was interested in was that the Majlis should be convened without delay and the fate of his cherished Agreement be decided.

The War Office were weary of Curzon's pressure to keep their forces in Iran. They were afraid of direct conflict with the Bolsheviks and eager to evacuate Norperforce quickly and, if possible, with honour. They sent Ironside, a tough soldier and an expert in dealing with critical situations, to command Norperforce. He quickly toppled Starosselski, with Norman's support and cooperation. Sepahdar was put in Moshir's place – Moshir had resigned rather than put the Cossacks under British officers – and an Iranian desk officer was made nominal commander of the Cossacks, whereas in reality they were led and drilled by Colonel Smyth and his men.

December 1920 and January 1921 were highly critical months. Sepahdar in the end agreed with the Taimurtash-Zia-Norman plan to raise an Iranian force under the command of British military advisers, but Curzon reneged on his promise to put up the money. Norperforce was set to leave in the spring; the Gilan insurgents were threatening to march to Tehran; the radicals in the capital had become popular and audacious; and the British legation was losing influence fast, not least with the Shah. There was serious talk of moving the capital to Isfahan or Shiraz.

The Foreign Office began to explore the possibility of either trying to bring in a strong no-nonsense government led by someone like Ain al-Dawleh or Farmanfarma, or, failing that, trying to defend the centre and south by creating a government there of the Shah backed by tribal forces, which they would indirectly control. India still insisted on abandonment of the Agreement, which Norman kept recommending, thereby pushing Curzon into further anger and unreason.

It was in this chaotic situation that Firuz decided to test his luck in trying to form a strong government, receiving some encouragement (although no commitment) from the Foreign Office, and went back to Iran via Mesopotamia. At the same time, and with the Cossacks effectively under his command, Ironside felt that a military dictatorship might save the situation from chaos and/or 'Bolshevism', along with British honour. Zia and his Committee of Iron, on the other hand, were looking for any opportunity to bring on a strong and reforming government, preferably their own. Smyth had known and worked with Mas'ud and Kazem of the gendarmerie, who were intimate lieutenants of Zia in the Committee of Iron. They all decided to bring the Cossacks to Tehran for a putsch before Norperforce's departure, which was set for April 1921.

They looked for a commander to lead the march, and approached Amir-Movassaq (later General Nakhjavan), who turned them down. They settled on Reza Khan. In February, Ironside was suddenly summoned to the Cairo Conference and felt that he had to act before leaving. He saw the Shah with Norman, and told him to bring Reza into 'a position of power' (the euphemism used by Ullman, who has seen Ironside's manuscript diary), which the Shah refused to do. Ironside then told Norman of his plan, which Norman did not endorse.

The Coup-makers needed a pretext for sending the Cossacks to Tehran. Being unaware of this, Norman, a few days before, had suggested to Smyth that perhaps some five or six hundred of the drilled and polished Qazvin Cossacks be sent to Tehran, and their rowdy and undisciplined colleagues sent back to be similarly drilled and polished. The Shah had approved the idea in principle. Taking advantage of this, Smyth and Zia pressured Sardar Homayun, the nominal commander of the Cossacks, to order the march of the full force – a couple of thousand strong. When the Shah heard about this, he rightly connected it to Ironside's suggestion to him, a couple of days before, of bringing Reza 'to a position of power'. He told Homayun to reverse the order, but Ironside and Smyth ignored this even after Norman intervened.

At this point Norman threw in his lot with the Coup-makers. When it became clear that the Cossacks were definitely coming, he was persuaded to cooperate with the Coup by Smart, Haig, Huddleston and probably Havard as well, making himself scarce so the Shah and Sepahdar could not contact him, neutralizing the police, and letting Smart arrange the diversion of sending a joint deputation to Mehrabad, instead of meeting resistance from the gendarmes. That is how the Coup succeeded without a fight, and Zia became prime minister.

Within a couple of weeks the Foreign Office had a fairly reasonable picture of what had happened, even though Norman in his correspondence denied any role by Ironside, himself or any other British officer or diplomat in organizing it. But Curzon did not have the slightest interest in the new government: it had been brought on by a Coup which had been made behind his back; Zia had committed the unforgivable sin of abrogating the 1919 Agreement, and had put men like Firuz in jail. Worst of all, he had Norman's backing, and the hated

India Office and War Office felt Zia should be given a chance, or at least moral support. Curzon gave them precisely nothing.

When Norperforce departed, Norman was left with no power, either moral or material, with which to defend Zia's government. Reza was aware of this, and Zia's arrogance and tactlessness had left him with little domestic support, only the goodwill of nationalist intellectuals, which was of little help in sustaining him in power. On the other hand, the astute and manipulative Reza posed as a loyal servant of the Shah and of the country who had no political ambition. He persuaded the Shah to dismiss Zia, and, although he tried, Norman could not prevent his fall from office.

Thus the turn of the tide began again, from chaos towards arbitrary rule, so familiar from the country's ancient history.

Notes

1   Norman to Curzon, 1/3/21 (although received by the Foreign Office on 26/4/1), F.O. 416/68.

2   See *ibid.*; the memoirs of Colonel Qahremani, Cossack officer and eyewitness, in Malek al-Sho'ra Bahar, *Tarikh-e Mokhtasar-e Ahzab-e Siyasi*, vol. 1, (Tehran: Amir Kabir, 1978), chapter 20; Mohammad Ali Jamalzadeh, 'Taqrirat-e Sayyed Zia and His "Black Book"', part 2, *Ayandeh*, vol. 7, June 1981 (this source is important because it contains notes taken from Zia's own account after his exile to Europe); General Amir Ahmadi,, *Khaterart-e Nakhostin Sepahbod-e Iran*, (ed.) Gholamhussein Zargarinezhad (Tehran: Mo'assehseh-ye Pazhuhesh-ha va Motale'at-e Farhangi, 1994), part 2; Hossein Makki, *Tarikh-e Bistsaleh-ye Iran*, vol. 1 (Tehran: Elmi, 1995), chapter 2.

3   See Sayyed Zia in Hossein Kay Ostovan, *Siyasat-e Movazeneh-ye Manfi*, vol. 1, (Tehran: Kay Ostovan, 1948), p. 77; Jamalzadeh 'Taqrirat-e Sayyed Zia', part 2; Amir Ahmadi, *Khaterat*, vol. 1.

4   See Jamalzadeh, 'Taqrirat-e Sayyed Zia'; Ja'far Mehdi-niya, *Zendegi-ye Siyasi-ye Sayyed Zia al-Din Tabatab'i* (Tehran: Mehdi-niya, 1990), part 2; Bahar, *Tarikh-e Mokhtasar*, chapter 6; Makki, *Tarikh-e Bistsaleh*, vol. 1, chapter 2.

5   See Jamalzadeh, 'Taqrirat-e Sayyed Zia', p. 209.

6   See Bahar, *Tarikh-e Mokhtasar*, vol. 1, p. 91.

7   Noman to Curzon, 1/3/21, F.O. 416/68.

8   *Ibid.*

9   See 'Yaddasht-ha-ye Khaterati-ye, Adib al-Saltaneh Sami'i', *Ayandeh*, vol. 7, February 1981, pp. 872–73.

10 Norman to Curzon, 1/3/21, F. O. 416/68.

11 *Ibid.*

12 See Sami'i, 'Yaddasht-ha', p. 874.

13 See Jamalzadeh, 'Taqrirat-e Sayyed Zia', parts 2 and 3, *Ayandeh*, June and July, 1981.

14 See Sami'i, '*Yaddasht-ha*', p. 785; Jamalzadeh, 'Taqrirat-e Sayyed Zia', parts 2 and 3; Makki, *Tarikh-e Bistsaleh*, vol. 1, chapter 2.

15 Norman to Curzon, 1/3/21.

16 Jamalzadeh, 'Taqrirat-e Sayyed Zia', parts 2 and 3.

17 See General Hassan Arfa, *Under Five Shahs* (London: John Murray, 1964), chapter 5.

18 See Jamalzadeh, 'Taqrirat-e Sayyed Zia', part 3; Mehdi-niya, *Zendegi-ye Siyasi-ye Sayyed Zia*, part 2.

19 Norman to Curzon, 1/3/21.

20 *Ibid.*

21   Jamalzadeh, 'Taqrirat-e Sayyed Zia', part 3. The same figure is also indirectly quoted from Zia by Donald Wilber. See his *Riza Shah Pahlavi, The Resurrection and Reconstruction of Iran* (New York: Exposition Press, 1975), chapter III. Bahar, in *Tarikh-e Mokhtasar*, p. 90, quotes the figure of 80,000 tomans.

22   Norman to Curzon, 1/3/21.

23   *Ibid.* Zia himself – in Jamalzadeh, 'Taqrirat-e Sayyed Zia, part 3' – says that he asked, and obtained, 'full powers' from the Shah.

24   Norman to Curzon, 21/2/21, *British Documents on Foreign Policy*, vol. xiii, no. 681.

25   Minute by G. P. Churchill, 22/2/21, F.O. 371/6401.

26   Haldane to War Office, 23/2/21, F.O. 371/6409.

27   See Minutes, 'Persia: Political Situation' (35), F.O. 371/6409.

28   Minute by Lancelot Oliphant, 22/2/21, F.O. 371/6401.

29   Minute by Churchill, 'Persia: Political Situation' (37), F.O. 371/6409.

30   Dickson to Curzon, 14/5/21, F.O. 371/6427.

31   Norman's formal letter to Dickson, 25/2/21, F.O. 371/6427.

32   Norman's private letter to Dickson, 25/2/21, F.O. 371/6427.

33   Dickson to Radcliffe, 8/10/21, F.O. 371/6427.

34   Dickson to Curzon, 14/5/21, 371/6427.

35   Norman to F.O., 2/3/21, F.O. 371/6427.

36   Memorandum by Oliphant, 5/5/21, F.O. 371/6427.

37   Norman to F.O., 2/3/21; Yahya Dawlat-Abadi, *Hayat-e Yahya*, vol. 4, chapter 25; Mehdi-niya, *Zendegi-ye Siyasi*, Part 2.

37a Caldwell to Dickson, 1/3/21, F.O. 371/6427.

38   Norman to Curzon, 25/2/21, *BDFP*, vol. xiii, no. 683; Norman to Curzon, 26/2/21, *ibid.*, no. 685.

39   *Ibid.*, no. 685.

40   Curzon to Norman, 28/2/21, *ibid.*, no. 687.

41   Dickson to Curzon, 14/5/21, F.O.371/6427.

42   Norman to Curzon, 3/3/21, F.O., 371/6401.

43   Memorandum by Oliphant, 4/3/21, F.O. 371/6401.

44   Curzon to Norman, 3/3/21, *BDFP*, no. 689.

45   Note by Oliphant, 2/3/21, quoted in Curzon to Norman, 14/3/21, n.2, *ibid.*, 696.

46   Stokes (Tiflis) to Curzon, 3/3/21, F.O. 371/6409.

47   See Mosaddeq's and Zia's exchanges on this in the fourteenth Majlis debate, in Kay Ostovan, *Siyasat-e Movazeneh-ye Manfi*, vol. 1.

48   See Jamalzadeh, 'Taqrirat-e Sayyed Zia', part 3.

49   Norman to Curzon, 26/2/21, *BDFP*, no. 684; Norman to Curzon, 3/3/21, ibid, no. 688; Norman to Curzon, 12/3/21, no. 695.

50   Curzon to Norman, 14/3/21, *ibid.*, no. 696.

51   The Shah to the King, 6/3/21, *ibid.*, no. 691.

52   The King to the Shah, 10/3/21, *ibid.*, no. 693.

53   I.O. to F.O., 6/5/21, F.O. 371/6404.

54   F.O. to I.O., 12/5/21, F.O. 371/6404.

55   Curzon to Norman, 25/5/21, F.O. 371/6404.

55a See Gordon Waterfield, *Professional Diplomat: Sir Percy Loraine* (London: John Murray, 1973), pp. 55–56.

55b See 'Persia. Political Situation (95)', 11/6/21, F. O. 371/6404. See also the Foreign Office paper, 11/6/21, entitled 'Persia' and written by G. P. Churchill, which summarises and reviews Anglo–Iranian relations, F.O. 371/6404.

56   Cox to Winston Churchill, 15/5/21, F.O. 371/6404.

57   The full text appears in several Persian sources. See for example Makki, *Tarikh-e Bistsaleh*, vol. l, p. 386.

58   *Ibid.*, pp. 384–88.

59 See Waterfield, *Professional Diplomat*, chapter 6.

60 The full text of both public statements appear in a few Persian sources. See, for example, Abdollah Mostawfi, *Sharh-e Zendegani-ye Man* (Tehran: Zavvar, 1964), vol. 3, p. 217.

61 For the full text of Zia's statement, see *ibid.*, pp. 217–20; for a summary of Zia's statement see Norman to Curzon, 28/2/21, *BDFP*, no. 686.

61a For the full text of Reza's statement see Mostawfi, *Sharh-e Zendegani*, pp. 222–23. The above passage is on p. 223, emphasis in the original.

62 See *Divan-e Aref*, (ed.) Abdorrahman Saif-e Azad (Tehran: Amir Kabir, 1963), pp. 411–13.

63 See *Kolhyiat-e Eshqi*, (ed.) Ali Akbar Moshir Salimi, first edition (Tehran: n.p., n. d.), pp. 302–05.

64 See *ibid.*, p. 396–402.

65 See *Divan-e Kamel-e Iraj Mirza*, (ed.), Mohammad Ja'far Mahjub, sixth edition, (USA: Sherkat-e Ketab, 1989), p. 213.

66 See Homa Katouzian, *Sadeq Hedayat, The Life and Legend of an Iranian Writer*, (London and New York: I. B. Tauris, 1991), 'Sadeq Hedayat va Marg-e Nevisandeh', in *Sadeq Hedayat va Marg-e Nevisandeh, va Panj Maqaleh-ye Digar* (Tehran: Nashr-e Markaz, 1993).

67 See *Divan-e Aref*, p. 300.

10

Reza Khan and the end of chaos

The post-revolutionary chaos reached its height in 1918–21, when it became increasingly clear that, in spite of the best intentions of many of its leaders, the system born out of the Constitutional Revolution did not bring stability either in the centre of politics or in the provinces. There were growing fears of disintegration.

The years 1921–25 were a time of dual sovereignty and power struggle between the three main political trends in the country: the forces of chaos; their antithesis, the forces of dictatorship (and later arbitrary government); and the constitutionalists, both conservative and democratic, who wished to have order without arbitrary rule, but did not know how to achieve it and quarrelled greatly among themselves. But given that they, and the classes they represented, were all in favour of ending the chaos, it was relatively easy to close this troubled chapter once there was the will – of which Reza Khan had plenty – and the military instrument, which he quickly created. On the other hand, because it was the forces favouring dictatorship (which later turned into arbitrary rule) which stamped out the chaos, constitutionalism did not have much chance of survival, and did not, in fact, survive.

What is remarkable, and true to the pattern of Iranian history, is the speed at which chaos was turned into subjugation. It had been a feature of Iranian society that an arbitrary regime which one day seemed to be eternal the next day could be overthrown, if for some reason the public felt it had lost its grip. By the same logic, a state of chaos that might have persisted even for decades could be ended almost abruptly, once the will was there to end it. The last striking example of this had been when Aqa Mohammad managed to stamp out decades of chaos and disintegration within a few years (see chapter one).

The immediate reasons behind these cyclical phenomena were twofold: the hatred of arbitrary rule and a massive rush to bring it down when a visible crack appeared in its edifice; and the hatred of chaos – of decentralised and widespread lawlessness – together with public support for restoring order once the necessary will and instruments were there to suppress the chaos. Shah Esma'il I, Shah Abbas I, Nader Shah, and Aqa Mohammad Khan were welcomed when they stamped out chaos, at least for some time. Both arbitrary rule and chaos were the products of an arbitrary society. These apparent opposites were in fact two sides of the same coin (see chapter one). To use Hegelian-Marxian jargon – although the idea is as old as Heraclitus – they made up the Iranian society's 'thesis' and 'antithesis', for which, however, a 'synthesis' had not been found.

Reza Khan

More than twenty years ago I made the following summary assessment of Reza Khan's personality (when very few Iranians thought well of him) to which I still adhere: "Reza Khan was an intelligent, hard-working, forthright and ruthless man, with an astonishingly powerful memory and a high degree of self-confidence that, with success, degenerated into arrogance. He was essentially a nationalist, who was pragmatic and ruthless in using whatever method he thought necessary to achieve personal and national objectives. On several occasions his iron will helped save his life, or a cause that otherwise might have been lost. He successfully combined a short temper and directness to the point of rudeness, even obscenity, with an ability to hold views, plans and even personal grudges very close to his chest. He had no time for freedom, but before becoming Shah pretended to operate within a framework of law and order. Although not democratic, there was an element of populism in his behaviour. Like his main rival and adversary, Sayyed Hasan Mudarris (some of whose personal qualities he must have secretly admired), he was contemptuous of the old nobility and regarded them as incapable of saving the situation. At one time Mudarris remarked that there were only two men of political courage and real masculinity left in the country: Reza Khan and himself."[i]

Reza's birth, childhood and upbringing, and much else about him before he marched the Cossacks to Tehran, are not known with any certainty. His official birthday was March 1878, but he might have been older, and certainly looked older than 63 when he abdicated.[1] His father, Dadash-baig of the Palani clan, was an officer of the Savad Kuh *Fawj*, but there is debate on whether he was the same Dadash-baig who is photographed as the jailer of Mirza Reza Kermani – before he assassinated Naser al-Din Shah – when he was imprisoned by Kamran Mirza, the governor of Tehran.[2] If it is true, however, that Reza Khan's father died before the child was one year old, he could not have been the same Dadash-baig, because Mirza Reza's arrest and imprisonment occurred many years later. On the other hand, Reza's mother married again after the death of his father, and the second husband – as was apparently confirmed by Reza himself – was also called Dadash-baig.[3] The latter might well have been the jailer of Mirza Reza.

Traditionally, it was believed that his father was a military stable boy, but a recent source describes him as an officer in the *Fawj*. It is clear from all sources, however, that he and his son Reza were, and were treated as, poor relations by the rest of the family.[4] His mother – variously named in the sources as Nush-afarin, Sekineh and Zahra[5] – was Dadash-baig's second wife, of a Georgian Muslim family who had emigrated to Iran after the separation of Georgia from Iran early in the nineteenth century. She married again, as mentioned above, but died when Reza was about seven years old. A maternal uncle who, according to Bahar, was a dressmaker in the Cossack Barracks *(Qazzaqkhaneh)*, brought up the boy. It was through him that, as a young teenager, Reza was accepted in the Cossack force as a trooper.[6]

There is a vested interest in portraying Reza's background, on the one hand, as being mean and even base, and on the other, as being that of a thriving urban middle-class family of the time. Whatever his family background, the evidence is that even when he was a high-ranking Cossack officer Reza Khan was not very literate and of lower culture, as were a number of Cossack officers.[7] His literacy and knowledge of the world improved rapidly as he rose to higher position and accumulated experience in military organization and leadership, but certain deeply rooted cultural limitations remained with him all his life.

Reza became known as Reza Maxim when, as an NCO, he distinguished himself in using the machine-gun of that name. He fought against the Constitutionalists as a Cossack soldier; he later fought with Constitutionalist armies led by Farmanfarma and Sardar Bahador (Sardar As'ad III); still later, he fought with the Cossacks on the side of the Russians and against the forces of the pro-German Provisional Government – the *Melliyun* – during the First World War.

Reza first entered history when he carried out Starosselski's order under Filartov to overthrow Clergé, the pro-Kerensky commander of the Cossacks sent from Russia after the overthrow of Tsarism (see chapter five). In a recently published memoir it is said that, at the same time, Reza Khan had tried to make a deal with the German chargé d'affaires in Tehran. Kahhalzadeh, a staunch supporter of Reza Khan/Shah, has claimed that, through him, Reza had contacted Zimmer, the German chargé, and had asked for German help to 'rid the country of the Russians and the British'. In a fairly elaborate story, the author claims that Zimmer sent a special agent with a letter to the German foreign ministry to report on Reza Khan's advances and ask for their support. The letter was written in cipher, but the German chargé informed the author (then in his late 'teens, and Persian secretary at their legation) of its contents. The matter was reported to the Kaiser himself, and an encouraging reply was sent to Zimmer in Tehran. And, according to Kahhalzadeh himself, the only tangible result of all this, apparently, was Reza's cooperation with Starosselski to get rid of Clergé![8] (See chapter five.)

In its details the story is unlikely to be true. But it is possible, and consistent with Reza's character, that he had tried and probably managed to establish some sort of contact with the German charge. The idea is reinforced by an important remark made by General Dickson, in a private letter to Curzon after his return to London in May 1921:

> ... Reza Khan, Sayyid Zia's military chief, is a man with whom I am well acquainted. He was disloyal to one of his chiefs, Colonel Clergé, at the time of the 1918 emeute; last spring when the problem of bringing the Cossacks

into the proposed uniform force was engaging serious attention, he made an offer to me to betray his Russian officers ...[9]

This shows that, at least before the Coup, Reza Khan's overriding concern was self-promotion, rather than a nationalist fervour to rid the country of the British and the Russians. That is probably why he agreed to cooperate with the Coup-makers while others – almost certainly Amir-Movassaq – declined the offer.

Another document which has recently come to light is part of the unpublished memoirs (in Persian translation) of Ardeshirji Reporter, the representative of Parsi Indians in Iran. A fervent admirer of Reza Shah and his nationalism, Reporter wrote that he had first met Reza Khan in 1920, at the house of a leading Zoroastrian merchant, Arbab Jamshid. Reza had told him of a plan of the Russian Cossack officers to occupy the capital in the name of protecting the Shah from Bolshevism. Reporter goes on to add:

> At this stage began my close cooperation with General Ironside on the orders of the War Office in London and the Viceroy of India. I had a high regard for Reza Khan's views about the Cossack force, and eventually introduced him to Ironside.[10]

Documents quoted in the previous chapter showed that, as late as three weeks before the Coup, the Viceroy was in favour of denouncing the Agreement, handing over of Cossacks and even the SPR's to Iran, and letting the Iranians control their own destiny. There was not the slightest hint of a military Coup. As for the War Office, we only have Reporter's word that they had told him to work with Ironside. It is not impossible, and would be consistent with his ambition, that Reza Khan had come into contact with Reporter, and that Reporter had 'introduced' him to Ironside. Yet the Cossacks, and Reza Khan among them, were first disarmed and held at Aqababa when they retreated from a long campaign in Gilan, on Ironside's orders when he was in Qazvin. And before that event, Ironside had not yet arrived in Iran. In other words, Reza was in Aqababa shortly after Ironside's arrival, and if Reporter did mention him to Ironside, he must have done so some time after that. Hence he could not have done so – at Arbab Jamshid's home or anywhere else – *in Tehran*. Besides, as shown in chapter nine, the military leader of the Coup was found after some searching in which Smyth, Zia, Mas'ud and Kazem were involved, and Reza was not the first man they approached. It follows that the impression given by Reporter as being the 'discoverer' of Reza Khan (in connection with the Coup) is, to say the least, highly exaggerated.

Naturally, Reza Khan himself believed, as he openly said to Mosaddeq, Dawlat-Abadi, Taqizadeh and a couple of other notables, that 'the British brought me to power', adding, 'but I served my country'. This is Dawlat-Abadi's version. Mosaddeq's is that Reza Khan told them: 'The British brought me to power, but they did not know whom they were dealing with.'[11] Even this elaboration implies much the same thing. Reza passed on this story as a legacy to his son, Mohammad Reza Shah, and it added to the general Iranian belief in the superhuman powers of the British. As late as May 1953, seven months after Mosaddeq had broken off diplomatic relations with Britain, and a couple of months before the 1953 Coup, the Shah, knowing that Britain had been trying to bring down Mosaddeq's government almost since its inception, sent a message to the Foreign Office via the State Department:

> He [the Shah] is reported to be harping about the theme that the British had thrown out the Qajar dynasty, had brought in his father and had thrown his father out. Now they could keep him in power or remove him as they saw fit. If they desired that he should stay and that the crown should retain the powers given to it by the Constitution he should be informed. If on the other hand they wished him to go he should be told immediately so that he could leave quietly. Did the British wish to substitute another Shah for himself or to abolish the monarchy? Were they behind the present efforts to deprive him of his power and prestige?[12]

Reza Khan's perception of the role of the British in the 1921 Coup made such an impression on his mind that anyone else's contact with them provoked his strong suspicion that a plot was in the making. For example, after Amir Ahmadi met Sir Percy Loraine briefly at Loraine's invitation, when he was commander of Army Division West, Reza Shah turned Amir Ahmadi, his only lieutenant-general and the sole remaining one of the four men with whom he had taken an oath of loyalty just before the Coup, into a nonentity and put him under police surveillance.[13] He was lucky to survive, as so many did not. But the matter went beyond fear of contact with the British: under Reza Shah all private contact with foreigners was forbidden. The only reason that has ever been offered for the arrest and murder of Firuz, many years after he had been out of office, is that he had had a meeting with the French minister in Tehran.[14] According to Taqizadeh, Reza Shah had ordered General Jahanbani's arrest in the late 1930s (thereby disgracing the whole of the Jahanbani clan), because he had had lunch at the French legation.[14a]

Reza's growing suspiciousness in later years had another, more realistic, cause. When it suited him, he had broken his own word to many he had worked with. It was, therefore, quite natural for him to expect this from others, be they General Amir Eqtedar, Colonel Puladin, General Amir Tamasebi, General Shaibani, Brigadier Dargahi, Sraem al-Dawleh, Firuz, Taimurtash, Asadi, Davar, Sardar As'ad III, Farajollah Bahrami, Foroughi, Taqizadeh, Adl al-Molk (Hossein Dadgar), Zainul'abedin Rahnema. These and many others who served him well ended up being, killed, jailed, banished, exiled or disgraced. Ironically, he did not suspect the one powerful and important man – General Mohammad Hossien Ayrom – who really was disloyal to him and, having got to know him very well, fed his suspicions against others until he felt he had amassed a large enough fortune to flee before he was caught. He left the country deceitfully, never to return.[14b]

Reza Khan was highly intelligent and astute, possibly even a genius. He had an exceptionally powerful memory, was quick to learn and to adapt, and was physically and psychologically courageous. In the end, when he saw he had no choice but to abdicate, he did so with reasonable courage and resolution, even though the public who had so feared him saw it as cowardice.[15] In fact, his most important, and initially positive, trait was his supreme and unshakeable self-confidence. But easy and rapid success – together with the absolute power of the ruler, and the extraordinary subservience and sycophancy of the ruled in Iran's arbitrary society – turned this into self-delusion.

Both to Iranians and to foreigners, Reza seemed very different from the old school politicians and the Qajar 'aristocracy', because he appeared to be open and forthright in his responses to questions and situations. This was partly because he did not belong to the old social and political culture, so he was not expected to observe its norms and became too successful to be bound by it. Otherwise he could be extremely duplicitous, both to foreigners and Iranians. For example, he ordered the arrest and (within a few months) murder in jail of Sardar As'ad III, his devoted personal friend and minister of war, the day after they had played a game of cards together in very good spirits.[15a] Firuz, the minister of finance, was suddenly arrested when he was leaving a public meeting in the company of the Shah himself.[15b]

Reza Khan was a nationalist of the new type, that is, inspired by the Aryanist and pan-Persian ideology which had increasingly gripped modern Iranians since the end of the First World War. He was tutored in that ideology by the younger politicians and intellectuals who gathered round him, particularly Farajollah Bahrami (Dabir-e A'zam), who was for many years his private secretary (*chef de cabinet*). Reza was no foreign country's agent. If anything, he was xenophobic, certainly in regard to the great European powers, and this grew stronger with time. Altogether, his qualities were virtually unique for stamping out the country's chaos in the shortest possible time.

End of chaos

Chaos in most regions and provinces was put down even before Reza Khan became Shah. Other, relatively minor, rebellions which surged up over in the few years following his coronation were more often a backlash against the arbitrariness with which Reza's army divisions behaved towards nomads, ethnic communities and provincial magnates. In the first couple of years, not only the ruthless suppression of rebellion and brigandry, but also subjugation of regional magnates and notables, was very popular at least with the urban public. The matter was extremely urgent. There had been so much chaos for so long, causing so much social insecurity and economic damage, and putting the very existence of the country in doubt, that suppressing it was the only achievement of Reza Khan and Reza Shah to be acknowledged and admired by friend and foe alike. In 1925, in the constitutent assembly called to make him Shah, Solaiman Morza (Eskandari) objected – not to Reza being made Shah but to the creation of a new dynasty – but emphasized that:

> No one doubts that on many occasions I have defended his [Reza's] services in stamping out the *Moluk al-Tavayefi* system, his centralization of power, his destruction of rebels and those who did not recognise the central power ...[15c]

More than a month before, in his speech in the Majlis against the motion for making Reza Khan temporary head of state, Taqizadeh stated that his most important reason for supporting Reza's government was 'the security which it has created'.[15d] But, Mosaddeq, who delivered the longest and most impassioned speech against the same motion, went much further:

> I doubt if there is anyone who is unaware of the services that he [Reza Khan] has rendered to the country. The situation in this country was such that, as we all know, if someone wished to travel he did not have security, and if someone was a landlord he had no security, and if he had an estate, he had to employ a few riflemen to protect his produce. But since he [Reza] has held the reins he has rendered service to the country's security, which I doubt have escaped anybody's notice. And, for the sake of protecting my own home, my own family and my own people, I naturally wish to see the man called Reza Khan Pahlavi be prime minister in this country. Because I wish to see security and stability; and it is true that, in the past couple of years, because of that man we have had such a thing, and so we have been able to get on with public works, and serving the interest of the society ... And thank God that, due to the blessing of his being, we would now like to get on with some fundamental work ...[15e]

As discussed below, there was some criticism, even at the centre, of the attempts by provincial army divisions to dominate provincial life, but they were mostly muted and few and far between. The credit was thus rightly given to Reza Khan for stamping out the chaos, which might have cost the country its integrity in the absence of any other way of dealing with it. Indeed, as Mosaddeq implied, it was the rapid and successful ending of chaos that provided the opportunity for increased public and private investment and a steady increase in national income, exactly as happened after the Qajars had stamped out several decades of chaos at the end of the eighteenth century.

As early as December 1920, when Moshaver al-Mamalek's negotiations in Moscow ended with a draft agreement, the writing was on the wall for the Gilan Insurgents, although very few people saw it at the time. The signing of the Irano–

Soviet agreement by Zia, the departure of Norperforce in April, and the fall of Zia, who was believed by the Gilan rebels and their Soviet allies to be a British agent, dissolved Soviet support for the Gilan Republic. Kuchik, on the other hand, who had a solid social base, once again entered an alliance with them.

Important as they certainly were, neither the withdrawal of Soviet backing nor the enhanced strength of the Cossacks was sufficient to bring about the collapse of the Republic and the quick rout of Kuchik and his allies. It was at least of equal importance that the Gilan rebels, as well as the general public, knew that they were no longer facing a foreign or foreign-led army, and that the general consensus was to put an end to the chaos. For all these reasons, the outcome was that Ehsanollah Khan and Khalu Ghorban defected, one to the Soviet Union, the other to Reza Khan; Kuchik froze to death while on retreat; his head was cut off and put on display in Rasht for a while, then sent to Tehran, where it was buried on Reza's orders.[16]

By the time Norperforce left and Zia fell, however, the Gilan rebellion looked less ominous than the revolt of Colonel Mohammad Taqi Khan Pesyan, the gendarmerie chief of Khorasan. This educated man of considerable military ability and promise had, like most gendarmes, sided with the provisional government during the First World War. Towards the end of the War he had visited Berlin and received further military training, and, upon return, had been appointed to lead and reorganize the Khorasan gendarmerie, at about the same time that the British East Persian Field Cordon was pulling out. Peyan was a modern nationalist, like many of those who tutored Reza Khan, but his nationalist sentiments were tempered by his solid educational and cultural roots, and the traditional gendarme respect for constitutional government. In the end he became a reluctant rebel, his greatest tragedy being perhaps (even more than Khiyabani's) that he himself was firmly in favour of putting an end to the chaos.

Just after the 1921 Coup Pesyan arrested Qavam, Vosuq's brother and governor-general of Khorasan, confiscated a good deal of his property in favour of the provincial government and contemptuously packed him off as a prisoner to Tehran. This was in keeping with Zia's policy elsewhere, and, like many other gendarme officers, Pesyan regarded Zia as a nationalist leader and saviour. Sarem al-Dawleh, the governor-general of the west, was likewise arrested. Mokhber al-Saltaneh, the governor-general of Azerbaijan, would have been arrested but for a hitch, after which his arrest was felt to be unnecessary. Mosaddeq was invited by Zia to cooperate, but, when he defied him, orders were sent for his arrest. He gave them the slip, and hid until Zia had fallen.[16a]

The difference was that there had been a longstanding feud between Qavam and Pesyan, both strong men with little respect for each other. Qavam thought of Pesyan as a modernist upstart, while Pesyan saw Qavam as a financially corrupt reactionary. When Zia fell, many, like Pesyan, saw it as a foreign conspiracy and the return of reaction. These included his devoted friends, the poets Aref and Iraj (see chapter nine). But to Pesyan's disgust and horror, the head of the new 'pro-foreign and anti-nationalist reaction' was none other than Qavam.

There were thus two reinforcing motives behind Pesyan's rejection of the change, although the personal motive must have been as strong as the public consideration. The matter dragged on between June and October 1921, with a bewildered Pesyan – apparently anxious about the issue of constitutional legiti-macy – at one moment appearing to rebel and take over the administration of Khorasan, and then relenting and pleading loyalty to the centre – excluding Qavam. He had 6000 well-trained gendarmes under his command who were passionately devoted to him, whereas not even half that force existed in Tehran. In the end, Reza sent a force of several hundred Cossacks, led not by himself but by Hossein Aqa (Khoza'i). They camped at a safe distance, and entered Mashad in triumph only after the colonel had fallen in a battle with tribal forces mobilized by Qavam's government. To make matters worse, Tehran was still embroiled in the campaign in Gilan against Kuchik and his allies, and there was even fear of Khorasan and Gilan getting together against Tehran.

In the end, Qavam sent word to the khans of north and south Khorasan, especially Sardar Mo'azzaz-e Bojnurdi and Amir Shokat al-Molk (later Ebrahim Alam), to put Pesyan down as a rebel. This was consistent with age-old tradi-tion, but it was effective largely because the khans were themselves alarmed at the colonel's centralizing and modernizing policy, not least his determination to collect land tax efficiently. Pesyan tried to come to an understanding with Shokat al-Molk, but before that could be reached he hurried up to the north with a small force to meet the Shadlu Kurds of Sardar Mo'azzaz, where he was killed in battle.[17]

Pesyan's was the only serious and dangerous challenge by the armed forces to the central government of Reza Khan and Reza Shah. It came very soon after the Coup, when there was much confusion about who stood where in Iranian politics. Hence, at the time and for some time to come, it was not sufficiently understood that the real winner of that conflict was Reza, whose public position had almost looked like a benevolent onlooker. The conflict of Qavam, the conservative constitutionalist, with Pesyan, the nationalist constitutionalist, bolstered the fortunes of Reza Khan, the nationalist anti-constitutionalist. There may well be a certain historical imperative in the conflicts of men such as Lafay-ette, Brissot, Robespierre, Danton, Dumouriez, Baras, Siéyès, and many other potential winners, having to pave the way for a Corsican general to establish strong government. In Iran at least, that seems to be consistent with the behav-iour of the traditional constitutionalist politicians – conservative, liberal, Democrat and Socialist – who, by persistent feuding among themselves, soon made possible Reza's meteoric rise to absolute, although not yet arbitrary, power.

Once Kuchik and Pesyan were put out of the way (almost at the same time), the coast was clear not only for stamping out provincial rebellion and brigandry, but also for subjugating the people of the provinces – nomadic and sedentary as well as urban – to a degree unknown in living memory (see chapter eleven). The most important of these activities were the overthrow of Sardar Mo'zzaz-e Bojnurdi in northern Khorasan, and of Eqbal al-Sataneh-ye Maku'i in Azerbaijan; the putting down, at long last, of the rebellion of Isma'il Aqa, chief of the Kurdish tribe of Shakkak in Azerbaijan, and of smaller scale revolts in the west, Loristan and the central southern regions.

By all accounts, Sardar Mo'azzaz was not a rebel. It was his forces who had killed Pesyan in battle, and there was no conflict between him and the army as long as Major- General Hossein Aqa (Khoza'i) was in command of the Eastern Division. His forbears, as chiefs of the Kurdish tribe of Shadlu, had been the official Keepers of the Frontier (*Sarhad-dar* for the ancient *Marzban*) of northern Khorasan. Then it was decided that the army itself should keep the frontier, and, without a fight, the Sardar agreed to go and live in Tehran in respectable banishment. But the army failed to stem the periodic plunders of nomadic Torkamans from across the border, and so the Sardar was honourably returned there to keep the peace. The army even agreed to defray some of his official costs against the arrears of his tax obligation.[18]

This was the position until Hossein Aqa was replaced by Brigadier Jan Mohammad Khan (Amir Ala'i/Davallu), son of Mirza Ahmad Khan Ala al-Dawleh, whose flogging of the two sugar merchants had triggered the Constitutional Revolution, and who had been subsequently assassinated over his quarrel with Shuster's tax collectors (see chapter three). Jan Mohammad himself was widely believed to have raped the young officer Habib Maikadeh (son of Mirza Solaiman Khan), driving him to suicide.[19] Shortly after taking up command in Mashad, Jan Mohammad sent for the Sardar, who voluntarily went to the provincial capital and was put in prison. At the same time, Major-General Amir Eqtedar (Mahmud Aqa Ansari), who was very close to Reza Khan and currently minister of the interior in his cabinet, was arrested in Tehran on suspicion that he had been in touch with Ahmad Shah (who was still Shah of Iran), to try and entice him to come back. Sir Percy Loraine thought the matter serious enough to report Amir Eqtedar's arrest for 'treason' to London.[19a] It was later proved, even to Reza Khan himself, that the charge had been baseless, and Amir Eqtedar was released.

Before that happened, however, it was believed that Amir Eqtedar had contacted the Shah on behalf of Sardar Mo'zzaz. Jan Mohammad had the Sardar and three of his relatives hanged in public, and severely put down the minor rebellion it provoked, even though the rebels gave up before Jan Mohammad himself had got there. That was followed by the looting of the Sardar's wealth and property. All available accounts of the incident maintain that Jan Mohammad's zeal to loot the Sardar's fabulous wealth had been the prime motive for his execution of Sardar Mo'zzaz.[20] The pattern was familiar from bygone ages.

Eqbal al-Saltaneh-ye Maku'i, the Khan of Maku, was the traditional *Sarhad-dar* of the North Western frontier and, according to Taqizadeh, the richest man in Iran after Zel al-Soltan and Khaz'al.[20a] He had sided with Mohammad Ali Shah

in 1908 and, like many provincial great khans, had enjoyed a degree of
autonomy in his area after the revolution although he was not in revolt against
the central government. Indeed, at one stage, after the Coup, his forces had
collaborated with government troops in a large and successful operation against
Isma'il Aqa Simko. On the other hand, he had his own local force, and ruled in
the tribal region much as the Sardar of Bojnurd did in northern Khorasan, the
Amir of Qa'enat (Alam) in southern Khorasan, and the Vali of Poshtkuh in the
south-west. Modern centralization meant that such militias should be brought
under effective control of the central government, though less force might have
been used to do so, at least when there was no resistance.

The Khan of Maku was asked by General Amir Tahmasebi, commander of
the North Western (Azerbaijan) Division, to go to Tabriz and he submitted. He
was killed, nonetheless, and his fabulous wealth was looted and sent to Tehran.
The official story – like those of Taimurtash, Sardar As'ad and others in years to
come – was that he had died of a heart attack in prison. Unlike many others in
the army, Amir Tahmasebi was not a private expropriator and did send the
Khan's treasure to Tehran. Such was the spectre of chaos and fear of disintegration at the time that few politicians of any tendency would challenge such
methods. In this case, however, a strong protest was made in the Majlis on the
grounds that the Khan of Maku's treasure had been personally appropriated by
Reza Khan himself.[21]

Amir Mo'ayyed, of Savad Kuh's Rastpay tribe, had carried out a similar traditional function in Mazandarn, and supplied the *Fawj* of Savd Kuh, to which Reza
Khan's father had belonged. Just before the fall of Vosuq in June 1920, the Amir
– invariably described as a patriot in contemporary Persian sources – had joined
forces with the Gilan rebels, but had not been active since Moshir's government. In the summer of 1920, forces led by Ahmad Aqa (Amir Ahmadi) were
sent to subdue him. He resisted and retreated to the forests, but submitted soon
afterwards as the result of a peace offer by the government, which obliged him
to take up residence in Tehran, and made his two sons officers in the new army.
A couple of years later his sons were executed on the charge of attempting to
desert. The Amir died of a broken heart, and his wealth and property, including
vast estates in Mazandaran, were personally appropriated by Reza Khan.[22]

The Vali of Poshtkuh, another traditional *Sarhad-dar,* was driven into exile
into Iraq, and all his wealth and estates appropriated, at the same time as the fall
of Khaz'al, to whom he was close (see chapter eleven). The only *Sarhad-dar* to
survive with his wealth and property intact was the very cautious and diplomatic
Amir of Qa'enat (Ebrahim Alam). He lived in Tehran as a Majlis deputy and
minister, and made sure he was constantly on the right side of Reza, especially
after he became Shah. Alam had confided to people close to him that he stayed
in Tehran because he might otherwise fall under suspicion and be destroyed.
His manager, personal friend and the father-in-law of his daughter, Mohammad
Vali Khan Asadi (Mesbah al-Saltaneh), was executed in 1935, after the riots in
Mashad protesting against the government order that all the country's men

should wear the European bowler hat. Sawlat al-Dawleh, the Ilkhan of the Qahqa'i federation of tribes, also submitted and went to Tehran as a Majlis deputy, but was later interned, together with his eldest son, and was killed or died of natural causes (it is not clear which) in prison.

Simko ('Semitqu') was a hardened rebel, who had long been responsible for repeated plunder and massacre. On a peaceful occasion when he met Reza Khan through the good offices of Amir Tahmasebi, he had told Bahrami – Reza's devoted private secretary – that he had become a rebel after his brother had been killed by a government official (long before Reza Khan's time) because Simko had not managed to raise the whole of the ransom money demanded for his release. According to another, more reliable, account, Ebrahim Aqa Shakkak, Simko's brother, had been given a solemn pledge of official immunity, but had been killed on arrival in Tabriz (a sequence of events not unfamiliar in Iranian history).[23] Nevertheless, Simko was, and remained, an incorrigible rebel, who resorted to killing, looting and brigandry. A couple of times a peaceful settlement had been reached, both before and under Reza, but broke down on both occasions, for reasons that cannot be established. He was eventually defeated and killed in action.

The operations of General Ahmad Aqa (Amir-Ahmadi) in the west and south-west were numerous, of smaller scale but involved ruthless atrocities. The scale of the atrocities became legendary even in Tehran, where hardly a voice of criticism was raised against such operations for fear of being accused of defending disorder and working for British imperialism. Amir Ahmadi subsequently became known as 'The Butcher of Loristan'. To give some indication of the style of operations there and elsewhere, it would be best to quote from Amir Ahmadi's own memoirs, which he wrote long after he had retired from the army. These memoirs were discovered in manuscript after the revolution of 1977–79, and were subsequently published. According to Ahmadi, when General Khoza'i took over the Loristan army from him, he summoned two former rebels who had been pacified by Ahmadi, together with twelve other notables of Khorram-Abad who were law-abiding and included Mo'in al-Saltaneh, former governor of the town. Khoza'i pretended that he was going to Tehran and asked them to see him off to Borujerd. There they lunched together. Afterwards, the general ordered 13 sets of gallows to be erected and had them all hanged:

> He first orders the two former rebels … to be hanged. Then he says, 'Take the others as well'. It turns out that they have erected one set of gallows too many. He says, 'Take Mo'in al-Saltaneh as well so the remaining gallows is not left idle'. At first, these people think that Khoza'i is having them on, because they knew they were innocent, but when they see he is serious they beseech and beg of him [to spare them]. But the general pays no attention, saying that Sardar Sepah [Reza Khan] must know that I am not lax. If Ahmad Aqa Khan [Ahmadi] hanged four men, I can hang fourteen in one day.

This, according to Ahmadi, had very negative consequences for the army and the central government:

> This legend-like news reached Tehran and provided a pretext for Sardar Sepah's opponents. They said the Jackboots hanged the people en masse. The Sardar summoned Khoza'i and asked him for an explanation. But Khoza'i had said that, to establish security, harshness is necessary. The action of General Khoza'i in killing these men without cause, and even without a mock trial, led the people of Loristan (who were beginning to tend towards the central government) to turn away from the army, and the fire of hatred and vengeance was kindled in their hearts.[24]

The accuracy of this account is impossible to know. But it is consistent with tales of army atrocities in regions and provinces, and certainly with Ahmadi's own reputation.

The new army and the campaign for republicanism

Reza Khan's premiership

It took only two years and a few months, from June 1921 to November 1923, for Reza Khan to become prime minister as well as minister of war and chief of the army. Interim events were typical of politicians of the old school, even though many of them – both conservative and popular – were becoming increasingly alarmed at the growing autonomy of Sardar Sepah and his army. There were no fewer than five ministries in this short period; Qavam twice (June 1921–February 1922; June 1922–February 1923); Moshir twice (February–May 1922; July–November 1923); and Mostawfi (February–July 1923).

The traditional politicians were still busy fighting among themselves and accusing one another of being some foreign power's agent, or a reactionary, Bolshevik, atheist, etc. Most of these appellations were either untrue or highly exaggerated. The acrimony increased the conviction of younger nationalists and modernists that the traditional group was utterly incapable of improving the national situation. On the other hand, Reza was heavily engaged in creating his army and increasing his spending – both legal and illegal – on extending and improving its size, weaponry, organization and training. At the same time, he cultivated friendships across the political spectrum, posed as an honest broker, and made himself appear indispensable as the keeper of order and stability.

He also established excellent relations with foreign envoys, especially the British minister, Loraine, and the Soviet minister, Rotstein. The latter was soon replaced by Shumiyatsky, an even greater admirer of the 'bourgeois nationalist' Reza Khan who, it seemed to him, was trying to put down the feudal reactionaries, many of whom were also agents of British imperialism. Reza was able to manipulate many on the road to power. And the fact that he managed to mislead and obtain the support of both the British and Soviet envoys – and therefore their governments, although the Foreign Office was more cautious and hesitant – is one of the most notable examples of his rich talent for self-interested diplomacy.

Loraine sent glowing reports on Reza both in his private letters – for example to Norman and Marling[25] – and his official reports, and it is clear that he was trying to change London's untrusting attitude towards Reza Khan. To give one example, in a lengthy assessment of the situation dispatched to Curzon in May 1923, Loraine was critical of the Shah and traditional politicians for their constant wrangling and inefficiency, while he presented Reza as a forthright, energetic and efficient leader who was the only one doing any good for the country:

> There is a very genuine element of patriotism underlying all that Reza Khan does. And there is no doubt in my mind in regard to the sincerity of his desire to raise up Persia out of the present state of disintegration, to establish law & order throughout her borders, & to earn for her the respect of her neighbours.

On the other hand, Loraine misread Reza Khan's agenda in some important respects, and was not inclined to correct this when Reza later became mistrusted by many Iranian observers:

> It is in the power of Reza Khan to become P[rime] M[inister] & rule as dictator, even to overthrow the Kajar dynasty ... but the fact that he has abstained from all of them pretty well disposes of any idea that he is solely actuated by personal ambition.[26]

As soon as the revolts of Gilan and Khorasan were put down, Sardar Sepah moved quickly to consolidate his hold over the armed forces. The first task was to dispense with the gendarmerie as an independent force. The idea of creating a unified force by merging the existing militias (see previous chapters) was a familiar one. The significant difference now was that Reza wanted, and managed, to submerge the gendarmes – most of whom were better trained, more educated, and more law-abiding – into the Cossack force and under Cossack commanders. The new unified army (*qoshun*) was, in fact, an enlarged Cossack force, with all the top ranks and posts going to Reza Khan's Cossack lieutenants such as Ahmadi, Khoza'i, Tamasebi, Ansari, Khodayari and Yazdan-panah.[27] Qavam, who was a shrewd politician, became aware of the danger of Reza as early as October 1921. But by the time the gendarmes were subjugated, Mosaddeq, Qavam's finance minister, had alienated many of the magnates by trying to collect taxes, and by cutting stipends and privy purses, including that of the heir-designate. The government fell in January 1922, at least in part, as a result of the unpopularity of Mosaddeq's measures.[28]

The urbane and disinterested Moshir, who took over from Qavam, was much more suited to Sardar Sepah's ambitions and designs. At the same time, the

Shah, who had been eager for a long time to visit Europe again, left Tehran, with his brother standing in as regent in his absence. No sooner had Moshir become prime minister, than Reza, his minister of war, annexed the two highly lucrative offices of the wheat and bread supply (*ghalleh va nan*) and state lands (*khalesehjat*), to the war ministry. They were headed by one of his generals, and their incomes were directly appropriated for the army.[29]

The subjugation of the gendarmerie led to a small but spirited resistance. Within a couple of weeks, the gendarme Major Lahuti Khan – a poet and young activist of the Constitutional Revolution – rebelled and occupied Tabriz with a small gendarme force. Reza shrewdly sent Brigadier Shaibani, the able former gendarme major who had not resisted the Coup, to put them down. They were outnumbered, and Lahuti crossed the border to the Soviet Union, where he lived the rest of his life, and became a leading political and literary figure in Tajikestan.[30] After that, the ascendancy of Reza and the Cossacks was complete and undisputed.

During the following two years, until Reza Khan became prime minister, there were four main tendencies among the politicians and Majlis deputies. Modarres and his followers had discerned Reza Khan's ambitions sooner than the others, and believed that only a man such as Qavam could stand up to him. The popular constitutionalists were in favour of Moshir and Mostawfi, although they greatly appreciated Reza Khan's role in bringing stability and order to the provinces. Old Democrats and Socialists, rather inconsistently, put equal emphasis on civil liberties and stability and modernization, and closely associated the latter with Reza Khan. Lastly, radical nationalists and modernists, like the Socialists, regarded the first group as reactionary and the second group as lacking resolve and energy. Thus radical nationalists as well as old Democrats and Socialists increasingly looked to Reza Khan as their man. They all supported the campaign for a republic in 1923, while popular constitutionalists sat on the fence and the Modarres group opposed it. These two groups united completely only when Reza Khan moved to overthrow the Qajars and establish his own dynasty, but by then it was too late.

Moshir's cabinet fell after only four months, when Reza Khan sent him an insulting message because he had refused to ban a newspaper which had criticized 'some army officers who abused their office'.[31] Moshir refused to withdraw his resignation, even when the Majlis asked him to and Reza Khan said that his message had been misunderstood. It took more than a month for Modarres to arrange a majority for Qavam to take over. But there were complaints about the financial encroachments of the army, as noted above. There was also anger at the muzzling of the press by the martial law administration, still in force since the Coup, and run by Amir Eqtedar. This led to a motion of censure in the Majlis by a Modarres supporter against the government. In his long speech in support of this motion, Mo'tamed al-Tojjar attacked press censorship, illegal imprisonment of journalists, and the effective control of the army in matters regarding police and public finance:

Enemies of the country's freedom and independence are constantly active and continuously extend their schemes. And there would soon come the day that heads would fall together with hats: not only constitutionalism but even the country's independence will go with the wind. Without any legal procedures they ban newspapers and jail, banish and torture their editors ... The constitution has defined ministerial responsibilities, and has made every minister responsible for his own department ...[32]

Modarres spoke next. In the guise of criticizing the previous speaker's 'pessimism', he pointed out that the Majlis had been effective in dealing with a number of important issues. Yet he added, in his usual blunt manner, that at that moment security matters were 'in the hands of someone who leaves most of us unhappy'. The previous speaker should not have spoken in 'a coded way'. The Majlis had full powers and could sack whomever it liked. Yet he ended with a conciliatory gesture:

The minister of war has some benefits and some costs ... But I still think that his benefits are fundamental, and his costs less important. We must try to remove his costs so that the country may enjoy his benefits.[33]

Reza Khan resigned, was persuaded to change his mind, and relented over both issues. Martial law was lifted, and the revenue departments were handed back to the treasury. But the changes did not last very long. And when, in October 1923, Reza Khan himself became prime minister, his freedom of action in these matters vastly increased.

Qavam's government fell in the following February, although Reza Khan's direct share in it was relatively small. Solaiman Mirza (later Eskandari) hated him, and now more specifically because the Soviet Union did not like him. This was partly because they thought he was a reactionary, but mainly because he had been negotiating to give northern Iran's oil concession to an American oil company, although this got nowhere. There were also problems regarding the Soviet fishing company which had the monopoly concession of fishing in the Iranian parts of the Caspian. According to Bahar, Solaiman Mirza used the Shah's influence in the Majlis – he always wished to be popular – to bring down Qavam and replace him by Mostawfi.

Mostawfi was honest, fairly pro-Soviet, although not a Socialist, highly popular but rather ineffectual. At that moment, no-one could have better suited Reza Khan's purpose as prime minister. That was exactly the fear of Modarres and his parliamentary group, who could usually muster a majority in the fourth Majlis. At the end of June 1923, Modarres's campaign sufficiently annoyed Mostawfi – who had little love for office – to resign, after delivering a hard-hitting speech against his opponents, although Qavam did not allow that to pass entirely unanswered. Modarres openly compared Mostawfi to a jewel-studded sword that was useful for peaceful purposes, and Qavam to a sharp sabre that was needed for war.[34] Reza, no doubt, did not miss the implication of these words. The socialist, modernist and nationalist intellectuals and journalists (as well as the Soviet legation) saw it all as the work of the devil – the presumed alliance of the British and the reactionaries – and showered abuse on Modarres, Qavam, Firuz and other leading members of the group.[35] At any rate, Modarres did not manage to bring Qavam back into power, and Moshir took over as a compromise candidate.

Moshir was almost as popular as Mostawfi, though he was more able and effective. But he was not the type who could control Reza Khan, and Modarres still hoped to bring in a Qavam ministry. From Reza Khan's point of view that had to be avoided at all costs, especially as he now felt that – besides the devotion of his expanding army in the provinces – he had enough support among civilian notables and Majlis deputies in the capital to seek to become prime minister.

The life of the fourth Majlis came to an end soon after Moshir took office in June 1923. It took almost six months before all the deputies of the fifth Majlis were returned. When that happened, Moshir's cabinet had already fallen, and Reza had at last become prime minister. It was Reza Khan who drove Moshir out of office, but he knew that Qavam, backed by Modarres, was waiting in the wings. There followed the bizarre episode, in October 1923, of the confession by Sardar Entesar, (later Mozaffar A'lam) of the Khiyabani episode (see chapter five). He confessed that, when Qavam had been prime minister fourteen months before, he had tried to use him to organize Reza's assassination by a group of disaffected gendarme officers.

And so the drama unfolded. Towards the end of the summer of 1923, a new group of active politicians was formed, describing itself as 'Independent Democrats of Iran'. It was led by Sayyed Mohammad Tadayyon, Adl al-Molk (later Hossien Dadgar, an erstwhile member of the Committee of Iron and also of Zia's cabinet), the Bahrami brothers (Dabir-e A'azam and Ehy' al-Saltaneh), Zainula'bedin Rahnema, editor of the semi-official and pro-Reza Khan newspaper *Iran*, and other officials and activists, and began a campaign for Reza's premiership. They were staunch supporters of Reza, to the point of adulation, and wooed Solaiman Mirza and his Socialists for an alliance. At the same time, Ali Akbar Davar, the future minister of justice and finance, was leading a group of 'young radicals' who – to use Loraine's words – advocated that Sardar Sepah 'should appoint some energetic young Prime Minister' to implement progressive policies. The Sardar had recommended that Davar go ahead with his plan to form a 'Young Persian' party. 'The newspapers are beginning to advocate a dictatorship', added Loraine in his report.[36]

The 'Young Persian' party must be the Young Iran Club (*Klub-e Iran-e Javan*) who were later told by Reza Khan that their nationalist and modernist aims were impeccable, but that they should close their club – as they duly did – because he himself would implement all their objectives.[37]

The Independent Democrats were much more important. They began to campaign openly for a Sardar Sepah ministry, and easily brought Davar into line with that objective. They informed and enticed Loraine, in order to forestall his suspicions, and did the same with Shumiyatsky. Reporting on their campaign to Curzon, Loraine wrote approvingly:

> They would include none of the 'effete and corrupt aristocracy' in the Cabinet, but at the same time they would arrange matters with the Firman Firma [Farmanfarma] family and perhaps Qawam es Sultaneh, to avoid their opposition.[38]

Loraine's report was sent on 2 October. Five days later, Qavam was arrested on the assassination charge. Sardar Entesar had confessed that, some time in the August of the previous year, Qavam had asked him if he knew of 'any means of reforming the ministry of war', and he had replied that he knew a number of dissatisfied ex-gendarme officers who were ready for action. The two men then concluded that the officers in question should be organized by Sardar Entesar to assassinate Reza. Some steps were taken, but somehow the whole scheme collapsed in the end without any action going ahead.[39]

The full account, serialized at the time by *Iran* and *Setareh-ye Iran* newspapers (both of them Reza Khan partisans), reads more like an unconvincing detective story. It is now virtually impossible to know for certain whether the allegations had any basis, and, if so, what it was. Whatever the truth, Entesar's arrest and confessions were used to neutralize Qavam, bring down Moshir's government, and frighten the Shah into appointing Reza Khan as prime minister before the new Majlis had met. Qavam was arrested on 7 October, although he was released on 21 October as a result of the Shah's intervention. This was followed by a cabinet resolution, and Reza Khan's declaration that he did not wish to press his own personal case against Qavam. The government resigned the same day, and Qavam was exiled to Europe under armed guards the following day. A couple of days later, the Shah issued a *farman* which made Reza prime minister, in a cabinet that included Solaiman Mirza and Adl al-Molk. A few days after that, the Shah left for Europe, never to return.[40]

Earlier in that same month of October, Loraine sent a long report to Curzon, critical of the Shah, favourable to Reza Khan, and describing the Shah's fear of him:

> The principal cause of the Shah's anxiety is the rapid growth of the power of Sirdar Sepah, the Minister of War, which His Majesty feels to be over-shadowing that of the throne and the dynasty.

But Loraine did not share the Shah's fears:

> The fact of the matter is of course that Sirdar Sepah is an energetic and determined man who is engaged resolutely in carrying out a fairly definite policy, whereas the Shah and the Civil Government are carrying on in the

old and not very commendable methods of government ... It thus comes
about that Sirdar Sepah, thanks to his comparative singleness of thought
and action, becomes the real and dominant power in Persia ... [T]he Shah
is thoroughly alarmed and an atmosphere of suspicion and distrust has
been grown up between him and his powerful Minister of War. He has
assured me ... that he had never opposed or intrigued against Sirdar
Sepah, but on the contrary had for the sake of peace given way to him all
along the line.

Yet the Shah was 'fearful of being dispossessed of his throne and of even
becoming the victim of personal violence':

The Shah thus feels that his own position is untenable and that the only
solution is for him to absent himself, to pay another visit to Europe, and
thus to escape fresh and possibly final humiliations. If things go fairly well
... His Majesty would contemplate returning to Persia in due course; but
he thinks that if any radical change was to take place it would be better for
the country and for himself that he should be out of the way when that
happens ... I have done my best to extricate His Majesty from this morbid
state of mind, but I cannot flatter myself that I have achieved any measure
of success or changed him from his purpose ...[41]

The Shah's fears proved to have been justified, but it is difficult to see how
the final demise of the Qajar's could have been avoided. The country was badly
in need of stability, reorganization and modernization. The existing framework
had proven to be incapable of addressing such problems, at least with the
urgency most leaders of public opinion felt was necessary. What might possibly
have been avoided was going to the other extreme, with too much concentration of power and the eventual restoration of arbitrary rule.

Loraine's reference to the newspaper's demand for a dictatorship must have
included Davar's articles in his newspaper *Mard-e Azad.*

In those articles, Davar had been highly critical of the Majlis and had advocated a dictator. A recently published document cogently illuminates the
thinking of the young and educated modern nationalists at the time, but is
unusual in its warning against the dangers of purely personal rule. This is
contained in a letter by Abolhasan Hakim (Hakim al-Molk's much younger
brother) to his friend Mahmud Afshar. They had belonged to the same circle of
young nationalists in Switzerland. Among other things, this group had led an
active press campaign against the 1919 Agreement, in which Davar had played a
leading part (see chapter five). Afshar had since returned to Iran, but Hakim was
still in Switzerland. He wrote the letter in November 1923, shortly after Reza
Khan had formed his cabinet.

The existing political framework, he writes, is incapable of solving any of the
urgent problems of 'Iran, those destitute people of Iran, those hungry people

spread across the whole of Iran'. He refers to Davar's articles in *Mard-e Azad* in favour of a dictatorship. He says that he too believes that 'this kind of constitutional government is useless for Iran, and will get nowhere'. He believes that 'force' must be used to reduce the power of the magnates (*gardankoloft-ha*), and to construct roads, establish factories, etc. Yet he disagrees with Davar, he says, because he thinks that 'the dictatorship of one person over a nation is wrong and would never be beneficial, especially if he happens to be uneducated as well'. Instead of 'a single dictator', he proposes the dictatorship of a competent and well-meaning 'elite', who would limit liberties

> to the extent that the people would need and understand. This is the only remedy, but we may in fact end up with a dictator in the wrong way. And that will be the day of Iran's eternal demise, although what I say may be no more than a babble.[41a]

It is clear that what Hakim meant by '*personal* dictatorship' was arbitrary rule, just as his reference to 'this kind of constitutional government' was to chaotic trends. He was thinking of a European-style dictatorship run by an elite, although – as with democracy – a particular person was inevitably at its head. Such regimes were also based on the consent of the influential social classes, had a binding legal framework, and were not arbitrary. Davar's own view must have been along the same lines, thinking that Reza Khan was needed to create such a strong centralized regime. At the time, it is extremely unlikely that he and others like him ever thought that Reza Khan's rule would quickly become so personal, and so arbitrary, as to lead to their own elimination.

Reza Khan for president

Sardar Sepah became prime minister late in October 1923. In March 1924, just before the *Nawruz*, a vigorous campaign was launched for the declaration of a republic, and it was obvious who would be president. Most modernists, centralists, nationalists and socialists were behind the campaign, including Tadayyon, Adl al-Molk, the Bahrami brothers, Zia'al-Va'ezin, Solaiman Mirza, Mirza Karim Khan Rashti and Aref-e Qazvini. The army played the key role in supplying much of the money and manpower needed to run the campaign, especially in the provinces. In the meantime, the new Majlis had been formally opened, and the army had ensured the return of a substantial pro-Reza Khan majority. Reza himself had told both Davar and Loraine that he had arranged for the former's return from Loristan as a Majlis deputy.[42] Months before that, in February 1923, the general officer commanding the Khorasan Division had told the provincial police chief that Reza Khan wished the elections to be delayed as much as possible, and 'Amir Lashkar himself added that Persia would be better without a parliament'.[42a]

Bahar has a long and humorous poem entitled 'The Republic Saga' (Jomhuri-nameh), written in the wake of the campaign's collapse, which describes its various stages and those involved in it. This was printed and distributed anonymously. It was believed to have been the work of Eshqi, who was publishing signed and much more scathing poems and articles against the proposed republic, which quickly led to his assassination by two police agents.[43]

The republic was opposed, although not very openly, by conservative religious leaders, for fear of further modernization and secularization, especially in view of recent developments in Turkey. It is clear, however, that the opposition of the Modarres group, and Eshqi, who defected to Modarres over the issue, was because they saw it as the first step in Reza Khan becoming Shah, and then arbitrary ruler. For example, Bahar wrote in 'The Republic Saga':

> Zia' al-Va'ezin, that silly midget,
> Is constantly shouting for a republic,
> What republic[?], I am surprised at him
> Who seems to be unaware of the motive of the Bloke,
> That he wishes to succeed the Qajar,
> Just as did that man of the Afshars [Nader Shah] ...[44]

And he wrote in another, much shorter, poem:

> In the guise of republicanism,
> He [Reza Khan] is knocking at the door of *Shahi,*
> We are ignorant and the greedy enemy is canny.[45]

Inevitably, the word went round that the idea had been approved in London, and that the Soviet legation was being duped into buying it as a progressive move. Eshqi went so far as to insist that the whole thing was a British plot.[46] Even the otherwise politically sophisticated Bahar was not immune:

> The idea has been approved in London
> That quickly summoned Sir Percy Loraine
> In case Shumyiatski became suspicious,
> We'd send him that duplicitous wanderer,
> Karim [Khan-e] Rashti, the conjuring devil.[47]

In fact, London had nothing to do with the matter. Loraine and the legation were neutral, although Loraine's heart must have been with the republicans because it had been won over by Reza Khan. The Soviet legation, and their government, were delighted, since they saw Reza as 'representative of bourgeois democratic dictatorship', and his adversaries as 'feudal reactionary agents of British imperialism'.[48]

The campaign collapsed, largely because the campaigners were in too much of a hurry, but also because Modarres played his hand astutely. When he was physically attacked in the Majlis by a zealous campaigner (Farajullah Bahrami's brother), the bazaar struck; there was a massive demonstration in front of the Majlis, and then bloodshed, because Reza Khan ordered the Majlis Guard to attack the crowd. Reza was severely rebuked by the Majlis speaker (Mo'tamen al-Molk) because he himself, as head of the legislature, and not Reza Khan was supreme commander of the Guard.[49]

The Shah had become increasingly unpopular, especially after his recent journey to Europe, and was commonly being described as 'Ahmad the Wondering Trader' (*Ahmad-e Allaf*). There was an upsurge in his popularity after these events. Seizing the moment, he sent a telegram to the Majlis that he no longer had confidence in Reza Khan, and sought their advice for a new government. Reza Khan resigned, and went to one of his estates near Damavand. The Independent Democrat group (known in the Majlis as the *Tjaddod* faction), issued dire statements that the country would be lost without Reza Khan.[50] Ali Dashti wrote a leading article in his newspaper, entitled 'the motherland's father went'.[51]

Reza Khan's generals commanding the army divisions in the provinces began to issue threatening statements, and two of them – Ahmad Aqa and Hossein Aqa – openly threatened to march on Tehran. The Tajaddod, Socialist and other factions, who now made up the Majlis majority, voted for Reza to return, and sent a heavyweight delegation which included Mostawfi, Moshir Solaiman Mirza and Musaddiq, to bring him back with ceremony.[51a]

Reza Khan returned. As it happened, the leading ulama who had been recently exiled from the *atabat* had just been allowed to return. Reza Khan had first heard the news from Loraine before his resignation, with marked satisfaction.[51b] He now hurried to Qom to see them off, and they advised him to abandon the republican campaign. That he did, and redoubled his efforts to look like the defender of the faith by organizing official religious congregations, with himself leading various processions in the annual mourning for the martyrs of Karbela. He was duly rewarded by the religious establishment, who ceremoniously delivered to him a gift of jewels from the treasury of the sacred shrines,[52] and also acquiesced when he made a bid to become Shah and establish a dynasty.

The bizarre *saqqa-khaneh* episode occurred in July 1924. Suddenly the news went around Tehran that a *saqqa-khaneh* (religiously-endowed fountain for drinking water) had performed a miracle by instantly blinding a 'Babi' (probably intended to mean Baha'i), who had allegedly spat in, or poisoned, the water. Passion-play demonstrations quickly followed. The American vice-consul went to watch them and took photographs. The angry crowd, who did not know who he was (except that he was a Christian), mobbed and injured him. He later died, or was battered to death, in hospital. Martial law was immediately declared, and several people were arrested.

The conspiracy legend, which was later elaborated and widely believed for many decades, was that the whole thing had been organized by the British in order to stop the Americans from getting a concession for north Iran oil. It was somehow overlooked that, for the legend to be true, the American vice-consul must have been a British agent agreeing to let himself be killed in the process. At the time, however, each side accused the other of having organized the shameful incident.

The government and their supporters blamed the opposition, specifically the royal court, as well as some Tehran ulama and – possibly – Modarres and his group. The opposition saw the incident as a plot by the government, intended both to discredit them (especially in the eyes of the foreigners) and to declare martial law. Only two weeks before the *Saqqa-khaneh* incident, the fiery young poet Eshqi had been assassinated by two police agents in broad daylight. Bahar has described the *Saqqa-khaneh* incident in detail and propounded the opposition view at length, although he also relates the views of the government and its supporters.[53] In a long telegram – recently come to light – by the prince regent to his brother Ahmad Shah in Paris, it is claimed that 'the people of Tehran did not kill the American consul, it was Armenian soldiers. [As for] the real instigator, what is manifest requires no explanation [as the Persian expression has it]'.[54] This refers specifically to the vice-consul's death. But the document in question is incomplete, and excludes parts that could have contained the regent's report on who might have instigated the movement itself. Some of the slogans of the demonstrators were thinly disguised attacks on Reza Khan.[54a] The text quoted above gives the impression that the regent had been in sympathy with the demonstrators, although not with the killing of the vice-consul.

Whoever organized the incident, its ramifications for the opposition, both inside and outside the Majlis, were most unwelcome, even though Modarres and other opposition deputies repudiated it. Martial law was declared, and many opposition activists and supporters were arrested or banished. Modarres and his group tabled a motion of censure. This so disturbed Sardar Sepah's supporters that they organized a large demonstration against Modarres outside the Majlis on the day the motion was to be debated. The Sardar himself was very angry when he arrived at the Majlis. The atmosphere was so charged that, in the end, the opposition left the Majlis without proposing the motion, although they did not withdraw it. A vote of confidence in the government was nevertheless passed, although the cabinet resigned the following day. Sardar Sepah introduced his new cabinet three weeks later.[55]

Khaz'al and the last line of resistance

Khaz'al Khan, the Shaikh of Mohammarh (later Khorramshahr) was the hereditary governor-general of the south-western province of Arabistan (so-called under the Qajars, but previously and later known as Khuzistan). In 1914, Sir Percy Cox had persuaded Khaz'al to enter a formal agreement with Britain to safeguard British interests in his part of the Persian Gulf in return for a guarantee of his position. He was consequently regarded by many of the Tehran politicians and activists as a British lackey. In the following years of chaos his power increased, and he had become a semi-autonomous ruler of the province. He had money, tribal support and British connections, and was therefore a much harder nut for Reza Khan to crack than any of the other provincial magnates. He, too, was understandably anxious about Sardar Sepah's increasing hegemony.

In November 1923, when Khaz'al Khan had seen the Shah off as he was crossing the border for Europe, the Shah had told him about his fears of Sardar Sepah's ambitions in the same way as he had spoken openly to Loraine. Then came the Shah's telegram of April 1924 – mentioned above – about his loss of confidence in Reza Khan. In the following summer, Khaz'al brought together some regional magnates and tribal heads – the Vali of Poshtkuh, heads of the Khamseh federation of tribes, and many of the local Arab tribal leaders – in a coalition to resist Reza. They described themselves as the Committee of the Rising for [the country's] Happiness (*Komiteh-ye Qiyam-e Sa'adat*), and sent telegrams and statements to Tehran. Their statements demanded constitutional government and the return of the Shah, who they said had been forced to remain in Europe. They also attacked military violations of the people's rights in the provinces, and 'the massacres of Loristan'; demanded Reza Khan's dismissal; and described the Prince Regent as the legitimate fount of authority. It was all in the name of the law, justice and the constitution, and 'in the illustrious name of His Majesty Soltan Ahmad Shah, the constitutional monarch':

> Letters and telegrams of complaint are censored in the capital and do not reach the authorities. Furthermore, any unfortunate person who, trying to recover his usurped rights, would plead for justice, would be charged with rebellion and sedition ... Now we openly and humbly inform those respected beings [the Majlis deputies] that the law-breaking deeds of Sardar Sepah have angered the Bakhtiyari and southern tribes and clans, and beseech them to put aside him who is no more than a law-breaking usurper ...

> It is our duty to defend and protect [constitutionalism], and stop the traitors and criminals freely dispensing with it and re-establishing the apparatus of arbitrary rule and injustice once again ... and stop Reza Khan from trampling the principles of democratic government (*hokumat-e melli*) under foot by arbitrary actions, and turning the country backwards towards arbitrary government ... Long live the Shah-an-Shah of Iran – Immortal be Iran. 11 October, 1924.[56]

Outside the circle of the royal court and the Modarres group, virtually all the politicians and political activists, as well as the Soviet government and legation, thought that this was a British plot to overthrow Reza Khan and impose a reactionary regime of their own agents, although Reza himself was soon to know better. In later years, when he became increasingly unpopular, and so was widely believed to be a British agent, this theory was suitably amended. It was now believed that the British had enticed Khaz'al into rebellion, and then delivered him to Reza Khan, who was now their preferred agent. Thus one serious news-paper wrote:

> The plan of Sardar Sepah and the foreign [i.e. British] politics behind him was to provoke the Shaikh and foment a rebellion in Khuzistan so they could send a force there and arrest the Shaikh, who was an impediment for the coming to power [i.e. becoming Shah] of Sardar Sepah, was a supporter of the royal court, and believed that Ahmad Shah should return.[57]

Makki's version of the theory is the most comprehensive: the British had brought Reza Khan to power to centralize the government in Iran (because it served their interest) and were now trying to remove the remaining impediments for his accession. Fearing Soviet suspicion and interference, however, they deceived the Shaikh into taking action, then withdrew their support from him and thus brought down Khaz'al, while the Soviet Union applauded.

What in fact happened was that the opposition to Reza Khan had pulled their resources together to try and stem the flood tide of his power by making use of the Shah's legitimacy. The exact sequence of events, and degree of combination and commitment, is difficult to ascertain. The movement seems to have been initiated in Tehran, because in his letter of April 1924, before the movement was declared, Modarres wrote that 'this plan, of course, has been designed here, but it must be applied prudently'.[58] The Shaikh was in contact with Modarres and his parliamentary group – apart from Modarres himself, Khaz'al corresponded with Qavam al-Dawleh, a leading figure in the Majlis opposition – as well as the Prince Regent.

The Shah must have learned about the movement at some stage, but it is not clear if Khaz'al or someone else in his group had directly sought the Shah's support. The Prince Regent wrote an encouraging letter to Khaz'al, all in the name of the Shah and for protection of the constitution, and said that the bearer would discuss matters with the Shaikh in detail.[59] On balance, it appears that the Shah and the court did not have the courage to commit themselves firmly to such a movement, but would go along with it if – as turned out not to be the case – there was a very good chance of success. Modarres, on the other hand, did have that courage (and imprudence), but lacked the means to be effective. In a letter to Khaz'al he even wrote, with typical bluntness:

> I have, on two or three occasions, mentioned in my letters that the people of Tehran generally do not think well of you; that you do not have a good reputation in the country; and that all the people have a sense of hatred and dislike towards you. Therefore if you would like your past to be forgotten, you will have to compensate for it with good deeds ... This is

the day on which you are being put to the test ... If you pass it well your wrongdoings will be inevitably mitigated ... Otherwise it is not possible to deceive the people of Tehran with words alone.[60]

In reply to the petition sent to the Majlis by the movement in the south, the Majlis firmly stood behind the government and, late in October, in a letter and a telegram signed by Mo'tamen himself as head of the Legislature, told them not to revolt against the central government.[61] Respectable popular constitutionalists like Mo'tamen were not Reza's men; they were weary of the chaos that Iran's brand of constitutionalism had created, and would not back any move against the central authority (see chapter one for the theoretical, and chapters two to eight for the practical background to this).

Reza Khan moved quickly, neutralized the Bakhtiyaris through the good offices of Sardar As'ad III, his devoted follower among the first-ranking Bakhtiyari khans, and then moved to Isfahan.[61a] He sent a telegram to Khaz'al that Khaz'al should either apologize to him and relent publicly, or take the full consequences.[62]

Khaz'al and his remaining associates could muster an army of 25,000 men, which was no less than Reza Khan could throw in the region at the time. In fact, the army he had amassed at the foot of the Loristan elevations was 15,000 strong. But Khaz'al did not dare to go into action without British approval. The British government was in no mood to go to war on Khaz'al's behalf, which, in any case, would have been publicly condemned in Iran and almost everywhere else, if not also in Britain. As it happened, Loraine had been honeymooning in Egypt, and arrived in Jerusalem to face piles of telegrams: the Foreign Office were not prepared to stand firmly by the Shaikh, and Reza Khan was demanding the Shaikh's submission.

Loraine rushed through Baghdad to Ahvaz and, after lengthy discussions, he convinced Khaz'al to desist and to apologize to Reza Khan. In return, he promised to intervene with Reza Khan to halt the advance of his troops into Khuzistan. The Shaikh sent an apology,[63] but, realizing that the danger had passed, Reza Khan paid little attention to Loraine's representations on the Shaikh's behalf. He let the troops pour into Khuzistan, and demanded that Khaz'al should surrender unconditionally and go straight to Tehran. The Foreign Office was very unhappy at Reza Khan's intransigence, but there was little they could do except use Loraine's diplomatic skills combined with some subtle bluffing. It worked for the time being. Khaz'al and Reza met and were reconciled in the presence of Loraine. Typically, they even swore an oath of friendship on the Qur'an. Reza said that Khaz'al would remain as governor in Ahvaz, and that the troops would be withdrawn in the spring. After a short while, when he had triumphantly returned to Tehran (but not before a pilgrimage to the shrines in Iraq), he broke all his pledges and had Khaz'al arrested and sent to Tehran. Khaz'al's estates and treasures were confiscated, and he was confined to the capital until some years later, when he was murdered at his home in Tehran.[64]

The fall of the Qajars

It took another year to bring down the Qajars and inaugurate the Pahlavi monarchy. Reza Kahn's triumph over the provincial rebels, khans and magnates was now complete, but some resistance remained at the centre. To campaign for a republic – at least as a first step – had had the support of the nationalists and modernists, the goodwill of the Soviet Union, and the neutrality of the British government. To try and become Shah, Reza Khan could alienate some of his modernist supporters, particularly the Socialists, the Soviet Union, and possibly (in his thinking) Britain as well. The ulama would be easier to bring into line if he kept up his demonstrations of official piety, because they saw much more danger in a republican system than in a Pahlavi monarchy. But the constitutionalist opposition would now include popular politicians such as Mostawfi, Moshir, Mosaddeq and others. This is the view which emerges with the benefit of hindsight (except that Britain remained neutral in the matter), but it could have been predicted without much difficulty in 1925, when the campaign for replacing the Qajars was launched.

Sardar Sepah continued his good relations with the Soviet embassy and the British legation. The former saw him as a modernizing and progressive leader who, *ipso facto*, was *not* in the pockets of the British, and they could have no better proof of all this than Reza Kahn's overthrow of Khaz'al.[65] Reza Khan, of course, realized that it was much more important to retain Loraine's goodwill, partly because the British presence in and around the country was still broader and stronger than any other foreign power, but mainly because he believed in the English magic wand, and was convinced that, through the 1921 Coup, they had brought him to power.

Already in January 1925, several of Reza Khan's supporters tested Loraine's opinion about the removal of the Shah. Loraine was under the impression, as he reported to the Foreign Office, that Reza Khan's 'present idea is to put [an] old man or [a] minor on throne, but that he does not aspire to throne himself'. However, in his reply to Reza Khan's supporters, Loraine had 'refused to express an opinion on a matter which His Majesty's Government regards as purely internal affair.'[66] The Foreign Office commented:

> The Shah has done nothing to earn him the gratitude or support of H.M.G. We should avoid taking any hand in the internal intrigues reported by Sir P. Loraine. His attitude … is entirely correct.[67]

Reza Khan intensified his efforts to reassure the religious establishment of his good Islamic intentions, and extended his contacts with important religious leaders. The recently published diaries of his valet at the time, Solaiman Behbudi (who became Master of Ceremony at Mohammad Reza Shah's court), reveal the extent and importance of these contacts. It was not only turbaned politicians such as Sayyed Mohammad Tadayyon, Zia' al-Va'zin (later Sayyed Ebrahim Zia) and Sayyed Ya'qub Shirazi (later Anvar), his active and open supporters, who were among his frequent callers and visitors. They included such influential ulama as Imam Jom'eh-ye Kho'i, Hajj Aqa Jamal Isfahani, Sayyed Mohammad Behbahani, Sayyed Abolqasem Kashani, Hajj Sayyed Nasrollah Akhavi (Taqavi), Ayatollah-Zadeh Isfahani, Ayatollh-zadeh Shirazi and others.[68]

Popular and respected constitutionalists had so far avoided open opposition to Reza Khan, though there is contemporary evidence that they were far from happy with the danger of military dictatorship and lack of respect for lawful government. Yet Mo'tamen's uncharacteristic explosion over Reza's order to the Majlis Guard to attack the crowd had been an exception which proved the rule. Already before Khaz'al's downfall, Reza had arranged an informal council which met with him regularly every week at the home of one of its members. It consisted of Mostawfi, Moshir, Mosaddeq, Taqizadeh, Dawlat-Abadi and Ala, as well as Forughi and Mokhber. The former six were Majlis deputies, known as the Independents (*monfaredin*), who sometimes voted with the government and sometimes with the opposition. The latter two were in the government.[69]

Reza Khan knew that if he had these men, especially the first five of them, behind any legislative proposal, he would have little difficulty in both getting it through the Majlis and winning over public opinion. In a meeting of January 1925, he openly told this personal council that he could not work with the Shah and the regent, and that ways must be found of removing them.[70] This caused much embarrassment, and in a following meeting Moshir said, on his colleagues' behalf, that such a thing would be unconstitutional. Accepting the verdict with visible annoyance, Reza said that since he felt his position to be insecure, he demanded that the Majlis would formally name him as the army supreme commander. They agreed, and induced Modarres also to agree. Modarres was politically close to men like Mostawfi and Moshir and would not oppose them on a basic issue. Besides, as a good tactician (though poor strategist) he knew that he would lose badly. But he did not agree until Reza Khan personally met him at his home and asked for his support, for he was as vain and open as Reza was secretive and cunning. The motion passed through the Majlis without a hitch in February.[71]

The Majlis was now solidly in Reza's hands, because of the efficient manipulations of Davar, Taimurtash and Firuz (even though the latter two had now joined the cabinet). Although essentially pro-Reza, Davar had been manoeuvring between factions in the previous Majlis. Taimurtash and Firuz – the latter more than the former – had followed Modarres's lead, but – the former before the latter – defected to Reza when it became clear that, to use Loraine's phrase, he was 'the winning horse'. Together with Davar, they formed a new triumvirate to run the parliamentary and civil politics of the country, centred on Reza Khan's leadership. Their role in organizing and managing the move for the abolition of the Qajars and establishment of the Pahlavis was extremely important.

As the summer of 1925 began, it looked as if there were no more impediments to Reza's ascendancy to the supreme position in the land. The court, led by the regent, was acutely aware of this and tried, as before, to induce the fright-ened Shah to return. A couple of months earlier, the opposition had sent a special envoy (Rahimzadeh Safavi) to France to try and instil enough courage in the Shah to come back to Iran. He carried letters and messages from the regent and Modarres, among others.[71a] There is little doubt that had the Shah gone back, he would have become a rallying point for many, not least the popular constitutionalists, who were against Reza's assumption of supreme power. It would hardly have affected Reza's position as prime minister and army chief, but his possible bid to become Shah would have had to take a different form, and would have had much more difficulty in succeeding.

Loraine's trust in Reza Khan's words once again led him into an error of judgement. He wired London in July that the government were 'fairly unanimous in desiring his [the Shah's] return in order to preserve the monarchy, though they recognize he will be of no use to the country'. He thought that the regent was 'of stronger character and may one day become Shah ...' Oliphant minuted:

> The Shah is a miserable and contemptible individual whose repeated state-ments that he is about to return to Persia no longer carry conviction with anyone. His younger brother the Vali Ahd [i.e. the regent] is a far better person; and the Persians being monarchical by nature, Reza Khan will be wise if he works with, not against the Vali Ahd'.[72]

It is clear that even as late as July 1925 the Foreign Office was unaware of Reza Khan's intention to bid to found his own dynasty. The reason was that, in a society such as Britain in which legitimacy was of utmost importance, it was difficult to believe that someone with Reza Khan's background would even think of such a thing only four years after leading a military Coup at the head of two thousand Cossacks. They did not understand the logic of Iranian history, its cycles of arbitrary rule-chaos-arbitrary rule, and the fact that 'legitimacy' belonged to whoever managed to capture power (see chapter one). That is also why, in November, when the Majlis removed the Qajars and declared Reza Khan as 'temporary head of state' pending the decision of the constituent assembly, Lancelot Oliphant was still far from convinced of Reza's success. He wrote in minutes:

> It is difficult for anyone who remembers the old regime to believe that the old Princes and their supporters can tamely accept such a usurper. Even if it appears to work at first, it will be surprising if a reaction does not follow ... There are difficult times ahead.[73]

Oliphant had no idea – and perhaps could not even contemplate the possibility – that no less than Farmanfarma and his son Firuz had been leading many of 'the old princes' in favour of the campaign to bring down Ahmad Shah and put Reza Khan in his place.

In mid-September, the Shah's supporters were still trying to get him back to the country in the hope of resisting what was fast becoming inevitable. The Shah sent a telegram to Reza Khan himself, as prime minister, informing him that, on 2 October, he would take a French liner and return home via Bombay.[73a] Yet the Shah would not go back unless he was sure that the British were not determined to overthrow him, as he suspected. Having sent a telegram to the regent 'asking for advice', the regent then sent a message to the British legation seeking 'Sir P. Loraine's personal opinion'. Havard replied that Loraine 'declined to be involved in this purely internal question.'

This must have convinced the Shah that the British planned the overthrow of his dynasty, and been an important factor in his decision not to return. Decades later, Mohammad Reza Shah's unjustified suspicion that America and Britain were behind the revolution of 1979–79 contributed significantly to his downfall. However, the Foreign Office commented on Loraine's report, sardonically:

> The Shah has got another attack of cold feet, and as usual, asks for British advice, which he would probably ignore even if rendered. Sir P. Loraine acted wisely.[74]

This was a month before the Majlis voted to dislodge the Qajars and instal Reza Khan in their place. Meanwhile, all the main Majlis factions other than the Modarres group and the Independents had been brought into line by the new triumvirate. Solaiman Mirza and his Socialists, although they had joyfully supported the campaign for a republic, were having pangs of political conscience regarding the establishment of a new *dynasty*. The Majlis vote, at any rate, would make Reza Khan 'temporary head of state', but Reza promised Solaiman that the ensuing constituent assembly would confer the title of Shah on himself for life. Even the ever-optimistic Loraine thought that it might be the first step towards declaring a republic, as the Soviet Union also hoped.[75] Solaiman's group therefore fell into line over the crucial Majlis vote, but could do little more later apart from Solaiman himself arguing against the establishment of a new dynasty in the constituent assembly of 1926. He was the only one (see chapter eleven).[76]

The Majlis vote was taken on 31 October. There had been a bread riot in Tehran in late September, and each side accused the other of having been behind it. The Soviet Persian broadcast passed negative comments on it,[77] which meant that they thought it was an anti-Reza Khan plot. One of the crowd's slogans outside the Majlis was, 'We want bread; we don't want the Shah', prompting Modarres to advise them to shout 'We want bread; we also want the Shah'. It was just after the bread riot that the regent sought Loraine's advice on the Shah's return. Once again there were mutual recriminations.

 Barely a week or two later, meetings began to be held in the capital, and telegrams poured in from the provinces calling for the removal of the Qajars. In the

evening of 29 October there was a lengthy debate in the Majlis on the report of
its Complaints' Committee about the communications received from the public
for the abolition of the Qajar dynasty. Bahar delivered a reasoned and tempered
speech on behalf of the opposition. Assassins had come there to kill him, but
not for that reason, and, in a case of mistaken identity, they killed a pro-Reza
Khan journalist instead. The assassination squad had been sent by Dargahi (the
chief of police) before it was known that Bahar would speak that night.[78] The
idea was to terrorize any remaining vestige of opposition. On that or the
following night, Davar arranged for 84 out of the 100 or so deputies to be
summoned to Sardar Sepah's house and, one by one, asked them to sign the
motion, which was tabled and approved on 31 October. They included a few
members of the Modarres faction as well.[79] Of those who had been invited, only
Dawlat-Abadi protested and refused to sign.[79a]

Modarres and the Independents tried to use delaying tactics to buy a little
time, but it did not work, and would not have been effective even if it had
succeeded. It was a procedural point that, since the Majlis speaker (Mosatawfi)
had resigned, the election of a new speaker took precedence over all other business. In fact, Mostawfi had resigned precisely in order to avoid chairing that
meeting. But this enabled his deputy (Taddayon), a leading pro-Reza Khan
figure, to chair the meeting and overrule Modarres's objection. Modarres used
the rejection of the procedural objection to declare the proceedings illegal, and
stormed out of the House without delivering a formal speech. The four men
who delivered speeches against the motion – Taqizadeh, Mosaddeq, Dawlat-
Abadi and Ala – were all members of the Independents as well as of Reza's
personal council (the other Independents simply stayed away). All had some
praise for Reza's achievements, especially the order and security which he had
brought to the country; none of them defended the Qajars, and all of them
stressed law and constitutional government.[80]

The move had strong backing from nationalists, modernists and Socialists
(though with the hesitation mentioned about a new dynasty), and among the
army and the higher civil service. The religious establishment did not campaign
for it, but neither did they oppose it, and a significant number of the ulama and,
especially, ulama-types, voted for it in the constituent assembly, which was held
in December (see chapter eleven).[81]

It is difficult to know how widely the event was supported among the general
public at the time. But in the elections for the sixth Majlis only the Tehran elections (held in June 1926) were free, and not a single deputy who had voted for
change of dynasty – including Solaiman, a longstanding darling of the Tehran
electorate – was elected. Instead, the voters elected those, like Modarres,
Mosaddeq, and Taqizadeh, who had formally opposed it, and others, like
Mostawfi, Moshir and Mo'tamen, who were known to have been opposed to
it.[82]

The response in the provinces was far from enthusiastic. The British legation
in Tehran had instructed its consulates in various towns and cities to remain

completely neutral during and after the event, and regard it as a purely internal Iranian affair. They simply asked them to send reports of the public response to the great change. Altogether, there were 13 short reports. In Isfahan, 'Population apparently entirely disinterested'. In Mashad, there was little enthusiasm for the celebrations, and the public regarded the change of dynasty 'as British triumph and Russian defeat'. In Tabriz, there was indifference by 'mass of population'. In Shiraz, a 'chilly reception'; the people saying that the telegrams sent earlier to demand the change of dynasty were the 'work of a small clique'. In Kerman, 'no one dared express any unfavourable opinion', although they thought it was the Qajar's own fault, but were apprehensive at a 'further strengthening of military power'. In Rasht, there was 'no excitement', in Bushire, quiet dissent, while in Yazd, the change 'appears to be popular'. Only in Sistan was the news received 'with every expression of rejoicing on the part of military and civilian'.[83]

On the whole, it appears that, with the urban public at large, the fall of the Qajars was not unpopular, but nor was the rise of the new dynasty popular. Yet this was the moment when Reza Khan/Shah was at the height of his popularity and enjoyed the broadest public support in the 20 years between 1921 and 1941. Nevertheless, had he not managed to succeed (or survive) in his earlier years, he would doubtless now be held as a great hero who had fallen victim to foreign imperialism and internal reaction'.[84] Such indeed are the ironies of Iranian history.

Notes

i See Homa Katouzian, 'Nationalist Trends in Iran, 1921–26', presented in May 1976 at the Middle East Centre, St Antony's College, Oxford, and subsequently published in *International Journal of Middle East Studies*, November 1979, p. 544. See also Katouzian, *The Political Economy of Modern Iran* (London and New York: Macmillan and New York University Press, 1981), p. 84.

1 See Reza Niyazmand, *Reza Shah: As Tavallod Ta Saltanat* (Bonyad-e Motale'at-e Iran, Washington and London: 1996); Donald N. Wilber, *Riza Shah Pahlavi: the Resurrection and Reconstruction of Iran* (New York: Exposition Press, 1975); see also Reader Bullard, *Letters From Tehran*, (ed.) E. C. Hodgkin (London and New York: I. B. Tauris, 1991), who felt that the Shah looked older than his official age. Abdollah Mostawfi (*Sharh-e Zendegani-ye Man*, vol. 3, Tehran: Zavvar, 1964) thought that Reza Shah had lived for 70 years.

2 See for example Niyazmand, *Reza Shah*; Malek al-Sho'ara Bahar, *Tarikh-e Mokhtasar-e Ahzab-e Siyasi dar Iran*, vol. 1 (Tehran: Jibi, 1978); Abdollah Mostawfi, *Sharh-e Zendegani-ye Man*, vol. 3. While this text was in preparation, a new biography of Reza Shah was published in Tehran. This adds little about Reza's general family background and childhood to sources already mentioned, but contains some new details. The book relies heavily on unpublished memoirs, especially those of General Hamzeh Pesyan on the earlier part of Reza's life. A further complication is that some of the direct quotations from these memoirs, and from Pesyan's in particular, seem to have been rewritten in contemporary style. See Najafqoli Pesyan and Khosraw Mo'tazed, *Az Savadkuh ta Zhohansburg* (Tehran: Sales, 1998).

3 See in particular, Mostawfi, *ibid.*, and Niyazmand, *Reza Shah*.

4 *Ibid.*

5 *Ibid.*, Pesyan and Mo'tazed, *Az Savadkuh*, and Hossein Makki, *Tarikh-e Bistsaleh-ye Iran*, vol. 2 (Tehran: Elmi, 1995).

6 See Bahar, *Tarikh-e Mokhtasar.*

7 See for example the photocopy of a letter written in 1918 in Reza's own hand, in Nasrollah Seifpour Fatemi, *A'ineh-ye Ebrat*, vol. 1 (London: Nashr-e Ketab, 1989).

8 See Abolqasem Kahhalzadeh, *Dideh-ha va Shenideh-ha, Khaterat-e Abolqasem Kahhalzadeh*, (ed.) Motreza Kamran (Tehran: Kamran, 1984), pp. 300–08.

9 Dickson to Curzon, 14/5/21, 371/6427.

10 See Mo'asseseh-ye Motale'at va Pazhuhesh-ha-ye Siyasi, *Zohur va Soqut-e Saltanet-e Pahlavi*, vol. 2, p. 151.

11 This was said at Mosaddeq's house in one of the weekly meetings of Reza Khan and the popular voluntary councillors he had chosen shortly before his final bid to become Shah (see also below). See Yahya Dawlat-Abadi's, *Hayat-e Yahya*, vol. 4, (Tehran: Attar & Ferdawsi, 1983), p. 343; Mohammad Mosaddeq, *Taqrirat-e Mosaddeq dar Zendan*, notes by Jalil Bozorgmehr, (ed.) Iraj Afshar (Tehran: Farhang-e Iranzamin, 1980).

12 British embassy in Washington to Sir R. Matkin, Foreign Office, 21/5/1953. For a photocopy of the document, see Doktor Karim Sanjabi, *Omid-ha va Na-omidi-ha*, (London: Nashr-e Ketab, 1989), p. 449. For the British government's attempts (in conjunction with the Shah and Iranian conservatives) to bring down Mosaddeq's government from the moment it took office, see 'Kushesh-ha-ye Sefarat-e Inglis bara-ye Ta'ine Nakhost Vazir-e Iran' in Homa Katouzian, *Estebdad, Demokrasi va Nehzat-e Melli*, second edition (Tehran: Nashr-e Markaz, 1996).

13 See Ahmad Amir Ahmadi, *Khaterat-e Nakhostin Sepahbod-e Iran, Gholamhossein Zargari-Nezhad*, (ed.), (Tehran: Mo'asseseh-ye Pazhuhesh va Motale'at-e Farhangi, 1994). Makki's account, which he claimed to have heard from Amir Ahmadi himself, is more chilling and dramatic than Amir Ahmadi's own memoirs. See his *Khaterat-e Siyasi-ye Hossein Makki*, Tehran: Elmi, 1989, pp. 92-94.

14 Nasrollah Seifpour Fatemi, *A'ineh-ye Ebrat*, vol. 2 (London: Nashr-e Ketab, 1990), chapter 55. Jalal Abdoh, prosecutor in the court which tried officials for political murders after Reza Shah's abdication, has given a detailed account of the killing of Firuz in Semnan and of its perpetrators. See his memoirs, *Chehel Sal dar Sahneh*, (ed.) Majid Tafreshi (Tehran: Rasa, 1989), vol. 1, pp. 171–72.

14a See Taqizadeh, *Zendegi-ye Tufani, Khaterat-e Sayyed Hasan Taqizadeh*, (ed.) Iraj Afshar (Tehran: Elmi, 1993), p. 364.

14b For Ayrom's amoral character and cunning machinations, see, for example, Ebrahim Khajeh Nuri, 'Ayrom', in *Bazigaran-e Asr-e Tala'i*, (Tehran: Jibi, 1978). For a long poetical account of Ayrom and his chilling work, see Bahar, 'Karnameh-ye Zendan' in *Divane Bahar*, (ed.) Mohammad Malekzadeh, vol. 2 (Tehran: Amir Kabir, 1957).

15 For differing accounts of the Shah's attitude and behaviour at the time of his abdication, see Hossein Makki, *Tarikh-e Bistsaleh*, vols. 7 and 8; Gholamhossein Mirza Saleh, (ed.), *Reza Shah* (Tehran:Tarh-e Naw, 1993); Baqer Aqeli, *Zok' al-Molk-e Forughi va Shahrivar-e 1320* (Tehran: Elmi, 1988); Nasrollah Entezam, *Khaterat-e Nasrullah Entezam, Shahrivar-e 1320 as Didgah-e Darbar*, Mohammad Reza Abbasi and Behruz Tayarani (eds.), (Tehran: Sazman-e Asnad-e Melli-ye Iran, 1992).

15a See for example Fatemi, *A'ineh-ye Ebrat*, vol. 2, chapter 35. See also Iraj Afshar (ed.), *Khaterat-e Sardar As'ad Bakhtiyari* (Tehran: Asatir, 1993).

15b See Mokhber al-Saltaneh (Hedayat) *Khaterat va Khatarat* (Tehran: Zavvar, 1984), p. 385. See also Baqer Aqeli, *Nosrat al-Dawleh Firuz* (Tehran: Nashr-e Mamak, 1994).

15c See Makki, *Tarikh-e Bistsaleh*, vol. 3, p. 591.

15d See Hossein Makki, *Doktor Mosaddeq va Notq-ha-ye Tarikhi-ye U* (Tehran: Elmi, 1985), p. 130.

15e Makki, *ibid.*, p. 139

16 Ebrahim Fakhra'i, *Sardar-e Jangal* (Tehran: Javidan, 1978), pp. 389–91, includes a picture

of Kuchik's head on public display; 'Khaterat-e Solaiman Behbudi', in Gholamhussein Mirza Saleh (ed.), *Reza Shah*, p. 12. For detailed accounts of the fall of the Gilan republic, see Fakhra'i, *Sardar-e Jangal*, and Cosroe Chaqueri, *The Soviet Socialist Republic of Iran*, (Pittsburgh: Pittsburgh University Press, 1995).

16a See for example Mohammad Musaddiq, *Mudaddiq's Memoirs*, (ed.) Homa Katouzian, tr. S.H. Amin and H. Katouzian (London: Jebheh, 1988); Ja'far Mehdi-niya, *Zendegi-ye Siyasi-ye Sayyed Zia al-Din Tabataba'i* (Tehran: Mehdi-niya, 1991).

17 There are various accounts of Pesyan's revolt in contemporary sources. For a traditional approach, see Ali Azari, *Qiyam-e Kolonel Mohammad Taqi Khan Pesyan*, (Tehran: Safi'ali Shah, 1973). For modern studies and documentation, see Mehrdad Bahar, *Darbareh-ye Qiyam-e Zhandarmeri-ye Khorasan beh Rahbari-ye Kolonel Mohammad Taqi Khan-e Pesyan* (Tehran: Mo'in, 1990); Kaveh Bayat, *Enqelab-e Khorasan*, (Tehran, 1991) *Mo'assehseh-ye Pazhuhesh-ha va Motale'at-e Farhangi*, (Tehran, 1991); Stephanie Cronin, 'An Experiment in Revolutionary Nationalism: The Rebellion of Colonel Muhammad Taqi Khan Pesyan, April–October 1921', *Middle Eastern Studies*, 33, 4, October 1997, and The *Army and the Creation of the Pahlavi State, 1910-1926* (London and New York: I.B. Tauris, 1997).

18 See Bahar, *Tarikh-e Mokhtasar*, vol. 2; Makki, *Tarikh-e Bistsaleh*, vol. 3; Cronin, *The Army and the Creation of the Pahlavi State*.

19 See for example Aref's moving poem of lamentation for Habib Maikadeh in *Divan-e Aref*, (ed.) Saif-e Azad (Tehran: Amir Kabir), 1963, pp. 263–64.

19a Loraine to Foreign Office, 20/1/25, FO 371/10840.

20 See for example, Bahar, *Tarikh-e Mokhtasar-e Ahzab-e Siyasi dar Iran*, vol. 2, (Tehran: Amir Kabir, 1984); Makki, *Tarikh-e Bistsaleh*, vol. 3.

20a See Afshar (ed.), *Zendegi-ye Tufani*, p. 160.

21 See Bahar, *Tarikh-e Mokhtasar*, vol. 2; Mostawfi, *Sharh-e Zendegani*, vol. 3;

22 See *ibid.*; Makki, *Tarikh-e Bistsaleh*, vol. 3; Dawlat-Abadi, *Hayat-e Yahya*, vol. 4.

23 See 'Amir Tahmasebi', in Khajeh-Nuri, *Bazigaran*, 'Esma'il Aqa Simko', 'Ja'far Aqa Shakkak', and 'Hosseinqoli Khan Nezam al-Saltaneh', in Mehdi Bamdad, *Sharh-e Hal-e Rejal-e Iran* (Tehran: Zavvar, 1992); Ahmad Kasravi, *Tarikh-e Hijdah Saleh-ye Azerbaijan* (Tehran: Amir Kabir, 1992). Mokhber al-Saltaneh, *Khaterat va Khatarat*.

24 Amir-Ahmadi, *Khaterat*, vol. 1, pp. 261–62. See also Cronin, *The Army and the Creation of the Pahlavi State in Iran*.

25 For Loraine's private letters to Foreign Office friends about the Iranian situation, see Gordon Waterfield, *Professional Diploma: Sir Percy Loraine* (London: John Murray, 1973), chapter 7.

26 Loraine to Curzon, 21/5/23, F.O. 248/1369. This was followed by similar assessments in Loraine's dispatches of 23/5/23, 24/5/23 and 28/5/22, F.O. 371/1369.

27 See Bahar, *Tarikh-e Mokhtasar*, vol. 1; *Cronin, The Army and the Creation of the Pahlavi State*.

28 See Homa Katouzian (ed.), *Mussadiq's Memoirs* (London: Jebheh, 1988), Book 1; Bahar, *Tarikh-e Mokhtasar*, vol. 1; Makki, *Tarikh-e Bistsaleh*, vol. 1, chapter 28; Baqer Aqeli, *Mirza Ahmad Khan Qavam al-Saltaneh* (Tehran: Javidan, 1988), chapter 4; *idem, Ruzshomar-e Tarikh-e Iran*, (Tehran: Nashr-e Goftar, 1995), p. 165.

29 See Aqeli, *ibid.*, p. 166; Bahar, *Tarikh-e Mokhtasar*, vol. 1.

30 For the full story of Lahuti's revolt, see Kaveh Bayat, *Kudeta-ye Lahuti, Tabriz, Bahman 1300* (Tehran: Shirazeh, 1997). See also Mokhber al Saltaneh, *Khaterat va Khatarat*, Makki, *Tarikh-e Bistsaleh*, vol. 2; Cronin, *The Army and the Creation of the Pahlavi State*.

31 See Bahar, *Tarikh-e Mokhtasar*, vol. 1, p. 209.

32 For the full text of the speech, see *ibid.*, pp. 230-233.

33 See the full text of the speech, *ibid.*, pp. 233–34.

34 See Homa Katouzian, 'Nationalist Trends in Iran, 1921–1926'. Aqeli, *Mirza Ahmad Khan Qavam al-Saltaneh*, chapter 5.

35 See for example *Kolliyat-e Mosavvar-e Eshqi*, (ed.) Ali Akbar Moshir Salimi, first edition (Tehran: n.p., n.d.); *Divan-e Farrokhi Yazdi*, (ed.), Hossein Makki,(Tehran: Amir Kabir, 1978).

36   Loraine to Curzon, ?/9/23 (minutes are dated 20/9/23), F.O. 248/1369.
37   See Ali Akbar Siyasi, *Gozaresh-e Yek Zendegi* (London: Siyasi, 1988).
38   Loraine to Curzon, 2/10/23, F.O. 248/1369.
39   See the long document, 'Terror activities against the War Minister (Sardar Sepah)', apparently a free summary translation of Persian press reports, F.O. 248/1369.
40   See Bahar, *Tarikh-e Mokhtasar*, vol. 2; Makki, *Tarikh-e Bistsaleh*, vol. 2; Mostawfi, *Sharh-e Zendegani*, vol. 3; Aqeli, *Ruzshoma*, pp. 179–80.
41   Loraine to Curzon, 6/10/23, F.O. 248/1369.
41a   See Mahmud Afshar, *Nameh-ha-ye Dustan*, (ed.) Iraj Afshar (Tehran: Bonyad-e; Mawqufat-e Doktor Mahmud Afshar, 1996), pp. 147–60.
42   Loraine to Curzon, 2/10/23, F.O. 248/1369.
42a   Colonel Prideaux in Meshed to the British legation in Tehran, 12/2/23, FO 248/1369.
43   See Malekzadeh, *Divan-e Bahar*, vol. 1, pp. 359–66. *Kolliyat-e Eshqi*, Books VI and VIII.
44   Malekzadeh, *Divan-e Bahar*, vol. 1, p. 361.
45   See his *mosammast-e movashshah*, *ibid.*, pp. 357–58.
46   For a full account of the republic campaign as a British plot, see Moshir Salimi, *Kolliyat-e Eshqi*, the *mathnav* about John Bull and the Republic, pp. 277–80.
47   See Malekzadeh, *Divan-e Bahar*, vol. 1, p. 363.
48   See further Katouzian, *The Political Economy*, chapter 5.
49   See Fatemi, *A'ineh-ye Ebrat*, vol. 2; Mostawfi, *Sharh-e Zendegani*, vol. 3; Dawlat-Abiadi, *Hayat-e Yahya*, vol. 4; Bahar, *Tarikh-e Mokhtasr*, vol. 2; Malekzadeh, *Divan-e Bahar*, vol. 1.
50   See the full text of the long communiqué in Behbudi, *Reza Shah*, (ed.) Mirza Saleh, pp. 498–501.
51   Quoted in Bahar, *Tarikh-e Mokhtasar*, vol. 2, pp. 667.
51 a Makki, *Tarikh-e Bistsaleh*, vol. 2, p. 576.
51b   Two months previously, he himself had said to Loraine that it would be better if they returned or otherwise they could make trouble for him. See Loraine to Foreign Office, 15/11/23, F.O. 248/1369.
52   See for example Bahar, *Tarikh-e Mokhtasar*, vol. 2, and Makki, *Tarikh-e Bistsaleh*, vols. 2 and 3. See in particular, the letter of the famous *Marja'*, Mirza Hossein Na'ini in Makki, vol. 3, p. 46.
53   See Bahar, *Tarikh-e Mokhtasar*, vol. 2, pp. 115–30.
54   For the text of a part of the latter (written down in Persian from the original telegram in Latin) see Fatemi, *A'ineh-ye Ebrat*, vol. 1, pp. 707–08.
54a   For example: 'This unprincipled Babi/has rebelled against the people'. See also Katouzian, *Political Economy*, p. 99.
55   See Ebrahim Khajeh-Nuri, *Modarres* (Tehran: Javidan, 1978); Sayyed Sadr al-Din Taher, *et. al.*, *Modarres* (Tehran: Bonyad-e Enqelab-e Islami-ye Iran, 1987); Bahar, *Tarikh-e Mokhtasar*, vol. 2.
56   For the text of two of their statements, see Makki, *Tarikh-e Bistsaleh*, vol. 3, pp. 103–04.
57   Quoted from *Qiyam-e Iran* in Makki, *ibid.*, p. 179.
58   *Ibid.*, p. 188.
59   For the full text of the letter see *ibid.*, pp. 186–87.
60   See Katouzian, 'Nationalist Trends', p. 546.
61   For the full text of the letter and the telegram, see Makki, *Tarikh-e Bistsaleh*, vol. 3, pp. 183–84.
61a   See Bahar, *Tarikh-e Mokhtasar*, vol. 2, pp. 154–55.
62   Immediately after the event, *Safarnameh-ye Khuzistan* was published by a victorious Reza Khan (the text was ghost-written by Bahrami). It is a triumphalist account and contains open attacks on the Shah, but also includes many of the telegrams exchanged between Reza and Khaz'al. It has been reprinted in its entirety in Makki, *Tarikh-e Bistsaleh*, vol. 3, pp. 198–314.
63   For the text of his telegram, see *ibid.*, p. 245.

64　The full story of the fall of Khaz'al is long. For British documentation see Waterfield, *Professional Diplomat*, and Houshang Sabahi, *British Policy in Persia, 1918–1925* (London: Frank Cass, 1990), both of which quote the relevant Foreign Office documents. For Iranian documentation, see Reza Khan, *Safarnameh-ye Khuzistan*. Makki, *Tarikh-e Bistsaleh*, vol. 3.

65　See for example contemporary Soviet broadcasts in Persian quoted in Makki, *Tarikh-e Bistsaleh*, vol. 3, 316–17; E. H. Carr, *The Bolshevik Revolution*, (Harmondsworth: Penguin, 1966), vol. iii.

66　Loraine to F.O., quoted in 'PERSIA', Foreign Office minutes, 23/1/25, F.O. 371/10840.

67　*Ibid.*

68　See Khaterat-e Behbudi in Mirza Saleh, *Reza Shah*.

69　See Dawlat-Abadi, *Hayat-e Yahya*, vol. 4; Homa Katouzian, *Musaddiq and the Struggle for Power in Iran*, second edition (London and New York: I. B. Tauris, 1998).

70　See Dawlat-Abadi, *Hayat-e Yahya*, vol. 4, p. 338; Bahar, *Tarikh-e Mokhtasar*, vol. 2, p. 205; Foreign Office minutes, 23/1/25, F.O. 371/10840.

71　See Bahar, *Tarikh-e Mokhtasar*, vol. 2, pp. 203–10, including the text of the Majlis motion; Makki, *Tarikh-e Bistsaleh*, vol. 3, pp. 253–63; Dawlat-Abadi, *Hayat-e Yahya*, vol. 4, pp. 338–44.

71a　See for example Bahar, *Tarikh-e Mokhtasar*, vol. 2, pp. 190–200, for the text of Rahimzadeh's reports back to Tehran.

72　'PERSIA', Foreign Office minutes, 7/7/25, F.O. 371/10840.

73　'PERSIA', Foreign Office minutes, 11/11/25, F.O. 371/10840.

73a　See Bahar, *Tarikh-e Mokhtasar*, vol. 2, pp. 263–64, for the texts of the Shah's telegram of 16 September, and Reza Khan's ceremonious reply of three days later.

74　'PERSIA', Foreign Office minutes, 29/9/25, F.O. 371/10840.

75　'PERSIA', Foreign Office minutes, 11/11/25, 371/10840; Katouzian, *Political Economy*, chapter 5.

76　See Solaiman Mirza's speech in Makki, *Tarikh-e Bistsaleh*, vol. 3, pp. 559–601.

77　See Bahar, *Tarikh-e Mokhtasar*, vol. 2, pp. 276–77.

78　See *ibid.*; Makki, *Tarikh-e Bistsaleh*, vol. 3; Dawlat-Abadi, *Hayat-e Yahya*, vol. 4; Fatemi, *A'iyneh-ye Ebrat*, vol. 1. See also Bahar's moving poetical reflections on the assassination attempt in Malekzadeh, *Divan-e Bahar*, vols. 1 and 2.

79　For eyewitness accounts of the event, see Bahar, *Tarikh-e Mokhtasar*, vol. 2; and Dawlat-Abadi, *Hayat-e Yahya*, vol. 4.

79a　See his own account, *ibid.*

80　For the full text of the speeches, see for example Makki, *Doktor Mosaddeq va Notq-ha*.

81　For the list of all participants in the constituent assembly as well as its full proceedings, Makki, *Tarikh-e Bistsaleh*, vol. 3.

82　For the list of the new Tehran deputies, see Aqeli, *Ruzshomar*, p. 210.

83　Various consular reports to Loraine, 3-8/11/25, F.O. 248/1372.

84　See Katouzian, *The Political Economy*, chapter, 3, n. 1, p. 51.

11

Reza Shah and
modern arbitrary rule

Reza Shah in 1926

To analyse the most important features of Reza Shah's rule, it would be helpful to recapitulate in a few words how the country had arrived at the Pahlavi State in 1926. Iran had seen increasing disorder, revolution and chaos for a quarter of a century since the death of Naser al-Din (chapters 2–9 above) when the 1921 Coup had rapidly brought it growing order, which in its turn had been helpful to the promotion of trade and investment. There was nationalist optimism among the urban young, in general, and the growing ranks of modern middle classes, in particular, about the future.

Revolution and subsequent changes in Russia had saved the country from the most arrogant and selfish imperialism in the region. No development of any kind might have been probable if the Tsarist yoke had not been lifted off Iran's neck as if by the hand of Providence. The experience of the 1919 agreement had burnt British fingers so badly that Curzon's policy of patrimonial interference had been replaced by a much more cautious attitude, almost one of regarding Iran as a buffer state.[1]

After the Coup the Foreign Office was decidedly chilly towards the new regime, despite Norman's efforts to gain approval for Zia. The fall of Zia led to the hostility of the British legation as well, when Norman described Reza Khan as an 'astute peasant' (see chapter 9, above). Shortly afterwards, Loraine replaced Norman and set about to repair the strained relations between the two countries. He quickly reached the conclusion that Britain should not cause trouble for Reza Khan. Curzon was cautious in accepting Loraine's judgement so that he even warned the latter that Reza Khan was 'quite capable of talking sweet and acting sour'.[2] Loraine persisted, arguing that Reza Khan was the only man capable of saving Iran from chaos, which he thought was both good for her and for Britain. Gradually, the Foreign Office came round to acquiescing in Reza Kahn's rise to power. Yet they might well have tried to defend Khaz'al if domestic (British) and international factors were not strongly against it.

When, at the end of September 1926, Loraine's term came to an end, Harold Nicolson who was holding the fort at the Legation before the arrival of R. H. Clive, the new minister, sent a long dispatch to Sir Austin Chamberlain, then Foreign Secretary, proposing a fundamental review of British policy. While he was full of praise for Loraine's efforts, he felt that some of his predictions had not been borne out by the facts. The Shah was not popular, he continued, and 'the fact that we are identified with the Shah increases our unpopularity'. 'The Majlis and the nationalists [i.e. *mellyiun*] are hostile', he wired, adding that 'the republicans regard us as identified with Reza Shah'.

He observed acutely that 'the Old Persia was a loose-knit pyramid resting on its base. The new Persia is a pyramid equally loose but resting on its apex; as such it is easier to overthrow' by domestic forces hostile to it. He realised that a British policy of 'active assistance' (to forces critical to Reza Khan) would not be welcome by Iranians. He also realised that there should not be a drastic change of British policy, but suggested a more critical attitude than that of Loraine:

> That having no illusion regarding the Shah's capacity we should continue to afford him our support and friendship: that we should at the same time discreetly widen the basis of our sympathy by cultivating a better understanding with the Majlis, and particularly with the nationalist party [i.e. the *melliyun*].[3]

Although it is less acute and prophetic, Nicolson's analysis in 1926, before Reza Shah's rule began to become comprehensively arbitrary, reminds the reader remarkably of Martin Herz's analysis of Mohammad Reza Shah's in 1964, when the period of his arbitrary rule had just begun.[3a]. Neither of them was listened to, no doubt for many reasons, including the absence of a real alternative movement.

Chamberlain's response to Nicolson's dispatch (which was communicated to Clive) was equally long and assertive. He was opposed to any interference, even of a very sympathetic nature. The British government 'have recognised and do recognise the independent and sovereign status of Persia, and are therefore unable, as they are unwilling, to intervene actively or directly in the course of events in Persia, or in shaping the institutions or policy of that country'. There might be domestic opposition to the present regime in Iran. That is an internal matter, though this should not debar 'His Majesty's Legation, to stimulate and encourage such elements in Persia as may be sincerely striving for the welfare of the country and its betterment'. Iran's relations with her neighbours (notably the Soviet Union) were also her own affair so long as it was not anti-British:

> Were Persia to fall ... under the domination of a foreign and possibly hostile power ... it might cause [the British government] to adopt a more active policy. They do not, however, seek for themselves such a dominant policy, nor do they wish to assume the responsibility of administering one single square mile of Persian territory, and they are convinced that the best way to avoid these pitfalls lies firmly in the policy of good relations indicated above.[4]

The British non-interference policy might not have been fully justified by events, Chamberlain went on to say, but he was 'convinced of its essential soundness and the desirability of adhering to it so long as possible':

> It is for this reason that my predecessors and I have not opposed the policy of centralisation initiated and followed by Reza Shah; that His Majesty's Government did not raise objection to the direct control of Arabistan [Khuzistan] by the Central Government; that they withdrew from the ports on the Persian Gulf their troops … For the same reason His Majesty's Government agreed to compromise on the basis of a most generous reduction of their monetary claims against the Persian Government.[5]

Such was the British foreign policy framework for relations with Iran, though the belief was already beginning to spread that Reza Shah was a paid agent of Britain, largely by those whose real grievance against him was his dictatorial rule. The Shah himself, on the other hand, suspected that Britain was behind any unpalatable event that happened in the country. A few months before the above correspondence, Salar al-Dawleh, Mohammad Ali Shah's brother, had once again led a Kurdish force in revolt, having entered the country from Iraqi Kurdish territory, as he had done before where Iraq was under Turkish rule. The Shah was convinced that the revolt had been a British plot, despite the fact that Salar had been arrested when he had retreated back into Iraq.[6]

As a matter of fact, the British role and power in the country continuously declined during Reza Shah's reign until 1941 when, together with the Soviet Union, they invaded Iran and put an end to Reza Shah's rule.

Back in 1926, Reza Shah had beaten all opposition on the way to becoming Shah. He was in direct control of the army that had been largely his own creation, and enjoyed its complete loyalty. He had the Majlis majority and most of the journalists on his side, and the support of many of them was still genuine. Many, if not most, middle and upper class young people were looking forward to a period of peace, prosperity and modernisation. He was almost idolised by young and foreign educated men like Ali Akbar Siyasi who, together with like-minded people, set up the Young Iran Club, but were quickly advised by the Shah to close it down, since he himself would implement their ideas (see chapter 10 above).[6a]

Of even more practical importance was the admiration, support, good will, or at least acquiescence or submission, of large sections of every establishment and elite of the society. Leading Qajar noblemen either actively supported and joined the regime or passively submitted to it. Important Tehran ulama such as the Behbahanis, the Ashtiyanis, the Imam Jom'eh clan, and others in the provinces – e.g. Ayatullah-zadeh-ye Khorasani (also known as Aqa-zadeh), son of the great Khorasani, who was very influential in Mashad – supported the change of dynasty. Leading bazaar merchants, some of whom – such as Amin al-Zarb (Mahdavi) and Mo'in al-Tojjar (Bushehri) – were important politicians in their own right, had been backing Reza for some time.

Men like Mostawfi, Moshir, Taqizadeh, Mosaddeq, etc., were not in favour of the change of dynasty, because they predicted that it would end the constitutional regime. But they were not against Reza himself. Some of them even swallowed their pride and worked with him for a period, while the others simply withdrew from politics. Most of their constituents among the young and younger intellectual and educated elite quickly and quietly accepted the change and provided the core of the administrative civil service during Reza Shah's rule.

Iranians, like many other peoples, are good at jumping on the bandwagon. Often it is not merely out of regard for material self-interest, but also as an emotional response to the tide of popular opinion, coupled with the habit of uncritical acceptance or rejection, as opposed to critical support or constructive opposition. Yet, in the case of Reza Khan there was no sudden conversion on the part of large numbers of people. It was a relatively slow process that was due to his establishment of peace in the country, plus the glaring absence of a real alternative for a strong, stable and modernising government.

Mokhber al-Saltaneh was a self-regarding man. He wrote his memoirs when Reza Shah was very unpopular in Iran, and he himself was critical of the later period of Reza's rule. Yet he wrote that in 1926 when the Shah asked him if he now had 'faith' in him, he had answered in the affirmative.[7]. Bahar wrote a *qasideh* on the occasion of the Shah's accession, in which he described him as the foremost leader and commander (*qa'ed*) of Iran, it being the term that was later used in Pakistan in the case of Jinnah. It was no cheap defection, as Bahar could have defected with real profit only a couple of months earlier. It was a genuine peace offering, especially as the poem, while very positive in tone, makes it clear that the poet's change of heart is conditional[8] (see further below).

The most informative single document regarding Reza Shah's position among the commanding heights of the society at the time of his succession is the proceedings of the constituent assembly. Voting was secret, and no one voted against the motion for the change of dynasty. There were three abstentions, while twelve members were not attending when the vote was taken. The event itself is quite comparable to the large countrywide assembly in Moghan Steppe, called by Nader a hundred and nienty years before, in effect to acknowledge the fact that he was master of the country. Excepting Solaiman Mirza's qualms about creating a new dynasty as opposed to a Shah for life, no one spoke against the motion, and almost the whole of the assembly's time was taken up by discussions on legal details and niceties.

Among the members of the Assembly there were such magnates of the Tehran ulama as Imam Jom'eh-ye Kho'i, Hajj Aqa Jamal Isafahani and Sayyed Mohammad Behbahani, although they did not attend the meetings regularly and did not partake in the voting. Others such as Ayatollh-zadeh-ye Khorasani, Ayatollah-zadeh-ye Shirazi, the Imam Jom'eh of Shiraz, Sayyed Abolqasem

Kashani, etc., attended more regularly, and most of them were present at the time of voting. Kashani was quite active in the discussions.

Leading and influential merchants were present. They included Hajj Mohammad Hossein Amin al-Zarb and Hajj Mohammad Taqi Bonakdar who had played such important roles in the Constitutional Revolution. Apart from Solaiman Mirza, there were other old radical Democrats in the Assembly: Sadeq Sadeq (Mostashar al-Dawleh II) was elected chairman. Another member was Hajj Mohammad ali Badamchi, one of the two or three closest lieutenants of Khiyabani and a leading figure in his revolt (see chapter 5 above).[9] Another famous constitutionalist figure was Mirza Mehdi Malek-zadeh, son of Malek al-Motekallemin who had been killed in Bagh-e Shah on Mohammad Ali's order.

Two well known and active members of Sayyed Zia's Committee of Iron – Soltan Mohammad Khan Ameri and Adl al-Molk (Hossein Dadgar), both of whom had later been included in Zia's small cabinet – were among the constituents. So were some of those who had recently defected from the camp of Modarres, including Shokrollah Khan Qavam al-Dawleh, Mirza Hashem Ashtiyani and Sayyed Abolhasan Hayerizadeh.

Landlords and provincial magnates included Qavam al-Molk-e Shirazi, Sadrdar Fakher (Reza Hekmat), Moshar al-Dawleh (Nezam al-Din Hekmat), Ali Asghar Hekmat, Mortezaqoli Khan Bayat, Mohammad Khan Mo'azzami, Lotfollah Liqvani and Mohammad Vali Khan Asadi (Mesbah al-Saltaneh) who was very close to Amir Shokat al-Molk (Ebrahim Alam). The religious minorities were represented by well known figures such as Arbab Kaikhosraw (Zorastrian), Alex Aqayan and Alexander Tomaniantz (Christian), and Haim, the Jewish deputy and community leader who was later to be executed on the Shah's order for unknown reasons.

There were more than two hundred and seventy representatives, and therefore many of the old pro-Reza activists were there. Davar, Taimurtash, the Bahrami brothers, Rail, Tadayyon, Sayyed Ya'ub (Anvar), Rahnema, his brother Tajaddod and others.[10] Never before or since could Reza claim such a broad support among the country's various influential elites.

The failure of political compromise

The life of the Majlis had come to an end, and Forughi had been holding the fort as acting prime minister while the constituent assembly put the ceremonial touches to the change of dynasty. After that, the Shah confirmed Forughi in his post, pending the assembly of the sixth Majlis. The Majlis elections were controlled everywhere except in Tehran, which – as mentioned in the previous chapter – returned candidates who had not supported the constitutional change. Vosuq (who had not been a deputy in the fifth Majlis) was among those elected for Tehran, and Modarres must have been helpful towards it.

At this point Modarres thought of establishing a dialogue with the new Shah. He still had a considerable popular following, and carried a good deal of weight within the political establishment. Once or twice before he had entered a deal with Reza, but these attempts proved to be abortive. This time he negotiated with Firuz, Taimurtash and, eventually, the Shah himself. There is no record of the negotiations, though Loraine was of the opinion that the Shah had abolished the office of Military Government of Tehran 'under pressure from Modarres'.[11] The evidence strongly suggests that Modarres was hoping for a settlement whereby the Shah would have the army and security forces as well as a considerable amount of say in civil administration, but would leave some real role for the Majlis. That included some role for Modarres himself in deciding the composition of the cabinet.

They decided on a cabinet headed by Mostawfi. The two most important appointments were those of Vosuq as minister of finance and Taqizadeh as minister of foreign affairs. As it happened Taqizadeh declined the offer and went to America on an official mission. But the British Foreign Office was not pleased to hear about his appointment before they knew that it had fallen through. They even thought that it was 'presumably a sop to Russia'.[12] Apart from suspecting him of having pro-Soviet tendencies, they also remembered his 'lurid past':

> Taqizadeh has had a lurid past, but when last in London in 1924 he seemed to have sobered down considerably. It remains to be seen whether he will turn out to be pro-Russian.[13]

There can be little doubt that Vosuq's appointment was the work of Modarres, though Lorraine felt that it was due to Vosuq's own popularity. Even Taqizadeh might have been recommended, or approved of, by Modarres, though it is not quite clear why he declined the offer.[13a] Loraine reported that there were strong rumours, which he himself believed, that Mostawfi's cabinet would be short lived, and would be followed by one headed by Vosuq. It is extremely doubtful if the Shah would have agreed to that, even putting aside the great taint of the 1919 agreement, because Vosuq was a strong personality. But it is possible that Modarres had pushed for Vosuq first for premiership, and then nominated Mostawfi as fall back.

Moatawfi was reluctant to accept office, and he told Mokhber that he had been pressured by Modarres to co-operate.[14] Modarres is likely to have told these men that though they had lost the game they should not give up all hope and withdraw from politics, which is what some of them soon did. He certainly told Poet-Laureate Bahar, a close political confidant, that they should work for a rapprochement, and try to make sure that the Shah's power did not become absolute. Bahar wrote later that Modarres had told them that they had done what they could, and 'now we should go along with the Shah and the state, hoping that they would serve the country'. 'And that is exactly what happened' added Bahar, 'and we gave up our opposition' to Reza Shah.[15]

Mosaddeq did not accept this argument. He declined Mostawfi's offer of the post of the foreign minister, arguing that it was not possible to work with the Shah.[15a] It is not clear whether the offer was made for this care-taker cabinet before the Majlis was assembled, or for the new cabinet which he presented to the newly assembled sixth Majlis, in September 1926. This cabinet included Vosuq as minister of justice, and Forughi minister of war, and Mosaddeq vehemently opposed it because of their inclusion in it, though most of his speech was about Vosuq and the 1919 agreement (see chapter 5, above). And it was in that debate that Modarres showed in his reply to Mosaddeq that he had been party to a deal:

> After all that has happened we would like to use these men in the service of the country. After all this chaos [*enqelabat*] we would like to use them to do important things. [Hardly anyone would be left if we said] Vosuq al-Dawleh is no good, his brother [Qavam, who had been exiled by Reza] is no good, I am no good, my brother ... and so on and so forth.[16]

Then, in a brief diversion, he revealed the logic of his new policy towards the Shah:

> If I could manage to serve a *constitutional* monarch I would do it; if not [i. e. if he was not constitutional] I would fight him. Today our agenda is the constitution. We should act according to that ... And the constitution is our [ultimate] ruler and should be applied without exception[17] (emphasis added).

It cost Modarres much popularity. It was easy to criticise him publicly, as some newspapers did, for defending Vosuq,[18] because this would certainly not offend the Shah. Yet the real reason for his loss of popularity was because, to a politically immature public, it looked as if he was compromising his principles. In twentieth century Iranian politics compromise (*sazesh*) at best meant 'collaborationism', and at worst was seen as 'selling out' to the other side (see chapter 2, above). There were only two choices left to the dissenters: either surrender unconditionally and sell out to the other side when it was evidently unbeatable, or suffer martyrdom socially, politically, or even physically. This left little room for politics. The attitude was rooted in the ancient pre-political culture of the country, regardless of the political and constitutional forms that had now been adopted from Europe (see chapter 1, above).

Mostawfi's new cabinet had been introduced to the Majlis in September when the above speeches were made. By November, Nicolson reporting the terrorist attempt on Modarres' life to Chamberlain said that, having lost much popularity because of his rapprochement with the Shah, he had lately become popular again since he had said that government must be constitutional:

I have already, in my despatch of 10th September last, indicated how the *6th Majlis had reacted against the supremacy of Mudarris imagining that he was but an agent of the Shah.* The former has of late succeeded in regaining a large portion of his influence by adopting an arrogantly domocratic [sic] attitude and in a recent speech he stated baldly that he For his part would only support the Shah so long as His Majesty acted constitutionally.[18a] (emphasis added).

The strategy of Modarres did not pay off because the Shah did not keep his end of the bargain. A couple of times Mostawfi tried to resign but was pressured by Modarres and others to hold on. He definitely resigned late in May 1927, and could no longer be persuaded to remain in office. The semi-official *Iran* expressed surprise and regret at his resignation.[19] He met with Mosaddeq shortly after his resignation and told him that he had told Mokhber, his successor: 'I sank into the mud up to my chin; make sure you don't drown in it right up to your head'.[20] It is clear, at least with hindsight, that if the Shah could not reach a *modus operandi* with the self-respecting but flexible and disinterested Mostawfi as prime minister, there could be little hope for anyone else.

Clearly, Modarres saw it that way when he opposed Mokhber al-Saltaneh (Hedayat)'s appointment as the new prime minister.[21] In a long speech he implied that he was not opposing Hedayat's premiership as such, but was unhappy about the political situation in general. The speech was interspersed with references to democracy (*hokumat-e melli*), and the will of the people (*eradeh-ye mellat*) as expressed by their representatives in the Majlis. 'In a country which has a democratic regime', he said, 'everything must be done – directly or indirectly – by the will of the people'.[21a] And he went on to emphasise that 'everything that is done in a democratic country must be done by the will of the people, and the vote of the National Consultative Assembly'.[22]

The failure, once again, of the attempt to compromise might have led to confrontation as on the previous occasions. But Modarres was no longer in a position to take on Reza Shah, and other popular leaders simply did not have the stomach to fight. A few months earlier, in late October 1926, two or three hired assassins had tried to kill the Sayyed, early in the morning, as he was going to teach at the Sepahsalar College. He survived. There was a popular outcry, and friend and foe alike displayed much indignation in the Majlis. Even Davar said that the motive must have been political. Few believed that the Shah had not known about the attempt, both then and later.[23] Yet the co-operation of Modarres with the government continued so long as Mostawfi remained prime minister.

The seventh Majlis election in 1928 saw the end of any independence by that body until the Shah abdicated in 1941. This time the Tehran elections were controlled as well. Taimurtash had offered Mosaddeq the possibility of an agreement, whereby out of the twelve deputies for Tehran, six would be from '*mellat*' and the other six from '*dawlet*.' The six members from '*mellat*' – suggested by Taimurtash himself – were Mostawfi, Moshir, Mo'tamen, Modarres, Mosaddeq and Taqizadeh. Mosaddeq had replied that deputies should be elected by voters.[24] In the end, the government put the names of the first three on the list of those elected for Tehran, but they resigned. There was a rumour that Modarres had said to the Prefect of the Police, 'If all those who voted for me two years before had changed their mind, whatever happened to the vote that I cast for myself'. It may not be true but it indicates the public view of the elections.

Soon afterwards, he was arrested and banished to Khaf, at the edge of the desert in Khorasan, and a decade later was taken to the nearby Kashmar where, for no apparent reason, he was killed by a special police team sent for the purpose from Tehran. The man in charge of his murder, Kazem Jahansuzi, had also headed the team who killed Abdohossein Diba, whom the Shah had dismissed as the court's chief accountant, put on trial for bribery, and banished to Malayer. There was even less apparent reason for that, except that he had been appointed by Taimutrtash.[25]

By 1928, the Shah's dictatorship was turning to autocracy (i. e. absolute but not yet arbitrary power), and arbitrary rule began to replace it fast. During the rise of dictatorship, which dated back to Reza Khan's premiership, there had of course been growing deviations from some basic tenets of the country's constitution, the dictatorial government intensifying into absolute and autocratic rule. But government was still constitutional *in so far as it was not purely personal*, and there was still a considerable amount of ministerial discretion and parliamentary argument, check and balance. This after all is what distinguishes a dictatorship, even autocratic government, from arbitrary rule.

There had of course been much arbitrary behaviour, especially in the regions and provinces, in the earlier period. But it had not been systematic, and had not yet begun to spread to the centre before the seventh Majlis. In 1929, Firuz, who was minister of finance, was suddenly and inexplicably arrested, while he was leaving a public gathering side by side with the Shah himself. The fall of Firuz in 1929 was the first ominous sign that thenceforth no one was immune from arbitrary arrest. The fall and murder in jail of Taimurtash in 1933 made that fact clear and unexceptionable. At the very time of his death, the Judicial Physician (corresponding to the forensic expert in modern coroner's courts) had told Golsha'iyan, the prosecutor – after they had both formally visited the corpse of Taimurtash in jail, before burial – that the man had been poisoned.[25a]

Sardar As'ad III quickly followed him both in prison and in death. And it was no longer felt even that a sham trial was necessary. When, early in 1937, Davar committed suicide for fear of a similar fate (Firuz had been re-arrested shortly before it, and was to be murdered shortly after) hardly any one of any past stature and independence was left in the government and at the court.[26] Many other faithful defenders and leading pillars of the Pahlavi regime were killed, disgraced, jailed and/or banished, for example, Abdolhossein Diba, Forughi, Farajollh Bahrami (Dabir-e A'zam), Hossein Dadgar (Adl al-Molk), General

Habibollah Shaibani and General Amanollh Jahanbani, General Amir-khosravi, Qasem Sur Esrafil, and so on.

When the Allies invaded Iran in 1941, the Shah was all on his own. There were very few men of any real standing, either civilian or military, who felt committed to him and his rule. These developments will be discussed in more detail in the following section.

Reza Shah's rule: a general assessment

Reza Shah's rule may be looked at and analysed from different angles, although any serious analysis must pay careful attention to the facts. Immediately after his fall, the attack against him was concentrated on his 'dictatorship'. Sometime later, particularly as the oil crisis began to flare up from 1948 onwards, the emphasis shifted to the foreign connection, especially as few – of *any* political persuasion – had any serious doubt that he had secretly collaborated with Britain in making the 1933 oil agreement. Still later, in the heydays of neo-anti-imperialism – of Vietnam, third worldism, the dependency theory, etc. – the perception of Reza Shah as a foreign agent became absolute and all pervading. The official view, on the other hand, was that Reza had saved Iran from certain disintegration, had restored her to her ancient glory, and had brought compre-hensive European modernisation to the country. Neither view stands a close as well as dispassionate analysis, although he did in fact save the country from chaos; did contribute to modernisation with mixed results; and he did conclude a new oil agreement which was harmful to the country's interest.

We have already shown that he was not a foreign agent. Regarding the other matters – modernisation, nationalism and 'dictatorship' – assessments would be different depending on two inter-connected criteria. First, the critic's view of the basic, long-term problems of Iranian society; secondly, his evaluation of the consequences of Reza Shah's rule in relation to those problems, as well as the more recent issues of state building, modernisation and development.

The assessment presented here is based on the long-term view of the society discussed in the previous chapters (against the theoretical framework set in chapter 1), and the meaning of modernisation and development suggested below. Accordingly, it is presented under three headings: arbitrary rule, nation-alism and pseudo-modernism. In the case of Reza Shah – as also of Mohammad Reza Shah, in the last phase of his rule (1963–1979) – the three aspects are inseparable, but it will be argued that the most important aspect was arbitrary government. For without that, the other aspects would have had much more positive and much less negative effects.

To give but one significant example, nationalism and modernism in Kemalist Turkey would not have been so relatively successful if they had been pursued by an arbitrary ruler, as opposed to a dictatorial and autocratic regime, which was based in law, was subject to some checks and balances, and had a definite social base (see further below). At the time of Ataruk's rise, Turkey enjoyed considerably greater political development than Iran. And although it cannot be argued that Reza Shah's arbitrary rule was inevitable, it is true that his rule was more likely to end up that way than was Ataturk's in Turkey. Indeed, such an outcome is consistent with the theory and long-term historical evidence presented in chapter 1. However, that is why Kemalist Turkey had enjoyed continuous legitimacy even from its critics, whereas Reza Shah's regime lost its legitimacy while its founder was still in power.

Arbitrary rule

Analytically, Reza Shah's rule in the 1920's, although growingly dictatorial, was not yet unconstitutional. The point is fine, though very important, and so it needs a short explanation. Any dictatorship was certainly contrary to the constitution of 1906 and its supplements, as it was a basically *democratic* constitution. On the other hand, constitutional – as opposed to arbitrary – rule does not necessarily have to be democratic. Therefore, authoritarian or dictatorial governments, although obviously undemocratic, are not unconstitutional. In a dictatorship, power is concentrated and government is not representative in a popular sense. Yet power is shared by a ruling elite, who (even if indirectly) represent the influential social classes. Government is not by personal fiat, and though the laws may be harsh, restrictive and elitist, both constitutional and judicial laws are normally observed. By the same token, the state is held to be legitimate at least by some – usually powerful – social classes who, despite internal conflicts of interest, are loyal to it, as they see their own broad interest in its survival. Ataturk's Turkey was an example of a third-world modern dictatorship of its time.

This is what Reza Shah's rule looked like at the beginning of the eighth Majlis. Hedayat (Mokhber al-Saltaneh) was prime minister. Men like the triumvirate of Taimurtash, Firuz and Davar, as well as Forughi, Sardar As'ad III, Taqizadeh, Sarem al-Dawleh (Mas'ud), Navvab (the old Democrat leader), etc., were in the government, although not all of them in the cabinet. In 1928, when a large number of ulama gathered in Qom to protest against the implementation of the military conscription law, Hedayat, Taimurtash, the Imam Jom'eh of Tehran and his brother Zahir al-Islam went and humoured them, thus avoiding a major crisis.[27]

But seven years later when a religious congregation in Mashad protested at the Shah's compulsory order to the male population to wear the European bowler hat, the Shah ordered them to be ruthlessly suppressed (see further below under 'pseudo-modernism'). Forughi was then prime minister. Mohammad Vali Asadi, the father of Forughi's sons-in-law, who was the trustee of Imam Reza's shrine – a post which was in the Shah's gift – was accused of having had a hand in the protestations, was summarily tried and convicted by a local military court and executed forthwith without leave to appeal.[28] He had been a former manager of the estates, and was a close confidant, of Amir Shokat al-Molk (Ebrahim Alam), whose daughter was married to Asadi's son, and he had voted both in the Majlis and in the constituent assembly for Reza Khan to become Shah. That incident led to Foroughi's downfall and disgrace.

A few months later, all women were ordered to take their veils off without the right to wear a scarf, on pain of persecution and arrest. They were allowed only to wear expensive and exclusive European hats which had been imported for the purpose. These are examples of pseudo-modernism which we shall discuss further below in that context. But they would not have been possible without absolute and arbitrary power such that no one in the land could raise one word of criticism or even advice with respect to any and all of the Shah's decisions. Hedayat (Mokhber) wrote in his memoirs

> In this period the immunity of some Majlis deputies – Javad Imami, Isma'l Araqi, E'tesam-zadeh and Reza Rafi [all of them old pro-Reza Khan campaigners] – was withdrawn [and so they went to jail]. As soon as anyone so much as mentioned the Shah's name they would grab him and ask him what he meant. Sometimes they would make a story for it, and this would help to line the pockets of the police agents. 'The hand of bureaucracy was extended to every vice/ there was no talk of virtue except in secret advice' [a Persian verse] ... *We have reached the point that the Shah expects to be worshipped*[29] ... (emphasis added).

And about ministerial power and responsibility:

> Under [Reza Shah] Pahlavi, no one had any independent power. Every business had to be reported to the Shah, and every order issued by him had to be carried out. Unless there is some degree of independence, responsibility would be meaningless ... and there would be no statesmen with a will of his own.[29a]

The Shah's power became absolute and arbitrary, but the new arbitrary rule was different from the traditional in three important respects. First, modern technology made the application of arbitrary rule much more effective and comprehensive than before. There was literally nowhere to hide. There was a modern police force and – more importantly – modern standing army and gendarmerie all at the Shah's command. Nomads could no longer feel immune well inside their usual habitat as they had done in the past. On the contrary, they were disarmed, moved from their own territory or region in harsh conditions, and forced to settle in strange environments. Almost all of the survivors returned to nomadic life after Reza Shah abdicated. There was also an urban political police, an important part of whose work was to inform on the people's harmless gossip about the Shah or his policies, and this could result in grave consequences for anyone caught off-guard. Even in high society, whenever someone uttered the slightest word of criticism, he would be strongly suspected of being an *agent provocateur,* and would be met with heavy and uneasy silence ...

The second important difference between the modern and the traditional arbitrary rule arose precisely from the fact that it had been re-established after the Constitutional Revolution. Since there was now a systematic body of civil, criminal and administrative laws, and a large judicial and administrative body to implement them, they were usually observed down to the slightest detail when there was no reason of state for breaking them. The government and country being new to a modern legal and administrative system, sometimes incredible procedures were used for the strict observation of the law. For example, when the Shah's senior wife and queen (mother of the crown prince) wished to import a box of chocolate free of customs' charges, the cabinet had to pass a resolution to waive the tariff in that single case.[30] And yet, as noted above, at the same time and place powerful ministers could be killed in jail without the slightest ceremony.

This is perhaps an extreme example in an otherwise unimportant case. But, in general, procedures were followed down to the minutest details, which had been copied from a European source, in administrative, civil and criminal cases. In 1934, the ministry of foreign affairs could not release from the customs the foreign wines it had imported to entertain important European guests, because the ministry of finance was demanding 9000 tomans customs charges from it which it did not have in its coffers.[30a]

The administrative and judicial systems were themselves expensive and highly time consuming, and only a small minority – perhaps not much more than 5 per cent of the total population – had real access to them. A more substantial example of contradiction arising from arbitrary rule and modernisation was the situation in jails, especially with respect to political prisoners. Torture as well as official murder took place in prisons whenever the Shah ordered or allowed it or it was understood that it would have his approval. On the other hand, the prisons had been built and organised by Swedish advisers, and the system that governed the rights and duties of the wardens, prisoners and visitors was, for its time, quite humane and advanced.[31]

The third important difference with traditional arbitrary rule was that there no longer was any recognised facility for mediation or cooling-off. In chapter 1 above, it was mentioned that traditional arbitrary rule had created some safeguards against harsh and unjust decisions, especially those regarding life and death. One was personal intervention by respectable elders and officials, which sometimes worked at least in helping reduce the harshness of the punishment. The other was taking sanctuary – not just in sacred shrines, but even in the royal stables – which often afforded time to reduce the ruler's wrath or suspicion. Under Naser al-Din, British and Russian envoys occasionally intervened on behalf of would-be victims such as Abbas Mirza Molk-Ara (see chapter 1, above). More effectively than that, the later Qajars had become sensitive to potential European criticism of frequent harsh and unjust punishments.

Neither mediation nor sanctuary was available under modern arbitrary rule. Nor was Reza Shah [unlike his son, later] sensitive to such European responses to the extent of making some allowance for them. Hardly anyone dared to plead for clemency with Reza Shah for fear of turning his anger and suspicion towards himself. Hedayat – who was both prime minister and an old, respected, and obviously harmless man – tried it a couple of times and only succeeded in a minor case. When the brothers Zaiol'abedin Rahnema and Reza Tajaddod, Farajollah Bahrami and Ali Dashti were arrested – no one knew for what possible reason – Hedayat pleaded clemency for them. All the four men, it may be recalled, had been leading enthusiastic campaigners for Reza Khan, and had remained loyal supporters of his regime. The Shah allowed Rahnema and Tajaddod to leave the country and go to Baghdad at their own expense, and banished the other two.[31a]

As mentioned above, when Foroughi, as prime minister, tried to save Asadi's life after the Mashad protests over the European hat, he himself was dismissed in disgrace. When, in his hour of need in August 1941, the Shah turned to him for help, he was still angry about his mediation for Asadi's life, saying 'Foroughi is a trustworthy man; only that Asadi corrupted him'.[32] Farajollah Bahrami (Dabir-e A'zam) had almost hero-worshiped Reza Khan as his private secretary, speechwriter and tutor in modern Iranian nationalist feeling and thinking. As governor-general of Khorasan the Shah ordered his dismissal for unknown reasons, and later had him arrested apparently because of a false report that he had spoken with the German embassy on the telephone. Hedayat's intervention was successful in this minor case (as mentioned before). When the Shah allowed Bahrami to be banished, he told Hedayat 'I won't kill him'. He had used the same expression – 'I won't kill him' – once before to Hedayat, when he had ordered the dismissal and arrest of Sarem al-Dawleh, the governor-general of Fars, though apparently Hedayat had not intervened in that case.[33]

According to Taqizadeh, when Davar meekly tried to intervene on Taimurtash's behalf, the Shah 'gave him a look and said, Open those ears of yours or I will have you destroyed (*ma'dumat mikonam*). Reza Shah used the word 'destroyed' regularly. He said the same thing to me in the case of Sawlat al-Dawleh, paramount chief of the Qashqa'i nomads ... [He said] these people must be destroyed'.[33a]

So much for the near impossibility of mediation under Reza Shah, as compared with traditional arbitrary government As for use of sanctuary, it was only once used by the crowd in Mashad during the protests against the compulsory European hat with consequences that were mentioned above.

The 1933 oil agreement caused more harm to the country and the Shah himself than any other single product of his arbitrary rule. The subject has been discussed by this and other authors in some detail.[34] Here we shall just concentrate on the decisive role that arbitrary decision taking played in bringing that agreement about. Differences between Iran and the Anglo-Persian Oil

Company dated back to Vosuq's premiership. Shortly afterwards, under Moshir, Armitage Smith negotiated and settled Iran's outstanding claims with the Company in 1920 (see chapter 6, above). In the 1920's there was growing awareness of the injustice of the D'arcy concession which had been granted by a feeble arbitrary ruler when the country and government were almost in a state of chaos (see chapter 2, above).

Systematic negotiation between Iran and the Company began early under Reza Shah. At first Taimurtash was wholly in charge of the negotiations which he conducted with skill and honesty. Later, when the Shah began to grow suspicious of him, Firuz, Davar, Taqizadeh – and still later – Foroughi and Hossein Ala were also brought into the search for a new settlement. At one stage, the Company chairman, Sir John (later, Lord) Cadman offered to Iran 20 percent of the shares in the company's entire global operations in return for the extension of the concessionary period. The Iranians did not take this up, and it was quickly withdrawn. The conflict dragged until 1932 when, very unexpectedly, the company declared Iran's royalty as a sum, which was about a quarter of the previous year.

The Shah fell into a great rage, thinking – perhaps rightly – that the Company had used this tactic as a blackmailing device, although it might also have been intended as a provocation, a hole into which the Shah hurriedly stepped. The first act of arbitrary behaviour in this regard was that he ordered the cabinet to annul the D'arcy concession without any discussion, any study, any preparation at all.[35] Britain then took the matter to the League of Nations, and the League advised the two sides to negotiate for a settlement. Cadman then went to Tehran, but his negotiations with the ministers (which, says Taqizadeh, were being reported hourly to the Shah) did not succeed. He then decided to return to London, but – it is not known for what possible reason – the Shah got cold feet, pretended that he did not know why a settlement had not been agreed, and asked Cadman to try again. The final settlement was made in his own presence when Cadman insisted on the extension of the concessionary period for thirty-three years.[36]

The Shah's second arbitrary decision in this case was to agree with that there and then, without consultation with the ministers and other experts, although Taqizadeh reports that the Shah did try to resist the demand for extension, and that he gave in with great reluctance.[37] As mentioned above, it is not known for what *definite* reason he asked Cadman not to leave, and surrendered over the extension of the concessionary period. It is clear that fear of British retaliation was the factor behind it. But, as Taqizadeh maintains,[38] it is difficult to know what it was. It may have been imagined. And if it was real – in the sense of receiving an open threat – there was still time to study it and then making the best possible response. The whole thing, after all, could have been avoided if the Shah had not arbitrarily ordered the abrogation of the D'arcy agreement, as British retaliation would well have been anticipated. Taqizadeh speaks of his own and Davar's deep depression resulting from this decision.

This is a stark example of the harm done by personal rule. Without it, neither would the concession have been abrogated in a hurry nor would the 1933 agreement have been made in equal haste. For decades, almost every one believed that that was all a show, and that the Shah had been working for the British all the while. Indeed many believed that the British made the 1921 Coup so that one day Reza Shah would enter the new oil agreement. They did not explain why it had to wait for twelve years, six years of which were wasted in useless negotiations.

Another major example of arbitrary behaviour was the Shah's enforced purchase, at nominal prices, of agricultural property. The Shah's appetite for land and building was insatiable, and he acquired much of them from landlords, big merchants and state property. It became a legend in its own time, to the extent that a French newspaper described Reza as a land-eating animal. Unlike most others, Taqizadeh was not very critical of the Shah's appropriation of property, at least when he came to write his memoirs. Perhaps this was because many, including Reza Shah, believed that he had a hand in encouraging those criticisms of the Shah in the French press. However that may be, he nevertheless wrote in his memoirs that the Shah 'took the whole of Mazandaran. He liked to take for himself any agricultural property that was good and valuable'.[39]

Abbasqoli Golsha'iyan wrote in his diary that when the generals were reporting on Soviet advances in northern Iran to the war cabinet late in August 1941, 'Suddenly the Shah said something that really resulted in surprise and regret: "What happens to our estates then, all of these areas are our property"'.[40] When he abdicated and left the country he owned about ten per cent of the country's agricultural property, but including the most productive cash crop producing estates, so that both their value and their income was much more than ten per cent of the total. At the time, countless poems and articles written against him poured out of press and poetry. In a poem that was much shorter and milder than the others, Bahar called him 'Reza the Thief'.[41] Weakness of private property had always been both a cause and a consequence of arbirary rule in Iranian history (see chapter 1 above).

Ali Dashti had been back in royal favour now for many years, and had been made a Majlis deputy, like all the others, with the Shah's approval. The Shah, though abdicated, was still in the country when, in a long Majlis speech, Dashti accused him of having stolen some of the Crown Jewels (this was a common belief but apparently had no foundation) and said that the people's property must be returned to them:

If ten days hence it turned out that some of these jewels were missing, would the government accept the responsibility for it ... and answer for the Crown Jewels?

With respect to violations of private property:

The right of private property is one of the oldest and most noble rights in civilised societies. But it was violated in these last twenty years to the utmost limit ... They have taken the people's property by force and it must be returned to them ... It is surprising that this violation of private property was done by government departments as well ...

Regarding the Shah's fortune:

Another important question is that while the Shah has handed over all his liquid as well as illiquid assets [to Mohammad Reza], the government merely discussed the illiquid assets in the Majlis ... I have heard, and there is a public rumour, that the Shah has seventy to eighty million [tomans] worth of liquid assets. But he has only transferred twenty four million tomans to the present Shah ...

... What about the moneys which are deposited outside Iran, in American, London and German banks? *They* will not give you anything for these letters of transfer. What will happen to *those* moneys?[42] (emphasis added).

Arbitrary rule inevitably results in an overly suspicious social and psychological atmosphere. Such an atmosphere is both a cause and a consequence of the general conspiratorial outlook – of acute unpredictability and insecurity, and of distrust and fear, alike by the ruler and the ruled – characteristic of life in an arbitrary regime (see chapte 1 above). This seems to have been stronger in Reza Shah than, say, in Fath'ali and Naser al-Din, but even that might have been due to relative differences in the circumstances rather than in the basic nature of these individuals.

The evidence of his extreme suspiciousness is abounding, and much that has been so far said about the fate of politicians and civil and military officials is a part of it. Here, two specific examples will be given which happened almost at the same time. Mohammad Hasan Mirza Qajar, the old Prince Regent, had settled in England since his expulsion from Iran. His young son Hamid Mirza had gone to school in England and had one day played the part of Caliban in an amateur dramatisation of Shakespeare's *Tempest*. Passing a comment on this, the *Daily Mirror* had said that he 'might have played a still more important part if the politics of Persia had been a little different'.[43]

The Shah took this light-hearted comment by a newspaper to mean that 'the British' were trying to restore the Qajars to the Iranian throne. There was a vehement press campaign – described by one newspaper as 'The Tempest of Feeling' – implicitly against Britain, but most openly against the Qajars:

The news of the appearance of this paragraph ... was followed by an outburst in the whole of Tehran press against the Qajar dynasty, including 'the cruelty of Agha Mahomed [sic] Khan the Eunuch, the ... voluptuous life of Fath Ali Shah, the indolence of Mahomed Shah, the love of all sorts of pleasures of Naser-ed-Din Shah, the apathy and sloth of Muzaffar-ed-Din Shah, the grossness and treachery of Muhammad Ali Shah and finally the idleness and love of money of Ahmed Shah'.[44]

These rulers had both oppressed the people and sold the country out to the foreigners, but all that had been changed by 'the great ruler who had come to the throne eight years before and had restored Persia to the pinnacles of glory and prosperity which were her birthright'.

Terribly alarmed, the Qajar clan living in Iran asked Nosrat al-Saltaneh – Ahmad Shah's young and favourite uncle cited in earlier chapters – to write to the press on their behalf and reaffirm their loyalty to Reza Shah. In his letter published in *Ettela'at,* the Qajar prince 'stated that none of the Qajars in Persia took any part in politics, and that they were all entirely loyal to the present regime, which was the best thing that had ever happened to Persia'. Yet the letter did not succeed in stopping the press campaign, which continued for some time.[45]

The other example is the fate of Taqizadeh. After signing the 1933 agreement against his own will, neither he nor the Shah wanted him to remain in the cabinet, and 'I was telling myself that one day I would leave Iran because of Reza Shah, and would never return'.[46] The Shah did not want him in the cabinet either, because he would sometimes take decisions before asking the court first.[47] His close friend Baqer Kazemi (Mohazzeb al-Dawleh), foreign minister in the new cabinet, managed to gain approval for him to become Iranian minister in Paris. After sometime at that post, some French newspapers wrote critical articles on the political situation in Iran, and Taqizadeh was blamed for not having managed to stop it through representation to the French government (in 1938 something similar happened again, and the French government explained that it was unable to punish the offending newspapers. The Shah broke diplomatic relations and cut off all other ties with France, to the point of repatriating the Iranian students there before they had completed their courses).

Taqizadeh had to relinquish his post, and went to Berlin to treat a chronic ailment. He did not contemplate returning to Iran, having in mind the fate of Taimurtash and Sardar As'ad among the others. 'The Shah's real intention', he wrote at the close of is life 'was for me to return to Iran. But I did not go back.'[48] In Germany, he noticed that the rumour of being out of favour threatened to ostracise him in the European as well as Iranian community, and make it difficult to earn his living. He wrote a couple of letters to the Shah's private secretary and each time was completely reassured on the Shah's behalf that all was absolutely well.[49] Yet the reactions and responses of his contacts in Europe remained as cool as ever. In despair, he wrote a personal letter to his old friend Forughi, shortly before the latter's own fall and disgrace, asking him to talk to the Shah personally and find out what his true feelings were. Forughi did that, and the result was as bad as Taqizadeh had suspected all along, but there was now an additional cause for the Shah's wrath and suspicion. He wrote that the

Shah had indeed been angry about the French newspapers' affair, but the article on the newly coined words,

> rekindled and confirmed the suspicions, not only making [the Shah's] sentiments towards yourself hot and heavy, but leading to anger against those who have published your article, which anger still continues.[50]

There now was an additional source for the royal anger, of which Taqizadeh had had no suspicion. An Academy (*Farhangestan*) had been set up to purge and purify the Persian language of loan-words, and especially those of Arabic origin. Almost all individuals of high culture (some of whom were even obliged to be members of it) were critical of this academy's proceedings on purely literary grounds. Each time the replacements for existing words were voted by the Academy, they would then be sent for the Shah's approval before they would officially come into force.[50a] Now the ministry of culture and education had just launched a literary and cultural magazine, and the minister himself – Ali Asghar Hekmat – had written to Taqizadeh and begged him for contributions. In response, Taqizadeh had written an article in which he had been critical – on literary grounds – of the procedure followed by that Academy. The minister had liked the article so much that – besides publishing it in the next issue – he had written to Taqizadeh and congratulated him for it.[51] Fortunately for him, he was out of the country when another 'tempest of feeling' broke out. This made it virtually impossible for Taqizadeh to return to Iran. He subsequently got a job at the University of London, and was made Iranian minister (later, ambassador) in London after the Shah's abdication.

The grave mistakes that led to the country's invasion by the allies were many, and arbitrary rule had much to do both with their being made, and with other wrong decision when disaster struck. It is not surprising that the Shah tried to use the rising German power as a countervailing force, and it could well have paid off if it had been pursued with wisdom and flexibility. The British had hurt and humiliated him badly, and imposed another unjust concession on the country. Apart from that, as Taqizadeh attests, the Shah saw British conspiracy everywhere. For example, long before the new oil agreement, Taqizadeh had got his approval to convert some of the country's foreign reserves into gold, but the Shah had suddenly been gripped with fear that the British would prevent it or possibly confiscate the gold on its way to Iran. He had been pleasantly surprised and relieved when Taqizadeh had told him that the deal had been made and the passage was trouble free.[52]

However, the continuation of the pro-German policy after the war broke out, and more especially after Germany had attacked the Soviet Union despite doing all it could to please them, would obviously lead to disaster. Britain and the Soviet Union were the two great powers in the region, and once they were both on the same side in the war, it was foolish in the extreme to give them any reason or excuse for invading the country. Once again it was personal rule, together with the supreme sense of self-confidence which it brings, that was behind the blunders. Germany attacked the Soviet Union on 22 June 1941, and the allies invaded Iran almost exactly two months later. The Shah waited until the eleventh hour, then became defiant and tried to put up a fight, then agreed to a cease-fire and complete co-operation with the allies, and finally abdicated out of the fear that the British might deliver him to the Soviets.[53]

Neither the invasion nor his abdication was inevitable. Turkey conducted a genuinely neutral policy and remained unscathed, despite having been a German ally in the First World War, despite having been defeated and dismembered by Britain and France in that war, and despite its suspicions of the Soviet Union. General Franco had won the Spanish civil war largely through German and Italian support. Yet he refused to give any assistance to the Axis powers despite great pressure from them. It is not difficult to know how – only where – Franco would have ended up if he had not been shrewd enough to observe strict neutrality.

Once the allies came, of course, there was hardly any choice for the Shah but to abdicate. The people's great fear of him suddenly gave way to relief, ridicule, abuse and wish for vengeance. It would have been very difficult to keep him on the throne even if the allies had wished to do so. The public outcry against him was very strong. Neither the loyal Forughi nor the Majlis deputies believed that the Shah would genuinely keep to a promise to observe constitutional government, many of them fearing that they would pay for their reformist demands handsomely the minute he was in a position to renege on his commitment.[54] Apart from that, it would not have been possible for him to try and play the role of constitutional monarch under the allies' watchful eyes (even if he wanted to) because of the irresistible pressures for the rectification of the injustices committed before, which directly implicated him. And if the allies had tried to keep him by sheer force, they would have earned the dual hatred of the people for both invading their country and keeping Reza Shah as their ruler. Indeed the Iranians' only source of satisfaction with, even gratitude to, the allies was the Shah's abdication.

Golsha'iyan – always a high offical under Reza Shah, and then minister of finance – wrote in his diaries at the time that, before the coming of war to Iran, they all worried about what would happen to the country (and, no doubt, themselves too) after Reza Shah died or was killed, i.e. assassinated, because he was so unpopular that no one expected him to last much longer:

> Because no one could anticipate abdication, and given the way he ruled, it was anticipated that if he did not die of natural causes [soon], he would definitely be killed; and the country would have been plunged into a terrible chaos and revolt – except in this way [i.e. abdication in consequence of the Allied invasion] which was beyond anybody's imagination.[54a]

It is clear from all this that when it was said above that the Shah's abdication was not inevitable, it meant that it would not have been so had he enjoyed a certain amount of legitimacy, and a reasonable social base among his own people. He could even have survived his war policy mistakes with that kind of domestic support, because he was ready to co-operate with the allies after they came, and it would *not* have been in their interest to bring him down *against* popular wishes. With the fall of arbitrary government the pattern of chaotic and disintegrative trends was repeated once again both in the centre of politics and in the provinces. Hence many of those who had celebrated the Shah's departure began to feel nostalgic for his rule after a few years. This was in keeping with the age-old cycle of arbitrary rule chaos-arbitrary rule.

Official Nationalism

In what follows the term 'nationalism' does *not* refer to its wider, popular, meaning of love for one's country and culture, and wish for her independence and development, nor even to a reasonable degree of pride in her historical achievements (so long as it does not denigrate other peoples and races, and does not entirely overlook the shortcomings of one's own). In other words, 'nationalism' here does *not* refer to patriotic feelings – in Sir Walter Scott's verse, 'This is my own, my native land' – described in Persian by *'mihan-parsi'* and similar terms. On the contrary, it refers to the European ideology, the origins of which are in the counter-enlightenment movement of the eighteenth century, and which, having developed in the nineteenth and early twentieth century, found its purest expressions in Fascist Italy and Nazi Germany.

Reza Shah's nationalism had two sides to it: the intellectual and the practical. He was no theorist, of course, and his rudimentary knowledge of ancient Iranian history he had acquired from the nationalist intellectuals, the closest one of whom to himself had been Farajollah Bahrami, before being sacked and banished (see above and chapter 10).

The intellectual origins of modern Iranian nationalism, in its historical context, were briefly discussed in chapter 3 above. It was born, firstly, of intellectual awareness of the nationalist ideas and history of Europe; secondly, of an intellectual awakening to ancient Iranian history; and thirdly, of a psychology of the downtrodden, which combines – at one and the same time – anger and self-reproach with millenarian ideals and an exaggerated sense of self-importance.

But before it became an official creed, it was still an intellectual concept, an almost artistic interpretation of the ancient glories, the present failures, and the high hopes for the future. It was still largely a nationalism, not of rulers but of the ruled, a new and dynamic wave with a firm sentimental base among the discontented modern intellectuals.[55] It was motivated by a sense of anger and shame because of cultural decline, economic backwardness and political impotence, and propelled by the real and imagined achievements of ancient Persia. It was opposed to European imperialism, but also captivated and mesmerised by modern European culture and power. It was contemptuous, sometimes even ashamed, of the existing norms and traditions, including many a great Iranian heritage – in some cases, including classical Persian poetry – but was proud instead of the romanticised glories of ancient Iran. It was embarrassed by the ordinary people and their ways, and self-conscious of what Europeans might think of 'us' because of 'them', but it was romantically proud of Cyrus and 'the Aryan race'. It was thus both Europeanist and anti-imperialist, both self-glorifying and self-denigrating.[56]

It is impossible to imagine that young intellectual nationalists like Eshqi, Taqi Arani or Hedayat would have been capable of the kind of things to other people (briefly described below) which were done under Reza Shah's official nationalism. Indeed Eshqi fell out with it in the early days and lost his life in the process. Arani turned to Marxism and died in jail. Hedayat shunned the state, and attacked the crude manifestations of official nationalism, particularly the official Academy – mild criticism of whose work got Taqizadeh in deep trouble – and the official Society for the Development of Minds, which put out official propaganda. Further than that, he wrote unpublishable fiction against it, and against the regime, for example, in the short story, 'The Patriot'.[57] This official nationalism was combined with pseudo-modernism – indeed the latter was an aspect of the former – and was applied by arbitrary methods.

The various theoretical features and practical consequences of official nationalism were briefly as follows. At the cultural level, it claimed that the Iranian 'nation' – for which, for want of an equivalet term, the traditional term *'mellat'* was used[57a] – was of a single homogeneous race and had a single language. This as, we shall see shortly below, was contrary to the facts. Apart from that, it propagated a self-righteous version of Iranian history which was openly and emphatically anti-Arab and anti-Turk, while Turkic speakers probably outnumbered the Persian speaking population.

Except in the propaganda material put out against the Qajars, the long tradition of arbitrary rule to the continuing problems of Iranian history were entirely ignored. The new generations did not learn, for example, that Abbas I – who certainly was a very able ruler and had saved the country from chaos – had not left for himself a single able-bodied son to succeed the throne. That his grandson and heir had been incarcerated in the women's quarters until his accession, whence he had emerged to indulge in injustice and misrule. And that a form of punishment under him (Abbas) was to order the standing cannibal guard (the *zendeh-khar* of an official clan) to eat the condemned man alive. (This does not mean that history should be written on the basis of present day criteria of justice, propriety and morality. On the contrary, it means that it should be exposed as it has in fact been, rather than in a propagandist fashion and consistent with contemporary norms and values).

A practical consequence of the above – which brought together the nationalist, pseudo-modernist and arbitrary aspects of the regime in a lurid way – was the fight against the other (both Iranian and non-Iranian) languages, economic and social discrimination against the non-Persian speaking provinces, and the military onslaught on nomadic life and culture. By the late 1920s hardly any trace had been left of any nomadic rebellion and brigandry, and – moreover – the nomads had been largely disarmed. It was precisely after such pacification that extreme force was used to break the tribes up and 'settle' them in strange environments, which often led to large-scale deaths in the process. Those in charge of these operations looked upon the nomads almost in the same way as American whites viewed the native Americans in the nineteenth century. Soltan Ali Soltani who had been a Majlis deputy for many years under Reza Shah, said in a long speech a couple of months after the Shah's abdication:

> The Qashqa'i, Kohgiluyeh, Bakhtiyari and other nomads ... not only has their property been looted, but group after group of these tribes have been executed without trial. Only in one case, they killed several groups of [Kohgiluyeh nomads] whom they failed to find guilty in military courts, claiming that they were trying to escape ... They killed 97 people of the Bahmani tribe ... in one day, including a thirteen year old boy, and they jailed four hundred of them in Ahvaz, of whom three hundred died ... They brought khans of the Boyr Ahmads to Tehran with the pledge of immunity, and then killed them saying they were rebels ... The way they settled the tribes was the way of execution and annihilation, not education and reform. And it is precisely this approach that has sapped the strength of the Iranian society and weakened the hope of national unity.[57b]

Since the Majlis speaker was constantly interrupting his speech, Soltani left the rostrum and the chamber in anger, shouting 'May arbitrary rule be uprooted from its very foundations'.

Iran is a plateau and a cultural region, which now makes up a number of independent countries, including that which is known by this name. This cultural region was not always ruled by a unified state or empire. And when it was, it was not always ruled by the people of the Iranian hinterland. It had once been ruled by the Hellenic Seleucids; by Muslim Arabs; and by peoples of Turkic and Mongolian origin, before it was reunited by the Safavids at the turn of the fifteenth century. It was disunited once again in the eighteenth century, and lost territory to outside powers in the nineteenth, until its present borders (more or less) were established in the latter half of the nineteenth century.

As mentioned above, Iran is both geographically and historically a cultural region which contains parts or the whole of a number of countries. The group of Iranian languages – of which New Persian is the most widespread – includes many living and dead languages and vernaculars, ranging from the ancient Avestan, Soghdian, Khotani, Parthian and Pahlavi, etc., to the classical and modern Dari, Tajiki, Persian, Kurdish, etc. These languages are more or less related to each other, and make up a family in the network of the Indo-European languages. Apart from Dari and Tajiki (which, as it happens, are spoken outside present-day Iran), none of these other languages and vernaculars can be comprehended by modern Persian speakers. It is Perhaps worth emphasising the point: modern Persian speakers understand Dari and Tajiki which are spoken outside of present-day Iran, but do not understand Kurdish, which is an Iranian language spoken inside the country. They do not even understand the dialects of their own language which are spoken in the Caspian provinces.

There is thus a distinction between Iranianism in general, and Persianism in particular, although neither does Persianism refer to a monolithic tradition. Hence the uniformities and diversities of the broader Iranian culture, to which all the peoples of the Iranian region have made important contributions. Iranian languages were spoken at different times and/or in different regions, and, later, some Turkic dialects were added to them. In post-Islamic times, the mother-tongue of Iran's rulers was often Turkic, but Persian was almost invariably the cultural and administrative language, indeed it was a lingua franca which some-times was used from Anatolia to Turkistan and Bengal.

Massive evidence of this broader Iranianism – which remained alive even during centuries of political disunity, mainly through the media of the Persian language and literature – is provided by classical Persian literature. Let us give but two examples here of what may take volumes to document comprehensively. The great twelfth century Persian poet Khaqani was a native of Shirvan, in the Caucasus, from a Christian mother to whom he was exceptionally attached. When he received the news of the sacking of Outer Khorasan, which was then a part of the eastern Seljuk empire, and was about as far away from his native land as central Europe, he wrote two long and mighty *qasidehs* mourning the catastrophe.

The second example is from Sa'di. He wrote in his *Goleatan* (or *Gulistan*) that when he visited Kashghar, the Khwarazmian Central Asian city (now in China), he met in the college a youthful scholar who was reading Zamakhshari's classic introduction to Arabic grammar. He quoted a short Arabic poem to the boy and was told to translate it into Persian so he would understand its meaning. And when he told the boy that he was a native of Shiraz, he asked him to quote something from Sa'di. Next day when he was leaving the city, the boy learned that he was Sa'di, and there followed a moving farewell scene.

Until the twentieth century, speaking other languages than Persian had not been a source either of pride or of shame – much less, contempt or persecution – although Persian had been the language of high literature, to which peoples of all the linguistic groups had contributed.

However, under Reza Shah, and in pursuit of the Pan-Persianist policies of the state, the existence of Arabic-speaking communities in the country's South-west was all but denied. Azerbaijani and other Turkic dialects were forbidden to be printed, or otherwise published and publicised in writing. The Kurdish language was officially described as a dialect of Persian. That, too, was forbidden to be printed and published. The provincial governors, military commanders and administrators were mostly selected from Persian speakers, many of whom, even in the lower ranks, were sent directly from Tehran itself, and sometimes behaved towards the local people as if they were running an occupied territory. There was general discrimination against all the provinces in the interest of Tehran, and against all the non-Persian speaking provinces in favour of Persian speakers.

This policy created deep divisions, frustrations and resentments across the country. It made the non-Persian speakers, for the first time in history, to begin to regard themselves as subjects of discrimination because of their ethnic and/ or linguistic origins. It dealt a blow to the broader sense of Iranianism which had always existed, and for which the Persian language and literature had provided the oldest, strongest and most widespread channels. As a result, when the lid was taken off in 1941 (as also decades after that, in 1979), the centrifugal nomadic, linguistic, ethnic and provincial forces burst into the open and threatened the unity and integrity of Iranian culture and society.[58]

This policy is sometimes defended on the argument that it was necessary for building a nation-state. But the claim does not stand examination either from the point of view of *the methods employed* or *the results obtained*. The further spread of the Persian language in the non-Persian speaking regions could well have been achieved with much greater ease and consent, rather than contempt and persecution. 'Nation-state building' was a product of post-Renaissance Europe. England was probably the first modern nation state, and yet there was not, and there has not been, any contempt for, or persecution of, the people of Wales for speaking or writing their language. Nor did the Italians persecute the people of southern Tyrol for speaking German after it was given to them by the peace of Versailles. Nowhere in Western Europe did they build a nation state by wholesale denials of the existence of various communities and languages. India did not become a nation state by persecuting ethnic and linguistic minorities, the separation of most of its Muslims on independence being entirely due to religious requirements.

So much for *the means and methods* of official nationalism. As for *the results*, we have already mentioned the resentment, alienation and sense of oppression, which was highly divisive and led to perennial provincial and nomadic revolts whenever the circumstances allowed it. A nation state is far from a deeply divided and scarred society in which it is simply denied that other languages and ethnic groups exist, and persecution is used to 'prove' the point. The confusion of European nation state building for what happened in Iran under the two Pahlavis is, among other things, typical of the general pseudo-modernist approach that was misunderstood often for modernisation. It was not due to Reza Shah alone. He applied the ideology of the nationalist-modernist elite, to which he himself had been converted.

Pseudo-modernism

In 1978, I wrote a brief note on the concepts of modernism and pseudo-modernism, before the term and concept of postmodernism had been invented. I cannot describe myself as a postmodernist if only because the term conveys different, even contradictory, meanings, although I regard some of the critical views of some of the early postmodernists as worthy of serious consideration. However, as will be clear, I had not yet even read any of the structuralists and poststructuralists when I wrote the following note on modernism:

"Modernism is a synthetic vision of both science and society, which has gradually emerged from European developments in the past two centuries. It is a general attitude which reduces science to mechanistic or technological universal laws, and social progress to the purely quantitative growth of output and technology. In this respect, the modernist vision is not ideological, for a mechanistic and universal attitude to science, and purely quantitative and technological aspirations for society, may be contained and pursued within conflicting ideological frameworks. Ideological beliefs and aspirations do matter a great deal, but conflicting ideological theories and policies can be (and, indeed, have been) formulated within the spirit and vision of this European modernism.

An aspect of this broad modernism which is most relevant to the present study is the way in which European (including American) thinkers, statesmen, journalists, and so on, have tended to study, approach, and report on the countries of what is now known as the third world by an *uncritical* application of techniques, theories, methods and aspirations drawn from the experience of advanced countries ... The problem has two interrelated sides to it. First, a mechanistic and universal view of modern science automatically excludes a search for those social and historical features of the developing countries which, with the aid of modern scientific *methods* and progressive *values,* could result in fruitful analyses of the relevant problems, and attempts at their solution. And, secondly, the exclusion from theory and policy of such important indigenous values, techniques, institutions and historical perspectives produces results which are often irrelevant – they are analogous to laboratory tests based on incorrect specifications of the problem.

It has now become fashionable among many non-European (including Iranian) intellectuals to claim that 'outsiders' are incapable of understanding their cultural and social problems, although, curiously enough, they do not normally extend their claim to the case of those 'outsiders' who have the 'right' ideological colourings ... I do not agree with this trend, and in particular see no inherent reason why 'outsiders', of whatever nationality, should be incapable of meaningful studies of the developing countries. For if it is merely a question of prejudice, then that is not necessarily determined by a person's nationality; and if, as I believe, it is a question of irrelevant generalisations from *existing* knowledge and experience everywhere in the world, and the related universality of scientific laws, then there is no reason why anyone could not formulate relevant theories and policies, by an appropriate application of those methods and ideas which have thus far developed science and society in the advanced countries. The problem, I repeat, has its roots in an implicit belief in the *homogeneity* of scientific laws, which (though contrary to the spirit of founders of modern science and society) have created their own problems in the advanced countries themselves."

This was my note on *modernism* in 1978, and my further note on *pseudo-modernism* immediately followed it:

"Indeed many intellectuals and political leaders of the third world itself are voluntary victims of a *superficial* version of this European modernism – that is, of pseudo-modernism. The modernism to which we have briefly referred is a product of certain developments in advanced countries even tough it is subject to criticism within its own context. Pseudo-modernism in the third world, however, is the product of this product: it is characteristic of men and women in those societies that – regardless of *formal* ideological divisions – are alienated from the culture and history of their own society ... but unlike the European modernists themselves, they seldom have a real *understanding* of European ideas, values and techniques. Thus, third world pseudo-modernism combines the European modernist's lack of regard for specific features of third world societies with a lack of proper understanding of modern scientific methods and social development, their scope, limit and implications, and whence they have emerged. That is how modern technology (which is often confused with modern science) is seen as omnipotent, and capable of performing miracles which would solve any and all socio-economic problems once purchased and installed; why traditional social values and production techniques are regarded as inherent symbols, indeed causes, of backwardness, and sources of national embarrassment; and why industrialisation is viewed not as an objective but as an object, and the installation of a modern steel plant not as a means but an end in itself ..."[59]

So much for my 'definitions' of modernism and pseudo-modernism. As is clear from the above, this pseudo-modernism, which affected almost every aspect of the society and economy, may be observed from the history of many, if nor most, third world countries, although there have been different variations around the trend in different countries, and different intensities of application and experience. It was far from a unique experience to Iran under the two Pahlavis, though it naturally had its own local aspects. *The most important of these was that it was combined with arbitrary rule.*

Modern constitutionalists of the late nineteenth century and beyond had had two overriding objectives: lawful government, and modernisation. Indeed they thought that once lawful government was established, modernisation would be an easy task (see chapters 1 and 2 above). The meaning and implications of modernisation are not even yet wholly clear, but those modern constitutionalists certainly longed for modern industry, modern administration modern education and health services, modernised cities, modern roads, and the like. But perhaps the biggest prizes they looked for was first a railway and, second, a national bank, which were seen as symbols of progress and 'civilisation' (*tamaddon*), a term which was regularly used for decades well into the twentieth century to refer to modern European development.

A beginning was made, notably in education, even before the onset of revolution. It was taken relatively much further than that between then and the early 20's, when the framework of a modern administration, including judicial courts, came into being, and there was civil, administrative as well as judicial legislation. Some private investment was made in modern manufacturing. There was more progress in education, where modern boy schools increased, and some girl schools were founded; and there was an expansion of higher education, especially in medicine, law and politics. This was briefly discussed in chapter 3 above, as part of the positive achievements of the revolution.

It was not possible to go further than that in the midst of the growing chaos; indeed it was no mean achievement in those circumstances. Reza Shah's termination of chaos, as we have seen, not only saved the country from possible disintegration, but by bringing stability and security helped agriculture and trade, and made it both desirable and profitable to invest in urban manufacturing, whether traditional or modern.

But it went further than that especially as the regime that had stamped out disorder belonged to the nationalist-modernist elite. The facts and statistics of economic development have been discussed in a number of studies, and need not detain us long in a book that is essentially about state and society.[60] Using the growing revenues form oil, which – though not colossal – were extremely helpful as one of the two major sources of foreign exchange, a considerable amount of state investment was made in infrastructure and industry, although little was done for agriculture and the rural society.

Bank Melli was founded and given the monopoly of note issue, and it acted as a state bank which provided commercial services. Later on, one or two other state banks, notably the Army Bank (*Bank Sepah*) were founded. By 1940 construction of the Trans-Iranian railway had been completed, costing the colossal amount of $150 million. The costs far outweighed any *economic* benefit brought by it. Road construction, instead, would have been considerably cheaper in the local currency, besides making huge savings in foreign exchange. But it must be remembered that, in the eyes of the nationalist-modernists, railways were a most prestigious desideratum, a source of great national pride. Indeed, even now, it is sometimes difficult to discuss the subject of that particular railway project rationally with modern-minded Iranians, who seem to think that a rationally critical evaluation of an economic project is tantamount to rejecting 'civilisation' itself.

The construction of new motor roads between the major cities, and improvement of some of the existing roads elsewhere, began earlier, and was to continue in the 1930s, though at a declining rate. State students were selected strictly on academic merits and sent to Western European countries – mainly Germany, France and Belgium – to study medicine, law, engineering, pure sciences history and languages. There was a decline in this project also in the 1930s. But, at the same time, the university of Tehran was founded by bringing the existing colleges and faculties – e. g. the School of Law and Political Science, which had been founded before the Constitutional Revolution – together with newly created faculties in one central university. In addition, a teachers' training college – the *Danesh-sara-ye Ali* – was founded in Tehran, along the lines of the French *écoles normale*.

Modern primary and secondary schools grew relatively rapidly, but mainly in Tehran and other main cities and towns. They were largely non-fee paying state schools, thus making it possible for the lower urban classes to make use of them, but only those children who did not have to make their living, especially beyond the ages of 10 or 12. Modern urban middle classes began to send their daughters to school almost without exception, but there was some participation by the more traditional classes as well. Again, the rural society was almost completely excluded. The main problem was that almost the whole of state investment was put in costly and prolonged academic education, and not much was done for a faster expansion of literacy. By the end of Reza Shah's rule Iran's illiteracy rate was between 85 and 90 per cent.

Population grew steadily but not too fast. There was a small shift of the population from the rural to the urban sector, and a larger one from small towns to the big cities, particularly Tehran. This led to the growth of urban employment. Some of the bigger cities were modernised, at least in terms of looks and basic facilities, but at the cost of the unnecessary destruction of some buildings and structures, largely out of the fear that to Europeans they might look backward. But sanitary conditions were relatively improved and health services expanded, though they were still out of reach of most of the people.

The army expanded fast with positive as well as negative results. By the time the Shah abdicated, a small air force, and a smaller navy had also come into being. It consistently took a large share of the government budget. It became larger than was necessary to keep the peace, but it performed very badly when it came to defending the country's borders. It is true that the allied armies were much stronger. But the flight of the forces before them, and the unauthorised order for general demobilisation by the army leaders in the capital reflected the gap between reality and myth about the Shah's army.

The bureaucracy also grew fast, though it built on the foundations laid before and – especially – after the Constitutional Revolution. The expansion of the 1920s was generally needed for the extension of the administration, and a reasonable centralisation of the state. But in the 1930s it went well beyond that, when over-bureaucratisation of the administration was justified only by the over-centralisation of the state.

Davar's reform of the justice departments and the courts was typical of his energy and dedication. The trouble was that the new structure was far more suitable for functioning in France than in Iran of that period. It was not the new laws that were necessarily alien, if only because most of the civil code, and a good deal of the criminal laws, were based on the existing traditions. It was the structure, hierarchy and procedures, which made the system expensive, time-wasting, remote and out of the reach of the vast majority of people. Nonetheless, it was one of the finest and most enduring achievements of the period.

To the question, 'Whether or not all these developments were useful', the answer is, 'Almost all of them were useful if the alternative was to do nothing at all'. But, even in those circumstances, more useful, more relevant, and more appropriate polices might have been pursued, if ideological passions had not dominated the decision making process. It is nevertheless true that, with regard to industry and infrastructure – including transport, education and health – the country was considerably better off in 1941 than it had been in 1921.

It was from the end of the 1920s that *étatisme* began to get out of hand and make matters worse both for economic efficiency and for social justice.

The purchase and distribution of important commodities, particularly wheat, became a state monopoly. The implications of that for the prices and, therefore, the incomes of both peasants and landlords are clear. Internal tariffs were imposed on goods moving from one part of the country to another, even from one city to another. Anyone wishing to leave or enter the main cities and towns had to obtain an internal passport from the police. The two acts of 1931 and 1932 made foreign trade the sole monopoly of the state, both increasing costs to the consumer and alienating the merchant community. The growing state companies to replace the merchants, in the end, became a great source of headache even for Davar himself, the honest and very able minister of finance who created them.

Yet, even back in 1928, there were some basic flaws in decision taking which tended to create waste and inefficiency. The railways were constructed not from economic considerations, but because of the wish to have a railway network, *a wish that was by no mean exclusive to Reza Shah and the ruling elite, but was shared by many modern and traditional middle classes.*[61] Yet, true to the traditional dichotomy of *mellat* and *dawlat*, it led to the wholly unjustified suspicion that Reza Shah constructed the railways on direct orders from Britain for potential strategic use against the Soviet Union. It is not well known that there were at least some British and Soviet suspicions, each thinking that the other side might be behind it. Thus, commenting on Loraine's report of his conversation with the Shah about Iranian relations with Britain and the Soviet Union, the Foreign Office noted:

The suggestion that Russia will oppose a north-south axis for the railway through fear of attack by Great Britain throws a new light on the question.

If this is really the case, we need not fear – as a trap set by Russia – the proposed line from Mohammareh [later, Khorramshahr] to Tehran, although an extension thence to the Caspian would still be risky.[62]

As noted above, there was a strong psychological side to pseudo-modernism in Iran and similar countries, reacting to European achievements in an unrealistic way, which itself arose from a misunderstanding of the nature, causes and processes of those achievements. But where there was arbitrary government, it made it much easier to give vent to the passionate psychological urge for looking like Europeans with almost no control at all.

The two following examples show both the psychology behind pseudo-modernist decisions, and how arbitrary power was applied to enforce them. The first example concerns the entertainment of foreign guests complete with modern European toilets and bathrooms. In November 1934, the British minister reported the stories to the Foreign Office, adding that 'they may seem too trivial to report, but they may have a bearing upon the difficulty which I am having in seeing the M.F.A. [Minister of Foreign Affairs] and in obtaining a farewell audience of the Shah'. The first story is about modern European toilets for Swedish guests:

> Waterclosets [sic] are the great excitement here at present. It seems likely that the Shah discovered this useful apparatus in the course of his Turkish travels. In any case the imminent advent of the Belgian Special Ambr [Ambassador] and the Crown Prince and Princess of Sweden has aroused H[is]M[ajesty] to a sense of the inadequacy of the Persian privy. The *sous-chef du protocole* was suddenly summoned the other day and ordered to see to it that water closets in the European style should be installed wherever the Swedish Royal party were likely to descend in the course of their journey from the frontier to the capital. Next day a lorry left Tehran heavily loaded with all the sanitary fittings which the meagre resources of Tehran could furnish. Considerable uncertainty was displayed as to where these famous European inventions were to be erected.

The British minister's second story in the same dispatch was similar in its psychological implications, except that it also involved arbitrary behaviour of a most humiliating kind towards a grand family, the Qaragozlus, the family of Naser al-Molk-e Hamadani, the late former prime minister and Regent, and Hossein Ala's father-in-law:

> The Belgian Mission provided a similar problem. The family of Qarago-zlou share with their relative, the present Persian Minister in London [Hossein Ala], a handsome house in the middle of Tehran. The Shah ordered them to place this house at the disposal of M[onsieur] Ithier and his suite of seven or eight Belgian ladies and gentlemen, but not only must

they offer their house; it must also be made suitable for its high destiny at the expense of the Qaragozlous; water closets and bathrooms must be put in and a new and more handsome front gate provided. The house has for the last fortnight been turned topsy-turvy by plumbers and the garden when recently visited by a member of my staff was adorned with baths and sanitary apparatus dumped indiscriminately among the flower beds but the fateful day is arriving and only the original Persian bath situated in a cellar under the front door is likely to be available for the ablutions of the Belgians.

The report is completed by the British minister's account of other current preoccupations in regard to European visitors:

Assad Khan, the amiable *Chef du Protocole,* is frankly in despair and very nearly off his head. Large consigmenta of glass and china for the banquets are being held up in the customs house and the Minister of Finance refuses to release them until the Minister of F[oreign] A[ffairs] has paid the necessary duty. 3000 tomans worth of wine is also being held to ransom for 9000 tomans which the M [i.e.Ministery of] F[oreign] A[ffaris] cannot find anywhere. On top of these anxieties the poor man is having to arrange for the reception by the Shah of Ministers from Finland and Austria who have inopportunely arrived to present their letters. The Finish Minister's case is complicated by the fact that nobody in Tehran can produce the score of the Finnish national anthemn [sic] though the Danish Chargé d'Affaires is believed to be able to whistle the tune.[63]

The second example is the banning of *chadors* as well as any scarves worn by women. The prelude to this was the bloody clash of troops in Mashad, mentioned above, with those who had taken *bast,* protesting against the state's order that all men must wear the European bowler hat, which is often thought – although incorrectly – to have been a protest against the banning of women's head-dresses.

Up till then, and for some time afterwards, it was strictly a matter of social propriety for all men – regardless of rank and class – to cover their heads in public, that is, in open places as well as indoors, and even at home, when they had visitors. There were a variety of different hats and head-dresses which reflected social rank and profession. At the beginnings of Reza Khan's rule a hat fashioned after his own military cap (which had been adapted from the French military and police cap) became in vogue among politicians and state officials, and was compulsory for military officers. This was later made compulsory for all men, and the compulsion was generally taken in good humour. The officially registered and recognised ulama and preachers could wear the turban.

Suddenly in the summer of 1935 the Shah ordered all men to wear the bowler hat, which was European *par excellence,* and which no one except for a few had even seen before. There was revulsion, and the non-violent resistance in Mashad, was put down by bloodshed, followed by the execution of Asadi, and Forughi's dismissal and disgrace (see further above). Mokhber al-Saltaneh (Hedayat) had been retired for some time, but still had occasional private audiences with the Shah. He wrote in his memoirs:

> In an audience, the Shah took my [European bowler] hat off and said, Now what do you think of this. I said it certainly protects one from the sun and the rain, but that [Pahlavi] hat which we had before had a better name. Agitated, His Majesty paced up and down and said, *All I am trying to do is for us to look like [the Europeans] so they would not laugh at us.* I replied that no doubt he had thought this to be expedient, but said to myself, It is what is under the hat, and irrelevant emulations, which they laugh at (emphasis added).[64]

The above quotation makes plain the only reason behind the enforced change of hats, that is, to stop the Europeans 'laughing at us'. It was certainly not a policy for liberating Iranian men, as the enforced removal of the *chador* and scarves is often explained on the ground that it was meant to liberate Iranian women. This was the background to the latter event, which no one dared to protest against in public. Women were suddenly ordered to take off their *chador,* which covered their heads as well as body. The effect for most women – and almost all of those above forty – was as if in 1936 European women had been suddenly ordered to go out topless into the street. The subject of removing the *chador* was not new. All modern, and some not so modern, intellectuals had been campaigning for its *voluntary* removal for decades, and articles and poems (for example by Eshqi and Iraj) had been written for making it legally possible and socially acceptable. No one had dreamed that it would or should be done by force, *without permission even of wearing a scarf.*

Some modern middle class women had already taken off the *chador* in indoor gatherings and parties, and many girls were going to school without it. One major problem for most urban women was that they simply lacked the sartorial culture of appearing in public without a bodily cover, and in any case it was very expensive for them at the time. They also lacked the culture of public hair-do, and – apart from that – would have felt much less shy if they could cover their hair with a scarf.

Perhaps the worst aspect of the order from the women's point of view was that they were not even allowed to wear a scarf. Only imported European hats were allowed which only upper class women had both the money and culture to wear. Compulsory district parties were ordered in which men had to bring their wives without the *chador.* Scarves were being torn off women's heads by the police in streets and alleys. There was much social and cultural violence and some physical suicides.[65]

If the idea were 'the liberation of women', then it would have been far better achieved without official violence, making it easy for women to reduce and/or remove their head gears gradually. This way it created deep scars among the vast majority of people, not least among women themselves. The result was that, outside the modern middle class women, almost all of them put their *chador*'s back after the abdication. The main motive force was 'so the Europeans would not laugh at us', the instrument for its realisation was arbitrary power.

Reza Shah: a brief appraisal

It is characteristic of Iran's politics and history that the subject of Reza Shah still arouses strong passions seventy years after his accession and fifty years after his demise. Here we shall attempt a summing up regardless of opinions – whether 'pro' or 'anti' – that arise from spheres other than dispassionate social and historical analysis.

Until some time after the revolution of 1977–79, there were extremely few Iranians of whatever rank, class and income who were not convinced that Reza Shah had been put on the throne by the British, and that he had extended the oil concession voluntarily as their agent. Even if there were some – and there were a few – who tried to justify this on the argument that it had been inevitable, and that the Shah had also had positive consequences for Iran, they still believed that Britain had been his master. As early as 1976 I argued that he was a very able man, and a product of the post-revolutionary chaos, and rise of modern Iranian nationalism.[65a] In 1978, I further argued that Reza was *not* an agent of Britain or anywhere else – if anything, he was anti-British almost from the beginning – and that the people began to believe he was one because of the great unpopularity he brought onto himself by arbitrary as well as harsh behaviour.[65b]

Reza Shah's detractors have described him as 'a stable boy' (*bachcheh mehtar*) for decades, while his admirers – who have been increasing only since a few years after the revolution of 1977–79 – have put forward a genealogy through a respectable line of military officers. They both seem to exaggerate. At a more serious level, he has been attacked for lack of legitimacy, for being a usurper, as he was not of royal descent. But he was not a usurper from the standpoint of Iranian history and society, which had always lacked a continuous aristocracy, and where rebellion was always justified by its success (see chapter 1, above). And, in any case, the constituent assembly that established the Pahlavi dynasty in 1926, by secret ballot and without a single vote against, represented the commanding heights of the society, and the provinces of the country. Once again, it was his harsh and arbitrary behaviour which lost him his legitimacy.

His power and popularity in the early years was neither due to British support (as it happens, he enjoyed more Soviet support at the time) nor, primarily, due to the loyalty of the army. It arose from the fact that he appeared as a fresh and forthright leader who – unlike the traditional politicians, whether popular or conservative – was capable of stamping out chaos, save the country from disintegration, and bring peace and stability, without which social and economic development of any kind would not have been possible. Most of the politicians themselves acknowledged that and supported him for it.

His admirers have often compared him with Nader Shah. There is some resemblance but, if anything, he fares better. Contrary to popular Iranian thinking, Nader saw himself *not* as a modern Iranian nationalist, but an Asiatic conqueror, in the image of Taimur the Lame, 'Tamerlane' (as the latter had seen himself in that of Gengiz Khan), and was hoping to create a vast Asian empire, of which Mashad was the central and capital city. His troops plundered both Iranian and foreign lands, and his extremely high taxes brought ruin to the people and the economy.[66] He was extremely cruel, and he died a universally hated man. But, after a while, the great chaos that ensued his demise (itself the inevitable product of his harsh and arbitrary rule) made people pray for his return. Like Nader, Reza Shah had very few friends when he fell from power, but after a few years of *relative* chaos many began to look upon the stability under his rule with nostalgia. The chaos was relatively limited because – as Golsh'iyan (quoted above) observed at the time – the Shah had fallen not by assassination, but by abdication enforced by the great powers who had occupied the country.

It is not surprising that an extremely favourable but not very realistic image of Nader Shah was fostered in the Pahlavi era. But, in addition to stamping out the chaos, Reza Shah brought peace and stability to the country that made both public and private economic activity possible, although his later polices of *etatisme*, etc., had negative effects. His public investments, especially in building a modern infrastructure, had no match in anything that Nader ever did for reconstructing the economy and society, even though its pseudo-modernist approach, psychology and method was unnecessarily wasteful.

Most of the things which went *excessively* wrong under his rule – be it a harmful foreign agreement, a highly wasteful investment project, or the forceful imposition of hats on men, and prohibition of wearing scarves by women – would have been avoided if his power had not been arbitrary. If Reza Shah's rule had remained firm but constitutional – even if not necessarily democratic – as in his early years, he would have gone down in Iranian history as a great leader, as did Ataturk in the history of Turkey.

The question is sometimes posed as to whether the country would have been better or worse off without Reza Shah. The answer is that if there had been no letting off of chaos and disintegration without him, then it was better that he took over the realm, for persistent chaos is worse than harsh and arbitrary government. But those who pose this question miss the main point. Reza Shah did save the country from chaos and disintegration, which was absolutely necessary. But firm government did not require arbitrary rule as well as great injustice and corruption. This indeed was recipe for chaos after the Shah's fall, which is exactly what followed it. The firm government of Reza Shah's early years was probably the only available root to saving the country from chaos and disintegration at the time. But his arbitrary rule was totally unnecessary. On the contrary, it was counterproductive and did unnecessary but highly effective damage, both to him and to the state and society.

Notes

1 See the long telegram by Harold Nicolson to Sir Austin Chamberlain, *British Documents on Foreign Policy*, vol. xiii, no. 447; and the long telegram by Chamberlain to R. H. Clive, *ibid.*, no. 458.

2 Gordon Waterfield, *Professional Diplomat, Sir Percy Loraine*, London: John Murray, 1973, p. 79. The quotation is directly from a telegram by Curzon to Loraine.

3 Nicolson to Chamberlain, *BDFP*, vol. xiii, no. 447.

3a See Appendix to this book and Homa Katouzian, 'Problems of Democracy and the Public Sphere in Modern Iran', *Comparative Studies of Southern Asia, Africa and the Middle East*, XVIII, 2, 1998.

4 Chamberlain to Clive, *ibid.*, no. 458.

5 *Ibid.*

6 Nicolson to Chamberlain, n. 7.

6a See Ali Akbar Siyasi, *Gozaresh-e Yek Zendegi*, London: Siyasi, 1988.

7 See Mokhber al-Saltaneh (Mehdiqoli Hedayat), *Khaterat va Khatarat*, Tehran: Zavvar, 1984, p. 371.

8 See his *qasideh* 'Din va Dawlat', *Divan-e Bahar*, ed. Mohammad Malekzadeh, vol. 1, Tehran: 1956, pp. 403–405. See also a following *qasideh*, a better poem, towards the end of which he praises the new Shah, 'Sepid Rud', pp. 650–653.

9 For Badamchi's radical democratic credentials, see, for example, his long article in *Iran-shahr*, no. 14, 1926 (special issue on Shaikh Moahammad Khiyabani), reprinted in *Entesharat-e Iranshahr*, Tehran: Eqbql, 1972. See further, Homa Katouzian, *The Revolt of Shaykh Muhammad Khiyabni*, *IRAN*, Journal of the British Institute of Persian Studies, 1999.

10 For the complete minutes of the constituent assembly, see Hossein Makki, *Tarikh-e Bist-saleh-ye Iran*, Tehran: Elmi, 1995, vol. 3, pp. 547–655.

11 Loraine to Chamberlain, 11/3/26, F.O. 371/11481.

12 Foreign Office minutes, 14/6/26, F.O. 371/11481.

13 Foreign Office minutes, 17/6/26, F.O. 371/11481.

13a Taqizadeh says in his memoirs that he was visiting his German wife's family in Berlin at the time on his way to Philadelphia as the head of Iran's delegation to attend the celebrations for the 150th of American independence. He declined the offer of becoming foreign minister, which he had received via wire from Tehran, and when they insisted, he wired 'either ask me to go to America or I shall not come back to Tehran at all'. Clearly, he could have accepted the post and gone to America as well. See Iraj Afhsar, ed., *Zendegi-ye Tufani, Khaterat-e Sayyed Hasan Taqizadeh*, Tehran: Elmi, 1993, 205–206.

14 See Mokhber al-Saltaneh, *Khaterat va Khatarat*, p. 370.

15 See Makki, *Tarikh-e Bistsaleh-ye Iran*, vol. 5, pp. 144–145. The whole of Bahar's series of articles in *Khandan-iha* have been reprinted in this source.

15a See Mohammad Mosaddeq, *Musaddiq's Memoirs*, ed. and intro. Homa Katouzian, tr. S. H. Amin and H. Katouzian, London: Jebheh, 1988.

16 See Hossein Makki, *Doktor Mosaddeq va Notqha-ye Tarikhi-ye U*, Tehran: Elmi, 1985, pp. 204-205.

17 *Ibid.*, p. 205.

18 See, for example, the article by the *Hablolmatin* newspaper quoted in *ibid.*, p. 199.

18a Nicolson to Chamberlain, 4/11/26, F.O. 371/11481.

19 See Makki, *Tarikh-e Bistsaleh*, vol. 4, p. 270.

20 See Homa Katouzian, *Musaddiq and the Stuggle for Power in Iran*, London and New York: I.B.Tauris, second edition, 1981, p. 30.

21 See Makki, *Tarikh-e Bistsaleh*, vol. 4, pp. 272–281.

21a *Ibid.*, p. 273.

22 *Ibid.*, p. 278.

23 For the assassination attempt, see, for example, Ebrahim Khajeh Nuri, 'Teror-e Modarres' in *Sayyed Hasan Modarres*, Tehran:Javidan, 1979. For the text of speeches in the Majlis condemning the attempt, see Hossein Makki, *Tarikh-e Bistsaleh*, vol. 4, pp. 187–217.

24 See Katouzian, *Musaddiq and the Struggle for Power* ..., chapter 3. See further, Hossein Kay-Ostovan, *Siyasat-e Movazeneh-ye Manfi*, vol. 1, p. 22; Iraj Afshar, ed., *Mosaddeq va Mas'el-e Hoquq va Siyasat*, Tehran: Zamineh, 1979, pp. 115–116.

25 See Shaikh al-Islam Malayeri's Majlis speech (in 1941) for the circumstances of the murder of Modarres in Khajeh Nuri, *Modarres*. See further, Makki, *Tarikh-e Bistsaleh*, vol. 4, for details both on the case of Modarres and Diba. See further, Jalal Abdoh – who was public prosecutor in the trial of the official death squads – *Chehl Sal dar Sahneh*, ed. Majid Tafreshi, Tehran: Rasa, 1989.

25a Golsha'iyan writes – in his note of October 1933 on the incident – that after he and Dr. Qezel-Ayagh left the prison and went to the criminal court offices the doctor was 'so unwell that he fell down on the chair':

> He then asked for sweetened hot water (*qandaq*) and drank it. After a long pause, he said I'll tell you something but for God's sake don't tell anybody. I said, What? He said Taimurtash didn't die [of natural causes], but he's been poisoned. I expressed surprise. He said, I am not mistaken, he has definitely been killed. I said, Why then did you certify that he has died of natural causes?. He said, Do you want me to end up like him too? ... The poor man had had a fit in the evening. Next day when I went to see how he was, he begged me saying, Make sure nobody hears of this or my whole family will go with the wind ... I have noted this affair [here] but I wonder what would happen to my and the poor doctor's whole existence if one day it falls into other people's hands.

See 'Yaddasht-ha-ye Golsha'iyan', in *Yaddasht-ha-ye Doktor Qasem Ghani*, ed. Cyrus Ghani, vol. II, London: Ghani, 1984, pp. 519–520.

26 The sources on these events are numerous. See, For example, 'Taimurtash' and 'Davar' in Ebrahim Khajeh Nuri, *Bazigaran-e Asr-e Tal'i*, Tehran: Jibi, 1978. Iraj Afshar, ed., *Zendegani-ye Tufani: Khaterat-e Sayyed Hasan Taqizadeh*, Tehran: Elmi, 1993. Nasrollh Siafpur Fatemi, *Ayeneh-ye Ebrat*, vol. 2, London: Jebheh, 1990. Abolhasan Ebtehaj, *Khaterat-e Abolhasan Ebtehaj*, vol. 1, London: Alireza Arouzi, 1991. Makki, *Tarikh-e Bistsaleh*, vols. 5 and 6 .

27 For a detailed description of the events, see Makki, *Tarikh-e Bistsaleh*, vol. 4, pp. 379–414. For the account of government discussions and handling of the crisis, see Mokhber al-Saltaneh, *Khterat va Khatarat*, pp. 375–378.

28 See, for example, Baqer Aqeli, *Zuka' al-Molk-e Forughi va Shahrivar-e 1320*, Tehran: Elmi, 1988. Makki, *Tarikh-e Bistsale*, vol. 6, and further notes below.

29 Mokhber al-Saltaneh, *Khaterat va Khatarat*, p. 397.

29a *Ibid.*, p. 402. See further Homa Katouzian, 'The Pahlavi Regime in Iran' in H. E. Chehabi and Juan J. Linz, eds., *Sultanistic Regimes*, Baltimore and London: The Johns Hopkins University Press, 1998.

30 See Reza Sheikholeslami, 'In the Reign of Reza Shah Pahlavi', Courts and Countries VII–VIII, in *Encyclopædia Iranica*.

30a British minister to the Foreign Office, 3/11/34, FO 248/1393.

31 See Homa Katouzian, ed. and intro., *Khaterat-e Siyasi-ye Khalil Maleki*, second edition, Tehran: Enteshar, 1988. *Note added to the proofs:* See further, Ervand Abrahamian, *Tortured Confessions, Prisons and Public Recantation in Modern Iran*, Berkely: University of California Press, 1999.

31a See Mokhber al-Saltaneh, *Khaterat va Khatarat*, p. 412.

32 See 'Yaddasht-ha-ye Abbasqoli Golsha'iyan', p. 549.

33 See Mokhber al-Saltaneh, *Khaterat va Khatarat*, pp. 383 and 412. See further on the fate of Bahrami, Saifpur Fatemi, *A'ineh-ye Ebrat*, vol. 2, chapter 42.

33a See Taqizadeh, *Zendegi-ye Tufani*, pp. 232–233.

34 See, for example, Mostafa Fateh *Panjah Sal Naft-e Iran*, Tehran: Chehr, 1956. Abolfazl Lesani, *Tala-ye Siyah ya Bala-ye Iran*, Tehran: Amir Kabir, 1978. Homa Katouzian, *The Political Economy of Modern Iran*, London and New York; Macmillan and New York University Press, 1981, and *Musaddiq and the Struggle for Power*. R. W. Ferrier, *The History of the British Petroleum Company*, vol. 1, *The Developing Years 1901–1932*, Cambridge: Cambridge University Press, 1982.

35 For events immediately leading up to the cancellation of the concession, see especially, Mokhber al-Saltaneh, *Khaterat va Khatarat*, and Taqizadeh, *Zendegi-ye Tufani*.

36 See especially, Taqizadeh, *ibid.*, and Fateh, *Panjah Sal Naft*.

37 See Taqizadeh, *Zendegi-ye Tufani*, and Makki, *Tarikh-e Bistsal-e*, vol. 5.

38 Taqizadeh, *Zendegani-ye Tufani*, p. 241.

39 See *ibid.*, p. 365.

40 See 'Yaddasht-ha -ye Golsh'iyan', p. 562. Golsha'iyan's diaries are a unique source for following the events and gauging the atmosphere at the time of the allied invasion in 1941, especially because they were written at the time by a cautious and temperate eyewitness who was a loyal senior minister.

41 See Homa Katouzain 'Tanz-e Dawreh-ye Hedayat', *Iranshenasi*, part 2, winter 1998. There were countless such poems. See, for example, those quoted in full in *Makki, Tarikh-e Bistsaleh*, vol. 8, especially the *qasideh* by Hamidi Shirazi entitled 'Bearing the Crown Is One Thing, Worshipping Money Is Another', pp. 160–162.

42 For the text of Dashti's long speech in the Majlis (22/8/41), see 'Dashti' in Khajeh-Nuri, *Bazigaran-e 'Asr-e Tala'i*, 187–191. See another long Majlis speech by him against arbitrary rule and corruption in Makki, *Tarikh-e Bistsaleh*, vol. 8, pp. 151–156. He was far from the only deputy with such complaints and suspicions. See further, *ibid.*, pp. 176–244, and Aqeli, *Zoka' al-Molk-e Forughi*, pp. 144–178.

43 R. H. Hoare (Tehran) to Sir John Simon (London), 1/2/1934, F.O. 248/1392.

44 *Ibid.*

45 *Ibid.*

46 See Taqizadeh, *Zendegi-ye Tufani*, p. 242. See also Mokhber al-Saltaneh, *Khaterat va Khatarat*, p. 401.

47 See Taqizadeh, *Zendegi-ye Tufani*, Appendix pp. 556–561, for letters of warning and admonition from the Shah's private secretary to Taqizadeh regarding such decisions.

48 See *ibid.*, p. 262.

49 See *ibid.*, Appendix pp. 562–568 for the letters exchanged between Taqizadeh and the Shah's private secretary Hossein Shokuh (Shokuh al-Molk).

50 See the full text of his letter, Forughi's reply, and Taqizadeh's reply to him in *Zendegi-ye Tufani*, Appendix pp. 569–576.

50a For an angry denunciation of their new 'dictionary' see Sadeq Hedayat, 'Farhang-e Farhangestan' in *Alaviyeh Khanom va Velengari*, Tehran: Amir Kabir, 1963. Mokhber al-Saltaneh says that he suggested a better alternative for a newly-coined word but was told by the Academy that it had already been approved by the Shah, and so had to remain. He adds, 'Some of the choices of the Academy were indeed scandalous and were being made fun of'. See *Khaterat va Khatarat*, p. 411.

51 See Hekmat's glowing letter to Taqizadeh in *Zendegani-ye Tufani ... Taqizadeh*, p. 593.

52 *Ibid.*, p. 246.

53 There are a few good primary Iranian sources on the invasion and abdication which, once studied critically together, give a realistic picture of the events seen from the Iranain side. They include, Aqeli, *Zoka' al-Molk-e Forughi*, and *The Memoirs of Mohammad*

Sa' ed Maragheh'ii (Tehran: Namak, 1994), 'Yaddasht-ha-ye Golsha'iyan', Mohammad Reza Abbasi and Berhruz Tayarani, eds., *Khaterat-e Nasrollah Entezam: Shahriver-e 1320 az Did-e Darbar*, Tehran:Asnad-e Melli-ye Iran, 1992, Makki, *Tarikh-e Bistsaleh*, vols. 7 and 8. See, for a summary account and analysis of the subject, Katouzian *Musaddiq and the Struggle*, chapters 3 and 4. For a good single primary British source, which includes a detailed description and appraisal of the events, see Reader Bullard's annual report to Anthony Eden, 26/5/42, FO 371/34–31443.

54   See Reader Bullard *ibid*. See also the full text of Forughi's Broadcast to the Nation (5/10/41) in Makki *Tarikh-e Bistsaleh*, vol. 8, pp. 179–185.

54a See Golsha'iyan's 'Yaddasht-ha', p. 604.

55   It is spread all over the collected poetical works of Aref-e Qazvini, Mohammad Reza Eshqi, Farrokhi Yazdi and Vahid-e Dastgerdi, although its echoes may be found in the works of almost all the leading modern writers, poets and journalists, even including the Poet-Laureate Bahar.

56   See further, Homa Katouzian, *Sadeq Hedayat, The Life and Legend of an Iranian Writer*, London and New York: I. B. Tauris, 1991, chapter 5, and *Musaddiq and the Stuggle for Power*, chapter 18.

57   See Katouzian *Sadeq Hedayat*, chapter 6, and *Sadeq Hedayat va Marg-e Nevisandeh*, second edition, Tehran: Nashr-e Markaz, 1995, chapter 3.

57a See Homa Katouzian, 'Mellat, Melli, Melligera va Nasionalism' in *Estebdad, Demokrasi va Nehzat-e Melli*, second edition, Tehran: Nashr-e Markaz, 1996.

57b For the full text of the speech, see 'The proceedings of the Majlis on Sunday 13 December 1941', in Kuhi Kermani, *Az Shahrivar 1320 ta Faje'eh-ye Azerbaijan*, vol. 1, Tehran: Kuhi, n. d., 222–229.

58   See further, Homa Katouzian, 'Problems of Political Development in Iran: Democracy, Dictatorship or Arbitrary Rule', *British Journal of Middle Eastern Studies*, May 1996.

59   See Katouzian *The political Economy of Modern Iran*, pp. 101–103 for the quotations, both on modernism and pseudo-modernism.

60   See, for example, Julian Bharier, *Economic Development in Iran 1900–1970*, London: Oxford University Press, 1971; Katouzian, *The Political Economy of Modern Iran*, chapters 6 and 7. Amin Banani, *The Modernisation of Iran*, Stanford: Stanford University Press, 1961. Donald Wilber, *Riza Shah Pahlavi, The Resurrection and Reconstruction of Iran*, New York: Exposition Press, 1975. Sa'id Nafisi, *Tarikh-e Mo'aser-e Iran: Az Kudeta-ye Sevvom-e Esfand-e 1299 ta Bist-va-chahrom-e Shahrivar Mah-e 1320*, Tehran: Forughi, 1966.

61   For an extended discussion of these points, see Katouzian, *Musaddiq and the Struggle*, chapter 3, and *Political Economy of Modern Iran*, chapter, 6.

62   Foreign Office minutes, 2/3/26, F.O. 371/11481.

63   British minister (Tehran) to the Foreign Office, 3/11/34, 248/1393.

64   Mokhber al-Saltaneh, *Khaterat va Khatarat*, p. 407.

65   For documents showing official coercion and persecution in this matter, see Sazman-e Madark-e Farhangi-ye Enqelab-e Islami, *Vaqeh'eh-ye Kashf-e Hejab*, Tehran: Mo'asseseh-ye Pazhuhesh-ha va Motal'eat-e Farhangi, 1992.

65a See 'Nationalist Trends in Iran, 1921–1926', *International Journal of Middle East Studies*, 1979, first presented to a seminar of St. Antony's College, Oxford in June 1976.

65b See *The Political Economy of Modern Iran*, chapters 5 and 6.

66   See Lawrence Lockhart, *Nadir Shah*, London: Luzac, 1938. See further his *The Fall of the Safavid Dynasty and the Afghan Occupation of Persia*, Cambridge: Cambridge University Press, 1958.

Appendix

Martin Herz's Analysis of the Political Situation in 1964

A remarkable analysis of the political situation in Iran in the mid-1960s is contained in Martin F. Herz's *A View from Tehran: A Diplomatist Looks at the Shah's Regime in June 1964*, Institute for the Study of Diplomacy (Georgetown University, Washington, 1979).

The late Mr (later Ambassador) Herz was counsellor for political affairs at the American Embassy in Tehran when he sent this dispatch to the Department of State. Significantly, he labelled it as 'Some Intangible Factors in Iranian Politics'. It would be difficult to exaggerate the breadth of information and – especially – depth of insight in this unusually long diplomatic dispatch. While he points out that the Shah had been thoroughly successful in the recent power struggles against the National Front, the Amini group and the religious leadership, he observes that he lacks a social base, and that his rule lacks a firm basis even among its beneficiaries. Here is a passage from the dispatch which is particularly relevant to our present analysis:

> Since the opposition is weak, divided and dispirited, the regime ought to be feeling happy and secure, particularly as it has important political assets in its favour. But one of the remarkable factors in the present situation is that the regime has so few convinced supporters. Evidence of this is to be found at every turn: prominent members of the New Iran Party who express the belief, quietly and privately, that their party is a sham and a fraud and that no political party can be expected to do useful work as long as the Shah's heavy hand rests on the decision-making process; hand-picked Majlis members who deplore 'American Support' for a regime which they call a travesty of democracy; civil adjutants of the Shah, who belong to his most devoted supporters, yet who express the belief that Iran will never be able to solve its problems as long as there is no freedom of expression, no delegation of authority, and so little selection of personnel for merit; prominent judges who declare, with surprising lack of circumspection, that the anti-corruption campaign cannot get anywhere as long as it is known that certain people are immune from prosecution; military officers who tip off the National Front regarding actions planned against its demonstrators; Foreign Ministry officials who privately advise against courses of action they are officially urging on the U.S. with respect to the treatment of opposition spokesmen in the United States. These are not members of the opposition. They are members of the Establishment who, even while loyal to the Shah, are suffering from a profound malaise, from lack of conviction in what they are doing, from doubts about whether the regime deserves to endure.

> Here, and not in particular activities of the opposition, lies the real weakness of the present regime, for even a militant minority in charge of the apparatus of government could create respect in the rest of a country ... Even when ample allowance is made for the ungovernable nature of the Iranian middle class ...

there remains the fact that the Shah's regime is regarded as a highly unpopular dictatorship not only by its opponents but, far more significantly, by its proponents as well ... (pp.6–7).

From Herz's own analysis it is clear that what he describes – for want of a more accurate terminology – as 'a highly unpopular dictatorship', is what we have called arbitrary government.

Herz nevertheless investigates the question as to how the regime does not collapse, and mentions a few factors, but says that in the opinion of 'an intelligent Iranian', the SAVAK, the oil revenues and, above all, American support for the regime are the pillars on which it stands. He points out that the belief in unqualified American support is incorrect, and so is the faith in 'American Omnipotence', but the fact that they are held with conviction in Iran performs the expected function. It is best to quote him directly on this point:

It is the Americans, he [the intelligent Iranian] is apt to say, who are propping up the regime, implying (or stating outright) that without our support the Shah and his government would be swept away in short order. While this is a fantastic oversimplification of the situation, it is an important intangible factor in the present political equation in Iran. We are not referring here to the perennial accusations we hear from opposition elements who wish the United States to fight their battles for them. There is good reason to believe that the Shah himself occasionally believes this myth, as we have had authoritative reports of his profound worries at the beginning of the Kennedy Administration and again, especially, when Ngo Dinh Diem was removed from power ... Prime Ministers are widely believed to be chosen by the United States, and even otherwise well-informed Iranians – such as the present Finance Minister before he came to office – have entirely exaggerated notions about the extent of American assistance to the Shah's regime.

Herz goes on to say that 'The Myth of American Omnipotence' which was held by rightist tendencies in the United States existed more in Iran than in the USA:

Parliamentary deputies, who had just been elected at the fiat of the Shah, have asked officers of the American Embassy whether they would think it advisable for them to make a speech criticising a particular aspect of the government. Candidates or would-be candidates for Prime Minister come to advertise their assets and their availability. Whether people are invited, or not invited, by the American Ambassador or his ranking subordinates, is a matter of profound concern to them as though it were an indication of their future political prospects in Iran ... By being given credit today for power to influence the situation in Iran that we do not actually possess, however we of course also incur the blame for the deficiencies that we are in no position to prevent or remedy. This is another important intangible factor in the situation.

What was true in 1964 when the regime had just embarked on its arbitrary phase, and oil revenues had just started to flow steadily and at a relatively high rate, was scarcely less true in 1977, when there was hardly anyone even among the regime's highest beneficiaries that felt any commitment towards it. And the belief, shared by the Shah himself, that the United States had decided to remove him from power played a decisive role in emboldening the revolutionary movement against the regime.

Index